T. Y. LIN was born in Foochow, China, and reared in Peking. He obtained his B.S. in Civil Engineering from Tangshan College, Chiaotung University, China. After receiving his Masters degree from the University of California, Berkeley, Professor Lin returned to China where he was engineer and chief design engineer for various Chinese Government Railways. He came back to teach at the University of California in 1946. Professor Lin served as chairman of the Division of Structural Engineering and Structural Mechanics and as director of the Structural Engineering Laboratory at the university from 1960 to 1963.

Author of over 50 technical papers and co-author of DESIGN OF STEEL STRUCTURES, Professor Lin was awarded a Fulbright fellowship in 1953, for advanced research on prestressed concrete in Belgium, and is a recipient of the ASCE Wellington Award for a paper on Long Span Bridge Loadings. He was General Chairman of the World Conference on Prestressed Concrete, held in San Francisco in 1957; Head of the United States Delegation to Observe Concrete Engineering in the U.S.S.R. in 1958; and Vice-president of the International Federation for Prestressing from 1958 to 1962.

Professor Lin is director of T. Y. Lin and Associates, and T. Y. Lin and Associates International, consulting structural engineers, which have served as consultants to the Government of Venezuela, the U.S. Department of Defense, the State of California Division of Architecture, Commonwealth of Puerto Rico, General Dynamics and General Motors Corporation, and have designed numerous outstanding structures of prestressed concrete throughout the world.

ssed Concrete Structures

Design of

Prestressed Concrete Structures

SECOND EDITION

T.-Y. Lin, PROFESSOR OF CIVIL ENGINEERING
UNIVERSITY OF CALIFORNIA

John Wiley & Sons, Inc., New York · London

To engineers who, rather than
blindly following the codes of practice,
seek to apply the laws of nature

preface

The development of prestressed concrete can perhaps be best described by this parody, which I presented before the World Conference on Prestressed Concrete in San Francisco, 1957.

All the world's a stage,
And all engineering techniques merely players:
They have their exits and their entrances.
Prestressed concrete, like others, plays a part,
Its acts being seven ages. At first the infant,
Stressing and compressing in the inventor's arms.
Then the curious schoolboy, fondly created
By imaginative engineers for wealthy customers;
Successfully built but costs a lot of dough. Then the lover,
Whose course never runs smooth, embraced by some,
Shunned by others, especially building officials. Now the soldier,
Produced en masse the world over, quick to fight
Against any material, not only in strength, but in economy as well.
Soon the justice—codes and specifications set up to abide,
Formulas and tables to help you decide. No more fun to the pioneers,
But so prestressed concrete plays its part. The sixth age
Shifts to refined research and yet bolder designs,
Undreamed of by predecessors and men in ivory towers.
Last scene of all, in common use and hence in oblivion,
Ends this eventful history of prestressed concrete
As one of engineering methods and materials
Like timber, like steel, like reinforced concrete,
Like everything else.

When I wrote the first edition of this book, prestressed concrete in the United States had barely entered its fourth stage—the beginning of mass production. Now it has emerged from the fifth stage and into the sixth. This rapid advance has made possible a rather thorough revision of the first edition.

In this second edition, the basic theory of flexure remains practically unchanged. However, the method of load-balancing, which I developed, offers a new approach and greatly simplifies the design of statically indeterminate structures. I recommend that this method be used side-by-side with the working-load and the ultimate-load methods, forming a tripod for prestressed-concrete design.

The chapter on materials has been brought up to date. The problems of shear and bond, so little known when the first edition was written, are now based on substantial data so that reasonable results can be obtained, though still somewhat empirically. Combined axial load and bending is added to compression members in Chapter 14, wherein pre-tensioned piles are also discussed in detail.

Chapter 15 presents the economics and layouts for bridges and buildings. Five comprehensive design examples follow in Chapter 16, including a complete design for a pre-tensioned section, a preliminary design for a typical continuous building frame, and a precast bridge made continuous by placing nonprestressed reinforcement over the piers. These examples reflect some of the latest developments in American practice.

Since building codes and bridge specifications are now available, they are discussed in Chapter 17 and included in the Appendixes. In Chapter 18, special topics are presented: fire resistance, durability, fatigue strength, dynamic behavior, and torsional strength of prestressed concrete. Applications to railroad ties, pavement, and masts are briefly mentioned.

It is indeed my wish that this revised edition will help to advance prestressed concrete not only as a major material but also as a new concept in structural engineering.

The checking of the manuscript, particularly the examples, by Mr. Christopher Lau is hereby gratefully acknowledged.

Berkeley, California   T. Y. LIN
June, 1963

contents

introduction

1

1-1 Development of Prestressed Concrete

Prestressing means the intentional creation of permanent stresses in a structure or assembly, for the purpose of improving its behavior and strength under various service conditions.

The basic principle of prestressing was applied to construction perhaps centuries ago, when ropes or metal bands were wound around wooden staves to form barrels (Fig. 1-1). When the bands were tightened, they were under tensile prestress which in turn created compressive prestress between the staves and thus enabled them to resist hoop tension produced by internal liquid pressure. In other words, the bands and the staves were both prestressed before they were subjected to any service loads.

The same principle, however, was not applied to concrete until about 1886, when P. H. Jackson, an engineer of San Francisco, California, obtained patents for tightening steel tie rods in artificial stones and concrete arches to serve as floor slabs. Around 1888, C. E. W. Doehring

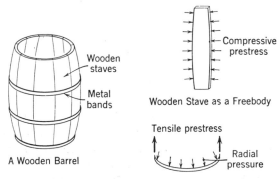

Fig. 1-1. Principle of prestressing applied to barrel construction.

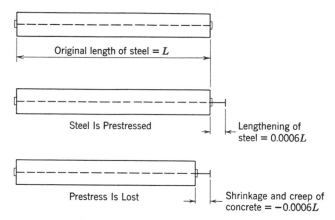

Fig. 1-2. Prestressing concrete with ordinary structural steel.

of Germany independently secured a patent for concrete reinforced with metal that had tensile stress applied to it before the slab was loaded. These applications were based on the conception that concrete, though strong in compression, was quite weak in tension, and prestressing the steel against the concrete would put the concrete under compressive stress which could be utilized to counterbalance any tensile stress produced by dead or live loads.

These first patented methods were not successful because the low prestress then produced in the steel was soon lost as a result of the shrinkage and creep of concrete. Consider an ordinary structural steel bar prestressed to a working stress of 18,000 psi (Fig. 1-2). If the modulus of elasticity of steel is 30,000,000 psi, the unit lengthening of the bar is given by

$$\delta = \frac{f}{E}$$
$$= \frac{18,000}{30,000,000}$$
$$= 0.0006$$

Since eventual shrinkage and creep often induce comparable amounts of shortening in concrete, this initial unit lengthening of steel could be entirely lost in the course of time. At best, only a small portion of the prestress could be retained, and the method cannot compete economically with conventional reinforcement of concrete.

In 1908, C. R. Steiner of the United States suggested the possibility of retightening the reinforcing rods after some shrinkage and creep of concrete had taken place, in order to recover some of the losses. In

1925, R. E. Dill of Nebraska tried high-strength steel bars coated to prevent bond with concrete. After the concrete had set, the steel rods were tensioned and anchored to the concrete by means of nuts. But these methods were not applied to any appreciable extent, chiefly for economic reasons.

Modern development of prestressed concrete is credited to E. Freyssinet of France, who in 1928 started using high-strength steel wires for pre-stressing. Such wires, with an ultimate strength as high as 250,000 psi and a yield point over 180,000 psi, are prestressed to about 150,000 psi, creating a unit strain of (Fig. 1-3)

$$\delta = \frac{f}{E}$$
$$= \frac{150,000}{30,000,000}$$
$$= 0.0050$$

Assuming a total loss of 0.0008 due to shrinkage and creep of concrete and other causes, a net strain of $0.0050 - 0.0008 = 0.0042$ would still be left in the wires, which is equivalent to a stress of

$$f = E\delta$$
$$= 30,000,000 \times 0.0042$$
$$= 126,000 \text{ psi}$$

Although Freyssinet also tried the scheme of pre-tensioning where the steel was bonded to the concrete without end anchorage, practical

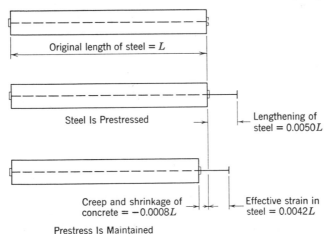

Fig. 1-3. Prestressing concrete with high-tensile steel.

Fig. 1-4. Three-inch prestressed concrete shells cantilever 90-ft—Grandstand for Hippodromo Caracas, Venezuela (Architect Arthur Froehlich, Structural Engineer Henry M. Layne, Consultant T. Y. Lin and Associates).

application of this method was first made by E. Hoyer of Germany. The Hoyer system consists of stretching wires between two buttresses several hundred feet apart, putting shutters between the units, placing the concrete, and cutting the wires after the concrete has hardened. This method enables several units to be cast between two buttresses.

Wide application of prestressed concrete was not possible until reliable and economical methods of tensioning and of end anchorage were devised. In 1939, Freyssinet developed conical wedges for end anchorages and designed double-acting jacks which tensioned the wires and then thrust the male cones into the female cones for anchoring them (Fig. 3-10, p. 71). In 1940, Professor G. Magnel of Belgium developed the Magnel system, wherein two wires were stretched at a time and anchored with a simple metal wedge at each end (Fig. 3-9, p. 71). About that time, prestressed concrete began to acquire importance, though it did not actually come to the fore until about 1945. Perhaps the shortage of steel in Europe during the war had given it some impetus, since much less steel is needed for prestressed concrete than for conventional types of construction. But it must also be realized that time was needed to prove and improve the serviceability, economy, and safety of prestressed concrete as well as to acquaint engineers and builders with a new method of design and construction.

Although France and Belgium led the development of prestressed concrete, England, Germany, Switzerland, Holland, Soviet Russia, and Italy quickly followed. About 80% of all concrete bridges now being built in Germany are of prestressed concrete. Soviet Russia produced 3,000,000 cubic meters of prestressed concrete for buildings in 1960.

Prestressed concrete in the United States followed a different course of development. Instead of linear prestressing, a name given to prestressed concrete beams and slabs, circular prestressing especially as applied to storage tanks took the lead. This was performed almost entirely by the Preload Company, which developed special wire winding machines and which, from 1935 to 1963, built about one thousand prestressed-concrete tanks throughout this country and other parts of the world.

Linear prestressing did not start in this country until 1949, when construction of the famed Philadelphia Walnut Lane Bridge was begun.

Fig. 1-5. Precast prestressed concrete girders and columns form rigid frames for 62-ft span garage, University of California, Berkeley (Architect Anshen and Allen, Structural Engineer T. Y. Lin and Associates International).

Fig. 1-6. Prestressed slabs and girders of Humble Oil Garage, Houston, Texas, has typical bay 63 × 28 ft and carries heavy machinery on roof up to 700 psf (Architect Welton Becket & Associates, Structural Engineer Stacey and Skinner, Consultant T. Y. Lin and Associates).

The Bureau of Public Roads survey showed that for the years 1957–60, 2052 prestressed concrete bridges were authorized for construction, totaling a length of 68 miles, with an aggregate cost of 290 million dollars and comprising 12% of all new highway bridges both in length and in cost.

The growth of prestressed concrete in the United States has so far been along the lines of precast pretensioned products, essentially for bridges and buildings. While there was only one such plant in 1950, there were 34 in 1954. A survey by the Prestressed Concrete Institute indicated at least 229 plants operating in 1961. The total volume of precast prestressed products is estimated to be over 2,000,000 cu yd in 1962, of which it can be roughly estimated that 50% went to bridges and the remaining to buildings, and other construction projects.[1] The volume of concrete post-tensioned in place in the United States cannot be reliably estimated, but it is known to constitute only a fraction of the precast volume.

While it is yet impossible to determine the number of buildings in the United States that embodied prestressed concrete, it seems safe to say that several thousand are being built each year. However, compared to the total volume of building construction, it represents only a small portion, probably not over 1% of the structural costs. This percentage seems rather low when compared to Denmark, for example, where 44% of the buildings in 1961 embodied some type of prestressed concrete components.

While bridges are more easily standardized by federal and state agencies

Fig. 1-7. Fifteen-story apartment building, Long Beach, California—7½-inch concrete slabs are post-tensioned to span 28′ 6″ while center shaft walls are post-tensioned vertically to resist earthquakes (Architect James R. Wilde, Structural Engineer T. Y. Lin and Associates).

thus helping to develop prestressed-concrete construction, it will take time to fully develop building products and designs for the individual architects and engineers. It is believed that, with the incorporation of prestressed concrete into building codes and a general understanding of prestressed design and construction, a faster rate of growth is expected for buildings from now on.

Impending development of prestressed concrete in the United States may well lie in the application of post-tensioning to buildings and bridges, including the combination of pre-tensioning, post-tensioning, and conventional reinforcing to structures and structural components. This will come when our engineers and architects realize the potentialities and possibilities of prestressing and have mastered the theory and the practice of its design and detailing.

Outside the field of tanks, bridges, and buildings, prestressed concrete has been occasionally applied to dams, by anchoring prestressed steel bars to the foundation, or by jacking the dam against it.[2] Piles, posts, and pipes all have been constructed of prestressed concrete. In certain structures, it is possible to prestress the concrete without using prestressing tendons. For example, the Freyssinet method of arch compensation introduces compensating stresses in the arch rib by a system of hydraulic jacks inserted in the arch. Such stresses are intended to neutralize the effects of shrinkage, rib shortening, and temperature drop in the arch. The Plougastel Bridge near Brest, with 3 spans of 612 ft each, is an example of such application.[3]

The basic principle of prestressing is not limited to structures in concrete; it has been applied to steel construction as well. When two plates are joined together by hot-driven rivets or high-tensile bolts, the connectors are highly prestressed in tension and the plates in compression, thus enabling the plates to carry tensile loads between them. The Sciotoville bridge, of 720-ft spans, had its members prestressed in bending during erection in order to neutralize the secondary stresses due to live and dead loads.[4] A continuous truss prestressed with high-tensile wires was built into the airplane hangars at Brussels, Belgium, and two similar ones were tested at the University of Ghent.[5]

Whether prestressing is applied to steel or concrete, its ultimate purpose is twofold: first, to induce desirable strains and stresses in the structure; second, to counterbalance undesirable strains and stresses. In prestressed concrete, the steel is pre-elongated so as to avoid excessive lengthening under service load, while the concrete is precompressed so as to prevent cracks under tensile stress. Thus an ideal combination of the two materials is achieved. The basic desirability of prestressed concrete is almost self-evident, but its widespread application will eventually depend on the

Fig. 1-8. Thirteen-story apartment building with all slabs post-tensioned on the ground being lifted into position; 8-inch lightweight concrete spans 28-ft; San Francisco. (Owner George Belcher, Engineer August Waegeman, Consultant T. Y. Lin and Associates).

development of new methods of design and execution which will enhance its economy relative to more conventional types of structures.

The progress of prestressed concrete, both in research and in development, is perhaps best indicated by the growth of its technical societies and their publications. In the United States, the Prestressed Concrete Institute formed in 1954 now has a membership of 900, and publishes the *PCItems* and the *PCI Journal*. Proceedings of the World Conference on Prestressed Concrete in San Francisco 1957, and Proceedings of Western Conferences on Prestressed Concrete Buildings held in California 1960, included valuable papers on all phases of the subject. The International Federation for Prestressing with its headquarters in London has 32 membership countries and has published hundreds of papers of their congresses held in London 1953, in Amsterdam 1955, in Berlin 1958, and in Rome 1962.

Fig. 1-9. Twenty-two-story Nob Hill Apartment Building, San Francisco—all floors are of post-tensioned concrete slabs 8-inch thick spanning 30 ft from elevator shafts to exterior walls (Architect John Carl Warnecke and Associates; Structural Engineer T. Y. Lin and Associates International).

1-2   General Principles of Prestressed Concrete

One of the best definitions of prestressed concrete is given by the ACI Committee on Prestressed Concrete.

Prestressed concrete: Concrete in which there have been introduced internal stresses of such magnitude and distribution that the stresses resulting from given external loadings are counteracted to a desired degree. In reinforced-concrete members the prestress is commonly introduced by tensioning the steel reinforcement.

It might be added that prestressed concrete, in the broader sense of the term, might also include cases where the stresses resulting from internal strains are counteracted to a certain degree, such as in arch compensation. This book, however, will deal essentially with prestressed-concrete structures as defined by the ACI Committee, and will limit itself to prestressing as introduced by the tensioning of steel reinforcement. This is at present by far the most common form of prestressed concrete.

Fig. 1-10. Methodist Church of Glendale, California, has post-tensioned folded plates and precast post-tensioned columns 60-ft high (Architect Flewelling and Moody, Structural Engineer Carl B. Johnson, Consultant T. Y. Lin and Associates).

Fig. 1-11. An all-precast nine-story office building under construction, University of California, Davis; 90-ft columns, floor panels, and exterior walls are all of precast pre-tensioned concrete (Architect Gardner A. Dailey; Structural Engineer T. Y. Lin and Associates International).

Three different concepts may be applied to explain and analyze the basic behavior of this form of prestressed concrete. It is important that a designer understands all three concepts so that he can proportion and design prestressed concrete structures with intelligence and efficiency. These will be explained as follows.

First Concept—Prestressing to Transform Concrete into an Elastic Material. This concept treats concrete as an elastic material and is probably still the most common viewpoint among engineers. It is credited to Eugene Freyssinet who visualized prestressed concrete as essentially *concrete* which is transformed from a brittle material into an elastic one by the precompression given to it. Concrete which is weak in tension and strong in compression is compressed (generally by steel under high tension) so that the brittle concrete would be able to withstand tensile stresses. From this concept the criterion of no tensile stresses was born. It is generally believed that if there are no tensile stresses in the concrete, there can be no cracks, and the concrete is no longer a brittle material but becomes an elastic material.

From this standpoint concrete is visualized as being subject to two systems of forces: internal prestress and external load, with the tensile stresses due to the external load counteracted by the compressive stresses due to the prestress. Similarly, the cracking of concrete due to load is prevented or delayed by the precompression produced by the tendons. So long as there are no cracks, the stresses, strains, and deflections of the concrete due to the two systems of forces can be considered separately and superimposed if necessary.

In its simplest form, let us consider a simple rectangular beam prestressed by a tendon* through its centroidal axis (Fig. 1-13) and loaded by external loads. Owing to the prestress F, a uniform stress of

$$f = \frac{F}{A} \tag{1-1}$$

will be produced across the section which has an area A. If M is the external moment at a section due to the load on and the weight of the beam,

Fig. 1-12. Setting precast prestressed concrete 180-ton spans for 24-mile Lake Pontchartrain Bridge, Louisiana (Palmer and Baker, Mobile, Alabama).

* See Appendix A for definition of tendon.

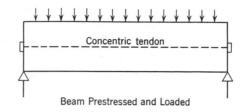

Beam Prestressed and Loaded

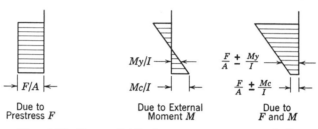

| Due to Prestress F | Due to External Moment M | Due to F and M |

Fig. 1-13. Stress distribution across a concentrically prestressed-concrete section.

then the stress at any point across that section due to M is

$$f = \frac{My}{I} \tag{1-2}$$

where y is the distance from the centroidal axis and I is the moment of inertia of the section. Thus the resulting stress distribution is given by

$$f = \frac{F}{A} \pm \frac{My}{I} \tag{1-3}$$

as shown in Fig. 1-13.

The solution is slightly more complicated when the tendon is placed eccentrically with respect to the centroid of the concrete section, Fig. 1-14. Owing to an eccentric prestress, the concrete is subject to a moment as well as a direct load. The moment produced by the prestress is Fe, and the stresses due to this moment are

$$f = \frac{Fey}{I} \tag{1-4}$$

Thus, the resulting stress distribution is given by

$$f = \frac{F}{A} \pm \frac{Fey}{I} \pm \frac{My}{I} \tag{1-5}$$

as shown in the figure.

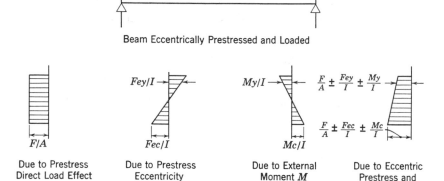

Beam Eccentrically Prestressed and Loaded

F/A	Fec/I	Mc/I	
Due to Prestress Direct Load Effect	Due to Prestress Eccentricity	Due to External Moment M	Due to Eccentric Prestress and External M

Fig. 1-14. Stress distribution across an eccentrically prestressed-concrete section.

EXAMPLE 1-1

A prestressed-concrete rectangular beam 20 in. by 30 in. has a simple span of 24 ft and is loaded by a uniform load of 3 k/ft including its own weight, Fig. 1-15. The prestressing tendon is located as shown and produces an effective prestress of 360 k. Compute fiber stresses in the concrete at the midspan section.

Solution. Using formula 1-5, we have $F = 360$ k, $A = 20 \times 30 = 600$ in.^{2} (neglecting any hole due to the tendon), $e = 6$ in., $I = bd^3/12 = 20 \times 30^3/12 = 45,000$ in.^{4}; $y = 15$ in. for extreme fibers.

$$M = 3 \times 24^2/8 = 216 \text{ k-ft}$$

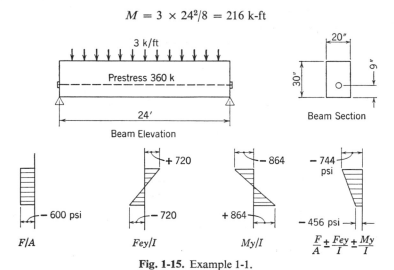

F/A	Fey/I	My/I	$\dfrac{F}{A} \pm \dfrac{Fey}{I} \pm \dfrac{My}{I}$

Fig. 1-15. Example 1-1.

Therefore

$$f = \frac{F}{A} \pm \frac{Fey}{I} \pm \frac{My}{I}$$

$$= \frac{-360,000}{600} \pm \frac{360,000 \times 6 \times 15}{45,000} \pm \frac{216 \times 12,000 \times 15}{45,000}$$

$$= -600 \pm 720 \pm 864$$

$$= -600 + 720 - 864 = -744 \text{ psi for top fiber}$$

$$= -600 - 720 + 864 = -456 \text{ psi for bottom fiber}$$

The resulting stress distribution is shown in Fig. 1-15.

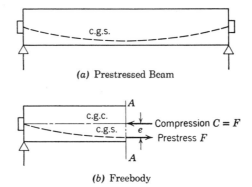

(a) Prestressed Beam

(b) Freebody

Fig. 1-16. Effect of prestress.

When the tendons are curved or bent, Fig. 1–16(*a*), it is often convenient to take either the left or the right portion of the member as a freebody in order to evaluate the effect of the prestressing force *F*. Thus, in Fig. 1-16(*b*), equilibrium of horizontal forces indicates that the compression in the

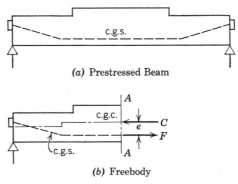

(a) Prestressed Beam

(b) Freebody

Fig. 1-17. Effect of variations away from section.

concrete equals the prestress in the steel F, and the stresses in the concrete due to eccentric force F is given by,

$$f = \frac{F}{A} \pm \frac{Fec}{I}$$

Thus, concrete stresses f at a section are dependent only on the magnitude and location of F at that section, regardless of how the tendon profile may vary elsewhere along the beam. For example, if section A-A of the beam in Fig. 1-17 is identical with section A-A in Fig. 1-16, the concrete stresses due to prestress F with eccentricity e are identical for the two sections, regardless of variations in the shape of the beam or the cable profile away from the section. (This is true only for the statically determinate members wherein external reactions are not affected by the internal prestressing. See Chapters 10 and 11 for statically indeterminate systems.)

EXAMPLE 1-2

A concrete beam with the same span, loading, section, and prestress as in example 1-1 has a parabolically curved tendon as shown, Fig. 1-18. Compute the extreme fiber stresses at midspan.

Solution. The beam section at midspan is shown in the figure and is identical with the section in Fig. 1-15 for example 1-1. Hence exactly the same calculation for example 1-1 will apply, and the extreme fiber stresses are also the same.

$$\text{Top fiber} \quad -744 \text{ psi (compression)}$$
$$\text{Bottom fiber} \quad -456 \text{ psi (compression)}$$

Second Concept—Prestressing for Combination of High-Strength Steel with Concrete. This concept is to consider prestressed concrete as a combination of steel and concrete, similar to reinforced concrete, with steel taking tension and concrete taking compression so that the two materials form a resisting couple against the external moment, Fig. 1-19. This is often an easy concept for engineers familiar with reinforced concrete where the steel supplies a tensile force and the concrete supplies a compressive force, the two forces forming a couple with a lever arm between them. Few engineers realize, however, that similar behavior exists in prestressed concrete.

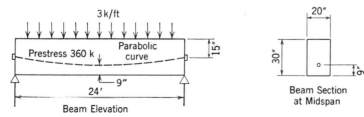

Fig. 1-18. Example 1-2.

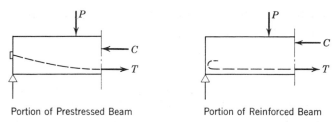

Fig. 1-19. Internal resisting moment in prestressed- and reinforced-concrete beams.

In prestressed concrete, high-tensile steel is used which will have to be elongated a great deal before its strength is fully utilized. If the high-tensile steel is simply buried in the concrete, as in ordinary concrete reinforcement, the surrounding concrete will have to crack very seriously before the full strength of the steel is developed, Fig. 1-20. Hence it is necessary to prestretch the steel with respect to the concrete. By prestretching and anchoring the steel against the concrete, we produce desirable stresses and strains in both materials: compressive stresses and strains in concrete, and tensile stresses and strains in steel. This combined action permits the safe and economical utilization of the two materials which cannot be achieved by simply burying steel in the concrete as is done for ordinary reinforced concrete. There were isolated instances where medium-strength steel was used as simple reinforcement without prestressing while the steel was specially corrugated for bond, in order to distribute the cracks. This process avoids the expenses for prestretching and anchoring but cannot be applied to high-tensile steel and does not have the desirable effects of precompressing the concrete and of reducing the deflections.

From this point of view, prestressed concrete is no longer a strange type of design. It is rather an extension and modification of the applications of reinforced concrete to include steels of higher strength. From this point of view, prestressed concrete cannot perform miracles beyond the capacity of the strength of its materials. Although much ingenuity can be exercised in the proper and economic design of prestressed-concrete structures,

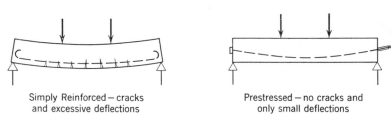

Simply Reinforced — cracks
and excessive deflections

Prestressed — no cracks and
only small deflections

Fig. 1-20. Concrete beam using high-tensile steel.

there is absolutely no magic method to avoid the eventual necessity of carrying an external moment by an internal couple. And that internal resisting couple must be supplied by the steel in tension and the concrete in compression, whether it be prestressed or reinforced concrete. This concept has been well utilized to determine the ultimate strength of prestressed concrete beams and is also applicable to their elastic behavior as brought out primarily by the author (see Chapter 6, reference 1).

Once the engineer sees this viewpoint, he understands the basic similarity between prestressed and reinforced concrete. Then much of the complexity of prestressing disappears, and the design of prestressed concrete can be intelligently accomplished and not performed by groping in the dark among a lot of complicated and confusing formulas.

The following example illustrates a simple application of the above principle in the analysis of prestressed-concrete beams; more extensive treatment will be presented in Chapter 6.

EXAMPLE 1-3

Solve the problem stated in example 1-2 by applying the principle of the internal resisting couple.

Solution. Take one half of the beam as a freebody, thus exposing the internal couple, Fig. 1-21. The external moment at the section is

$$M = \frac{wL^2}{8}$$

$$= \frac{3 \times 24^2}{8}$$

$$= 216 \text{ k-ft}$$

The internal couple is furnished by the forces $C = T = 360$ k, which must act with a lever arm of

$$\frac{216}{360} \times 12 = 7.2 \text{ in.}$$

Since T acts at 9 in. from the bottom, C must be acting at 16.2 in. from it. Thus the center of the compressive force C is located.

So far we have been dealing only with statics, the validity of which is not

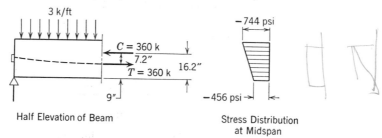

Half Elevation of Beam

Stress Distribution at Midspan

Fig. 1-21. Example 1-3.

subject to any question. Now, if desired, the stress distribution in the concrete can be obtained by the usual elastic theory, since the center of the compressive force is already known. For $C = 360,000$ lb acting with an eccentricity of $16.2 - 15 = 1.2$ in.,

$$f = \frac{F}{A} \pm \frac{Mc}{I}$$
$$= \frac{-360,000}{600} \pm \frac{360,000 \times 1.2 \times 15}{45,000}$$
$$= -600 \mp 144$$
$$= -744 \text{ psi for top fiber}$$
$$= -456 \text{ psi for bottom fiber}$$

Third Concept—Prestressing to Achieve Load Balancing. This concept is to visualize prestressing primarily as an attempt to balance the loads on a member. This concept was essentially developed by the author, although undoubtedly also utilized by other engineers to a lesser degree.

In the overall design of a prestressed concrete structure, the effect of prestressing is essentially viewed as the balancing of gravity loads so that members under bending such as slabs, beams, and girders will not be subjected to flexural stresses under a given loading condition. This enables the transformation of a flexural member into a member under direct stress and thus greatly simplifies both the design and analysis of otherwise complicated structures.

The application of this concept requires taking the concrete as a free-body, and replacing the tendons with forces acting on the concrete.

Take, for example, a simple beam prestressed with a parabolic tendon (Fig. 1-22) if

$F =$ prestressing force
$L =$ length of span
$h =$ sag of parabola

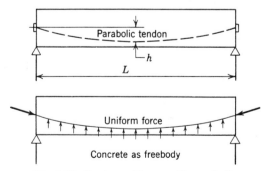

Fig. 1-22. Prestressed beam with parabolic tendon.

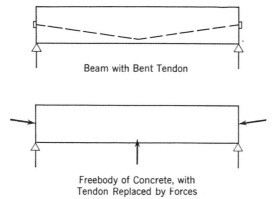

Beam with Bent Tendon

Freebody of Concrete, with
Tendon Replaced by Forces

Fig. 1-23. Prestressed beam with bent
tendon.

The upward uniform force is given by

$$w = \frac{8Fh}{L^2}$$

Thus, for a given downward uniform load w, the transverse load on the
beam is balanced, and the beam is subjected only to the axial force F,
which produces uniform stresses in concrete, $f = F/A$. The change in
stresses from this balanced condition can easily be computed by the
ordinary formulas in mechanics, $f = Mc/I$.

For a beam with bent tendon, Fig. 1-23, the load from the tendon on the
concrete can easily be determined by statics. This approach, while unnecessarily cumbersome for some simple cases, often becomes very effective for
complicated structures, such as continuous beams, rigid frames, flat and
waffle slabs, and some thin shells, which will be explained more fully in
Chapter 11. When further extended, it can be used for the design and
analysis of self-anchored, prestressed-concrete bridges, when the force
from the steel cable on the concrete roadway and girders can be predetermined, and the stresses in the concrete analyzed without much difficulty.

EXAMPLE 1-4

Solve the problem in example 1-2 by the method of load balancing taking
the concrete as freebody, isolated from the tendon or steel, Fig. 1-24.

Solution. The upward uniform force from the tendon on the concrete is

$$w = \frac{8Fh}{L^2}$$

$$= \frac{8 \times 360 \times (6/12)}{24^2}$$

$$= 2.5 \text{ k/ft}$$

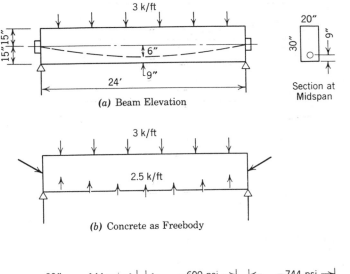

(a) Beam Elevation

Section at Midspan

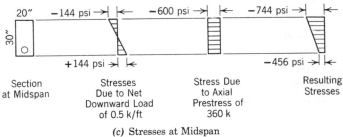

(b) Concrete as Freebody

Section at Midspan

Stresses Due to Net Downward Load of 0.5 k/ft

Stress Due to Axial Prestress of 360 k

Resulting Stresses

(c) Stresses at Midspan

Fig. 1-24. Example 1-4.

Hence the net downward load on the concrete beam is $3 - 2.5 = 0.5$ k/ft, and the moment at midspan due to that load is

$$M = \frac{wL^2}{8} = \frac{0.5 \times 24^2}{8}$$

$$= 36 \text{ k-ft}$$

The fiber stresses due to that moment are

$$f = \frac{Mc}{I} = \frac{6M}{bd^2}$$

$$= \frac{6 \times 36 \times 12{,}000}{20 \times 30^2}$$

$$= 144 \text{ psi (compression top fiber; tension bottom fiber)}$$

The fiber stress due to the direct load effect of the prestress is very nearly

$$\frac{F}{A} = \frac{-360,000}{20 \times 30}$$

$$= -600 \text{ psi compression}$$

The resulting stresses are

$$-144 - 600 = -744 \text{ top fiber comp.}$$
$$+144 - 600 = -456 \text{ bottom fiber comp.}$$

the same as in examples 1-2 and 1-3.

1-3 Classification and Types

Prestressed-concrete structures can be classified in a number of ways, depending upon their features of design and construction. These will be discussed as follows.

Externally or Internally Prestressed. Although this book is devoted to the design of prestressed-concrete structures internally prestressed, presumably with high-tensile steel, it must be mentioned that it is sometimes possible to prestress a concrete structure by adjusting its external reactions. The method of arch compensation was mentioned previously, where a concrete arch was prestressed by jacking against its abutments. Theoretically, a simple concrete beam can also be externally prestressed by jacking at the proper places to produce compression in the bottom fibers and tension in the top fibers, Fig. 1-25, thus even dispensing with steel reinforcement in the beam. Such an ideal arrangement, however, cannot be easily accomplished in practice, because, even if abutments favorable for such a layout are obtainable, shrinkage and creep in concrete may completely offset the artificial strains unless they can be readjusted. Besides, such a site would probably be better suited for an arch bridge.

For a statically indeterminate structure, like a continuous beam, it is possible to adjust the level of the supports, by inserting jacks, for example, so as to produce the most desirable reactions, Fig. 1-26. This is sometimes practical, though it must be kept in mind that shrinkage and creep in

Fig. 1-25. Prestressing a simple concrete beam by jacking against abutments.

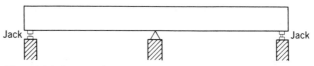

Fig. 1-26. Prestressing a continuous beam by jacking its reactions.

concrete will modify the effects of such prestress so that they must be taken into account or else the prestress must be adjusted from time to time.

Linear or Circular Prestressing. Circular prestressing is a term applied to prestressed circular structures, such as round tanks, silos, and pipes, where the prestressing tendons are wound around in circles. This topic is discussed in Chapter 13. As distinguished from circular prestressing, the term linear prestressing is often employed to include all other structures such as beams and slabs. The prestressing tendons in linearly prestressed structures are not necessarily straight; they can be either bent or curved, but they do not go round and round in circles as in circular prestressing.

Pre-Tensioning and Post-Tensioning. The term pre-tensioning is used to describe any method of prestressing in which the tendons are tensioned before the concrete is placed. It is evident that the tendons must be temporarily anchored against some abutments or stressing beds when tensioned and the prestress transferred to the concrete after it has set. This procedure is employed in precasting plants or laboratories where permanent beds are provided for such tensioning; it is also applied in the field where abutments can be economically constructed. In contrast to pre-tensioning, post-tensioning is a method of prestressing in which the tendon is tensioned after the concrete has hardened. Thus the prestressing is almost always performed against the hardened concrete, and the tendons are anchored against it immediately after prestressing. This method can be applied to members either precast or cast in place.

End-Anchored or Non-End-Anchored Tendons. When post-tensioned, the tendons are anchored at their ends by means of mechanical devices to transmit the prestress to the concrete. Such a member is termed end-anchored. Occasionally, though rarely, a post-tensioned member may have its tendons held by grout with no mechanical end anchorage. In pre-tensioning, the tendons generally have their prestress transmitted to the concrete simply by their bond action near the ends. The effectiveness of such stress transmission is limited to wires and strands of small size. More recently, anchorages have been developed for pre-tensioning so as to permit the use of tendons of larger diameter. Different types of end anchorages will be discussed in Chapter 3.

Bonded or Unbonded Tendons. Bonded tendons denote those bonded throughout their length to the surrounding concrete. Non-end-anchored tendons are necessarily bonded ones; end-anchored tendons may be either bonded or unbonded to the concrete. In general, the bonding of post-tensioned tendons is accomplished by subsequent grouting; if unbonded, protection of the tendons from corrosion must be provided by galvanizing, greasing, or some other means. Sometimes, bonded tendons may be purposely unbonded along certain portions of their length.

Precast, Cast-in-Place, Composite Construction. Precasting involves the placing of concrete away from its final position, the members being cast either in a permanent plant or somewhere near the site of the structure, and eventually erected at the final location. Precasting permits better control in mass production and is often economical. Cast-in-place concrete requires more form and falsework per unit of product but saves the cost of transportation and erection, and it is a necessity for large and heavy members. In between these two methods of construction, there are tilt-up wall panels and lift slabs which are constructed at places near or within the structure and then erected to their final position; no transportation is involved for these. Oftentimes, it is economical to precast part of a member, erect it, and then cast the remaining portion in place. This procedure is called composite construction. The precast elements in a structure of composite construction can be more easily joined together than those in a totally precast structure. By composite construction, it is possible to save much of the form and falsework required for total cast-in-place construction. However, the suitability of each type must be studied with respect to the particular conditions of a given structure.

Partial or Full Prestressing. A further distinction between the types of prestressing is sometimes made depending on the degree of prestressing to which a concrete member is subject. When a member is designed so that under the working load there are no tensile stresses in it, then the concrete is said to be fully prestressed. If some tensile stresses will be produced in the member under working load, then it is termed partially prestressed. For partial prestressing, additional mild-steel bars are frequently provided to reinforce the portion under tension. In practice, it is often difficult to classify a structure as being partially or fully prestressed since much will depend on the magnitude of the working load used in design. For example, highway bridges in this country are always designed for full prestressing, though actually they are subject to tensile stresses during the passage of heavy vehicles. On the other hand, roof beams designed for partial prestressing may never be subject to tensile stresses since the assumed live loads may never act on them.

1-4   Stages of Loading

One of the considerations peculiar to prestressed concrete is the plurality of stages of loading to which a member or structure is often subjected. Some of these stages of loading occur also in nonprestressed structures, but others exist only because of prestressing. For a cast-in-place structure, prestressed concrete has to be designed for at least two stages; the initial stage during prestressing and the final stage under external loadings. For precast members, a third stage, that of handling and transportation, has to be investigated. During each of these three stages, there are again different periods when the member or structure may be under different loading conditions. These will now be analyzed.

Initial Stage.   The member or structure is under prestress but is not subjected to any superimposed external loads. This stage can be further subdivided into the following periods, some of which may not be important and therefore may be neglected in certain designs.

Before Prestressing.   Before the concrete is prestressed, it is quite weak in carrying load; hence the yielding of its supports must be prevented. Provision must be made for the shrinkage of concrete if it might occur. When it is desirable to minimize or eliminate cracks in prestressed concrete, careful curing before the transfer of prestress is very important. Drying or sudden change in temperature must be avoided. Cracks may or may not be closed by the application of prestress, depending on many factors. Shrinkage cracks will destroy the capacity of the concrete to carry tensile stresses and may be objectionable.

During Prestressing.   This is a critical test for the strength of the tendons. Often, the maximum stress to which the tendons will be subject throughout their life occurs at that period. It occasionally happens that an individual wire may be broken during prestressing, owing to defects in its manufacture. But this break is seldom significant, since there are often many wires in a member. If a bar is broken in a member with only a few bars, it should be properly replaced. For concrete, the prestressing operations impose a severe test on the bearing strength at the anchorages. Since the concrete is not aged at this period while the prestress is at its maximum, crushing of the concrete at the anchorages is possible if its quality is inferior or if the concrete is honeycombed. Again, unsymmetrical and concentrated prestress from the tendons may produce overstresses in the concrete. Therefore the order of prestressing the various tendons must often be studied beforehand.

At Transfer of Prestress.   For pre-tensioned members, the transfer of prestress is accomplished in one operation and within a short period. For post-tensioned members, the transfer is often gradual, the prestress in the tendons being transferred to the concrete one by one. In both cases there is no external load on the member except its own weight. Thus the initial prestress, with little loss as yet taking place, imposes a serious condition on the concrete and often controls the design of the member. For economic reasons the design of a prestressed member often takes into account the weight of the member itself in holding down the cambering effect of prestressing. This is done on the assumption of a given condition of support for the member. If that condition is not realized in practice, failure of the member might result. For example, the weight of a simply supported prestressed girder is expected to exert a maximum positive moment at midspan which counteracts the negative moment due to prestressing. If the girder is cast and prestressed on soft ground without suitable pedestals at the ends, the expected positive moment may be absent and the prestressing may produce excessive tensile stresses on top fibers of the girder, resulting in its failure.

Decentering and Retensioning. If a member is cast and prestressed in place, it generally becomes self-supporting during or after prestressing. Thus the falsework can be removed after prestressing, and no new condition of loading is imposed on the structure. Some concrete structures are retensioned, that is, prestressed in two or more stages. Then the stresses at various stages of tensioning must be studied.

Intermediate Stage. This is the stage during transportation and erection. It occurs only for precast members when they are transported to the site and erected in position. It is highly important to ensure that the members are properly supported and handled at all times. For example, a simple beam designed to be supported at the ends will easily break if lifted at midspan, Fig. 1-27. Figure 1-28 shows a correct way to lift a prestressed simple beam.

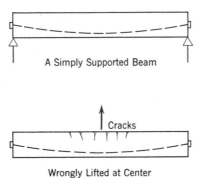

A Simply Supported Beam

Cracks

Wrongly Lifted at Center

Fig. 1-27. Failure of beam due to careless handling.

Fig. 1-28. Erecting a prestressed single-tee girder (Concrete Industries, Australia, Ltd.).

Not only during the erection of the member itself, but also when adding the superimposed dead loads, such as roofing or flooring, attention must be paid to the conditions of support and loading. This is especially true for a cantilever layout, when partial loading may result in more serious bending than a full loading, Fig. 1-29.

Final Stage. This is the stage when the actual working loads come on the structure. As for other types of construction, the designer must consider various combinations of live loads on different portions of the structure with lateral loads such as wind and earthquake forces, and with strain loads such as those produced by settlement of supports and temperature effects. For prestressed-concrete structures, especially those of unconventional types, it is often necessary to investigate their cracking and

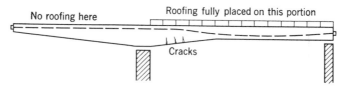

Fig. 1-29. Cracking of beam due to wrong sequence in adding superimposed load.

ultimate loads, their behavior under the actual sustained load in addition to the working load. These will be discussed as follows.

Sustained Load. The camber or deflection of a prestressed member under its actual sustained load (which often consists only of the dead load) is often the controlling factor in design, since the effect of flexural creep will eventually magnify its value. Hence it is often desirable to limit the camber or deflection under sustained load.

Working Load. To design for the working load is a check on excessive stresses and strains. It is not necessarily a guarantee of sufficient strength to carry overloads. However, an engineer familiar with the strength of prestressed-concrete structures may often design conventional types and proportions solely on the basis of working-load computations.

Cracking Load. Cracking in a prestressed-concrete member signifies a sudden change in the bond and shearing stresses. It is sometimes a measure of the fatigue strength. For certain structures, such as tanks and pipes, the commencement of cracks presents a critical situation. For structures subject to corrosive influences, for unbonded tendons where cracks are more objectionable, or for structures where cracking may result in excessive deflections, an investigation of the cracking load seems important.

Ultimate Load. Structures designed on the basis of working stresses may not always possess a sufficient margin for overloads. This is true, for example, of prestressed-concrete members under direct tensile loads. Since it is desirable that a structure does possess a certain minimum overload capacity, it is often necessary to determine its ultimate strength. In general, the ultimate strength of a structure is defined by the maximum load it can carry before collapsing. However, before this load is reached, permanent yielding of some parts of the structure may already have developed. Although any strength beyond the point of permanent yielding may serve as additional guarantee against total collapse, some engineers consider such strength as not usable and prefer to design on the basis of usable strength rather than the ultimate strength. However, ultimate strength is more easily computed and is more commonly accepted as a criterion for design.

In addition to the above normal loading conditions, some structures may be subject to repeated loads of appreciable magnitude which might result in fatigue failures. Some structures may be under heavy loads of long duration, resulting in excessive deformations due to creep, while others may be under such light external loads that the camber produced by prestressing may become too pronounced as time goes on. Still others may be subject to undesirable vibrations under dynamic loads. Under a sudden impact load or under the action of earthquakes, the energy absorption capacity of the member as indicated by its ductility may be of prime importance. These are special conditions which the engineer must consider for his individual case.

The above discussion outlines the relatively new and complex problems encountered in the design of prestressed-concrete as compared with reinforced-concrete structures. It is unfortunate that the design of prestressed concrete is more complicated, but the difficulty is by no means excessive. The new problems must be understood and solved. Ignorance of the situation might result in tragic failures such as are experienced by careless practitioners in almost any new field of endeavor.

With some experience in design, many of the loading stages mentioned above are automatically eliminated from consideration by inspection. Calculations will actually have to be made for only one or two controlling conditions. Besides, as will be shown in later chapters, calculations can be greatly simplified if the correct methods of approach and analysis are chosen. It is the observation of the author that an engineer who belittles the complications of prestressed-concrete design will encounter problems beyond his expectations, while the majority of engineers will find it not as difficult as they may imagine.

1-5   Prestressed vs. Reinforced Concrete

As it is assumed that readers are already acquainted with reinforced concrete, it will be interesting to compare prestressed concrete with it. The most outstanding difference between the two is the employment of materials of higher strength for prestressed concrete. In order to utilize the full strength of the high-tensile steel, it is necessary to resort to prestressing to prestretch it. Prestressing the steel and anchoring it against the concrete produces desirable strains and stresses which serve to reduce or eliminate cracks in concrete. Thus the entire section of the concrete becomes effective in prestressed concrete, whereas only the portion of section above the neutral axis is supposed to act in the case of reinforced concrete.

The use of curved tendons will help to carry some of the shear in a member. In addition, precompression in the concrete tends to reduce the diagonal tension. Thus it is possible to use a smaller section in prestressed concrete to carry the same amount of external shear in a beam.

High-strength concrete, which cannot be economically utilized in reinforced-concrete construction, is found to be desirable and even necessary with prestressed concrete. In reinforced concrete, using concrete of high strength will result in a smaller section calling for more reinforcement and will end with a more costly design. In prestressed concrete, high-strength concrete is required to match with high-strength steel in order to yield economical proportions. Stronger concrete is also necessary to resist high stresses at the anchorages and to give strength to the thinner sections so frequently employed for prestressed concrete.

Each material or method of construction has its own field of application. When welding was first developed in the 1930's, some engineers were overenthusiastic and believed that it would replace riveting altogether, which it has not done even yet.' Prestressed concrete is likely to have a similar course of development. Not for a long time will it be used in as great quantity as reinforced concrete. But a new type of construction, basically sound in its strength and economy, is likely to have a rapid rate of growth and to be adaptable to new and unprecedented situations and requirements.

The advantages and disadvantages of prestressed concrete as compared with reinforced concrete will now be discussed with respect to their serviceability, safety, and economy.

Serviceability. Prestressed-concrete design is more suitable for structures of long spans and those carrying heavy loads, principally because of the higher strengths of materials employed. Prestressed structures are more slender and hence more adaptable to artistic treatment. They yield more clearance where it is needed. They do not crack under working loads, and whatever cracks may be developed under overloads will be closed up as soon as the load is removed, unless the load is excessive. Under dead load, the deflection is reduced, owing to the cambering effect of prestress. This becomes an important consideration for such structures as long cantilevers. Under live load, the deflection is also smaller because of the effectiveness of the entire uncracked concrete section, which has a moment of inertia two to three times that of the cracked section. Prestressed elements are more adaptable to precasting because of the lighter weight.

So far as serviceability is concerned, the only shortcoming of prestressed concrete is its lack of weight. Although seldom encountered in practice, there are situations where weight and mass are desired instead of strength. For these situations, plain or reinforced concrete could often serve just as well and at lower cost.

Safety. It is difficult to say that one type of structure is safer than another. The safety of a structure depends more on its design and construction than on its type. However, certain inherent safety features in prestressed concrete may be mentioned. There is partial testing of both the steel and the concrete during prestressing operations. For many structures, during prestressing, both the steel and the concrete are subjected to the highest stresses that will exist in them during their life of service. Hence, if the materials can stand prestressing, they are likely to possess sufficient strength for the service loads.

When properly designed by the present conventional methods, pre-stressed-concrete structures have overload capacities similar to and per-haps slightly higher than those of reinforced concrete. For the usual designs, they deflect appreciably before ultimate failure, thus giving ample warning before impending collapse. The ability to resist shock and impact loads and repeated working loads has been shown to be as good in prestressed as in reinforced concrete. The resistance to corrosion is better than that of reinforced concrete for the same amount of cover, owing to the nonexistence of cracks. If cracks should occur, corrosion can be more serious in prestressed concrete. Regarding fire resistance, high-tensile steel is more sensitive to high temperatures, but, for the same amount of mini-mum cover, prestressed tendons can have a greater average cover because of the spread and curvature of the individual tendons. These problems are discussed in Chapter 16.

Prestressed-concrete members do require more care in design, construc-tion, and erection than those of ordinary concrete, because of the higher strength, smaller section, and sometimes delicate design features involved. Although prestressed-concrete construction has been practiced only since the late 1940's, it is possible to conclude from experience that the life of such structures can be as long as if not longer than that of reinforced concrete.

Economics. From an economic point of view, it is at once evident that smaller quantities of materials, both steel and concrete, are required to carry the same loads, since the materials are of higher strength. There is also a definite saving in stirrups, since shear in prestressed concrete is reduced by the inclination of the tendons, and the diagonal tension is further minimized by the presence of prestress. The reduced weight of the member will help in economizing the sections; the smaller dead load and depth of members will result in saving materials from other portions of the structure. In precast members, a reduction of weight saves handling and transportation costs.

In spite of the above economies possible with prestressed concrete, its use cannot be advocated for all conditions. First of all, the stronger materials will have a higher unit cost. More auxiliary materials are required for prestressing, such as end anchorages, conduits, and grouts. More complicated formwork is also needed, since nonrectangular shapes are often necessary for prestressed concrete. More labor is required to place 1 lb of steel in prestressed concrete, especially when the amount of work involved is small. More attention to design is involved, and more supervision is necessary; the amount of additional work will depend on the experience of the engineer and the construction crew, but it will not be serious if the same typical design is repeated many times.

From the above discussion, it can be concluded that prestressed-concrete design is more likely to be economical when the same unit is repeated many times or when heavy dead loads on long spans are encountered. It should also find suitable application when combined with precasting or semi-precasting such as composite or lift-slab construction. Each structure must be considered individually. The availability of good designers, of experienced crews, of pre-tensioning factories, and of competitive bidding often helps to tip the balance in favor of prestressed concrete.

References

1 "Prestress: Steady Growth Period Ahead," *Concrete Products*, January 1963, p. 50.
2 "Dams of Prestressed Concrete," *Eng. News-Rec.*, April 5, 1945, p. 456.
3 C. B. McCullough and E. S. Thayer, *Elastic Arch Bridges*, John Wiley & Sons, New York, 1931, (out of print).
4 G. A. Hool and W. S. Kinne, *Movable and Long Span Steel Bridges*, McGraw-Hill Book Co., New York, 1943.
5 G. Magnel and H. Lambotte, "Essai de deux poutres jumelées en acier précomprimé de 21.20 mètres de portée," *Précontrainte Prestressing*, No. 2, 1953.

2

materials ·

2-1   Concrete, Strength Requirements

Stronger concrete is usually required for prestressed than for reinforced work. Present practice in this country calls for 28-day cylinder strength of 4000 to 5000 psi for prestressed concrete, while the corresponding value for reinforced concrete is around 2500 psi. The usual cube strength specified for prestressed concrete in Europe is about 450 kg/cm², based on 10-, 15-, or 20-cm cubes at 28 days. If cube strength is taken as 1.25 times the cylinder strength, this would correspond to

$$450 \times 14.2/1.25 = 5100 \text{ psi cylinder strength}$$

Although the above are the usual values, strengths differing from these are occasionally specified.

   Higher strength is necessary in prestressed concrete for several reasons. First, in order to minimize their cost, commercial anchorages for pre-stressing steel are always designed on the basis of high-strength concrete. Hence weaker concrete either will require special anchorages or may fail under the application of prestress. Such failures may take place in bearing or in bond between steel and concrete, or in tension near the anchorages. Next, concrete of high compressive strength offers high resistance in tension and shear, as well as in bond and bearing, and is desirable for prestressed-concrete structures whose various portions are under higher stresses than ordinary reinforced concrete. Another factor is that high-strength concrete is less liable to the shrinkage cracks which sometimes occur in low-strength concrete before the application of prestress. It also has a higher modulus of elasticity and smaller creep strain, resulting in smaller loss of prestress in the steel.

   Experience has shown that 4000- to 5000-psi strength will generally work out to be the most economical mix for prestressed concrete. Al-though the strength of concrete to be specified for each job must be considered individually, there are some evident reasons why the economical mix usually falls within a certain range. Concrete strength of 4000 to 5000 psi can be obtained without excessive labor or cement. The cost of 5000-psi concrete averages about 15% higher than that of 2500-psi concrete, while it has 100% higher strength, which can be well utilized and is often seriously needed in prestressed structures. To obtain strength much greater than 5000 psi, on the other hand, not only will cost more but also will call for careful design and control of the mixing, placing, and curing of concrete which cannot be easily achieved in the field.

To attain a strength of 5000 psi, it is necessary to use a water-cement ratio of not much more than 0.45 by weight. In order to facilitate placing, a slump of 2 to 4 in. would be needed, unless more than ordinary vibration is to be applied. To obtain 3-in. slump with water-cement ratio of 0.45 would require about 8 bags of cement per cu yd of concrete. If careful vibration is possible, concrete with $\frac{1}{2}$-in. or zero slump can be employed, and 7 bags of cement per cu yd may be quite sufficient. Since excessive cement tends to increase shrinkage, a lower cement factor is desirable. To this end, good vibration is advised whenever possible, and proper admixtures to increase the workability can sometimes be advantageously employed.

Not only should high-strength concrete be specified for prestressed work, but, when called for, such strength should be more closely attained in the field than for reinforced concrete. It will be shown later (in Chapter 14) that the usual factor of safety against ultimate compressive failure in concrete is around 2.5, which is certainly a sufficient factor but is not as excessive as in reinforced concrete, where the factor is more nearly 3.5. For this, as well as for other reasons mentioned previously, care should be exercised to produce as good concrete as called for in the design. However, it is also evident that, with a factor of safety of 2.5, it would be no cause for alarm if the concrete in the structure should possess a strength 10 or 20% below the required value. In fact, many engineers believe that, if the concrete is not crushed under the application of prestress, it should be able to stand any subsequent loadings, since the strength of concrete usually increases with age and since excessive overloads are very rare except for some structures.

The above discussion is not intended to encourage careless concreting in the field. Indeed, more parts of a prestressed-concrete member are subjected to high stresses than of a reinforced one. Consider a simple prestressed beam, for example. While the top fibers are highly compressed under heavy external loads, the bottom fibers are under high compression at the transfer of prestress. While the midspan sections resist the heaviest bending moments, the end sections carry and distribute the prestressing force. Hence, in a prestressed member, it is more important to secure uniformity of strength, whereas in reinforced concrete the critical sections are relatively limited. It would be foolish to tear down a structure just because its concrete did not test up to the specified strength, but the engineer should use reasonable precautions to obtain good and strong concrete.

It is general practice to specify a lower strength of concrete at transfer than its 28-day strength. This is desirable in order to permit early transfer of prestress to the concrete. At transfer, the concrete is not subject to external overloads, and strength is necessary only to guard against anchorage failure and excessive creep, hence a smaller factor of safety is considered sufficient. For example, in pre-tensioning work, a strength of 3500 psi at transfer is often sufficient for a specified 28-day strength of 5000 psi.

Direct tensile strength in concrete is a highly variable item, generally ranging from $0.06f_c'$ to $0.10f_c'$, and may be zero if cracks have developed as the result of shrinkage or other reasons. Modulus of rupture in concrete is known to be higher than its direct tensile strength, varying from about $0.15f_c'$ for 3000-psi concrete to $0.10f_c'$ for 6000-psi concrete. Direct shearing strength, not often used in design, ranges from $0.50f_c'$ to $0.70f_c'$. Beam shear produces the principal tensile stress, whose limiting value is commonly gaged on the basis of direct tensile strength in concrete.

2-2 Concrete, Strain Characteristics

In prestressed concrete, it is important to know the strains produced as well as the stresses. This is necessary to estimate the loss of prestress in steel and to provide for other effects of concrete shortening. For the purpose of discussion, such strains can be classified into four types: elastic strains, lateral strains, creep strains, and shrinkage strains.

Elastic Strains. The term elastic strains is perhaps a little ambiguous, since the stress-strain curve for concrete is seldom a straight line even at normal levels of stress, Fig. 2-1. Neither are the strains entirely recoverable. But, eliminating the creep strains from consideration, the lower portion of the instantaneous stress-strain curve, being relatively straight, may be conveniently called elastic. It is then possible to obtain values for the modulus of elasticity of concrete. The modulus varies with several factors,[1,2] notably the strength of concrete, the age of concrete, the properties of aggregates and cement, and the definition of modulus of elasticity itself, whether tangent, initial, or secant modulus. Furthermore, the modulus may vary with the speed of load application and with the type of specimen, whether a cylinder or a beam. Hence it is almost impossible to predict with any accuracy the value of the modulus for a given concrete.

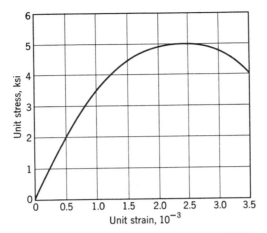

Fig. 2-1. Typical stress-strain curve for 5000-
psi concrete.

As an average value for concrete at 28 days old, and for compressive
stress up to about $0.40f_c'$, the secant modulus has been approximated by
the following empirical formulas.

A. The ACI Code for Reinforced Concrete specifies the following
empirical formula:
$$E_c = 1000f_c' \tag{2-1}$$

which is a simple approximation but apparently close enough only for f_c'
around 3000 psi, the usual strength for reinforced concrete. For concrete

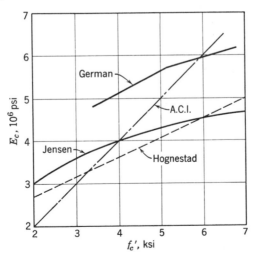

Fig. 2-2. Empirical formulas for E_c.

of higher strength, such as employed for prestressed construction, this formula seems to yield values of E_c somewhat too high.

B. Empirical formula proposed by Jensen:

$$E_c = \frac{6 \times 10^6}{1 + (2000/f_c')} \tag{2-2}$$

which gives more correct values for f_c' around 5000 psi.

C. Empirical formula proposed by Hognestad:

$$E_c = 1,800,000 + 460f_c' \tag{2-3}$$

which gives results similar to the last one.

D. Instead of a formula, German specifications for prestressed concrete give the following set of values.

Cube Strength kg/cm²	Corresponding Cylinder Strength, psi	Modulus of Elasticity, psi
300	3400	4,800,000
450	5100	5,700,000
600	6800	6,200,000

Plotting the above four proposals in Fig. 2-2, we can see that those of Jensen and Hognestad come quite close together but the ACI and the German values are relatively high. It is believed that the German values were intended to represent modulus used for computing instantaneous beam deflections while the others were based on measured strains from cylinder specimens. Authorities differ on the relation between the two kinds of moduli. Some tests indicate the agreement of these two values; others tend to show that the modulus for beams is higher than that for cylinders. Not too much work has been done for the modulus of elasticity of concrete in tension, but it is generally assumed that, before cracking, the average modulus over a length of several inches is the same as in compression, although the local modulus in tension is known to vary greatly,

Lateral Strains. Lateral strains are computed by Poisson's ratio.[2] Owing to Poisson's ratio effect, the loss of prestress is slightly decreased in biaxial prestressing. Poisson's ratio varies from 0.15 to 0.22 for concrete, averaging about 0.17.

Creep Strains. Creep of concrete is defined as its time-dependent deformation resulting from the presence of stress. A great deal of work has been done in this country on the creep or plastic flow of concrete.[3,4]

A brief summary of a comprehensive investigation carried out at the University of California extending over a period of 30 years is now presented.[5] For specimens of 4-in. diameter loaded in compression to 800 psi at 28 days and thereafter stored in air at 50% relative humidity and 70°F, the findings are:

1. Creep continued over the entire period, but the rate of change at the later ages was very small. Of the total creep in 20 years, 18–35% occurred in the first two weeks of loading, 40–70% within 3 months, and 60–83% within 1 year. The average values were 25, 55, and 76% respectively. Typical creep-time ratio curves with upper and lower limits are shown in Fig. 2-3 (from reference 5).

2. Creep increased with a higher water-cement ratio and with a lower aggregate-cement ratio, but was not directly proportional to the total water content of the mix.

3. Creep of concrete was appreciably greater for type IV (low-heat) than for the type I (normal) Portland cement. For type IV cement the creep was greater for the coarse grind than for the fine, but the reverse was true for the type I cement.

4. Creep of concrete was greatest for crushed sandstone aggregate, followed in descending order by basalt, gravel, granite, quartz, and limestone. The creep for sandstone concrete was more than double that for limestone concrete.

For ages from 28 to 90 days at time of loading, for stresses from 300 to 1200 psi, for storage conditions which ranged from air at 50% relative humidity to immersion in water, and for specimen diameters from 4 to 10 in., the following statements apply.

1. The older the specimen at the time of loading, the more complete the

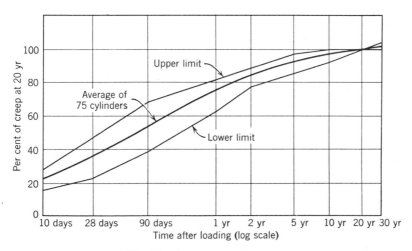

Fig. 2-3. Creep-time ratio curves.

hydration of cement, the less the creep. Those loaded at 90 days had less creep than those at 28 days, by roughly 10%.

2. The creep per unit of stress was only slightly greater at the high stresses than at the low stresses.

3. The total amount of creep strain at the end of 20 years ranged from 1 to 5 times the instantaneous deformations (averaging about 3 times) while the combined shrinkage or swelling and creep ranged from 1 to 11 times the instantaneous deformations, the low values occurring for storage in water or fog and for limestone aggregates.

4. The creep in air at 50% relative humidity was about 1.4 times that in air at 70% relative humidity and about 3 times that for storage in water.

5. Creep decreased as the size of specimen increased.

Only a limited amount of data is available concerning the creep of concrete under high stress.[6] Some of these data seem to indicate that when the sustained stress is in excess of about $\frac{1}{3}$ of the ultimate strength of concrete, the rate of increase of strain with stress tends to get higher. It is possible that this increase can become quite pronounced as the stress approaches the ultimate strength of the concrete.

Upon the removal of the sustained stress, part of the creep can be recovered in the course of time.[3] Generally, it takes a longer time to recover the creep than for the creep to take place. For the limited amount of data available, it can be stated that roughly 80 to 90% of the creep will recover during the same length of time that creep has been allowed to take place.

While most of the creep tests were run on axially loaded specimens, it is generally assumed that such data can be applied to the flexural creep of beams and slabs by considering each fiber as an axially loaded prism.

In Europe, the term creep coefficient C_c is employed to indicate the total strain δ_t (instantaneous plus creep strain) after a lengthy period of constant stress to the instantaneous strain δ_i immediately obtained upon the application of stress,[7] thus

$$C_c = \frac{\delta_t}{\delta_i}$$

This coefficient varies widely as reported from different tests, essentially because of the difficulty of separating shrinkage from creep. For purposes of design, it is considered safe to take C_c as around 3.0. For post-tensioned members, where the prestress is applied late, the coefficient could be a little less; for pre-tensioned members, where the prestress is applied at an early age, the coefficient could be a little more.

This same term, creep coefficient, is sometimes used to denote the ratio of the creep strain δ_c (excluding the instantaneous strain) to the instantaneous strain δ_i, thus

$$C_c = \frac{\delta_c}{\delta_i}$$

Hence care should be exercised to find out the exact meaning of "creep coefficient" whenever the term is employed. Using the first definition, the creep coefficient is about 2.5 at the end of one year for the curve in Fig. 2-3; using the second definition, that same coefficient is only 1.5.

Of the total amount of creep strain, it can be roughly estimated that about $\frac{1}{4}$ takes place within the first 2 weeks after application of prestress, another $\frac{1}{4}$ within 2 to 3 months, another $\frac{1}{4}$ within a year, and the last $\frac{1}{4}$ in the course of many years, Fig. 2-3.

There is good reason to believe that, for smaller members, creep as well as shrinkage takes place faster than for larger members. Upon the removal of stress, part of the creep can be recovered in the course of time. Again, owing to the difficulty of separating shrinkage from creep, the amount and speed of such recovery have not been accurately measured.

Shrinkage Strains. As distinguished from creep, shrinkage in concrete is its contraction due to drying and chemical changes dependent on time and on moisture conditions, but not on stresses. At least a portion of the shrinkage resulting from drying of the concrete is recoverable upon the restoration of the lost water. The magnitude of shrinkage strain also varies with many factors, and it may range from 0.0000 to 0.0010 and beyond. At one extreme, if the concrete is stored under water or under very wet conditions, the shrinkage may be zero. There may even be expansion for some types of aggregates and cements. At the other extreme, for a combination of certain cements and aggregates, and with the concrete stored under very dry conditions, as much as 0.0010 can be expected. Reference 5 lists test results showing the magnitude of shrinkage and its rate of occurrence as affected by various factors. Fig. 2-4 shows some typical shrinkage-time ratio curves taken from that reference.

Shrinkage of concrete is somewhat proportional to the amount of water employed in the mix. Hence, if minimum shrinkage is desired, the water-cement ratio and the proportion of cement paste should be kept to a minimum. Thus aggregates of larger size, well graded for minimum void, will need a smaller amount of cement paste, and shrinkage will be smaller.

The quality of the aggregates is also an important consideration. Harder and denser aggregates of low absorption and high modulus of elasticity will exhibit smaller shrinkage. Concrete containing hard limestone is believed to have smaller shrinkage than that containing granite, basalt, and sandstone of equal grade, approximately in that order. The

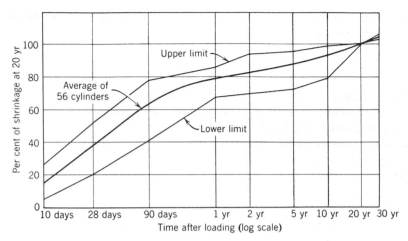

Fig. 2-4. Drying shrinkage-time ratio curves.

chemical composition of cement also affects the amount of shrinkage. For example, shrinkage is relatively small for cements high in tricalcium silicate and low in the alkalies and the oxides of sodium and potassium.

The amount of shrinkage varies widely, depending on the individual conditions. For the purpose of design, an average value of shrinkage strain would be about 0.0002 to 0.0004 for the usual concrete mixtures employed in prestressed construction. The rate of shrinkage depends chiefly on the weather conditions. Actual structures exposed to weather show measurable seasonal changes in the shrinkage of concrete—swelling during rainy seasons and shrinking during dry ones. If the concrete is left dry, there is reason to believe that most of the shrinkage would take place during the first 2 or 3 months. If it is always wet, there may be no shrinkage at all. When stored in air at 50% relative humidity and 70°F, there were indications[5] that the rate of occurrence of shrinkage is comparable to that of creep and that the magnitude of shrinkage is often similar to that of creep produced by a sustained stress of about 600 psi.

2-3   Concrete, Special Manufacturing Techniques

Most of the techniques for manufacturing good concrete, whether for plain or reinforced work, can be applied to prestressed concrete. However, they must be investigated for a few factors peculiar to prestressed concrete. First, they must not decrease the high strength required; next, they must not appreciably increase the shrinkage and creep; they must not produce adverse effects, such as inducing corrosion in the high-tensile wires.

Compacting the concrete by vibration is usually desirable and necessary. Either internal or external vibration may be used. In order to produce high-strength concrete without using an excessive amount of mortar, a low water-cement ratio and a low-slump concrete must be chosen. Such concrete cannot be well placed without compaction. There are only a few isolated applications in which concrete of high slump is employed and compaction may be dispensed with. But it will be found preferable to use at least a small amount of compaction for corners and around reinforcements and anchorages.

Good curing of concrete is most important. Too early drying of concrete may result in shrinkage cracks before the application of prestress. Besides, only by careful curing can the specified high strength be attained in concrete. In order to hasten the hardening process, steam curing is often resorted to in the precasting factory; it can also be employed in the field where the amount of work involved justifies the installation. When field work of casting must be carried out in cold weather, steam can profitably be used to raise the temperature of the ingredients and the placed concrete in order that high strength may be attained within a reasonable time.

Early hardening of the concrete is often desirable, either to speed plant production or to hasten field construction. Early high-strength concrete can be produced by any one of a number of techniques or combinations of techniques.[9] High early-strength cement or steam curing is commonly employed. Admixtures to accelerate the strength should be employed with caution. For example, calcium chloride, the most commonly used accelerator, even applied in normal amounts, will increase shrinkage. There is also some evidence that it may cause corrosion, which could be serious for the prestressing wires. When accelerators are used, care must also be taken not to have the initial set take place too soon.

Wetting admixtures to improve the workability of concrete may be found to be profitable, since they may permit easy placing of high-strength concrete without too high a cement content. Some of these admixtures tend to increase the shrinkage and may offset the advantage of saving cement. Each must be judged on its own merits in conjunction with the nature of the aggregates and cement. Air entrainment of 3 to 5% improves workability and reduces bleeding. When well-recognized, air-entraining agents are employed, there is no evidence of increased shrinkage or creep. Hence proper application of air entrainment is considered beneficial for prestressed concrete.

Concrete blocks have been frequently manufactured for prestressed beams.[10] Breaking up a beam into blocks reduces the individual weight and facilitates casting and handling. These blocks can be mass produced in a plant where rigid inspection and control can be effected. However, the high cost of labor involved in the handling and placing of the blocks may often offset the economy of obtained in their manufacturing.

For the joints between the blocks, two methods are employed. One is to grind the concrete surface for perfect bearing. This is usually a costly procedure. Another is to put mortars or grouts in between. By using high-early-strength cement for the grouts and applying a slight tension to the tendons to tighten the joints, a good bearing can be obtained. Full prestress is to be applied only after a few days.

Clay tiles of 10,000-psi strength have been prestressed to form beams and columns.[11] The use of ceramics of high strength, although not likely to be economical for massive structures, may prove desirable for light structures such as airplanes. Where resistance to high temperatures or to acid attacks is required, prestressed ceramics may prove to be an ideal material for certain structures.

2-4   Lightweight Aggregate Concrete

Since about 1955, lightweight concrete has been gaining in application to prestressed construction, especially in California. The main reason for using lightweight concrete is to reduce the weight of the structure, thus minimizing both the concrete and the steel required for carrying the load. This is especially important when the dead load is the major portion of the load on the structure, or when the weight of the member is a factor to be considered for transportation or erection.

It used to be a task to produce lightweight concrete of sufficient strength for prestressing, but this is no longer true. With experience in control and design of lightweight concrete mixes, 28-day cylinder strength of 5000 psi can generally be obtained with no difficulty, while 6000–7000 psi or more can be reached if desired. Strength at 1-day transfer of 3500 or 4000 psi is frequently attained by the use of high-early-strength cement and steam curing.

Data giving the physical and mechanical properties of lightweight concrete made with aggregates throughout the country are given in a paper by Shideler.[12] Those related to aggregates in the states of Texas and California are presented in two other papers.[13,14] While these test series did not yield identical values, some general observations can be made from them. When quantitative values are desired for a particular lightweight aggregate used in a given locality, it will be necessary to examine the aggregate and compare it with similar ones in the series, bearing in mind that exact values for either lightweight or regular weight concrete can be obtained only when extensive tests have been conducted for that particular aggregate, and the field conditions are under perfect control.

Fortunately, a certain amount of tolerance is permissible so that when properly designed and built, prestressed, lightweight concrete will behave satisfactorily.

One objection against lightweight concrete for prestressing is its low modulus of elasticity, which indicates more elastic shortening under the same unit stress. This means that there is a slightly higher loss of prestress in the steel. It also means that for cast-in-place structures, a greater elastic movement will take place under the application of the prestress. As a rough approximation, it may be said that the E_c for lightweight concrete averages about 55% the E_c for regular weight concrete. For f_c' between 3000 and 6000 psi, using 60% of Hognestad's formula for E_c (p. 38), we get a fairly good approximation,

$$E_c = 1,000,000 = 250f_c'$$

where $f_c' = $ cylinder strength of concrete at the time E_c is measured. However, E_c values may easily vary 20% either way from those given by the above formula, depending on various factors, especially the nature of the lightweight aggregate.

Poisson's ratio for lightweight concrete is apparently comparable to that for sand and gravel concrete; values between 0.15 and 0.25 have been reported with an average value of 0.19.[12]

Modulus of rupture for lightweight concrete averages about $0.15f_c'$ for 3000 psi strength and $0.12f_c'$ for 4500 psi strength, which are comparable to that for sand and gravel concrete. There was some evidence that, for much higher strength concrete, the modulus of rupture for lightweight concrete is lower than that for sand and gravel concrete.

The unit weight of lightweight concrete varies considerably, between 90 and 110 pcf. The addition of fine, natural sand would somewhat increase the unit weight and is also known to increase the workability and strength of the mix.

The shrinkage of lightweight concrete is apparently comparable to that of similar sand and gravel concrete.[13] However, some tests showed that it was slightly higher by 6–38%;[12] while other tests indicated that it was much lower.[14] Hence it is concluded that each lightweight aggregate must be studied by itself, but the chances are that they will have no more shrinkage than sand and gravel concrete.

Total creep strain in lightweight concrete is again comparable to that in sand and gravel concrete for specimens under the same sustained stress. Some have higher creep while others have less, probably by a maximum of some 20%, one way or the other. For detailed information, readers are referred to references 12, 13, and 14.

2-5   Self-stressing Cement

Types of cements that expand chemically after setting and during hardening are known as expansive or self-stressing cements. When these cements are used to make concrete with embedded steel, the steel is elongated by the expansion of the concrete. Thus the steel is prestressed in tension, which in turn produces compressive prestress in the concrete, resulting in what is known as chemical prestressing or self-stressed concrete.

Modern development of expansive cement started in France about 1940.[15] Its use for self-stressing has been investigated intensively in U.S.S.R. since 1953.[16] At the University of California, Berkeley, studies were directed toward the use of calcium sulfoaluminate admixtures for expansive cements in 1956, and their practical chemistry, manufacture, and potentials were analyzed and described in a paper by Klein and Troxell.[17] The physical properties of one such expansive cement were then further investigated, and results were presented in a paper by Klein, Karby, and Polivka,[18] while pilotary effort to study the structural possibilities of such expansive cement, when used for prestressing concrete, was described in another paper by Lin and Klein.[19] The testing of a self-stressed slab is shown in Fig. 2-5.

When concrete made with expanding cement is unrestrained, the amount of expansion produced by the chemical reaction between the cement and water could amount to 3–5%, and the concrete would then disintegrate by itself. When restrained either internally or externally with steel or other means, the amount of expansion can be controlled. By applying restraint in one direction, the growth in the other two orthogonal directions can be limited because of the crystalline nature of the hardened paste. The Russian self-stressing cement requires hydrothermal curing resulting in a quick setting, while the component developed in California requires water or fog curing under normal temperatures.

When high-tensile steel is used to produce the prestress, say corresponding to tensile stress at 150,000 psi and an E_s of 27,000,000 psi, an expansion of

$$\frac{150,000}{27,000,000} = 0.55\%$$

is required. For other stress levels, varying amounts of expansion will be required. For proper development of the bond between steel and concrete, mechanical end-anchorages might be necessary unless the steel has sufficient corrugation to transfer the stress.

Because of the expansion in all three directions, it seems difficult to use the cement for complicated structures cast in place, such as buildings.

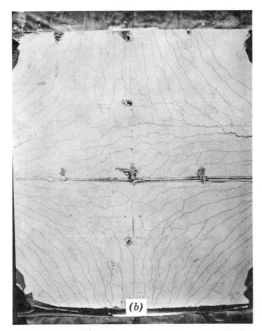

Fig. 2-5. (*a*) A concrete slab 6-ft square and 2-in. thick self-stressed by expanding cement is tested with air pressure applied through plastic bag placed under slab (University of California, Berkeley). Crack pattern is shown in (*b*). Slab supported at four corners.

However, for pressure pipes and pavements, where prestressing in at least two directions is desired, this type of chemical prestressing can easily be more economical than mechanical prestressing; this is also true for precast slabs, walls, and shells. However, no immediate economy is seen in the making of beams which require eccentric prestressing. Unless the beam soffit is precast by itself, curvature of the beam may result from steel embedded eccentrically in the beam.

Expanding cement has been successfully applied for many interesting projects, especially in France. When a concrete block of expanding cement is cast as the keystone for a concrete arch, it serves as a jack, producing the desired arch compensation to balance rib shrinkage and shortening. When used for underpinning buildings, it tends to lift the structure without jacking. It can be used for pressure grouting or for producing concrete pavements and slabs with no shrinkage joints.

While many problems remain yet unsolved concerning the use of expanding cement for self-stressing, such as the chemical and physical stability and exact control of the stresses and strains, extensive applications of expansive cement may not be too far in the future.

2-6   Steels for Prestressing

High-tensile steel is almost the universal material for producing prestress and supplying the tensile force in prestressed concrete. The obvious approach toward the production of high-tensile steel is by alloying, which permits the manufacture of such steels under normal operation. Carbon is an extremely economical element for alloying, since it is cheap and easy to handle.[20] Other alloys include manganese and silicon. Other approaches are by controlled cooling of the steels after rolling and by heat treatment such as quenching and tempering. Beneficial results have been obtained by quenching from the rolling heat at a given temperature and also by interrupting the quench at a given temperature.

The most common method for increasing the tensile strength of steel for prestressing is by cold-drawing, high-tensile steel bars through a series of dyes. The process of cold-drawing tends to realign the crystals, and the strength is increased by each drawing so that the smaller the diameter of the wires, the higher their ultimate unit strength. The ductility of wires, however, is somewhat decreased as a result of cold-drawing. A curve giving the typical variation of strength with diameter is shown in Fig. 2-6. The actual strength, of course, will vary with the composition and manufacture of the steel.

High-tensile steel for prestressing usually takes one of three forms: wires, strands, or bars. For post-tensioning, wires are widely employed;

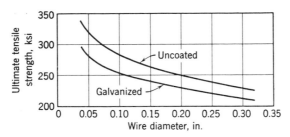

Fig. 2-6. Typical variation of wire strength with diameter.

they are grouped, in parallel, into cables. Strands are fabricated in the factory by twisting wires together, thus decreasing the number of units to be handled in the tensioning operations. Strands, as well as high-tensile rods, are also used for post-tensioning.

For pre-tensioning, 7-wire strands are almost exclusively used in the United States and have replaced much of wire pre-tensioning in other countries. Although strands cost slightly more than wires of the same tensile strength, its better bonding characteristics make it especially suitable for pre-tensioning.

While the ultimate strength of high-tensile steel can be easily determined by testing, its elastic limit or its yield point cannot be so simply ascertained, since it has neither a yield point nor a definite proportional limit. Various arbitrary methods have been proposed for defining the yield point of high-tensile steel, such as the 0.1% set, 0.2% set, 0.7% strain, or 1.0% strain. The more commonly accepted methods are probably the 0.2% set and the 1.0% strain.

2-7   Steel Wires

Wires for prestressing generally conform to ASTM Specification A-421 for "Uncoated Stress-relieved Wire for Prestressed Concrete." They are made from rods produced by the open hearth or electric-furnace process. After cold-drawn to size, wires are stress-relieved by a continuous heat treatment to produce the prescribed mechanical properties. The ladle analysis of the steel, according to ASTM A-421, shall conform to the following ranges.

Carbon	0.72–0.93%
Manganese	0.40–1.10%
Phosphorus, max.	0.040%
Sulfur, max.	0.050%
Silicon	0.10–0.35%

The tensile strength and the minimum yield strength (measured by the 1.0% total-elongation method) are prescribed in the following table, for the common sizes of wires.

TABLE 2-1

Tensile and Yield Strength for Prestressing Wires

Nom. Diameter in.	Remarks	Area, Sq in.	Min. Tensile Strength, psi	Min. Yield Point, psi
0.192	Gage No. 6	0.02895	250,000	200,000
0.196	5 mm	0.03017	250,000	200,000
0.250	$\frac{1}{4}$ in.	0.04909	240,000	192,000
0.276	7 mm	0.05983	235,000	188,000

A typical stress-strain curve for a stress-relieved $\frac{1}{4}$-in. wire conforming to the ASTM A-421 is shown in Fig. 2-7, with a typical modulus of elasticity between 28,000,000 and 30,000,000 psi. The specified minimum elongation in 10 in. is 4.0%, while a typical elongation at rupture is more likely from 5 to 6%.

Curves for a bar and for a 7-wire strand are also shown in Fig. 2-7. They are considered to be sufficiently accurate for the purposes of structural design. For computing exact elongations, it is advised that accurate stress-strain relationships be obtained from the manufacturer or by actual testing of specimens.

Wires are supplied in drums. They are cut to length and assembled either at the plant or in the field. Drum diameters are made as big as practicable, at least 5 to 6 ft, so that wires may be wound around them with the least permanent set. However, most wires when unwound from the drums do have a slight permanent set and require some straightening. Some wires also need a certain amount of degreasing and cleaning before placement, in order to ensure good bond with concrete. Loose rust or scale should be removed, but a firmly adherent rust film is considered advantageous in improving the bond.

In continental Europe, smooth wires 2 and 3 (sometimes 2.5) mm in diameter and corrugated wires of 4 and 5 mm are employed in pre-tensioning work. Small wires possess higher unit strength and furnish better bond, which is often vital in pre-tensioning. In order to save labor and anchorage costs, larger wires are preferred for post-tensioning. For the common systems, such as the Freyssinet and the Magnel, the anchorages are manufactured for the 5- and 7-mm wires. Such wires still possess high strength and there are fewer units to handle. Hence they have become popular and almost monopolize the post-tensioning field.

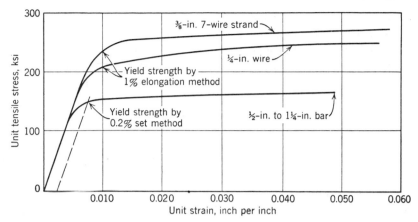

Fig. 2-7. Typical stress-strain curve for prestressing steels.

In England, wires are based on the British Imperial Gauge, No. 2 of which has a diameter of 0.276 in., exactly 7 mm, while No. 6 has a diameter of 0.192 in., which is very close to 5 mm. Hence gage Nos. 2 and 6 are sometimes called for in post-tensioning, while the exact equivalents of 7 and 5 mm (0.276 and 0.196 in., respectively) are also frequently employed. In Germany, corrugated wires with oval cross section are widely used for post-tensioning. These wires have areas of 20, 30, 35, and 40 mm², with Oval 40 having a major diameter of 11 mm and a minor diameter of 4.5 mm.

In this country, wires are manufactured according to the U.S. Steel Wire Gage, No. 2 of which has a diameter of 0.2625 in. and No. 6 has a diameter of 0.1920 in. Neither of these is the exact equivalent of the millimeter counterparts. Hence, when the European types of anchorages are adopted, 0.276-in. and 0.196-in. wires are often specified. For post-tensioning systems developed in the United States, ¼-in. wires have been most commonly incorporated. Where mechanical end anchorages are provided, ⅜-in. wires have been successfully employed for pretensioning.

2-8 Steel Strands

Strands for prestressing generally conform to ASTM Specification A-416 for "Uncoated Seven-wire Stress-relieved for Prestressed Concrete." While these specifications were intended for pre-tensioned, bonded, prestressed-concrete construction, they are also applicable to post-tensioned construction, whether of the bonded or the unbonded type. These seven-wire strands all have a center wire slightly larger than the outer six wires which enclose it tightly in a helix with a uniform pitch between 12 and 16 times the nominal diameter of the strand. After stranding, all strands are subjected to a stress-relieving continuous heat treatment to produce the prescribed mechanical properties.

Seven-wire strands commonly used for prestressing conform to the ASTM A-416 Specifications, having a guaranteed minimum ultimate strength of 250,000 psi. Their properties are listed in Appendix B-2. Since 1962, a stronger steel known as the 270K grade is being produced by various companies, with a guaranteed minimum ultimate strength of 270,000 psi. For the same nominal size, the 270K grade has more steel area than the ASTM A-416 grade and is about 15% stronger (see Appendix B-2).

A typical stress-strain curve for a stress-relieved $\frac{3}{8}$-in. 7-wire strand (ASTM A-416 grade) is shown in Fig. 2-7, which is also typical for strands of all sizes. For approximate calculations, a modulus of elasticity of 27,000,000 psi is often used for ASTM A-416 grade and 28,000,000 psi for 270K grade. The specified minimum elongation of the strand is 3.5% in a gage length of 24 in. at initial rupture, although typical values are usually in the range of 6%. When these strands are galvanized, they are about 15% weaker.

For post-tensioning, strands considerably larger than those listed in Table 2-1, up to $1\frac{11}{16}$ in. in diameter and above, are often employed. These strands possess lower unit strength since the wires are larger and more in number. When uncoated, the ultimate strength is about 220,000 psi, and when galvanized, it is around 200,000 psi. A typical set of such strands is listed in Appendix B under the Roebling System. The modulus of elasticity of these strands, when prestretched, ranges between 24,000,000 and 26,000,000 psi.

Recently, 3-wire stress-relieved strands up to $\frac{5}{16}$ in. in diameter are produced by the Leschen Wire Rope Division, H. K. Porter Co. of St. Louis, Missouri. These strands have the same diameter, steel area, and ultimate strength requirements as the corresponding 7-wire strands.

As fabricated, wire strands are several thousand feet long. When unwinding strands, care must be taken not to pull them. Strands can best be laid out by rolling them along the path. Pulling them might result in kinking and permanent twisting of the strands, which would be very difficult to undo.

2-9 Steel Bars

ASTM Specifications A-322 and A-29 are often applied to high-strength alloy steel bars. It is usually required that all such bars be proof-stressed to 90% of the guaranteed ultimate strength. Although the actual ultimate strength often reaches 160,000 psi, the specified minimum is generally set at 145,000 psi. A typical stress-strain curve for these bars is shown in Fig. 2-7 from which it can be noticed that a constant modulus of elasticity exists only for a limited range (up to about 80,000 psi stress) with a value between 25,000,000 and 28,000,000 psi.

The yield strength of high tensile bars is often defined by the 0.2% set method, as indicated in Fig. 2-7, where a line parallel to the initial tangent is drawn from the 0.002 strain, and its intersection with the curve is defined as the yield-strength point. Most specifications would call for a minimum yield strength at 130,000 psi, though actual values are often higher. Minimum elongation at rupture in 20 diameters length is specified at 4%, with minimum reduction of area at rupture at 25%. Common sizes and properties of high-tensile rods for prestressing are listed in Appendix B-8.

High-tensile bars are available with length up to 80 ft. Because of difficulty in shipping, the length may have to be further limited. But sleeve couplers are available to splice the bars to any desired length. These couplers have tapered threads in order to develop very nearly the full strength of the bars. They have outside diameters about twice that of the bar and a length about 4 times its diameter.

Auxiliary reinforcement using nonprestressed steel is commonly employed in prestressed construction. Steel of almost any strength will serve the purpose when properly designed. Generally, reinforcing bars conform to ASTM Specifications A-15, A-16, and A-305, and welded wire mesh conforms to ASTM Specification A-185.

2-10 Fiberglass Tendons

Fiberglass is manufactured by drawing fluid glass into fine filaments. The possible use of fiberglass for prestressing has been under investigation for some years.[21,22,23]

Although fiberglass has not yet been commercially applied in prestressed-concrete construction, it does possess certain superior qualities that indicate high promise for prestressing. An ultimate tensile strength of 1,000,000 psi is quite commonly obtained. Values as high as 5,000,000 psi have been reported for individual silica fibres 0.00012 in. in diameter, it being known that the strength varies approximately inversely as the diameter of the fiber.

Fiberglass can be made in three forms: parallel chords, twisted strands, and parallel fibers embedded in plastic. The last form in the shape of fiberglass rods is considered most suitable for prestressing because of its relative simplicity for handling, gripping, and anchoring. At Princeton

University, three types of resin have been tried out as bonding agents in the manufacture of fiberglass rods: polyester, epoxy, and polyamide resins. To date, the rods laminated with epoxy resins have appeared to be superior. A short-duration tensile strength has been obtained in excess of 220,000 psi, based on the gross area of the rod.

Another advantage of fiberglass is its low modulus of elasticity, which ranges from 6,000,000 to 10,000,000 psi. With its high stress and low modulus, the percentage of loss of prestress would be quite small. Other advantages claimed for this material are high resistance to acids and alkalies and the ability to withstand high temperature. However, some major problems must be solved before it can be applied in practice.

1. The static fatigue limit, that is, the long-time ultimate strength of fiberglass rods as opposed to the short-time ultimate strength. This is an important problem since it is known that the duration of loading has a pronounced effect on the ultimate strength.

2. The dynamic fatigue limit of fiberglass or fiberglass rods, although there is some evidence to indicate that this may not be a serious problem.

3. The chemical stability of fiberglass such as its reaction to the surrounding concrete, especially under wet conditions.

4. The best methods of fabricating cords from fiberglass to obtain an even distribution of stress so as to increase the ratio of the strength of cords to the strength of individual fibers. The minimizing of shearing deformation of the laminating material, since such deformation could result in the breaking of the outer fibers with an inner core of fibers remaining intact.

5. The design of suitable end anchorages, since the brittle material is liable to fail in the grip under the effect of stress concentrations and combined stresses.

If these problems can be solved, there still remains a last hurdle: the economics of the application of the material in competition with high-tensile steel, which is being produced in large quantities and at relatively low cost. On the other hand, it is conceivable that the special properties of fiberglass might make it desirable in special situations.

2-11 Auxiliary Materials—Grouting

Among the special auxiliary materials required for prestressed concrete are those for the provision of proper conduits for the tendons. For pre-tensioning, no such conduits are necessary. For post-tensioning, there are two types of conduits, one for bonded, another for unbonded prestressing.

When the tendons are to be bonded, generally by grouting, the conduits can be made of aluminum, steel, tin, or other metal sheathing or tubes.

For small cables, corrugated sheet-metal pipes are often employed. For example, the Freyssinet system employs metal hose with outside diameters varying from $1\frac{1}{8}$ to $1\frac{5}{8}$ in. for 8 to 18 wires, with thickness of hose about $\frac{1}{16}$ in.

It is also possible to form the duct by withdrawing steel tubing or rod before the concrete hardens. More frequently, the duct is formed by withdrawing extractable rubber cores buried in the concrete. Several hours after the completion of concreting, these cores can be withdrawn without much effort, because the lateral shrinkage of the rubber under a pull helps to tear the rubber away from the surrounding concrete. In order that the rubber cores may remain straight during concreting, they are stiffened internally by inserting steel pipes or rods into axial holes provided in the rubber. To maintain the cores in position during concreting, transverse steel rods are placed under and over them at 3- to 4-ft intervals. For the Magnel system, for example, rubber cores approximately $2\frac{1}{8}$ by 2 in. and $2\frac{1}{8}$ by 3 in., to accommodate 0.196-in. wires, are obtainable; $2\frac{1}{2}$ in. by $2\frac{1}{2}$ in. and $2\frac{1}{2}$ in. by $3\frac{1}{2}$ in. cores are used for 0.276-in. wires. The combinations of these sizes make possible various numbers of wires in a cable. Sometimes, rubber tubes inflated from their normal diameter can be substituted for the above rubber cores. These tubes can then be deflated and withdrawn.

When the tendons are to be unbonded, plastic or heavy paper sheathing is frequently used, and the tendons are properly greased to facilitate tensioning and to prevent corrosion. Rust inhibitors are usually added to the grease together with additional compounds to ensure its uniform consistency in extremes of temperature. Asbestos fibres are often added to the grease to hold it together during application. Plastic or paper sheathing should be wound with wires or tapes at frequent intervals. Plastic tubes of the split type should be properly overlapped and taped along the seams, so as to seal them against any leakage of mortars, which might bind the tendons to the tubes. When papers are spirally wrapped around the tendons, care should be exercised in wrapping so as to avoid jamming of the papers when the tendons are tensioned.

For bonding the tendons to the concrete after tensioning (in the case of post-tensioning), cement grout is injected, which also serves to protect the steel against corrosion. Entry for the grout into the cableway is provided by means of holes in the anchorage heads and cones, or pipes buried in the concrete members. The injection can be applied at one end of the member until it is forced out of the other end. For longer members, it can be applied at both ends until forced out of a center vent. Either ordinary portland cement or high-early-strength cement may be used for the grout. Coarse sand is preferred for bond and strength, but sufficient fineness is necessary considering the limited space through which the grout has to pass. To ensure good bond for small conduits, grouting under pressure is desirable; however, care should be taken to ensure that the bursting effect of the pressure on the walls of the cable enclosure can be safely resisted. Machines for mixing and injecting the grouts are commercially available.

Where larger space between the wires is obtained, such as in a Magnel cable, a 1:1 cement-sand mix is often used with a water-cement ratio of about 0.5 by volume, and a pressure of a few psi may be sufficient for short cables. Where the space is limited, as in a Freyssinet or Strescon cable, neat cement paste with about the same water-cement ratio should be employed. When it is desired to save cement on a big job, fine sand of $\frac{1}{64}$-in. grain size can be added. The water : cement : sand proportion should be about $1.0 : 1.3 : 0.7$ by volume. Grouting pressure generally ranges from 80 to 100 psi. After the grout has discharged from the far end, that end is plugged and the pressure is again applied at the injecting end to compact the grout. It is also good practice to wash the cables with water before grouting is started, the excess water being removed with compressed air.

Because of the difficulties frequently encountered during grouting, the procedures and problems were discussed at length in several papers presented at the Third Congress of the Federation de la Precontrainte held at Berlin, 1958. These papers are summarized by G. F. Janssonius in his general report on "Progress in Site Techniques," also published in the proceedings of the above Congress. Readers are referred to a paper by Professor Milos Polivka[24] presented at the FIP-RILEM Symposium on Injection Grout for Prestressed Concrete held at Trondheim, Norway, 1961. This paper describes in detail the materials and techniques used for grouting.

The Prestressed Concrete Institute has published its "Tentative Recommended Practices for Grouting Post-tensioned Prestressed Concrete" in its Journal June 1960. "A Report of Field Experience in Grouting Post-tensioning Cables" also appears in the August 1962 issue of the *PIC Journal*.

References

1 S. Walker, "Modulus of Elasticity of Concrete," *Proc. Am. Soc. Test. Mat.*, Part II, 1919.
2 R. E. Davis and G. E. Troxell, "Modulus of Elasticity and Poisson's Ratio for Concrete and the Influence of Age and Other Factors upon These Values," *Proc. Am. Soc. Test. Mat.*, 1929. Also see A. D. Ross, "Experiments on the Creep of

Concrete under Two-Dimensional Stressing," *Magazine of Concrete Research*, June 1954.

3   R. E. Davis and H. E. Davis, "Flow of Concrete under Action of Sustained Loads," *J. Am. Conc. Inst.*, March 1931 (*Proc.*, Vol. 27), pp. 837–901.

4   H. R. Staley and D. Peabody, Jr., "Shrinkage and Plastic Flow of Prestressed Concrete," *J. Am. Conc. Inst.*, January 1946 (*Proc.*, Vol. 42), pp. 229–244.

5   G. E. Troxell, J. M. Raphael, and R. E. Davis, "Long-time Creep and Shrinkage Tests of Plain and Reinforced Concrete," *Proc. Am. Soc. Test. Mat.*, 1958.

6   "Creep of Concrete under High Intensity Loading," *Concrete Laboratory Report* No. C-820, Division of Engineering Laboratories, Bureau of Reclamation, U.S. Dept. of the Interior, April 10, 1956.

7   G. Magnel, "Creep of Steel and Concrete in Relation to Prestressed Concrete," *J. Am. Conc. Inst.*, February 1948 (*Proc.*, Vol. 44), pp. 485–500; also *Prestressed Concrete*, McGraw-Hill Book Co., New York, 1954.

8   R. E. Davis and G. E. Troxell, "Properties of Concrete and Their Influence on Prestressed Design," *J. Am. Conc. Inst.*, January 1954 (*Proc.*, Vol. 50), pp. 381–391.

9   P. Klieger, "Early High-strength Concrete for Prestressing," *Proceedings World Conference on Prestressed Concrete*, San Francisco, 1957.

10 R. H. Bryan, "New Designs Cut Prestressed Block-Beam Cost," *Eng. News-Rec.*, April 22, 1954, p. 32.

11 "Prestressed-Tile Roof and Girders Make All-Tile Building Possible," *Eng. News-Rec.*, April 15, 1954, p. 39.

12 J. J. Shideler, "Lightweight Aggregate Concrete for Structural Use," *J. Am. Conc. Inst.*, October 1957, (*Proc.*, Vol. 54), p. 299–328.

13 T. R. Jones, Jr. and H. K. Stephenson, "Properties of Lightweight Related to Prestressing," *Proceedings World Conference on Prestressed Concrete*, San Francisco, 1957.

14 C. H. Best and M. Polivka, "Creep of Lightweight Concrete," *Magazine of Concrete Research*, November 1959, pp. 129–134.

15 H. Lossier, "L'Autocontrainte des betons par les cimente expansifs," *Memoires Societe des Ingenieurs Civils de France*, March, April 1949, pp. 189–225; also, H. Lossier, "The Self-stressing of Concrete by Expanding Cement," *C.A.C.A.*, London.

16 V. V. Mikhailov, "New Developments in Self-stressed Concrete," *Proceedings World Conference on Prestressed Concrete*, San Francisco, 1957.

17 A. Klein and G. E. Troxell, "Studies of Calcium Sulfoaluminate Admixtures for Expansive Cements," *ASTM* (*Proc.*, Vol. 58), 1958, pp. 986–1008.

18 A. Klein, T. Karby, and M. Polivka, "Properties of an Expansive Cement for Chemical Prestressing," *J. Am. Conc. Inst.*, June 1961.

19 T. Y. Lin, and A. Klein, "Chemical Prestressing of Concrete Elements Using Expanding Cements," *J. Am. Conc. Inst.*, 1963.

20 Alois Legat, "Metallurgical, Metallographical and Economic Problems in the Manufacture of Prestressed Reinforcing Steels," extract of final report of *RILEM Symposium*, Liege, July 1958.

21 I. A. Rubinsky and A. Rubinsky, "A Preliminary Investigation of the Use of Fiberglas for Prestressed Concrete," *Magazine of Concrete Research*, pp. 71–78, September 1954.

22 Frank J. Maguire, III, *Report on Further Investigation Concerning the Feasibility of the Use of Fiberglass Tendons in Prestressed Concrete Construction*, M.S. Thesis, Princeton University, 1960.

23   Von Stanislaw Kajfasz, "Technische Probleme bei der Verwendung von Glasfaser als Bewehrung fuer Spannbeton," *Papers Third Congress of the Federation Internationale de la Precontrainte*, Berlin, 1958.
24   Milos Polivka, "Grouts for Post-tensioned Prestressed Concrete Members," *Journal of the Prestressed Concrete Institute*, 1961.

prestressing systems;   *3*
end anchorages

3-1 Introduction

On account of the existence of different systems and their patents for tensioning and anchoring the tendons, the situation appears a little confusing to a beginner in the design and application of prestressed concrete. Actually, present practice in this country does not require of the designer a thorough knowledge of the details of all systems or even of the system that he intends to use for his particular job. In order to encourage competitive bidding, the engineer often specifies only the amount of effective prestressing force required so that the bid is open to all systems of prestressing. However, he should have a general knowledge of the methods available and keep it in mind while dimensioning his members so that the tendons of several systems can be well accommodated. Sometimes he must compute the actual size and number of tendons for his members in order to obtain feasible arrangements and an accurate estimate of the quantities of materials. A knowledge of the details of end anchorages and the tensioning jacks is required to design the ends of his members so as to be ready to house the anchorages and to receive the jacks.

In the United States alone, there are well over one hundred patents and patents pending on various systems of prestressing.[1] Many of these patents have never been commercially or economically applied, but many others are still being developed. It would now take the job of a specialized lawyer in addition to a specialized engineer to look into the matter, or to apply for and obtain a new patent. The situation is further complicated by the development of similar methods in other countries having reciprocal patent arrangements with ours, although, in general, any patents obtained abroad must be at least registered in this country before being effective here. These problems, however, are only for the inventors to worry about. The practicing engineer, who simply wants to design some structures of prestressed concrete, is free to specify and design for any system without studying the intrigues of patent rights. In fact, the owner of the structure would not have to pay any direct royalty to the patent holder. The royalty is indirectly included in the bid price for the supplying of prestressing steel and anchorages, which sometimes also includes the furnishing of equipment for prestressing and some technical supervision for jacking. Owing to the keen competition already existing in this country in the field of prestressing, the matter of patent royalty is not a serious cost item for the owner. In order to bid on a structure embodying prestressed concrete, the general contractor usually approaches the various prestressing concerns for sub-bids. Thus the standard method of bidding applicable to reinforcing steel and other trades is extended to prestressing work.

In some other countries, the conditions are different. In Germany, for example, there is a tendency not to accept any general contractor for a job employing prestressed concrete unless he himself has devised a system of prestressing. As a result, each contractor is forced to devise some system of his own, and he tends to charge an excessive royalty for his method if his competitors want to use it. In France and Belgium, for historic and other reasons, one or two prestressing systems are much more widely applied than the others; hence the direction of growth tends toward the development of these particular systems rather than a multiple approach.

The basic principles of prestressing cannot be patented, but the details of its application can. There are some patents on the methods of construction, such as special production of prestressed slabs or pipes, using processes different from the ordinary. Fortunately, these patents are based more on the construction procedures than on the design features and seldom affect the designing work of the engineer. Furthermore, it is not good policy for an engineer to try to hold a monopoly on his design. Hence engineers are seldom obstructed from using any design in prestressed concrete.

The so-called prestressing system comprises essentially a method of stressing the steel combined with a method of anchoring it to the concrete, including perhaps some other details of operation.[2] Hence most of the patents on prestressed concrete are based on either or both of the following two operational details: (1) the methods of applying the prestress; (2) the details of end anchorages. In addition to these, sometimes the size and number of wires also form part of the patented process, although most patents contain a variety of combinations of these. Linear-prestressing systems known to the author are grouped and classified in Table 3-1. Systems for circular prestressing will be discussed in Chapter 13.

Since it is almost impossible and perhaps also unnecessary to discuss all these systems, only the more prominent and common ones will be described in this chapter. The eventual success of each system will depend on a number of conditions, the chief criterion being its economy and

TABLE 3-1

Linear Prestressing Systems

Type	Classification	Description		Name of System	Country of Origin
Pre-tensioning	Methods of stressing	Against buttresses or stressing beds		Hoyer	Germany
		Against central steel tube		Shorer Chalos	U.S. France
		Continuous stressing against molds		Continuous wire winding	U.S.S.R.
		Electric current to heat steel		Electrothermal	U.S.S.R.
	Methods of anchoring	During prestressing	Wires	Various wedges	
			Strands	Strandvise	U.S.
		For transfer of prestress	Bond, for strands and small wires		Europe, U.S.
			Corrugated clips, for big wires	Dorland	U.S.
Post-tensioning	Methods of stressing	Steel against concrete		Most systems	
		Concrete against concrete		Leonhardt	Germany
				Billner	U.S.
		Expanding cement		Lossier	France
		Electrical prestressing		Billner	U.S.
		Bending steel beams		Preflex	Belgium
	Methods of anchoring	Wires, by frictional grips		Freyssinet	France
				Magnel	Belgium
				Morandi	Italy
				Holzmann	Germany
				Preload	U.S.
		Wires, by bearing		B.B.R.V.	Switzerland
				General prestressing or Prescon	U.S.
				Texas P.I.	U.S.
		Wires, by loops and combination of methods		Billner	U.S.
				Monierbau	Germany
				Huttenwerk Rheinhausen	Germany
				Leoba	Germany
				Leonhardt	Germany
		Bars, by bearing and by grips		Lee-McCall	England
				Stressteel	U.S.
				Stress rods	U.S.
				Finsterwalder	Germany
				Dywidag	Germany
				Karig	Germany
				Polensky and Zollner	Germany
				Wets	Belgium
				Bakker	Holland
		Strands, by bearing		Roebling	U.S.
				Wayss and Freytag	Germany
		Strands, by friction grips		CCL	England
				Freyssinet	U.S.
				Anderson	U.S.
				Atlas	U.S.

convenience. It is difficult to predict whether new and better systems, or major improvements of existing ones, may not be developed in the future, but it does seem that most of the practical ideas have been embodied, in one form or another, in the systems mentioned.

3-2 Pre-tensioning Systems and End Anchorages

A simple way of stressing a pre-tensioned member is to pull the tendons between two bulkheads anchored against the ends of a stressing bed. After the concrete hardens, the tendons are cut loose from the bulkheads and the prestress is transferred to the concrete. Such stressing beds are often used in a laboratory and sometimes in a prestressing factory. For this set-up, both the bulkheads and the bed must be designed to resist the prestress and its eccentricity.

For mass production of pre-tensioned members, an extension of the above method often known as the Hoyer system is generally used. It consists of stretching the wires between two bulkheads some distance apart, say several hundred feet, Fig. 3-1. The bulkheads can be independently anchored to the ground, or they can be connected by a long stressing bed. Such a bed is costly, but it can serve two additional purposes if properly designed. First, intermediate bulkheads can be inserted in the bed so that shorter wires can be tensioned. Secondly, the bed can be designed to resist vertical loads, thus permitting the prestressing of bent tendons.

With this Hoyer process, several members can be produced along one line, by providing shuttering between the members and concreting them separately. When the concrete has set sufficiently to carry the prestress, the wires are freed from the bulkheads, and the prestress is transferred to the members through bond between steel and concrete or through special pre-tensioning anchorages at the ends of members. This long-line production method is economical and is used in almost all pre-tensioning factories in the United States. Various means have been devised for deflecting the tendons up and down along the length of the bed. One method is shown in Fig. 3-2.

Devices for gripping the pre-tensioning wires to the bulkheads are usually made on the wedge and friction principles.[3] A typical split cone wedge is shown in Fig. 3-3a, made from a tapered conical pin. The pin, drilled axially and tapped, is cut in half longitudinally to form a pair of wedges. These grips can be used for single wires as well as for twisted wire strands. Another grip is shown in Fig. 3-3b, made from a conical pin on which a flat surface has been machined and serrated. The pin fits into a conical hole in a block and holds the wire between the serrated face and the block. In addition, there are quick release grips, which are more

Fig. 3-1. A pre-tensioning yard in the United States (Algonquin plant, Material Service Division of General Dynamics, Illinois).

complicated and more costly, but effect a great saving in time. If the wires are to be held in tension only for short periods, these quick-release grips may be found to be more economical. Quick-release grips for holding strands have also been manufactured in this country, for example, the Strandvises, Fig. 3-4, by the Reliable Electric Company of Illinois, and the Europa

Fig. 3-2. Deflecting tendons (harping) in a pre-tensioning bed, Ben C. Gerwick, Inc., Petaluma, Calif.

anchor grips distributed by the International Prestressing Corporation in Los Angeles.

The dependence on bond to transmit prestress between steel and concrete necessitates the use of small wires to ensure good anchorages. Wires greater than about $\frac{1}{8}$ in. are used only if they are waved along their length or if they are corrugated. In any case, a certain length of transfer is required to develop the bond. Should there be insufficient length of transfer, for example, when cracks occur near the end of a beam, the bond may be broken and the wires may slip. A more reliable method is to add mechanical end anchorage to the pre-tensioned wires. One method developed in San Diego, California, is the Dorland anchorage, which can be gripped on to the wires or strands at any point, thus supplying positive mechanical anchorage in addition to the bond. The clips are gripped to the tendon under high pressure, and the edges of the clips are then welded together at several points. It should be noted that such anchorage makes possible the use of bigger tendons and sometimes permits an earlier transfer of prestress, resulting in considerable economy in the laying and stressing operations.

The Shorer system[3] involves an ingenious feature, doing away with

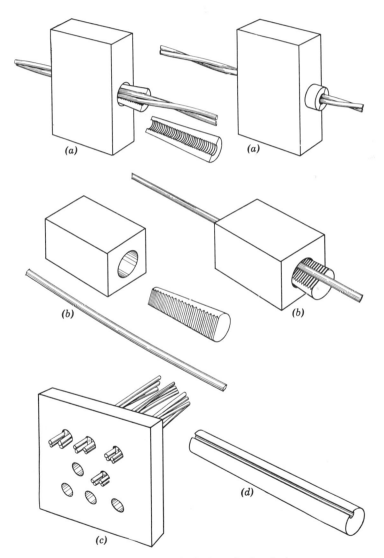

Fig. 3-3. Some typical wire gripping devices.

Fig. 3-4. Assembly of a strandvise for gripping pre-tensioning strands (Reliable Electric Co., Franklin Park, Illinois).

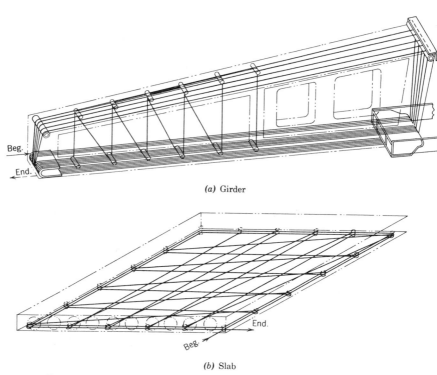

(a) Girder

(b) Slab

Fig. 3-5. Different types of continuous prestressing in the U.S.S.R.[5]

stressing beds and bulkheads. In their stead, a central tube of high-strength steel carries the prestress from the surrounding wires, and the entire assembly is placed in position and concreted. After the concrete has set and attained a certain strength, the tube is removed and the prestress is transferred to the concrete by bond. The hole left by the tube is then filled with grout. This method has not found wide application in this country. In France, the method is credited to Chalos and is known as the Chalos system.

As a direct contrast to the long-line method, the individual mold method for pre-tensioning has found wide application in the U.S.S.R. and is occasionally used in the United States and Germany. Instead of moving the process to the product as in the case of the long-line method, the product is moved to the process when using the individual mold method, which is somewhat similar to the assembly-line method in automobile production.

The individual mold method adapts itself to relatively complicated patterns of the path of prestressing, such as prestressing in two directions for slabs or for trusses. It is also convenient for small products such as railway ties. Fig. 3-5 shows different types of continuous prestressing used in the U.S.S.R. for girders, slabs, railway ties, and trusses. The continuous

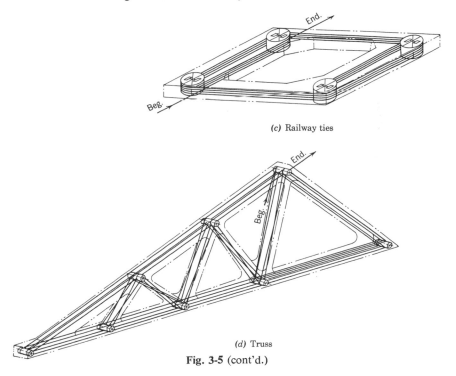

(c) Railway ties

(d) Truss

Fig. 3-5 (cont'd.)

Fig. 3-6. A pre-tensioning plant in the U.S.S.R. with machine in foreground.

prestressing is essentially carried out by two types of machines: one has a turntable with a stationary feeder head, Fig. 3-6, and the other consists of a stationary table with a movable feeder head. The prestressing wire is fed to the mold under controlled tension force and is laid out in a predetermined pattern as it is weaved around steel pegs fixed to the mold.[5,6]

In the United States, the individual mold method is being used by the Material Service Division of General Dynamics to produce large hollow-core sections known as Dynacores (Fig. 16-1). In this method pretensioning is applied to the section both longitudinally and transversely.

3-3 Post-Tensioning, Tensioning Methods

The methods of tensioning can be classified under four groups: (1) mechanical prestressing by means of jacks; (2) electrical prestressing by application of heat; (3) chemical prestressing by means of expanding cement; (4) miscellaneous.

Mechanical Prestressing. In both pre-tensioning and post-tensioning, the most common method for stressing the tendons is jacking. In post-tensioning, jacks are used to pull the steel against the hardened concrete;

in pre-tensioning, to pull it against some bulkheads or molds. Hydraulic jacks are often used, because of their high capacity and the relatively small force required to apply the pressure. Occasionally, screwjacks are used when the force to be exerted does not exceed about 5 tons. Levers may be found convenient only when very small wires are to be tensioned individually.

When hydraulic jacks are employed, one or two rams are worked by one pump unit with a control valve in the pipe circuit, Fig. 3-7. The capacity of jacks varies greatly, from about 3 tons up to 100 tons or more. A strand of $1\frac{1}{2}$-in. nominal diameter may require an initial tensioning of 90 tons; it may then be desirable to have two jacks of 60-ton rated capacity for the tensioning, for an ample margin of safety, Fig. 3-8. For some prestressing systems, jacks are specially designed and rated to perform the job of tensioning particular cables containing a given number and size of wires. For some systems, any jack of sufficient capacity can be employed, provided suitable grip for the tendon is available. Care must be taken to see

Fig. 3-7. Electric pump operating a hydraulic jack to stress a Prescon cable (note the insertion of shims).

Fig. 3-8. Two rams, each of 60-ton rated capacity, apply a prestress of 85 tons on a 1½-in. Roebling cable.

that the jack can be properly mounted on the end bearing plates, and that there is enough room at the tensioning ends to accommodate the jacks.

It is not possible to compile all the data necessary for designing each system of prestressing. New systems are being developed and existing ones are being modified from time to time. Engineers interested in a particular system should obtain the company's pamphlets or consult its representatives for particular details. In order to facilitate such consultation, the addresses of some prestressing systems in this country are listed in Appendix B.

Systems of jacking vary from pulling one or two wires up to several hundred wires at a time. The Clifford-Gilbert system in England employs a small screwjack weighing about 20 lb which pulls one wire at a time and can be easily handled. In the Magnel system, tensioning is carried out by a

Fig. 3-9. The Magnel jack, stressing two wires at a time.

hydraulic jack which pulls two wires at a time by means of a temporary wire grip, Fig. 3-9. The jacks are designed for both 0.196-in. and 0.276-in. wires. The frame for the jack is made big enough so that several pairs of wires may be tensioned with the jack remaining in the same working position.

The Freyssinet double-acting jack pulls up to 18 wires or 12 strands at a time, Fig. 3-10. The wires are wedged around the jack casing and are stretched by the main ram which reacts against the embedded anchorage. When the required tension is reached, an inner piston pushes the plug into the anchorage to secure the wires; the pressure on the main ram and that on the inner piston are then released gradually, and the jack is removed

Jacks for the Roebling system are fitted with threaded bars to be screwed

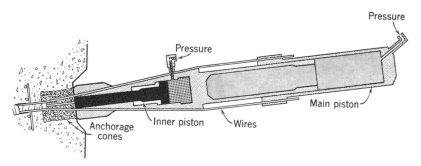

Fig. 3-10. The Freyssinet double-acting jack.

Fig. 3-11. Jacking Stressteel bars for a bridge girder (courtesy Stressteel Corp.).

into the strand fitting for tensioning. Jacks for the Lee-McCall or Stressteel system are provided with an adjustable connector to accommodate various bar diameters, Fig. 3-11.

Some hints regarding the practice of jacking may be helpful for designers as well as for supervising engineers. In order to minimize creep in steel and also to reduce frictional loss of prestress, tendons are sometimes jacked a few per cent above their specified initial prestress. Overjacking is also necessary to compensate for slippage and take-up in the anchorage at the release of jacking pressure. When tendons are long or appreciably curved, jacking should be done from two ends. During the process of jacking, anchorage screw nuts and wedges should be run all the way home and seated moderately tight against the end plates. This may help to avoid serious damages in the event of a wire breakage or a sudden failure of the jacks.

Pressure gages for jacks are calibrated either to read the pressure on the piston or to read directly the amount of tension applied to the tendon. It is usual practice to measure the elongation of steel to be checked against the gage indications. The amount of frictional loss can be estimated from the discrepancy between the measured and the expected elongations.

When several tendons in a member are to be tensioned in succession, care should be taken to pull them in the proper order so that no serious eccentric loading will result during the process. If necessary, some tendons may have to be tensioned in two steps so as to reduce the eccentric loading on the member during tensioning.

Instead of being attached to the steel, the jacks are sometimes inserted between two portions of concrete to force them apart, one against the other. Notably, this procedure is used in two systems: the Leonhardt system of Germany, and the Billner system of the United States. In the Leonhardt system,[7] one reinforced-concrete anchor block is poured at each end of a structural portion, and prestressing cables are wound around the blocks to be stressed all at once by hydraulic jacks inserted between the blocks and the main body of the structure, Fig. 3-12. The advantage of this method lies in the reduction of the number of stressing operations. But naturally much heavier jacks are required. In order to reduce the cost of the heavy jacks, built-in ones of reinforced concrete are made on the job. They are eventually left in the structure.

The reinforced-concrete jack of the Leonhardt system is made of several metal cylinders serving as pistons. The ends of the cylinders are filled with concrete and fixed horizontally to the vertical surface of the anchorage block. Over each piston is placed an outer metal sleeve surrounded by a

Fig. 3-12. Continuous cable and end jacking blocks for the Leonhardt system.

coil of heavy reinforcing steel, which forms the cylinder. These jacks are interconnected by tubes and actuated by water pressure which forces the end blocks away from the major portion of the structure, thus prestressing the entire structure in one operation. When the desired elongation of the cables has been attained, cement grout is pumped in to fill the jacks and the gap left by the jacking is filled with concrete. Elongation of the wires around the loop is facilitated by special wax lubrication between the wires and the contact surface. The lubricant melts under pressure and offers very little friction during tensioning.

In contrast to the Leonhardt system, which is specifically designed for large structures, the Billner system[8] is better suited to small ones. In the Billner system, the member is cast in two portions, split at the midspan. Jacks separated by a comblike partition are inserted between the two portions. Concrete is cast on both sides of the partition, forming two separate units. The prestressing wires pass through the slots provided in the partition plate and are not bonded to the concrete except at the ends. In this system, jacking is done near the midspan and between the concrete; hence the end anchorages only have to perform the task of anchoring, which is simply achieved by looping the tendons around the concrete. In spite of the saving of the more expensive end anchorages otherwise required for post-tensioning, this method has not yet been found to be commercially economical.

Electrical Prestressing. The electrical method of prestressing[9] dispenses with the use of jacks altogether. The steel is lengthened by heating with electricity. This electrical process is a post-tensioning method where the concrete is allowed to harden fully before the application of prestress. It employs smooth reinforcing bars coated with thermoplastic material such as sulfur or low-melting alloys and buried in the concrete like ordinary reinforcing bars but with protruding threaded ends. After the concrete has set, an electric current of low voltage but high amperage is passed through the bars. When the steel bars heat and elongate, the nuts on the protruding ends are tightened against heavy washers. When the bars cool, the prestress is developed and the bond is restored by the resolidification of the coating.

This method, as originally developed, was intended for steel bars stretched to about 28,000 psi, which requires a temperature of about 250°F. Owing to the high percentage of loss of prestress for steel with such a low prestress, and to other expenses involved in the process, this method has been found to be uneconomical in competition with prestressing using high-tensile steel. It has not been applied to high-tensile steel because a much higher temperature would be required for its prestressing. Such a high temperature could involve a number of complications, including possible damage to some physical properties of high-tensile steel.

In Russia, on the other hand, the electrothermal method of pre-tensioning prestressing has found wide usage in pre-tensioning. Electric current is used to heat and expand prestressing steel, which is then held at the ends. As the steel cools and tends to shrink, it is stressed. A combination of electrical and mechanical stressing is also employed in the U.S.S.R.[10]

Chemical Prestressing. As described previously, the chemical reactions taken place in expansive cements can stress the embedded steel which in turn compresses the concrete. This is often termed self-stressing, but can also be called chemical prestressing. Readers are referred to section 2-5 for details.

Miscellaneous. Still another method of prestressing, not belonging to any of the above groups, was developed and applied in Belgium; it is known as the "Preflex" method.[11] The procedure consists of loading a high-tensile steel beam in the factory with a load equal to that anticipated in use. While the beam bends considerably under this load, its tensile flange is clothed with concrete of high compressive strength. After the concrete hardens, the load on the beam is removed, and the concrete is compressed as the beam regains a measure of its original shape. Then the beam is transported to the site to form a part of the structure, generally with the top flange and the web then also encased in concrete. Thus a composite section is obtained combining the strength of high-tensile steel with the rigidity of concrete. A series of tests (on Preflex beams) were carried out at the Lehigh University.

3-4 Post-Tensioning Anchorages for Wires by Wedge Action

There are essentially three principles by which steel wires are anchored to concrete.

1. *By the principle of wedge action producing a frictional grip on the wires.*
2. *By direct bearing from rivet or bolt heads formed at the end of the wires.*
3. *By looping the wires around the concrete.*

Several dependable systems have been developed based on the principles of wedge action and of direct bearing. Little can be said about the relative advantages of these two principles, the superiority of each system depending on the method of application rather than on the principle itself. The last method, looping the wires around the concrete, has not been widely applied, although it also has its advantages.

Fig. 3-13. A set of Freyssinet anchorage cylinder and cone.

Two popular prestressing systems anchor their wires by wedge action: the Freyssinet system and the Magnel system. The Freyssinet system makes use of concrete cylinders and cones reinforced with steel wires, Fig. 3-13. Each anchorage unit consists of a cylinder with a conical interior through which the wires pass, and against the walls of which the wires are wedged by a conical plug lined longitudinally with grooves to receive them. The cylinder is buried flush with the face of the concrete and serves to transmit the reaction of the jack as well as the prestress of the wires to the concrete (see Fig. 3-10). After the completion of prestressing, grout is injected through a hole at the center of the conical plug.

The Freyssinet cones are made for wires of 5-mm (0.196-in.) diameter, with the number of wires ranging from 2 through 8, 10, 12 and up to 18 per cable, 12 and 18 wires being most common. The outside dimensions of a 12-wire anchorage are about $3\frac{3}{4}$ in. for diameter and 4 in. for length; of an 18-wire anchorage, about $4\frac{3}{4}$ in. for diameter and $4\frac{3}{4}$ in. for length. Cones are made also for 7-mm (0.276-in.) wires, with 12 wires per cable. For exact dimensions of various units see Appendix B and also consult catalogues of the Freyssinet Company.

The Magnel system, also known as the Magnel-Blaton system, uses rectangular sandwich plates of steel which have tapered notches to receive the wedges. Wires of 0.196 or 0.276 in. are gripped between the grooves of the wedges and the sandwich plate, Fig. 3-14. The most commonly used plates are those for 8 wires, but plates for 2, 4, or 6 wires are also available.

Each cable is formed of 1 to 8 of these plates laid one against the other, which react against a cast-steel distributing plate interposed between them and the concrete. The entire anchorage assembly is usually laid after the setting of the concrete, with the steel distribution plates cemented to the concrete at proper angles. These plates may be cast into the member at the proper place during concreting if desired.

The number of wires for the Magnel cable varies from 2 to 64 per cable for both sizes of wires. At intervals of several feet the wires are spaced by grilles made of thin, mild-steel strips. In order to resist the transverse component of curved tendons, the grilles are sometimes stiffened with blocks placed along the center of the grilles. The cable can be encased in a light metal sheath which is concreted into the structure. More often it is drawn into performed ducts made by means of extractable rubber cores. In some jobs, the wires are placed outside the concrete, thus avoiding the use of rubber cores or metal sheathing; then the cable is wrapped with cement mortar for protection.

A typical Magnel cable of twenty-four 0.196-in. wires consists of 6 layers with 4 wires per layer. The outside dimensions of the grilles for such a cable are about 2 in. by $2\frac{1}{2}$ in. The end anchorages consist of 3 sandwich plates bearing on a distribution plate about 7 in. by 10 in., with a maximum thickness of about $1\frac{1}{2}$ in.

The Preload Company of the United States developed an anchorage in which the wires are gripped by split cones wedged in the holes of a heavy distribution plate, similar to pre-tensioning bulkheads. Holzmann of

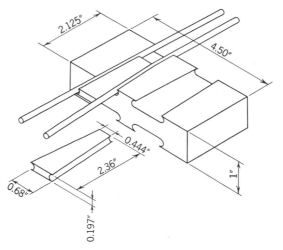

Fig. 3-14. A Magnel sandwich plate with wedges (for 0.196-in. wires).

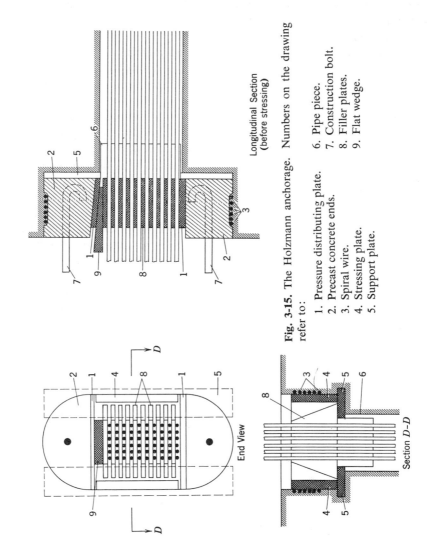

Fig. 3-15. The Holzmann anchorage. Numbers on the drawing refer to:

1. Pressure distributing plate.
2. Precast concrete ends.
3. Spiral wire.
4. Stressing plate.
5. Support plate.
6. Pipe piece.
7. Construction bolt.
8. Filler plates.
9. Flat wedge.

Longitudinal Section (before stressing)

End View

Section D–D

Germany developed another system, in which the ends of the prestressing wires are wrapped around with spiral wires holding the prestressing wires in hoop tension. By this system, only one set of wedges is required to hold many wires, Fig. 3-15. In Italy, the Morandi system makes use of cables of 16 wires, with every pair of wires anchored individually by a small conical wedge. These latter methods have not been applied in the United States.

3-5   Post-Tensioning Anchorages for Wires by Direct Bearing

Several systems employing cold-formed rivet heads for direct bearing at the ends of stressing wires are used throughout the United States. These systems have special head-forming machines for the purpose. One of these is the Prescon system (Appendix B). By this method, rivet heads are cold-formed at the proper place for high-tensile wires of $\frac{1}{4}$-in. diameter. Static tests on these heads have shown that the full strength of the wire can be developed. If the wires are grouted, there being practically no change in stress at the ends, no danger of fatigue failure is expected. Even if the wires are not grouted, since extreme variations of stress do not exist at the ends, the possibility of failure under repeated loads is not believed to be serious.

The Prescon system uses cables of 2 to 42 wires arranged in parallel. The wires are threaded through a stressing washer at each end, Fig. 3-16, before having their heads formed. A hole is provided in the stressing washer to permit grouting. The stressing jack has a special stressing collar which is screwed over the stressing washer and pumped to give the required

Fig. 3-16. End anchorage, Prescon system.

Fig. 3-17. Complete P.I. assembly. Left to right: pulling rod, stressing adapter, stressing assembly (contained within adapter), grouting nipple, anchorage assembly split holding rings, bearing plates.

elongation. A slight excess elongation will enable the shims to be inserted more easily. Then the jack is relieved to transmit the pressure to the shims. The height of the shims must be calculated for each particular case, depending on the length and modulus of elasticity of the wire, the amount of prestress, and the frictional force along the cable. After completion of the prestressing operations, the entire end anchorage is enclosed with concrete for protection against corrosion and fire. In order to minimize handling of individual wires in the field, they are made into cables in the plant and shipped to the site ready for installation.

If the cables are used for bonded work, metal hose is required. In order to permit the passage of grout, the inside diameter of the hose is at least $\frac{1}{4}$ in. greater than required to house the wires. For unbonded work, grease is applied to the wires, which are then wrapped with heavy papers into a cable. For a 6-wire unit, the cable has a diameter of $\frac{3}{4}$ in., and the stressing washer has a diameter of about 2 in. and a thickness of $\frac{3}{4}$ in. and bears against the steel shims which rest on a 5 in. by $4\frac{1}{2}$ in. steel plate $\frac{1}{2}$ in. thick. For the nonstressed ends, the wire head bears directly on the steel bearing plate without the shims. Both the stressing washer and the bearing plate are made of high-strength steel, such as plow steel.

The General Prestressing System supplied by Western Concrete Structures of Los Angeles is practically identical with the Prescon System. The BBRV system developed in Switzerland, and distributed by Ryerson in the United States, is also similar to the Prescon; Appendix B shows the end anchorage.

The Texas P.I. (Texas Prestressing Incorporated) system differs from the Prescon system in that two rivet heads instead of one are formed on the wire at the stressing end, Fig. 3-17. The first head at the end of the wire is used for pulling and the second one for anchoring. After tensioning, the extruding portion is cut off up to the second rivet head. By employing two heads, long shims and thick concrete coverage at the ends sometimes required for the Prescon system are eliminated. Since it is necessary to pull the second rivet head through the bearing plate, its anchorage to the plate requires special hardware such as shown in the figure. The usual wire size is also $\frac{1}{4}$ in. for the Texas P.I. system, and the number of wires per cable varies from 4 to 12. A typical bearing plate for a 6-wire unit is 5 in. by 5 in. by $\frac{1}{2}$ in. thick, with an accompanying split-holding ring $3\frac{1}{2}$ in. in diameter by $\frac{1}{2}$ in. thick.

In certain systems the wires are connected to a short rod of high-tensile steel which can be anchored by nuts and washers. In Germany, three such systems were developed, differing in the method of connecting the wires to the end rod. In the Leoba system, a short tee is formed at one end of the stub, around which the wires are looped. The Monierbau system spreads the wires in a steel cone and anchors them with zinc or lead, as in the case of Roebling anchorage for strands, described later in the chapter. The Huettenwerk Rheinhausen system uses a cylinder for connection. For the Leonhardt and the Billner systems, the wires loop around the concrete and bear directly on it (see Fig. 3-11).

3-6 Post-Tensioning Anchorages for Bars

A suitable end anchorage for high-tensile steel bars in prestressed concrete was developed by Donovan Lee of England where it is known as the Lee-McCall system. In this country it is known as the Stressteel system. The ends of the bars are threaded and anchored with nuts on washers and bearing plates. The essential point is the proper threading of the ends to take a special nut capable of developing as nearly as possible the full strength of the bar. By using tapered threads, about 98% of the bar strength is developed, Fig. 3-18.

Only a short length of the bar is threaded at the untensioned end, sufficient to receive the nut resting on a washer. For the jacking end, a long threaded end is required; the total length of thread is such that, after tensioning to the full value, the nut will be turned to the very bottom of the taper so as to develop the full strength of the bar. If, owing to non-uniformity of material or construction, the bar has to be lengthened more than the calculated amount in order to obtain the desired prestress, split washer shims may be inserted between the nut and the regular washer.

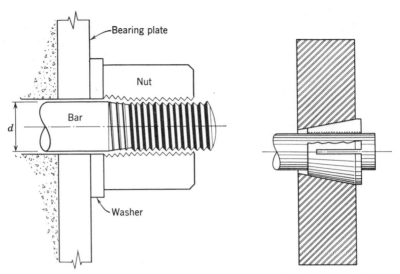

Fig. 3-18. End anchorage for the Lee-McCall or Stressteel system.

Fig. 3-19. Wedge for anchoring rods.

Over-tensioning will be necessary if because of friction or for other reasons the bar cannot be lengthened to the predicted amount under the desired prestress.

During jacking, an adapter from the jack screws into the threaded end of the bar to apply the pull. Since the jacking force for each bar is never more than 60 or 70% of its ultimate strength, the net section at the root of thread is not critical during jacking. However, as mentioned previously, it is a good safety measure to keep the nut near the washer at all times during the process of jacking. After completion of the prestressing operations, the protruding threaded ends can be either cut off or buried in concrete together with the anchorage plates.

The bars can be either bonded or unbonded to the concrete. If unbonded, they can be encased in flexible metal tubing or coated with grease and wrapped with heavy paper. They are then placed and supported in the forms before concreting. If bonded, the bars can be placed either before or after the pouring of concrete. For prepouring placement, flexible metal tubes with inside diameter about $\frac{1}{4}$ in. greater than the bar size are used to facilitate grouting. For post-pouring placement, hole-forming cores such as inflated rubber or rubber with stiffening bars can be employed.

The hexagonal nuts for the bars have a short diameter equal to about twice the bar diameter and a thickness about 1.6 times the bar diameter.

The standard and split washers are made of $\frac{3}{16}$-in. and 14-gage metal. The anchorage plates differ in size and can accommodate 1 to 3 bars per plate. The plates have a thickness of $\frac{5}{8}$ to $1\frac{1}{2}$ in. and an area per bar equal to about $(5d)^2$, where d is the bar diameter. If sleeve couplers are used to splice the bars, it is necessary to provide enough space near the couplers to permit movement during the tensioning process.

More recently, wedge anchorage has been developed for these large bars, using wedge anchors and wedge plates, Fig. 3-19. The advantage of the wedge anchorage is its convenience in gripping the bar at any point along its length, whereas the threaded anchorage is limited to the threaded portion and requires the use of shims for adjustments.

Bars with similar characteristics and anchorages are also supplied by the Rods, Inc. of Berkeley, California, known under the tradename of Stressrods. Rods, Inc., has developed a scissor jack which enables the pulling and holding of two rods against each other so as to develop continuity or coupling in a limited space, Fig. 3-20.

In other countries, similar methods of anchorage for high-tensile bars have been devised. They differ in detail from the Lee-McCall or Stressteel system, but thread and nuts bearing against washers are employed in all

Fig. 3-20. Scissor jack for prestressing two rods one against the other and coupling them together (courtesy Rods, Inc., Berkeley, Calif.).

methods. In Germany alone, four such methods have been developed, namely, the Dywidag, Finsterwalder, Karig, and Polensky and Zollner systems; in Belgium, the Wets system; in Holland, the Bakker system. These will not be described here.

3-7 Post-Tensioning Anchorages for Strands

For pre-tensioning, wire strands can be gripped by strand vises mentioned in section 3-2. For post-tensioning, the first commercial strand anchorages in this country were those of the Roebling system. The Roebling system uses anchorages similar to those long employed for rope suspenders of suspension bridges. The ends of the wires of a strand are spread into a bushing and buried with zinc poured in a conical funnel of cast-steel tube, Fig. 3-21. The outer end of the tube is threaded both inside and outside. During prestressing, a threaded rod on the jack is attached to the inside of the tube in order to pull the cable. After the cable is pulled to its desired elongation and stress, the nut threaded to the outside of the tube is turned tight to bear against the bearing plate, which in turn rests on the concrete. A small length of pipe is embedded in the concrete to house the fittings before prestressing and also to transmit, through bond, part of the prestress from the bearing plate to the concrete. The same anchorage is used on the unjacked end with the nut bearing on the plate previous to tensioning.

A second type of the Roebling anchorage consists of a long threaded stud at the prestressing end, to which are attached both the jack adapter and the anchoring nut. The nut is turned tight after the cable is jacked to its desired prestress. For both types, the amount of lengthening must be figured out beforehand to make sure that the threaded portion is long

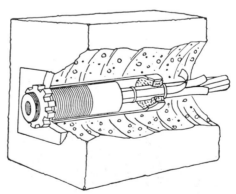

Fig. 3-21. End anchorage for the Roebling system.

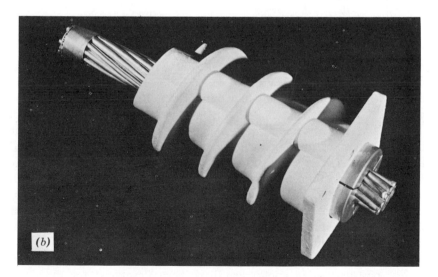

Fig. 3-22. CCL anchorages for strands. (*a*) Anchorage for 7 strands. (*b*) Anchorage for an $1\frac{1}{8}$-inch strand.

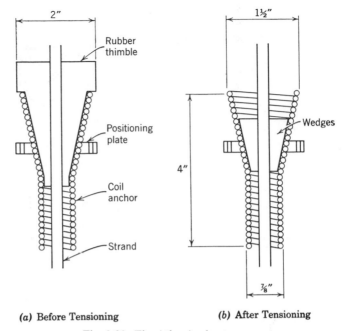

(a) Before Tensioning   *(b)* After Tensioning

Fig. 3-23. The Atlas Anchorage.

enough for the anchorage. If the length of the threaded portion is insufficient, special split washers must be added for bearing. In other cases, the entire threaded portion is hidden within the pipe before jacking. Then the pipe must be large enough to house the jack adapter for tensioning.

While the CCL (Cable Covers Limited) also includes anchorages for 8 and 12 wires of 0.276-in. diameter, its strand anchorage is of special interest because of its compactness, Fig. 3-22. At present, it offers only the 1⅛-in. strand with a minimum ultimate strength of 80 tons and an initial prestress of 60 tons. The anchorage consists of a spheroidal graphite casting, cast into the concrete. Strand is fit into the inside taper of the casting with three segmental wedges; the teeth of the wedges are machined to provide a positive mechanical anchorage.

Since ½-in. strands are widely used for pre-tensioning in the United States, post-tensioning anchorages have been developed for them. A new Freyssinet anchorage for 12½-in. strands will provide an ultimate strength of 432 kips (Appendix B), and a working effective force of about 260 kips. Similar anchorages for strands are provided by the Anderson system.

Single strand post-tensioning using greased wrapping is provided by the Atlas system Fig. 3-23. A ½-in. strand will supply a prestress of about 20 kips and is suitable for slabs and similar components. This system requires no pockets around the end anchorages and permits flexible length in the field to make up for construction discrepancies.

3-8 Comparison of Systems

It is very difficult to compare the advantages of various systems of prestressing. Speaking in general, established systems that have been proved by tests and service can all be considered safe ones. That does not preclude the possibility that newer and perhaps better systems may be developed. Any new system, however, should be subjected to adequate tests before it can be adopted in practice.

Owing to the manner in which prestressed concrete has developed, any "prestressing system" generally embodies several essential features, some of which are also adopted by other systems in one form or another. For example, the methods of providing the conduits, the size, number, and arrangement of wires, and the basic principles of jacking and of anchoring are common to many methods. The essential difference between the systems, then, lies usually in the following three features: the material for producing the prestress, the details of jacking process, and the method of anchoring.

First of all, there is the choice between pre-tensioning and post-tensioning. When a pre-tensioning plant is accessible, and the precast member can be conveniently transported, pre-tensioning will generally be found to be the cheaper, because of the saving in end anchorages, in conduits, and in grouting, and because of the centralization of the production process. If a plant is too far away, the cost of transportation may be excessive. If a plant has to be established just for one job, the costs may be prohibitive unless the job is big enough to justify such an establishment. Long and heavy members can best be poured in place or cast in blocks to be post-tensioned at the site, and pre-tensioning may not be economical.

In the United States, pre-tensioning using small wires has proved to be relatively uneconomical and has given way to the widespread adoption of wire strands. Seven-wire strands up to $\frac{1}{2}$-in. diameter have been successfully employed. Since strands anchor themselves quite well through bond with concrete, anchorages for pre-tensioning have not been found necessary except for short beams and cantilevers.

One important shortcoming in pre-tensioning was the fact that its application had been limited to the employment of straight wires tensioned between two bulkheads. Hence advantage could not be taken of the curving and bending of cables so beneficial to many beam layouts. In modern pre-tensioning plants in the United States, however, provisions are made so that pre-tensioning wires can be bent at almost any point. Heavy girders using bent-up wires anchored to the beds at the points of bending were built for the New Northam Bridge, Southampton, England, in 1954.

For post-tensioning, the members can be either precast or cast in place. There is a further choice between bonded and unbonded reinforcing. Most present-day systems permit the use of either the bonded or the unbonded type. Certain systems yield a slightly better bond than others, depending on the passage provided for grouting and the bonding perimeter afforded per unit of prestressing force. For other systems, the tendons can be more easily greased and wrapped for unbonded reinforcing. When competition is keen between systems, the choice of the bonded or the unbonded type may decide the economy of one system as against the others.

Another important decision is the choice of proper materials for prestressing, whether wires, strands, or bars. Wires possess higher unit strength than the others; strands and bars mean fewer units for handling. The strength of strands is close to that of wires, but strands cost more per pound. Bars possess the least strength; but they are easier to handle and cheaper to anchor.

Anchorages for strands are more costly, but the percentage cost of anchorages decreases with the length of tendons. Bars require splices for longer length, whereas strands and wires can be supplied without splice for almost any length of tendon. These are some of the inherent advantages and disadvantages of each material. Once the choice of materials is made, the choice of prestressing systems is further narrowed down. In the United States, only two or three systems are available for strands or bars, though several systems are employed for wires. Since the choice of materials almost automatically dictates the choice of prestressing systems and tends to eliminate competition, it is common practice not to commit the design to any one material. This is often achieved by specifying the amount of effective prestress instead of the material and area of the tendons.

The final decision is often an economic one, that is, which system will work out the cheapest. There are some basic advantages to each system. For example, when fewer wires are stretched per operation, smaller jacks will be needed; they are easier to handle but take more time for the total tensioning. Systems where the jacking is done all at once demand jacks of much greater capacity, which are naturally more costly and more cumbersome to move.

For any particular structure at a given time and location, one system will come out to be the most economical. This is usually the result of the surrounding conditions as much as the inherent advantages of that system.

The availability of service from the system's representatives, the accessibility of materials and equipments, the acquaintance of the designing engineer with a particular system, and the desirability and ability of the system to get that job often form the deciding factors. Most surviving popular systems possess a number of merits of their own, but the economy of each system will vary with each job.

Finally, an engineer designing for any particular system should refer to the latest pamphlets issued by the respective companies for details so that his structure may be designed accordingly. It is also possible that the representatives or licensees of a system will be able to furnish special advice as to how the structure can be suitably detailed. The engineer can learn much from such advice, although he should always depend on his own judgment for the final decision. In order that engineers in this country may conveniently get in touch with the various system representatives, a list of the head offices is given in Appendix B.

References

1 C. Dobell, "Patents and Code Relating to Prestressed Concrete," *J. Am. Conc. Inst.*, May 1950 (*Proc.*, Vol. 46), pp. 713–724.
2 T. Germundsson, "Prestressed Concrete Construction Procedures," *J. Am. Conc. Inst.*, June 1950 (*Proc.*, Vol. 46), pp. 857–875.
3 *Plant for Prestressing Concrete*, Ministry of Works, London.
4 H. Shorer, "Prestressed Concrete, Design Principles and Reinforcing Units," *J. Am. Conc., Inst.*, June 1943 (*Proc.*, Vol 39), pp. 493–528.
5 V. V. Mikhailov, "Automation in the Production of Prestressing Units," *Proceedings World Conference on Prestressed Concrete*, San Francisco, 1957.
6 T. Y. Lin, et al, *A Report on the Visit of an American Delegation to Observe Concrete and Prestressed Concrete Engineering in the U.S.S.R.*, Portland Cement Association, 1958.
7 F. Leonhardt, "Continuous Bridge Girder Prestressed in a Single Operation," *Civil Engineering* January 1953, pp. 42–45.
8 K. P. Billner, "Prestressing of Reinforced Concrete," *Précontrainte Prestressing*, No. 1, 1951, pp. 5–13.
9 K. P. Bilner and R. W. Carlson, "Electrical Prestressing of Reinforcing Steel," *J. Am. Conc. Inst.*, June 1943 (*Proc.*, Vol. 39), pp. 585–592.
10 V. V. Mikhailov, "Recent Developments in Automatic Manufacture of Prestressed Members in the USSR," *P.C.I. Journal*, September 1961.
11 L. Baes and A. Lipski, "La Poutre préflex," *Précontrainte Prestressing*, No. 1, 1953.

4

loss of prestress; friction

4-1 Elastic Shortening of Concrete

Let us first consider pre-tensioned concrete. As the prestress is transferred to the concrete, the member shortens and the prestressed steel shortens with it. Hence there is a loss of prestress in the steel. Considering only the axial shortening of concrete produced by prestressing (the effect of bending of concrete will be considered in section 4-5), we have

$$\text{Unit shortening } \delta = \frac{f_c}{E_c}$$

$$= \frac{F_0}{A_c E_c}$$

where F_0 is the total prestress just after transfer, that is, after the shortening has taken place. Loss of prestress in steel is

$$\Delta f_s = E_s \delta = \frac{E_s F_0}{A_c E_c} = \frac{n F_0}{A_c} \qquad (4\text{-}1)$$

The value of F_0, being the prestress after transfer, may not be known exactly. But exactness is not necessary in the estimation of F_0, because the loss due to this shortening is only a few per cent of the total prestress, hence an error of a few per cent in the estimation will have no practical significance. It must be further remembered that the value of E_c cannot be accurately predicted either. However, since the value of the initial prestress F_i is usually known, a theoretical solution can be obtained by the elastic theory. Using the transformed-section method, with $A_t = A_c + nA_s$, we have

$$\delta = \frac{F_i}{A_c E_c + A_s E_s}$$

$$\Delta f_s = E_s \delta = \frac{E_s F_i}{A_c E_c + A_s E_s}$$

$$= \frac{nF_i}{A_c + nA_s}$$

$$\Delta f_s = \frac{nF_i}{A_t} \tag{4-2}$$

EXAMPLE 4-1

A straight pre-tensioned concrete member 40 ft long, with a cross section of 15 in. by 15 in., is concentrically prestressed with 1.2 sq in. of steel wires which are anchored to the bulkheads with a stress of 150,000 psi (Fig. 4-1). If $E_c = 5,000,000$ psi and $E_s = 30,000,000$ psi, compute the loss of prestress due to the elastic shortening of concrete at the transfer of prestress.

Solution. Using formula 4-1 and a prestress of $150,000 \times 1.2 = 180,000$ lb, we have

$$\Delta f_s = \frac{nF_0}{A_c} = \frac{6 \times 180,000}{225} = 4800 \text{ psi}$$

indicating a loss of $4800/150,000 = 3.2\%$.

Note that, theoretically, an A_c of $225 - 1.2 = 223.8$ sq in. could have been used, but most of the time the gross concrete area can be employed with little error.

If a more exact solution is desired, formula 4-2 yields

$$\Delta f_s = \frac{nF_i}{A_c + nA_s} = \frac{6 \times 180,000}{223.8 + 6 \times 1.2} = 4660 \text{ psi}$$

indicating a loss of $4660/150,000 = 3.1\%$ only slightly different from the above approximate solution.

For post-tensioning, the problem is different. If we have only a single tendon in a post-tensioned member, the concrete shortens as that tendon

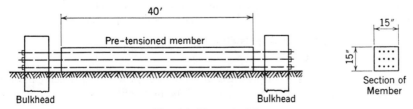

Fig. 4-1. Example 4-1.

is jacked against the concrete. Since the force in the cable is measured after the elastic shortening of the concrete has taken place, no loss in prestress due to that shortening need be accounted for.

If we have more than one tendon and the tendons are stressed in succession, then the prestress is gradually applied to the concrete, the shortening of concrete increases as each cable is tightened against it, and the loss of prestress due to elastic shortening differs in the tendons. The tendon that is first tensioned would suffer the maximum amount of loss due to the shortening of concrete by the subsequent application of prestress from all the other tendons. The tendon that is tensioned last will not suffer any loss due to the elastic concrete shortening, since all that shortening will have already taken place when the prestress in the last tendon is being measured. The computation of such losses can be made quite complicated. But, for all practical purposes, it is accurate enough to determine the loss for the first cable and use half of that value for the average loss of all the cables. This is shown in example 4-2.

EXAMPLE 4-2

Consider the same member as in example 4-1, but post-tensioned instead of pre-tensioned. Assume that the 1.2 sq in. of steel is made up of 4 tendons with 0.3 sq in. per tendon. The tendons are tensioned one after another to the stress of 150,000 psi. Compute the loss of prestress due to the elastic shortening of concrete.

Solution.   The loss of prestress in the first tendon will be due to the shortening of concrete as caused by the prestress in the other 3 tendons. Although the prestress differs in the 3 tendons, it will be close enough to assume a value of 150,000 psi for them all. Hence the force causing the shortening is

$$3 \times 0.3 \times 150,000 = 135,000 \text{ lb}$$

The loss of prestress is given by formula 4-1

$$f_s = \frac{nF_0}{A_c} = \frac{6 \times 135,000}{225} = 3600 \text{ psi}$$

Note that it is again unnecessary to use the more exact formula 4-2; neither is it necessary to use the net concrete area for A_c, although theoretically it would be more accurate.

Similarly, the loss in the second tendon is 2400 psi, in the third tendon 1200 psi, and the last tendon has no loss. The average loss for the 4 tendons will be

$$\frac{3600 + 2400 + 1200}{4} = 1800 \text{ psi}$$

indicating an average loss of prestress of $1800/150,000 = 1.2\%$, which can also be obtained by using one-half of the loss of the first cable,

$$3600/2 = 1800 \text{ psi}$$

The above method of computation assumes that the tendons are stretched in succession and that each is stressed to the same value as indicated by a manometer or a dynamometer. It is entirely possible to jack the tendons to different initial prestresses, taking into account the respective amount of loss, so that all the tendons would end up with the same prestress after deducting their losses. Considering the above example, if the first cable should be tensioned to a stress of 153,600 psi, the second to 152,400, the third to 151,200, and the last to 150,000, then, at the completion of the prestressing process, all the tendons would be stressed to 150,000 psi. Such a procedure, although theoretically desirable, is seldom carried out because of the additional complications involved in the field. When there are many tendons and the elastic shortening of concrete is appreciable, it is sometimes desirable to divide the tendons into three or four groups; each group will be given a different amount of over-tensioning according to its order in the jacking sequence.

In actual practice, either of the following two methods is used.

1. Stress all tendons to the specified initial prestress (e.g., to 150,000 psi in example 4-2), and allow for the average loss in the design (e.g., 1800 psi in example 4-2).

2. Stress all tendons to a value above the specified initial prestress by the magnitude of the average loss (e.g., to $150,000 + 1800 = 151,800$ psi in example 4-2). Then, when designing, the loss due to the elastic shortening of concrete is not to be considered again.

If the loss due to this source is not significant, the first method is followed. If the steel can stand some overtensioning, and if a high effective prestress is desired, the second procedure can be adopted.

The above discussion refers to the case when the prestress in the tendons is measured by manometer or dynamometer and only approximately checked by elongation measurements. At other times, prestress is measured by the amount of elongation, the gages being used merely as a check. The preference for one or the other depends on many factors: the personal practice of the engineer, the accuracy of the different instruments available, the constancy of the modulus of elasticity of steel, the amount of friction in the tendons, as well as the system of prestressing employed. In the previous discussion, when the gages are used as the final means of measuring, it is evident that if the tendons are tensioned to the same initial stress they will eventually possess different effective prestresses, and hence different effective elongations, although their elongations may not vary by more than 2 or 3% and may not be easily detectable. In other words, the tendons are supposedly stretched to the same initial elongation, but, as the concrete shortens gradually, the tendons that are stretched earlier lose more of their tensile strains and therefore lose more of their tensile stresses.

If, on the other hand, the eventual elongations are used as the measure of stress, the problem would be different. Consider the Prescon system, for example, where wedges with length equal to the computed elongation are inserted at the anchorages; the elongation of each tendon relative to the concrete is kept constant at all times. Hence any loss of prestress due to the shortening of concrete would be uniform for all tendons irrespective of their order of tensioning. This means that the wires will have different initial prestresses, that the initial elongation of the tendons will be different, but that the eventual elongations will be the same for all. For such a system, if the tendons are stressed to the same initial prestress, they will have varying effective prestress, and the wedges will have to vary in length. The difference in length, however, is seldom more than 2 or 3% and is hardly noticeable.

4-2 Creep and Shrinkage in Concrete

The amounts and nature of shrinkage and creep having been discussed in sections 2-2 and 2-4, we shall now consider their effect on the loss of prestress. First, let us consider creep. Since the amount of creep ranges from 1 to 5 times the elastic shortening, it is obviously an important item. Furthermore, although the loss due to elastic shortening can be counter-balanced for post-tensioned members, the loss due to creep cannot be easily compensated for. It is not possible to over-tension the wires excessively in order to allow for such loss, because that would mean very high initial stresses in the steel which might increase its creep or approach its yield point. If the steel is unbonded or not yet bonded to the concrete, it is sometimes possible to retension the steel after some of the losses have taken place. But this might be expensive and undesirable.

It is known that the failure of early efforts at prestressing was attributed largely to the lack of knowledge concerning creep in concrete. In fact, it is still one of the main sources of loss, and a serious one, if the prestress in the steel is low and the compression in the concrete is high.

Assuming a prestress in the concrete of 1000 psi for $E_c = 5,000,000$ psi $E_s = 30,000,000$ psi, and a creep equal to twice the elastic strain, the loss of prestress in the steel due to creep in concrete is

$$\Delta f_s = 2\frac{f_c E_s}{E_c} = 2nf_c = 2 \times 6 \times 1000$$
$$= 12,000 \text{ psi}$$

For an initial prestress of 150,000 psi in the steel, this is a loss of 12,000/ 150,000 = 8%.

So far as creep due to prestress is concerned, the amount of prestress producing the creep can be assumed to be constant in computing the losses. Actually the prestress decreases as creep takes place, but it may not be necessary to split hairs in a practical design.

A more complicated problem is to determine the deflection of beams resulting from flexural creep. Here not only the deflection due to prestress is affected by creep, but also the deflection due to external load is similarly affected. Hence the eventual deflection of a prestressed beam will depend on the duration of the external load, which often cannot be well predicted. Of course, the same holds true for the deflection of ordinary reinforced-concrete beams. And the magnitude may or may not be significant, depending on the specific conditions.

Since the age of concrete at transfer affects the amount of creep, it is generally true that pre-tensioned members will have more loss than post-tensioned ones. This is because transfer of prestress usually takes place earlier in pre-tensioned members.

Shrinkage of concrete, as discussed in sections 2-2 and 2-4, varies widely. For ordinary prestressed concrete, an average value of shrinkage strain of 0.0003 appears to be about right. The corresponding loss of prestress in steel with a value of $E_s = 30,000,000$ psi is given by

$$\Delta f_s = \delta_s E_s = 0.0003 \times 30,000,000 = 9000 \text{ psi}$$

For an initial steel stress of 150,000, this means a loss of 6%.

The amount of shrinkage varies greatly with the proximity of the concrete to water and the time of application of prestress. Prestress was applied to a certain concrete tank after most of the shrinkage had taken place, and it was found that, when the tank was later filled with water, the restoration of water content to the concrete resulted in considerable expansion which balanced all the creep. On the other hand, if the concrete is prestressed early, before shrinkage has taken place, and then subjected to a very dry atmosphere, the loss of prestress due to shrinkage could be excessive.

The British First Report on Prestressed Concrete, for example, recommends a total shrinkage of 0.0003 for pre-tensioning. For transfer at 2 to 3 weeks, a shrinkage of 0.0002 is considered sufficient. For creep in concrete, a strain of 0.0000004 for each psi of stress is recommended for pre-tensioning, and 0.0000003 for post-tensioning applied at about 2 to 3 weeks of age. Test results in this country conducted on concrete of lower strength indicated creep up to 0.0000015 per psi in the course of 20 years (see Chapter 2, reference 5).

For pre-tensioning, the amount of shrinkage is independent of the age at transfer. The total shrinkage starting from the setting of concrete must be considered. The amount of creep, however, would be less if the transfer took place later.

German Specifications DIN 4227, Spannbeton, 1953, specify the following.

	Ratio of Creep Strain to Elastic Strain	Shrinkage Strain
1. Under water	0.5–1.0k	0
2. In very moist air	1.5–2.0k	0.0001
3. In ordinary atmosphere	2.0–3.0k	0.0002
4. In dry air	2.5–4.0k	0.0003

In the above, the value k varies with the ratio $f_{ci}'/f_{c\infty}'$ (f_{ci}' = strength of concrete at time of load application, and $f_{c\infty}'$ = strength at infinite time), as follows:

$f_{ci}'/f_{c\infty}'$	k
0.65	1.50
0.75	1.00
0.85	0.75
1.00	0.50

Since the coefficient of expansion of steel is nearly the same as that for concrete, there is practically no loss of prestress due to temperature drop if the two materials are subject to the same changes. However, because of the heat of setting of the cement, the eventual temperature drop in concrete after the dissipation of heat can result in loss of prestress. German specifications mentioned that, if the prestress is introduced before the concrete has hardened, the equivalent fall in temperature should be assumed to be 45°F; if the prestress is introduced after the concrete has hardened, the equivalent temperature fall may range from 10° to 40°F, depending on the hardness of concrete at the time of prestressing.

Except for very massive structures, the heat of setting is almost entirely dissipated within the first week after placing. Hence no such loss needs to be considered in post-tensioning work where the prestress is seldom applied before the concrete is 1 or 2 weeks old. Furthermore, if, during prestressing, the steel has the same temperature as the concrete, there will be no loss due to a temperature drop. For pre-tensioning work, if the steel is tensioned at one temperature and the concrete sets at a higher temperature there will be a loss of prestress. Assuming a difference of 20°F, for a coefficient of expansion of concrete of 0.000006, the shrinkage strain amounts to nearly

$$0.000006 \times 20 = 0.0001$$

This means a loss of prestress in the steel of

$$30,000,000 \times 0.0001 = 3000 \text{ psi}$$

which is about 2% for an initial prestress of 150,000 psi.

4-3 Stress Relaxation in Steel

Stress relaxation in steel, also termed as creep, is the loss of its stress when it is prestressed and maintained at a constant strain for a period of time. It is sometimes measured by the amount of lengthening when maintained under a constant stress for a period of time. The two methods give about the same results when the relaxation is not excessive, but the constant-strain method is more often employed as a basis for measurement, because of its similarity to the actual conditions in prestressed concrete. Relaxation varies with steel of different compositions and treatments; hence exact values can be determined only by test for each individual case if previous data are not available.

Approximate stress-relaxation characteristics, however, are known for most of the prestressing steels now in the market. Speaking in general, the percentage of creep increases with increasing stress, and when a steel is under low stress, the creep is negligible.[1] Typical curves giving the relation[2] between creep and initial stress level in two types of steel[2] are shown in Fig. 4-2. The "as-drawn" cold-drawn wire has a relaxation amounting to about 3% of the initial stress when stressed to about $0.50f_s'$. This stress loss increases almost as a straight line until it reaches 12% at an initial stress equal to $0.90f_s'$. The stress-relieved wire has less loss at initial stresses below $0.70f_s'$. Above $0.70f_s'$, the stress loss of stress-relieved wires increases rapidly and reaches about 16% when stressed to $0.80f_s'$. For initial stresses above $0.80f_s'$, the percentage of stress loss remains approximately constant at 16% provided the rate of loading is such that the initial stress is reached in over 4 minutes. When the initial stress is reached in 2 minutes, higher losses are observed, as indicated by the light lines in Fig. 4-2. (For details of these wires and the tests, readers are referred to reference 2.) In the above discussions, the ultimate tensile strength refers to the *actual* ultimate strength of the wire, which is often 10% or more higher than the specified minimum guaranteed ultimate strength. Hence when a steel is stressed to 80% of the specified ultimate, it may actually be stressed to only 70% of the actual ultimate strength. Galvanized wires have about the same creep characteristics as the stress-relieved wires. They have practially no creep when used within 55% of the ultimate strength, but should preferably not be subjected to any stress above $0.60f_s'$ without carefully considering the effect of creep. Creep in stress-relieved

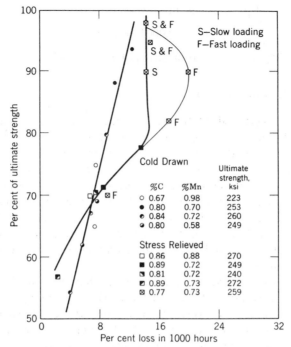

Fig. 4-2. Per cent loss in 1000 hours. Relaxation of prestressing wires.

strands has been determined by W. O. Everling of the United States Steel Corporation, Cleveland, Ohio, 1953–1955. In general, their characteristics are similar to those of stress-relieved wires. For high-tensile bars, some limited tests seemed to show that, for stress up to about $0.60f_s'$, creep is not more than 3%.

While creep in steel is a function of time, there is evidence to show that under the ordinary working stress for high-tensile steel (see Chapter 2, reference 7), creep takes place mostly during the first few days. Under constant strain, creep ceases entirely after about 2 weeks. If the steel is stressed to a few per cent above its initial prestress and that overstress is maintained for a few minutes, the eventual creep can be greatly lessened, and it practically stops in about 3 days.

For most kinds of steel now in the market, stressed to the usual allowable values, the percentage of creep varies from 1 to 5%, and an average of 3% should be a fair guess. It is best for the engineer to know the creep characteristics of his steel and to take at least the ordinary precautions to minimize creep. If no precautions are taken, creep may occasionally become excessive.

Theoretically, it is possible to stress the steel to a certain level and hold it there for a few days until most of the creep has taken place. In practice, retensioning or aftertensioning is sometimes employed, that is, retightening the steel after most of its creep has taken place. But the expense and inconvenience involved in such operations can be justified only under special circumstances.

The question has sometimes been raised as to the possibility of excessive creep under repeated loads. But, so far as available evidence from fatigue tests show, no such creep need be feared for the ordinary range and duration of stress to which the wire is subject. There has also been some question as to the difference in creep between bonded and unbonded steel. Although no experimental data are available on this, it appears that creep in steel is dependent on its own properties, and not on its bond with concrete.

Some authors have attempted to define a "creep limit" for steel. Professor Campus suggested two possible limits.[3] The absolute or theoretical creep limit for a steel is defined as the highest stress that can be applied to it and maintained for a few days without producing any noticeable creep. Since this limit is difficult to determine, a conventional creep limit is proposed and defined as the stress that will not produce more than 1% creep in the steel. Tests have also been performed to determine these creep limits for certain steels.

4-4   Loss Due to Anchorage Take-Up

For most systems of post-tensioning, when a tendon is tensioned to its full value, the jack is released and the prestress is transferred to the anchorage. The anchorage fixtures that are subject to stresses at this transfer will tend to deform, thus allowing the tendon to slacken slightly. Friction wedges employed to hold the wires will slip a little distance before the wires can be firmly gripped. The amount of slippage depends on the type of wedge and the stress in the wires, an average value being around 0.1 in. For direct bearing anchorages, the heads and nuts are subject to a slight deformation at the release of the jack. An average value for such deformations may be only about 0.03 in. If long shims are required to hold the elongated wires in place, there will be a deformation in the shims at transfer of prestress. As an example, a shim 1 ft long may deform 0.01 in.

When tensioning heavy strands, the high force in the end fixtures of the strands may produce some slippage in the wires. In the Roebling system, for example, this deformation may be as much as 0.2 in. for the $1\frac{11}{16}$-in. strands. Then it would be best to retighten all the strands after such losses have taken place if accurate prestress is to be attained.

A general formula for computing the loss of prestress due to anchorage deformation Δ_a is

$$\Delta f_s = \frac{\Delta_a E_s}{L} \tag{4-3}$$

Since this loss of prestress is caused by a fixed total amount of shortening, the percentage of loss is higher for short wires than for long ones. Hence it is quite difficult to tension short wires accurately, especially for systems of prestressing whose anchorage losses are relatively large. For example, the total elongation for a 10-ft tendon at 150,000 psi is about

$$\frac{150,000 \times 10 \times 12}{30,000,000} = 0.6 \text{ in.}$$

and a loss of 0.1 in. would be a loss of 17%. On the other hand, for a wire of 100 ft, a loss of only 1.7% would be caused by such slippage, and it can be easily allowed for in the design, or counterbalanced by slight overtensioning.

4-5 Loss Due to Bending of Member

Loss of prestress due to a uniform shortening of the member under axial stress was discussed in sections 4-1 and 4-2. When a member bends, further changes in the prestress may occur: there may be either a loss or a gain in prestress, depending on the direction of bending and the location of the tendon. If there are several tendons and they are placed at different levels, the change of prestress in them will differ. Then it may be convenient to consider only the centroid of all the tendons (the c.g.s. line) to get an average value of the change in prestress.

This change in prestress will depend on the type of prestressing: whether pre- or post-tensioned, whether bonded or unbonded. Before the tendon is bonded to the concrete, bending of the member will affect the prestress in the tendon. Neglecting frictional effects, any strain in the tendon will be stretched out along its entire length, and the prestress in the tendon will be uniformly modified. After the tendon is bonded to the concrete, any further bending of the beam will only affect the stress in the tendon locally but will not change its "prestress."

Consider a simple beam, where the tendon is bonded to the concrete either by pre-tensioning or by grouting after post-tensioning, Fig. 4-3. Before any load is applied to the beam, it possesses a camber, as shown. Then an external load is applied and the beam deflects downward. The external load produces bending moment in the beam. Bending in the beam changes the unit stresses, hence the unit strains, in the tendon. The stress in the tendon near the mid-span changes quite a bit, but that at the end does not change at all since there is no change in bending moment at the ends. If the "prestress" from the steel on the concrete is considered to be force applied at the ends, the change in "stress" along the length is not considered as a change in "prestress." After the tendon is bonded to the concrete, the steel and concrete form one section, and any change in stress due to bending of the section is easily computed by the transformed section method. Hence, it is convenient to say that "prestress" does not change as the result of bending of a beam after the bonding of steel to concrete, although the stress in the tendon does change.

The same is true of pre-tensioned members bending under prestress and their own weight. Again referring to Fig. 4-3, after the transfer of prestress, the beam bends upward and the wires shorten because of that bending. For the same reason as discussed above, that shortening of the wires due to bending is not considered a loss of prestress, just as the eventual lengthening under load is not considered a gain in prestress. In both cases, the prestress considered is the prestress at the ends of the members, which does not change under bending.

For post-tensioned bonded beams before grouting, the bending of the member will affect the prestress in the steel. Referring to Fig. 4-4, suppose that the cables are tensioned one by one and the beam cambers upward gradually as more cables are tensioned. Then the cables that are tensioned first will lose some of their prestress due to this bending, in addition to the

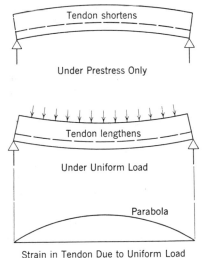

Fig. 4-3. Variation of strain in a bonded tendon.

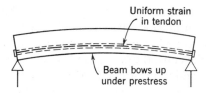

Fig. 4-4. Post-tensioned member before grouting.

elastic shortening of concrete due to axial precompression. In general, these losses will be small and can be neglected. But when the camber is appreciable, it may be desirable to retension the cables after completing the first round of tensioning or to allow for such losses in the design. Since it is the curvature of the beam at the time of grouting that determines the length of the tendons, the effect of creep in concrete will exaggerate the curvature and should be taken into account when allowing for such changes in prestress.

For post-tensioned unbonded simple beams there may be a loss of prestress due to upward bowing caused by prestressing, and there will be a gain in prestress when the beam is fully loaded. If the tendons are permitted to slide freely within the concrete they will lengthen and shorten along their entire length as the beam bends. If a tendon does not remain at a constant distance from the c.g.c. line (center of gravity of concrete section), the computation of the change in length will be quite complicated. Fortunately, the loss or gain due to this source is ordinarily not more than 2 or 3 % and for all practical purposes can be approximately estimated and allowed for.

EXAMPLE 4-3

A concrete beam 8 in. by 18 in. deep is prestressed with an unbonded tendon through the lower third point, Fig. 4-5, with a total initial prestress of 144,000 lb. Compute the loss of prestress in the tendon due to the bowing up of the beam under prestress, neglecting the weight of the beam itself. $E_s = 30,000,000$, $E_c = 4,000,000$ psi. Beam is simply supported.

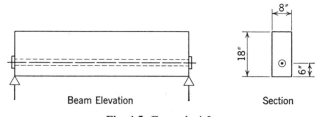

Beam Elevation   Section

Fig. 4-5. Example 4-3.

Solution. Owing to the eccentric prestress, the beam is under a uniform bending moment of

$$144,000 \times 3 \text{ in.} = 432,000 \text{ in.-lb}$$

The concrete fiber stress at the level of the cable due to this bending is

$$f = \frac{My}{I} = \frac{432,000 \times 3}{(8 \times 18^3)/12} = 333 \text{ psi compression}$$

(Note that stress due to the axial prestress of 144,000 lb is not included here; also, the gross area of the concrete is used for simplicity.)

Unit compressive strain along the level of the tendon is therefore

$$333/4,000,000 = 0.000083$$

Corresponding loss of prestress in steel is

$$0.000083 \times 30,000,000 = 2500 \text{ psi}$$

However, if the beam is left under the action of prestress alone, the creep of concrete will tend to increase the camber and will result in further loss of prestress. On the other hand, if the prestress in the tendon is measured after the bowing of the beam has taken place, this loss due to bending of beam need not be considered.

4-6 Frictional Loss, Practical Considerations

Valuable and extensive research work has been carried out to determine the frictional loss of prestress in prestressed concrete,[4,5] so that now it is possible to estimate such losses within the practical requirement of accuracy. First of all, it is known that there is some friction in the jacking and anchoring system so that the stress existing in the tendon is less than that indicated by the pressure gage. This is especially true for some systems whose wires change direction at the anchorage. This friction in the jacking and anchoring system is generally small though not insignificant. It can be determined for each case, if desired, and an overtension can be applied to the jack so that the calculated prestress will exist in the tendon. It must be remembered, though, that the amount of overtensioning is limited by the yield point, the creep limit, and the strength of the wires.

More serious frictional loss occurs between the tendon and its surrounding material, whether concrete or sheathing, and whether lubricated or not. This frictional loss can be conveniently considered in two parts: the length effect and the curvature effect. The length effect is the amount of friction that would be encountered if the tendon is a straight one, that is, one that is not purposely bent or curved. Since in practice the duct for the tendon cannot be perfectly straight, some friction will exist between the tendon and its surrounding material even though the tendon is meant to be straight. This is sometimes described as the wobbling effect of the duct and is dependent on the length and stress of the tendon, the coefficient of friction between the contact materials, and the workmanship and method used in aligning and obtaining the duct. Some approximate values for these losses are given in section 205, Appendix D.

The loss of prestress due to curvature effect results from the intended curvature of the tendons in addition to the unintended wobble of the duct. This loss is again dependent on the coefficient of friction between the contact materials and the pressure exerted by the tendon on the concrete. The coefficient of friction, in turn, depends on the smoothness and nature of the surfaces in contact, the amount and nature of lubricants, and sometimes the length of contact. The pressure between the tendon and concrete is dependent on the stress in the tendon and the total change in angle.

For multiple wires arranged in one duct, there are other sources of friction around curves. If the wires in one duct are tensioned in succession, those tensioned later may be subject to excessive friction because the radial component of the tension in the outer wires will tend to press against the inner wires. It would be desirable to tension the inner wires first, but in a tendon with reversed curves there is little choice to make. If wire separators are employed in the duct they may be disarranged, as the units are tensioned successively, and thus produce additional friction. These are individual points which may sometimes be significant, depending on the existing conditions.

The Cement and Concrete Association of England has conducted extensive experiments in an effort to determine the coefficient of friction and the wobble effect for computing the frictional loss in the Freyssinet, the Magnel, and the Lee-McCall systems.[4] It is also pointed out that μ and K will depend on a number of factors: the type of steel used, whether wires, strands, or rods; the kind of surface, whether indented or corrugated, whether rusted or cleaned or galvanized. The amount of vibration used in placing the concrete will affect the straightness of the ducts; so will the overall size of the duct and its excess over the enclosed steel, and the spacing of the supports for the tendons or the duct-forming material. Individual values vary greatly, and the readers are referred to reference 4 if more accurate information is desired. As an example, for Freyssinet cables in light metal sheathing, the K value can be as high as 0.0050 if heavy vibration is applied to the concrete and light-gage metal is used for sheathing without adequate supports.

Additional frictional coefficients have been determined by Dr. Leonhardt for different stressing wires and strands on various underlays.[6] He also mentioned many factors that cannot be predetermined, such as thin sheet metal casings which may be worn through so that the wires slide against the concrete, or the lateral binding of wires in curved sections, or the uneven movement of the separators due to the elongation of wires. Some of his values are tabulated in Table 4-1, but they are intended only as a guide for the normal conditions.

The coefficient of friction depends a great deal on the care exercised in construction. For unbonded reinforcement, lubricants can be used to advantage. Cables well greased and carefully wrapped in plastic

TABLE 4-1

Frictional Coefficients μ for Stressing Wires on Various Underlays
(Dr. F. Leonhardt)

Type of Wire	Underlay	μ
Drawn wires, 0.196-in. diameter	Smoothly finished concrete	0.29–0.31
	Roughly finished concrete	0.35–0.44
	New black sheet metal	0.16–0.22
Two 0.079-in. wire strands	Smoothly finished concrete	0.38–0.40
	Roughly finished concrete	0.40–0.46
	New black sheet metal	0.19–0.22
Seven 0.099-in. wire strands	Black sheet metal	0.20–0.25
	Paraffin, under pressure of 30 psi	0.10
	Paraffin, under pressure of 700 psi	0.02–0.025

tubes will have little friction, but if mortar leaks through openings in the tube, the cables may be tightly stuck. For bonded reinforcement, where lubricants may occasionally be employed, they must be applied very carefully in order not to destroy the eventual bond to be effected by grouting. Water-soluble oils have been successfully employed to reduce the friction while tensioning, and the lubricant is flushed off with water afterwards.

There are several methods of overcoming the frictional loss in tendons. One method is to overtension them. When friction is not excessive, the amount of overtension is usually made to equal the maximum frictional loss. The amount of wire lengthening corresponding to that overtension and the estimated friction can also be computed to serve as a check. This amount of overtension required for overcoming friction is not cumulative over that required for overcoming anchorage losses or for minimizing creep in steel. It is sufficient to take the greatest of the three required values and overtension for that amount. This is because in all three cases

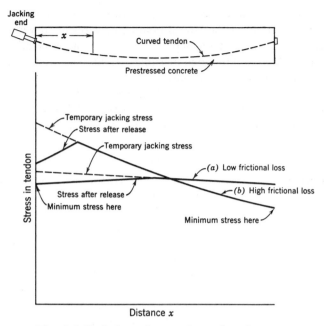

Fig. 4-6. Variation of stress in tendon due to frictional force.

the overtensioning consists of an overstretching and a subsequent release-back. It must be noted that, if most of the friction exists near the jacking end, overtensioning to balance that friction will not produce any over-stretching of the main portion of the tendon and hence will not serve to minimize creep to any extent.

The effect of overtensioning with a subsequent release-back is to put the frictional difference in the reverse direction. Thus, after releasing, the variation of stress along the tendon takes some shape as in Fig. 4-6. When the frictional loss is a high percentage of the prestress, it cannot be totally overcome by overtensioning (curve *b*, Fig. 4-6), since the maximum amount of tensioning is limited by the strength or the yield point of the tendon. The portion of the loss that has not been overcome must then be allowed for in the design.

Jacking from both ends, of course, is another means for reducing frictional loss. It involves more work in the field but is often resorted to when the tendons are long or when the angles of bending are large. For a simple beam, where the critical point is its midspan, tensioning from both ends will not appreciably affect the controlling prestress at the midspan though it might change the beam deflection quite a bit.

4-7 Frictional Loss, Theoretical Considerations

The basic theory of frictional loss of a cable around a curve is well known in physics. In its simple form, it can be derived as follows. Consider an infinitesimal length dx of a prestressing tendon whose centroid follows the arc of a circle of radius R, Fig. 4-7, then the change in angle of the tendon as it goes around that length dx is

$$d\theta = \frac{dx}{R}$$

For this infinitesimal length dx, the stress in the tendon may be considered constant and equal to $F;$ then the normal component of pressure produced by the stress F bending around an angle $d\theta$ is given by

$$N = F\,d\theta = \frac{F\,dx}{R}$$

The amount of frictional loss dF around the length dx is given by the pressure times a coefficient of friction μ, thus,

$$dF = -\mu N$$
$$= \frac{-\mu F\,dx}{R} = -\mu F\,d\theta$$

Transposing, we have

$$\frac{dF}{F} = -\mu\,d\theta$$

Integrating this on both sides, we have

$$\log_e F = -\mu\theta$$

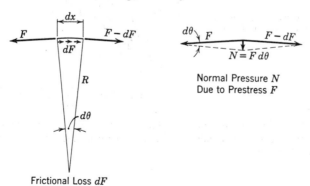

Frictional Loss dF

Fig. 4-7. Frictional loss along length dx.

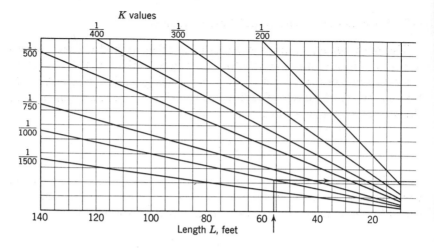

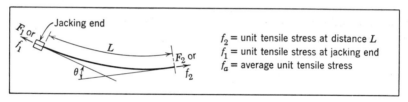

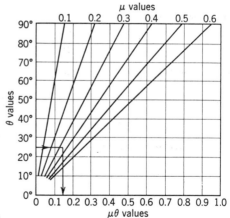

EXAMPLE: Given: $L = 56$ ft., $\theta = 25°$.
Assume $K = 0.0010$, $\mu = 0.35$,
$f_2 = 155$ ksi. From small chart,
determine $\mu\theta = 0.15$. Enter large
chart at $L = 56$ and follow
indicated path. To obtain f_2 of
155 ksi, required f_1 is 191 ksi.
Average stress f_a is 173 ksi.

Fig. 4-8. Chart for solution of equation 4-6a (from *Criteria for Prestressed Concrete Bridges*, Bureau of Public Roads, adapted from chart by the Freyssinet Company, New York).

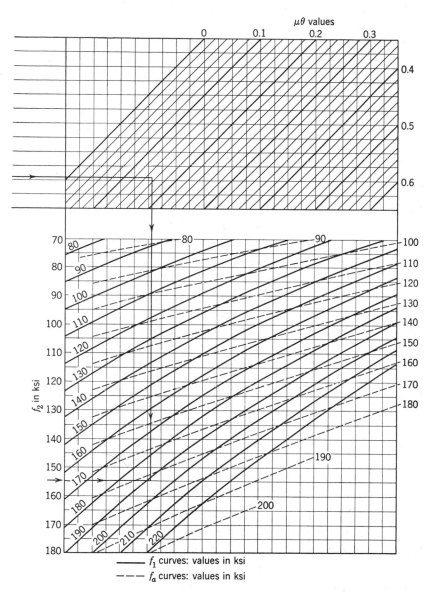

Fig. 4-8 (contd.)

Using the limits F_1 and F_2, we have the conventional friction formula

$$F_2 = F_1 e^{-\mu\theta} = F_1 e^{-\mu L/R} \qquad (4\text{-}4)$$

since $\theta = L/R$ for a section of constant R.

For tendons with a succession of curves of varying radii, it is necessary to apply this formula to the different sections in order to obtain the total loss.

The above formula can also be applied to compute frictional loss due to wobble or length effect. Substituting the loss KL for $\mu\theta$ in formula 4-4, we have

$$\log_e F = -KL \qquad F_2 = F_1 e^{-KL} \qquad (4\text{-}5)$$

If it is intended to combine the length and curvature effect, we can simply write

$$\log_e F = -\mu\theta - KL$$

For limits F_1 and F_2,

$$F_2 = F_1 e^{-\mu\theta - KL} \qquad (4\text{-}6)$$

Or, in terms of unit stresses,

$$f_2 = f_1 e^{-\mu\theta - KL} \qquad (4\text{-}6a)$$

These formulas are theoretically correct and take into account the decrease in tension and hence the decrease in the pressure as the tendon bends around the curve and gradually loses its stress due to friction. A chart is given in Fig. 4-8 for the solution of equation 4-6a. If, however, the total difference between the tension in the tendon at the start and that at the end of the curve is not excessive (say not more than 15 or 20%), an approximate formula using the initial tension for the entire curve will be close enough. On this assumption, a simpler formula can be derived in place of the above exponential form. If the normal pressure is assumed to be constant, the total frictional loss around a curve with angle θ and length L is, Fig. 4-9,

$$F_2 - F_1 = -\mu F_1 \theta = -\frac{\mu F_1 L}{R} \qquad (4\text{-}7)$$

For length or wobble effect, we can again substitute KL for $\mu\theta$, thus,

$$F_2 - F_1 = -KLF_1 \qquad (4\text{-}8)$$

To compute the total loss due to both curvature and length effect, the above two formulas can be combined, giving

$$F_2 - F_1 = -\mu F_1 \theta - KLF_1$$

Transposing terms, we have

$$\frac{F_2 - F_1}{F_1} = -KL - \mu\theta = -\left(K + \frac{\mu}{R}\right)L \qquad (4\text{-}9)$$

The loss of prestress for the entire length of a tendon can be considered from section to section, with each section consisting of either a

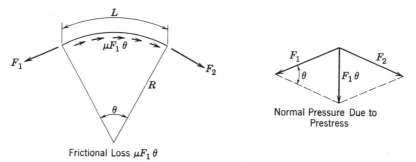

Frictional Loss $\mu F_1 \theta$

Normal Pressure Due to Prestress

Fig. 4-9. Approximate frictional loss along circular curve.

straight line or a simple circular curve. The reduced stress at the end of a segment can be used to compute the frictional loss for the next segment, etc.

Since, for practically all prestressed-concrete members, the depth is small compared with the length, the projected length of tendon measured along the axis of the member can be used when computing frictional losses. Similarly, the angular change θ is given by the transverse deviation of the tendon divided by its projected length, both referred to the axis of the member.

EXAMPLE 4-4

A prestressed-concrete beam is continuous over two spans, Fig. 4-10, and its curved tendon is to be tensioned from both ends. Compute the percentage loss of prestress due to friction, from one end to the center of the beam (A to E). The coefficient of friction between the cable and the duct is taken as 0.4, and the average "wobble" or length effect is represented by $K = 0.0008$ per ft.

Solution 1. A simple approximate solution will first be presented. Using formula 4-9,

$$\frac{F_2 - F_1}{F_1} = -KL - \mu\theta$$
$$= -0.0008 \times 70 - 0.4(0.167 + 0.100)$$
$$= -0.056 - 0.107$$
$$= -0.163$$

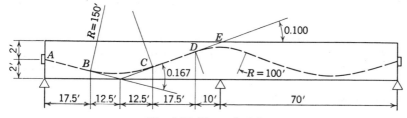

Fig. 4-10. Example 4-4.

Solution 2. The above solution does not take into account the gradual reduction of stress from A toward E. A more exact solution would be to divide the tendon into 4 portions from A to E, and consider each portion after the loss has been deducted from the preceding portions. Thus, for stress at $A = F_1$,

$$AB, \text{ length effect: } KL = 0.0008 \times 17.5 = 0.014$$
$$\text{Stress at } B = 1 - 0.014 = 0.986F_1$$
$$BC, \text{ length effect: } KL = 0.0008 \times 25 = 0.020$$
$$\text{Curvature effect: } \mu\theta = 0.4 \times 0.167 = 0.067$$
$$\text{Total: } 0.020 + 0.067 = 0.087$$

Using the reduced stress at B of 0.986, the loss is $0.087 \times 0.986 = 0.086$.

$$\text{Stress at } C = 0.986 - 0.086 = 0.900F_1$$
$$CD, \text{ length effect: } KL = 0.0008 \times 17.5 = 0.014$$

Using the reduced stress of 0.900 at C, the loss is $0.014 \times 0.900 = 0.013$.

$$\text{Stress at } D = 0.900 - 0.013 = 0.887F_1$$
$$DE, \text{ length effect: } KL = 0.0008 \times 10 = 0.008$$
$$\text{Curvature effect: } \mu\theta = 0.4 \times 0.100 = 0.040$$
$$\text{Total: } 0.008 + 0.040 = 0.048$$
$$\text{Loss} = 0.048 \times 0.887 = 0.043$$
$$\text{Stress at } E = 0.887 - 0.043 = 0.844F_1$$
$$\text{Total loss from } A \text{ to } E = 1 - 0.844 = 0.156 = 15.6\%$$

This computation can be tabulated in order to simplify the work. It can be further noticed that this second method yields a loss only slightly less than the first approximate method.

Solution 3. A still more exact solution is to use the conventional friction formula 4-6, which takes into account not only the variation of stress from segment to segment but also that from point to point all along the cable. The solution is tabulated as shown.

Segment	L	KL	θ	$\mu\theta$	$KL + \mu\theta$	$e^{-KL-\mu\theta}$	Stress at End of Segment
AB	17.5	0.014	0	0	0.014	0.986	$0.986F_1$
BC	25	0.020	0.167	0.067	0.087	0.916	$0.903F_1$
CD	17.5	0.014	0	0	0.014	0.986	$0.890F_1$
DE	10	0.008	0.100	0.040	0.048	0.953	$0.848F_1$

The total frictional loss from A to E is given as

$$1 - 0.848 = 0.152 = 15.2\%$$

4-8   Total Amount of Losses

Initial prestress in steel minus the losses is known as the *effective* or the design *prestress*. The total amount of losses to be assumed in design will depend on the basis on which the initial prestress is measured. First, there is the *temporary maximum jacking stress* to which a tendon may be subject for the purpose of minimizing creep in steel or for balancing frictional losses. Then there is a slight release from that maximum stress back to the normal *jacking stress*.

As soon as the prestress is transferred to the concrete, anchorage loss will take place. The *jacking stress* minus the anchorage loss will be the stress at anchorage after release and is frequently called the *initial prestress*. For post-tensioning, losses due to elastic shortening will gradually take place, if there are other tendons yet to be tensioned. This elastic shortening of concrete may be considered in two parts: that due to direct axial shortening and that due to elastic bending, as discussed in sections 4-1 and 4-5. For pre-tensioning, the entire amount of loss due to elastic shortening will occur at the transfer of prestress.

Depending on the definition of the term *initial prestress*, the amount of losses to be deducted will differ. If the jacking stress minus the anchorage loss is taken as the initial prestress, as described in the previous paragraph, then the losses to be deducted will include the elastic shortening and creep and shrinkage in concrete plus the creep in steel. This seems to be the most common practice. If the jacking stress itself is taken as the initial prestress, then anchorage losses must be deducted as well. If the stress after the elastic shortening of concrete is taken as the initial prestress, then the shrinkage and creep in concrete and the creep in steel will be the only losses. For points away from the jacking end, the effect of friction must be considered in addition. Frictional force along the tendon may either increase or decrease the stress, as discussed in section 4-6.

The magnitude of losses can be expressed in four ways:

1. In unit strains. This is most convenient for losses such as creep, shrinkage, and elastic shortenings of concrete.

2. In total strains. This is more convenient for the anchorage losses.

3. In unit stresses. All losses when expressed in strains can be transformed into unit stresses in steel, if the modulus of elasticity of steel is known.

4. In percentage of prestress. Losses due to creep in steel and friction can be most easily expressed in this way. Other losses expressed in unit stresses can be easily transformed into percentages of the initial prestress. This often conveys a better picture of the significance of the losses.

It is difficult to generalize the amount of loss of prestress, because it is dependent on so many factors: the properties of concrete and steel, curing and moisture conditions, magnitude and time of application of prestress, and the process of prestressing. For average steel and concrete properties, cured under average air conditions, the tabulated percentages may be taken as representative of the average losses.

	Pre-Tensioning, %	Post-Tensioning, %
Elastic shortening and bending of concrete	3	1
Creep of concrete	6	5
Shrinkage of concrete	7	6
Creep in steel	2	3
Total loss	18	15

The table assumes that proper overtensioning has been applied to reduce creep in steel and to overcome friction and anchorage losses. Any frictional loss not overcome must be considered in addition. The common allowance for loss of prestress is 15% for post-tensioning and about 18% for pre-tensioning. Such allowance is seen to be not too far from the probable values. It must be borne in mind, however, that, when conditions deviate from the average, different allowances should be made accordingly. For example, when the average prestress in a member (F_e/A_c) is high, say about 1000 psi, these losses should be increased to about 25% for pretensioning and 20% for post-tensioning. When the average prestress is low, say about 250 psi, the above losses should be reduced to 14% for pre-tensioning and 12% for post-tensioning. That is why an understanding and analysis of the sources of loss are of prime importance to the designing engineer.

EXAMPLE 4-5

A post-tensioned concrete beam, Fig. 4-11, with a cable of 24 parallel wires (total steel area = 1.20 sq in.) is tensioned with 2 wires at a time. The jacking stress is to be measured by jack gage pressure. The wires are to be stressed from

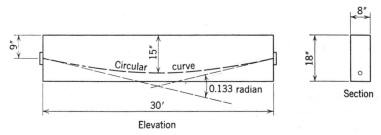

Fig. 4-11. Example 4-5.

one end to a value of f_1 to overcome frictional loss, then released to a value of f_2 so that immediately after anchoring an initial prestress of 120,000 psi would be obtained. Compute f_1 and f_2. Then compute the final design stress in the steel after all losses have taken place. Assume the following:

1. Coefficient of friction $\mu = 0.6$ between steel and concrete, K for length effect $= 0.0010$.

2. Deformation of anchorage and slippage of wires estimated at 0.05 in. per end. $E_s = 30,000,000$ psi.

3. Elastic shortening of concrete to be computed for $E_c = 4,000,000$ psi. Neglect shortening of steel due to bending of beam.

4. Creep coefficient of concrete $= 2.2$.

5. Shrinkage of concrete $= 0.0002$.

6. Creep of steel $= 3\%$ of initial steel stress.

Solution. 1. The percentage loss of prestress due to friction is given by

$$\text{Length effect} = KL = 30 \times 0.0010 = 0.30 \, .o\%$$

$$\text{Curvature effect} = \mu\theta = 0.6 \times 0.133 = 0.08$$

$$\text{Total } 0.03 + 0.08 = 0.11$$

Hence it is necessary to tension the steel to

$$f_1' = 120,000/(1 - 0.11) = 135,000 \text{ psi}$$

at one end in order to overcome the friction and obtain a stress of 120,000 psi at the unjacked end. Note that, should the frictional loss be more than 20 or 30%, it may be desirable to apply formula 4-6.

2. The anchorage slippage of 0.05 in. occurs only on one end since the unjacked end would have its slippage taking place before the release of jack. The loss in unit strain is given by

$$0.05/360 = 0.00014$$

and the loss in steel stress is

$$0.00014 \times 30,000,000 = 4200 \text{ psi}$$

Hence, by tensioning the steel to $f_1 = 135,000$ psi and then releasing it to $f_2 = 124,200$ psi for anchoring, the minimum stress after anchoring will be 120,000 psi. This minimum stress will occur at both ends of the beam.

3. Since the wires are tensioned, two by two, the first pair will lose some stress due to the elastic shortening of concrete under the action of the subsequent 11 pairs, and the amount will be approximately

$$\frac{\frac{11}{12} \times 120,000 \times 1.20 \times 30,000,000}{4,000,000 \times 18 \times 8} = 6800 \text{ psi}$$

The average loss for all the wires will be $6800/2 = 3400$ psi.

4. The total stress in the steel is very nearly 144,000 lb, for which the elastic shortening of concrete is

$$\frac{144,000}{4,000,000 \times 18 \times 8} = 0.00025$$

Creep of concrete $= (2.2 - 1)0.00025 = 0.00030$, which corresponds to a stress of

$$0.00030 \times 30{,}000{,}000 = 9000 \text{ psi in the steel}$$

5. For shrinkage of 0.0002, the loss in the steel stress is

$$0.0002 \times 30{,}000{,}000 = 6000 \text{ psi}$$

6. Creep of steel at 3% of 120,000 = 3600 psi
The total loss can now be summarized:

	Stress Loss	Percentage Loss
Elastic shortening	3,400	3
Creep of concrete	9,000	7
Shrinkage of concrete	6,000	5
Creep in steel	3,600	3
Total	22,000 psi	18%

4-9   Elongation of Tendons

It is often necessary to compute the elongation of a tendon caused by prestressing. When fabricating the anchorage parts in the Roebling and Stressteel systems, the expected amount of elongation must be known approximately. For the Prescon and Texas P.I. systems it must be known rather accurately. For all systems the measured elongation is compared to the expected value, thus serving as a check on the accuracy of the gage readings or on the magnitude of frictional loss along the length of the tendon. The computation of such elongation is discussed in two parts as follows.

Neglecting Frictional Loss along Tendon. If a tendon has uniform stress f_s along its entire length L, the amount of elongation is given by

$$\Delta_s = \delta_s L = f_s L/E_s = FL/E_s A_s \tag{4-10}$$

For prestress exceeding the proportional limit of the tendon, this formula may not be applicable, and it may be necessary to refer to the stress-strain diagram for the corresponding value of δ_s.

Before any tendon is tensioned, there almost always exists in it a certain amount of slack. For systems requiring shim plates, such as the Prescon system, that slack must be allowed for when computing the length of the shims. In addition, it may be desirable to allow for the shrinkage and elastic shortening of concrete at the time of tensioning. Hence the length of the shims must equal the elastic elongation of the tendon plus the slack in the tendon plus the shortening of concrete at transfer. Conversely, the elastic elongation of the tendon must be computed by deducting the initial slack and the elastic shortening of concrete from the apparent elongation.

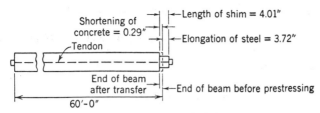

Fig. 4-12. Example 4-6.

It is not easy to determine the slack in a tendon accurately, hence the usual practice is to give the tendon some initial tension f_{s1} and measure the elongation Δ_s thereafter. Then, neglecting any shortening of the concrete, the total elastic elongation of the tendon can be computed by

$$\text{Elastic elongation} = \frac{f_s}{f_s - f_{s1}} \Delta_s \qquad (4\text{-}11)$$

EXAMPLE 4-6

A Prescon cable, 60 ft long, Fig. 4-12, is to be tensioned from one end to an initial prestress of 150,000 psi immediately after transfer. Assume that there is no slack in the cable, that the shrinkage of concrete is 0.0002 at time of transfer, and that the average compression in concrete is 800 psi along the length of the tendon. $E_c = 3,800,000$ psi; $E_s = 29,000,000$ psi. Compute the length of shims required, neglecting any elastic shortening of the shims and any friction along the tendon.

Solution. From equation 4-10, the elastic elongation of steel is

$$\Delta_s = f_s L / E_s = 150,000 \times 60 \times 12/29,000,000 = 3.72 \text{ in.}$$

Shortening of concrete due to shrinkage is

$$0.0002 \times 60 \times 12 = 0.14 \text{ in.}$$

Elastic shortening of concrete is

$$800 \times 60 \times 12/3,800,000 = 0.15 \text{ in.}$$

Length of shims required is

$$3.72 + 0.14 + 0.15 = 4.01 \text{ in.}$$

If shims of 4.01 in. are inserted in the anchorage, there should remain an initial prestress of 150,000 psi in the steel immediately after transfer.

EXAMPLE 4-7

Eighteen 0.196-in. wires in a Freyssinet cable, 80 ft long, are tensioned initially to a total stress of 3000 lb. What additional elongation of the wires as measured therefrom is required to obtain an initial prestress of 160,000 psi? $E_s = 28,000,000$ psi. Assume no shortening of concrete during the tensioning process and neglect friction.

Solution.

$$A_s = 18 \times 0.03 = 0.54 \text{ sq in.}$$
$$f_{s1} = 3000/0.54 = 5500 \text{ psi}$$

Total elastic elongation of tendon from 0 to 160,000 psi is

$$f_s L / E_s = 160{,}000 \times 80 \times 12 / 28{,}000{,}000 = 5.48 \text{ in.}$$

From equation 4-11,

$$5.48 = \frac{f_s}{f_s - f_{s1}} \Delta_s$$

$$= \frac{160{,}000}{160{,}000 - 5500} \Delta_s$$

$$\Delta_s = 5.28 \text{ in.}$$

Thus, with zero reading taken at a total stress of 3000 lb, an elongation of 5.28 in. must be obtained for a prestress of 160,000 psi.

Considering Frictional Loss along Tendon. It was shown in section 4-7 that, for a curved tendon with a constant radius R, the stress at any point away from the jacking end is

$$F_2 = F_1 e^{-(\mu\theta + KL)}$$

The average stress F_a for the entire length of curve with stress varying from F_1 to F_2 can be shown to be

$$F_a = F_2 \frac{e^{\mu\theta + KL} - 1}{\mu\theta + KL} \tag{4-12}$$

This equation is solved graphically in Fig. 4-8, where the dotted lines give the values of $f_a = F_a / A_s$.

The total lengthening for length L is given by

$$\Delta_s = \frac{F_a L}{E_s A_s} = \frac{F_2 L}{E_s A_s} \frac{e^{\mu\theta + KL} - 1}{\mu\theta + KL} \tag{4-13}$$

If only an approximate solution is desired, the medium value of F_1 and F_2 can be used in computing the elongation; thus

$$\Delta_s = \frac{F_1 + F_2}{2} \frac{L}{E_s A_s} \tag{4-13}$$

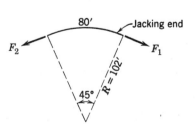

Fig. 4-13. Example 4-8.

EXAMPLE 4-8

A tendon 80 ft long is tensioned along a circular curve with $R = 102$ ft, Fig. 4-13. For a unit stress of 180,000 psi applied at the jacking end, a total elongation of 4.80 in. is obtained. $E_s = 30{,}000{,}000$ psi. Compute the stress f_2 at the far end of the tendon.

Solution. 1. Approximate solution. Average stress in the tendon is given by

$$f_a = \Delta_s E_s / L = 4.80 \times 30{,}000{,}000 / (80 \times 12)$$

$$= 150{,}000 \text{ psi}$$

Since the maximum stress is 180,000 psi, the minimum stress f_2 must be 120,000 psi, assuming uniform decrease in the stress.

2. Exact solution. Using Fig. 4-8, enter the diagram with $f_1 = 180$ ksi and $f_a = 150$ ksi. At the intersection of these two curves, read $f_2 = 125$ ksi.

References

1 D. D. Magura, M. A. Sozen, and C. P. Siess, "A Study of Stress Relaxation in Prestressing Reinforcement," *Structural Research Series*, No. 237, Univ. of Illinois, 1962; also. G. T. Spare, "Prestressing Wires—Stress-Relaxation and Stress-Corrosion up to Date," *Wire and Wire Products*, December 1954.

2 W. O. Everling, "Prestressing Steel under High Stress," *Proceedings World Conference on Prestressed Concrete*, San Francisco, 1957.

3 "Prestressed Concrete," *Proceedings of the Conference Held in 1949*, Institution of Civil Engineers, London, p. 29.

4 E. H. Cooley, *Friction in Post-Tensioned Prestressing Systems*, and *Estimation of Friction in Prestressed Concrete*, Cement and Concrete Assn., London, 1953.

5 T. Y. Lin, "Cable Friction in Post-tensioning," *Journal of the Structural Division, ASCE*, November 1956.

6 F. Leonhardt, "Continuous Prestressed Concrete Beams," *J. Am. Conc. Inst.*, March, 1953 (*Proc.*, Vol. 49), p. 617.

5

analysis of sections for flexure

5-1 Introduction and Sign Conventions

Differentiation can be made between the *analysis* and *design* of pre-stressed sections for flexure. By *analysis* is meant the determination of stresses in the steel and concrete when the form and size of a section are already given or assumed. This is obviously a simpler operation than the *design* of the section, which involves the choice of a suitable section out of many possible shapes and dimensions. In actual practice, it is often necessary to first perform the process of design when assuming a section, and then to analyze that assumed section. But, for the purpose of study, it is easier to learn first the methods of analysis and then those of design. This reversal of order is desirable in the study of pre-stressed as well as reinforced concrete.

This chapter will be devoted to the first part, the *analysis*; the next chapter will deal with *design*. The discussion is limited to the analysis of sections for flexure, meaning members under bending, such as beams and slabs. Only the effect of moment is considered here; that of shear and bond is treated in Chapter 7.

A rather controversial point in the analysis of prestressed-concrete beams has been the choice of a proper system of sign conventions. Many authors have used positive sign (+) for compressive stresses and negative sign (−) for tensile stresses, basing their convention on the idea that prestressed-concrete beams are normally under compression and hence the plus sign should be employed to denote that state of stress. The author prefers to maintain the common sign convention as used for the design of other structures; that is, minus for compressive and plus for tensile stresses. Throughout this treatise, plus will stand for tension and minus for compression, whether we are talking of stresses in steel or concrete, prestressed or reinforced. When the sense of the stress is self-evident, signs will be omitted.

5-2   Stresses in Concrete Due to Prestress

Some of the basic principles of stress computation for prestressed concrete have already been mentioned in section 1-2. They will be discussed
in greater detail here. First of all, let us consider the effect of prestress.
According to present practice, stresses in concrete due to prestress are
always computed by the elastic theory. Consider the prestress F existing at
the time under discussion, whether it be the initial or the final value. If F
is applied at the centroid of the concrete section, and if the section under
consideration is sufficiently far from the point of application of the prestress,
then, by St. Venant's principle, the unit stress in concrete is uniform across
that section and is given by the usual formula,

$$f = \frac{F}{A}$$

where A is the area of that concrete section.

For a pre-tensioned member, when the prestress in the steel is transferred from the bulkheads to the concrete, Fig. 5-1, the force that was
resisted by the bulkheads is not transferred to both the steel and the concrete in the member. The release of the resistance from the bulkheads is
equivalent to the application of an opposite force F_i to the member. Using
the transformed section method, and with A_c = net sectional area of concrete, the compressive stress produced in the concrete is

$$f_c = \frac{F_i}{A_c + nA_s} = \frac{F_i}{A_t} \tag{5-1}$$

while that induced in the steel is

$$\Delta f_s = n f_c = \frac{nF_i}{A_c + nA_s} = \frac{nF_i}{A_t} \tag{5-2}$$

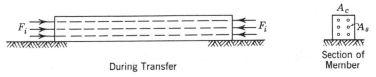

Fig. 5-1. Transfer of concentric prestress in a pre-tensioned member.

which represents the immediate reduction of the prestress in the steel as a result of the transfer.

Although this method of computation is correct according to the elastic theory, the usual practice is not to follow such a procedure, but rather to consider the prestress in the steel being reduced by a loss resulting from elastic shortening of concrete and approximated by

$$\Delta f_s = \frac{nF_i}{A_c} \quad \text{or} \quad \frac{nF_i}{A_g} \tag{5-3}$$

which differs a little from formula 5-2 but is close enough for all practical purposes, since the total amount of reduction is only about 2 or 3% and the value of n cannot be accurately known anyway.

After the transfer of prestress, further losses will occur owing to the creep and shrinkage in concrete. Theoretically, all such losses should be calculated on the basis of a transformed section, taking into consideration the area of steel. But, again, that is seldom done, the practice being simply to allow for the losses by an approximate percentage. In other words, the simple formula $f = F/A$ is always used, with the value of F estimated for the given condition, and the gross area of concrete used for A. For a post-tensioned member, the same reasoning holds true. Suppose that there are several tendons in the member prestressed in succession. Every tendon that is tensioned becomes part of the section. The effect of tensioning any subsequent tendon on the stresses in the previously tensioned ones should be calculated on the basis of a transformed section. Theoretically, there will be a different transformed section after the tensioning of every tendon. However, such refinements are not justified, and the usual procedure is simply to use the formula $f = F/A$, with F based on the initial prestress in the steel.

EXAMPLE 5-1

A pre-tensioned member, similar to that shown in Fig. 5-1, has a section of 8 in. by 12 in. It is concentrically prestressed with 0.8 sq in. of high-tensile steel wire, which is anchored to the bulkheads of a unit stress of 150,000 psi. Assuming that $n = 6$, compute the stresses in the concrete and steel immediately after transfer.

Solution 1. An exact theoretical solution. Using the elastic theory, we have

$$f_c = \frac{F_i}{A_c + nA_s} = \frac{F_i}{A_g + (n-1)A_s}$$

$$= \frac{0.8 \times 150,000}{12 \times 8 + 5 \times 0.8} = 1200 \text{ psi}$$

$$nf_c = 6 \times 1200 = 7200 \text{ psi}$$

Stress in steel after transfer $= 150,000 - 7200 = 142,800$ psi.

Solution 2. An approximate solution. The loss of prestress in steel due to elastic shortening of concrete is estimated by

$$= n \frac{F_i}{A_g}$$

$$= 6 \frac{120,000}{8 \times 12} = 7500 \text{ psi}$$

Stress in steel after loss $= 150,000 - 7500 = 142,500$ psi. Stress in concrete is

$$f_c = \frac{142,500 \times 0.8}{96} = 1190 \text{ psi}$$

Note that, in this second solution, the approximations introduced are: (1) using gross area of concrete instead of net area, (2) using the initial stress in steel instead of the reduced stress. But the answers are very nearly the same for both solutions. The second method is more convenient and is usually followed.

Next, suppose that the prestress F is applied to the concrete section with an eccentricity e, Fig. 5-2; then it is possible to resolve the prestress into two components: a concentric load F through the centroid, and a moment Fe. By the usual elastic theory, the fiber stress at any point due to moment Fe is given by the formula

$$f = \frac{My}{I} = \frac{Fey}{I} \tag{5-4}$$

Then the resultant fiber stress due to the eccentric prestress is given by

$$f = \frac{F}{A} \pm \frac{Fey}{I} \tag{5-5}$$

The question again arises as to what section should be considered when computing the values of e and I, whether the gross or the net concrete

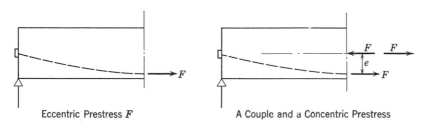

Eccentric Prestress F A Couple and a Concentric Prestress

Fig. 5-2. Eccentric prestress on a section.

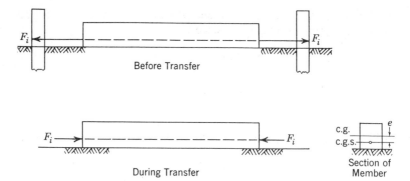

Fig. 5-3. Transfer of eccentric prestress in a pre-tensioned member.

section or the transformed section, and what prestress F to be used in the formula, the initial or the reduced value. Consider a pre-tensioned member, Fig. 5-3. The steel has already been bonded to the concrete; the release of the force from the bulkhead is equivalent to the application of an eccentric force to the composite member; hence the force should be the total F_i, and I should be the moment of inertia of the transformed section, and e should be measured from the centroidal axis of that transformed section. However, in practice, this procedure is seldom followed. Instead, the gross or net concrete section is considered, and either the initial or the reduced prestress is applied. The error is negligible in most cases.

EXAMPLE 5-2

A pre-tensioned member similar to that shown in Fig. 5-3 has a section of 8 in. by 12 in. deep. It is eccentrically prestressed with 0.8 sq in. of high-tensile steel wire which is anchored to the bulkheads at a unit stress of 150,000 psi. The c.g.s. is 4 in. above the bottom fiber. Assuming that $n = 6$, compute the stresses in the concrete immediately after transfer.

Solution 1. An exact theoretical solution. Using the elastic theory, the

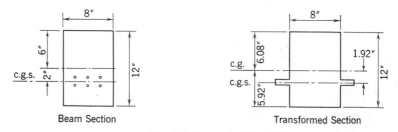

Fig. 5-4. Example 5-2.

centroid of the transformed section and its moment of inertia are obtained as follows. Referring to Fig. 5-4, for $(n - 1)A_s = 5 \times 0.8 = 4$ sq in.,

$$y_0 = \frac{4 \times 2}{96 + 4} = 0.08 \text{ in.}$$

$$I_t = \frac{8 \times 12^3}{12} + 96 \times 0.08^2 + 4 \times 1.92^2$$

$$= 1152 + 0.6 + 14.7$$

$$= 1167.3 \text{ in.}^4$$

Top fiber stress $= \dfrac{F_i}{A_t} + \dfrac{F_i e y}{I_t}$ ~*Comp*

$$= \frac{-120,000}{100} + \frac{120,000 \times 1.92 \times 6.08}{1167.3}$$

$$= -1200 + 1200$$

$$= 0$$

Bottom fiber stress $= \dfrac{-120,000}{100} - \dfrac{120,000 \times 1.92 \times 5.92}{1167.3}$

$$= -1200 - 1170$$

$$= -2370 \text{ psi} \qquad .7200 \checkmark$$

Solution 2. An approximate solution. The loss of prestress can be approximately computed, as in example 5-1, to be 7500 psi in the steel. Hence the reduced prestress is 142,500 psi or 114,000 lb. Extreme fiber stresses in the concrete can be computed to be

$$f_c = \frac{F}{A} \pm \frac{Fey}{I}$$

$$= \frac{-114,000}{96} \pm \frac{114,000 \times 2 \times 6}{(8 \times 12^3)/12}$$

$$= -1187 \pm 1187$$

$$= 0 \text{ in the top fiber}$$

$$= -2374 \text{ psi in the bottom fiber}$$

The approximations here introduced are: using an approximate value of reduced prestress, and using the gross area of concrete. This second solution, although approximate, is more often used because of its simplicity.

Now consider a pre-tensioned curved member as in Fig. 5-5. If the transfer of prestress is considered as a force F_i applied at each end, the eccentricity and the moment of inertia will vary for each section. If the exact method of elastic analysis is preferred, different I's and e's will have to be computed for different sections. If an approximate method is permitted, a constant I based on the gross concrete area would suffice

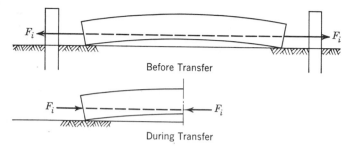

Fig. 5-5. Transfer of prestress in a curved pre-tensioned member.

for all sections, and the eccentricity can be readily measured from the mid-depth of the section.

For a post-tensioned member before being bonded, the prestress F to be used in the stress computations is again the initial prestress minus the estimated losses. For the value of I, either the net or the gross concrete section is used, although, theoretically, the net section is the correct one. After the steel is bonded to the concrete, any loss that takes place actually happens to the section as a whole. However, for the sake of simplicity, a rigorous analysis based on the transformed section is seldom made. Instead, the reduced prestress is estimated and the stresses in the concrete are computed for that reduced prestress acting on the net concrete section (gross concrete section may sometimes be conveniently used). Stresses produced by external loads, however, are often computed on the basis of the transformed section if accuracy is desired; otherwise, gross section is used for the computation. The permissible simplifications for each case will depend to a large degree on the degree of accuracy required and the time available for computation.

EXAMPLE 5-3

A post-tensioned beam has a midspan cross section with a duct of 2 in. by 3 in. to house the wires, as shown in Fig. 5-6. It is prestressed with 0.8 sq in. of steel to an initial stress of 150,000 psi. Immediately after transfer the stress is reduced by 5% owing to anchorage loss and elastic shortening of concrete. Compute the stresses in the concrete at transfer.

Solution 1.   Using net section of concrete. The centroid and I of the net concrete section are computed as follows

$$A_c = 96 - 6 = 90 \text{ sq in.}$$

$$y_0 = \frac{6 \times 3}{96 - 6} = 0.2 \text{ in.}$$

$$I = \frac{8 \times 12^3}{12} + 96 \times 0.2^2 - \frac{2 \times 3^3}{12} - 6 \times 3.2^2$$

$$= 1152 + 3.8 - 4.5 - 61.5$$

$$= 1090$$

Total prestress in steel $= 150{,}000 \times 0.8 \times 95\% = 114{,}000$ lb

$$f_c = \frac{-114{,}000}{90} \pm \frac{114{,}000 \times 3.2 \times 5.8}{1090}$$

$$= -1270 + 1940 = +670 \text{ psi for top fiber}$$

$$f_c = -1270 - 2070 = -3340 \text{ psi for bottom fiber}$$

Solution 2. Using gross section of concrete. An approximate solution using the gross concrete section would give results not so close in this case:

$$f_c = \frac{-114{,}000}{96} \pm \frac{114{,}000 \times 3 \times 6}{(8 \times 12^3)/12}$$

$$= -1187 \pm 1783$$

$$= +596 \text{ psi for top fiber}$$

$$= -2970 \text{ psi for bottom fiber}$$

If the eccentricity does not occur along one of the principal axes of the section, it is necessary to further resolve the moment into two component moments along the two principal axes, Fig. 5-7; then the stress at any point is given by

$$f = \frac{F}{A} \pm \frac{Fe_x x}{I_x} \pm \frac{Fe_y y}{I_y}$$

Since concrete is not a really elastic material, the above elastic theory is not exact. But, within working loads, it is considered an accepted form of computation. When the stresses are excessively high, the elastic theory may no longer be nearly correct.

The above method further assumes that the concrete section has not cracked. If it has, the cracked portion has to be computed or estimated, and computations made accordingly. The computation for cracked section in concrete is always complicated. Fortunately, such a condition is seldom met with in actual design of prestressed concrete. In general, any

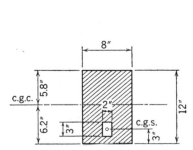

Fig. 5-6. Example 5-3.

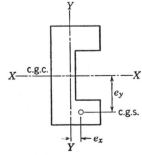

Fig. 5-7. Eccentricity of prestress in two directions.

high-tensile stresses produced by prestress are counterbalanced by compressive stresses due to the weight of the member itself, so that in reality no cracks exist under the combined action of the prestress and the beam's own weight. Hence the entire concrete section can be considered as effective, even though, at certain stages of the computation, high-tensile stresses may appear on paper.

During post-tensioning operations, concrete may be subjected to abnormal stresses. Suppose that there is one tendon at each corner of a square concrete section. When all four tendons are tensioned, the entire concrete section will be under uniform compression. But when only one tendon is fully tensioned, there will exist high tensile stress as well as high compressive stress in the concrete. If two jacks are available, it may be desirable to tension two diagonally opposite tendons at the same time. Sometimes it may be necessary to tension the tendons in steps, that is, to tension them only partially and to retension them after others have been tensioned. Computation for stresses during tensioning is also made on the elastic theory. It is believed that the elastic theory is sufficiently accurate up to the point of cracking, although it can hardly be used to predict the ultimate strength under prestress if it should be desirable to determine such strength.

5-3 Stresses in Concrete Due to Loads

Stresses in concrete produced by external bending moment, whether due to the beam's own weight or to any externally applied loads, are computed by the usual elastic theory.

$$f = \frac{My}{I} \tag{5-6}$$

For a pre-tensioned beam, steel is always bonded to the concrete before any external moment is applied. Hence the section resisting external moment is the combined section. In other words, the values of y and I should be computed on the basis of a transformed section, considering both steel and concrete. For approximation, however, either the gross or the net section of concrete alone can be used in the calculations; the magnitude of error so involved can be estimated and should not be serious except in special cases.

When the beam is post-tensioned and bonded, for any load applied after the bonding has taken place, the transformed section should be used as for pre-tensioned beams. However, if the load or the weight of the beam itself is applied before bonding takes place, it acts on the net concrete section, which should hence be the basis for stress computation. For post-tensioned unbonded beams, the net concrete section is the proper one for all stress computations. It should be borne in mind, though, that when the beam is unbonded, any bending of the beam may change the overall prestress in the steel, the effect of which can be separately computed or estimated as discussed in section 4-5.

Often, only the resulting stresses in concrete due to both prestress and loads are desired, instead of their separate values. They are given by the following formula, a combination of 5-5 and 5-6.

$$f = \frac{F}{A} \pm \frac{Fey}{I} \pm \frac{My}{I}$$

$$= \frac{F}{A}\left(1 \pm \frac{ey}{r^2}\right) \pm \frac{My}{I}$$

$$= \frac{F}{A} \pm (Fe \pm M)\frac{y}{I} \tag{5-7}$$

Any of these three forms may be used, whichever happens to be the most convenient. But, to be strictly correct, the section used in computing y and I must correspond to the actual section at the application of the force. It quite frequently happens that the prestress F acts on the net concrete section, while the external loads act on the transformed section. Judgment should be exercised in deciding whether refinement is necessary or whether approximation is permissible for each particular case.

When prestress eccentricity and external moments exist along two principal axes, the general elastic formula can be used.

$$f = \frac{F}{A} \pm \frac{Fe_x x}{I_x} \pm \frac{Fe_y y}{I_y} \pm \frac{M_x x}{I_x} \pm \frac{M_y y}{I_y}$$

$$= \frac{F}{A} \pm (Fe_x \pm M_x)\frac{x}{I_x} \pm (Fe_y \pm M_y)\frac{y}{I_y} \tag{5-8}$$

EXAMPLE 5-4

A post-tensioned bonded concrete beam, Fig. 5-8, has a prestress of 350 kips in the steel immediately after prestressing, which eventually reduces to 300 kips. The beam carries two live loads of 10 kips each in addition to its own weight of 300 plf. Compute the extreme fiber stresses at midspan, (a) under the initial condition with full prestress and no live load, and (b) under the final condition, after the losses have taken place, and with full live load.

Solution. To be theoretically exact, the net concrete section should be used up to the time of grouting, after which the transformed section should be considered. This is not deemed necessary, and an approximate but sufficiently exact solution is given below, using the gross section of concrete at all times that is,

$$I = 12 \times 24^3/12 = 13,800 \text{ in.}^4$$

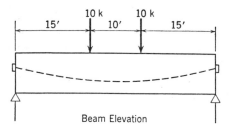
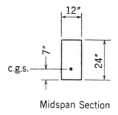

Beam Elevation   Midspan Section

Fig. 5-8. Example 5-4.

1. *Initial condition.* Dead-load moment at midspan, assuming that the beam is simply supported after prestressing:

$$M = \frac{wL^2}{8} = \frac{300 \times 40^2}{8} = 60,000 \text{ ft-lb}$$

$$f = \frac{F}{A} \pm \frac{Fey}{I} \pm \frac{My}{I}$$

$$= \frac{-350,000}{288} \pm \frac{350,000 \times 5 \times 12}{13,800} \pm \frac{60,000 \times 12 \times 12}{13,800}$$

$$= -1215 + 1520 - 625 = -320 \text{ psi, top fiber}$$

$$= -1215 - 1520 + 625 = -2110 \text{ psi, bottom fiber}$$

2. *Final condition.* Live-load moment at midspan = 150,000 ft-lb; therefore, total external moment = 210,000 ft-lb, while the prestress is reduced to 300,000 lb; hence,

$$f = \frac{-300,000}{288} \pm \frac{300,000 \times 5 \times 12}{13,800} \pm \frac{210,000 \times 12 \times 12}{13,800}$$

$$= -1040 + 1300 - 2190 = -1930 \text{ psi, top fiber}$$

$$= -1040 - 1300 + 2190 = -150 \text{ psi, bottom fiber}$$

Example 5-4 describes the conventional method of stress analysis for prestressed concrete, but it will be recalled that in section 1-2 another method of approach is described in which the center of pressure C in the concrete is set at distance a from the center of prestress T in the steel such that

$$Ta = Ca = M \qquad (5\text{-}9)$$

By this method, the stresses in concrete are not treated as being produced by prestress and external moments separately, but are determined by the magnitude and location of the center of pressure C, Fig. 5-9. Most beams do not carry axial load, therefore, C equals T and is located at a distance from T.

$$a = M/T$$

Since the value of T is the value of F in a prestressed beam it is quite accurately known. Thus the computation of a for a given moment M is simply a matter of statics. Once the center of pressure C is located for a concrete section, the distribution of stresses can be determined either by the elastic theory or by the plastic theory. Generally the elastic theory is followed, in which case we have, since

$$C = T = F, \qquad f = \frac{C}{A} \pm \frac{Cey}{I} = \frac{F}{A} \pm \frac{Fey}{I} \qquad (5\text{-}10)$$

where e is the eccentricity of C, not of F.

Following this approach, a prestressed beam is considered similar to a reinforced-concrete beam with the steel supplying the tensile force T, and the concrete supplying the compressive force C. C and T together form a couple resisting the external moment. Hence the value of A and I to be used in the above formula should be the net section of the concrete, and not the composite section. If a beam has conduits grouted for bond, the stress in the grout is actually different from that in the adjacent concrete, and an exact theoretical solution would be quite involved. Under such conditions it is advisable to use the gross section of concrete for all computations for the sake of simplicity. Only when investigating the stresses before grouting should the net concrete section be used.

It can be noted that formula 5-10 is only a different form of formula 5-7, with e measured to C, thus combining the effect of M with the eccentricity of F. Although the formulas are in fact identical, the approaches are different. By following this second approach, all the inaccuracies are thrown into the estimation of the effective prestress in steel, which can generally be estimated within 5%. After that, the location of C is a simple problem in statics, and the distribution of C across the section can be easily computed or visualized. This method of approach will be further explained in the next chapter on the design of beam sections.

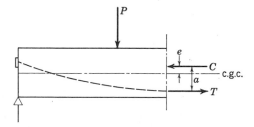

Fig. 5-9. Internal resisting couple C-T with arm a.

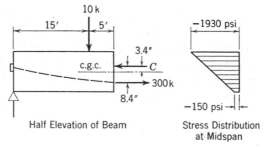

Half Elevation of Beam   Stress Distribution
                              at Midspan

Fig. 5-10. Example 5-5.

EXAMPLE 5-5

For the same problem as in example 5-4, compute the concrete stresses under the final loading conditions by locating the center of pressure C for the concrete section.

Solution.   Referring to Fig. 5-10, a is computed by

$$a = (210 \times 12)/300 = 8.4 \text{ in.}$$

Hence e for C is $8.4 - 5 = 3.4$ in. Since $C = F = 300,000$ lb.

$$f = \frac{C}{A} \pm \frac{Cey}{I}$$

$$= \frac{-300,000}{288} \pm \frac{300,000 \times 3.4 \times 12}{13,800}$$

$$= -1040 - 890 = -1930 \text{ psi, top fiber}$$

$$= -1040 + 890 = -150 \text{ psi, bottom fiber}$$

Also, by inspection, since the center of pressure is near the third point, the stress distribution should be nearly triangular as is shown. By comparing this solution with that for example 5-4, the directness and simplicity of this method seem to be evident.

5-4   Stresses in Steel Due to Loads

In prestressed concrete, prestress in the steel is measured during tensioning operations, then the losses are computed or estimated as described in Chapter 4. When dead and live loads are applied to the member, minor changes in stress will be induced in the steel. In a reinforced-concrete beam, steel stresses are assumed to be directly proportional to the external bending moment. When there is no moment, there is no stress. When the moment increases, the steel stresses increase in direct proportion. This is not true for a prestressed-concrete beam, whose resistance to external moment is furnished by a lengthening of the lever arm between the resisting forces C and T which remain relatively unchanged in magnitude.

In order to get a clear understanding of the behavior of a prestressed-concrete beam, it will be interesting to first study the variation of steel stress as the load increases. For the midspan section of a simple beam, the variation of steel stress with load on the beam is shown in Fig. 5-11. Along the X-axis is plotted the load on the beam, and along the Y-axis is plotted the stress in the steel. As prestress is applied to the steel, the stress in the steel changes from A to B, where B is at the level of f_0, which is the initial prestress in the steel after losses due to anchorage and elastic shortening have taken place.

Immediately after transfer, no load will yet be carried by the beam if it is supported on its falsework and if it is not cambered upward by the prestress. As the falsework is removed, the beam carries its own weight and deflects downward slightly, thus changing the stress in the steel, increasing it from B to C. When the dead weight of the beam is relatively light, then it can be bowed upward during the course of the transfer of prestress. The beam may actually begin to carry load when the average prestress in the steel is somewhere at B'. There may be a sudden breakaway of the beam's soffit from the falsework so that the weight of the beam is at once transferred to be carried by the beam itself, or the weight may be transferred gradually, depending on the actual conditions of support.

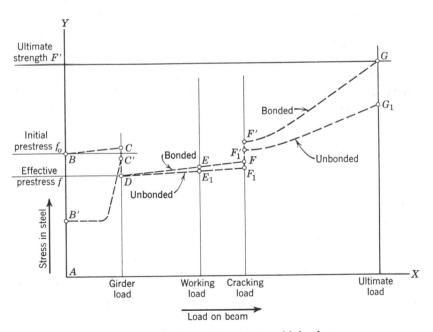

Fig. 5-11. Variation of steel stress with load.

But, in any event, the stress in steel will increase from B' up to point C'. The stress at C' is slightly lower than f_0 by virtue of the loss of prestress in the steel as caused by the upward bending of the beam. Consider now that the losses of prestress take place so that the stress in the steel drops from C or C' to some point D, representing the effective prestress f for the beam. Actually, the losses will not take place all at once but will continue for some length of time. However, for convenience in discussion, let us assume that all the losses take place before the application of superimposed dead and live loads.

Now let us add live load on the beam until the full-design working load is on it. The beam will bend and deflect downward, and stress in the steel will increase. For a bonded beam, such increase can be simply computed by the usual elastic theory,

$$f_s = n f_c = n \frac{M y}{I}$$

where I and y correspond to the transformed section, and n is the modular ratio of steel to concrete. Since the maximum change in concrete stresses at the level of steel is not more than about 2000 psi in most cases, the corresponding change of stress in steel is limited to $2000n$, or 12,000 psi for a value of $n = 6$. This stage is represented by the line DE in Fig. 5-11. It is significant to note that, in prestressed concrete, the variation in steel stress for working loads is limited to a range of about 12,000 psi even though the prestress is probably as high as 140,000 psi.

If the beam is overloaded, beyond its working load and up to the point of cracking, the increase in steel stress still follows the same elastic theory. Hence the line DE is prolonged to point F. This would represent a tensile stress in the concrete around 600 psi, indicating an increase in steel stress of about $6 \times 600 = 3600$ psi from E to F.

When the section cracks, there is a sudden increase of stress in the steel, from F to F' for the bonded beam. After cracking, the stress in the steel will increase faster with the load. As the load is further increased, the section will gradually approach its ultimate strength, the lever arm for the internal C-T couple cannot be increased any more, and increase in load is accompanied by a proportional increase in steel stress. This continues up to the point of failure. From the results of various tests, it is known that the stress in the steel approaches very nearly its ultimate strength at the rupture of the beam provided compression failure does does not start in the concrete and failure of the beam is not produced by shear or bond. Hence the stress curve can be approximately drawn as from F' to G.

The computation of steel stress beyond cracking and up to the ultimate load is a complicated problem which cannot be accurately solved until more test data are available. But it must be pointed out that between the two points, F' and G, there is one point when the steel ceases to be elastic, elastic in the sense that no appreciable permanent set is caused by the external load. This point is considered by some engineers to be the limit to which a structure, such as a bridge or a building, should ever be subjected. If it can be conveniently determined, it may be a more significant criterion for design than the cracking or ultimate load used at present.

If the beam is unbonded, the stress in the steel will be different from the bonded beam. Assuming that the same effective prestress is obtained before the addition of any external load, we can discuss the stress in an unbonded tendon as follows: Starting from point D, when load is added to the beam, the beam bends while the steel slips with respect to the concrete. Owing to this slip, the usual method of a composite steel and concrete section no longer applies. Before cracking of the concrete, stress in the concrete due to any external moment M is given by

$$f = \frac{My}{I}$$

where I and y refer to those for the net concrete section. But it must be remembered that the stress in the steel changes as load is applied, Fig. 5-12. Hence the question becomes more complicated.

At the section of maximum moment, the stress in an unbonded tendon will increase more slowly than that in a bonded tendon. This is because any strain in an unbonded tendon will be distributed throughout its entire length. Hence, as the load is increased to the working or the cracking load, the steel stress will increase from D to E_1, F_1, and F_1',

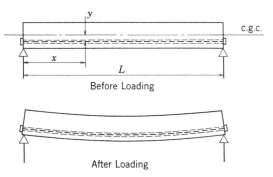

Fig. 5-12. Change of cable length in an unbonded beam.

below E, F, and F', respectively, Fig. 5-11. To compute the average strain for the cable, it is necessary to determine the total lengthening of the tendon due to moments in the beam. This can be done by integrating the strain along the entire length. Let M be the moment at any point of an unbonded beam; the unit strain in concrete at any point is given by

$$\delta = \frac{f}{E} = \frac{My}{E_c I}$$

The total strain along the cable is then

$$\Delta = \int \delta \, dx = \int \frac{My}{E_c I} \, dx$$

The average strain is

$$\frac{\Delta}{L} = \int \frac{My}{LE_c I} \, dx$$

The average stress is

$$f_s = E_s \frac{\Delta}{L} = \int \frac{MyE_s}{LE_c I} \, dx = \frac{n}{L} \int \frac{My}{I} \, dx \qquad (5\text{-}10)$$

If y and I are constant and M is an integrable form of x, the solution of this integral is simple. Otherwise, it will be easier to use a graphical or an approximate integration.

After cracks have developed in the unbonded beam, stress in the steel increases more rapidly with the load, but again it does not increase as fast as that at the maximum moment section in a similar bonded beam. In an unbonded beam, it is generally not possible to develop the ultimate strength of the steel at the rupture of the beam. Thus the stress curve is shown going up from F_1' to G_1, with G_1 below G by an appreciable amount. It is evident that the ultimate load for an unbonded beam is less than that for a corresponding bonded one, although there may be very little difference between the cracking loads for the two beams. There is a tendency for the unbonded beams to develop large cracks before rupture. These large cracks tend to concentrate strains at some localized sections in the concrete, thus lowering its ultimate strength. Therefore, the strength of unbonded beams may be appreciably increased by the addition of nonprestressed bonded reinforcements, which tend to spread the cracks and to limit their size, as well as to contribute toward the tensile force in the ultimate resisting couple.

EXAMPLE 5-6

A post-tensioned simple beam on a span of 40 ft is shown in Fig. 5-13. It carries a superimposed load of 750 plf in addition to its own weight of 300 plf. The initial prestress in the steel is 138,000 psi, reducing to 120,000 psi after

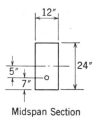

Midspan Section

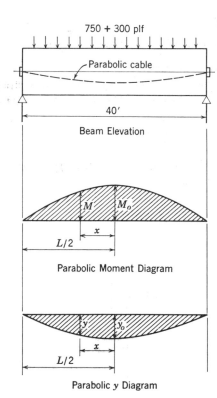

750 + 300 plf

Parabolic cable

40'

Beam Elevation

Parabolic Moment Diagram

M M_o

x

$L/2$

Parabolic *y* Diagram

y y_o

x

$L/2$

Fig. 5-13. Example 5-6.

deducting all losses and assuming no bending of the beam. The parabolic cable has an area of 2.5 sq in., $n = 6$. Compute the stress in the steel at midspan, assuming: (1) the steel is bonded by grouting; (2) the steel is unbonded and entirely free to slip.

Solution 1. Moment at midspan due to dead and live loads is

$$\frac{wL^2}{8} = \frac{(300 + 750)40^2}{8}$$

$$= +210,000 \text{ ft-lb}$$

Moment at midspan due to prestress is

$$2.5 \times 120,000 \times \tfrac{5}{12} = -125,000 \text{ ft-lb}$$

Net moment at midspan is $210,000 - 125,000 = 85,000$ ft-lb. Stress in concrete at the level of steel due to bending, using I of gross concrete section, is

$$= \frac{My}{I} = \frac{85,000 \times 12 \times 5}{13,800} = 370 \text{ psi}$$

Stress in steel is thus increased by

$$f_s = nf_c = 6 \times 370 = 2220 \text{ psi}$$

Resultant stress in steel = 122,220 psi at midspan.

Solution 2. If the cable is unbonded and free to slip, the average strain or stress must be obtained for the whole length of cable as given by formula 5-10,

$$f_s = \frac{n}{L} \int \frac{My}{I} \, dx$$

Using y_0 and M_0 for those at midspan and measuring x from the midspan, we can express y and M in terms of x, thus,

$$M = M_0 \left[1 - \left(\frac{x}{L/2} \right)^2 \right]$$

$$y = y_0 \left[1 - \left(\frac{x}{L/2} \right)^2 \right]$$

$$f_s = \frac{n}{LI} \int_{-L/2}^{+L/2} M_0 y_0 \left[1 - \left(\frac{x}{L/2} \right)^2 \right]^2 dx$$

$$= \frac{nM_0 y_0}{LI} \left[x - \frac{2}{3} \frac{x^3}{(L/2)^2} + \frac{x^5}{5(L/2)^4} \right]_{-L/2}^{+L/2}$$

$$= \frac{8}{15} \left(\frac{nM_0 y_0}{I} \right)$$

which is $\frac{8}{15}$ of the stress for midspan of the bonded beam, or $\frac{8}{15}(2220) = 1180$ psi.

Resultant stress in steel is $120,000 + 1180 = 121,180$ psi throughout the entire cable. In this calculation, the I of the gross concrete section is used and the effect of the increase in the steel stress on the concrete stresses is also neglected. But these are errors of the second order. Since the change in steel stress is relatively small, exact computations are seldom required in an actual design problem.

5-5   Cracking Moment

The moment producing first hair cracks in a prestressed concrete beam is computed by the elastic theory, assuming that cracking starts when the tensile stress in the extreme fiber of concrete reaches its modulus of rupture. Questions have been raised as to the correctness of this method. First, some engineers believed that concrete under prestress became a complex substance whose behavior could not be predicted by the elastic theory with any accuracy.[1] Then it was further questioned whether the usual bending test for modulus of rupture could give values to represent the tensile strength of concrete in a prestressed beam. However, most available test data seem to indicate that the elastic theory is sufficiently accurate up to the point of cracking, and the method is currently used.

Attention must be paid to the fact that the modulus of rupture is only a measure of the beginning of hair cracks which are often invisible to the naked eye. A tensile stress higher than the modulus is necessary to produce visible cracks. On the other hand, if the concrete has been previously cracked by overloading, shrinkage, or other causes, cracks may reappear at the slightest tensile stress. If the beam is made of concrete blocks, the cracking strength will depend on the tensile strength of the joining material.

Referring to formula 5-7, if f' is the modulus of rupture, it is seen that, when

$$-\frac{F}{A} - \frac{Fec}{I} + \frac{Mc}{I} = f'$$

cracks are supposed to start. Transposing terms, we have the value of cracking moment given by

$$M = Fe + \frac{FI}{Ac} + \frac{f'I}{c} \tag{5-11}$$

where $f'I/c$ gives the resisting moment due to modulus of rupture of concrete, Fe the resisting moment due to the eccentricity of prestress, and FI/Ac that due to the direct compression of the prestress.

Formula 5-11 can be derived from another approach. When the center of pressure in the concrete is at the top kern point, there will be zero stress in the bottom fiber. The resisting moment is given by the prestress F times its lever arm measured to the top kern point, (see Appendix A for definition of kern points k_t and k_b), Fig. 5-14, thus,

$$M_1 = F\left(e + \frac{r^2}{c}\right)$$

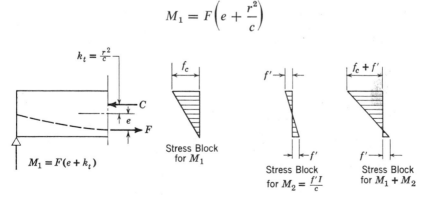

Fig. 5-14. Cracking moment.

Additional moment resisted by the concrete up to its modulus of rupture is $M_2 = f_t I/c$. Hence the total moment at cracking is given by

$$M = M_1 + M_2 = F\left(e + \frac{r^2}{c}\right) + \frac{f'I}{c} \qquad (5\text{-}12)$$

which can be seen to be identical with formula 5-11.

In order to be theoretically correct when applying the above two formulas, care must be exercised in choosing the proper section for the computation of I, r, e, and c. For computing the term $f'I/c$, the transformed section should be used for bonded beams, while the net concrete section should be used for unbonded beams (proper modification being made for the value of prestress due to bending of the beam as explained in section 4-5). For the term $F\left(e + \frac{r^2}{c}\right)$, either the gross or the net section should be considered, depending on the computation of the effective prestress F. For a practical problem, these refinements are often unnecessary, and it will be easier to use one section for all the computations. In order to simplify the computations, the gross section of the concrete is most often used. If the area of holes is an important portion of the gross area, then net area may be used. If the percentage of steel is high, the transformed area may be preferred. The engineer must use his own discretion in choosing a method of solution consistent with the degree of accuracy required for his particular problem.

EXAMPLE 5-7

For the problem given in example 5-6, compute the total dead and live uniform load that can be carried by the beam, (1) for zero tensile stress in the bottom fibers, (2) for cracking in the bottom fibers at a modulus of rupture of 600 psi, and assuming concrete to take tension up to that value.

Solution 1.   Considering the critical midspan section and using the gross concrete section for all computations, k_t is readily computed to be at 4 in. above the mid-depth, Fig. 5-15. To obtain zero stress in the bottom fibers, the center

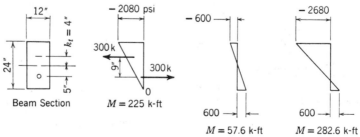

Fig. 5-15. Example 5-7.

of pressure must be located at the top kern point. Hence the resisting moment is given by the prestress multiplied by the lever arm, thus

$$F(e + k_t) = 300(5 + 4)/12 = 225 \text{ k-ft}$$

Solution 2. Additional moment carried by the section up to beginning of cracks is

$$\frac{f'I}{c} = \frac{600 \times 13,800}{12}$$

$$= 690,000 \text{ in.-lb}$$

$$= 57.6 \text{ k-ft}$$

Total moment at cracking is $225 + 57.6 = 282.6$ k-ft, which can also be obtained directly by applying formula 5-11 or 5-12.

5-6 Ultimate Moment

Exact analysis for the ultimate strength of a prestressed-concrete section under flexure is a complicated theoretical problem, because both steel and concrete are generally stressed beyond their elastic range. However, for the purpose of practical design, where an accuracy of 5-10% is considered sufficient, relatively simple procedures can be developed.

Many tests have been run, and many papers written, on the ultimate flexural strength of prestressed concrete sections. Worthy of special mention are the group of papers on this thesis[2] presented before the First International Congress on Prestressed Concrete held in London, October 1953, and another summary paper presented at the Third Congress of the International Federation for Prestressing.[3] In the United states, laboratory investigations carried out at the University of Illinois and the Portland Cement Association gave the results of extensive tests, together with definite recommendations.[4,5,6] Although formulas for ultimate strength proposed by various authors seem to differ greatly on the surface, they generally yield values within a few per cent of one another. Hence it can be concluded that the ultimate strength of prestressed concrete under flexure can be predicted with sufficient accuracy.

A simple method for determining ultimate flexural strength is presented herewith, based on the results of the aforementioned tests as well as others. This method is limited to the following conditions.

1. The failure is primarily a flexural failure, with no shear bond, or anchorage failure which might decrease the strength of the section.
2. The beams are bonded. Unbonded beams possess different ultimate strength and are discussed later.

3. The beams are statically determinate. Although the discussions apply equally well to individual sections of continuous beams, the ultimate strength of continuous beams as a whole is explained by the plastic hinge theory to be discussed in Chapter 10.

4. The load considered is the ultimate load obtained as the result of a short static test. Impact, fatigue, or long-time loadings are not considered.

Of the methods proposed for determining the ultimate flexural strength of prestressed-concrete sections, some are purely empirical and others highly theoretical. The empirical methods are generally simple but are limited only to the conditions which were encountered in the tests. The theoretical ones are intended for research studies and hence unnecessarily complicated for the designer. For the purpose of design, a rational approach is presented in the following, consistent with test results, but neglecting refinements so that reasonably correct values can be obtained with the minimum amount of effort. The method is based on the simple principle of a resisting couple in a prestressed beam, as that in any other beam. At the ultimate load, the couple is made of two forces, T' and C', acting with a lever arm a'. The steel supplies the tensile force T', and the concrete, the compressive force C'.

Before going any further with the method, let us first study the modes of failure of prestressed-beam sections. The failure of a section may start either in the steel or in the concrete, and may end up in one or the other. The most general case is that of an under-reinforced section, where the failure starts with the excessive elongation of steel and ends with the crushing of concrete. This type of failure occurs in both prestressed- and reinforced-concrete beams, when they are under-reinforced. Only in some rare instances may fracture of steel occur in such beams; that happens, for example, when the compressive flange is restrained and possesses a higher actual strength. A relatively uncommon mode of failure is that of an over-reinforced section, where the concrete is crushed before the steel is stressed into the plastic range. Hence there is only a limited amount of deflection before rupture, and a brittle mode of failure is obtained. This is similar to an over-reinforced nonprestressed-concrete beam. Another unusual mode of failure is that of a too lightly reinforced section, where failure may occur by the breaking of the steel immediately following the cracking of concrete. This happens when the tensile force in the concrete is suddenly transferred to the steel whose area is too small to absorb that additional tension.

There is no sharp line of demarcation between the percentage of reinforcement for an over-reinforced beam and that for an under-reinforced one. The transition from one type to another takes place gradually as the percentage of steel is varied. For the materials presently used in pre-stressed work, the normal reinforcement ranges between 0.3% and 0.8%. Such ratios of reinforcement almost always end in plastic failure and can be termed as under-reinforced ratios. If the ratio is over 1%, sudden crushing of concrete without substantial elongation of steel will be likely to take place. If it is less than about 0.15%, breaking of the wires following cracking of concrete may occur.

A proper definition of the percentage of steel p cannot be easily given for prestressed sections because of their irregular shapes. For certain purposes, the ratio p is A_s/A_c, where A_c refers to the total area of concrete. For ultimate strength it is not the total concrete area but the concrete area in the compressive flange that matters; hence p will be more indicative of the relative strength of concrete and steel if it is expressed in terms of A_s/bd, where b is the width or average width of the compressive flange and d the effective depth. Similarly, for investigating the minimum percentage of steel to prevent sudden fracture at cracking, the width of the tensile flange is the proper value for b.

Under-Reinforced Bonded Beams. For under-reinforced bonded beams, the steel is almost always stressed to its ultimate strength at the point of rupture. In fact, there are some test data which seem to show that the steel was stressed even beyond its ultimate strength. Though this does not seem to be possible, it might perhaps be explained by the fact that the group strength of wires forced to fail together at one section of a beam might be higher than the tested strength of the specimens, since, during specimen tests, only the strength of the weakest link is recorded. Other engineers believe that the tensile resistance in the concrete contributes toward the ultimate strength, although such participation is not likely to be significant. For the purpose of practical design, it will be sufficiently accurate to assume that the steel is stressed to the ultimate strength at the rupture of under-reinforced beams.

If it is assumed that the steel is stressed to its ultimate strength at the rupture of the beam, the computation of the ultimate resisting moment is a relatively simple matter and can be carried out as follows. Referring to Fig. 5-16, the ultimate compressive force in the concrete C' equals the ultimate tensile force in the steel T', thus,

$$C' = T' = A_s f_s' \qquad (5\text{-}13)$$

Let a' be the lever arm between the forces C' and T'; then the ultimate resisting moment is given by

$$M' = T'a' = A_s f_s' a' \qquad (5\text{-}14)$$

To determine the lever arm a', it is only necessary to locate the center of pressure C'. There are many plastic theories for the distribution of

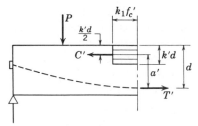

Fig. 5-16.

compressive stress in concrete at failure,[7] assuming the stress block to take the shape of a rectangle, trapezoid, parabola, etc. Although the actual stress distribution is a very interesting problem for research, for the purpose of design, any of these methods would be sufficiently accurate, because they would yield nearly the same lever arm a', seldom differing by more than 5%.

Choosing the simplest stress block, a rectangle, for the ultimate compression in concrete, the depth to the ultimate neutral axis $k'd$ is computed by

$$C' = k_1 f_c' k' bd$$

where $k_1 f_c'$, is the average compressive stress in concrete at rupture. Hence,

$$k'd = \frac{C'}{k_1 f_c' b} = \frac{A_s f_s'}{k_1 f_c' b} \tag{5-15}$$

$$k' = \frac{A_s f_s'}{k_1 f_c' bd} \tag{5-16}$$

These formulas apply if the compressive flange has a uniform width b at failure.

Locating C' at the center of the rectangular stress block, we have the lever arm

$$a' = d - k'd/2$$
$$= d\left(1 - \frac{k'}{2}\right) \tag{5-17}$$

Hence, the ultimate resisting moment is

$$M' = A_s f_s' d\left(1 - \frac{k'}{2}\right) \tag{5-18}$$

Now the determination of the value of k_1 deserves some comments. According to Whitney's plastic theory of reinforced-concrete beams, k_1 should be 0.85, based on cylinder strength. According to some authors in Europe, k_1 should be 0.60 to 0.70 based on the cube strength; since cube strength is 25% higher than cylinder strength, this would give approximately 0.75 to 0.88 for k_1 based on the cylinder strength. The important thing for the designer to see is the fact that variation of the value of k_1 does not appreciably affect the lever arm a'. Hence it is considered accurate enough to adopt some approximate value, such as 0.85 for k_1. Since the center of pressure C' is actually located slightly above the middle of $k'd$, we are on the safe side when assuming a rectangular stress block. Using 0.85 for k_1, formula 5-16 can be written as

$$k' = \frac{A_s f_s'}{0.85 f_c' bd} \qquad (5\text{-}19)$$

By substituting this expression for k' into equation 5-18, we have

$$M' = A_s f_s' d \left(1 - \frac{A_s f_s'}{2 \times 0.85 f_c' bd}\right) \qquad (5\text{-}20)$$

For a rectangular section, we can let $p = A_s/bd$. Then, using f_{su} for f_s', we have the following formula:

$$M' = A_s f_{su} d \left(1 - \frac{0.59 p f_{su}}{f_c'}\right) \qquad (5\text{-}21)$$

which is almost identical to that given in the Building Code Requirements of the Prestressed Concrete Institute (Appendix D) and as first proposed by the ACI-ASCE Recommendations.[8] In order to illustrate the computation of ultimate strength in beam sections by this method, two examples will be given. Example 5-8 deals with a rectangular section, while example 5-9 has a T section.

EXAMPLE 5-8
A rectangular section 12 in. by 24 in. deep is prestressed with 1.5 sq in. of steel wires to an initial stress of 150,000 psi. The c.g.s. of the wires is 4 in. above the bottom fiber of the beam, Fig. 5-17; $f_s' = 240,000$ psi; $f_c' = 5000$ psi. Estimate the ultimate resisting moment of the section.
Solution. Assuming that the wires will be stressed to their ultimate strength, the total T' at rupture is

$$1.5 \times 240{,}000 = 360{,}000 \text{ lb}$$

Assuming that the average stress in concrete is $0.85 f_c' = 4250$ psi, the depth to neutral axis $k'd$ is, from formula 5-19,

$$k'd = \frac{360{,}000}{4250 \times 12} = 7.0 \text{ in.}$$

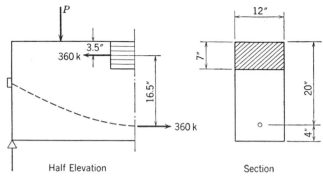

Fig. 5-17. Example 5-8.

The center of pressure C is located at $7/2 = 3.5$ in. from the top. Hence the tensile force T in the wires has a lever arm of $20 - 3.5 = 16.5$ in., and the ultimate resisting moment is, from formula 5-14,

$$360,000 \times 16.5 = 5,940,000 \text{ in.-lb}$$

For a more exact solution, see example 5-10.

EXAMPLE 5-9

A T-section is shown in Fig. 5-18, with 1.5 sq in. of wires prestressed to 150,000 psi; $f_s' = 240,000$ psi; $f_c' = 5000$ psi. Estimate the ultimate resisting moment.

Solution. This being a T-section, formulas 5-16 and 5-19 do not directly apply. But similar procedure can be followed. Assuming the average stress in concrete to be $0.85f_c' = 4250$ psi, and the steel stressed to its ultimate strength of $1.5 \times 240,000 = 360,000$ lb, the total compressive area required for concrete is

$$360,000/4250 = 85 \text{ sq in.}$$

The flange supplies an area of 60 sq in., leaving an area of 25 sq in. to be supplied by the web. Thus the neutral axis is located $25/5 = 5$ in. below the flange.

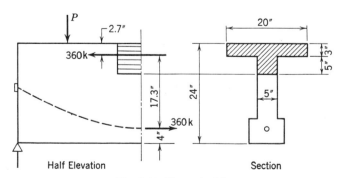

Fig. 5-18. Example 5-9.

If only an approximate solution is desired, the effect of compression in the web can be neglected and the center of pressure can be located at mid-depth of the flange, 1.5 in. below the top. Then the lever arm for the steel is 18.5 in., and the ultimate resisting moment is

$$360,000 \times 18.5 = 6,660,000 \text{ in.-lb}$$

If a more exact solution is desired, still based on a rectangular stress block, the center of pressure C' can be located at the centroid of the compressive area, thus:

$$\frac{20 \times 3 \times 1.5 + 5 \times 5 \times 5.5}{20 \times 3 + 5 \times 5} = 2.7 \text{ in.}$$

$$a' = 20 - 2.7 \text{ in.} = 17.3 \text{ in.}$$

$$M' = 360,000 \times 17.3 = 6,220,000 \text{ in.-lb}$$

A word of caution is perhaps in order with regard to the possible error that might result from the simple assumption of a rectangular stress block. When accurate values are desired, a more refined stress distribution for concrete should be used, such as a trapezoidal block or other stress blocks.[7] More exact location of the neutral axis could then be obtained, as well as a more exact determination of the stress in the steel at alternate load. This is especially true for over-reinforced beams which are discussed subsequently.

Over-Reinforced Bonded Beams. The above method assumes that the ultimate strength of the steel can be developed at the rupture of the beam. But when a section is over-reinforced, the neutral axis at rupture will be low, and compressive failure will take place in the concrete before the ultimate strength in the steel is developed. In such a case, to determine the stress of steel at rupture of the beam (termed f_{su}), it is necessary to study the strain relations in the section and relate them to the stress-strain diagram of steel. This is done as follows.

The maximum strain of concrete at failure is believed to vary between 0.003 and 0.004. Tests at the University of Illinois gave an average value of 0.0034 for the strain of the top fiber of concrete at failure. Assuming that plane section remains plane at rupture (which was also found to be approximately correct by the University of Illinois tests), we can obtain the strain of steel at rupture of beam to be

$$e_{s2} = 0.0034 \frac{d - k'd}{k'd} = 0.0034 \frac{1 - k'}{k'}$$

That strain in the steel is in addition to the prestressed strain in the steel e_{s1} at the time when concrete strain is zero on the top fiber, Fig. 5-19. The total strain e_s is given by $e_{s2} + e_{s1}$. From the stress-strain diagram of

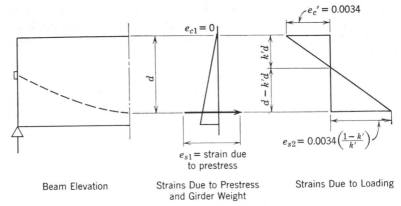

Fig. 5-19. Strains in steel and concrete at rupture.

steel, the corresponding stress f_{su} can be obtained. If that stress f_{su} is near the ultimate value f_s', the section is not over-reinforced, and the previous method using the ultimate strength of steel is accurate enough. If f_{su} is appreciably lower than f_s', the solution has to be modified. To obtain the actual value of f_{su} at rupture, a method of trial and error can be followed, repeating the above process, until the assumed and computed values of f_{su} agree within limits. This procedure will be illustrated in the following example.

EXAMPLE 5-10

For the same section as in example 5-8, compute the ultimate resisting moment. Assume that the high-tensile wires have a stress-strain diagram as shown for the $\frac{1}{4}$-in. wire in Fig. 2-5. Use the trial-and-error method.

Solution. Corresponding to the first trial in example 5-8, assuming a stress of $f_{su} = 240,000$ psi in steel, the neutral axis at rupture was located at 7 in. from

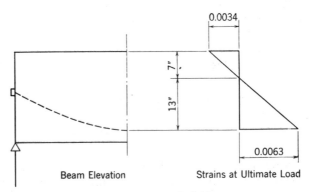

Fig. 5-20. Example 5-10.

the top. If the maximum concrete strain is assumed to be 0.0034, the strain in the steel can be obtained from the simple relation shown in Fig. 5-20.

$$e_{s2} = 0.0034 \times \frac{13}{7} = 0.0063$$

If the effective prestress in the steel is assumed to be 126,000 psi, for $E_s = 30,000,000$ psi, this indicates a strain of 0.0042. Thus the total strain at failure is $0.0063 + 0.0042 = 0.0105$, which corresponds to a stress of $f_{su} = 210,000$ psi not 240,000 psi as previously assumed.

Next assuming a stress of $f_{su} = 210,000$ psi in the steel,

$$T' = 1.5 \times 210,000 = 315,000 \text{ lb}$$

$$k'd = \frac{315,000}{4250 \times 12} = 6.2 \text{ in.}$$

$$e_{s2} = 0.0034 \frac{13.8}{6.2} = 0.0075$$

$$e = 0.0075 + 0.0042 = 0.0117$$

which corresponds to $f_{su} = 212,000$ psi. This is close enough to the assumed value. Hence the ultimate moment is

$$1.5 \times 212,000 \times (20 - 6.2/2) = 5,380,000 \text{ in.-lb}$$

which is about 9% lower than the more approximate value obtained in example 5-8.

In the above example, it is seen that $f_{su} = 0.91 f'_s$ which means that about 91% of the ultimate strength of steel is developed at rupture. Appreciable elongation of steel and consequently considerable deflection and cracking of the beam would have taken place before rupture. This is not considered as a seriously over-reinforced beam although the ultimate deflection would be much greater if the percentage of steel were lowered. A beam would be really over-reinforced when the value of k' was greater than about 0.5. Such a condition can be readily detected by equating the concrete strength above the mid-depth to about 85% of the ultimate strength of the steel reinforcement. For a rectangular section, we have

$$0.85 f'_s A_s = 0.5 \times 0.85 f'_c bd$$

$$p = A_s/bd = 0.5 f'_c / f'_s$$

For $f'_c = 5000$, $f'_s = 250,000$ psi, we have $p = 1\%$ as the limiting value.

The PCI Code Requirements (Appendix D) and the ACI-ASCE Recommendations[8] both give a limiting value of

$$p = \frac{0.3 f'_c}{f_{su}}$$

Assuming $f_{su} = 0.85f_s'$, we have $\rho = 0.353f_c'/f_s'$. Although this seems to be a safe limitation, there is no doubt that a rectangular beam is beginning to become over-reinforced when this percentage is reached.

Again, there is no abrupt change from an under-reinforced beam to an over-reinforced one. The change in mode of failure is a gradual one as the percentages of steel are increased. It must be further noted that these formulas should be modified if some of the tendons are positioned far away from the c.g.s. of the section, since the stress in such tendons will be quite different at the rupture of the section.

Unbonded Beams.   An accurate calculation for the ultimate strength of unbonded beams is more difficult than for that of bonded ones, because the stress in the steel at rupture of the beam cannot be closely computed. Also there have not been sufficient data on the ultimate strength of unbonded beams to establish definitely a reliable method of computation. It is agreed, however, that unbonded beams are weaker than the corresponding bonded ones in their ultimate strength, the difference being placed at 10–30%.

Explanations can be offered for the lower strength of unbonded beams. First, since the tendon is free to slip, the strain in a tendon is more or less equalized along its length, and the strain at the critical section is lessened. Hence the stress in the tendon is increased only slowly so that, when the crushing strain has been reached in the concrete, stress in the steel is often far below its ultimate strength. When there are no cracks in the beam, stress in steel can be computed as in solution 2, example 5-6. As soon as part of the beam cracks or is stretched into the plastic range, the stress cannot be conveniently calculated. For the purpose of design, however, it may be possible to estimate the stress in the steel at the rupture of the beam and to compute the corresponding lever arm so as to approximate the ultimate resisting moment. Until further test data are available, such estimation may often err by 10–15%. Fortunately, unbonded beams are not often used where ultimate strength is a controlling factor, and they are generally designed for the working loads by the elastic theory rather than for the ultimate load.

Another reason for the lower ultimate strength of unbonded beams is the appearance of a few large cracks in the concrete instead of many small ones well distributed. Such wide cracks tend to concentrate the strains in the concrete at these sections, thus resulting in early failure.

Some tests tend to prove that the ultimate strength of unbonded beams can be materially increased by the addition of nonprestressed steel. Such increase is attributed to the resistance of the nonprestressed steel itself as well as to its effect in distributing and limiting the cracks in the concrete. This will be discussed in Chapter 11.

A general formula for f_{su}, the stress in steel at ultimate load, in an unbonded beam is

$$f_{su} = f_e + f_{sa}$$

where f_e is the effective prestress in the steel, and f_{sa} is the additional stress in the steel produced as a result of beam bending up to the ultimate load. The ACI-ASCE Tentative Recommendations[8] give an empirical formula, with f_{sa} assumed at 15,000 psi, thus

$$f_{su} = f_e + 15,000$$

Tests at the University of Illinois (Fig. 117, reference 6) showed f_{sa} varying from about 10,000 to 80,000 psi; those at the Portland Cement Association showed f_{sa} between 40,000 and 60,000 psi (p. 615, reference 5). Limited tests at the University of California indicated f_{sa} varying from 30,000 psi to 80,000 psi, with the higher values of f_{sa} occurring for the curved tendons, where frictional force probably restricted the free slipping of the wires, and for the beams, which had a sizable amount of nonprestressed steel.

5-7 Composite Sections

In prestressed-concrete construction, it is often advantageous to precast part of a section (either by pre-tensioning or by post-tensioning), lift it to position, and cast the remainder of the section in place. The precast and cast-in-place portions thus act together (with stirrups if necessary) and form a composite section. Members of composite sections laid side by side may be eventually connected together by transverse prestressing, while such members laid end to end may be further prestressed longitudinally in order to attain continuity. These points will be discussed in later chapters. We shall first describe here the basic method of analysis commonly employed for such composite sections.

Figure 5-21 shows a composite section at the midspan of a simply supported beam, whose lower stem is precast and lifted into position with the top slab cast in place resting directly on the stem. If no temporary intermediate support is furnished, the weight of both the slab and the

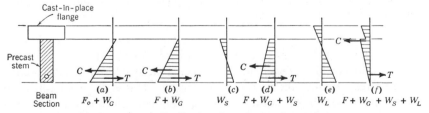

Fig. 5-21. Stress distribution for a composite section.

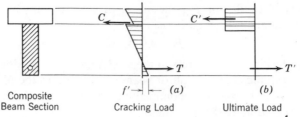

Fig. 5-22. Stress distributions for cracking and ultimate loads.

stem will be carried by the stem acting alone. After the slab concrete has hardened, the composite section will carry any live or dead load that may be added on to it.

In the same figure, stress distributions are shown for various stages of loading. These are discussed as follows.

(*a*) Owing to the initial prestress and the weight of the stem, there will be heavy compression in the lower fibers and possibly some small tension in the top fibers. The tensile force T in the steel and the compressive force C in the concrete form a resisting couple with a small lever arm between them.

(*b*) After losses have taken place in the prestress, the effective prestress together with the weight of the stem will result in a slightly lower compression in the bottom fibers and some small tension or compression in the top fibers. The C–T couple will act with a slightly greater lever arm.

(*c*) Owing to the addition of the slab, its weight produces additional moment and stresses as shown.

(*d*) Owing to the effective prestress plus the weight of the stem and slab, we can add (*b*) to (*c*), and a somewhat smaller compression is found to exist at the bottom fibers and some compression at the top fibers. The lever arm for the C–T couple further increases.

(*e*) Stresses resulting from live load moment are shown, the moment being resisted by the composite section.

(*f*) Adding (*d*) to (*e*), we have stress block as in (*f*), with slight tension or compression in the bottom fibers, but with high compressive stresses in the top fibers of the stem and the slab. The couple T and C now acts with an appreciable lever arm.

The above shows the stress distribution under working load conditions. For overloads, the stress distributions are shown in Fig. 5-22. For the load producing first cracks, it is assumed that the lower fibers reach a tensile stress equal to the modulus of rupture. This is obtained when the live-load stresses shown in Fig. 5-21(*e*) are big enough to result in a stress distribution as shown in Fig. 5-22(*a*), computed by the elastic theory.

Under the ultimate moment, however, the elastic theory is no longer nearly correct. As an approximation, the ultimate resisting moment is best represented by a tensile force T' almost equal to the ultimate strength of the steel acting with a compressive force C' supplied by the concrete. If failure in bond and shear is prevented, the ultimate strength of a composite section can be estimated by a method similar to that previously described for a simple prestressed section. It must be emphasized, however, that a composite section may fail in horizontal shear between the precast and the cast-in-place portions, unless proper stirrups or connectors are provided.

The above describes a simple case of composite action; there are many possible variations. First, the precast portion may be supported on falsework while the cast-in-place slab is being poured or placed, the falsework being removed only after the hardening of the slab concrete. This will permit the entire composite section to resist the moment produced by the weight of the slab. It is also possible to prop up the falsework so that the stem will carry practically no moment by itself. Then the moments due to the weight of the stem will also be carried by the composite section. Since the composite section has a greater section modulus than the stem alone, the resulting stresses will be more favorable. The desirability of such methods depends on the cost of falsework for the particular structure.

Another variation happens when the cast-in-place slab overlaps with the precast portion as shown in Fig. 5-23. Here, the stresses in the concrete between levels M and N will follow two different variations, as shown in (c); one for the precast and another for the cast-in-place portion. At the ultimate range, however, they will all be stressed to the maximum and the difference will be hardly noticeable. Then the section can be analyzed as if it were a simple one, Fig. 5-23(d).

If the precast portion is only a small part of the whole section, it may

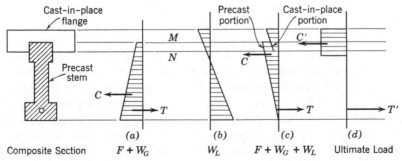

Fig. 5-23. Stress distribution for a special composite section.

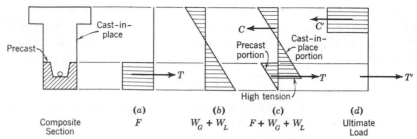

Fig. 5-24. Stress distribution for a special (Udall) composite section.

be prestressed for direct tension only, or with a slight eccentricity of prestress. One method used in England (known as the Udall system), Fig. 5-24, employs both prestressed and nonprestressed wires in the groove of precast blocks, with the major top portion cast in place so as to be well bonded to the wires. For such a construction, high tension may exist in the bottom fibers of the cast-in-place portion (*c*), resulting in cracks under working load. But the ultimate strength in flexure is not affected by the tensile stresses (*d*).

In other instances, the section is prestressed in two stages. Only part of the tendons are prestressed first in order to hold the stem together. The remaining tendons are prestressed after the slab has been cast and has hardened; otherwise the tendons may be partially prestressed first, to be fully prestressed later. If the process of retensioning is not too costly, this may result in an economical design. The stress distribution must be studied for the various stages, but the allowable stresses need not be the same as for an ordinary simple section. In certain instances, considerable tension may be permitted.

When differential shrinkage and creep between the precast and the in-place portions are considered, high stresses are obtained. The usual practice of neglecting such stresses can be justified on the grounds that the ultimate strength of the section is seldom affected by these stresses. However, the elastic behavior, such as camber and deflection, may be seriously modified. In practice, the in-place portion will have more shrinkage, since shrinkage of the precast portion has mostly taken place; but the precast portion will have more creep because it is usually under higher compression due to prestress. If the higher shrinkage in the in-place portion is just about balanced by the higher creep in the precast portion, it would be possible to neglect both. It often happens, however, that the shrinkage of the in-place portion is more serious, especially when the concrete has a high water-cement ratio. In this case the in-place concrete may crack, or the entire composite member may be forced to deflect downward.

EXAMPLE 5-11

The midspan section of a composite beam is shown in Fig. 5-25. The precast stem 12 in. by 36 in. deep is post-tensioned with an initial force of 550 kips, Fig. 5-25(a). The effective prestress after losses is taken as 480 kips. Moment due to the weight of that precast section is 200 k-ft at midspan. After it is erected in place, the top slab of 6 in. by 36 in. wide is to be cast in place producing a moment of 100 k-ft. After the slab concrete has hardened, the composite section is to carry a maximum live load moment of 550 k-ft. Compute stresses in the section at various stages. $A_s = 3.7$ sq in. $f_s' = 240,000$ psi. $f_c' = 5000$ psi. Estimate the ultimate moment.

Solution. C.g.c. of the composite section is located at 25 in. from the bottom fiber. The area and moment of inertia of the rectangular and the composite sections are computed and listed below:

	Rectangular Section	Composite Section
Area, sq in.	432	648
I, in.^{4}	46,600	111,000

(a) Immediately after prestressing, the stresses in the rectangular section will be

$$f = \frac{F}{A} \pm \frac{(M - Fe)c}{I}$$

$$= \frac{-550,000}{432} \pm \frac{(200,000 \times 12 - 550,000 \times 10)18}{46,600}$$

$$= -1270 \pm 1200$$

$$= -70 \text{ psi top fiber}$$

$$= -2470 \text{ psi bottom fiber}$$

(b) After loss of prestress, the stresses will be

$$f = \frac{-480,000}{432} \pm \frac{(200,000 \times 12 - 480,000 \times 10)18}{46,600}$$

$$= -1110 \pm 930$$

$$= -180 \text{ psi top fiber}$$

$$= -2040 \text{ psi bottom fiber}$$

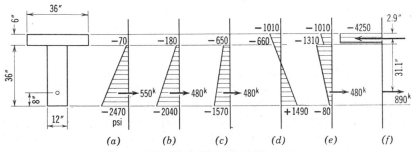

Fig. 5-25. Example 5-11.

(c) After pouring of top slab, the stresses will be

$$f = \frac{-480,000}{432} \pm \frac{(300,000 \times 12 - 480,000 \times 10)18}{46,000}$$

$$= -1110 \pm 460$$

$$= -650 \text{ psi top fiber}$$

$$= -1570 \text{ psi bottom fiber}$$

(d) The live load acts on the composite section, producing stresses,

$$f = \frac{-550,000 \times 12 \times 17}{111,000} = -1010 \text{ psi top fiber of composite section}$$

$$f = \frac{550,000 \times 12 \times 25}{111,000} = +1490 \text{ psi bottom fiber}$$

By proportioning, the stress at top fiber of the rectangular portion is found to be −660 psi due to this live load.

(e) The combined stresses due to prestress and dead and live loads are given in Fig. 5-25(e), which yields −80 psi for bottom fiber and −1310 psi for top fiber of the rectangular section.

(f) The ultimate moment capacity of the section can be estimated as follows. Assume that ultimate strength of steel is developed; then total tensile force is

$$3.7 \times 240,000 = 890,000 \text{ lb}$$

Area of compression concrete, for an average stress of $0.85f_c' = 4250$ psi, is

$$\frac{890,000}{4250} = 210 \text{ sq in.}$$

or a width of $210/36 = 5.8$ in. The center of compressive force is about $5.8/2 = 2.9$ in. from top; hence the lever arm for the resisting moment is $42 - 2.9 - 8 = 31.1$ in., and the ultimate moment capacity is

$$890,000 \times 31.1/12,000 = 2310 \text{ k-ft}$$

The total applied dead and live load moment is only 850 k-ft, indicating a factor of safety of $2310/850 = 2.7$.

5-8   Flexural Behavior and Ultimate Strength at Transfer

While extensive studies have been made, both analytically and experimentally, of the behavior of prestressed-concrete beams under the final conditions of loading, only a limited amount of investigation has been carried out to determine the behavior at transfer.[9] The term "at transfer" is used here in a broad sense to mean that the beam is under little or no external positive moment or under an external negative moment which increases the eccentricity of prestress. Such knowledge is of importance when a beam is subjected to reversal of moments during stressing and erecting operations, or under service conditions. When appreciable cracking may occur, reinforcing bars should be provided to control the cracks or to increase the strength. The design for these bars will be discussed later in section 9-6.

The elastic stresses due to prestress have been discussed in section 5-2, while those due to external loads were discussed in section 5-3. The combined stresses due to prestress and loading are given by the well-known formula 5-7,

$$f = \frac{F}{A} \pm \frac{Fey}{I} \pm \frac{My}{I}$$

When the moment is negative, acting to increase the eccentricity of prestress, it is only necessary to insert the proper sign for the third term My/I in formula 5-7, as illustrated in example 5-12.

EXAMPLE 5-12

A post-tensioned bonded beam (as in example 5-4) with a transfer prestress of $F_t = 350$ kips is being wrongly picked up at its midspan point, Fig. 5-26. Compute the critical fiber stresses.

Solution. Compute the external moment due to beam's own weight of $w = 300$ plf, on a cantilever of 20 ft span,

$$-M = \frac{wL^2}{2} = \frac{300 \times 20^2}{2} = 60,000 \text{ ft-lb}$$

The fiber stresses at midspan are computed as follows and shown in Fig. 5-26.

$$f = \frac{F}{A} \pm \frac{Fey}{I} \pm \frac{My}{I}$$
$$= \frac{-350,000}{288} \pm \frac{350,000 \times 5 \times 12}{13,800} \pm \frac{-60,000 \times 12 \times 12}{13,800}$$
$$= -1215 + 1520 + 625 = +930 \text{ psi top fiber}$$
$$= -1215 - 1520 - 625 = -3360 \text{ psi bottom fiber}$$

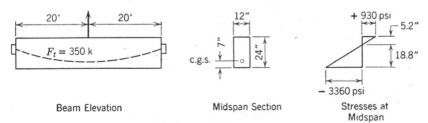

Beam Elevation   Midspan Section   Stresses at Midspan

Fig. 5-26. Example 5-12.

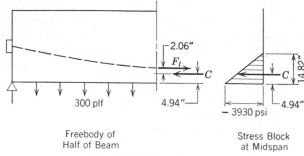

Freebody of
Half of Beam

Stress Block
at Midspan

Fig. 5-27. Example 5-13.

These stresses indicate possible cracking for the top fibers and high compression for the bottom fibers. If cracking does occur, the stress distribution would be modified and the bottom compression further aggravated. Also note that as the bottom fiber is compressed, the prestress $F_t = 350k$ is somewhat reduced, but this will not be discussed here.

It is sometimes more convenient to compute the fiber stresses by locating the center of pressure C, and then apply formula 5-10, using the increased eccentricity e.

$$f = \frac{F}{A} \pm \frac{Fey}{I}$$

Thus example 5-12 can be solved in a manner similar to example 5-5. When cracking occurs, locating the center of pressure C will yield a simple solution as illustrated in the next example.

EXAMPLE 5-13
For the beam picked up at midspan point in example 5-12, if the top fiber cracks and the concrete is assumed not to take any tension, compute the bottom fiber stress.

Solution. Assuming prestress F_t to remain at $350k$, with an external negative moment of 60 k-ft, the center of pressure C will be moved downward by

$$\frac{M}{F_t} = \frac{60 \times 12}{350} = 2.06 \text{ in.}$$

locating it at 4.94 in. above the bottom fiber, Fig. 5-27. Assuming a triangular stress block, the height of the triangle is

$$3 \times 4.94 = 14.82 \text{ in.}$$

and the bottom fiber stress is

$$\frac{-350,000}{14.82 \times 12} \times 2 = -3930 \text{ psi}$$

When the center of pressure C moves further downward, the bottom portion of the beam will be stressed into the plastic range. Then it will be a better approximation to assume a rectangular or a trapezoidal stress block for the determination of the stress values. This is illustrated in example 5-14.

EXAMPLE 5-14
Assuming the beam in example 5-13 is picked up suddenly at midspan so that an impact factor of 100% is considered, compute the maximum stress.

Solution. The external moment will be doubled as a result of 100% impact, thus,

$$-M = 2 \times 60,000 = 120,000 \text{ ft-lb}$$

and the C location will be moved downward by (still considering $F_t = 350k$)

$$2 \times 2.06 \text{ in.} = 4.12 \text{ in.}$$

or located 2.88 in. above the bottom fiber. A triangular stress block will yield a high maximum stress of $2 \times 350,000/(8.64 \times 12) = 6750$ psi. Assuming a rectangular stress block, we have, Fig. 5-28,

$$\frac{350,000}{5.76 \times 12} = 5050 \text{ psi}$$

Note that trapezoidal stress block, using Jensen's theory, will give a more accurate answer,[9] but will not be attempted here.

The three foregoing examples illustrate stress distributions in beams at transfer before cracking, after cracking, and near ultimate. The permissible stress values both in tension and in compression will depend on many factors, such as the shape of the section, the magnitude and location of the prestress, the chances of misplacement of the tendons, the probability of adverse moments, and the seriousness of cracking. Meanwhile, values specified in the codes may be used as a reference (Appendixes D and E).

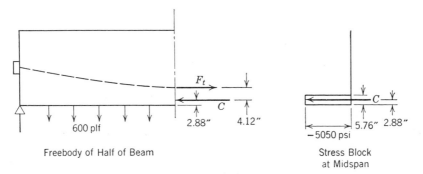

Freebody of Half of Beam   Stress Block at Midspan

Fig. 5-28. Example 5-14.

References

1   G. L. Rogers, "Validity of Certain Assumptions in the Mechanics of Prestressed Concrete," *J. Am. Conc. Inst.*, December 1953 (*Proc.*, Vol. 49), pp. 317–330.
2   *International Federation of Prestressing, Preliminary Publications*, First International Congress, London, October 1953.
3   G. S. Ramaswamy and S. K. Narayana, "The Ultimate Flexural Strength of Post-tensioned Grouted Rectangular Beams," *Papers, Third Congress of the International Federation of Prestressing*, Berlin, 1958.
4   D. F. Billet and J. H. Appleton, "Flexural Strength of Prestressed Concrete Beams," *J. Am. Conc. Inst.*, June 1954 (*Proc.*, Vol. 50), pp. 837–854.
5   J. R. Janney, E. Hognestad, and D. McHenry, "Ultimate Flexural Strength of Prestressed and Conventionally Reinforced Concrete Beams," *J. Am. Conc. Inst.*, February 1956 (*Proc.* Vol. 52), pp. 601–620.
6   J. Warwaruk, M. A. Sozen, C. P. Siess, "Strength and Behavior in Flexure of Prestressed Concrete Beams," Engineering Experiment Station *Bull. No. 464*, University of Illinois, 1962.
7   E. Hognestad, H. W. Hanson, and D. McHenry, "Concrete Stress Distribution in Ultimate Strength Design," *J. Am. Conc. Inst.*, December 1955 (*Proc.* Vol. 52), pp. 455–479.
8   "Tentative Recommendations for Prestressed Concrete," *J. Am. Conc. Inst.*, January 1958 (*Proc.* Vol. 54), pp. 545–578.
9   A. C. Scordelis, T. Y. Lin, and H. R. May, "Flexural Strength of Prestressed Concrete Beams at Transfer," *Proceedings World Conference on Prestressed Concrete*, San Francisco, 1957.

design of sections for flexure 6

6-1 Preliminary Design

Preliminary design of prestressed-concrete sections for flexure can be performed by a very simple procedure, based on a knowledge of the internal C–T couple acting in the section. In practice the depth h of the section is either given, known, or assumed, as is the total moment M_T on the section. Under the working load, the lever arm for the internal couple could vary between 30 to 80% of the overall height h and averages about $0.65h$. Hence the required effective prestress F can be computed from the equation

$$F = T = \frac{M_T}{0.65h} \tag{6-1}$$

if we assume the lever arm to be $0.65h$, Fig. 6-1. If the effective unit prestress is f_s for the steel, then the area of steel required is

$$A_s = \frac{F}{f_s} = \frac{M_T}{0.65hf_s} \tag{6-2}$$

The total prestress $A_s f_s$ is also the force C on the section. This force will produce an average unit stress on the concrete of

$$\frac{C}{A_c} = \frac{T}{A_c} = \frac{A_s f_s}{A_c}$$

For preliminary design, this average stress can be assumed to be about 50% of the maximum allowable stress f_c, under the working load. Hence,

$$\frac{A_s f_s}{A_c} = 0.50 f_c$$

$$A_c = \frac{A_s f_s}{0.50 f_c} \tag{6-3}$$

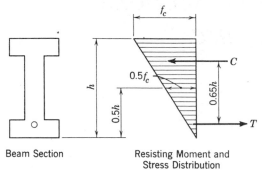

Beam Section   Resisting Moment and
                            Stress Distribution

Fig. 6-1. Preliminary design of a beam section.

Note that in the above procedure the only approximations made are the coefficients of 0.65 and 0.50. These coefficients vary widely, depending on the shape of the section. However, with some experience and knowledge, they can be closely approximated for each particular section, and the preliminary design can be made rather accurately.

The above procedure is based on the design for working load, with little or no tension in the concrete. Preliminary designs can also be made on the basis of ultimate strength theories with proper load factors. Such an alternative procedure will be discussed in section 6-8.

EXAMPLE 6-1

Make a preliminary design for a section of a prestressed-concrete beam to resist a total moment of 320 k-ft. The overall depth of the section is given as 36 in. The effective prestress for steel is 125,000 psi, and allowable stress for concrete under working load is −1600 psi.

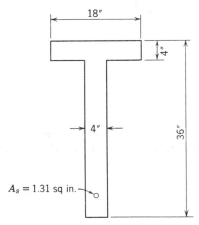

Fig. 6-2. Example 6-1.

Solution.   From equations 6-1, 6-2, and 6-3,

$$F = T = M_T/0.65h$$
$$= (320 \times 12)/(0.65 \times 36) = 164 \text{ k}$$
$$A_s = F/f_s = 164/125 = 1.31 \text{ sq in.}$$
$$A_c = 164/(0.5 \times 1.60) = 205 \text{ sq in.}$$

Now a preliminary section can be sketched with a total concrete area of about 205 sq in., a height of 36 in., and a steel area of 1.31 sq in. Such a section is shown in Fig. 6-2. A T-section is chosen here because it is an economical shape when M_G/M_T ratio is large.

In estimating the depth of a prestressed section, an approximate rule is to use 70% of the corresponding depth for conventional reinforced-concrete construction. Some other empirical rules are also available. For example, the thickness of prestressed slabs may vary from $L/35$ for heavy loads to $L/55$ for light loads. The depth of beams of the usual proportions can be approximated by the following formula.

$$h = k\sqrt{M}$$

where h = depth of beam in inches
   M = maximum bending moment in k-ft
   k = a coefficient varying from 1.5 to 2.0

It is needless to add that such empirical rules apply only under the average conditions and should be used merely as a preliminary guide.

A more accurate preliminary design can be made if the girder moment M_G is known in addition to the total moment M_T. When M_G is much greater than 20 to 30% of M_T, the initial condition under M_G generally will not control the design, and the preliminary design needs be made only for M_T. When M_G is small relative to M_T, then the c.g.s. cannot be located too far outside the kern point, and the design is controlled by $M_L = M_T - M_G$. In this case, the resisting lever arm for M_L is given approximately by $k_t + k_b$, which averages about 0.50h. Hence the total effective prestress required is

$$F = \frac{M_L}{0.50h} \tag{6-4}$$

When M_G/M_T is small, this equation should be used instead of equation 6-1. Equation 6-3 is still applicable.

EXAMPLE 6-2

Make a preliminary design for the beam section in example 6-1, with $M_T = 320$ k-ft, $M_G = 40$ k-ft, $h = 36$ in., $f_s = 125{,}000$ psi, and $f_c = -1600$ psi.

Solution. Since M_G is only 12% of M_T, it is not likely that the c.g.s. can be located much outside the kern. Hence it will be more nearly correct to apply equation 6-4. Thus,

$$M_L = M_T - M_G = 320 - 40$$
$$= 280 \text{ k-ft}$$
$$F = M_L/0.50h = 280 \times 12/(0.50 \times 36)$$
$$= 187 \text{ k}$$

Applying the first part of formula 6-2 and also formula 6-3, we have

$$A_s = F/f_s = 187/125$$
$$= 1.50 \text{ sq in.}$$
$$A_c = A_s f_s/0.50f_c = 187/(0.50 \times 1.60)$$
$$= 234 \text{ sq in.}$$

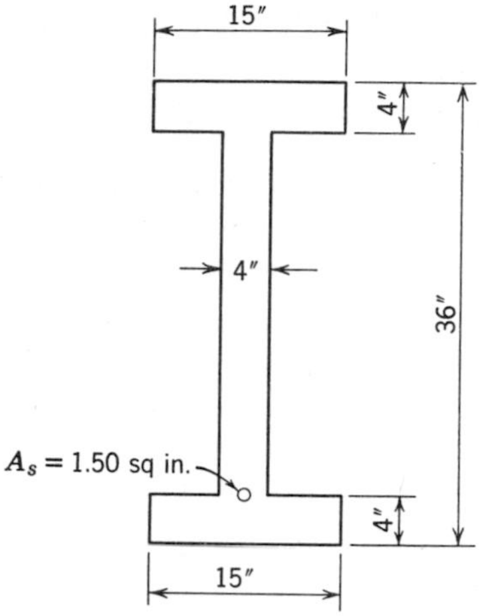

Now a preliminary section can be sketched with a total concrete area of about 234 sq in., a height of 36 in., and a steel area of 1.50 sq in., as shown in Fig. 6-3. An I-section is chosen because it is a suitable form when the M_G/M_T ratio is small.

Fig. 6-3. Example 6-2.

When it is not known whether M_T or M_L should govern the design, one convenient way is to apply both equations 6-1 and 6-4, and use the greater of the two values of F. For example, if $M_G = 80$ k-ft in example 6-1, we have, from equation 6-1,

$$F = M_T/0.65h$$
$$= (320 \times 12)/(0.65 \times 36)$$
$$= 164 \text{ k}$$

From equation 6-4 we have

$$F = M_L/0.50h$$
$$= [(320 - 80)12]/(0.50 \times 36)$$
$$= 160 \text{ k}$$

$F = 164$ k controls the design.

6-2   Elastic Design, General Concepts

There is a prevailing impression that the design of prestressed-concrete sections is much more complicated than that of reinforced ones. This is not true if the procedure recommended in this chapter is followed. However, the design of a section is based on a knowledge of its analysis. Hence readers must be familiar with the methods of analysis discussed

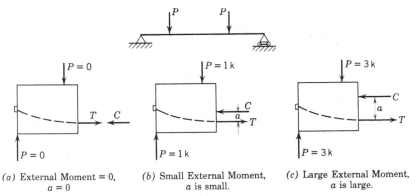

(a) External Moment = 0, (b) Small External Moment, (c) Large External Moment,
    $a = 0$ a is small. a is large.

Fig. 6-4. Variable a in a prestressed-concrete beam.

in the previous chapter before they can master the methods of design.

The method of preliminary design presented in section 6-1 is based on the fact that the section is governed by two controlling values of external bending moment: the total moment M_T, which controls the stresses under the action of the working loads; and the girder load moment M_G, which determines the location of the c.g.s. and the stresses at transfer.

It is desirable to reiterate here the basic concept of a resisting couple in a prestressed-concrete-beam section. From the law of statics, the internal resisting moment in a prestressed beam, as in a reinforced-concrete beam, must equal the external moment. That internal moment can be represented by a couple, C–T, for either the prestressed- or the reinforced-concrete-beam section, Figs. 6-4 and 6-5. T is the centroid of the prestress or tensile force in the steel; and C is the center of pressure or the center of compression on the concrete.

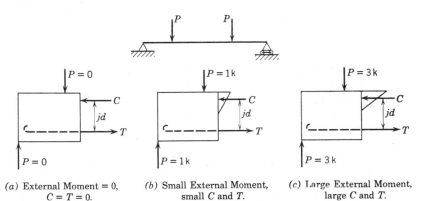

(a) External Moment = 0, (b) Small External Moment, (c) Large External Moment,
    $C = T = 0$.   small C and T.   large C and T.

Fig. 6-5. Constant jd in a reinforced-concrete beam.

There is, however, an essential difference between the behavior of a prestressed- and of a reinforced-concrete-beam section. The difference is explained as follows:

1. In a reinforced-concrete-beam section, as the external bending moment increases, the magnitude of the forces C and T is assumed to increase in direct proportion while the lever arm jd between the two forces remains unchanged, Fig. 6-5.

2. In a prestressed-concrete-beam section under working load, as the external bending moment increases, the magnitude of C and T remains practically constant while the lever arm a lengthens almost proportionately, Fig. 6-4.

Since the location of T remains fixed, we get a variable location of C in a prestressed section as the bending moment changes. For a given moment M, C can be easily located, since

$$Ca = Ta = M \tag{6-5}$$

$$a = M/C = M/T \tag{6-5a}$$

Thus, when $M = 0$, $a = 0$, and C must coincide with T, Fig. 6-4(a). When M is small, a is also small, Fig. 6-4(b). When M is large, a is also large, Fig. 6-4(c).

In a prestressed-concrete beam, the amount of initial prestress F_0 is measured and is rather accurately known. At the time of transfer of prestress, $T = F_0$. After all losses have taken place, $T = F$. Although the value of T does change as the beam bends under loading, the change is small within the working range and can either be taken into account or neglected in design.

Once the magnitude of T is known, the value of a can be computed from equation 6-5a for any value of M. The location of C can thus be determined. With the position and magnitude of C known, stress distribution across the concrete section can be obtained by the elastic or the plastic theory, although the elastic theory is usually followed.

It will be well to mention some of the simple relations between stress distribution and the location of C, according to the elastic theory, Fig. 6-6. If C coincides with the top or bottom kern point, stress distribution will be triangular, with zero stress at bottom or top fiber, respectively. If C falls within the kern, the entire section will be under compression; if outside the kern, some tension will exist. If C coincides with c.g.c., stress will be uniform over the entire concrete section. (See Appendix A for k_t and k_b, defining the kern.)

In the actual design of prestressed-concrete sections, similar to any other type of section, a certain amount of trial and error is inevitable.

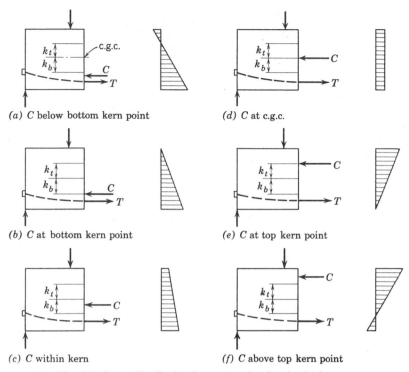

(a) *C* below bottom kern point   (d) *C* at c.g.c.

(b) *C* at bottom kern point   (e) *C* at top kern point

(c) *C* within kern   (f) *C* above top **kern** point

Fig. 6-6. Stress distribution in concrete by the elastic theory.

There is the general layout of the structure which must be chosen as a start but which may be modified as the process of design develops. There is the dead weight of the member which influences the design but which must be assumed before embarking on the moment calculations. There is the approximate shape of the concrete section, governed by both practical and theoretical considerations, which must be assumed for the trial. Because of these variables, it has been found that the best procedure is one of trial and error, guided by known relations which enable the final results to be obtained without excessive work.

When the shape of the section and the loadings are known, the amount and location of prestress can be solved by programs set up for digital computers to meet stress requirements at different points along a beam, resulting in saving of manual computation.

6-3 Elastic Design, No Tension in Concrete

In this section will be discussed the final flexural design of sections based on the elastic theory and allowing no tension in the concrete both at transfer and under working load. While allowing no tension is generally regarded as too conservative a criterion, it does help to simplify computation and hence will be discussed first. Two cases will be considered, one for small and one for large ratios of M_G/M_T.

Small Ratios of M_G/M_T. For the section obtained from the preliminary design, the values of M_G, k_t, k_b, A_c are computed. When the ratio of M_G/M_T is small, c.g.s. is located outside the kern just as much as the M_G will allow. Since no tension is permitted in the concrete, c.g.s. will be located below the kern by the amount of Fig. 6-7(*b*).

$$e - k_b = M_G/F_0 \qquad (6\text{-}6)$$

If c.g.s. is so located, C will be exactly at the bottom kern point for the given M_G, and the stresses at the top and bottom fibers will be

$$f_t = 0$$
$$f_b = \frac{F_0}{A_c}\frac{h}{c_t} \qquad (6\text{-}7)$$

Hence,

$$A_c = \frac{F_0 h}{f_b c_t} \qquad (6\text{-}7a)$$

If c.g.s. is located farther up, C will fall within the kern; then the top fibers will be under some compression, and the bottom fibers will be stressed less than given by equation 6-7. If c.g.s. is located farther below, C will fall outside the kern; then there will be some tension in the top fibers, and the bottom fibers will be stressed higher than given by equation 6-7.

With c.g.s. located as above, the available lever arm for the resisting moment is given by $e + k_t$, and the effective prestress F is given by

$$F = \frac{M_T}{e + k_t} \qquad (6\text{-}8)$$

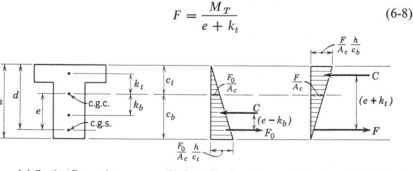

(*a*) Section Properties   (*b*) Just after Transfer   (*c*) Under Working Load
                          C at bottom kern point   C at top kern point

Fig. 6-7. Stress distribution, no tension in concrete (small ratios of M_G/M_T).

Under the action of this effective prestress F and the total moment M_T, C will be located at the top kern point, and the top and bottom fiber stresses are, Fig. 6-7(c),

$$f_b = 0$$

$$f_t = \frac{F}{A_c} \frac{h}{c_b} \tag{6-9}$$

Hence,

$$A_c = \frac{Fh}{f_t c_b} \tag{6-9a}$$

If F is smaller than the value given by equation 6-8, there will be tension in the bottom fibers, and the compressive stress in the top fibers will be greater than that given by equation 6-9; if F is greater, there will be some residual compression in the bottom fibers, and the compressive stress in the top fibers will be less than that indicated by equation 6-9.

If f_b or f_t exceeds the allowable value, it will be necessary to increase the area of concrete A_c, or to decrease the ratio of h/c_t or h/c_b, respectively. If f_b and f_t are both less than the respective allowable values, A_c can be decreased accordingly. Slight changes in the dimensions of the section may not affect the k_t, k_b, and other values. But if major changes are made, it may be desirable to go over the procedure once more to obtain a new location for the c.g.s. and compute new values for F and check over the required A_c.

To summarize the procedure of design, we have:

Step 1. From the preliminary design section, locate c.g.s. by

$$e - k_b = M_G/F_0$$

Step 2. With the above location of c.g.s., compute the effective prestress F (and then the initial prestress F_0) by

$$F = \frac{M_T}{e + k_t}$$

Step 3. Compute the required A_c by

$$A_c = F_0 h/f_b c_t$$

and

$$A_c = Fh/f_t c_b$$

Step 4. Revise the preliminary section to meet the above requirements for F and A_c. Repeat steps 1 through 4 if necessary.

From the above discussion, the following observations regarding the properties of a section can be made.

1. $e + k_t$ is a measure of the total moment-resisting capacity of the beam section. Hence, the greater this value, the more desirable is the section.

2. $e - k_b$ locates the c.g.s. for the section, and is determined by the value of M_G. Thus, within certain limits, the amount of M_G does not seriously affect the capacity of the section for carrying M_L.

3. h/c_b is the ratio of the maximum top fiber stress to the average stress on the section under working load. Thus, the smaller this ratio, the lower will be the maximum top fiber stress.

4. h/c_t is the ratio of the maximum bottom fiber stress to the average stress on the section at transfer. Hence, the smaller this ratio, the lower will be the maximum bottom fiber stress.

To facilitate design computations, properties of different sections are listed in Appendix C, Tables 1 through 6. Values of A_c, I, k_t, k_b, c_t, c_b, etc., are given in these tables. Properties for a rectangular section are included in Table 1 under the headings $b'/b = t/h = 1$, that is, section 1-q. By the use of these equations and the tables, it is possible to develop formulas which will give directly the required section modulus for a given shape. But for a practical design, it is generally preferable to follow a method of trial and error as we just outlined, because dimensioning and other practical considerations do not often permit keeping to an assumed shape of section.

EXAMPLE 6-3

For the preliminary section obtained in example 6-2, make a final design, allowing $f_b = -1.80$ ksi, $f_0 = 150$ ksi. Other given values were: $M_T = 320$ k-ft; $M_G = 40$ k-ft; $f_t = -1.60$ ksi; $f_s = 125$ ksi; $F = 187$ k. And the preliminary section is the same as in Fig. 6-3.

Solution. For the trial preliminary section, compute the properties as follows

$$A_c = 2 \times 4 \times 15 + 4 \times 28 = 232 \text{ sq in.}$$

$$I = \frac{15 \times 36^3}{12} - \frac{11 \times 28^3}{12}$$

$$= 58{,}200 - 20{,}100$$

$$= 38{,}100 \text{ in.}^4$$

$$r^2 = 38{,}100/232$$

$$= 164 \text{ in.}^2$$

$$k_t = k_b = 164/18 = 9.1 \text{ in.}$$

Step 1. For an assumed

$$F = 187 \text{ k}$$

$$F_0 = \frac{150}{125} 187 = 225 \text{ k}$$

c.g.s. should be located at $e - k_b$ below the bottom kern, where

$$e - k_b = \frac{M_G}{F_0} = \frac{40 \times 12}{225} = 2.1 \text{ in.}$$

$$e = 9.1 + 2.1 = 11.2 \text{ in.}$$

Step 2. Effective prestress required is recomputed as

$$F = \frac{M_T}{e + k_t} = \frac{320 \times 12}{11.2 + 9.1}$$

$$= 189 \text{ k}$$

$$F_0 = \frac{150}{125} 189 = 227 \text{ k}$$

Step 3. A_c required is

$$A_c = \frac{F_0 h}{f_b c_t}$$

$$= \frac{227 \times 36}{1.80 \times 18}$$

$$= 252 \text{ sq in. controlling}$$

$$A_c = \frac{Fh}{f_t c_b}$$

$$= \frac{189 \times 36}{1.60 \times 18}$$

$$= 236 \text{ sq in.}$$

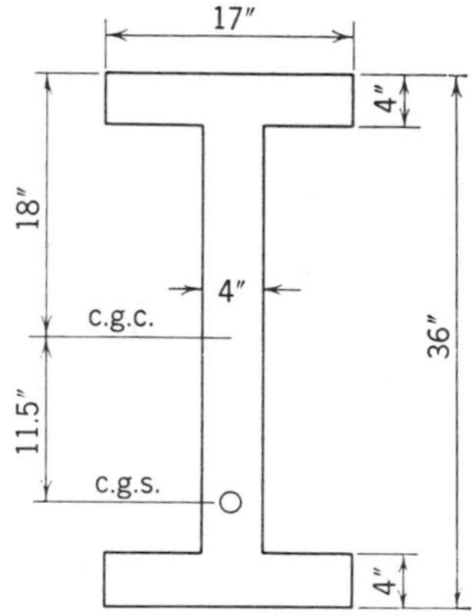

Fig. 6-8. Example 6-3.

Step 4. Try a new section as shown in Fig. 6-8, with $A_c = 248$ sq in. For this new section, $I = 42,200$ in.^{4}; $k_t = k_b = 9.4$ in.; $e - k_b = 2.1$ in.; $F = 320 \times 12/(11.5 + 9.4) = 184$ k; $F_0 = 221$ k; A_c required for bottom fiber $= 246$ sq in., for top fiber $= 230$ sq in. Hence the section seems to be quite satisfactory. And no further revision is needed.

Large Ratios of M_G/M_T. When the ratio of M_G/M_T is large, the value of $e - k_b$ computed from equation 6.6 may place c.g.s. outside of the practical limit, for example, below the section of the beam. Then it is necessary to place the c.g.s. only as low as practicable and design accordingly.

For such a condition, the bottom fiber stress is seldom critical. Under the initial condition, just after transfer, the bottom fiber stress is shown in Fig. 6-9(*b*) and is given by the formula

$$f_b = \frac{F_0}{A_c} + \frac{(F_0 e - M_G)c_b}{I}$$

$$= \frac{F_0}{A_c}\left(1 + \frac{e - (M_G/F_0)}{k_t}\right)$$

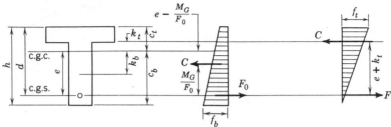

(a) Section Properties   (b) Just after Transfer,   (c) Under Working Load,
                              C above bottom kern point   C at top kern point

Fig. 6-9. Stress distribution, no tension in concrete (large ratios of M_G/M_I).

from which the required area A_c can be computed as

$$A_c = \frac{F_0}{f_b}\left(1 + \frac{e - (M_G/F_0)}{k_t}\right) \qquad (6\text{-}10)$$

The top fiber is always under some compression and does not control the design under this condition.

Under the working load, the stress distribution is the same as for the first case (small ratios), and is pictured in Fig. 6-9(c). The design is practically the same as before except that equation 6-10 should be used in place of equation 6-7a. For convenience, the procedure will be outlined as follows.

Step 1.   From the preliminary section, compute the theoretical location for c.g.s. by

$$e - k_b = M_G/F_0$$

If it is feasible to locate c.g.s. as indicated by this equation, follow the first procedure. If not, locate c.g.s. at the practical lower limit and proceed as follows.

Step 2.   Compute F (and then F_0) by

$$F = \frac{M_T}{e + k_t}$$

Step 3.   Compute the required area by equations 6-9a and 6-10.

$$A_c = Fh/f_t c_b$$
$$A_c = \frac{F_0}{f_b}\left(1 + \frac{e - (M_G/F_0)}{k_t}\right)$$

Step 4.   Use the greater of the two A_c's and the new value of F, and revise the preliminary section. Repeat steps 1 through 4 if necessary.

EXAMPLE 6-4

Make final design for the preliminary section obtained in example 6-1, $M_G = 210$ k-ft, allowing $f_b = -1.80$ ksi, $f_0 = 150$ ksi. Other values given were $M_T = 320$ k-ft; $h = 36$ in.; $f_s = 125$ ksi; $f_t = -1.60$ ksi. The preliminary section is shown in Fig. 6-10, with $A_c = 200$ sq in., $c_t = 13.5$ in., $c_b = 22.5$ in., $I = 26,000$ in.^{4}, $k_t = 5.8$ in., $k_b = 9.6$ in., $F = 164$ k, $F_0 = 164(150/125) = 197$ k.

Solution. *Step* 1.   Theoretical lowest location for c.g.s. is given by

$$e - k_b = M_G/F_0$$
$$= (210 \times 12)/197$$
$$= 12.8 \text{ in.}$$

indicating 12.8 in. below the bottom kern, or 0.1 in. above the bottom fiber, which is obviously impossible. Suppose that for practical reasons the c.g.s. has to be kept 3 in. above the bottom fiber to provide sufficient concrete protection. This problem then belongs to the second case, and we proceed as below.

Step 2.   The effective prestress required is, corresponding to a lever arm of $e + k_t = 22.5 - 3 + 5.8 = 25.3$ in.,

$$F = (320 \times 12)/25.3 = 152 \text{ k}$$
$$F_0 = 152(150/125) = 182 \text{ k}$$

Step 3.   Compute the area required by

$$A_c = \frac{Fh}{f_t c_b}$$
$$= \frac{152 \times 36}{1.60 \times 22.5}$$
$$= 152 \text{ sq in.}$$

$$A_c = \frac{F_0}{f_b}\left(1 + \frac{e - (M_G/F_0)}{k_t}\right)$$
$$= \frac{182}{1.80}\left(1 + \frac{19.5 - 210 \times 12/182}{5.8}\right)$$
$$= 199 \text{ sq in.}$$

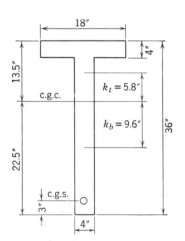

Fig. 6-10. Example 6-4. Trial section.

which indicates that the trial preliminary section with $A_c = 200$ sq in. is just about right for the stress in the bottom fibers, but much more than enough as far as the top fibers are concerned. In other words, if practical conditions permit, it may be desirable to reduce the concrete area in the top flange and to add concrete area to the bottom flange, to obtain a more economical section. The reader may try this out to see whether a better section is obtainable for this example.

6-4   Elastic Design, Remarks on Allowing Tension

In the preceding section we discussed the design of prestressed-concrete sections allowing no tensile stresses. This requirement may often be an extravagance that cannot be justified. When compared to reinforced concrete, where high tensile stresses and cracks are always present under working load, it seems only logical that at least some tensile stresses should be permitted in prestressed concrete. On the other hand, there are several reasons for limiting the tensile stresses in prestressed concrete. These are:

1. The existence of high tensile stress in prestressed concrete may indicate an insufficient factor of safety against ultimate failure. When high tensile stress exists in prestressed concrete, the working lever arm a for the resisting couple is a large ratio of h, Fig. 6-11, so that no substantial increase in the lever arm can take place in case of overloads. Thus the margin of safety may not be sufficient.

2. The existence of tensile stress may indicate an insufficient factor of safety against cracking and may easily result in cracking if the concrete has been previously cracked. Although cracking may not be significant under static load, it could be an important criterion when a member is subject to repeated loads. Cracking also signifies a change in the nature of bond and shearing stresses. Furthermore, it is sometimes believed that the small wires in prestressed concrete are more susceptible to corrosion in the event of permanent cracks, although opening of cracks under passing loads is seldom held as contributing to corrosion to any significant extent.

Since the original idea of prestressing concrete was to produce a new material out of concrete by putting it permanently under compression, it

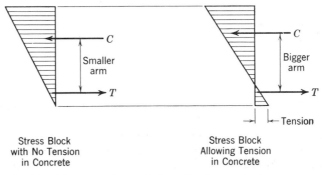

Fig. 6-11. Bigger arm for steel when allowing tension in concrete.

was more or less arbitrarily concluded that tensile stresses were not permitted under working loads. As more experience and knowledge was gained with the behavior of prestressed concrete, most engineers have now shifted to the opinion that a certain amount of tension is permissible. Thus the PCI Building Code Requirements (Appendix D) permit tensile stresses as follows.

1. *Stresses at transfer:*
   Tension in members without auxiliary reinforcement—$3\sqrt{f_{ci}'}$
   Tension in members with properly designed auxiliary reinforcement
   —no limit
2. *Stresses at design loads:*
   Tension in precompressed tensile zone of members not exposed to a corrosive environment and which contain bonded reinforcement to control cracking—$6\sqrt{f_{ci}'}$
   Tension in all other members—0
   Tension in excess of above limiting values may be permitted when shown to be not detrimental to proper structural behavior.

It is clear from the above that, while empirical limits are often specified for convenience in design and checking, the magnitude of permissible tensile stresses should vary with the conditions and cannot easily be fixed at one or two definite values.

When tensile stresses are permitted under working loads, the term "partial prestressing" is often employed, indicating that the concrete is only partially compressed by the prestress. It is the author's opinion that there is really no basic difference between partial and full prestress. The only difference is that, in partial prestressing, there exists a certain amount of tension in concrete under working loads. Since most structures are subject to occasional overloads, tensile stresses will actually exist in both partial and full prestressing, at one time or another. Hence there is no basic difference between them.

It is sometimes argued that the allowing of tension in concrete is a dangerous procedure, since the concrete might have cracked previously and could not take any tension. This is true if the tensile force in concrete is a significant portion of the tensile force in the steel, in which event it will be necessary to neglect tensile force furnished by the concrete, Fig. 6-12. On the other hand, if the tensile force in the concrete is only a small proportion of that in steel, the calculations will not be very different whether it is neglected or included.

In the following two sections, two methods of design will be presented, both allowing tension in the concrete. For the first method, tensile force in concrete will be neglected in the computation, assuming all concrete

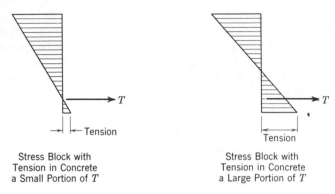

Stress Block with
Tension in Concrete
a Small Portion of T

Stress Block with
Tension in Concrete
a Large Portion of T

Fig. 6-12. Relative significance of tension in concrete.

under tension to be cracked. This is believed to be a safe method of design, provided that the tensile stress allowed in concrete is not excessive. The second method of design takes into account the tensile force in concrete, assuming uncracked sections. This gives a better representation of the actual stress distribution before cracking, but it is not conservative enough unless the portion of the tensile force taken by concrete is small or the cracking of concrete is prevented at all times. It is, however, a convenient method of design and gives practically the same results as the first method when the tensile force in concrete is relatively small.

6-5   Elastic Design, Allowing but Neglecting Tension

Small Ratios of M_G/M_T. Designing by this method will yield steel areas and sometimes concrete areas somewhat less than when tension is not allowed. It is usually best to make a design by the method in section 6-3, allowing no tension. This will give a fairly close section to start with. Using this as a trial section, the portion under compression or the uncracked portion at transfer can be assumed as in Fig. 6-13(a), with the allowable tensile stress on top fiber f_t' and the allowable compressive stress on bottom fiber f_b shown thereon. For this uncracked portion with depth h_1 compute the section properties, $A_{c1}, I_1, c_{t1}, c_{b1}, k_{t1}, k_{b1}$. The c.g.s. can now be located below the bottom kern of the uncracked portion by the amount of M_G/F_0.

Under the working load, if some tension f_b' is permitted in the bottom fibers, the uncracked portion with depth h_2 can be assumed as shown in Fig. 6-13(b). The properties of this second uncracked portion can be computed as $A_{c2}, I_2, c_{t2}, c_{b2}, k_{t2}, k_{b2}$. The center of compression is located at the top kern, and the total lever arm for the internal resisting moment

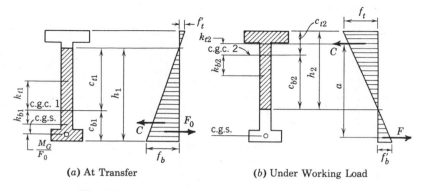

(a) At Transfer   (b) Under Working Load

Fig. 6-13. Allowing but neglecting tension in concrete.

is *a* as shown in the figure. Thus the required value of effective prestress is computed as

$$F = M_T/a \qquad (6\text{-}11)$$

The bottom fiber stress under the initial condition at transfer is given by

$$f_b = \frac{F_0 h_1}{A_{c1} c_{t1}} \qquad (6\text{-}12)$$

For an allowable stress of f_b, the required area A_{c1} is given by

$$A_{c1} = \frac{F_0 h_1}{f_b c_{t1}} \qquad (6\text{-}12a)$$

The top fiber stress under working load is given by

$$f_t = \frac{F h_2}{A_{c2} c_{b2}} \qquad (6\text{-}13)$$

and similarly, for an allowable stress of f_t, the required A_{c2} is

$$A_{c2} = \frac{F h_2}{f_t c_{b2}} \qquad (6\text{-}13a)$$

From these four equations, checking can be done either for the stresses produced or for the areas to be furnished.

Design by this method is illustrated in the following example.

EXAMPLE 6-5

Redesign the section in example 6-3, allowing tension in concrete: $f_t' = 0.30$ ksi, $f_b' = 0.24$ ksi. Other values given for the trial section were: $M_T = 320$ k-ft, $M_G = 40$ k-ft, $f_t = -1.60$ ksi, $f_b = -1.80$ ksi, $F = 184$ k, $F_o = 221$ k.

Solution. *Step* 1. Assuming the bottom fiber stress at transfer to be $f_b = -1.80$ ksi and the top fiber stress to be 0.30 ksi, the uncracked portion is shown

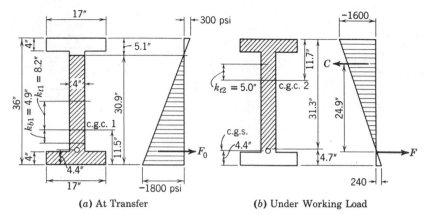

(a) At Transfer   (b) Under Working Load

Fig. 6-14. Example 6-5.

in Fig. 6-14 (a). Properties of the uncracked portion are:

$$A_{c1} = 4 \times 17 + 26.9 \times 4 = 68 + 108 = 176 \text{ sq in.}$$

$$c_{b1} = \frac{68 \times 2 + 108 \times 17.5}{176} = 11.5 \text{ in.}$$

$$I_1 = 68\left(\frac{4^2}{12} + 9.5^2\right) + 108\left(\frac{26.9^2}{12} + 6^2\right)$$

$$= 6200 + 10,400 = 16,600 \text{ in.}^4$$

$$r_1^2 = 16,600/176 = 94.3 \text{ in.}^2$$

$$k_{t1} = 94.3/11.5 = 8.2 \text{ in.}$$

$$k_{b1} = 94.3/19.4 = 4.9 \text{ in.}$$

$$M_G/F_0 = 40 \times 12/221 = 2.2 \text{ in.}$$

Hence c.g.s. can be located at $11.5 - 4.9 - 2.2 = 4.4$ in. above bottom fiber.

Step 2. Under working conditions, for a stress at top fiber of $f_t = -1.60$ ksi and at bottom fiber of $f_b' = 0.24$ ksi, the uncracked portion is shown in Fig. 6-14(b). Properties of the uncracked portion are:

$$A_{c2} = 4 \times 17 + 27.3 \times 4 = 68 + 109 = 177 \text{ sq in.}$$

$$c_{t2} = \frac{68 \times 2 + 109 \times 17.7}{177} = 11.7 \text{ in.}$$

$$I_2 = 68\left(\frac{4^2}{12} + 9.7^2\right) + 109\left(\frac{27.3^2}{12} + 6.0^2\right)$$

$$= 6470 + 10,700 = 17,200 \text{ in.}^4$$

$$r_2^2 = 17,200/177 = 97.0 \text{ in.}^2$$

$$k_{t2} = 97.0/19.6 = 5.0 \text{ in.}$$

Total lever arm $a = 36 - 4.4 - 11.7 + 5.0 = 24.9$ in.

$$F = M_T/a$$

$$= 320 \times 12/24.9$$

$$= 154 \text{ k}$$

$$F_0 = 154 \times 150/125 = 185 \text{ k}$$

Step 3.   Area A_{c1} required will be

$$A_{c1} = \frac{185 \times 30.9}{1.80 \times 19.4} = 164 \text{ sq in.}$$

A_{c1} furnished was 176 sq in., indicating a slight excess.   Area A_{c2} required will be

$$A_{c2} = \frac{154 \times 31.3}{1.60 \times 19.6} = 154 \text{ sq in.}$$

A_{c2} furnished was 177 sq in., again indicating an excess.   Hence a somewhat smaller section can be tried, and the above procedure repeated if desired.

Large Ratios of M_G/M_T.   In this case, the c.g.s. has to be located at the lowest practicable point.   At transfer, the stress distribution will be as shown in Fig. 6-9(*b*), and there will be no critical tensile stresses at the top fibres.   The area of concrete required is given by equation 6-10,

$$A_c = \frac{F_0}{f_b}\left(1 + \frac{e - (M_G/F_0)}{k_t}\right)$$

EXAMPLE 6-6

Revise the design for the section in example 6-4 allowing tension in concrete, $f_t' = 0.30$ ksi and $f_b' = 0.24$ ksi.   Other values given were: $M_T = 320$ k-ft; $M_G = 210$ k-ft; $F = 152$ k; $F_0 = 182$ k; $A_c = 200$ sq in.; $c_t = 13.5$ in.; $c_b = 22.5$ in.; $I = 26,000$ in.[4]; $k_t = 5.8$ in.; $k_b = 9.6$ in. (Fig. 6-15).

Solution.   Step 1.   Proceeding as in example 6-4, the theoretical lowest position for c.g.s. without producing tension in top fiber is given by

$$e - k_b = M_G/F_0$$

$$= (210 \times 12)/182$$

$$= 13.8 \text{ in.}$$

indicating 13.8 in. below the bottom kern, or 0.9 in. below the bottom fiber, which is not feasible.   Suppose that the c.g.s. is located at 3 in. above bottom fiber; then no tension will be in top fiber.

Step 2.   Under the working load, assuming the top fiber stress to be -1.60 ksi and the bottom fiber stress to be 0.24 ksi, the uncracked portion has a depth of 31.3 in., as shown in Fig. 6-15(*b*). Properties of the uncracked portion are:

$$A_{c2} = 4 \times 18 + 4 \times 27.3 = 72 + 109 = 181 \text{ sq in.}$$

$$c_{t2} = \frac{72 \times 2 + 109 \times 17.6}{181} = 11.4 \text{ in.}$$

$$I_2 = 72\left(\frac{4^2}{12} + 9.4^2\right) + 109\left(\frac{27.3^2}{12} + 6.3^2\right)$$

$$= 6480 + 11,100 = 17,600$$

$$k_{t2} = 17,600/(181 \times 19.9) = 4.9 \text{ in.}$$

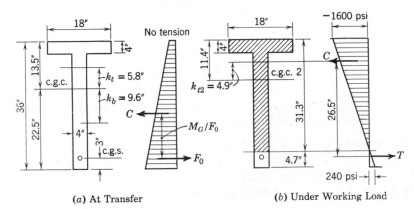

(*a*) At Transfer   (*b*) Under Working Load

Fig. 6-15. Example 6-6.

Total lever arm *a* for bending is

$$a = 36 - 3 - 11.4 + 4.9 = 26.5 \text{ in.}$$

$$F = (320 \times 12)/26.5 = 145 \text{ k}; \quad F_0 = 145\left(\frac{150}{125}\right) = 174 \text{ k}$$

Step 3. As governed by top fiber in compression,

$$A_{c2} = \frac{145 \times 31.3}{1.60 \times 19.9} = 143 \text{ sq in.}$$

As governed by the bottom fiber, using the entire section for $F_0 = 174$ k,

$$A_c = \frac{174}{1.80}\left(1 + \frac{19.5 - (210 \times 12/174)}{5.8}\right)$$

$$= 180 \text{ sq in.}$$

The above calculation shows that the top flange area can be reduced while the bottom flange area can be slightly increased, in order to obtain a more balanced section. Compare this with the solution for example 6-4.

6-6 Elastic Design, Allowing and Considering Tension

This method should be used only with caution. It may not always be a safe procedure when tension in concrete constitutes a major part of the total tensile force in resisting bending. It is, however, a convenient method and yields results comparable to those of the method in section 6-5 when the tensile force in concrete considered is only a small portion of the total tension. The method will be explained as follows.

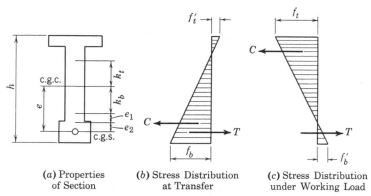

(a) Properties of Section   (b) Stress Distribution at Transfer   (c) Stress Distribution under Working Load

Fig. 6-16. Allowing and considering tension in concrete.

Small Ratios of M_G/M_T. If tensile stress f_t' is permitted in the top fibers, the center of compression C can be located below the bottom kern by the amount of

$$e_1 = f_t'I/F_0c_t = f_t'Ak_b/F_0 \qquad (6\text{-}14)$$

For a given moment M_G, the c.g.s. can be further located below C by the amount of

$$e_2 = M_G/F_0 \qquad (6\text{-}15)$$

Hence the maximum total amount that the c.g.s. can be located below the kern is given by

$$e_1 + e_2 = \frac{M_G + f_t'Ak_b}{F_0} \qquad (6\text{-}16)$$

The c.g.s. having been located at some value e below c.g.c., the lever arm a under working load is known. For an allowable tension in the bottom fiber, the moment carried by the concrete is

$$f_b'I/c_b = f_b'Ak_t$$

The net moment $M_T - f_b'Ak_t$ is to be carried by the prestress F with a lever arm acting up to the top kern point; hence the total arm is (Fig. 6-16).

$$a = k_t + e \qquad (6\text{-}17)$$

and the prestress F required is

$$F = \frac{M_T - f_b' A k_t}{a} \tag{6-18}$$

The bottom fiber stress at transfer is given by

$$f_b = \frac{F_0 h}{A_c c_t} + f_t' \frac{c_b}{c_t} \tag{6-19}$$

from which we have

$$A_c = \frac{F_0 h}{f_b c_t - f_t' c_b} \tag{6-19a}$$

Similarly, the top fiber stress under working load is given by

$$f_t = \frac{Fh}{A_c c_b} + f_b' \frac{c_t}{c_b} \tag{6-20}$$

from which

$$A_c = \frac{Fh}{f_t c_b - f_b' c_t} \tag{6-20a}$$

EXAMPLE 6-7

Redesign the beam section in example 6-3, allowing and considering tension in concrete. $f_t' = 0.30$ ksi, $f_b' = 0.24$ ksi. Other given values were: $M_T = 320$ k-ft; $M_G = 40$ k-ft; $f_t = -1.60$ ksi; $f_b = -1.80$ ksi; $F = 184$ k; $F_0 = 221$ k.

Solution.   *Step 1.*   From example 6-3, we have $k_t = k_b = 9.4$ in.; $A_c = 248$ sq in. Using equation 6-16, we have

$$e_1 + e_2 = \frac{40 \times 12 + 0.3 \times 248 \times 9.4}{221} = 5.3 \text{ in.}$$

Hence c.g.s. can be located 5.3 in. below the bottom kern, or 3.3 in. above the bottom fiber, Fig. 6-17.

Step 2.   The net moment to be carried by the prestress is

$$M_T - f_b' A k_t = 320 \times 12 - 0.240 \times 248 \times 9.4$$
$$= 3840 - 560 = 3280 \text{ k-in.}$$

For a resisting lever arm of $9.4 + 9.4 + 5.3 = 24.1$ in., the prestress required is

$$F = 3280/24.1 = 136 \text{ k}$$
$$F_0 = 136 \times 150/125 = 163 \text{ k}$$

Step 3.   To limit the bottom fibers to -1.80 ksi, we need

$$A_c = \frac{163 \times 36}{1.80 \times 18 - 0.30 \times 18}$$
$$= 218 \text{ sq in.}$$

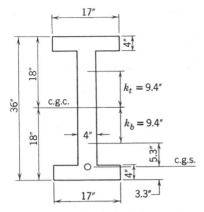

Fig. 6-17. Example 6-7.

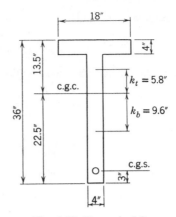

Fig. 6-18. Example 6-8.

To keep the top fibers to -1.60 ksi, we need

$$A_c = \frac{136 \times 36}{1.60 \times 18 - 0.24 \times 18}$$

$$= 200 \text{ sq in.}$$

which indicates that the trial section can be appreciably reduced and a new section tried over again.

Large Ratios of M_G/M_T.   When M_G/M_T is large, C will be within the kern at transfer, and the allowing of tension on top fiber will have no effect on the design. The c.g.s. has to be located within practical limits. Otherwise, the design is made as for the first case. This is illustrated in the next example.

EXAMPLE 6-8

Revise the design for the section in example 6-4 allowing and considering tension in concrete. Other values given were: $M_T = 320$ k-ft; $M_G = 210$ k-ft; $F = 152$ k; $F_0 = 182$ k; $A_c = 200$; $c_t = 13.5$ in.; $c_b = 22.5$ in.; $k_t = 5.8$ in.; $k_b = 9.6$ in. (Fig. 6-18).

Solution.   Step 1.   Referring to example 6-6, since the possible theoretical location for c.g.s. is 13.8 in. below the bottom kern (0.9 in. below bottom fiber) without producing tension in top fiber, whereas the practical location of c.g.s. has to be 3 in. above bottom fiber, no tension will exist in top fiber.

Step 2.   Net amount to be carried by prestress is

$$M_T - f_b' A k_t = 320 \times 12 - 0.240 \times 200 \times 5.8$$

$$= 3840 - 280 = 3560 \text{ k-in.}$$

The resisting lever arm is

$$36 - 3 - 13.5 + 5.8 = 25.3 \text{ in.}$$

The required prestress is

$$F = 3560/25.3 = 141 \text{ k}$$
$$F_0 = 141(150/125) = 169 \text{ k}$$

To keep the bottom fiber stress within limits, we can apply equation 6-10,

$$A_c = \frac{F_0}{f_b}\left(1 + \frac{e - (M_G/F_0)}{k_t}\right)$$

$$= \frac{169}{1.80}\left(1 + \frac{19.5 - (210 \times 12/169)}{5.8}\right)$$

$$= 168 \text{ sq in.}$$

To keep the top fiber stress within limit, we have, from equation 6-20a,

$$A_c = \frac{141 \times 36}{1.60 \times 22.5 - 0.24 \times 13.5}$$

$$= 155 \text{ sq in.}$$

The area furnished is 200 sq in., which can be reduced if desired.

6-7   Elastic Design, Composite Sections

As described previously, a composite section consists of a precast pre-stressed portion to be combined with another cast-in-place portion which usually forms part or all of the top flange of the beam. The design of composite sections is more complicated than that of simple ones because there are many possible combinations in the make-up of a composite section. Only a very common case will be treated here, leaving the possible variations to the designer after he has mastered the principles here presented.

In the case considered here the precast portion forms the lower flange and the web while part or the whole of the top flange is cast in place. Tension is usually permitted in the top flange at transfer and often also in the bottom flange under working load. Hence, formulas will be derived to include tensile stresses. These can be easily simplified when tensile stresses are not permitted. For such composite sections compressive stress in the cast-in-place portion is seldom critical and hence will be checked only at the end of the design. When the cast-in-place portion becomes the major part of the web, or when falseworks are employed to support the precast portion during casting, the method presented here has to be modified accordingly.

The procedure of design here presented follows closely the basic approach previously adopted for noncomposite sections. It is essentially a trial-and-error process, simplified by a systematic and fast converging

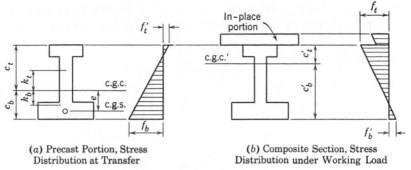

(a) Precast Portion, Stress
Distribution at Transfer

(b) Composite Section, Stress
Distribution under Working Load

Fig. 6-19. Elastic design of composite sections.

procedure and assisted by the use of some simple relations and formulas. One additional concept introduced for composite action is the reduction of moments on the composite section to equivalent moments on the precast portion. This is accomplished by the ratio of the section moduli of the two sections. Steps in the design and the formulas employed will now be explained.

Step 1. Location of c.g.s. For a given trial section, the c.g.s. must be so located that the precast portion will not be overstressed and yet will possess the optimum capacity in resisting the applied external moments. Thus, the c.g.s. must be situated as low as possible but not lower than given by the following value of eccentricity, Fig. 6-19(a),

$$e = k_b + e_1 + e_2$$

where

$$e_1 = \frac{f_t' I}{c_t F_0}$$

$$e_2 = \frac{M_G}{F_0}$$

where f_t' = allowable tension stress on top fiber of precast portion at transfer

I = moment of inertia of precast portion

c_t = distance to top fiber from c.g.c. of precast portion

Step 2. Compute the equivalent moment on the precast portion. For any moment M_C acting on the composite section, it will produce stresses on the precast portion as follows, Fig. 6-19(b),

$$f_t = \frac{M_C c_t'}{I'}$$

$$f_b = \frac{M_C c_b'}{I'}$$

where $I' = I$ of composite section, c_t' and $c_b' = $ distance to extreme fibers of the precast portion measured from c.g.c.' of the composite section. Let

$$m_t = \frac{I/c_t}{I'/c_t'}$$

and

$$m_b = \frac{I/c_b}{I'/c_b'}$$

We have

$$f_t = \frac{m_t M_C c_t}{I} = \frac{m_t M_C}{A_c k_b}$$

$$f_b = \frac{m_b M_C c_b}{I} = \frac{m_b M_C}{A_c k_t}$$

where $A_c = $ area of the precast section
  $k_b = $ bottom kern distance of precast section
  $k_t = $ top kern distance of precast section.

The above indicates that M_C can be modified by the coefficients m_t and m_b so that it can be reduced to equivalent moments for computation based on the precast-portion properties.

  Step 3.   Compute the amount of prestress required for the moments as follows. If $M_P = $ the total moment acting on the precast portion, and $f_b' = $ allowable tensile stress at the bottom fiber, we have

$$\frac{F}{A_c}\left(-1 - \frac{e}{k_t}\right) + \frac{M_P}{A_c k_t} + \frac{m_b M_C}{A_c k_t} = f_b'$$

$$F = \frac{M_P + m_b M_c - f_b' k_t A_c}{e + k_t} \tag{6-21}$$

or

$$F = \frac{M_P + m_b M_C}{e + k_t} \tag{6-21a}$$

if

$$f_b' = 0$$

from which compute the required initial prestress F_0. Revise the location of c.g.s. by this new value of F_0 if necessary.

  Step 4.   In order to limit the bottom fiber stress to the allowable value at transfer, we have

$$f_b = \frac{F_0}{A_c} + \frac{(F_0 e - M_G)}{A_c k_t}$$

from which

$$A_c = \frac{1}{f_b}\left[F_0 + \frac{F_0 e - M_G}{k_t}\right] \tag{6-22}$$

In order to limit the top fibers of the precast portion to within allowable compressive stress f_t under working load, we have

$$f_t = \frac{F}{A_c} + \frac{M_P + m_t M_C - Fe}{A_c k_b}$$

$$A_c = \frac{1}{f_t}\left[F + \frac{M_P + m_t M_C - Fe}{k_b}\right] \tag{6-23}$$

The greater of the two formulas will control the A_c required for the precast portion. The top fiber of the cast-in-place top flange can be computed by the formula $f = Mc/I$, using the applicable values.

EXAMPLE 6-9

The top flange of a composite section is given as a slab 4 in. thick and 60 in. wide cast in place. Design a precast section with a total depth of 36 in. (including the slab thickness) to carry the following moments: $M_T = 320$ k-ft, $M_G = 40$ k-ft, $M_P = 100$ k-ft, $M_C = 220$ k-ft. Allowable stresses are: $f_t = -1.60$ ksi, $f_b = -1.80$ ksi, $f_t' = 0.30$ ksi, $f_b' = 0.16$ ksi. Initial prestress = 150 ksi, effective prestress = 125 ksi.

To assume the section, make a preliminary design, assuming a lever arm of $0.65h$ for the prestressing force in resisting the total moment; we have

$$F = \frac{M_T}{0.65h}$$

$$= \frac{320 \times 12}{0.65 \times 36}$$

$$= 164 \text{ k}$$

$F_0 = 164 \times 150/125 = 197$ k. For an inverted T-section, the concrete area required can be approximated by

$$A_c = 1.5\frac{F_0}{f_b}$$

$$= 1.5\frac{197}{1.8}$$

$$= 164 \text{ sq in.}$$

From this preliminary section, a sketch of a trial section is shown, Fig. 6-20, and the design proceeds as follows.

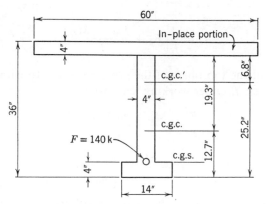

Fig. 6-20. Example 6-9.

For the precast portion, the section properties are

$$4 \times 14 = 56 \times 2 = 112$$
$$28 \times 4 = 112 \times 18 = 2016$$
$$A_c = \overline{168} \qquad \overline{2128} \div 168 = 12.7 \text{ in.} = c_b$$

$$56(4^2/12 + 10.7^2) = 6,500$$
$$112(28^2/12 + 5.3^2) = 10,450$$
$$\overline{16,950} \div 168 = 101 = r^2$$

$$k_t = 101/12.7 = 8.0 \text{ in.}$$

$$k_b = 101/19.3 = 5.2 \text{ in.}$$

For the composite section, the properties are

$$4 \times 60 = 240 \times 2 \quad = 480$$
$$168 \times 23.3 = 3920$$
$$\overline{408} \qquad \overline{4400} \div 408 = 10.8 \text{ in.}$$

$$240(4^2/12 + 8.8^2) \quad = 18,800$$
$$168(12.5^2) \qquad = 26,200$$
$$I \text{ of precast portion} = 16,950$$
$$\overline{62,000}$$

$$m_t = \frac{I/c_t}{I'/c_t{'}} = \frac{16,950/19.3}{62,000/6.8} = 0.10$$

$$m_b = \frac{I/c_b}{I'/c_b{'}} = \frac{16,950/12.7}{62,000/25.2} = 0.54$$

Step 1. Location of c.g.s.

$$e_1 = \frac{f_t'I}{c_t F_0}$$

$$= \frac{0.30 \times 16{,}950}{19.3 \times 197} = 1.3 \text{ in.}$$

$$e_2 = M_G/F_0$$

$$= (40 \times 12)/197 = 2.4 \text{ in.}$$

$$k_b = 5.2 \text{ in.}$$

$$e = 1.3 + 2.4 + 5.2 = 8.9 \text{ in.}$$

Thus c.g.s. can be located at $12.7 - 8.9 = 3.8$ in. above bottom fiber.

Step 2. As computed above,

$$m_t = 0.10$$

$$m_b = 0.54$$

Step 3. Compute the required F,

$$F = \frac{M_P + m_b M_C - f_b' k_t A_c}{e + k_t}$$

$$= \frac{(100 + 0.54 \times 220)12 - 0.16 \times 8.0 \times 168}{8.9 + 8.0}$$

$$= \frac{2430}{16.9}$$

$$= 144 \text{ k}$$

$$F_0 = 144 \times 150/125 = 173 \text{ k}$$

For $F_0 = 173$ k instead of 197 k, revise e_1 and e_2 as follows;

$$e_1 = 1.3 \times 197/173 = 1.5 \text{ in.}$$

$$e_2 = 2.3 \times 197/173 = 2.7 \text{ in.}$$

$$e = 5.2 + 1.5 + 2.7 = 9.4 \text{ in.}$$

which indicates that c.g.s. can be located at $12.7 - 9.4 = 3.3$ in. above bottom fiber. With new $e + k_t = 9.4 + 8.0 = 17.4$ in., F can be revised to be $144 \times 16.9/17.4 = 140$ k. $F_0 = 140 \times 150/125 = 168$ k.

Step 4. To keep bottom fiber within allowable stress f_b,

$$A_c = \frac{1}{f_b}\left(F_0 + \frac{F_0 e - M_G}{k_t}\right)$$

$$= \frac{1}{1.80}\left(168 + \frac{168 \times 9.4 - 40 \times 12}{8.0}\right)$$

$$= 170 \text{ sq in.}$$

To keep top fiber within allowable f_t,

$$A_c = \frac{1}{f_t}\left(F + \frac{M_P + m_t M_C - Fe}{k_b}\right)$$

$$= \frac{1}{1.60}\left(140 + \frac{(100 + 0.10 \times 220)12 - 140 \times 9.4}{5.2}\right)$$

$$= 106 \text{ sq in.}$$

The top fiber is not controlling in this case, and the A_c required for bottom fiber stress is 170 sq in., which is very close to the A_c of 168 sq in. furnished by the trial section. The design is considered satisfactory.

As pointed out in section 5-7, differential shrinkage and creep between the precast and the in-place portions of a composite section may produce high stresses. However, the usual practice is to ignore them in the process of design. Such practice can be justified on the basis that sections obtained by following the conventional procedure and using the allowable stresses generally result in fairly reasonable proportions. Another justification lies in the fact that the ultimate strength of composite sections is seldom much affected by shrinkage and creep. When deflections and camber are the controlling factors, the effect of differential shrinkage and creep should be carefully considered in design.

6-8   Ultimate Design

Only the ultimate design for simple sections with bonded tendons will be discussed here. Basically, the procedure is also applicable to the ultimate design of composite sections, the details of which will be left to the reader, however.

Preliminary Design. The amount of mathematics involved in the design of prestressed-concrete sections is less in ultimate design than in elastic design, since the ultimate flexural strength of sections can be expressed by simple semi-empirical formulas. For preliminary design, it can be assumed that the ultimate resisting moment of bonded prestressed sections is given by the ultimate strength of steel acting with a lever arm. This arm lever varies with the shape of section and generally ranges between $0.6h$ and $0.9h$, with a common value of $0.8h$. Hence the area of steel required is approximated by

$$A_s = \frac{M_T \times m}{0.80h \times f_s'} \tag{6-24}$$

where m = factor of safety or the load factor.

Assuming that the concrete on the compressive side is stressed to $0.85f_c'$, then the required ultimate concrete area under compression is

$$A_c' = \frac{M_T \times m}{0.80h \times 0.85f_c'} \qquad (6\text{-}25)$$

which is supplied by the compression flange (occasionally with the help of part of the web). The web area and the concrete area on the tension side are designed to provide the shear resistance and the encasement of steel, respectively. In addition, concrete on the precompressed tension side has to stand the prestress at transfer. For a preliminary design, these areas are often obtained by comparison with previous designs rather than by making any involved calculations.

The chief difficulty in ultimate design lies in the proper choice of the factor of safety or the load factor, which will be discussed in detail in Chapter 17. For the present it will be assumed that a load factor of 2 will be sufficient for steel and one of 2.5 for concrete. The application of the method is illustrated in the following example.

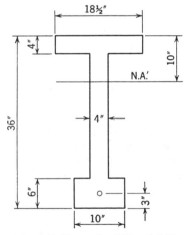

EXAMPLE 6-10

Make a preliminary design for a pre-stressed-concrete section 36 in. high to carry a total dead and live load moment of 320 k-ft, using steel with an ultimate strength of 220 ksi and concrete with $f_c' = 4$ ksi. Use ultimate design, and assume a bonded beam.

Solution. Using a load factor of 2 for steel, we have, from equation 6-24,

$$A_s = \frac{320 \times 12 \times 2}{0.80 \times 36 \times 220} = 1.21 \text{ sq in.}$$

Fig. 6-21. Examples 6-10 and 6-11.

Using a load factor of 2.5 for concrete, from equation 6-25,

$$A_c' = \frac{320 \times 12 \times 2.5}{0.80 \times 36 \times 0.85 \times 4} = 98 \text{ sq in.}$$

Thus a preliminary section can be sketched as in Fig. 6-21, providing an ultimate area of 98 sq in. under compression, assuming the ultimate neutral axis to be 10 in. below the top fiber. Note that the exact location of the ultimate neutral axis cannot and need not be obtained for a preliminary design but can be assumed to be about 30% of the effective depth of section.

Final Design. Although the above illustrates a preliminary design based on ultimate strength, a final design is more complicated in that the following factors must be considered.

1. Proper and accurate load factors must be chosen for steel and concrete, related to the design load and possible overloads for the particular structure.
2. Compressive stresses at transfer must be investigated for the tensile flange, generally by the elastic theory. In addition, the tensile flange should be capable of housing the steel properly.
3. The approximate location of the ultimate neutral axis may not be easily determined for certain sections.
4. Design of the web will depend on shear and other factors.
5. The effective lever arm for the internal resisting couple may have to be more accurately computed.
6. Checks for excessive deflection and overstresses may have to be performed.

In spite of these factors, a reasonably good final design for flexure can be made for bonded sections based on ultimate strength considerations. This is illustrated in the following example.

EXAMPLE 6-11

Make a final design for the beam in example 6-10, based on its ultimate strength.

Solution. A trial-and-error procedure is considered convenient for the purpose. Using the preliminary section obtained in example 6-10 as the first trial section, Fig. 6-21, we can proceed as follows.

With the ultimate axis 10 in. below top fiber, the centroid of the ultimate compressive force is located by

$$\frac{74 \times 2 + 24 \times 7}{74 + 24} = 3.2 \text{ in.}$$

or 3.2 in. from top fiber. With the c.g.s. located 3 in. above bottom fiber, the ultimate lever arm for the resisting moment is

$$36 - 3.2 - 3 = 29.8 \text{ in.}$$

Now the area of steel required may be recomputed as

$$A_s = \frac{320 \times 12 \times 2}{29.8 \times 220} = 1.17 \text{ sq in.}$$

which is very near to the preliminary value of 1.21 sq in., and no further trial is necessary. Design of the top flange may be done as in example 6-10. Tensile stress should also be checked in the top flange at transfer. Since the bottom flange is seldom controlled by ultimate strength considerations, it is usually checked for elastic stresses. The web, of course, has to be designed for shear, which will be discussed in Chapter 7.

Ultimate vs. Elastic Design.   At the present time, both the elastic and the ultimate designs are used for prestressed concrete, the majority of designers still following the elastic theory. It is difficult to state exact preference for one or the other. Each has its advantages and shortcomings. But, whichever method is used for design, the other one must often be applied for checking. For example, when the elastic theory is used in design, it is the practice to check for the ultimate strength of the section in order to find out whether it has sufficient reserve strength to carry overloads. When the ultimate design is used, the elastic theory must be applied to determine whether the section is overstressed under certain conditions of loading and whether the deflections are excessive. Overstressing is objectionable because it may result in undesirable cracks and creep and fatigue effects. When the design is of conventional types and proportions, such checking becomes unnecessary, because it is then generally known that designing by one method will yield safe results when checked by the other. This is, in fact, the reason why such checking is not required of reinforced-concrete structures designed by the usual codes. When we delve into new types and proportions, it is possible that elastic design alone might not yield a sufficiently safe structure under overloads, while the ultimate design by itself might give no guarantee against excessive overstress under working conditions. It is therefore deemed desirable to apply both the elastic and the ultimate methods, especially for structures of unusual proportions.

An understanding of both theories of design is also essential in forming judgment when designing structures. Sometimes, design based on one method will yield different proportions from those based on the other. In order to illustrate the point, let us compare a symmetrical I-section and its circumscribing rectangular section, example 6-12. Based on elastic design, allowing no tension in the concrete, the I-section will carry greater moment than the rectangular section; the rectangular section, however, has a higher ultimate strength. If strength is a more important consideration, the design can be based on ultimate strength. If tensile stress, cracking, creep, or deflection is a critical limit, elastic design should be followed. If both strength and stress are controlling criteria for a structure, we are forced to apply both methods to ensure safety and proper behavior, often at the sacrifice of some economy.

EXAMPLE 6-12
An I-section and another circumscribing rectangular section are both pre-stressed with 0.9 sq in. of steel, Fig. 6-22. $f_c' = 5$ ksi, $f_s = 125$ ksi, $f_s' = 250$ ksi.

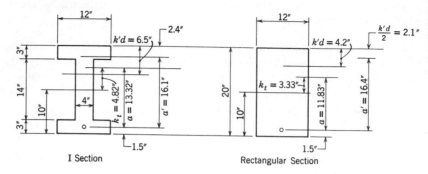

Fig. 6-22. Example 6-12.

Compute (*a*) the resisting moment capacity of each section by the elastic theory, allowing no tension in concrete; (*b*) the ultimate moment capacity of each section.

Solution. (*a*) For no tension in concrete, using formula 6-8, we have

	I-Section	Rectangular Section
Area, sq in.	128	240
I, in.^{4}	6170	8000
k_t, in.	4.82	3.33
Lever arm between c.g.s. and k_t, in.	13.32	11.83
Effective prestress, kips	112.5	112.5
Resisting moment, k-ft	125	111

(*b*) For the ultimate moment capacity, following the method in section 5-6, we have, assuming $k_1 f_c' = 4.5$ ksi,

	I-Section	Rectangular Section
$k'd$, in.	6.5	4.2
Ultimate distance of centroid of compression force from top fiber, in.	2.4	2.1
Ultimate lever arm a' for resisting couple, in.	16.1	16.4
Ultimate tension in steel, kips	225	225
Ultimate resisting moment k-ft	302	307

The above example illustrates that, when designed by the elastic theory, the I-section can carry greater moment; when designed by ultimate strength, the rectangular section carries the greater moment.

There is another case where the application of the elastic and the ultimate designs yields radically different results. Consider two sections of exactly the same steel and concrete dimensions, but one with bonded steel and the other unbonded (see section 5-6). By the elastic design, both sections will carry the same moment; but by the ultimate design, the unbonded section will carry much less moment. Which method should be used in design will depend on the particular conditions of the structure. When ultimate strength is an important consideration, the bonded section must be given preference. On the other hand, when excessive overloads are not likely, the bonded and unbonded sections can be considered equally satisfactory.

6-9 Shapes of Concrete Sections

Having studied both the elastic and ultimate designs, we are now ready to discuss the selection of the best shapes for prestressed concrete sections under flexure. The simplest form is the rectangular shape possessed by all solid slabs and used for some short-span beams. As far as formwork is concerned, the rectangular section is the most economical. But the kern distances are small, and the available lever arm for the steel is limited. Concrete near the centroidal axis and on the tension side is not effective in resisting moment, especially at the ultimate stage.

Hence other shapes are frequently used for prestressed concrete, Fig. 6-23:

1. The symmetrical I-section.
2. The unsymmetrical I-section.
3. The T-section.
4. The inverted T-section.
5. The box section.

The suitability of these shapes will depend on the particular requirements. The I-section has its concrete concentrated near the extreme fibers where it can most effectively furnish the compressive force, both at transfer of prestress and under working and ultimate loads. The more the concrete is concentrated near the extreme fibers, the greater will be the kern distances, and the greater will be the lever arm furnished for the internal resisting couple. However, this principle of concentrating the concrete in the extreme fibers cannot be carried too far, because the width and thickness of the flanges are governed by practical considerations, and the web must have a minimum thickness to carry the shear, to avoid buckling, and to permit proper placement of concrete.

If the M_G/M_T ratio is sufficiently large, there is little danger of overstressing the flanges at transfer, and concrete in the bottom flange can be accordingly diminished. This will result in an unsymmetrical I-section

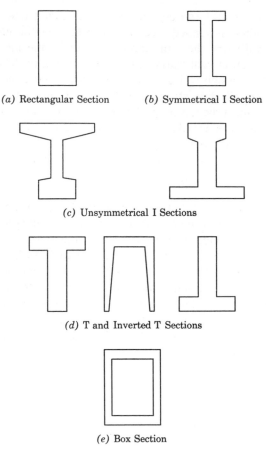

(a) Rectangular Section   (b) Symmetrical I Section

(c) Unsymmetrical I Sections

(d) T and Inverted T Sections

(e) Box Section

Fig. 6-23. Shapes of concrete sections.

which when carried to the fullest extent becomes a T-section. A T-section, similar to that for reinforced beams, is often most economical, since the concrete is concentrated at the top flange where it is most effective in supplying the compressive force. It may not be economically used, however, where the M_G/M_T ratio is small, because the center of pressure at transfer may lie below the bottom kern point. Then tensile stresses may result in the top flange and high compressive stresses in the bottom flange.

The unsymmetrical I-section with a bigger bottom flange, like a rail section, is not an economical one in carrying ultimate moment, since there is relatively little concrete on the compression flange. However, there is a great deal of material to resist the initial prestress. It can be economically used for certain composite sections, where the tension flange is precast and the compression flange is poured in place. This section requires very little girder moment to bring the center of pressure within the kern and hence is suitable when the M_G/M_T ratio is small. When carried to the extreme, this section becomes an inverted T-section.

The box section has the same properties as the I-section in resisting moment. In fact, their section properties are identical and both are listed in Table 6 of Appendix C. The adoption of one or the other will depend on the practical requirements of each structure.

The above discussion can be summarized as follows. For economy in steel and concrete it is best to put the concrete near the extreme fibers of the compression flange. When the M_G/M_T ratio is small, more concrete near the tension flange may be necessary. When the M_G/M_T ratio is large, there is little danger of overstressing at transfer, and concrete in the tension flange is required only to house the tendons properly.

In choosing the shapes, prime importance must be given to the simplicity of formwork. When the formwork is to be used only once, it may constitute the major cost of the beam, so that any irregular shapes for the purpose of saving concrete or steel may not be in the interest of overall

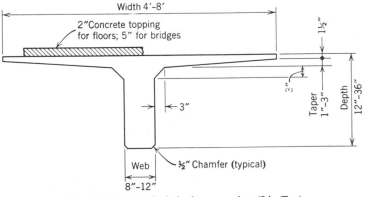

Fig. 6-24.(*a*) Typical single tee section (Lin Tee)

Table of Properties

(Width = 6′; web = 8″; taper = 2″; no topping)

Depth, in.	Area, in.²	I, in.⁴	c_b, in.
12	265	2360	9.2
16	297	6170	11.8
20	329	11,730	14.5
24	361	19,700	17.0
28	393	30,400	19.5
32	425	44,060	21.9
36	457	61,000	24.2

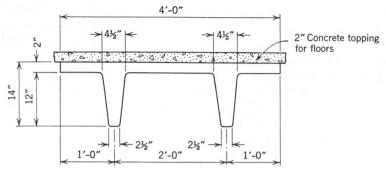

Fig. 6-24.(*b*) Typical double tee section.

Table of Properties

Topping	Area, in.^{2}	I, in.^{4}	c_b, in.
With 2″ topping	276	4456	11.74
Without topping	180	2862	10.00

economy. On the other hand, when the forms can be reused repeatedly, more complicated shapes may be justified.

For plants producing precast elements, it is often economical to construct forms that can be easily modified to suit different spans and depths. For example, by filling up the stems for the section in Fig. 6-24(*a*) and 6-24(*b*), several depths can be obtained. Again, by omitting the center

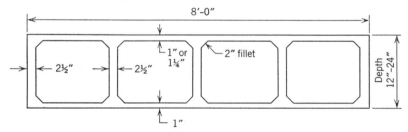

Fig. 6-24.(*c*) Typical Dynacore section (top and bottom flanges are transversely prestressed).

Table of Properties

(Top flange $= 1\frac{1}{4}″$ thick)

Depth, in.	Area, in.^{2}	I, in.^{4}	c_b, in.	Recommended Span Limits, ft	
				Roof	Floor
12″	370	7880	6.27	45	40
20″	470	21,100	10.39	70	60

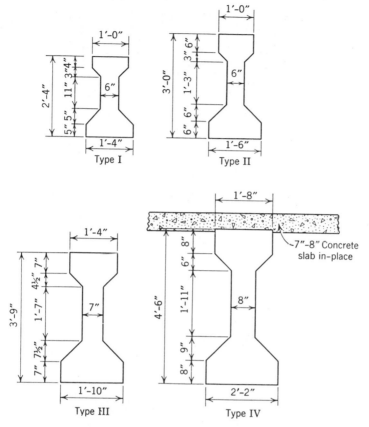

Fig. 6-24.(*d*) Standard AASHO-PCI Prestressed Concrete I-Beams for Highway Bridges.[2]

Table of Properties

(Without in-place slab)

Beam Type	Area, in.^{2}	I, in.^{4}	c_b, in.	Recommended Span Limits, ft
I	276	22,750	12.59	30–45
II	369	50,980	15.83	40–60
III	560	125,390	20.27	55–80
IV	789	260,730	24.73	70–100

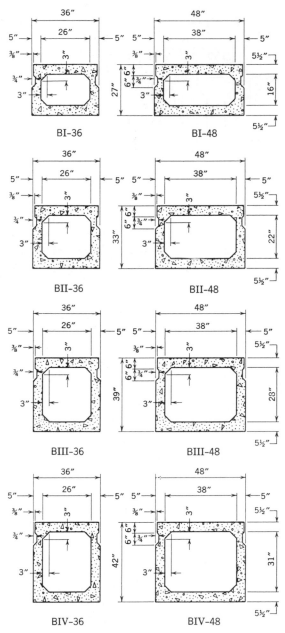

Fig. 6-24.(*e*) Standard AASHO-PCI Prestressed Concrete Box Beams for Highway Bridges.

Fig. 6-24 (*e*) continued

Table of Properties

Beam Type	Area, in.^{2}	I, in.^{4}	c_b, in.	Recommended Span Limits, ft Draped Strand	Recommended Span Limits, ft Straight Strand
BI-36	560.5	50,334	13.35	74	62
BI-48	692.5	65,941	13.37	73	63
BII-36	620.5	85,153	16.29	86	73
BII-48	752.5	110,499	16.33	86	74
BIII-36	680.5	131,145	19.25	97	83
BIII-48	812.5	168,367	19.29	96	83
BIV-36	710.5	158,644	20.73	103	87
BIV-48	842.5	203,088	20.78	103	88

portions of a tapered beam or decreasing the distance between the side forms, one set of forms can be made to fit many shorter spans.

Sections must be further designed to enable proper placement of concrete around the tendons and the corners. This is especially true when proper vibration cannot be ensured. The use of fillets at corners is often desirable. It is also common practice to taper the sides of the flanges. Such tapering will permit easier stripping of the formwork and easier placement of concrete.

Examples of some sections commonly used in the United States are shown in Fig. 6-24. A typical single tee section (often known as Lin Tee) for which a set of forms can be adjusted to suit several variables is shown in Fig. 6-24(*a*). The depth of the section can be set by raising the soffit. The width of the stem can be varied by spreading the two halves of the forms. The width and the thickness of the flange can be modified by changing the outside strips. When carefully designed, the 36-inch deep section can be used for floors up to 100 ft, roofs up to 120 ft, and highway bridges up to 70 ft. Some plants have steel forms to produce these tees up to a depth of 48 in. and a width of 10 ft.

Fig. 6-24(*b*) shows the double-tee section, commonly used for roofs and floors of buildings, up to about a 50-ft span. Note that by filling up the stems, smaller depths can be obtained.

Slab sections of about 8-in. thick, with round cores of about $5\frac{1}{2}$-in. diameter spaced at some 8-in. centers, are frequently used for short span roofs and floors where a flat soffit is desired. The Dynacore section recently developed, Fig. 6-24(*c*), has large rectangular cores and for 24-in. depth, can span up to 90 ft.

I-sections have been used for buildings with a poured-in-place slab so as to get composite action. For bridges, four such sections have been standardized by the Joint Committee of the AASHO-PCI, Fig. 6-24(*d*), which have also standardized 8 sections for prestressed box beams, Fig. 6-24(*e*), as well as 8 sections for prestressed cored slabs, Fig. 6-24(*f*).

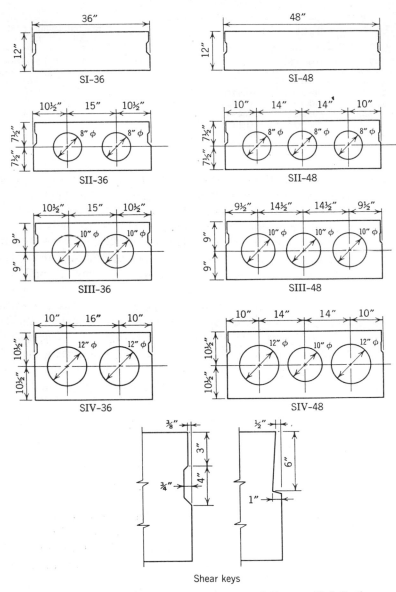

Shear keys

Fig. 6-24.(*f*) Standard AASHO-PCI Prestressed Concrete Slab Sections.

Fig. 6-24 (*f*) continued

Table of Section Properties

Type	Area, in.²	I, in.⁴	c_b, in.	Approximate Span, ft
SI-36 (12″ × 36″)	432	5184	6.0	20–29
SII-36 (15″ × 36″)	439.5	9725	7.5	27–38
SIII-36 (18″ × 36″)	491	16,514	9.0	34–46
SIV-36 (21″ × 36″)	530	25,747	10.5	41–54
SI-48 (12″ × 48″)	576	6912	6.0	20–29
SII-48 (15″ × 48″)	569	12,897	7.5	27–38
SIII-48 (18″ × 48″)	628	21,855	9.0	34–46
SIV-48 (21″ × 48″)	703	34,517	10.5	41–55

When cast in place, simplicity of formwork is of prime importance. Thus solid slabs with or without cores, and T-shapes with vertical or tapered sides, are often convenient. Only when the forms can be re-used many times would the I-shape and other complicated shapes be considered economical.

6-10 Arrangement of Steel

The arrangement of steel is governed by a basic principle: in order to obtain the maximum lever arm for the internal resisting moment, it must be placed as near the tensile edge as possible. This is the same for prestressed as for reinforced sections. But, for prestressed concrete, one more condition must be considered: the initial condition at the transfer of prestress. If the c.g.s. is very near the tensile edge, and if there is no significant girder moment to bring the center of pressure near or within the kern, Fig. 6-25, the tension flange may be overcompressed at transfer while the compression flange may be under high tensile stress. Hence

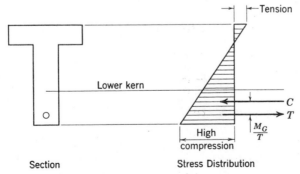

Section   Stress Distribution

Fig. 6-25. Girder moment insufficient to bring *C* within kern.

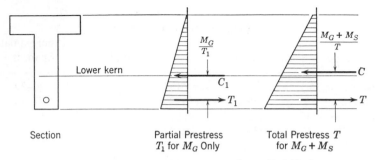

Section   Partial Prestress   Total Prestress T
                 T_1 for M_G Only   for $M_G + M_S$

Fig. 6-26. Prestressing in two stages to keep C within kern.

this brings up a special condition in prestressed concrete: a heavy moment is desirable at transfer so that the steel can be placed as near the edge as possible. However, no economy is achieved by adding unnecessary dead weight to the structure in order to enable a bigger lever arm for the steel, because whatever additional moment capacity was thus obtained would be used in carrying the additional dead load, although some additional reserve capacity is obtained for the ultimate range. Loads that will eventually have to be carried by the beam can be more economically put on the structure before transfer rather than after, because moments produced by such loads will permit the placement of steel nearer the tensile edge.

Another method sometimes used in order to permit placement of steel near the tensile edge is to prestress the structure in two or more stages; this is known as retensioning. At the first stage, when the moment on the beam is small, only a portion of the prestress will be applied; the total prestress will be applied only when additional dead load is placed on the beam producing heavier moment on the section, Fig. 6-26. Thus the center of pressure can be kept within the kern at all times, and excessive tension in the compression flange, as well as high compression in the tension flange, can be avoided.

For certain sections, the tendons are placed in the compression flange

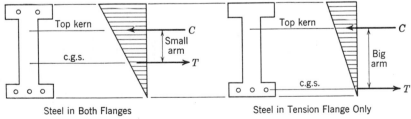

Steel in Both Flanges   Steel in Tension Flange Only

Fig. 6-27. Prestressing steel in both flanges reduces lever arm for resisting moment.

as well as in the tension flange, Fig. 6-27. Generally speaking, this is not an economical arrangement, because it will move the c.g.s. nearer to the c.g.c. and thereby decrease the resisting lever arm. At the ultimate range, tendons in the compressive flange will neutralize some of its compressive capacity, whereas only those in the tension flange are effective in resisting moment. However, under certain circumstances it may be necessary to put tendons in both flanges in spite of the resulting disadvantages. These conditions are:

1. When the member is to be subject to loads producing both $+M$ and $-M$ in the section.

2. When the member might be subject to unexpected moments of opposite sign, during its handling process.

3. When the M_G/M_T ratio is small and the tendons cannot be suitably grouped near the kern point. Then the tendons will be placed in both the tension and the compression flanges with the resulting c.g.s. lying near the kern.

The minimum concrete protection for tendons is governed by two requirements: first for fire resistance which is discussed in Chapter 16, then by corrosion protection which has been determined more or less by experience and practice. PCI Building Code Requirements specifies the following minimum thickness of concrete cover for prestressing steel, ducts, and nonprestressed steel.

	Cover, inches
Formed concrete surfaces in contact with ground	2
Beams and girders	
Prestressing steel and main reinforcing bars	$1\frac{1}{2}$
Stirrups and ties	1
Slabs and joists exposed to weather	1
Slabs and joists not exposed to weather	$\frac{3}{4}$

It is generally believed that the above protection is quite adequate if the cover concrete is prestressed and not subjected to cracking under sustained loading.

The minimum spacing of tendons is governed by several factors. First, the clear spacing between tendons, or between tendons and side forms, must be sufficient to permit easy passage of concrete. Here we may apply the general rule for reinforced concrete, which limits the clear distance to a minimum of $1\frac{1}{3}$ times the size of the maximum aggregates. This requirement may be reduced for prestressed concrete when good vibration can be ensured. Second, to properly develop the bond between steel and concrete, we may again apply the rule for reinforcing bars: the clear distance between bars should be at least the diameter of the bars for special anchorage and $1\frac{1}{2}$ times the diameter for ordinary anchorage, with a minimum of 1 in. These limitations may not be necessary for small wires and strands used in prestressed work, and they are often bundled together.

The PCI Building Code Requirements call for a minimum clear spacing at each end of the member of four times the diameter of individual wires or three times the diameter of strands, in order to properly develop the transfer bond. These values are conservative, and smaller distances apparently have been successfully employed. Along the middle portion of the span, bundling is always permitted.

Ducts may be arranged closely together vertically when provision is made to prevent the tendon from breaking through into an adjacent duct. When the tendons are sharply curved, the radial thrusts exerted on the concrete along the bends may be considerable. Horizontal disposition of ducts shall allow proper placement of concrete. When the tendons are placed outside of the concrete to be eventually covered with mortar, then only the problem of fire and corrosion protection need be considered.

To help dimension a beam section, the sizes of some tendons and their conduits are listed in Appendix B.

References

1 T. Y. Lin and A. C. Scordelis, "Selection and Design of Prestressed Concrete Beam Sections," *J. Am. Conc. Inst.*, November 1953 (*Proc.*, Vol. 49), pp. 209–224.
2 "Tentative Standards for Prestressed Concrete Piles, Slabs, I-beams, and Box Beams, and Interim Manual for Inspection of Such Construction," American Association of State Highway Officials, 1963.

shear; bond; bearing 7

7-1 Shear, General Considerations

The strength of prestressed-concrete beams in flexure is quite definitely known, but their strength in resisting shear or the combination of shear and flexure cannot be predicted with precision. Previous to about 1955, numerous prestressed-concrete beams had been tested for their strength in flexure, but very few in shear. Between 1955 and 1961, however, hundreds of specimens were actually tested to determine their strength in resisting shear or moment and shear, with or without web reinforcement.[1–8] Unfortunately, on account of the complexity of the problem and our inability to isolate the variables in our experiments and analyses, we cannot claim that we have solved the problem, even with this wealth of information now available to us.

This rather dim view of our knowledge concerning shear does not stop us from designing prestressed-concrete beams, just as our lack of knowledge concerning shear strength of reinforced-concrete beams does not stop us from designing them. In fact, it may be stated that prestressed-concrete beams possess greater reliability in shear resistance than rein-forced-concrete beams, because prestressing will usually prevent the occurrence of shrinkage cracks which could conceivably destroy the shear resistance of the reinforced-concrete beams, especially near the point of contraflexure. Since so many prestressed-concrete beams have been designed and built on the basis of some assumed theories for shear resistance, and since so very few have actually failed in shear, it may be concluded that our present method of design is a safe one. However, the degree of safety of the structures designed by our conventional methods may vary rather widely. Some of our designs may be too safe in shear, others not so safe, even though all have functioned safely under the usual service loads. Furthermore, we must be aware of the possibilities of shear failure when we get into types and proportions beyond the present scope of practice. Specifically, when we have very thin webs, when we have high depth/span ratio, when we have combined high moment and shear such as in continuous beams and cantilevers, when we have settlement of supports for deep beams, etc., our conventional method of shear design may not be safe enough.

A general picture of the shear in a prestressed-concrete beam will first be presented. Consider three beams carrying transverse loads as shown in Fig. 7-1. Beam (*a*) is prestressed by a straight tendon. Taking an arbitrary section *A–A*, the shear *V* at that section is carried entirely by the concrete, none by the tendon which is stressed in a direction perpendicular to the shear. Beam (*b*) is prestressed with an inclined tendon. Section *B–B* shows that the transverse component of the tendon carries part of the shear, leaving only a portion to be carried by the concrete, thus,

$$V_c = V - V_s$$

This may be compared to reinforced-concrete beams with bent-up bars where the inclined portion of the steel carries some of the shear. It must be noted that a horizontal tendon, though inclined to the axis of the beam, does not carry any vertical shear, as illustrated by section *C–C* in beam (*c*). Whenever the tendon is not perpendicular to the direction of shear, then it does assist in carrying the shear, for example, section *D–D*. It is interesting to note that, in some rare instances, the transverse component of the prestress increases the shear in concrete.

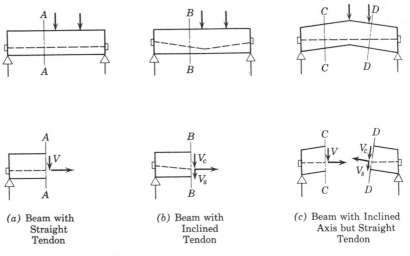

(*a*) Beam with
Straight
Tendon

(*b*) Beam with
Inclined
Tendon

(*c*) Beam with Inclined
Axis but Straight
Tendon

Fig. 7-1. Shear carried by concrete and tendons.

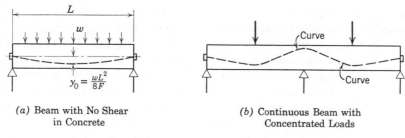

(a) Beam with No Shear
in Concrete

(b) Continuous Beam with
Concentrated Loads

Fig. 7-2. Varying inclination of tendons to carry shear.

By following the balanced load approach for prestressed concrete, it is possible to design a beam with no shear in the concrete under a given condition of loading. Take Fig. 7-2, for example; if the simple beam carrying a uniform load is prestressed by a parabolic cable with a sag equal to

$$y_0 = \frac{wL^2}{8F}$$

where F is the prestress in the cable, then the transverse component of the cable equals the shear at any point, and there is no shear to be carried by the concrete. For beams carrying concentrated loads, or for continuous beams over the intermediate supports, Fig. 7-2(b), the problem is more complicated since the tendon cannot be bent sharply to conform with the theoretically sudden change in shear at the point of concentration. It may be remarked, however, that the actual change in shear under a concentrated load is not likely to be as abrupt, although its form of variation is little known.

The amount of shear acting on the concrete having been determined, the next step is to compute the shear resistance of the concrete. It is generally believed that prestressed beams, similar to reinforced ones, practically never fail under direct shear or punching shear. They fail as a result of tensile stresses produced by shear, known as diagonal tension in reinforced concrete and as principal tension in prestressed concrete. Before cracking, prestressed concrete can be considered as made up of a homogeneous material; the computation of principal tensile stresses can thus be made by the usual method in strength of materials for the state of stress in a homogeneous body. Although the principal tensile stresses can be computed, the strength of concrete in resisting such stresses is not definitely known, since for concrete there are many theories of failure, of which the maximum tensile stress theory is only one. After the cracking of concrete, and with the addition of web reinforcement, the problem

becomes even more complicated. Tests on both reinforced- and prestressed-concrete beams have seemed to indicate that, when shear failure
occurs at a section, not only the shear but also the moment at that section
has effect on its ultimate strength. Thus the problem of shear strength is
complicated indeed, if a clear understanding is desired. For the purpose of
design, empirical methods are employed. They are relatively simple and
are presented in the following sections. For further investigation, readers
are referred to the references listed at the end of this chapter. It suffices
to mention at this point that there are essentially two types of shear
failures: one in which the cracking starts in the web as a result of high
principal tension, Fig. 7-3, and another in which vertical flexural cracks
occur first and gradually develop into inclined shear cracks, Fig. 7-4. The
first type will be treated in section 7-2, and the second in section 7-3.

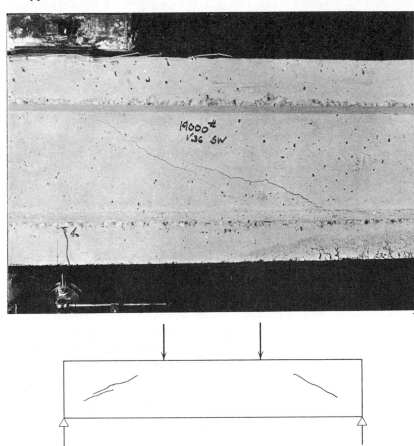

Fig. 7-3. Inclined tension crack originating in web.[3]

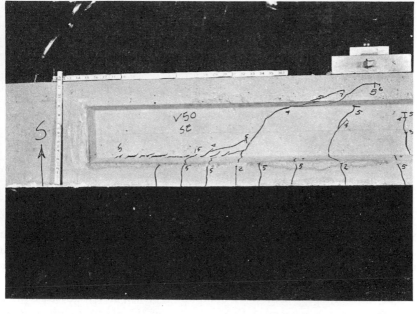

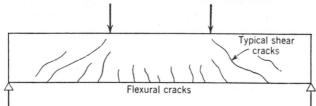

Fig. 7-4. Inclined tension crack originating from flexure crack.[3]

7-2   Shear, Principal Tensile Stress

Conventional design for shear in prestressed-concrete beams is based on the computation of the principal tensile stress in the web and the limitation of that stress to a certain specified value. The first part of this method, the computation of the principal tension based on the classical approach, is a correct procedure so long as the concrete has not cracked. The second part of this method, limiting the principal tension to a definite value, is not always an accurate approach, because there is evidence to show that the resistance of concrete to such principal tension is not a consistent value but varies with the magnitude of the axial compression.[9] It seems, however, that, when the axial compression is not too high, say less than about $0.50f_c'$, the resistance of concrete to its principal tensile

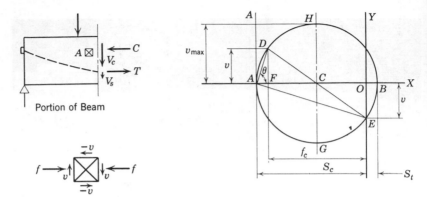

Portion of Beam

Element *A* from Above   Mohr's Circle of Stress for Element *A*

Fig. 7-5. State of stress in concrete.

stress is relatively consistent. Hence, the computation of principal tensile stress can be regarded as a proper criterion for the stress conditions within the working range, though it may not give a correct measure of safety when considering overloads or when the concrete has cracked.

The conventional method of computing principal tensile stress in a prestressed-concrete-beam section is based on the elastic theory and on the classical method for determining the state of stress at a point as explained in any treatise on mechanics of materials. The method can be outlined as follows.

1. From the total external shear V across the section, deduct the shear V_s carried by the tendon to obtain the shear V_c carried by the concrete, thus,

$$V_c = V - V_s \qquad (7\text{-}1)$$

Note again that occasionally, though rarely, $V_c = V + V_s$; this happens when the cable inclination is such that it adds to the shear on the concrete.

2. Compute the distribution of V_c across the concrete section by the usual formula, Fig 7-5,

$$v = V_c Q / I b$$

where v = shearing unit stress at any given level

Q = statical moment of the cross-sectional area above (or below) that level about the centroidal axis.

b = width of section at that level.

3. Compute the fiber stress distribution for that section due to external moment M, the prestress F, and its eccentricity e by the formula

$$f_c = \frac{F}{A} \pm \frac{Fec}{I} \pm \frac{Mc}{I}$$

4. The maximum principal tensile stress S_t corresponding to the above v and f_c is then given by the formula

$$S_t = \sqrt{v^2 + (f_c/2)^2} - (f_c/2) \tag{7-2}$$

Graphically it can be solved by Mohr's circle of stress* as shown in Fig. 7-5. One advantage of this graphical method lies in the indication of the plane of principal tension as shown in Fig. 7-5 and listed in the table. (Note: AA = plane perpendicular to AB.)

Plane	Shearing Stress	Normal Stress
AD = vertical plane	v	f_c
AE = horizontal plane	$-v$	0
AB = principal tensile plane	0	S_t
AA = principal compressive plane	0	S_c

It can be seen from the table that the angle between the principal tensile plane AB and the vertical plane AD is greater than 45°. Also note that the principal compressive stress, although somewhat greater than the compressive fiber stress, is seldom considered in design. It is considered sufficient to limit the compressive fiber stress to an allowable value. Similarly, no account is taken of the maximum shearing stresses which occur on planes at 45° to the principal planes, since it is the tension rather than shear that produces ultimate failure.

The greatest principal tensile stress does not necessarily occur at the centroidal axis, where the maximum vertical shearing stress exists. At some point, where f_c is diminished, equation 7-2 will often yield a higher principal tension even though v is not a maximum. For I-sections, the junction of the web with the tensile flange is frequently a critical point for computing the greatest principal tension. This is illustrated in the following example.

EXAMPLE 7-1

A prestressed-concrete beam section under the action of a given moment has a fiber stress distribution as shown in Fig. 7-6. The total vertical shear in the concrete at the section is 520 k. Compute and compare the principal tensile stresses at the centroidal axis N–N and the junction of the web with the lower flange M–M.

* Mohr's circle is constructed as follows:
Choose a pair of rectangular axes X-Y with origin at O. Measure OE equal to v. Measure OF equal to f_c and FD equal to v. Draw a circle with DE as diameter. Then OB is the principal tension, OA the principal compression, and $CG = CH$ = principal shear.

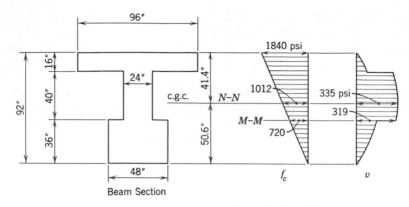

Fig. 7-6. Example 7-1.

Solution. I of the section about its centroidal axis is computed as 3,820,000 in.[4] Other values are listed separately for the two levels M–M and N–N as tabulated.

Section	M–M	N–N
Q, in.[3]	$36 \times 48 \times 32.6$ $= 56{,}200$	$14.6 \times 24 \times 7.3$ $+ 56{,}200 = 58{,}800$
$v = \dfrac{V_c Q}{Ib}$, psi	$\dfrac{520{,}000 \times 56{,}200}{3{,}820{,}000 \times 24}$ $= 319$	$\dfrac{520{,}000 \times 58{,}800}{3{,}820{,}000 \times 24}$ $= 335$
f_c, psi	720	1012
$S_t = \sqrt{v^2 + \left(\dfrac{f_c}{2}\right)^2} - \dfrac{f_c}{2}$	$\sqrt{319^2 + \left(\dfrac{720}{2}\right)^2} - \dfrac{720}{2}$ $= 121$	$\sqrt{334^2 + \left(\dfrac{1012}{2}\right)^2} - \dfrac{1012}{2}$ $= 100$

Instead of using equation 7-2 as above, S_t can be obtained directly from Fig. 7-7, using the curves plotted therein, or it can be measured graphically by constructing Mohr's circles as in Fig. 7-5. The same answers will be obtained by any of these methods.

In this example, the greatest principal tension occurs at M–M rather than the centroidal axis N–N where v is a maximum. As in most prestressed sections, the principal tension is much smaller than the vertical shearing stress.

The following example illustrates how principal tension may increase much faster than the increase in shear. This indicates that shear design for working load alone may not be sufficient, and the principal tension

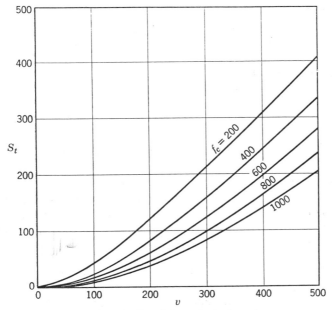

Fig. 7-7. Graph for principal tension.

as well as the effect of flexural cracking under ultimate load should be investigated.

EXAMPLE 7-2

For the beam section in example 7-1, suppose that the external load is increased by 25% so that the fiber stress distribution is shown in Fig. 7-8 and the total vertical shear in the concrete is 520 × 1.25 = 650 k. Compute the principal tensile stress at *M–M*.

Solution. The compressive fiber stress at *M–M* is computed to be 560 psi, assuming that cracks have not occurred at the bottom fiber for the tensile stress

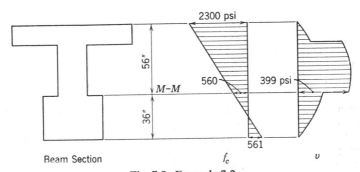

Fig. 7-8. Example 7-2.

of 561 psi. The unit vertical shearing stress is

$$v = \frac{V_c Q}{Ib} = \frac{650{,}000 \times 56{,}200}{3{,}820{,}000 \times 24} = 399 \text{ psi}$$

Hence the principal tensile stress at M–M is

$$S_t = \sqrt{v^2 + \left(\frac{f_c}{2}\right)^2} - \frac{f_c}{2}$$

$$= \sqrt{399^2 + \left(\frac{560}{2}\right)^2} - \frac{560}{2} = 208 \text{ psi}$$

By comparing this value with $S_t = 121$ psi in example 7-1, it is seen that, for this particular point, an increase of 72% in principal tension has taken place corresponding to a 25% increase in loading. Note that, in this example, V_s is assumed to be zero. If V_s is not zero, the percentage increase in the value of S_t will be still higher.

The limiting value for principal tensile stress in prestressed-concrete design has been set in a more or less arbitrary manner, and hence it varies from country to country and from time to time. Under the design load, the limiting principal tension ranges from $0.013f_c'$ to $0.033f_c'$ for beams without web reinforcement, and from $0.04f_c'$ to $0.10f_c'$ when sufficient web reinforcement is provided. Under ultimate load, it ranges from $0.045f_c'$ to $0.08f_c'$ without web reinforcement, and up to $0.11f_c'$ with web reinforcement.

The most reasonable provision is probably that contained in The British Standard Code of Practice[10] as follows (Table 7-1).

TABLE 7-1

Limiting Principal Tensile Stresses for Prestressed Concrete
(British Standard Code of Practice)

		Limiting Principal Tensile Stress, psi	
(1) Specified Cube Strength for Concrete, psi	(2) Approximate Cylinder Strength for Concrete psi	(3) At working load	(4) At ultimate load, in un-cracked sections
4500	3600	125	300
6000	4800	150	350
7500	6000	175	400

The British Code further states the following.

Where the principal tensile stress at working loads exceeds that given in column (3) above, shear reinforcement shall be introduced. The proportion of shear to be resisted by this reinforcement should be assumed to vary linearly with the principal tensile stress from a value of 0 for the stress in column (3) to 1.0 for a stress of 1.5 times that given. When the principal tensile stress exceeds 1.5 times that given in column (3), the whole of the shear should be carried by reinforcement. When the principal tensile stress under the ultimate load exceeds that given in column (4), the whole of the shear in excess of that resisted by tendons inclined to the neutral surface should be resisted by shear reinforcement acting at a stress not exceeding 80 per cent of the yield stress (or 0.2 per cent proof stress, where appropriate). Special consideration should be given to the shear resistance under ultimate load conditions where the section is cracked in bending.

It is the author's opinion that these British specifications represent fairly good and conservative guidance for shear design.

In both the ACI-ASCE Recommendations for Prestressed Concrete and the PCI Building Code Requirements, no reference is made to the limiting value of principal tension. The tendency in the United States is to base shear design on the ultimate strength, as will be discussed in the next section.

In composite construction, shearing stress v between precast and in-place portions is computed on the basis of the ordinary elastic theory,

$$v = \frac{VQ}{Ib}$$

where V = the total shear in lb applied after the in-place portion has been cast

Q = statical moment of the cross-sectional area of in-place portion taken about the centroidal axis of the composite section

I = moment of inertia of the composite section

b = width of the contact area between the precast and the in-place portions

Obviously, the shearing strength along the surface will depend on many factors. However, for purpose of design, empirical values have been set by various authorities. For example the PCI Code Requirements allows a value of 40 psi for a smooth surface without ties, and 160 psi for a roughened surface with adequate ties. While admittedly arbitrary in nature, these recommendations are considered conservative.

Generally speaking, no ties are required for composite slabs or panels where large contact areas are provided. For beams with a narrow strip of top flange to be made composite with in-place slabs, ties are almost always required. Although designed on the basis of shear resistance, a main function of the ties is to prevent the separation of the component elements in a direction normal to the contact surface. Hence ties should be provided if there is a danger of separation, regardless of the shearing stress.

Recent push-off tests at the Portland Cement Association[7] yielded some interesting values. It was indicated that the ultimate shearing stress for composite action (between 3000 psi slab concrete and 5000 psi girder concrete) was about 500 psi for a rough bonded surface and 300 psi for a smooth bonded surface. In addition to these values, approximately 175 psi shear capacity may be added for each per cent stirrup reinforcement crossing the joint. These tests also indicated, contrary to the traditional belief, that shear keys used with a rough bonded surface do not change the strength of the connection. This is explained by the fact that the slip movements required to develop the keys are greater than the movements for a bonded surface; therefore, one will fail before the other and the effects of the two are not additive.

7-3 Shear, Ultimate Strength

As discussed in the previous section, the conventional method for "analyzing" the principal tension, based on the state of stress in a homogeneous material, is a rational method of analysis as long as the concrete has not cracked. However, when applied for "designing," the members so proportioned will possess different factors of safety, since slight increases in loads may produce appreciable and varying increases in the principal tension while the resistance of concrete to principal tension may also change with the magnitude of the compressive fiber stress. Furthermore, after the cracking of concrete, whether produced by flexural or principal tension, the method of analysis is no longer applicable. Hence it is evident that shear design by stress analysis is not a satisfactory one, especially if the member is to be subjected to overloads.

In order to obtain more logical and accurate design for shear, particularly in structures of unusual proportions, it is necessary that design be based on their strength under overloads as well as on their stresses under the working loads.

In prestressed-concrete beams, cracks may be produced by either flexural or principal tension, Figs. 7-3, 7-4. For certain beams, generally those with low percentages of longitudinal reinforcement and with high moment-to-shear ratios, the flexure cracks will develop faster than the principal tension cracks, the steel will be highly stressed in the region of high bending moment, and final failure will occur by crushing of concrete above the flexural cracks. When the beams are over-reinforced but still subject to high moment rather than high shear, failure may occur by crushing of concrete while the steel is still in the elastic range.

When the shear is heavy, the principal tension cracks will develop faster than the flexural cracks; the presence of principal tension cracks will tend to reduce the compressive depth of concrete, and the beam will fail at a load lower than its capacity under pure flexure. Flexure cracks are not necessarily objectionable, unless they combine with and develop into principal tension cracks. Existing by themselves, flexure cracks do not indicate any imminent failure of the beam unless it is highly over-reinforced. On the other hand, when flexural cracks develop into inclined tension cracks, sudden and violent failure could result.

The strength of prestressed-concrete beams under combined moment and shear cannot be easily predicted. Qualitatively speaking, the strength varies with several factors, as follows.

1. It increases with the concrete area A_c and varies with the shape of the section.
2. It increases with the strength of concrete f_c'.
3. It increases with the percentage of steel.
4. It increases with the effective prestress in the steel.
5. It increases with the shear carried by the prestressed steel.
6. It increases with the amount of web reinforcement.

Because of the many factors involved, it has not been possible to set up any rational basis for the determination of the strength. As a result of 99 beams (all without web reinforcement) tested at the University of Illinois,[3] an empirical expression was derived and seems to represent a consistent and simple relationship applicable to the range of specimens tested. Here specimens were all simple beams with overall section of 6 in. by 12 in. deep, of rectangular and I shapes, both pre-tensioned and post-tensioned, on spans of 7 ft and 9 ft, and loaded at midspan or at two symmetrical points. The expression is

$$\frac{V_c}{b'd} = \frac{\sqrt{b/b'}}{(a/d)}\left[f_t + \frac{F_{se}}{A_c}\right]$$

where V_c = applied shear at inclined tension cracking load, lb
    b' = web thickness, which was 6-in. for rectangular beams, 3 in. or $1\frac{3}{4}$ in. for the I-beams
    d = effective depth of beam, varying from 8 to 11 in. top
    b = top flange width, all at 6-in.
    a = length of shear span, in. (distance from support to the load)
    f_t = assumed tensile strength of concrete set at 200 to 500 psi for concrete of various strength and mixes
    F_{se} = effective prestress force, lb
    A_c = gross area of cross section, in.[2]

This expression gives an apparent unit shearing stress at the start of inclined tension cracking, generally as a continuation of flexural cracks. This apparent stress $V_c/b'd$ is expressed as a function of three terms. First, a/d, the ratio of shear span to effective depth, ranging from 2.8 to 6.7, represents the relative effect of moment. Next, b/b', ranging from 1 to 3.4, represents the form factor. And finally $f_t + F_{se}/A_c$ represents the sum of the tensile strength of concrete and the average precompression in the concrete at the centroidal axis. This expression indicates that the shear at inclined tension cracking decreases in inverse ratio with an increase in the shear span; although this was true for the tested specimens, the trend is not expected to continue indefinitely. The range of eccentricity of the prestressing force in these tests varied from about 15 to 45 per cent of the overall depth of the beams, but apparently did not have any effect on the value of the inclined tension-cracking load, although its influence was felt through the change in the value of the effective depth d.

After the start of inclined tension cracking, there will usually be a further increase in the external load before reaching the ultimate. In the above test series, the ratio of measured ultimate load to the inclined tension-cracking load was found to be between 1.0 and 1.4, with the majority of the ratios below 1.2. Hence it may be concluded that it is desirable to use the start of inclined tension cracking as a critical limit, although some margin of safety still exists after the start of the cracking.

The ultimate shearing strength of prestressed-concrete slabs is an even more complicated problem, since it is intimately connected with the relative amount of moment in the slab as well as many other factors. A limited series of tests was performed on 15 such slabs 6-ft square supported along all four edges and centrally loaded.[6] An empirical equation was derived to represent the ultimate load as follows.

$$\frac{V_u}{bd} = \left(0.175 - 0.0000242 f_c' + 0.000020 \frac{F_e}{s}\right) f_c'$$

where V_u = ultimate punching shear load, lb

b = total perimeter of the four sides of the square area directly surrounding the punching collar

d = effective depth of the slab, from the compressive surface to the center of reinforcement

F_e = effective total prestress in each tendon prior to loading, lb

s = spacing of tendons, in.

This equation applies only to the limited test series with its particular combination of moment and shear. Major variables involved in the tests were concrete strength (2800 to 5200 psi), average initial prestress (250 to 500 psi), collar size for punching (13 to 16 in.), slab thickness (6 to 10 in.), and amount of collar recess (0, 1, 2, or 4 in.). It was also established that the amount of collar recess will appreciably decrease the resisting capacity of the slab, since the recess will reduce the compressive area of slab concrete which would otherwise effectively resist the punching shear.

7-4 Shear, Web Reinforcement

Since we do not well understand the behavior of prestressed or reinforced concrete beams without web reinforcement, it is obviously more difficult to analyze those with web reinforcement. Fortunately, fairly extensive series of tests have now been conducted,[5] and semi-empirical methods have been formulated so that design for shear can be properly made, at least conservatively, if not economically. Two cases will be treated separately: first, when the inclined cracks start in the web and then, when the flexural cracks gradually develop into inclined cracking. It is to be noted that the behavior of concrete before cracking is practically independent of the amount of web reinforcement (unless the reinforcement is prestressed), although the web reinforcement will play an important role after cracking. Hence all web reinforcement must be designed on the basis of cracked sections, and ultimate design is considered the logical approach.

Pure Web Shear. In this case, inclined cracking starts in the web and the purpose of web reinforcement is to limit the cracks so they do not become unsightly or result in gross distortion of adjacent portions thus causing failure. First the principal tension in the concrete is computed, as described in section 7-2. Then, if the concrete cracks, its tensile force is transferred to the stirrups. By the elastic design, it is often assumed that the stirrups will be stressed to an allowable value of $f_v = 20,000$ psi across the cracks. The procedure for this method can be outlined as follows.

1. For each section of the beam, compute the maximum principal tension S_t as in section 7-2, and the direction of the principal tensile plane, making an angle θ with the vertical plane, Fig. 7-9.

2. For vertical stirrups with spacing s, the force to be taken by each stirrup is the vertical component of the tensile force $S_t bs \cos \theta$, which is,

$$S_t bs$$

where b is the width of the beam at the point.

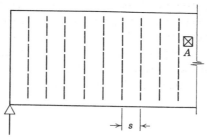

Portion of Beam with Web Reinforcement

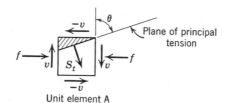

Unit element A

Fig. 7-9. Elastic design for web reinforcement.

3. Since the force supplied by each stirrup with area A_v at working stress f_v is $A_v f_v$, we can equate the resisting and working forces, obtaining

$$A_v f_v = S_t b s \quad \text{and} \quad s = \frac{A_v f_v}{S_t b} \qquad (7\text{-}3)$$

While this method is correct insofar as the limitation of cracks under working load is concerned, it may not insure a sufficient factor of safety against overloads. As was pointed in section 7-2, the principal tension often increases more rapidly then the external shear. Thus, if the shear is doubled, the stress in the stirrups may be more than doubled, and the design may not be safe. Hence it may be necessary to compute the principal tension under ultimate load conditions and provide stirrups to carry that tension at their yield point stress, probably not to exceed 40,000 psi. The following example illustrates how divergent stirrup designs are obtained by the working load and the ultimate load methods.

EXAMPLE 7-3

A prestressed-concrete beam has a rectangular section as shown in Fig. 7-10 and is subjected to a shear of 150 k under working loads. The effective prestress in the tendons totals 300 k and is inclined at an angle of arc sin $\alpha = \frac{1}{6}$. The fiber stress distribution under working load is 505 psi throughout. Half-inch U-stirrups are to be used ($A_v = 0.40$ sq in.), $f_v = 20,000$ psi, $f_v' = 40,000$ psi. (*a*) For the working-load conditions, determine the stirrup spacing, assuming all tension in the concrete to be carried by the stirrups; (*b*) For ultimate design with a load factor of 2, compute the stirrups spacing, assuming a different fiber stress distribution as shown.

Solution. (a) Under working load, shear carried by the tendons is

$$V_s = 300/6 = 50 \text{ k}$$

$$V_c = V - V_s$$

$$= 150 - 50 = 100 \text{ k}$$

Let us consider the state of stress at the centroidal axis,

$$v = \frac{3}{2}\frac{V}{A}$$

$$= \frac{3}{2}\left(\frac{100,000}{10 \times 60}\right)$$

$$= 250 \text{ psi}$$

For $f_c/2 = 252$ psi, and applying equation 7-2,

$$S_t = \sqrt{250^2 + 252^2} - 252$$

$$= 102 \text{ psi}$$

Applying equation 7-3, we have

$$S = \frac{A_v f_v}{S_t b}$$

$$= \frac{0.40 \times 20,000}{102 \times 10}$$

$$= 7.8 \text{ in.}$$

(b) For ultimate design with a load factor of 2, $V' = 2 \times 150 = 300$ k. Assuming V_s to remain at 50 k and using f_c at centroidal axis = 505 psi,

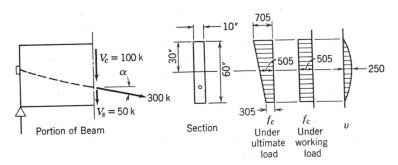

Fig. 7-10. Example 7-3.

we have

$$V_c' = 300 - 50 = 250 \text{ k}$$

$$v = \frac{3V_c'}{2A}$$

$$= \frac{3}{2}\left(\frac{250,000}{10 \times 60}\right)$$

$$= 625 \text{ psi}$$

$$S_t = \sqrt{625^2 + 252^2} - 252$$

$$= 418 \text{ psi}$$

Hence,

$$s = \frac{A_v f_v'}{S_t b}$$

$$= \frac{0.40 \times 40,000}{418 \times 10}$$

$$= 3.8 \text{ in.}$$

Note that the formula $v = \dfrac{3}{2}\dfrac{V_c'}{A_c}$ is too conservative, since redistribution of shear after cracking would certainly result in approximately

$$v = \frac{V_c'}{A}$$

Reference is made to Table 7-1, where principal tensile stresses as allowed by the British Standard Code of Practice are listed. It is apparent from example 7-3 that under most conditions, ultimate load will govern the design, in spite of the higher stresses permitted. British recommendation using 80% of the yield stress for ultimate design is considered to be too conservative, although this will depend on the load factors employed and the possibility of extreme overloads.

When the principal tensile stress is low, concrete is considered good enough to resist the tension. However, a nominal amount of stirrups will often be desirable for beam webs, especially if there is any chance of longitudinal cracks produced by shrinkage or along the location of the tendons. The amount of such stirrups may be computed by a rule of thumb, such as 0.25% of the web area recommended by the PCI Code Requirements. This may be excessive for members with thick webs, and may not be required at all if indicated by experience and common sense.

More or less arbitrary rules set up in the PCI Code Requirements, based on the ACI-ASCE Recommendations for Prestressed Concrete, assumed that prestressed concrete sections can resist shear better than equivalent reinforced concrete ones. Thus it calls for an area of web reinforcement one-half that of that required for reinforced concrete, with a stipulation that this factor be increased as the member approaches the condition of conventionally reinforced concrete. The formula follows.

$$A_v = \frac{1}{2} \frac{(V_u - V_c)s}{f_v' jd} \tag{7-4}$$

where A_v = area of web reinforcement at spacing s, placed perpendicular to the axis of the member

V_u = shear due to specified ultimate load and effect of prestressing

$V_c = 0.06 f_c'$ $b'jd$ but not more than $180\, b'jd$ (assume $j = \frac{7}{8}$);

b' = width of web

s = longitudinal spacing of web reinforcement

f_v' = yield strength of web reinforcement

In this formula, no mention is made of whether high moment exists with the shear. It is generally assumed that, if the moment is low and no flexural cracking occurs, concrete can carry a lot of shear and that this formula is amply safe. Example 7-4 indicates that this formula will yield much less stirrup steel than indicated by example 7-3. The value of d in the above formula is intended to be the effective depth to the centroid of the prestressing force, but it may be the overall height of the section if no flexural cracking occurs near the section under consideration. It is to be noted that radically different results are obtained by using the two different values of d.

EXAMPLE 7-4

Compute the stirrup spacing required for example 7-3, following the PCI Code Requirements. Assume $d = 40$ in.

$$V_u = 300 - 50 = 250 \text{ k}$$
$$V_c = 180 b'jd = 180 \times 10 \times \tfrac{7}{8} \times 40 = 63 \text{ k}$$
$$A_v = 0.4 \text{ sq in.}$$
$$f_v' = 40,000 \text{ psi}$$
$$jd = 40 \times \tfrac{7}{8} = 35 \text{ in.}$$
$$s = 2 \frac{A_v f_v' jd}{V_u - V_c} = \frac{2 \times 0.4 \times 40,000 \times 35}{250,000 - 63,000}$$
$$= 6.0 \text{ in.}$$

Note that if d is taken as 60 in., we will have

$$V_c = 180 \times 10 \times \tfrac{7}{8} \times 60 = 94 \text{ k}$$
$$jd = 60 \times \tfrac{7}{8} = 52.5 \text{ in.}$$
$$s = \frac{2 \times 0.4 \times 40,000 \times 52.5}{250,000 - 94,000}$$
$$= 10.7 \text{ in.}$$

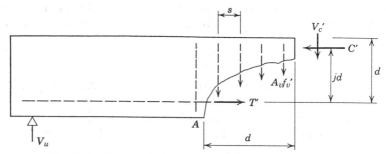

Fig. 7-11. Ultimate design for combined moment and shear.

Combined Moment and Shear. Under combined high moment and shear, flexural cracks develop into inclined tension cracking which could reduce the moment capacity and result in sudden and violent failure of the section if proper web reinforcement is not provided. The design for combined moment and shear can be best based on the ultimate strength behavior as illustrated in Fig. 7-11. Owing to high moment and shear, a flexural crack starting at point A will progress upward and eventually turn into an inclined crack. The web stirrups, each supplying a force of $A_v f_v'$ will be called into action as the crack progresses. At the ultimate load, the inclined crack will likely extend over a projected distance of at least d, and the number of stirrups intercepted by the crack will be d/s. Thus, static equilibrium requires that

$$V_u - V_c' = A_v f_v' d/s \qquad (7\text{-}5)$$

where V_u = ultimate external shear on the section minus the effect of prestress

V_c' = ultimate shear carried by the concrete in the compressive flange

A_v = area of each stirrup

f_v' = yield point stress of the stirrups

d = effective depth of the section

s = spacing of stirrups

The major difficulty in the above lies in the determination of V_c'. While V_c' will depend on the ultimate compressive area of the concrete and the amount of compression C' it can be approximated by the shear load producing flexural crack at a point d from the load.[5] It can be further assumed that any shear load in addition to that producing the flexural crack is to be carried by the web reinforcement. This does not take into account the shear capacity lost as a result of web cracking; nor does it consider the additional shear carried by the top flange after the inclined cracking. Equation 7-5 makes two further assumptions. One assumption is that all the stirrups are stressed to the yield point. This may not be exactly correct, since some of the intercepted stirrups may be stressed below the yield point. The other is that the projected distance of the inclined crack is d. This is a safe assumption since it has been found experimentally[5] that the distance is generally greater than d, and probably at least equal to $1.1d$.

An Empirical Method for Stirrup Design. An ultimate strength method proposed for the 1963 ACI Code follows an empirical approach based on the test results of the University of Illinois.[5] The method indicates that the yield strength in the stirrups extending over a distance d could be considered effective in transmitting the shear of $V_u - V_{ci}$; thus,

$$A_v f_v' d/s = V_u - V_{ci} \qquad (7\text{-}6)$$

where V_u is the ultimate load shear, and V_{ci} is the shear at the section when the vertical flexural crack starts to develop into an inclined one. A similar criterion is recommended for the case of web cracking initiating by itself without flexural cracking; thus,

$$A_v f_v' d/s = V_u - V_{cw} \qquad (7\text{-}7)$$

where V_{cw} is the shear at the section when web cracking starts by itself, without any flexural cracking.

The difficulty in this method lies in the determination of V_{ci} and V_{cw}, although they are given by empirical formulas in the ACI Code. As a conservative approximation, V_{ci} can be assumed to be the external shear corresponding to the cracking moment at the section for a tensile stress of $10\sqrt{f_c'}$, while V_{cw} can be assumed to be the external shear producing a principal tensile stress in the web of $4\sqrt{f_c'}$.

When using this method, it is suggested that the critical section for shear computation be taken at a distance d away from the theoretical point of maximum shear. In using formulas 7-6 and 7-7, the value of d need not be less than $0.8h$ in any case. The following example illustrates a solution by this method, wherein the 1963 ACI Code is applied in principle but not adhered to in detail. Readers are advised to study the example for an understanding of this approach to shear design. For an exact solution, it would be preferable to refer to the ACI Code, using its formulas and specified values.

EXAMPLE 7-5

A prestressed-concrete cantilever beam has a rectangular section, Fig. 7-12, and is subjected to a total shear of 150 k under working loads. The effective prestress in the tendons total 390 k and has a c.g.s. as shown. For a load factor of 2, design the web reinforcement considering possible web-cracking as

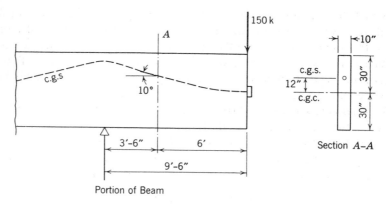

Portion of Beam

Fig. 7-12. Example 7-5.

well as combined-moment-and-shear failure. $f_c' = 5000$ psi; $f_v' = 40{,}000$ psi; use $\frac{5}{8}$-in. U-stirrups ($A_v = 0.62$ sq in.). Consider critical section at a distance, $d = 42$ in., from the support, and use the approximate method outlined above. Neglect weight of beam.

Solution. (*a*) Compute shear V_{cw} for web cracking at a principal tension $S_t = 4\sqrt{f_c'} = 283$ psi as follows. At the centroidal axis, compressive stress produced by a prestress of 384 k (horizontal component of 390 k at 10° inclination) is

$$f_c = \frac{384{,}000}{10 \times 60} = 640 \text{ psi}$$

and shear corresponding to $S_t = 283$ psi and $f_c = 640$ psi is

$$\sqrt{v^2 + (640/2)^2} - 640/2 = 283$$
$$v = 510 \text{ psi}$$

Shear carried by concrete at $v = 510$ psi is

$$V_c = \tfrac{2}{3} vA = \tfrac{2}{3} \times 510 \times 600$$
$$= 204 \text{ k}$$

Shear carried by vertical component of tendons is

$$V_s = 390 \sin 10° = 390 \times 0.173$$
$$= 67 \text{ k}$$

Total shear at web cracking is

$$V_c + V_s = 204 + 67 = 271 \text{ k}$$

(*b*) Compute shear V_{fc} for flange cracking prestress at extreme fiber tension of $10\sqrt{f_c'} = 707$ psi. For prestress component of 384 k with eccentricity of 12 in.

and compression at centroidal axis of 640 psi, the bending moment at flange cracking is

$$M_{fc} = Fe + \frac{(f_c + 10\sqrt{f_c'})bd^2}{6 \times 1000}$$

$$= 384 \times 12 + \frac{(640 + 707)10 \times 60^2}{6 \times 1000}$$

$$= 4610 + 8060$$

$$= 12,670 \text{ k-in.}$$

Total shear corresponding to $M = 12,670$ k-in. is

$$V_{fc} = 12,670/(6 \times 12) = 176 \text{ k}$$

(c) Since $V_{fc} = 176$ k is smaller than $V_{wc} = 271$ k, flange cracking will control the design. Web reinforcement will be designed to resist the excess of the ultimate shear over the shear at flange cracking, or

$$2 \times 150 - 176 = 124 \text{ k}$$

The actual value of d is 42 in., but it is reasonable to use at least $0.80h = 48$ in. for d; thus,

$$A_v f_v' d/s = 124$$

$$0.62 \times 40 \times 48/s = 124$$

$$s = 9.6 \text{ in.}$$

Hence a spacing of 9 in. or $9\frac{1}{2}$ in. can be adopted for the stirrup spacing from section A–A extending to the support. From A–A toward the end of cantilever, larger spacing can be adopted since the effect of bending moment is not so pronounced.

7-5 Flexural Bond at Intermediate Points

For post-tensioned concrete, bond is supplied by grouting. For pre-tensioned concrete, bond is secured directly when placing the concrete. When a bonded beam is subject to shear, bond stresses are produced. In order to design against bond failure, it is necessary to determine two things: first, the amount of bond stress existing between steel and concrete; second, the bond resistance between the two materials. Prestress transfer bond in pre-tensioning, where the end anchorage of the tendons is secured solely by bond, is discussed in the next section. Bond at intermediate points along the length of beam, whether pre-tensioned or post-tensioned, will now be discussed.

To determine the bond stress existing between concrete and the tendons, two stages have to be considered: before and after cracking of concrete. Before the cracking of concrete, bond stress can be calculated similar to

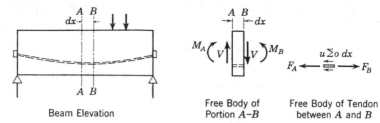

Fig. 7-13. Bond stress before cracking.

that for compressive steel in reinforced concrete. Consider a prestressed beam loaded externally, Fig. 7-13. To determine the bond stress, taking an elementary segment dx between sections A and B as a free body, we have

$$V\,dx = dM = M_B - M_A$$

Since $M_B = f_B I_t/y$ and $M_A = f_A I_t/y$, we have

$$V\,dx = \frac{f_B I_t}{y} - \frac{f_A I_t}{y}$$

which can be written as

$$V\,dx = \frac{I_t}{nA_s y}(nA_s f_B - nA_s f_A)$$

Since $nA_s f_B - nA_s f_A = F_B - F_A$, we have

$$V\,dx = \frac{I_t}{nA_s y}(F_B - F_A)$$

Taking the wires as a free body, we have

$$F_B - F_A = u\Sigma o\,dx$$

hence,

$$V\,dx = \frac{I_t}{nA_s y}(u\Sigma o\,dx)$$

Transposing,

$$u = \frac{nA_s y V}{\Sigma o I_t} \qquad (7\text{-}8)$$

For round wires, $A_s/\Sigma o = D/4$, we have

$$u = \frac{V y n D}{4 I_t} \qquad (7\text{-}9)$$

When wires are encased in metallic hoses, bond stress must be calculated for two contact areas: first, between wires and the grout; then between hoses and the concrete. For the latter computation, equation 7-8 and not 7-9 should be applied; A_s is the area of the encased wires, and Σo stands for the perimeter of the hoses. The same principle holds when considering a group of wires and computing the bond between the group and the surrounding grout or concrete.

EXAMPLE 7-6

A prestressed-concrete rectangular beam is post-tensioned and then grouted. The steel consists of three tendons, each made up of twelve $\frac{1}{4}$-in. wires ($A = 0.05$ sq in. per wire) encased in a thin metallic hose 1.25 in. in diameter. $E_c = 4 \times 10^6$ psi; $E_s = 28 \times 10^6$ psi. The beam spans 30 ft and carries a concentrated load as shown, Fig. 7-14. Compute the unit bond stress, (a) between each wire and the grout, (b) between the hose and the concrete.

Solution. Since the beam is grouted after being post-tensioned, no bond stress is produced by the weight of the beam. The maximum shear V to be used for computing bond is that due to live load only, thus,

$$V = 24,000 \text{ lb}$$

Instead of using the transformed section including the steel, it will be close enough to use the gross concrete section; hence,

$$I_t = I = \frac{9 \times 20^3}{12} = 6000 \text{ in.}^4$$

and y can be measured from the mid-depth of the section,

$$y = 8 \text{ in.}$$

(a) For bond stress between each wire and the grout, apply equation 7-9,

$$u = \frac{VynD}{4I_t}$$

Since $n = \frac{28}{4} = 7$, and $D = 0.25$, we have

$$u = \frac{24,000 \times 8 \times 7 \times 0.25}{4 \times 6000}$$

$$= 14 \text{ psi}$$

(b) For bond stress between the hoses and the concrete, we can compute either on the basis of one hose or of all three hoses, obtaining the same results.

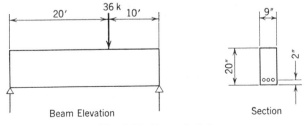

Beam Elevation · Section

Fig. 7-14. Example 7-6.

Considering one hose, we have $A_s = 12 \times 0.05 = 0.60$ sq in., and $\Sigma o = 1.25\pi = 3.92$ in. Applying equation 7-8,

$$u = \frac{nA_s y V}{\Sigma o I_t}$$

$$= \frac{7 \times 0.60 \times 8 \times 24{,}000}{3.92 \times 6000}$$

$$= 34 \text{ psi}$$

After the cracking of concrete, the problem is more complicated. First of all, it is known that bond stresses change suddenly at the cracks owing to the abrupt transfer of tension from concrete to steel at such points.[11] Thus there exists a varying bond stress near the cracks which cannot be easily determined. However, if it is assumed that the bond stress is uniform along the length, then a formula similar to that for tensile bars in reinforced-concrete beams can be applied.

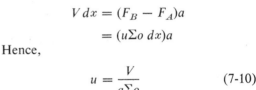

Referring to Fig. 7-15, again taking the element dx as a free body, we have

$$V \, dx = (F_B - F_A)a$$

$$= (u \Sigma o \, dx)a$$

Hence,

$$u = \frac{V}{a \Sigma o} \qquad (7\text{-}10)$$

Fig. 7-15. Bond stress after cracking.

In the ultimate range, the value of a can be approximated by $\frac{7}{8}d$ as for reinforced-concrete beams. Equation 7-10 gives a much higher bond stress than equation 7-8 or 7-9. This indicates that the bond stress increases suddenly when the section changes into a cracked one.

EXAMPLE 7-7

For the same beam as in example 7-6, compute the bond stress between the hoses and concrete, if the load is doubled and cracks have occurred on the tensile side.

$$\text{Shear } V = 2 \times 24{,}000 = 48{,}000 \text{ lb}$$

Assuming $a = \frac{7}{8}d = \frac{7}{8}(18) = 15.7$ in., we have, from equation 7-10, considering all three hoses,

$$u = \frac{V}{a \Sigma o}$$

$$= \frac{48{,}000}{15.7 \times 1.25 \times 3.14 \times 3}$$

$$= 260 \text{ psi}$$

indicating a very high value of bond stress. Comparing this with example 7–6, it is seen that, while the shear is only doubled, the unit bond stress is increased from 34 to 260 psi. This again illustrates the inadequacy of the elastic theory and the importance of investigating the ultimate strength of prestressed elements.

The existing bond stress having been determined, the next step is to find out the resisting unit bond strength between steel and concrete. This, obviously, depends on many factors, foremost of which are the surface and the form of steel and the strength of the adjoining concrete or grout. While many tests have been run for bond resistance of reinforcing bars, only a few data are available concerning the bond strength between prestressed steel and concrete.[12] Referring to ordinary reinforced concrete, it is seen that the bond strength varies from $0.08f_c'$ for plain bars to $0.30f_c'$ for new deformed bars.[13] For prestressing steel, ordinary plain wires have bond strength comparable to that of plain reinforcing bars, while corrugated wires (and perhaps waved wires) will have greater bond resistance. It is also known that twisted wire strands have higher bond than straight wires.

Besides the above bond stresses produced by shear, there are bond stresses produced by flexure alone, even in a region of zero shear. Consider, for example, a beam loaded at the third points of the span. The middle third of the beam has no shear but is under heavy bending moment. When that section begins to crack, stress in the steel right at the cracks necessarily differs from that away from the cracks. Thus there exists a rather high and varying bond stress adjacent to any cracks produced by flexure, whether there is shear or not. Such local bond stress is often high enough to result in failure of bond between steel and concrete near the cracks. However, this local bond failure may not be significant as far as the overall safety of the beam is concerned.

7-6 Prestress Transfer Bond in Pre-Tensioned Concrete

Nature of Bond and Length of Transfer. When tendons are pre-tensioned, their stress is often transferred to the concrete solely by bond between the two materials. Thus there is a length of transfer at each end of the tendons to perform the function of anchorage, when mechanical end anchorages are not provided. The condition of bond stress existing at these ends is radically different from that along the intermediate length of a beam. At intermediate points, the bond stress is produced by the external shear or by the existence of cracks. Where there are no cracks and no shear, the bond stress is zero. At anchorage, bond stress exists immediately after transfer. The stress in the tendons varies from zero at the exposed end to a full prestress at some distance inside the concrete. That distance is known as the length of transfer; and such bond stress is termed as prestress transfer bond.[12]

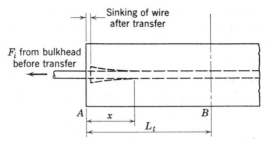

Fig. 7-16. Prestress transfer at end of pre-tensioned beam.

The nature of prestress transfer bond is entirely different from the flexural bond stress produced by shear or cracks. At intermediate points along a beam, the bond stress is resisted by adhesion between steel and concrete, aided by mechanical resistance provided by corrugations in the steel when deformed bars are used. At end anchorages, the pre-tensioned tendons almost always slip and sink into the concrete at the moment of transfer. This slippage destroys most of the adhesion for the length of transfer and part of the mechanical resistance of the corrugations, leaving the bond stress to be carried largely by friction between steel and concrete.

Immediately after transfer, at end A, Fig. 7-16, the wire will have zero stress and its diameter will be restored to the unstressed diameter. At B, the inner end of the length of transfer, the wire will have almost full prestress, and, owing to Poisson's ratio effect, its diameter will be smaller than the unstressed diameter. Thus along the length of transfer, there is an expansion of the wire diameter which produces radial pressure against the surrounding concrete. Frictional force resulting from this pressure serves to transmit the stress between steel and concrete. In other words, a sort of wedging action takes place within that length of transfer.

On the supposition of lateral expansion, Hoyer[14] has derived an equation giving the length of transfer, L_t, as

$$L_t = \frac{d}{2\mu}(1 + m_c)\left(\frac{n}{m_s} - \frac{f_i}{E_c}\right)\frac{f_e}{2f_i - f_e} \tag{7-11}$$

where m_c = Poisson's ratio for concrete
m_s = Poisson's ratio for steel
$n = E_s/E_c$
E_c = modulus of elasticity for concrete
f_i = initial prestress in steel
f_e = effective prestress in steel
μ = coefficient of friction between steel and concrete
d = diameter of wire

If we assume that $m_c = 0.1$, $m_s = 0.3$, $n = 6$, $E_c = 5,000,000$ psi, $f_i = 150,000$ psi, and $f_e = 125,000$ psi, we will reduce equation 7-11 to

$$L_t = 8d/\mu$$

It can be observed, therefore, that the length of transfer varies directly as the diameter of wire and inversely as the coefficient of friction, assuming this wedging action to be the only bonding force.

More recently, a similar elastic analysis has been made by Janney,[12] also based on the elastic theory of a thick-walled cylinder, considering only the frictional bonding phenomenon and neglecting the adhesion or mechanical bond due to corrugation. This analysis leads to the following formula, which gives the ratio of steel stress f_s/f_e at a distance x from the free end;

$$\log \frac{f_e - f_s}{f_e} = \frac{-4\mu m_s x}{d[1 + (1 + m_c)n]} \tag{7-12}$$

In order to show the variation of stress along the length of transfer, equation 7-12 is plotted in Fig. 7-17, giving f_s/f_e for wires of diameter

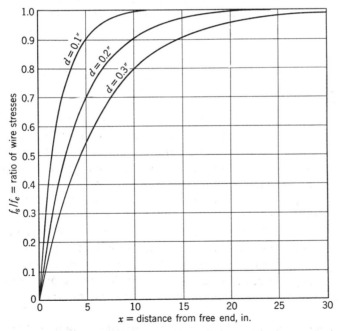

Fig. 7-17. Theoretical variation of wire stress along length of transfer. (From equation 7-12 with $\mu = 0.3$, $m_c = 0.1$, $m_s = 0.3$, $n = 6$.)

0.1, 0.2, and 0.3 in., with a coefficient of friction $\mu = 0.3$. Values of m_c, m_s, and n are again assumed to be 0.1, 0.3, and 6, respectively. It can be observed from equation 7-12 that the distance x required to develop a given ratio of f_s/f_e varies directly with the diameter of the wire and inversely with the coefficient of friction. Hence, for wires of other diameters and other coefficients of friction, the distance x for a given f_s/f_e can be proportionately obtained from these curves. The results given by this equation are necessarily approximate because only the frictional force is considered and because concrete is not élastic but plastic.

TABLE 7-2

Range of Transfer Length

Wire diameter, in.	Factory Pre-tensioned			Laboratory Pre-tensioned		
	Length of transfer for full stress, in.	Length for 80% stress build-up, in.	Stress build-up at 6 in. from end	Length of transfer for full stress, in.	Length for 80% stress build-up, in.	Stress build-up at 6 in. from end
0.08	6–13	4–9	30–100%			
0.02	6–32	5–26	0–100%	7–18	5–12	30–90%
0.276	12–45	8–30		12–23	8–13	40–60%

Actual tests by Janney[12] to measure the variation of steel stress along the length of transfer verified the above analysis in a qualitative manner, indicating that prestress transfer bond for wires is largely a result of friction between concrete and steel. However, the high stresses produced in the surrounding concrete indicated plastic behavior and the inaccuracy of formula 7-12, which is derived on the assumption of the elastic theory. Janney's tests indicated that, for 0.276-in. diameter lubricated wire pre-tensioned to 120,000 psi, the stress transfer was effected in 36 in., while 0.162-in diameter rusted wire has transfer length of 12 in.

Investigations carried out in Great Britain[15] on plain and indented wires of various sizes, pre-tensioned in both in the factories and in the research laboratory, yielded the following table for the range of transfer length.

This table seems to indicate that the transfer length of these wires averages about 100 diameters in the factory and about 60 diameters in the laboratory under controlled conditions.

In addition, these tests revealed the following.

1. Too great a concentration of prestressing wires can lead to the formation of horizontal shear cracks above the wires.

2. Sudden release of wires by flame cutting or other means leads to a great increase in the transfer length.

3. Change in transfer length with time after transfer is small.

4. Repeated loading tests show no increase in transfer length.

5. Higher concrete strength will appreciably decrease the transfer length.

While it is also known that rusted wires or stands perform better in bond than clean ones, careless rusting allowing localized pitting should be avoided.

The study of transfer length has been carried on by investigators in various countries, including Russia,[16] Japan,[17] and England.[18] In the United States, Lehigh University,[19] the Portland Cement Association,[20] and the University of Illinois[21] have performed experiments on the transfer length for 7-wire strands. Since strand provides a sizable amount of mechanical resistance in addition to friction, its transfer length is shorter than a smooth wire of the same size.

Figure 7-18 shows an end portion of a pre-tensioned beam wherein the stress in the tendon increases from zero to a maximum value f_{se}. Taking a length dx of the tendon as a freebody, Fig. 7-18(b), we have,

$$(f_s + df_s)A_s - f_sA_s = u\Sigma O \, dx$$

$$u = \frac{A_s}{\Sigma O}\frac{df_s}{dx} \tag{7-13}$$

The values of u will vary along the transfer length, with a maximum near the end. Tests at Lehigh University, for $\frac{7}{61}$-in. 7-wire strands pre-tensioned to an initial value of about 175 ksi, gave maximum values of u varying from 311 psi up to 1740 psi, with an average of about 960 psi. The length of transfer L_t was between 9 and 39 in., averaging 21 in.

Although it is known that the transfer length for strands increases with the size of strands, the exact relation is not too well known. In other words, the value of u may vary with the size of strands, as well as with other factors. As an approximation, it can be assumed that L_t varies directly with the diameter D and the effective prestress f_{se}. If it is further assumed that bond stress is uniform along the length of transfer, we can then use the usual formula for bond stress in reinforcing bars,

$$L_t = \frac{f_{se}D}{4u_{av}} \tag{7-14}$$

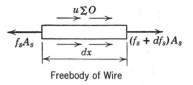

Freebody of Wire

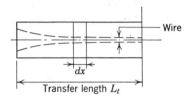

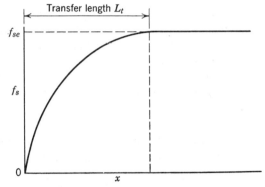

Fig. 7-18. Transfer length.

Lehigh University tests indicated u_{av} from 350 to 1500 psi, averaging about 780. If a fairly safe value for u_{av} at 500 psi is assumed for 7-wire strands and for $f_{se} = 150,000$ psi, we obtain

$$L_t = \frac{150,000\,D}{4 \times 500} = 75D \tag{7-15}$$

Design for Prestress Transfer by Bond. The design of prestressed members as affected by the transfer bond may be described in two parts. The first involves the distribution of prestress at the ends of members, since the prestress is not concentrated at the free end but is transferred gradually along a certain length. Hence the stress concentration at the free end is somewhat relieved, while the stress a few inches inside the free end may be more critical. Since a certain portion of the end of the member is not fully prestressed, its resistance to flexure, cracking, and shear must be determined accordingly, and additional reinforcing steel provided as necessary.

In prestressed beams, it is significant to avoid flexural cracking near the end portions. When concrete cracks under flexure, the bond stress in the vicinity of the cracks rises, and slip occurs over a small portion of the strand adjacent to the cracks. With continued increase in load, the high bond stress progresses as a wave from the original cracks toward the beam ends. If the peak of the high bond stress wave reaches the prestress transfer zone, the increase in steel stress resulting from the bond slip decreases the strand diameter, reduces the frictional bond resistance in wires which have little mechanical resistance, and general bond failure could result. For strands, the helical shape of the individual wires will provide mechanical resistance so that the beam can support additional load even after slip of the strand at the beam ends. The steel stress that can be developed varies with the size of the strand, the strand embedment length (the distance from the flexural crack to the free end of the beam), the pre-tensioning stress, the concrete strength, etc. Although locally variable, the embedment lengths L_u required to prevent general bond step of 7-wire strands have been determined experimentally[20] and are shown in Fig. 7-19. Hence it seems clear that if flexural cracks cannot occur near the end portion of the beam, there is no danger of the high bond stress wave reaching the prestress transfer zone, and there is no danger of beam failure resulting from bond slip. The failure of a beam resulting from bond slippage may be illustrated in Fig. 7-20, which shows the end portion of a pre-tensioned beam loaded to cracking near the end. The solid line in Fig. 7-20(b) indicates the stress in the tendons under normal loads before cracking, having a transfer length L_t. Under increased loading, when a crack occurs at C, the stress in the tendon is raised to a maximum stress of f_{su}, as shown by the dotted line. Thus there is a bond stress developed from C to B. If B reaches past point A, that is, if the bond length overlaps the transfer length, then the tendon could be pulled through the concrete.

The bond length L_b is a function of the stress differential $f_{su}-f_{se}$, of the bond stress u, the tendon diameter D, and other factors. Assuming uniform bond stress along the length L_b, and equating the total stress differential to the total bond stress, we have

$$(f_{su} - f_{se}) \frac{\pi D^2}{4} = u\pi D L_b$$

$$L_b = \frac{(f_{su} - f_{se})D}{4u} \tag{7-16}$$

To determine the value of u, it is noted that the bond stress at slippage is lower than that for the transfer length. Within the transfer length, the strand tends to expand and anchor to the concrete, while when strand is

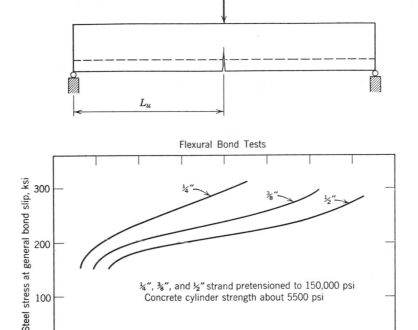

Fig. 7-19. Relation of steel stress at general bond slip to strand embedment length L_u.

stressed above f_{se}, it tends to contract and pull away from the concrete. Assuming a conservative value $u = 250$ psi for this bond length, and let $f_{su} = 250{,}000$ psi; $f_{se} = 150{,}000$ psi, we have

$$L_b = \frac{(250{,}000 - 150{,}000)D}{4 \times 250}$$

$$= 100\,D$$

Thus the total length L_u required to avoid pulling through is

$$L_u = L_t + L_b = 75D + 100D$$
$$= 175\,D \qquad (7\text{-}17)$$

This empirical formula will yield values of L_u smaller than those given in Fig. 7-19. This is because Fig. 7-19 gives the length required to prevent the first general bond slip. The general bond slip is in most cases arrested by mechanical interlock between the strand and the surrounding concrete, so that additional bond can be developed before the strand is pulled through.

The use of end anchors for strands could stop the pulling through, but it does not become effective until slip has occurred along the entire embedded length. Then the beam acts as a post-tensioned one without bond, and the ultimate moment resistance may not be much higher than those without anchors.

Based on the results of tests at the Portland Cement Association Laboratories[20] together with some additional data from the Association of American Railroads, the 1963 ACI Code has the following empirical formula for the minimum embedment length L in pre-tensioned flexural members using 7-wire strands with nominal diameter D:

$$L = (f_{su} - \tfrac{2}{3}f_{se})D \qquad (7\text{-}18)$$

where f_{su} and f_{se} are in ksi, while L and D are in inches. The embedment length is the distance from the flexural cracking to the end of the beam, or to the end of the bonding between the strand and the concrete if portion of the strand is unbonded.

Assuming $f_{su} = 250$ ksi and $f_{se} = 150$ ksi, we have

$$L = (250 - \tfrac{2}{3} \times 150)D = 150D \qquad (7\text{-}19)$$

which is not too different from equation 7-17.

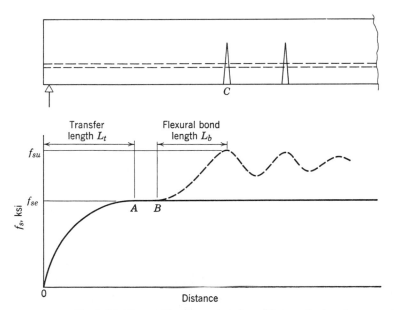

Fig. 7-20. Flexural bond overlapping with transfer length.

7-7 Bearing at Anchorage

For tendons with end anchorages, where the prestress is transferred to the concrete by direct bearing, various designs may be used for transmitting the prestress: steel plates, steel blocks, or reinforced-concrete ones.

The design of an anchorage consists of two parts: determining the bearing area required for concrete, and designing for the strength and detail of the anchorage itself. Stress analysis for any anchorage is a very complicated problem, because not only the elasticity but also the plasticity of concrete enters into the picture. As a result, anchorages are designed by experience, tests, and usage rather than by theory. Since anchorages are generally supplied by the prestressing companies which have their own standards for different tendons, the engineer does not have to design for them. Anchorages that have been successfully adopted are usually considered reliable, and no theoretical check on their stresses is necessary. For a new type of anchorage, the most reliable check is to run a test to determine its ultimate strength. A proper safety factor can then be applied to obtain the allowable load.

Sometimes it is necessary to design or to check the bearing areas for end anchorage, as governed by the allowable bearing in concrete. Since the cost of anchorage increases greatly if the allowable bearing stress is low, it has been the practice to use as high a bearing stress as is consistent with safety, much higher than permitted in reinforced concrete. This is true for practically all systems of prestressing. Besides reasons of economy, such high bearing stress can be justified on the following grounds.

1. The highest bearing stress that will ever exist at the anchorage occurs at transfer. As loss of prestress takes place, the bearing stress gradually diminishes.

2. The strength of concrete increases with time. Hence, if failure does not take place immediately at transfer, there is little possibility that it will happen later.

3. For bonded tendons with anchorages at the end of members, externally applied load will not increase the force on the anchorage. For unbonded tendons, the force on the anchorage will increase with load; but the increase is limited, hence a high factor of safety is not required.

The allowable bearing stress depends on several factors, such as the amount of reinforcement at the anchorage, the ratio of bearing to total area, and the method of stress computation. A value commonly allowed is $0.60f_c'$, assuming uniform bearing over the entire contact area. If the anchorage is rigid, the variation of pressure will be small over the contact area; if only a thin plate is used, high bearing pressure may exist near the tendons. If the anchorage simply bears on the end of concrete without being buried in it, the prestress is transferred entirely through bearing. If the anchorage is buried in the concrete, then part of the prestress may be transferred through bond along the sides of the anchorage. Take the Freyssinet cone, for example; it is believed that about a third of the prestress is transmitted through the sides.

Because of the strict economy followed in the design of end anchorages, it has not been unusual that when the concrete is poor it actually crushes under the application of the prestress. Hence it is important that concrete for prestressed work should be of high quality and should be carefully placed around the anchorages.

Besides supplying strength and rigidity, anchorage must be detailed to suit the dimensions of the jack and the ends of the beam. When both anchorages and jacks are supplied by the prestressing company, the designer will not have to worry about such details. If the thickness of the bearing plate has to be designed, a procedure similar to that used for designing column bearing plates may be followed. This consists of designing the critical section for bending at an allowable stress. Here, again, the allowable stress can be somewhat higher than ordinary, since there is no danger of overload or fatigue effect. The design for a Roebling anchorage is shown in the following example.

EXAMPLE 7-8

Compute the thickness required for the bearing plate to carry a Roebling cable $1\frac{1}{2}$ in. in diameter, with an initial tension of 170 k. Size of the plate is chosen as 10 in. square, being limited by jacking requirements. Compute the bearing pressure on concrete. $f_c' = 5000$ psi. Other details of the anchorage are shown in Fig. 7-21.

Solution. Allowable load carried by bond may be calculated as follows:

Area of contact $= 6.625\pi \times 16 = 333$ sq in.

Allowable bond stress assumed at $= 0.04 f_c' = 200$ psi.

Permissible load by bond $= 200 \times 333 = 67$ k.

Load to be carried by bearing $= 170 - 67 = 103$ k.

Bearing area $= 100 - 28$ (area of pipe) $= 72$ sq in.

Bearing stress $= 103,000/72 = 1430$ psi.

Assume allowable stress to be $0.60 f_c' = 3000$ psi, the stress of 1430 psi is evidently low. But it is not possible to reduce the bearing area because of jacking requirements in this case.

To compute the thickness of the plate, consider critical section Y–Y. Assuming uniform distribution of pressure, the lever arm of force from concrete on plate $= 2.8$ in., the lever arm of force from screw nut on plate $= 2.0$ in. The total force for half of the plate $= 103/2 = 51.5$ k.

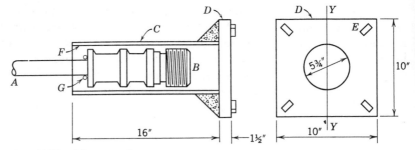

$A = 1\frac{1}{2}''$ Roebling strand.

$B =$ end fitting for above strand, in position before prestressing.

$C = 6''$ standard pipe 16″ long with 11/16″ holes for rods G to pass; holes to be sealed with mastic. Outside diameter $= 6.625''$.

$D = 1\frac{1}{2}'' \times 10'' \times 10''$ steel plate, with center hole slightly greater than inside of pipe.

$E = \frac{1}{2}'' \times \frac{1}{2}'' \times 1\frac{1}{4}''$ centering lugs for jack, welded to 2″ plate.

$F =$ paper packing.

$G =$ keeper rods 5/8″.

Fig. 7-21. Example 7-8.

Total bending moment

$$M = 51,500 \times (2.8 - 2.0)$$
$$= 41,200 \text{ in.-lb}$$

Section modulus of $Y-Y$, for net width $b = 4.25$ in.,

$$Z = bd^2/6$$
$$= 4.25d^2/6$$
$$= 0.708d^2$$

Allowing a high stress of 30,000 psi in the steel plate, we have

$$f = M/Z$$
$$30,000 = 41,200/0.708d^2$$
$$d = 1.4 \text{ in.}$$

Use a $1\frac{1}{2}$-in. plate.

7-8 Transverse Tension at End Block

The portion of a prestressed member surrounding the anchorages of the tendons is often termed the end block. Throughout the length of the end block, prestress is transferred from more or less concentrated areas and distributed through the entire beam section. The theoretical length of the end block is the distance through which this change takes place and is sometimes called the lead length. It is known from theoretical and experimental investigations that this lead is not more than the height of the beam and often is much smaller except for pre-tensioned beams with long transfer length

Referring to Fig. 7-22, the prestress at section A–A, whether horizontal or inclined, is applied as concentrated or somewhat distributed loads. At section B–B, the end of the lead length, the resistance from the beam consists of linearly distributed fiber stresses and corresponding shearing stresses as calculated by the usual beam theory. For the portion between sections A–A and B–B, the stress distribution is rather complicated. If we cut a longitudinal section X–X, and take a freebody as in Fig. 7-22(b), there will exist moment, shear, and a direct load on that section. These components of forces can be simply computed from statics, but their distribution along X–X cannot be easily determined. It is not possible to apply the usual beam theory assuming a plane section remaining plane, because that theory is far from being correct when applied to a short

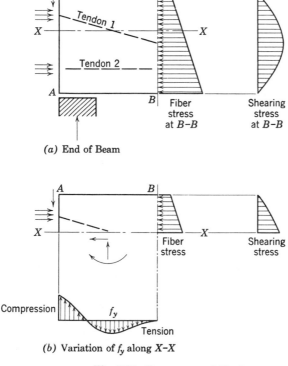

(*a*) End of Beam

(*b*) Variation of f_y along X–X

Fig. 7-22. Stresses at end block.

block like $A-A-B-B$. It can only be solved by the advanced theory of elasticity, which is complicated even for the simplest conditions of loading.

In order to simplify the solution, an assumption is made that the load is uniformly distributed across the width of the beam; thus, instead of a load concentrated at one point, we can assume a knife-edge load extending the entire width of the beam. Then the problem is reduced from a three- to a two-dimensional problem. On this assumption, and on the theory of elasticity, stress distributions within the end block have been solved, and tables and graphs are available for certain conditions of loading.[21] For these graphs, Fig. 7-23, it is convenient to express the stresses in terms of the average direct compression f, where

$$f = F/A$$

F = total axial prestress at end of beam, and A = cross-sectional area of beam.

In general, along any longitudinal section, such as $X-X$, in Fig. 7-22, the shearing stress is small and does not cause any trouble; only the transverse tensile stress f_y can be serious. Hence we are interested only in the variation of f_y.

Graphs in Fig. 7-23 are for rectangular sections and are intended to indicate the general nature of the tensile stresses in end blocks. Lines of equal f_y, also termed "isobars," are shown in the graphs. From these isobars, it can be observed that there are two general areas of tension. One area in the center of the section is termed the "bursting zone." It has a maximum tension along the line of the load and at some distance from it. Another area is on the sides of the load close to the end surface, termed the "spalling zone." This zone is subject to high tensile stresses but only over a small area.

Additional graphs are available in Guyon's *Prestressed Concrete*,[22] to which readers are referred. Even though these graphs are theoretically correct and some of them have been confirmed by photo-elasticity, their application to design is another problem. First, concrete is not a perfectly elastic material and will act plastically especially when part of it is over-stressed. Second, what should be the allowable tension in the concrete? Third, if the allowable tension is exceeded, how shall we design the reinforcing steel? Fourth, the pattern of forces applied at the end is often more complicated than can be handled by the theory of elasticity. Hence, though theory is needed in analysis, judgment must be exercised in design.

Guyon recommends that the allowable tensile stress be set at about a tenth of that for compression, that is, about $0.04f_c'$. Wherever the tension exceeds that value, steel reinforcement should be designed to take the entire amount of tension on the basis of the usual allowable stress in steel.

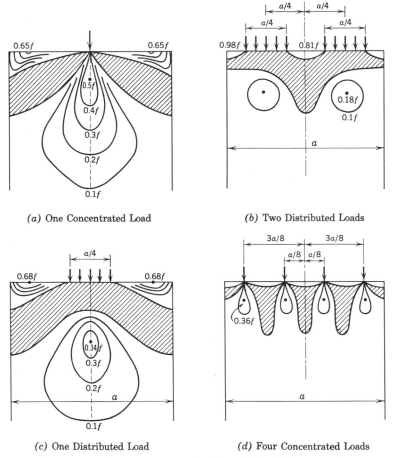

(a) One Concentrated Load   (b) Two Distributed Loads

(c) One Distributed Load   (d) Four Concentrated Loads

Fig. 7-23. Isobars for transverse tension in end block (in terms of average compression f). Shaded areas represent compressive zones. From Guyon's *Prestressed Concrete.*

In the spalling zone, the tensile stresses are very high and will generally exceed the allowable value. However, these stresses act on only a small area, and the total tensile force is therefore small. For most cases, it has been found sufficient to provide steel for a total transverse tension of $0.03F$. For post-tensioning, this steel is placed as close to the end as possible. Either wire mesh or steel bars may be used.

To carry the tension in the bursting zone, either stirrups or spiral steel may be used. For local reinforcement under the anchorage, $\frac{1}{4}$-in. spirals at 2-in. pitch or $\frac{3}{8}$-in. spirals at $1\frac{1}{2}$-in. pitch are sometimes adopted. For overall reinforcement, stirrups can be efficiently employed. A design of these stirrups is illustrated in example 7-9. It is fortunate that under ordinary conditions the number of stirrups required to resist the transverse tension is not excessive. Hence nominal amounts of reinforcement will suffice. However, longitudinal cracks have been produced by transverse tension when reinforcement was not provided or was insufficient.

EXAMPLE 7-9

The end of a prestressed beam is rectangular in section and is acted on by two prestressing tendons anchored as shown, Fig. 7-24. The initial prestress is 170 k per tendon. $f_c' = 4000$ psi. Design the reinforcement for the end block, allowing a maximum of 120 psi for the tension in the concrete.

Solution. Tensile stresses for the bursting zone can be obtained from Fig. 7-23(*b*). Critical tensile stresses exist through sections C–C and D–D of Fig. 7-24(*b*), and their variation is plotted in Fig. 7-24(*c*). The greatest tensile stress is given as 0.18*f*,

$$0.18f = 0.18 \left(\frac{2 \times 170,000}{10 \times 40} \right)$$
$$= 0.18 \times 850$$
$$= 153 \text{ psi}$$

Suppose that reinforcement is required for the portion whose tension exceeds 120 psi; then the shaded portion of about 5 in. would require reinforcement. Assuming an average tension of 140 psi for the 5-in. length, the total tensile force to be resisted by steel is

$$140 \times 5 \times 10 = 7000 \text{ lb}$$

For an allowable stress of 20,000 psi in the steel, the area of steel required is

$$A_s = \frac{7000}{20,000} = 0.35 \text{ sq in.}$$

Four $\frac{1}{2}$-in. U-stirrups will be provided as shown, giving a total area of 1.57 sq in. Note that computation such as this simply serves as a guide. Judgment must be exercised in design. Since the tension is not excessive, liberal provision of steel is possible without much additional cost.

If concrete around the anchorages is thin, it is desirable to add some spiral steel, such as $\frac{1}{4}$-in. wires at 2-in. pitch.

For the spalling zone, stresses as high as $0.98f = 0.98 \times 850 = 830$ psi exist. The total force, however, is small and can be approximated by an average of 400 psi over a length of 2 in., which amounts to

$$400 \times 2 \times 10 = 8000 \text{ lb}$$

Using the value of 0.03F as suggested, we would get

$$0.03 \times 340,000 = 10,200 \text{ lb}$$

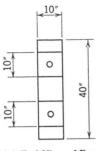

(a) End View of Beam

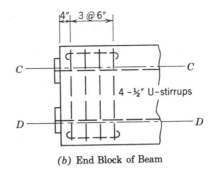

(b) End Block of Beam

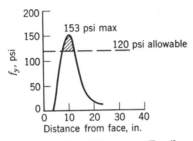

(c) ·Variation of Transverse Tensile
Stress along *C–C* or *D–D*

Fig. 7-24. Example 7-9.

showing not too bad an agreement in this problem. Steel required to resist
8000 lb is

$$8000/20,000 = 0.40 \text{ sq in.}$$

which is adequately provided by the $\frac{1}{2}$-in. stirrups.

While certain recent tests[23] confirmed the correctness of the several
classical theories for anchorage zone stresses, including Guyon's method
as outlined above, other tests[24] seem to indicate that the actual tensile
stresses and total transverse tensile forces could be two to three times
higher than the above described Guyon's method. Because of the many
variables involved in a problem of this kind, it is most difficult to be exact.
The AASHO Bridge Committee, after consultation with the PCI, has now
revised Article 1.13.15, of the 1961 AASHO Bridge Specifications
(Appendix E) to read as follows.

Article 1.13.15. End Zone of Concrete I-Beams.
For beams with post-tensioning tendons, end blocks shall be used to distribute
the concentrated prestressing forces at the anchorage. Where all tendons are
pretensioned wires or 7-wire strand, the use of end blocks will not be required.

End blocks shall have sufficient area to allow the spacing of the prestressing steel as specified in Article 1.13.16. Preferably, they shall be as wide as the narrower flange of the beam. They shall have a length at least equal to three-fourths of the depth of the beam and in any case 24 inches. In post-tensioned members a closely spaced grid of both vertical and horizontal bars shall be placed near the face of the end block to resist bursting and closely spaced reinforcement shall be placed both vertically and horizontally throughout the length of the block.

In pre-tensioned beams, vertical stirrups acting at a unit stress of 20,000 psi to resist at least 4 per cent of the total prestressing force shall be placed within the distance of $d/4$ of the end of the beam, the end stirrup to be as close to the end of the beam as practicable.

Studies at the Portland Cement Association Laboratories[25] indicated an empirical equation for the design of stirrups to control horizontal cracking in the ends of pre-tensioned I-girders,

$$A_t = 0.021 \frac{T}{f_s} \cdot \frac{h}{l_t} \tag{7-20}$$

where A_t = required total cross-sectional area of stirrups at the end of girder, to be uniformly distributed over a length equal to one-fifth of the girder depth

T = total effective prestress force, lb

f_s = allowable stress for the stirrups steel, psi

h = depth of girder, in.

l_t = length of transfer taken approximately assumed to be 50 times the strand diameter, in.

The above formula shows that the amount of end stirrups should vary directly with the depth of the section and inversely with the length of transfer. These conclusions are apparently quite logical and can be qualitatively justified.

References

1 Rene Walther, "The Shear Strength of Prestressed Concrete Beams," *Proceedings Third Congress of the International Federation for Prestressing*, Berlin, 1958.
2 R. H. Evans and A. H. H. Hosny, "The Shear Strength of Post-tensioned Prestressed Concrete Beams," *Proceedings Third Congress of the International Federation for Prestressing*, Berlin, 1958.
3 M. A. Sozen, "Strength in Shear of Prestressed Concrete Beams without Web Reinforcement," *Structural Research Series No. 139*, Univ. of Illinois, August 1957; also see J. G. MacGregor, "Effect of Draped Reinforcement on Behavior of Prestressed Concrete Beams," *Structural Research Series No. 154*, Univ. of Illinois, May 1958.
4 Rene E. Walther and Robert F. Warner, *Ultimate Strength Tests of Prestressed and Conventionally Reinforced Concrete Beams in Combined Bending and Shear*, Fritz Engineering Laboratory, Lehigh University, Institute of Research, September 1958.
5 J. G. MacGregor, M. A. Sozen, and C. P. Siess, "Strength and Behavior of Prestressed Concrete Beams with Web Reinforcement," *Structural Research Series No. 201*, Univ. of Illinois, August 1960, see also "Investigation of Prestressed Reinforced Concrete for Highway Bridges," *Eleventh Progress Report*, Univ. of Illinois, 1962.
6 A. C. Scordelis, T. Y. Lin, and H. R. May, "Shearing Strength of Prestressed Lift Slabs," *J. Am. Conc. Inst.* October 1958, pp. 485–506.

7 Norman W. Hanson, "Precast-prestressed Concrete Bridges—2. Horizontal Shear Connections," *Journal of the PCA Research and Development Laboratories*, Vol. 2, No. 2, 1960.

8 N. M. Hawkins, M. A. Sozen, and C. P. Siess, "Strength and Behavior of Two-span Continuous Prestressed Concrete Beams," *Structural Research Series No. 225*, Univ. of Illinois, September 1961.

9 B. Bresler and K. S. Pister, "Strength of Concrete under Combined Stresses," *J. Am. Conc. Inst.*, September 1958.

10 "The Structural Use of Prestressed Concrete in Buildings," *Bristish Standard Code of Practice*, The Council for Codes of Practice, British Standards Institution, 1959.

11 R. M. Mains, "Measurement of the Distribution of Tensile and Bond Stresses along Reinforcing Bars," *J. Am. Conc. Inst.*, November 1951 (*Proc.*, Vol. 47), pp. 225–252.

12 J. R. Janney, "Nature of Bond in Pre-Tensioned Prestressed Concrete," *J. Am. Conc. Inst.*, May 1954 (*Proc.*, Vol. 50), pp. 717–736. Also E. Hognestad and J. R. Janney, "The Ultimate Strength of Pre-Tensioned Prestressed Concrete Failing in Bond," *Magazine of Concrete Research*, June 1954.

13 A. P. Clark, "Bond of Concrete Reinforcing Bars," *J. Am. Conc. Inst.*, November 1949.

14 E. Hoyer and E. Friedrich, "Beitrag zur Frage der Haftspannung in Eisenbeton-bauteilen," *Beton und Eisen*, Berlin, 1939 (Vol. 38, No. 6), pp. 107–110. Also K. Billig, *Prestressed Concrete*, Van Nostrand Co., New York, 1953.

15 G. D. Base, "An Investigation of Transmission Length in Pre-tensioned Concrete," *Papers of Third Congress FIP*, Berlin, 1958.

16 E. H. Ratz, M. M. Holmjanski, and V. M. Kolner, "The Transmission of Prestress to Concrete by Bond," *Papers of Third Congress FIP*, Berlin, 1958.

17 T. Inomata and S. Kato, *The Bond Effect of Deformed Prestressed Concrete Wire at Prestressing*, Industrial Engineering Institute of Tokyo University, Tokyo, 1960.

18 R. H. Evans and A. Williams, "The Use of X-rays in Measuring Bond Stresses in Prestressed Concrete," *Proceedings World Conference on Prestressed Concrete*, San Francisco, 1957.

19 G. A. Dinsmore, P. L. Deutsch, and J. L. Montemayor, "Anchorage and Bond in Pretensioned Prestressed Concrete Members," *Fritz Laboratory Report 223–19*, Lehigh University, December 1958.

20 N. W. Hanson and P. H. Kaar, "Flexural Bond Tests of Pretensioned Prestressed Beams," *J. Am. Conc. Inst.*, January 1959, pp. 783–802.

21 R. W. Kenning, M. A. Sozen, and C. P. Siess, "A Study of Anchorage Bond in Prestressed Concrete," Univ. of Illinois, *Structural Research Series No. 251*. June 1962.

22 Y. Guyon, *Prestressed Concrete*, John Wiley & Sons, New York, 1960, see pp. 127–174.

23 J. Zielinski and R. E. Rowe, "An Investigation of the Stress Distribution in the Anchorage Zones of Post-tensioned Concrete Members," *Report No. 9, C.A.C.A.*, London, September 1960.

24 S. Ban, H. Muguruma, and Z. Ogaki, "Anchorage Zone Stress Distributions in Post-tensioned Concrete Members," *Proceedings World Conference on Prestressed Concrete*, San Francisco, 1957.

25 W. T. Marshall and Allan H. Mattock, "Control of Horizontal Cracking in the Ends of Pre-tensioned Prestressed Concrete Girders," J. Prestressed Conc. Inst., October 1962.

8

camber, deflections; cable layouts

8-1 Camber; Deflections

Before cracking, the deflections of prestressed-concrete beams can be predicted with greater precision than that of reinforced-concrete beams. Under working loads, prestressed-concrete beams do not crack; reinforced ones do. Since prestressed concrete is a more or less homogeneous elastic body which obeys quite closely the ordinary laws of flexure and shear, the deflections can be computed by methods available in elementary strength of materials.

As usually encountered for any concrete member, two difficulties still stand in the way when we wish to get an accurate prediction of the deflections. First, it is difficult to determine the value of E_c within an accuracy of 10% or even 20%. Tests on sample cylinders may not give the correct value of E_c, because E_c for beams may differ from that for cylinders. Besides, the value of E_c varies for different stress levels and changes with the age of concrete. The second difficulty lies in estimating the effect of creep on deflections.[1] The value of the creep coefficient as well as the duration and magnitude of the applied load cannot always be known in advance. However, for practical purposes, an accuracy of 10% or 20% is often sufficient, and that can be attained if all factors are carefully considered.

Deflections of prestressed beams differ from those of ordinary reinforced beams in the effect of prestress. While controlled deflections due to prestress can be advantageously utilized to produce desired cambers and to offset deflections due to loadings, there are also known cases where excessive cambers due to prestress have caused serious troubles. Cambers or deflections due to prestress can be computed by two methods. The first method is to take the concrete as a freebody separated from the tendons, which are replaced by a system of forces acting on the concrete, Fig. 8-1. This would necessitate the computation of proper components

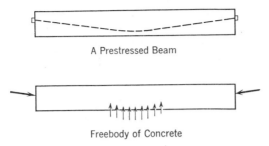

A Prestressed Beam

Freebody of Concrete

Fig. 8-1. Computation for deflection due to prestress.

of forces at the end anchorages plus transverse or radial forces at every bend of the tendons. This method is applicable to both simple and continuous beams. For the sake of simplicity, the following assumptions are usually made:

1. The gross section of concrete can often be used in computing the moment of inertia, although the net concrete section would be a more correct value.

2. The prestress producing deflection is somewhere between the initial and the final effective value. It is considered sufficiently accurate to assume a reasonable value for the purpose of computation.

3. The component of the prestress along the beam axis is assumed constant unless the inclination of the tendons becomes excessive. The component transverse to the beam is computed by the prestress times the tangent of the angle of bending unless the angle becomes unusually large.

4. Where the tendons bend suddenly, the transverse components may be assumed to be concentrated; where they form a flat curve, the transverse load may be assumed to be uniformly distributed along the bend.

5. All computations may be based on the c.g.s. line, the tendons being treated as a whole instead of individually.

6. Shearing deflections are small for ordinary proportions of prestressed beams and can be neglected.

The second method of computation is based on the same assumptions as above, but, without calculating the forces from the tendons on the concrete, a moment diagram produced by the tendons is directly drawn from the c.g.s. profile. For statically determinate beams the moment diagram is similar to the eccentricity profile of the c.g.s. line; hence it is only necessary to plot the eccentricity profile to another scale to obtain the moment diagram. Then the computation of deflections from the moment diagram is performed by any method given in elementary strength of materials. This procedure is often simpler than the first, since it does away with the computation of forces from the tendons. But when applied to statically indeterminate beams, it has to be modified because of moments produced by the redundant reactions as a result of prestressing, which will be explained in Chapter 10.

Acting simultaneously with the prestress is the weight of the beam itself, which will produce deflections depending on the conditions of support. Such deflections can again be computed by the usual elastic theory. The resultant deflections of the beam at transfer are obtained by summing algebraically the deflections due to prestress and those due to beam weight.

EXAMPLE 8-1

A concrete beam of 32-ft simple span, Fig. 8-2, is post-tensioned with 1.2 sq in. of high-tensile steel to an initial prestress of 140 ksi immediately after prestressing. Compute the initial deflection at midspan due to prestress and the beam's own weight, assuming $E_c = 4,000,000$ psi. Estimate the deflection after 3 months, assuming a creep coefficient of $C_c = 1.8$ and an effective prestress of 120 ksi at that time.

Solution.   Using the first method, take the concrete as a freebody and replace the tendon with forces acting on the concrete. The parabolic tendon with 6-in.

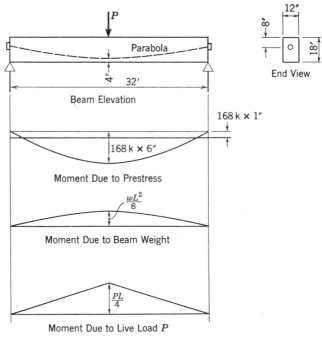

Fig. 8-2. Examples 8-1 and 8-2.

midordinate is replaced by a uniform load acting along the beam with intensity

$$w = \frac{8F6}{L^2} = \frac{8 \times 140{,}000 \times 1.2 \times 6}{32^2 \times 12} = 655 \text{ plf}$$

In addition, there will be two eccentric loads acting at the ends of the beam, each producing a moment of $140{,}000 \times 1.2 \times \frac{1}{12} = 14{,}000$ ft-lb.

Since the weight of the beam is 225 plf, the net uniform load on concrete is $655 - 225 = 430$ plf, which produces an upward deflection at midspan given by the usual deflection formula

$$\Delta = \frac{5wL^4}{384EI}$$

$$= \frac{5 \times 430 \times 32^4 \times 12^3}{384 \times 4{,}000{,}000 \times (12 \times 18^3)/12}$$

$$= 0.434 \text{ in.}$$

The end moments produce a downward deflection given by the formula

$$\Delta = \frac{ML^2}{8EI}$$

$$= \frac{140 \times 1.2 \times 1 \times 32^2 \times 12^2}{8 \times 4{,}000{,}000 \times (12 \times 18^3)/12}$$

$$= 0.133 \text{ in.}$$

Thus the net deflection due to prestress and beam weight is

$$0.434 - 0.133 = 0.301 \text{ in. upward}$$

If we follow the second method, it will not be necessary to compute the forces between the tendon and the concrete. Instead, the moment diagram is drawn from the eccentricity curve of the tendon, and the deflection computed therefrom. For convenience in computation, the moment diagram can be divided into two parts, a parabola and a rectangle (Fig. 8-2). By area-moment principles or any similar method, the upward deflection due to prestress can be computed to be

$$\Delta = \frac{5F6L^2}{48EI} - \frac{ML^2}{8EI}$$

$$= \frac{5 \times 140 \times 1.2 \times 6 \times 32^2 \times 12^2}{48 \times 4{,}000{,}000 \times (12 \times 18^3)/12} - \frac{140 \times 1.2 \times 1 \times 32^2 \times 12^2}{8 \times 4{,}000{,}000 \times (12 \times 18^3)/12}$$

$$= 0.661 - 0.133$$

$$= 0.528 \text{ in.}$$

Downward deflection due to beam weight of 225 plf is given by

$$\Delta = \frac{5WL^4}{384EI} = \frac{5 \times 225 \times 32^4 \times 12^3}{384 \times 4{,}000{,}000 \times (12 \times 18^3)/12} = 0.227 \text{ in.}$$

The resultant deflection is $0.528 - 0.227 = 0.301$ in. upward, the same answer as by the first method.

While the above gives the initial deflection, the eventual deflection should be modified by two factors: first, the loss of prestress, which tends to decrease the deflection; and second, the creep effect, which tends to increase the deflection. Since the prestress is reduced from 140 to 120 ksi, the deflection due to prestress can be modified by the factor 120/140. Then, for the creep effect, the net deflection should be increased by the coefficient 1.8. Thus, if the beam is not subject to external loads the eventual deflection after 3 months can be estimated as

$$\left(0.528 \times \frac{120}{140} - 0.227\right)1.8 = 0.407 \text{ in. upward}$$

The calculation for deflections due to external loads is similar to that for nonprestressed beams. So long as the concrete has not cracked, the beam can be treated as a homogeneous body and the usual elastic theory applied to it for deflection computations.

If the beam is bonded at the time of application of the load, the transformed section including steel should be used in computing the moment of inertia. If it is unbonded, to be theoretically correct, the net section of the concrete should be used and the effect of the change in prestress in the tendons under loading should be taken into account. For practical purposes, however, it will be close enough to consider the gross section of concrete in the computations and to neglect the change in prestress. This will simplify the procedure a great deal and will yield practically the same results. It must always be remembered that the greatest difficulties in arriving at correct deflections are the proper choice of a value for E_c and an accurate allowance for creep effect.

When the beam is loaded beyond its working load (or near its working load, for some cases), tensile stresses will exist in the beam. So long as the beam has not cracked, the elastic theory can still be applied for the computation of deflections. Although the tensile modulus of elasticity may be different from the compressive, the difference is not significant enough to alter the nature of deflection, since, at that stage, tension exists only in a small portion of the beam.

When cracks begin to occur in the beam, the nature of deflection will start to change. Even at the beginning of cracks, when they are still hair cracks hardly visible to the unaided eye, the effective section in resisting moment will be the cracked section instead of the entire concrete section. As the cracks extend deeper and deeper, the moment of inertia of the section will become smaller and smaller until eventually the cracked section may have a moment of inertia about one-half or one-third that of the uncracked section. Besides, the concrete will be under higher

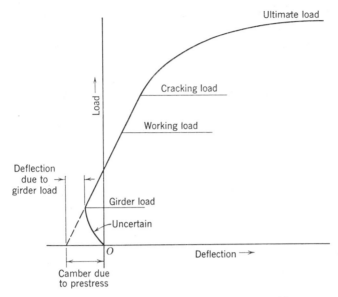

Fig. 8-3. Load deflection curve of a prestressed beam.

average stress and therefore will possess a lower average value of E_c. Hence the deflection of the section will increase much faster than before cracking. It must be noticed, however, that only the part of the beam subjected to higher moment has cracked, while the remaining portion under lower moments may still remain intact. Thus the deflection of the beam will increase faster as more cracks develop. This is shown graphically in Fig. 8-3.

Upon the removal of the applied load, the beam will return to its original position even though cracks have already developed, provided that the prestress in the steel has not suffered any losses due to the overload. There will, in general, be some residual deflection left in the beam, depending on the degree and duration of loading. Such residual deflection is often attributed to the plasticity of concrete and can amount to a few per cent of the total deflection upon the first application of the load, but will be hardly noticeable for the second and third similar applications. If the loading is sustained for some time, residual deflections will be produced as a result of creep but can be recovered in the course of time.

When cracks have developed to an appreciable degree, portions of the steel near and across the cracks may be stressed beyond the elastic or creep limit. In such cases, there will be loss of prestress upon the removal of the load. The amount of loss naturally depends on the degree of overload; if the amount of permanent deformation equals or exceeds the prestressed strain, the prestress can be entirely lost. Then, upon reloading, that section of the beam will behave like an unprestressed one reinforced with high-tensile steel. Cracks will appear much earlier, even though the ultimate load of rupture may not be decreased.

The above description of the deflections of beams applies to both bonded and unbonded beams. It is believed that unbonded beams are almost as strong as the bonded ones in so far as the elastic limit of steel is concerned. Bonded beams, however, can carry higher load before the eventual crushing of concrete.

After concrete has cracked, the cracks will reappear as soon as tensile stresses again exist in that portion. The tensile stress does not have to approach the modulus of rupture for the cracks to reappear. Hence, between the working load and the cracking load, the beam will deflect slightly more after it has been previously cracked.

EXAMPLE 8-2

For the beam in example 8-1, compute the center deflection due to a 10-k concentrated load applied at midspan, when the beam is 3 months old after prestressing.

Solution. If the beam is bonded, the moment of inertia for the section should be computed on the basis of the transformed section including steel, but it can be approximated by using the gross concrete section. Also note that the modulus of elasticity E_c may be greater at the time of application of load than at transfer, but will be assumed to be 4,000,000 psi for simplicity. Using the usual formula for deflection, we have

$$\Delta = \frac{PL^3}{48EI}$$

$$= \frac{10,000 \times 32^3 \times 12^3}{48 \times 4,000,000 \times (12 \times 18^3)/12}$$

$$= 0.505 \text{ in.}$$

which is the instantaneous downward deflection due to a load of 10 k. Since the deflection before the application of load was 0.407 in. upward, the resultant deflection is 0.505 − 0.407 = 0.098 in. downward. If the load is kept on for a time, the creep effect due to that load must be considered. Also, if the load is heavy enough to produce cracking, then the elastic theory for computing deflection can be used only as guidance for an approximation.

Experience has shown that it is difficult to predict cambers in prestressed concrete beams with any precision, because they vary not only with the E_c and creep of concrete, but also with age of concrete, actual support conditions, temperature and shrinkage differential between top and bottom fibers, and variation in properties between top and bottom concrete. It is generally necessary to get sufficient experience with the product of a particular plant before accurate prediction can be made. Lacking such reliable data, camber computation for pre-tensioned concrete with one-day strength of 4000 psi may be made on the basis of $E_c = 4,000,000$ psi for hard rock, and $E_c = 2,500,000$ psi for lightweight. These values should then be modified by the loss of prestress and the coefficient for flexural creep, which might be grossly approximated by the following table.

Age of Concrete	Ratio of Effective to Initial Steel Stress	Coefficient for Flexural Creep	
		Hard Rock	Lightweight
1-day	94%	1.0	1.0
3-day	91%	1.3	1.2
7-day	89%	1.6	1.3
30-day	86%	2.0	1.5
1-year	83%	2.5	1.8

For computing instantaneous deflection due to transient live load, a higher E_c should be assumed depending on the age of concrete, approximately as follows.

Age of Concrete	Modulus of Elasticity, psi	
	Hard Rock	Lightweight
1-day	4,000,000	2,500,000
7-day	4,500,000	3,000,000
30-day	5,000,000	3,400,000
1-year	5,500,000	3,800,000

This method can be quite inaccurate, when the loss of prestress is unusually high or low (as is true with certain lightweight concretes or with concrete under very high or very low prestress), when members having high span/depth ratio are subjected to a considerable initial camber, or when E_c and creep characteristics of the concrete are quite different from those given above. Under these conditions, it is advised that reliable values be obtained from available data and actual check on the members be made.

For pretensioned beams, the magnitude of prestress varies along the length of transfer at the ends. This variation can usually be neglected

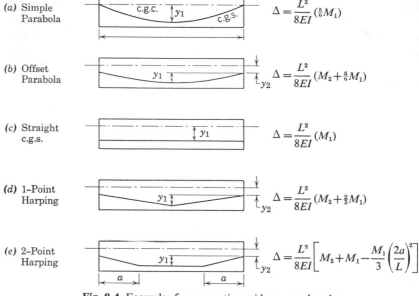

(a) Simple Parabola $\quad \Delta = \dfrac{L^2}{8EI}(\tfrac{5}{6}M_1)$

(b) Offset Parabola $\quad \Delta = \dfrac{L^2}{8EI}(M_2 + \tfrac{5}{6}M_1)$

(c) Straight c.g.s. $\quad \Delta = \dfrac{L^2}{8EI}(M_1)$

(d) 1-Point Harping $\quad \Delta = \dfrac{L^2}{8EI}(M_2 + \tfrac{2}{3}M_1)$

(e) 2-Point Harping $\quad \Delta = \dfrac{L^2}{8EI}\left[M_2 + M_1 - \dfrac{M_1}{3}\left(\dfrac{2a}{L}\right)^2\right]$

Fig. 8-4. Formulas for computing midspan camber due to prestress (simple beams).

in camber computations, but it may need to be taken into account when greater accuracy is desired.

It is good practice to balance the deflection resulting from dead load by the camber produced by the prestress whenever possible. When this is achieved, the flexural creep and the highly variable value of E_c will have little effect on the camber or deflection. Frequently, a designer can put a slight camber in the beam so that flexural creep tending to camber the beam upward will just about balance the downward deflection resulting from the loss of prestress. We should also note that if the initial camber is too small, sagging may eventually take place.

Some simple formulas are listed in Fig. 8-4 to help the computation of camber due to prestress. They are derived from the well-known moment-area principles. By isolating the value of M and grouping the terms L, E, and I together, arithmetical work is reduced, and checking of the answers made easier. In these formulas, the moment M at each section is computed by the prestress F (or more accurately the horizontal component of F) multiplied by the corresponding ordinate y as marked, thus

$$M_1 = Fy_1$$

and

$$M_2 = Fy_2$$

Accurate data are lacking concerning the deflection of prestressed concrete beams after cracking. Because of the slenderness of most of these beams, they can deflect considerably before ultimate collapse. Hence they are quite resilient in the plastic as well as in the elastic range and possess a high energy-absorption capacity. The ultimate angular rotation of a beam section may be approximated by locating the ultimate neutral axis and using a maximum unit compressive strain in the concrete of 0.34%. The ultimate deflection of a beam can be accurately determined by a summation procedure if the moment-curvature relationship is known for all sections of a beam. It is noted that when a beam fails, only a limited portion develops its full rotational capacity while most other portions will be subjected to smaller moments and hence smaller rotation.

8-2 Simple Beam Layout

The layout of a simple prestressed-concrete beam is controlled by two critical sections: the maximum moment and the end sections. After these sections are designed, intermediate ones can often be determined by inspection but should be separately investigated when necessary. The maximum moment section is controlled by two loading stages, the initial stage at transfer with minimum moment M_G acting on the beam and the working-load stage with maximum design moment M_T. The end sections are controlled by the area required for shear resistance, bearing plates, anchorage spacings, and jacking clearances. All intermediate sections are designed by one or more of the above requirements, depending on their respective distances from the above controlling sections. A common arrangement for post-tensioned members is to employ some shape, such as I or T, for the maximum moment section and to round it out into a simple rectangular shape near the ends. For pre-tensioned members, produced on a long line process, a uniform I, T, double-T, or cored section is employed throughout, in order to facilitate production. The design for individual sections having been explained in Chapters 5, 6, and 7, the general cable layout of simple beams will now be discussed.

The layout of a beam can be adjusted by varying both the concrete and the steel. The section of concrete can be varied as to its height, width, shape, and the curvature of its soffit or extrados. The steel can be varied occasionally in its area but mostly in its position relative to the centroidal axis of concrete. By adjusting these variables, many combinations of layout are possible to suit different loading conditions. This is quite different from the design of reinforced-concrete beams, where the usual layout is either a uniform rectangular section or a uniform T-section and the position of steel is always as near the bottom fibers as is possible.

Consider first the pre-tensioned beams, Fig. 8-5. Here straight cables are preferred, since they can be more easily tensioned between two abutments. Let us start with a straight cable in a straight beam of uniform

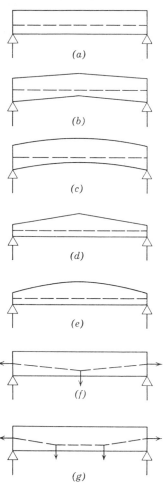

Fig. 8-5. Layouts for pre-tensioned beams.

section, (a). This is simple as far as form and workmanship are concerned. But such a section cannot often be economically designed, because of the conflicting requirements of the midspan and end sections. At the maximum moment section generally occurring at midspan, it is best to place the cable as near the bottom as possible in order to provide the maximum lever arm for the internal resisting moment. When the M_G at midspan is appreciable, it is possible to place the c.g.s. much below the kern without producing tension in the top fibers at transfer. The end section, however, presents an entirely different set of requirements. Since there is no external moment at the end, it is best to arrange the tendons so that the c.g.s. will coincide with the c.g.c. at the end section, so as to obtain a uniform stress distribution. In any case, it is necessary to place the c.g.s. within the kern if tensile stresses are not permitted at the ends, and not too far outside the kern if at all possible.

It is not possible to meet the conflicting requirements of both the midspan and the end sections by a layout such as (a). For example, if the c.g.s. is located all along the lower kern point, which is the lowest point permitted by the end section, a satisfactory lever arm is not yet attained for the internal resisting moment at midspan. If the c.g.s. is located below the kern, a bigger lever arm is obtained for resisting the moment at midspan, but stress distribution will be more unfavorable at the ends. Besides, too much camber may result from such a layout, since the entire length of the beam is subjected to negative bending due to prestress. In spite of these objections, this simple arrangement is often used, especially for short spans.

For a uniform concrete section and a straight cable, it is possible to get a more desirable layout than (*a*) by simply varying the soffit of the beam, as in Fig. 8-5(*b*) and (*c*); (*b*) has a bent soffit, while (*c*) has a curved one. For both layouts, the c.g.s. at midspan can be depressed as low as desired, while that at the ends can be kept near the c.g.c. If the soffit can be varied at will, it is possible to obtain a curvature that will best fit the given loading condition, for example, a parabolic soffit will suit a uniform loading. While these two layouts are efficient in resisting moment and favorable in stress distribution, they possess three disadvantages. First, the formwork is more complicated than in (*a*). Second, the curved or bent soffit is often impractical in a structure, for architectural or functional reasons. Third, they cannot be easily produced on a long-line pre-tensioning bed.

When it is possible to vary the extrados of concrete, a layout like Fig. 8-5(*d*) or (*e*) can be advantageously employed. These will give a favorable height at midspan, where it is most needed, and yet yield a concentric or nearly concentric prestress at end sections. Since the depth is reduced for the end sections, they must be checked for shear resistance. For (*d*), it should also be noted that the critical section may not be at midspan but rather at some point away from it where the depth has decreased appreciably while the external moment is still near the maximum. Beam (*d*), however, is simpler in formwork than (*e*), which has a curved extrados.

Most pre-tensioning plants in the United States have buried anchors along the stressing beds so that the tendons for a pre-tensioned beam can be bent, Fig. 8-5(*f*) and (*g*). It may be economical to do so, if the beam has to be of straight and uniform section, and if the M_G is heavy enough to warrant such additional expense of bending. Means must be provided to reduce the frictional loss of prestress produced by the bending of the tendons. For example, the tendons may be tensioned first from the ends and then bent at the harping points.

It is evident from the above discussion that many different layouts are possible. Only some basic forms are described here, the variations and combinations being left to the discretion of the designer. The correct layout for each structure will depend upon the local conditions and the practical requirements as well as upon theoretical considerations.

Most of the layouts for pre-tensioned beams can be used for post-tensioned ones as well. But, for post-tensioned beams, Fig. 8-6, it is not necessary to keep the tendons straight, since slightly bent or curved tendons can be as easily tensioned as straight ones. Thus, for a beam of straight and uniform section, the tendons are very often curved as in Fig. 8-6(*a*). Curving the tendons will permit favorable positions of c.g.s. to be obtained at both the end and midspan sections, and other points as well.

A combination of curved or bent tendons with curved or bent soffits is frequently used, Fig. 8-6(*b*), when straight soffits are not required. This will permit a smaller curvature in the tendons, thus reducing the friction.

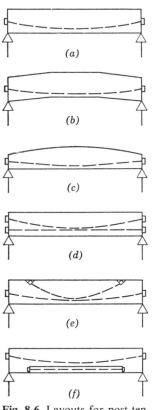

Fig. 8-6. Layouts for post-tensioned beams.

Curved or bent cables are also combined with beams of variable depth, as in (*c*). Combinations of straight and curved tendons are sometimes found convenient, as in (*d*).

Variable steel area along the length of a beam is occasionally preferred. This calls for special design of the beam and involves details which may offset its economy in weight of steel. In Fig. 8-6(*e*), some cables are bent upward and anchored at top flanges. In (*f*), some cables are stopped part way in the bottom flange. These arrangements will save some steel but may not be justified unless the saving is considerable as for very long spans carrying heavy loads.

8-3   Cable Profiles

It is stated in the previous section that the layout of simple beams is controlled by the maximum moment and end sections so that, after these two sections are designed, other sections can often be determined by inspection. It sometimes happens, however, that intermediate points along the beam may also be critical, and in many instances it would be desirable to determine the permissible and desirable profile for the tendons. To do this, a limiting zone for the location of c.g.s. is first obtained, then the tendons are arranged so that their centroid will lie within that zone.

The method described here is intended for simple beams, but it also serves as an introduction to the solution of more complicated layouts, such as cantilever and continuous spans, where cable location cannot be easily determined by inspection. The method is a graphical one, giving the limiting zone within which the c.g.s. must pass in order that no tensile stresses will be produced. Compressive stresses in concrete are not checked by this method. It is assumed that the layout of the concrete

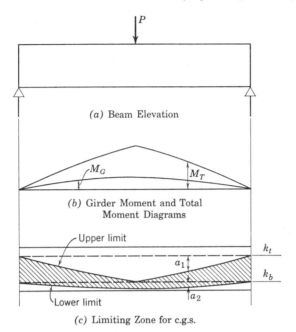

(a) Beam Elevation

(b) Girder Moment and Total
Moment Diagrams

(c) Limiting Zone for c.g.s.

Fig. 8-7. Location of limiting zone for c.g.s.

sections and the area of prestressing steel have already been determined.
Only the profile of the c.g.s. is to be located.

Referring to Fig. 8-7, having determined the layout of concrete sections, we proceed to compute their kern points, thus yielding two kern
lines, one top and one bottom, (c). Note that for variable sections, these
kern lines would be curved, although for convenience they are shown
straight in the figure.

For a beam loaded as shown in (a), the minimum and maximum moment diagrams for the girder load and for the total working load respectively are marked as M_G and M_T in (b). In order that, under the working
load, the center of pressure, the C-line, will not fall above the top kern
line, it is evident that the c.g.s. must be located below the top kern at
least a distance

$$a_1 = M_T/F \qquad (8\text{-}1)$$

If the c.g.s. falls above that upper limit at any point, then the C-line
corresponding to moment M_T and prestress F will fall above the top kern,
resulting in tension in the bottom fiber.

Similarly, in order that the C-line will not fall below the bottom kern
line, the c.g.s. line must not be positioned below the bottom kern by a

distance greater than

$$a_2 = M_G/F_0 \tag{8-2}$$

which gives the lower limit for the location of c.g.s. If the c.g.s. is positioned above that lower limit, it is seen that the C-line will be above the bottom kern and there will be no tension in the top fiber under the girder load and initial prestress F_0.

Thus, it becomes clear that the limiting zone for c.g.s. is given by the shaded area in Fig. 8-7(c), in order that no tension will exist both under the girder load and under the working load. The individual tendons, however, may be placed in any position so long as the c.g.s. of all the cables remains within the limiting zone.

The position and width of the limiting zone are often an indication of the adequacy and economy of design, Fig. 8-8. If some portion of the upper limit falls outside or too near the bottom fiber, in (*a*), either the prestress F or the depth of beam at that portion should be increased. On the other hand, if it falls too far above the bottom fiber, in (*b*), either the prestress or the beam depth can be reduced. If the lower limit crosses the upper limit, in (*c*), it means that no zone is available for the location of c.g.s., and either the prestress F or the beam depth must be increased or the girder moment must be increased to depress the lower limit if that can be done.

The application of the above graphical method is illustrated in example 8-3.

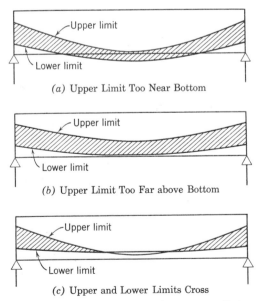

(*a*) Upper Limit Too Near Bottom

(*b*) Upper Limit Too Far above Bottom

(*c*) Upper and Lower Limits Cross

Fig. 8-8. Undesirable positions for c.g.s. zone limits.

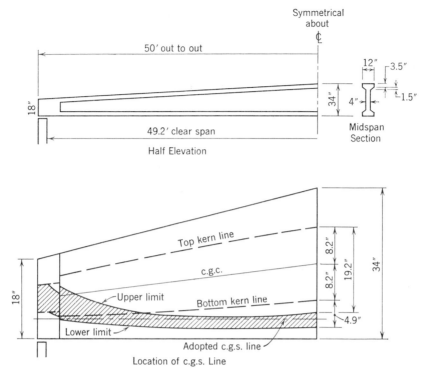

Fig. 8-9. Example 8-3.

EXAMPLE 8-3

Preliminary design for a 50-ft pre-tensioned beam gives a layout with tapered top flange and symmetrical I-sections as shown in Fig. 8-9. Ten steel wires of $\frac{3}{8}$-in. diameter with anchorages are used for prestressing. $f_0 = 130$ ksi, $f_s = 110$ ksi, $f_c' = 5000$ psi. Determine the position for the c.g.s. line. Live and superimposed dead load on the beam totals 450 plf, in addition to the weight of the beam itself. $M_G = 58$ k-ft and $M_T = 194$ k-ft at midspan.

Solution. To get an accurate graphical solution, 4 or 5 points should be calculated for half of the span, but only calculations for the midspan section will be shown here. Note that the sections near the end are of rectangular shape; hence there is a sudden jump in the kern lines at the junction. Also, theoretically, there is no external moment for the portions directly over the supports.

First, locate the kern lines. Values for the midspan section are as follows:

$$I \text{ of section} = 28{,}200 \text{ in.}^4$$

$$A \text{ of section} = 204 \text{ in.}^2$$

$$r^2 \text{ of section} = 140 \text{ in.}^2$$

$$k_t \text{ and } k_b = 140/17 = 8.2 \text{ in.}$$

With $F = 10 \times 0.11 \times 110 = 121$ kips, minimum resisting arm required for M_T is, from equation 8-1,

$$M_T/F = (194 \times 12)/121 = 19.2 \text{ in.}$$

which is measured down from the top kern line and located as shown.

For initial prestress $F_0 = 10 \times 0.11 \times 130 = 143$ k, the lever arm corresponding to $M_G = 58$ k-ft is, from equation 8-2,

$$M_G/F_0 = (58 \times 12)/143 = 4.9 \text{ in.}$$

These limiting points are calculated for several other sections, and the limiting zone is indicated by the shaded area. Straight tendons are preferred for pretensioning, while it is impossible to get a straight c.g.s. line within this shaded area. The best recourse in this design is perhaps to permit some tension near the supports and to reinforce the ends with some mild steel. Then it is possible to adopt a c.g.s. line as shown which will result in no tension in the bottom fibers under working loads but will have some tension in the top fibers near the supports. If such tension is to be avoided, it will be necessary to use a greater prestressing force, thus raising the upper limit of the zone and enabling a c.g.s. line to be located at about 6 in. from the bottom. Deflection of this beam at transfer should be computed to see whether the camber is excessive, but it will not be illustrated in this example.

The location of the c.g.s. line as just described is based on the elastic theory, allowing no tensile stress both at transfer and under the working loads. If some tension is permitted, then it is possible to place the c.g.s. line slightly outside the previous limiting zone. Referring to Fig. 8-10, for an allowable tensile stress of f_t' in the top fibers at transfer, we have

$$f_t' = \frac{Mc_t}{I}$$

$$= \frac{F_0 e_b c_t}{I} \tag{8-3}$$

where $e_b = $ the amount c.g.s. may fall below the lower limit. For an allowable tensile stress of f_b' in the bottom fibers under the working load,

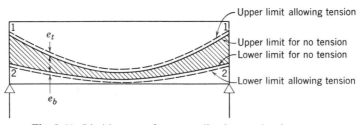

Fig. 8-10. Limiting zone for c.g.s. allowing tension in concrete.

we have

$$f_b' = \frac{Fe_t c_b}{I} \qquad (8\text{-}4)$$

where $e_t =$ the amount c.g.s. may rise above the upper limit. From equations 8-3 and 8-4, we can write

$$e_b = \frac{f_t' I}{F_0 c_t} = \frac{f_t' A k_b}{F_0} \qquad (8\text{-}5)$$

and

$$e_t = \frac{f_b' I}{F c_b} = \frac{f_b' A k_t}{F} \qquad (8\text{-}6)$$

Hence, the limiting zones for no tensile stresses can be extended to lines 1-1 and 2-2 if some tensile stresses are permitted, Fig. 8-10.

The above graphical method can also be applied when there are changes in the cross-sectional area of steel. It is only necessary to use the corresponding value of prestress existing at the particular point when computing the position of the limiting zone. Thus, at points of change in the steel area, there will be sudden jumps in the limiting lines. If the prestress is

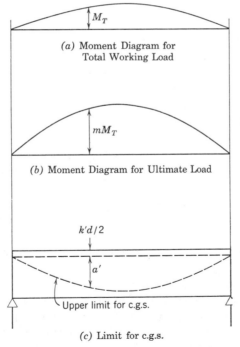

(a) Moment Diagram for
Total Working Load

(b) Moment Diagram for Ultimate Load

(c) Limit for c.g.s.

Fig. 8-11. Location of c.g.s. by ultimate design.

applied in two stages, two lower limits should be computed, each based on its own prestressing force. However, if too many complications are involved, the graphical method may not be efficient.

If ultimate-strength design is to be used, the c.g.s. line can also be located by a graphical method, Fig. 8-11. But, since ultimate design applies only to the maximum loading stage, the lower limit for the c.g.s. still has to be determined by the elastic theory or some other method. The upper limit, however, can be obtained by the ultimate theory as follows. If M_T is the total moment, and m the load factor, then the ultimate moment is mM_T, which is to be resisted by the ultimate strength of the steel (in the case of bonded reinforcement) with a level arm,

$$a' = \frac{mM_T}{A_s f_s'}$$

The line of pressure at ultimate load is located at $k'd/2$ below top fiber, where $k'd$ is obtained by

$$k'd = \frac{A_s f_s'}{k_1 f_c' b}$$

if a uniform width b is obtained for the top flange at the ultimate load.

8-4   Cantilever Beam Layout

Because of the balancing and reduction of moments, cantilever beams can be economically utilized in prestressed-concrete structures, especially for certain favorable span ratios and for long and heavy beams. The basic theories and methods for the design of cantilever beams are the same as those for simple beams. But the work of designing is more complicated, because of several factors which must be more carefully considered. These are

1. Certain portions of a cantilever are subjected to both positive and negative moments, depending on the position of live loads.

2. To obtain most severe loading conditions, partial loading of the spans must sometimes be considered.

3. In a cantilever, moments produced by loads on a certain portion are often counterbalanced by loads on other portions. Hence the moments are sensitive to changes in external load. Because of this, the sequence of the application of superimposed loads on the beam must be carefully considered and executed.

4. If the beam is precast, care must be exercised during erection and transportation of the beam. At all times the supporting conditions assumed in design must be realized for the beam. Even slight changes in the position of supports may affect the moments seriously.

5. Cantilever beams are more sensitive to temperature changes which might result in excessive deflections.

6. The ultimate capacity of cantilever beams may be relatively low if heavy partial loading is a possibility. The coexistence of high moment and shear at certain critical sections may also tend to reduce the ultimate strength in a cantilever.

In spite of the complications, cantilever beams are often used, because of their economy and their adaptability to certain structures. In fact, the above-mentioned complications should not be held against the use of cantilever beams. They only indicate that greater care must be exercised in their design and construction.

Two general layouts are possible for cantilevers: the single and the double cantilevers. Some typical layouts for the single cantilevers are shown in Fig. 8-12. (*a*) shows the layout for a short span with a short

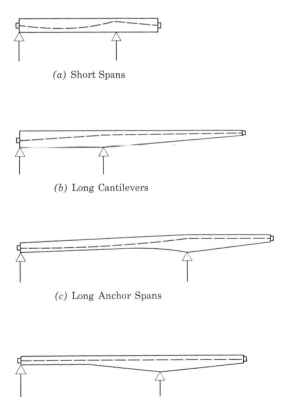

(*a*) Short Spans

(*b*) Long Cantilevers

(*c*) Long Anchor Spans

(*d*) Straight Tendons

Fig. 8-12. Typical layouts for single cantilevers.

cantilever, where a straight and uniform section may be the most economical. In such a design, it is only necessary to vary the c.g.s. profile so that it will conform with the requirements of the moment diagrams. When the cantilever span becomes longer, it is advisable to taper the beam as in (*b*). If the anchor span is short compared to the cantilever, it may be entirely subjected to negative moments, and the c.g.s. may have to be located above the c.g.c. at all points.

For longer anchor spans, it may be desirable to haunch them as in (*c*) and (*d*). Then the c.g.s. profile can be properly curved as in (*c*) or may remain practically straight as in (*d*) where conditions permit.

For short double cantilevers, a straight and uniform section can be adopted as shown in Fig. 8-13(*a*). When the cantilevers are long, they may be tapered as in (*b*). If the anchor span is long, it may be haunched as in (*c*). If the anchor span is short compared with the cantilevers, the c.g.s. line may lie near the top of the beam at all points, as in (*d*).

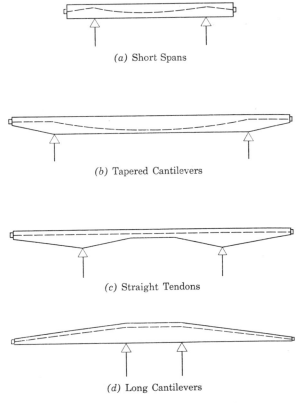

(*a*) Short Spans

(*b*) Tapered Cantilevers

(*c*) Straight Tendons

(*d*) Long Cantilevers

Fig. 8-13. Typical layouts for double cantilevers.

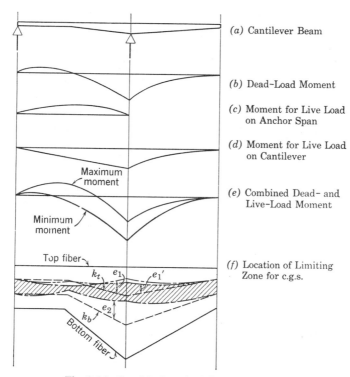

(a) Cantilever Beam

(b) Dead–Load Moment

(c) Moment for Live Load on Anchor Span

(d) Moment for Live Load on Cantilever

(e) Combined Dead- and Live-Load Moment

(f) Location of Limiting Zone for c.g.s.

Fig. 8-14. Graphical method for location c.g.s.

Cable location for cantilevers can be obtained graphically as for simple beams, except that more thought should be given to the possibilities of partial live loads and the reversal of moments. Figure 8-14(a) shows a cantilever beam. Assume that the beam is under the action of its own weight and the action of uniform live load on any portion. Moment due to dead weight of the beam is pictured in (b). Moment due to live load on the anchor span is shown in (c); that due to live load on the cantilever is shown in (d). For convenience in discussion, maximum moment will signify the greatest positive or the smallest negative moment, while minimum moment will mean the smallest positive or the greatest negative moments. So, for this beam, the maximum moment will be given by (b) + (c), and the minimum moments by (b) + (d). Both are plotted in (e).

In order to obtain the limiting zone for the c.g.s. line, first plot the top and bottom kern lines for the beam, k_t and k_b lines in (f). If no tension is permitted in the concrete, one limiting line is obtained by plotting from each kern line the permissible eccentricity e, with

$$e = M/F$$

274 design of prestressed concrete structures

Note that e may be plotted from either the k_t or the k_b line, whichever gives the more critical limit. But e due to $+M$ is always plotted downward, since it tends to shift the required c.g.s. line downward. By similar reasoning, e due to $-M$ is always plotted upward. In general the upper limit for the zone is plotted from the k_t line with a distance

$$e_1 = M_{max}/F$$

The lower limit for the zone is plotted from the k_b line with a distance

$$e_2 = M_{min}/F$$

Consideration should also be given to the action of dead load alone, since in this case we may have the initial prestress which is greater than the effective prestress and may impose a more critical situation. With the dead load acting alone, another limit is obtained by plotting from the k_t line a distance

$$e_1' = M_G/F_0$$

again plotting the $+M$ downward and the $-M$ upward. In this figure it is not necessary to plot e_1' from the k_b line, because evidently it will not be controlling. When plotted from the k_t line, it is seen that, for certain portions of the beam, e_1' will be controlling rather than e_1. The resulting limiting zone is shaded as in (f).

For long cantilevers carrying heavy loads, it is sometimes economical to cut off some of the prestressing wires at intermediate points. The number and location of cut-offs can also be established by a graphical method, which is the reverse of the above procedure and will be illustrated in example 8-4.

EXAMPLE 8-4

Compute the variation of steel area required along the 140-ft length of the cantilever roof girder having a layout as shown in Fig. 8-15. Given the following data.

1. Concrete: $f_c' = 5000$ psi, allowable $f_c = 2250$ psi for working load, and 2500 psi under initial prestress, allowable tension in concrete $= 0$ under working load.

2. Steel: $f_s = 240{,}000$ psi, initial prestress $= 150{,}000$ psi, final effective prestress $= 125{,}000$ psi.

3. Live load and superimposed dead load $= 1.60$ k per linear foot of girder, producing moment at support

$$wL^2/2 = 1.60 \times 140^2/2 = 15{,}700 \text{ k-ft}$$

4. Moments due to weight of girder: For the trial layout, the girder load moments are computed for various points on the cantilever, with a maximum of 15,200 k-ft at the support.

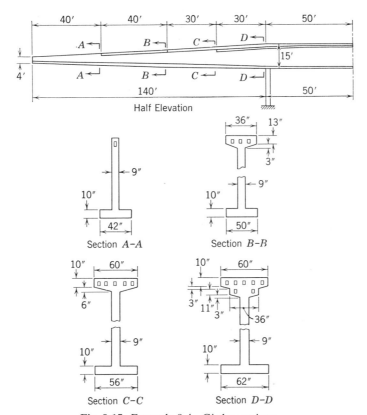

Fig. 8-15. Example 8-4. Girder sections.

Solution. After some preliminary investigation, it is found that, owing to the relatively heavy girder load moment, there will exist compressive stresses along most of the bottom flange. Hence it is not necessary to check for any tensile stress in the bottom flange except near the cantilevering end. For the given layout, the c.g.s. line is computed and plotted in Fig. 8-16. The resisting lever arm a_1 available for the internal resisting couple is measured from the c.g.s. line to the k_b line at each point. Corresponding to a_1, the minimum amount of prestress required is

$$F = M_T/a_1$$

and the steel area required is

$$A_s = F/125 = M_T/125a_1$$

Similarly, the maximum steel permitted without producing tension in the bottom fiber is

$$A_s = M_G/150a_2$$

where a_2 is the distance between the c.g.s. and the k_t lines.

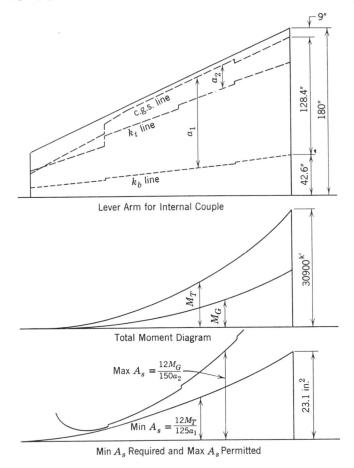

Lever Arm for Internal Couple

Total Moment Diagram

$$\text{Max } A_s = \frac{12M_G}{150a_2}$$

$$\text{Min } A_s = \frac{12M_T}{125a_1}$$

Min A_s Required and Max A_s Permitted

Fig. 8-16. Example 8-4.   Computation for A_s.

First, the M_T and M_G moment diagrams are drawn. Next the distances a_1 and a_2 between the c.g.s. line and the k_b and k_t lines are measured. Then the minimum and maximum A_s lines are computed by the above formulas. Several points may be necessary for an accurate determination of these curves, but only some sample computations will be illustrated here. At the support, the total moment is

$$M_T = 15{,}200 + 15{,}700 = 30{,}900 \text{ k-ft}$$

The c.g.s. is located 9 in. from the top, and the k_b is located 42.6 in. above the bottom fibers; hence the available lever arm a_1 is

$$a_1 = 180 - 42.6 - 9 = 128.4 \text{ in.}$$

The minimum area of steel required at the support is, therefore,

$$\min A_s = \frac{M_T}{125a_1} = \frac{30,900 \times 12}{125 \times 128.4} = 23.1 \text{ sq in.}$$

At 35 ft from the cantilevering end,

$$M_G = 600 \text{ k-ft}$$

a_2 is measured to be 10.5 in. The maximum steel area permitted at this point is

$$\max A_s = \frac{M_G}{150a_2} = \frac{600 \times 12}{150 \times 10.5} = 4.57 \text{ sq in.}$$

Similar computations are made for other points, and the curves are drawn as shown. It will be seen that the maximum A_s curve is actually required only for a short portion of the beam near the cantilevering end. Keeping as close as possible to the minimum A_s curve, but without crossing the maximum A_s curve, the adopted steel area may be tailored and cut off as desired.

The checking of compressive stresses in concrete and other design features will not be discussed here. Note that all moments are obviously negative in this solution, hence no particular attention has been paid to the signs of the moments.

One advantage of such a graphical solution is that it gives a visual presentation. The variations of the lever arm a_1 and a_2 and of the A_s curves both follow certain simple laws so that necessary modifications to suit changes in design can be easily made, either by shifting the c.g.s. location or by varying the steel areas.

8-5 Span-Depth Ratio Limitations

For reasons of economy and esthetics, higher span-depth ratios are almost always used for prestressed concrete than for reinforced concrete. Higher ratios are possible because deflection can be much better controlled in prestressed design. On the other hand, when these ratios get too high, camber and deflection become quite sensitive to variations in loadings, in properties of materials, in magnitude and location of prestress, and in temperature. Furthermore, the effects of vibration become more pronounced.

It is difficult to establish a simple set of span-depth ratio limitations because the proper limitation, for prestressed as for other types of construction, should vary with the nature and magnitude of the live load, the damping characteristics, the boundary conditions, the shape and variations of the section, the modulus of elasticity, and the length of span itself. In fact, if a structure is carefully investigated for possible camber, deflections, and vibrations, there is no reason to adhere to any set ratio. However, as a result of accumulated experience, the following values may be taken as a preliminary guide for building designs.

For cantilever solid slabs, a span-depth ratio of 18 for floors and 20 for roofs has been found to be satisfactory. But cantilevers are sensitive to deflections and vibrations, and greater care should be taken. For example, a camber in the anchor span would usually produce a dip in the cantilever

TABLE 8-1

Approximate Limits for Span-Depth Ratios

	Continuous Spans		Simple Spans	
	Roof	Floor	Roof	Floor
One-way solid slabs	52	48	48	44
Two-way solid slabs (supported on columns only)	48	44	44	40
Two-way waffle slabs (3′ waffles)	40	36	36	32
Two-way waffle slabs (12′ waffles)	36	32	32	28
One-way slabs with small cores	50	46	46	42
One-way slabs with large cores	48	44	44	40
Double tees and single tees (side by side)	44	40	40	36
Single tees (spaced 20-ft centers)	36	32	32	28

Generally speaking, when span-depth ratios are some 10% below the tabulated values, problems of camber, deflection, and vibration should not occur unless the loadings are extremely heavy and vibratory in nature. Occasionally, these ratios can be exceeded by 10% or more, if careful study would justify and ensure proper behavior.

The above values are intended for both hard-rock concrete and lightweight concrete, but should be reduced by about 5% for lightweight concrete having E_c less than 3,000,000 psi. For long spans (say, in excess of about 70 ft) and for heavy loads (say, line loads over 100 psf) the above values should be reduced by 5 to 10%. For in-place concrete in composite action with the precast elements, the total depth may be considered in computing the above span-depth ratios.

It should be emphasized that the above table is intended as a guide and should not be applied blindly, without considering the local conditions. For example, the degree of continuity (whether full or partial), the existence of rigid frame action, the reliability of the production and construction control, and the local temperature differential will all affect the ratio limitations.

The problem of objectionable vibration can be studied by determining the amplitude and the natural frequency of the structure.[2] Human sensitivity to vibration increases with the frequency and the amplitude. When vibration is produced by mechanical loading, the degree of damage is also proportional to the frequency and the amplitude. The synchronization of the applied loading with the natural frequency of the structure will, of course, amplify the vibration, whereas damping would help to minimize the effects.

Little experience has been obtained for railway bridges of prestressed concrete to justify any limitation on their span-depth ratios; the usual ratios have been in the range of 10 to 14 for box sections up to 100 ft or more. For simple-span highway bridges of the I-beam type, up to about 200 ft, a span-depth of 20 is considered conservative, 22 to 24 is normal, while 26 to 28 would be the critical limit. Box sections can have ratios about 5 to 10% higher than I-beams, while T-sections spaced far apart should have ratios about 5 to 10% lower than I beams. Again, there is no reason to believe that a fixed span-depth ratio will apply to all cases. The effect of continuity, of varying moment of inertia, etc., should be considered. The Union Oil Pedestrian Bridge, Fig. 11-22, has a structural depth of 27 in. spanning 102 ft (a span-depth ratio of 45), but was carefully designed to take care of camber, deflection, and vibrations. It has behaved in a very satisfactory manner since its completion in 1956.

References

1 S. L. Bugg, "Long-time Creep of Prestressed Concrete I-beams," *Technical Report R-212*, U.S. Naval Civil Engineering Laboratory, Port Hueneme, California, 1962.
2 "Vibrations in Buildings," *Building Research Station Digest*, No. 78, London, England, June 1955.

9 *partial prestress and nonprestressed reinforcements*

9-1 Partial Prestress and Beam Behavior

When prestressed concrete was introduced in the 1930's, the philosophy of design was to create a new material by putting concrete under compression so that there would never be any tension in it, at least not under working loads. In the later 1940's, observations on those earlier structures indicated that often extra strength existed in them. Therefore some engineers believed that a certain amount of tensile stresses could be permitted in design. In contrast to the earlier criterion of no tensile stress, which may be called "full prestressing," this later method of design allowing some tension is often termed "partial prestressing." As discussed in section 6-4, there is no basic difference between the two, because, although a structure may be designed for no tension under working loads, it will be subjected to tension under overloads. Therefore the difference is rather a matter of degree; tensile stresses will be higher and occur more frequently for the same structure if designed for partial prestressing rather than full prestressing.

In order to provide additional safety for partially prestressed concrete, nonprestressed reinforcements are often added to give higher ultimate strength to the beam, and to help carry the tensile stresses in the concrete. For these beams, some of the reinforcements are prestressed and others are not. This situation also lends itself to the use of the term "partial prestress," so that, sometimes, "partial prestress" may mean either or both of the following two conditions, although more frequently it is employed to denote the first condition only.

1. Tensile stresses are permitted in the concrete under working loads. Design on that basis is described in sections 6-4 through 6-6.

2. Nonprestressed reinforcements are employed in the member. This condition will be described in the following sections of this chapter.

An important advantage of partial prestressing is the decrease in the

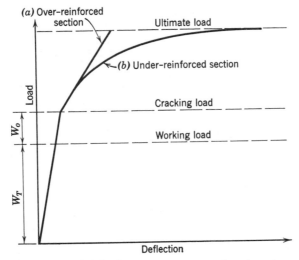

Fig. 9-1. Load-deflection curves, over- and under-reinforced sections.

amount of camber. Minimizing camber is important especially when the girder load or the dead load is relatively small compared to the total design load. Minimizing the initial camber also means decreasing the effect of flexural creep and easier control of the uniformity of camber.

In order to understand the design of partially prestressed beams, it is necessary to study the behavior of such beams with varying amount of reinforcement and subjected to varying amount of prestress.[1] The difference in behavior of over-reinforced and under-reinforced beams is seen by comparing curves (*a*) and (*b*) of Fig. 9-1. The difference in behavior of over-prestressed and under-prestressed beams is seen by comparing curves (*a*), (*b*), (*c*), and (*d*) in Fig. 9-2.

When a section is over-reinforced, Fig. 9-1, it will fail by compression in concrete before the steel is stressed beyond its elastic limit. Thus, the ultimate deformation of the steel and the ultimate deflection of the beam are rather small, and the failure is brittle. When seriously over-reinforced, even if the steel is not prestressed, the deflection of the beam before rupture will still be limited. When a section is under-reinforced, its deflection increases very appreciably before failure, thus giving ample warning of impending collapse. Failure starts in the excessive elongation of steel and ends in the gradual crushing of concrete on the compressive side.

In order to avoid sudden and brittle failures, and also for general economy in design, most beams are under-reinforced. When an under-reinforced section is designed for full prestressing, allowing no tension

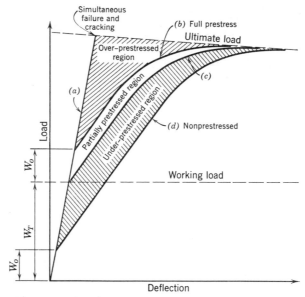

Fig. 9-2. Load-deflection curves for varying degrees of pre-stress (for under-reinforced sections of bonded beams).

in concrete under the working loads, the load-deflection relation is given by curve (*b*) of Fig. 9-2. Before cracking, the section will carry an additional load W_0 above the working load W_T, the magnitude of that additional load being

$$W_0 = k \, \frac{f'I}{c_b}$$

where k is a constant depending on the span length and end conditions, f' is the modulus of rupture, and c_b the distance from c.g.c. to the tensile extreme fibers.

If the same under-reinforced section with the same amount of steel is given somewhat smaller prestress so that cracking is reached just at the working load, the tensile stress being equal to the modulus of rupture under working load, the load-deflection relation will be given by curve (*c*), where the deflection corresponding to the cracked section starts at the working load. If the beam is not prestressed at all, but still reinforced with the same amount of steel, provided that the steel is bonded to the concrete, the beam will behave as in curve (*d*). It will start cracking as soon as load W_0 is reached, although its ultimate strength may not be greatly reduced.

If the beam is over-prestressed, it will crack only after the load exceeds $W_T + W_0$, and its load-deflection curve will fall between curves (*a*) and (*b*), Fig. 9-2. In the extreme case, when the beam is very much under-reinforced but highly over-prestressed, cracking and failure may take place simultaneously so that brittle failure occurs with sudden rupture in the steel. In principle, a partially prestressed beam may have a load-deflection curve lying anywhere between curves (*b*) and (*d*), depending on the amount of prestress. But, in practice, seldom is cracking permitted for prestressed concrete under working load; hence the actual load-deflection curve will usually fall between curves (*b*) and (*c*), and seldom below curve (*c*).

The desired amount of prestress will depend on the type of service to which the structure is to be subjected. For structures in which the possibility of cracking under working loads must be avoided and where overload might occur rather frequently, full prestress yielding load-deflection curve (*b*) is preferred. For structures which are seldom overloaded, such as certain types of buildings, partial prestress between curves (*b*) and (*c*) may be permitted. Some prestressing steel is saved by designing for partial prestress, but, if the same ultimate strength is desired, at least the same amount of total reinforcement must be used.

The area under the load-deflection curve is a measure of the ability of a beam to stand impact load and to absorb shocks. Hence it is seen that both the fully and the partially prestressed beams will supply a fairly large amount of resilience, while both the over-prestressed and the under-prestressed ones will supply appreciably less. The over-prestressed beams will possess less plastic energy, while the under-prestressed ones will absorb less elastic energy.

Partial prestress may be obtained by any of the following measures.

1. By using less steel for prestressing; this will save steel, but will also decrease the ultimate strength, which is almost directly proportional to the amount of steel.

2. By using the same amount of high-tensile steel, but leaving some nonprestressed; this will save some tensioning and anchorage, and may increase resilience at the sacrifice of earlier cracking and slightly smaller ultimate strength.

3. By using the same amount of steel, but tensioning them to a lower level; the effects of this are similar to those of method 2, but no end anchorages are saved.

4. By using less prestressed steel and adding some mild steel for reinforcing; this will give the desired ultimate strength and will result in greater resilience at the expense of earlier cracking.

The engineer must use his own judgment as to which method is desirable for his particular structure.

The advantages and disadvantages of partial prestress as compared to full prestress may be now summarized.

Advantages

1. Better control of camber.
2. Saving in the amount of prestressing steel.
3. Saving in the work of tensioning and of end anchorages.
4. Possible greater resilience in the structure.
5. Economical utilization of mild steel.

Disadvantages

1. Earlier appearance of cracks.
2. Greater deflection under overloads.
3. Higher principal tensile stress under working loads.
4. Slight decrease in ultimate flexural strength for the same amount of steel.

9-2   Uses of Nonprestressed Reinforcements

One of the more recent developments in prestressed concrete is the use of nonprestressed flange reinforcements.[2] These reinforcements can be made up of high-tensile wires, wire strands, bars, or merely ordinary mild-steel bars. When used in conjunction with prestressed steel, they form an effective combination, one supplementing the other. The prestressed steel balances a portion of the load, reduces the deflection, and supplies the major part of the strength, while the nonprestressed steel distributes the cracks, increases the ultimate strength, reinforces those portions not readily reached by prestressed steel, and provides additional safety for unexpected conditions of loading. With proper design, both economy and safety can be attained in many cases. Although not too many experiments are yet available regarding the exact behavior of such designs, the general nature is known and numerous structures have been built utilizing such combinations.

Nonprestressed reinforcements can be placed at various positions of a prestressed beam to serve different purposes and to help carry the loading at different stages. Often, one set of these reinforcements can serve to strengthen the beam in several ways. This will become evident upon examining the following functions performed by them.

1. To provide strength immediately after transfer of prestress:

A. When the compressive flange may be under some tension at transfer, nonprestressed steel will help to reinforce that flange against any possible fracture, Fig. 9-3(a). This design is often desirable when the beam's own weight is small compared to its live load. The use of such nonprestressed

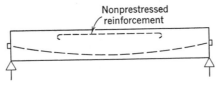

(a) To Carry Tension Due to Prestress
at Center of Span

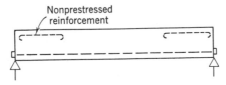

(b) To Carry Tension Due to Prestress
at Ends of Span

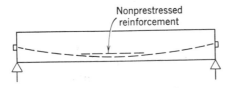

(c) To Carry Compression Due to Prestress

Fig. 9-3. Nonprestressed reinforcements to strengthen beam just after transfer of prestress.

steel will permit the placing of the prestressing steel nearer to the extreme tensile fibers, thus gaining a bigger lever arm for the resisting moment.

B. When straight tendons are used for straight beams, top flange at the ends of the beam may be subjected to tensile stresses. Nonprestressed reinforcements can be placed therein for reinforcement, Fig. 9-3(b).

C. When high compressive stresses are produced in the tensile flange by high prestressing, steel bars may be added to reinforce that flange, Fig. 9-3(c). Such bars will also tend to minimize creep in the concrete. On the other hand, when these bars are subjected to high compressive stresses, especially when considering the effect of creep and shrinkage, lateral expansion of the bars due to Poisson's ratio effect may have a tendency to split the surrounding concrete. German specifications call for a minimum cover of about 3 times the bar's diameter to prevent such splitting. The use of proper stirrups may also be helpful.

2. To reinforce certain portions of precast beams so as to be able to carry special or unexpected loads during handling and erection, Fig. 9-4. This may either permit easier handling of the beams or may prevent serious rupture in case of careless handling.

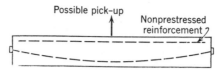

Fig. 9-4. Nonprestressed reinforcement to strengthen precast beam during handling and erection.

3. To reinforce the beam under working loads:

A. Either high-tensile or ordinary steel can be placed side by side with prestressed steel, Fig. 9-5(a). This will help to distribute cracks when they occur and also to increase the ultimate strength, especially when the prestressed steel is not bonded to the concrete. By preventing the formation of concentrated big cracks, both the flexural and shear resistance of the beams may be increased. Nonprestressed steel can often be economically employed because it has to be placed only over certain critical portions, while the prestressed steel generally has to extend the whole length of the beam.

B. Ordinary steel bars can be added to the compressive flange to reinforce it against high compression, Fig. 9-5(b). This is generally uneconomical but may be required under certain conditions.

The use of nonprestressed reinforcements is certainly not limited to simple spans. For cantilevers and continuous spans, where peak moments exist it is often economical to reinforce such portions with nonprestressed

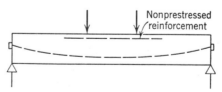

(a) To Distribute Cracks and Increase
Ultimate Strength

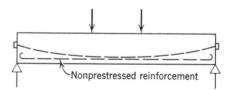

(b) To Reinforce Compression in Concrete

Fig. 9-5. Nonprestressed reinforcements to reinforce beams under working and ultimate loads.

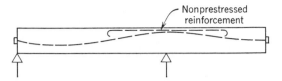

Fig. 9-6. Nonprestressed reinforcement to reinforce moment peaks in cantilevers.

steel, Fig. 9-6. Here, again, the use of some short length of ordinary steel may save some long prestressed steel, and economy is thereby achieved.

When prestressed and nonprestressed reinforcements are combined in a structure, the cooperation of the two should be carefully investigated. Most of the time, the nonprestressed steel will not be acting effectively until the cracks have formed. Its effect on the start of hair cracks and on the elastic deflection of the beam will be small. But after cracking occurs, such steel will distribute the cracks and prevent the formation of big ones which may sometimes be detrimental in producing diagonal tension cracks and compression failures. The ultimate strength of beams under both static and repeated loads can be materially increased by proper employment of nonprestressed steel.[3]

9-3 Nonprestressed Reinforcement—Elastic Stresses

It is difficult, if not impossible, to design nonprestressed reinforcement by the elastic theory, because, within the elastic range, the tensile stresses in the reinforcements are very small and the reinforcements are consequently ineffective, although in the ultimate range they are usually stressed to the yield point and function effectively. However, a study of the elastic stresses is significant in helping to understand the behavior of such beams and to design them properly. As discussed in section 9-2, nonprestressed steel can be placed on either or both sides of the beam: the tension side which is counter-compressed by prestressing, and the compression side which could be under tension before the application of external loads. Let us investigate the stresses in both sides together, as in Fig. 9-7.

Assume that there is no shrinkage of concrete; then there is no stress in the nonprestressed steel until prestress is transferred. At the transfer of prestress, the nonprestressed steel will have strains corresponding to the adjacent concrete, and stresses can be computed by the elastic theory with the usual formula

$$f_s = n \left[\frac{(M_G + F_0 e)y}{I_t} + \frac{F}{A} \right]$$

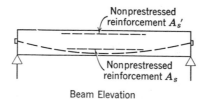

Beam Elevation

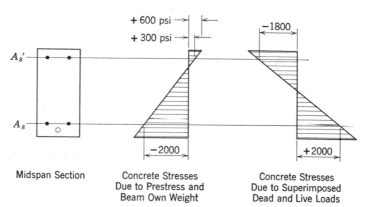

Midspan Section   Concrete Stresses   Concrete Stresses
                     Due to Prestress and   Due to Superimposed
                     Beam Own Weight   Dead and Live Loads

Fig. 9-7. Concrete stresses at levels of nonprestressed reinforcements.

Owing to creep in concrete, stresses in the steel will be modified by the creep coefficient so that they will increase from f_s to $C_c f_s$.

The above method can be assumed to apply equally to the tensile and to the compressive stresses in the steel. Thus both the tensile and the compressive stresses in the steel will be increased by the effect of creep in concrete, and both can be modified by the coefficient of creep applicable for the given duration of time.

Next, let us consider the effect of shrinkage in concrete due to which compressive stresses will be produced in steel to the amount of

$$f_s = \delta E_s$$

where δ is the unit shrinkage strain in the concrete. Thus the resulting stresses in the steel before the application of external loads is given by the formula

$$f_s = C_c n \left(\frac{(M_G + F_0 e)y}{I} + \frac{F}{A} \right) + \delta E_s \tag{9-1}$$

using proper signs for each of the items.

The approximate magnitudes of these stresses can be shown as below. Assuming that the concrete fiber at the level of the nonprestressed reinforcement A_s, Fig. 9-7, is stressed to -2000 psi, for a value of $n = 6$ and $C_c = 1.5$, the compressive stress in steel will be

$$-2000 \times 6 \times 1.5 = -18,000 \text{ psi}$$

Add to this the effect of a shrinkage strain of -0.0002, which will induce a compressive stress in the steel of

$$-0.0002 \times 30,000,000 = -6000 \text{ psi}$$

Hence the total stress in the steel A_s on the tension flange may be around $-18,000 - 6000 = -24,000$ psi. Thus the steel will be stressed appreciably in compression.

For the steel A_s' on the compression flange the stresses cannot be very high. Assuming a tensile stress of 600 psi in the extreme top fibers of concrete, there may be only about 300 psi tension at the level of steel. For the same creep and shrinkage as above, the resulting stress in the steel A_s' will be

$$(1.5 \times 300 \times 6) - 6000 = -3300 \text{ psi}$$

Hence this nonprestressed steel in the compression flange, which is intended to carry tension in that flange under girder loads, will probably be under compression instead. In other words, before the occurrence of cracks, such reinforcements may not serve their intended purpose at all.

Now, when the external load is applied on the beam, steel A_s' on the compression flange will be further compressed, while the steel A_s on the tensile side will be decompressed. These stresses can again be computed by the elastic theory, the effect of shrinkage and creep being taken into account if necessary. To get an idea of the magnitude of the elastic stresses produced by loading, assume a compression of about 1800 psi in the concrete fiber near the A_s', and a decompression of about 2000 psi in the concrete fiber at the A_s; we have, Fig. 9-7,

$$f_s = -3300 - 1800 \times 6 = -14,100 \text{ psi in } A_s'$$
$$f_s = -24,000 + 2000 \times 6 = -12,000 \text{ psi in } A_s$$

which indicates that the tensile steel A_s, which is intended to carry the tension under working loads, may actually still be under compression instead. Hence it is impossible to design such nonprestressed steel for working loads. Previous to cracking, they will not serve the intended function at all. They will increase the ultimate strength of the beam and minimize its deflection after cracking. For members whose serviceability is impaired by cracking, nonprestressed reinforcements cannot suitably be employed.

9-4   Nonprestressed Reinforcements, Ultimate Strength

It is shown in the previous section that nonprestressed reinforcements, when used in conjunction with prestressed ones, do not function effectively in carrying any tension within the elastic working range. Similar to bars in ordinary reinforced concrete beams, they act efficiently in tension only after the concrete has cracked. Before the cracking of concrete, their tensile stresses, if any, are limited. Since almost all prestressed beams are designed for no cracks within the working loads, the nonprestressed reinforcements are apparently useless under such conditions. The interesting phenomenon is that, though they do not serve within the working range, they are often as effective as the prestressed ones near the ultimate load. Thus, if the ultimate strength is of prime importance rather than the elastic strength, nonprestressed reinforcements can be profitably employed.

Figure 9-8 shows, for various reinforcements, the variation of stresses with strains produced by external loads. Consider first a prestressed wire with effective prestress of 125 ksi, elastic limit of 180 ksi, and ultimate

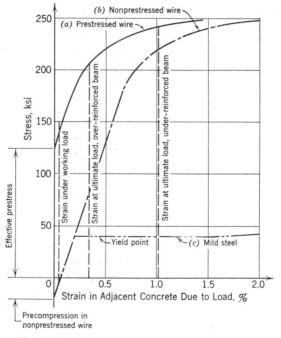

Fig. 9-8. Stress-strain diagrams of prestressed and nonprestressed steel.

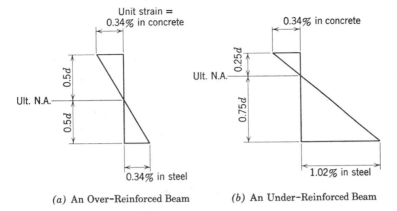

(a) An Over-Reinforced Beam (b) An Under-Reinforced Beam

Fig. 9-9. Strain relations at ultimate load for a bonded beam.

strength of 250 ksi. As the load on the beam increases, the strain and hence the stress increases as shown in curve (a). Next consider a non-prestressed wire of the same qualities embedded at the same level. Its stress-strain variation is given by curve (b). The wire will actually be precompressed during the transfer of prestress, so that, before any external load is applied to the beam, the wire will be under compression. If the amount of precompression is 20 ksi, the total difference in stress between this wire and the prestressed one is of the order of 145 ksi.

Under working load, producing a strain in the steel of about 0.05%, stress in the prestressed wire will be increased to 140 ksi, while that in the nonprestressed one will be changed to 5 ksi compression. Hence the nonprestressed wire is still not functioning at all.

Now, going into the ultimate range, let us refer to Fig. 9-9, which shows the conditions of strain in a prestressed bonded beam section at the ultimate load. In (a), we see that, for an average over-reinforced beam, the strain in steel at failure is about 0.34%. Figure 9-8 shows that, at this strain, the stress in the prestressed wire is about 207 ksi while that in the nonprestressed one is only 80 ksi. This means that the nonprestressed wire is picking up some stress but still has been worked only to about a third of its capacity, even at the ultimate load.

Figure 9-9(b) shows the strain relations of an average under-reinforced beam, with a strain in the steel amounting to about 1.02% at the ultimate load. Corresponding to this strain, it is seen from Fig. 9.8 that the pre-stressed wire will be stressed to about 243 ksi and the nonprestressed one to 222 ksi, the two values being quite close. This means that the non-prestressed wire is now almost as effective as the prestressed one. It can thus be concluded that, for an under-reinforced beam, the nonprestressed wires will be quite efficient in resisting the ultimate load, although under ordinary working loads it is hardly functioning at all.

The stress in a nonprestressed ordinary mild-steel bar can be studied by referring to curve (c), Fig. 9-8. Under ordinary working loads, the bar may be under some compression similar to the nonprestressed wire. But at the ultimate load, it will be stressed to its yield point for either an over-reinforced or an under-reinforced beam. In the latter case, it is possible that the bar may sometimes be stressed even beyond its yield point.

The above discussion has been confirmed by many tests, such as mentioned in the references for this chapter. Although the detailed behavior of nonprestressed reinforcements may still need experimental investigation before they can be definitely formulated, enough data are on hand to permit designs made within the usual range of accuracy desired in practice.

Having described the general behavior of nonprestressed steel in a prestressed beam, we can now proceed to the design of such beams on the basis of ultimate strength. It must again be remembered that ultimate strength is only one measure of the safety of a structure. High stresses and local strains, which may be detrimental if repeated often enough, and deflections and cracks, which may impair the serviceability of the structure long before the ultimate strength is reached, should be carefully studied in each case before a design can be adopted.

It is difficult to formulate a proper basis for the design of nonprestressed reinforcements in the compression flange, where they are needed to strengthen the beam during handling, since there is no way to predict exactly how the beam might be handled. A method for determining the ultimate strength of such prestressed sections, however, has been analyzed and tested.[4] Briefly speaking, it can be assumed that the nonprestressed steel will be worked to the yield point at the failure of the beam, with a lever arm which can be approximately estimated, if not carefully analyzed. For example, Fig. 9-10(a) shows one half of a beam which is being lifted at the midspan point. With half of the beam as a freebody and taking moments about point A, the c.g.s. of the prestressed steel, we can write, for conditions at failure,

Moment of tension in nonprestressed steel about A
= Moment of weight of member about A

assuming that the ultimate center of compression in concrete coincides with the c.g.s. A more accurate computation would require the determination of the actual center of compression at the ultimate moment.

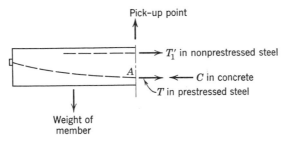

(a) Nonprestressed Steel in Compression Flange,
an Arbitrary Assumption for Design

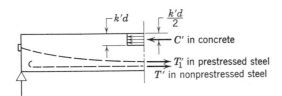

(b) Nonprestressed Steel in Tension Flange

Fig. 9-10. Ultimate design of nonprestressed steel.

More importantly, a proper factor of safety has to be chosen against the ultimate load capacity.[4]

The ultimate design of nonprestressed steel in the tension flange can be formulated as follows. Referring to Fig. 9-10(b), the total tension in the steel, both prestressed and nonprestressed, can be estimated. Corresponding to that total tension, the depth of compression in the concrete can be figured,

$$k'd = \frac{T' + T_1'}{k_1 f_c' b}$$

With the neutral axis thus located for the ultimate load, the ultimate tension in the steels can be obtained from diagrams and curves such as Figs. 9-8 and 9-9. Then $k'd$ can be revised, if necessary. The lever arms for the tensile forces, a' and a_1', are easily obtained and the ultimate moment computed,

$$M' = T'a' + T_1'a_1'$$

Then the allowable moment can be obtained from M' by using a proper factor of safety.

This procedure will be illustrated in the following example.

EXAMPLE 9-1

A prestressed concrete beam has a T section as shown, Fig. 9-11. It is prestressed with high tensile wires ($A_s = 1.06$ sq in.) and additionally reinforced

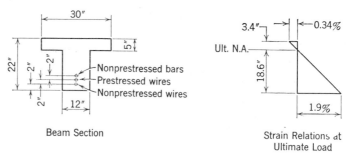

Fig. 9-11. Example 9-1.

with nonprestressed wires ($A_s = 0.47$ sq in.) and nonprestressed mild steel bars ($A_s = 1.32$ sq in.). The c.g.s. of each type of steel is shown in the figure. $f_c' = 5000$ psi; for wires, $f_s' = 250$ ksi, $f_s = 125$ ksi; for mild steel bars, $f_y = 40$ ksi. Estimate the ultimate flexural strength of the section, assuming no failure in shear or bond.

Solution. Assuming that at rupture the prestressed wires will be stressed to 250 ksi, the nonprestressed wires stressed to 230 ksi, and the mild steel to 40 ksi, then the total tensile force at rupture will be

$$250 \times 1.06 = 265 \text{ k}$$
$$230 \times 0.47 = 108 \text{ k}$$
$$40 \times 1.32 = \underline{53 \text{ k}}$$
$$\text{Total} = 426 \text{ k}$$

Assuming the average stress in concrete to be $0.85 f_c' = 4250$ psi, the ultimate depth of compression will be

$$k'd = \frac{426,000}{30 \times 4250}$$
$$= 3.4 \text{ in.}$$

For a concrete ultimate strain of 0.0034 or 0.34%, the ultimate strain in steel can be computed by a simple diagram as in the figure, thus,

$$(0.34/3.4) \times 18.6 = 1.9\%$$

corresponding to which the stresses in both the prestressed and the nonprestressed wires can be taken as 250 ksi (see Fig. 9-8).

Further revision of $k'd$ is deemed unnecessary; hence the resisting moments of the various steels, taken to the mid-depth of $k'd$, can be listed as below.

$$250 \times 1.06 \times 16.3 = 4320 \text{ k-in.}$$
$$250 \times 0.47 \times 18.3 = 2150 \text{ k-in.}$$
$$40 \times 1.32 \times 14.3 = \underline{750 \text{ k-in.}}$$
$$\text{Total} = 7220 \text{ k-in.} = 600 \text{ k-ft}$$

which is considered a rather close estimate of the ultimate resisting moment of the section. The design moment should be determined by applying a proper factor of safety to the ultimate moment. In addition, the stresses in the concrete and the amount of deflection under the working load should be investigated.

9-5 Nonprestressed Reinforcements for Transfer Strength

Section 5-8 discusses the stress conditions "at transfer," when there exists little external moment or when a negative moment is applied to adversely increase the eccentricity of prestress. This section will present the design of reinforcement to improve the behavior of such beams and to increase their ultimate strength.

To improve the behavior of these beams immediately after cracking, nonprestressed reinforcement can be added to limit the cracks. This is usually done by providing sufficient steel to replace the tensile force represented in the elastic stress block. Thus, referring to example 5-12, Fig. 5-26, the total tension is given by

$$930 \times 12 \times 5.2/2 = 29,000 \text{ lb}$$

Using an allowable stress of 20,000 psi, the required A_s is

$$29,000/20,000 = 1.45 \text{ sq in.}$$

This design approach is often improper, because the total tensile force in the stress block is quite sensitive to the change in the magnitude of the external moment. Since it is frequently impossible to accurately predict the external moment, the computed tension force may have little meaning. Furthermore, it is not easy to determine the actual stress in the reinforcement across the cracks, and using an arbitrary value such as 20,000 psi may not be satisfactory. However, when judiciously applied, this method can work well for the limitation and control of cracking.

The ultimate strength method is considered to be a more rational approach to the design of these reinforcements for resisting adverse moments. Using this method, the maximum adverse moment that can be expected is computed or estimated, using a suitable margin of safety in its estimation. Then the reinforcement is designed to resist this moment.

Under a high prestress, acting on the bottom flange, it is possible that a compression failure in the concrete could occur previous to the yielding of the top tensile steel (see Chapter 5, reference 9). Since such failures are relatively rare in practice, we will consider only tension failure resulting from the top steel reaching its yield point.

A freebody of one-half of a simple beam being picked up at midspan is shown in Fig. 9-12, which indicates the weight of the beam acting on the cantilever producing a negative moment at midspan. For the purpose of

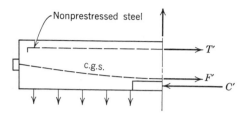

Fig. 9-12. Freebody of half beam reinforced for adverse moments.

design, this moment can be multiplied by factor of safety to obtain the ultimate negative moment M'. Other forces acting on the section are

T' = tension force in the nonprestressed top steel, assumed to be $A_s f_y$

F' = prestressing force under the ultimate moment, which is less than the effective prestress F_e owing to the compression in the concrete

C' = ultimate compressive force in concrete = $F' + T'$

As a rough approximation, we can neglect C' and F', and design the section like a conventionally reinforced concrete beam, thus,

$$M' = T'jd = A_s f_y jd$$

Hence,

$$A_s = \frac{M'}{f_y jd} \qquad (9\text{-}2)$$

For a more accurate answer, the magnitude and location of both C' and F' should be taken into account, considering the strain relations between the concrete and the steels (Chapter 5, reference 9).

EXAMPLE 9-2

Design the nonprestressed steel required for the top of the beam in example 5-14 to resist an ultimate moment of the beam's own weight plus 100% impact.

Solution. Using approximate formula 9-2, and assuming $j = 0.87$, $f_y = 40,000$ psi, we have, required steel area,

$$A_s = \frac{M'}{f_y jd} = \frac{120,000 \times 12}{40,000 \times 0.87 \times 22}$$

$$= 1.85 \text{ sq in.}$$

The effect of the tendons may either increase or decrease the above value of A_s and should be considered in many instances.

9-6   Tendons Stressed at Low Level

In order to meet the requirement of high ultimate strength, it is sometimes necessary to use an unusually large tendon area. If the tendons are fully prestressed, the concrete will be subjected to high stresses, and excessive camber will occur. Thus it becomes necessary to stress the steel to a low level of stress (example 9-3) or to stress only a portion of the steel and leave the remainder unstressed. The first alternative, when carried too far, could end up in a high percentage of loss of prestress, while the second alternative may not enable the unstressed steel to develop its ultimate stress. Both methods, however, are useful for certain conditions.

EXAMPLE 9-3

A pre-tensioned beam, with a section as shown, Fig. 9-13, is to be designed to resist a high ultimate moment of 1600 k-ft. Compute the amount of steel and determine its level of prestress. $M_G = $ 200 k-ft. $I = 73,800$ in.^{4}, $A = 680$ in.^{2}

Solution. Locate the c.g.s. at 5 in. above the bottom fiber, and assume a level arm of $a = 28$ in. We have for steel stressed to 230 ksi,

$$A_s = \frac{1600}{230} \times \frac{12}{28} = 2.98 \text{ sq in.}$$

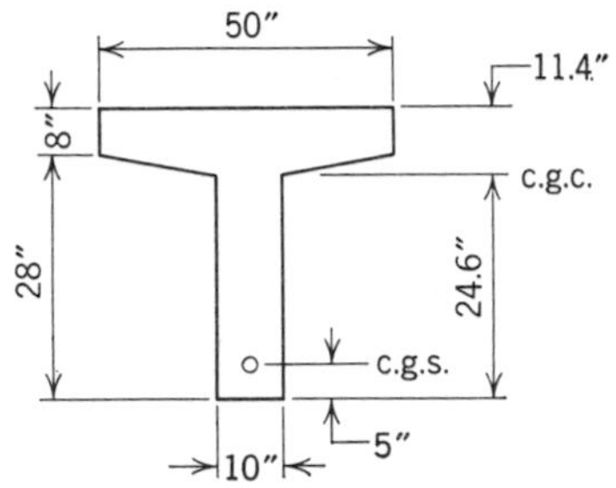

Fig. 9-13. Example 9-3.

Suppose it is desired to limit the top fiber tension to 200 psi and the bottom fiber compression to 2400 psi at transfer; we can compute the maximum total prestress F:

$$f = \frac{F}{A} \pm \frac{Fec}{I} + \frac{Mc}{I}$$

For top fiber,

$$200 = \frac{-F}{680} + \frac{F \times 19.6 \times 11.4}{73,800} - \frac{200 \times 12,000 \times 11.4}{73,800}$$

$$200 = -0.00147F + 0.00303F - 372$$

$$F = \frac{572}{0.00156} = 367,000 \text{ lb}$$

For bottom fiber,

$$-2400 = \frac{-F}{680} - \frac{F \times 19.6 \times 24.6}{73,800} + \frac{200 \times 12,000 \times 24.6}{73,800}$$

$$= -0.00147F - 0.00655F + 800$$

$$F = \frac{3200}{0.00802} = 399,000 \text{ lb}$$

Top fiber controls, $F = 367$ k.
For $A_s = 2.98$ in.^{2},

$$f_s = \frac{F}{A_s} = \frac{367}{2.98} = 123 \text{ ksi}$$

Hence it is only permissible to stress the steel to 123 ksi at transfer, instead of the usual 175 ksi. If the loss of prestress is 35 ksi, the percentage loss will be $35/123 = 28.4\%$.

9-7　Combination of Prestressed and Reinforced Concrete

While a combination of prestressed and reinforced concrete is evidenced in the use of nonprestressed reinforcement, the flexural strength is essentially supplied by the tendons, with the nonprestressed steel playing only a minor role. For certain types of construction, a full combination of prestressed and reinforced concrete could be the best design, making use of the advantages of both. Reinforced concrete has the advantage of simplicity in construction, monolithic in behavior, no camber, less creep, and reasonably high ultimate strength. Prestressed concrete utilizes high-strength steel economically, produces a favorable distribution of stress under certain conditions of loading, and controls deflection and cracking.

Certain structural elements and systems would favor pure reinforced concrete; others would favor pure prestressed concrete; still others, partially prestressed concrete. But some will be best designed with a combination of reinforced and prestressed concrete having the nonprestressed steel carrying perhaps 50% or more of the total ultimate load.

One occasion for the economical use of this combination would be the case of high live load to dead load ratio, when prestressing alone could produce excessive camber. Another case would be high added dead load requiring prestressing in stages which may be cumbersome. A third case would be the requirement of high ultimate strength to resist heavy blast loadings. There is also reason to believe that a heavy amount of nonprestressed steel used in conjunction with unbonded tendons will result in economy and in developing a high ultimate stress in the tendons.

For precast columns, prestressing will help control cracking during transportation and erection; it will contribute to the bending strength. Nonprestressed steel will increase both the axial load and the flexural capacity. Hence a combination may be the best solution for certain cases. The use of nonprestressed reinforcement for joineries and continuity is, of course, frequently a simple and economical solution.

There are new problems involved in this combination. First of all, shrinkage and creep due to prestressing will put the nonprestressed steel into compression. The nonprestressed steel does not act until the concrete cracks, and does not contribute toward the precracking strength. Hence if cracking could result in a primary or a secondary failure, nonprestressed steel may not be of any help. Another problem is the possibility of corrosion of the prestressing steel if the member cracks too early or too often. However, it is clear that this field has not been explored and may prove to be a fertile one, especially when different grades of steel and types of tendons are considered in combination.

References

1   P. W. Abeles, "How Much Prestress," *Eng. News-Rec.*, July 5, 1951, pp. 32–33. Also see reader's comment on p. 46, April 13, 1950, and on p. 10, Jan. 15, 1951.
2   P. W. Abeles, "The Use of High Strength Steel in Ordinary Reinforced and Prestressed Concrete Beams," *Preliminary Publications, Fourth Congress, Int. Assn. for Bridge and Structural Engg.*, 1952. Also supplement to above, *Final Report, Fourth Congress*, 1953.
3   P. W. Abeles, "Static and Fatigue Tests on Partially Prestressed Concrete Constructions," *J. Am. Conc. Inst.*, December 1954 (*Proc.*, Vol. 50), pp. 361–376.

10 *continuous beams*

10-1 Continuity, Pros and Cons

A simple comparison between the strength of a simply supported and a continuous beam will demonstrate the basic economy inherent in continuous construction of prestressed concrete. Consider a simple prestressed beam loaded with a uniformly distributed load of intensity w, Fig. 10-1(a). The total load w' that can be ultimately carried by the beam is determined by the ultimate moment capacity of the midspan section. If the ultimate tension developed in the tendon is T', acting with a lever arm a', then the ultimate resisting moment at midspan is $T'a'$. With one half of the span as a freebody, Fig. 10-1(b), and taking moment about the left support, we have

$$\frac{w'L^2}{8} = T'a'$$

$$w' = \frac{8T'a'}{L^2} \tag{10-1}$$

The moment diagram produced by the load w' is shown in Fig. 10-1(c). It should be noted that the ultimate load w' carried by the beam is controlled by the capacity of the midspan section and cannot be increased by any change in the end eccentricities of the c.g.s.

Now consider the intermediate span of a continuous beam, Fig. 10-2(a), with the same section, same span, and same prestressing steel as the simple beam of Fig. 10-1(a). Again with one half of the span as a freebody, Fig. 10-2(b), and taking moment about the left support, we have

$$\frac{w_c'L^2}{8} = 2T'a'$$

$$w_c' = \frac{16T'a'}{L^2} \tag{10-2}$$

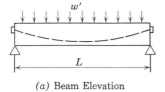

(a) Beam Elevation

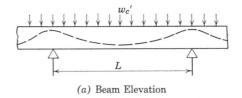

(a) Beam Elevation

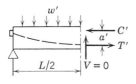

(b) Freebody of Half Span

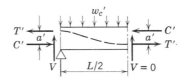

(b) Freebody of Half Span

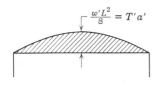

(c) Moment Diagram

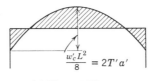

(c) Moment Diagram

Fig. 10-1. Load-carrying capacity of a simple beam.

Fig. 10-2. Load-carrying capacity of a continuous beam.

noting that there are two resisting moments, one at midspan and another over the support. Hence the load-carrying capacity is definitely affected by the position of c.g.s. over the intermediate support. The moment diagram produced by the load w_c' is now plotted in Fig. 10-2(c).

Comparing Fig. 10-1(c) with Fig. 10-2(c), or equation 10-1 with equation 10-2, it is readily seen that $w_c' = 2w'$. This means that twice the load on the simple span can be carried by the continuous span for the same amount of concrete and steel. This represents a very significant basic economy that should be realized by engineers designing prestressed concrete structures. Because of this strength inherent in continuous construction, it is possible to employ smaller concrete sections for the same load and span, thus reducing the dead weight of the structure and attaining all the resulting economies.

Although it is generally conceded that continuity is economical in reinforced concrete, it is seldom known that, from certain points of view, even greater economy can be attained in prestressed construction. In reinforced concrete, the negative steel often laps with the positive steel bars, and both sets of bars are extended for additional anchorage, thus canceling some of the economy of continuity. In prestressed concrete, the same cable for the $+M$ is bent over to the other side to resist the $-M$, with no loss of overlapping. In addition, continuity in prestressed concrete saves end anchorages otherwise required over the intermediate supports, thus resulting in further economy and convenience.

The above discussion refers to the ultimate capacity of continuous beams, but the same general principles hold true within the elastic range. For both the elastic and the plastic ranges, with one half of the beam a freebody, there are two resisting moments in a continuous beam, but only one in a simple beam. Within the elastic range, however, the two resisting moments acting on the beam may not have equal capacity. Then one of the moments will control the design stresses, and the elastic resisting capacity of the continuous may not be twice that of the simple beam.

Economical design of continuous prestressed beams can be achieved in several ways. Owing to the variation of moment along the beam, the concrete section and the amount of steel are often varied accordingly. The peaks of the negative moments can be reinforced with nonprestressed steel, thus reducing the amount of prestressing steel. Advantage can be taken of the redundant reactions to obtain favorable lines of pressure in the concrete, which will be discussed in sections 10-4 and 10-5. Designs can be based on the ultimate strength of such beams, applying the principles of limit design. Some of these, however, are more delicate problems which should be handled with care.

It is perhaps unnecessary to add that, as is true with other continuous structures, the deflections will be less than comparable simple spans. Hence, for continuous spans, smaller depth is sufficient not only for strength but also for rigidity.

Like any type of construction, there are advantages and also short-comings, which, under certain conditions, could outweigh the advantages. The choice of a particular type of design must be made after considering all the factors involved in the job. Disadvantages inherent in continuous prestressed concrete beams can be enumerated as follows.

1. Frictional loss in continuous tendons. This can be serious if there are many reversed curves, if the curves possess large deflection angles, or if the tendons are excessively long. Such loss can be minimized by using relatively straight cables in undulating or haunched beams. The usual

methods of overtensioning, of stressing from both ends, can also be used to reduce frictional losses, as discussed in Chapter 4.

2. Shortening of long continuous beams under prestress. This may produce excessive lateral force and moments in the supporting columns, if they are rigidly connected to the beams during prestressing. Provisions are usually made to permit movement at the beam bearings or rocking of the columns.

3. Secondary stresses. Secondary stresses due to prestressing, creep and shrinkage effects, temperature changes, and settlements of supports could be serious for continuous structures unless they are controlled or allowed for in the design. One interesting point in continuous prestressed structures is that these secondary stresses can often be utilized to good advantage so that they will add to the economy of the structure.

4. Concurrence of maximum moment and shear over supports. It is believed that the concurrence of maximum moment and shear at the same section may decrease the ultimate capacity of a beam. This happens over the supports of most continuous beams. Hence care must be taken to reinforce such points properly for both shear and moment if high ultimate strength is desired. The elastic strength, however, is not affected by such concurrence.

5. Reversal of moments. If live loads are much heavier than dead load, and if partial loadings on the spans are considered, continuous beams can be subjected to serious reversal of moments. This can sometimes be overcome by proper design, such as extensive use of nonprestressed steel in combination with prestressed concrete.

6. Moment peaks. Peaks of maximum negative moments may sometimes control the number of tendons required for the entire length of the beam. These peaks, however, can be strengthened by employing deeper sections or by adding prestressed and nonprestressed reinforcements over the portions where they are needed.

7. Difficulty in achieving continuity for precast elements. It is easy and natural to obtain continuity for cast-in-place construction, but continuity for precast elements cannot always be achieved without special effort. On account of difficulties in handling precast continuous beams, they are often precast as simple elements, to be made continuous after they are erected in place.

8. Difficulty in designing. It is more difficult to design continuous than simple structures. But, with the development of simpler methods, the design of continuous prestressed concrete beams can be made into a more or less routine procedure applying basic principles for continuous structures familiar to most engineers. These methods will be presented in the following sections, and later in Chapter 14.

10-2   Layouts for Continuous Beams

Several methods for providing continuity in prestressed concrete construction have been applied in practice.[1] These methods permit various layouts to be adopted, some of which are shown in Figs. 10-4 and 10-5 and will be described below. There are other methods and layouts that are perhaps less frequently used. Still other arrangements are being developed. But it is considered sufficient to present the more common methods, leaving the variability as well as the desirability of each to the judgment of the designer, who should of course take into account the particular conditions surrounding each structure when selecting his layout.

Continuous beams may be divided into two classes: fully continuous beams and partially continuous beams. For full continuity, all the tendons are prestressed in place and are generally continuous from one end to the other, although some can be anchored at intermediate points if found desirable. The concrete may be either poured in place or made of blocks assembled on falsework. The tendons may be encased in the concrete during pouring, threaded through preformed holes, or placed outside the webs. They may be either bonded or unbonded, depending on the requirements of the structure.

Precast elements can also be made fully continuous by coupling the tendons together with a high tensile rod and then stressing one or both of the tendons. A typical case is shown in Fig. 10-3. Some other typical layouts for full continuity are shown in Fig. 10-4:

(*a*) In (*a*) is shown a straight beam with curved tendons, which follows in general the tensile side of the beam. This layout is often used for slabs or short-span beams, where simple formwork is more important than the saving of steel and concrete. The main objections here are the heavy frictional loss and the difficulty of threading the tendons through when they are continuous over several spans.

(*b*) For longer spans and heavier loads, it will be more economical to haunch or curve the beams, as in (*b*). This will not only save concrete and steel but also permit the use of straight tendons, likewise positioned on the tensile side of the beam. However, it is often difficult to get the optimum eccentricities all along the beam if the tendons are to remain entirely straight.

(*c*) The best layout is often obtained with a compromise of the above two arrangements, using curved beams and slightly curved tendons at the same time, as in (*c*). This would permit optimum depth of beam as well as ideal position of steel at all points, while avoiding excessive frictional loss.

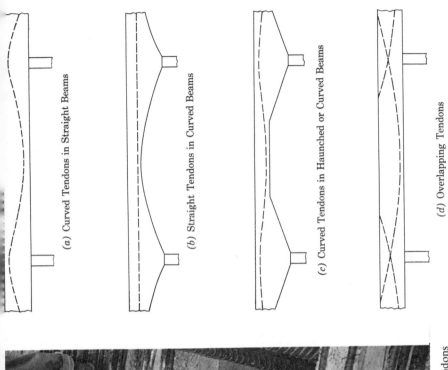

(a) Curved Tendons in Straight Beams

(b) Straight Tendons in Curved Beams

(c) Curved Tendons in Haunched or Curved Beams

(d) Overlapping Tendons

Fig. 10-4. Layouts for fully continuous beams.

Fig. 10-3. Precast members made continuous by coupling the tendons with high-tensile rods (Prescon system).

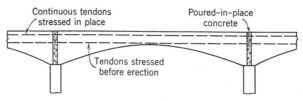

(*a*) Continuous Tendons Stressed after Erection

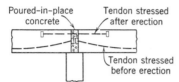

(*b*) Short Tendons Stressed over Supports

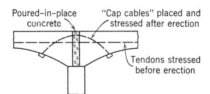

(*c*) Cap Cables over Supports

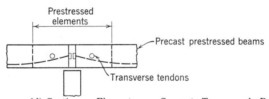

(*d*) Continuous Elements over Supports Transversely Prestressed

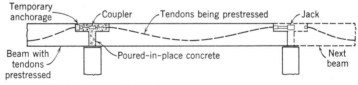

(*e*) Couplers over Supports

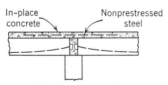

(*f*) Nonprestressed Steel over Supports

Fig. 10-5. Layouts for partially continuous beams.

(*d*) Cables protruding at intermediate points, as in (*d*), offer a possibility of varying prestressing force along the beam. The arrangement here shown has no reversed curves in the tendons, so that heavier cables and rods can be more easily threaded through and stressed with less frictional loss.

For partial continuity, each span is first precast as a simple beam, a sufficient amount of prestressed steel being used for handling and erection. Concrete blocks can also be used if desired. Generally, no falsework is required for erection. After the simple elements are erected in place, additional elements, sometimes nonprestressed, but often prestressed longitudinally or transversely, are inserted to provide continuity over the supports. These are termed partially continuous beams, Fig. 10-5.

(*a*) In (*a*) are shown continuous prestressed cables placed in conduits or grooves left in the structure. After erection, concrete is poured between the beams over the supports. When the concrete hardens, the continuous cables can be stressed to provide continuity. The construction is relatively simple, but economy in steel cannot be easily attained since the same cable area is provided throughout the entire length, whether needed or not.

(*b*) In (*b*) is shown a layout similar to (*a*), but with the continuous tendons placed over the supports only. This saves steel but requires more anchorages than the first layout. Moreover, the anchorages are located at intermediate points and are more difficult to tension.

(*c*) Another method of supplying continuity over the supports is to add the so-called cap cables, as in (*c*). These tendons, usually made of wires or small strands, can be conveniently stressed from the soffit of the beam, but they possess an appreciable curvature and hence corresponding frictional loss. It is not possible to thread big rods through the holes, unless the profile is made into a circular curve and the bars are prebent to a definite curvature.

(*d*) Still another way to provide continuity is to insert tensile elements over the supports, as in (*d*), and to attach them to the precast beams by transverse prestressing, which supplies a sort of bolt action clamping the elements together. These tying elements can be made of reinforced- or prestressed-concrete planks, and can be either precast or poured-in-place. Sometimes, the precast elements themselves can be cantilevered at the ends so that they overlap over the supports and transverse prestress is applied to hold them together, thus making them continuous under live load.

(*e*) Especially applicable to high-tensile bars, but also to other forms of tendons, is the use of couplers as a means of obtaining continuity, (*e*). This permits the stressing of tendons one span at a time, thus minimizing the frictional loss encountered when prestressing tendons running through several continuous spans. Suppose we erect the beams in (*e*) successively from left to right. After one beam is fully prestressed, the next beam is erected and its unstressed bar is connected to the stressed bar of the previous beam by a coupler. Then a jack is applied to the right end for tensioning. This method is also applicable to cast-in-place beams, provided the sequence of construction permits the insertion of jacks.

(*f*) Precast elements can be conveniently made continuous for live load by placing nonprestressed steel over the support (*f*).[2] This is especially true for composite construction where a topping will be concreted in place. If dead load continuity is desired, propping of the precast elements will be required.

10-3   Analysis, Elastic Theory

Tests on continuous prestressed-concrete beams have shown that the elastic theory can be applied with accuracy within the working range. Since there is little or no tensile stress in the beam under working loads, there are no cracks, and the beam behaves as a homogeneous elastic material, more so than an ordinary reinforced-concrete beam which usually is cracked in certain portions. By making proper allowance for shrinkage and creep, the elastic theory can be applied for all practical purposes to compute the deflections, strains, and stresses up to cracking. This is true for the effect of prestress as well as of dead and live loads.

The method of analysis presented here is based on the classical elastic theory. Fundamentally, the theory is applicable to all statically indeterminate structures of prestressed concrete, provided that consideration is given to the axial shortening effect in frames and similar structures. However, for simplicity, only fully continuous beams are referred to in the following, although most of the discussions apply to rigid frames, slabs, and partially continuous beams as well.

The analysis and design of continuous prestressed concrete structures are considered by most engineers to present a rather difficult problem. This is an erroneous impression. Undoubtedly, the design is more complicated than that of continuous reinforced-concrete structures or of statically determinate prestressed structures. But the basic theories involved are the same, and the additional complications are limited in nature. Hence a person who understands the analysis of statically indeterminate structures and the design of simple prestressed concrete beams can learn the design of continuous prestressed concrete beams with little difficulty.

Several methods are available for the analysis of prestressed continuous beams.[3,4,5] All of them are similar to those followed in the analysis of any statically indeterminate structures; they are all based on the same assumptions and yield the same answers. Hence only one method, which the author considers the simplest, will be discussed in this chapter. The method will be based on no involved mathematics, and only the following principles will be utilized.

1. Moment and shear diagrams for ordinary continuous beams.
2. Moment distribution method.[6,7]
3. Location of line of pressure in a prestressed-concrete beam.

Before starting on this method of analysis, let us examine first the difference between a continuous prestressed beam and a simple one. Owing to the application of external loads, the moments in a bonded continuous prestressed beam are computed by the elastic theory, like any other type of statically indeterminate structure. In an unbonded beam, the effect of change in prestress due to beam curvature should be added, although the magnitude is usually small and can be neglected. Owing to the application of prestress, the moments in a continuous beam are directly affected by the prestress and indirectly by the support reactions induced by the bending of the beam. In a simple beam, or any other statically determinate beam, no support reactions can be induced by prestressing.

Consider a prestressed simple beam, Fig. 10-6(*a*). No matter how much the beam is prestressed, only the internal stresses will be affected by prestressing. The external reactions, being determined by statics, will depend on the dead and live load (including the weight of the beam), but are not affected by the prestress. Without load on the beam, no matter how we prestress the beam internally, the external reactions will

(*a*) Beam Elevation

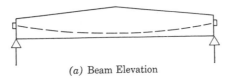

(*b*) Part of Beam as Free Body

Fig. 10-6. Moment in concrete due to prestressing in a simple beam.

be zero, hence the external moment will be zero. With no external moment on the beam, the internal resisting moment must be zero, hence the C-line (which is the line of pressure in the concrete) must coincide with the T-line in the steel (which is the c.g.s. line), as in (*b*). The C-line in the concrete being known, the moment in the concrete at any section can be determined by $M = Te = Ce$.

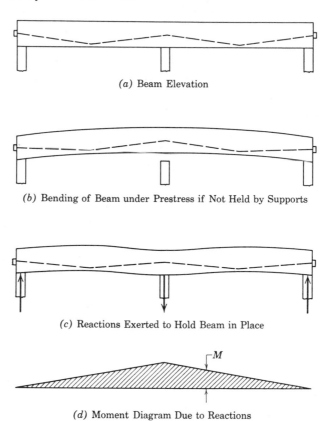

(*a*) Beam Elevation

(*b*) Bending of Beam under Prestress if Not Held by Supports

(*c*) Reactions Exerted to Hold Beam in Place

(*d*) Moment Diagram Due to Reactions

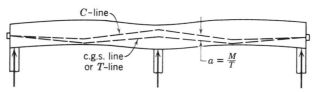

(*e*) Deviation of C-line from c.g.s. Line Due to Moment in (*d*)

Fig. 10-7. Moment in concrete due to prestressing in a continuous beam.

Next, let us consider a continuous prestressed-concrete beam, Fig. 10-7(a). When the beam is prestressed, it bends and deflects. The bending of the beam can be such that the beam will tend to deflect itself away from some of the supports, as in (b). If the beam is refrained from deflection at these supports, (c), reactions must be exerted on the beam to hold it there. Thus reactions are induced when a continuous beam is prestressed (unless, by intent or by chance, the prestress has no tendency to deflect the beam from any of its supports). These induced reactions produce moments in the beam, (d). To resist these moments, the C-line must be at a distance a from the T-line, (e), such that the internal resisting moment equals the external moment M caused by the reactions, that is,

$$a = \frac{M}{T}$$

Now, let us compare the simple beam with the continuous beam under the action of prestress, neglecting the weight of the beam and all other external loads. In the simple beam, the C-line coincides with the T-line. In the continuous beam, the C-line usually deviates from the T-line. In the simple beam, the stress distribution in the concrete at any section is given by the location of the T-line. In the continuous beam, it is given by the location of the C-line which does not coincide with the T-line. The difference between the two beams lies in the presence of external reactions and moments in the continuous beam, produced as a result of prestressing. Since the external moment is solely produced by the reactions, and since the reactions are only applied at the supports, the variation of moment between any two consecutive supports is a linear one. If T remains constant between the supports, then the deviation a, being directly proportional to M, also has to vary linearly, Fig. 10-7.

From another point of view, the difference between a simple and a continuous beam under prestress can be represented by the existence of "secondary moments." Once these moments over the supports are determined, they can be interpolated for any point along the beam. These moments are called secondary because they are by-products of prestressing and because they do not exist in a statically determinate beam. The term "secondary" is somewhat misleading, since sometimes the moments are not secondary in magnitude but play a most important part in the stresses and strength of the beam.

From this same point of view, the moment in the concrete given by the eccentricity of the prestress is designated as the primary moment, such as would exist if the beam were simple. On account of such primary moment acting on a continuous beam, the secondary moments caused by the induced reactions can be computed. The resulting moment due to prestress, then, is the algebraic sum of the primary and secondary moments.

The following gives a procedure for computing directly the resulting moments in the concrete sections over the supports, based on the moment distribution method. Once the resulting moments are obtained, the secondary moments can be computed from the relation

Secondary moment + Primary moment = Resulting moment

It is also possible to consider some reactions as redundant and solve for the values required to produce zero deflections at the supports. This can be done by the classical method of redundant reactions, and sometimes may be simple for a single redundancy. But this method and others will not be discussed here.

Before going any further, it would be well to summarize first the assumptions made for our method of design and analysis. These are the usual assumptions made for continuous prestressed-concrete beams, and their effects on the computed values are known to be negligible in most cases.

1. The eccentricities of the prestressing cables are small compared to the length of the members.

2. Frictional loss of prestress is negligible (where frictional loss is appreciable, it should be taken into account).

3. The same tendons run through the entire length of the member (varying steel areas can be included with some modifications, which will be evident to the designer once he learns the basic procedure presented herein).

As a result of the above assumptions, analysis can be made on the following bases.

1. The axial component of the prestress is constant for the member and is equal to the prestressing force F.

2. The primary moment M_1 at any section in the concrete is given by

$$M_1 = Fe_1$$

where e_1 is the eccentricity of the c.g.s. with respect to c.g.c.

On these bases, the procedure of analysis can be formulated as follows.

First treat the entire beam as if it had no supports. Plot the moment diagram for the concrete produced by the eccentricity of prestress. Compute the loading on the beam corresponding to that moment diagram; this is the loading produced by the steel on the concrete. Now, with this loading acting on the continuous beam as it is actually supported, compute

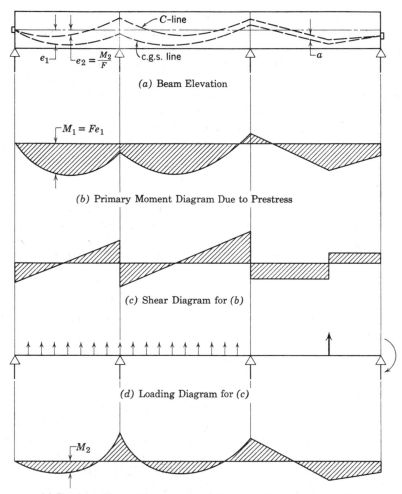

(a) Beam Elevation

(b) Primary Moment Diagram Due to Prestress

(c) Shear Diagram for *(b)*

(d) Loading Diagram for *(c)*

(e) Resulting Moment Diagram Due to Prestress, from Loading in *(d)*

Fig. 10-8. Computation of moments due to prestress in continuous beam.

the resulting moment by moment distribution or other similar method. Referring to Fig. 10-8, the various steps will be further outlined.

1. Plot the primary moment diagram for the entire continuous beam, as produced only by prestress eccentricity, as if there were no supports to the beam. This is simply given by the eccentricity curve plotted to some suitable scale, as in *(b)*, since $M_1 = Fe_1$, and F is a constant.

2. From the above moment diagram, plot the shear diagram corresponding to it, *(c)*. This can be done either graphically or algebraically.

3. From the above shear diagram plot the loading diagram corresponding to it, (*d*). This can also be done either graphically or algebraically.

4. Now, for the loading obtained above acting on the continuous beam with the actual supports, and including any singular moments such as might occur at the ends of the beam due to the eccentricity of c.g.s., compute the resulting moments M_2 by moment distribution, (*e*).

5. The *C*-line in (*a*) is now obtained by linearly transforming the c.g.s. line so that it will have new eccentricities e_2 over the supports corresponding to the resulting moments M_2, thus,

$$e_2 = M_2/F$$

Since the *C*-line deviates linearly from the c.g.s. line, it will have the same intrinsic shape as the c.g.s. line, and can be easily plotted. It is usually not necessary to compute the secondary moment, which is represented by the deviation between the *C*-line and the c.g.s. line. If desired, it can be computed by the simple relation

$$\text{Secondary moment} = M_2 - M_1$$

and the deviation *a* of the *C*-line from the c.g.s. line, Fig. 10-8(*a*), is given by

$$a = \frac{M_2 - M_1}{F}$$

Note that the above procedure involves only principles familiar to the engineer except perhaps the plotting of loading and shear diagram from given moment diagrams. While engineers can plot shear from loading diagrams and moment from shear diagrams, which is essentially a process of integration, most are not familiar with the reverse of the process, plotting shear from moment diagrams and loading from shear diagrams, which is essentially a process of differentiation. However, with a little experience, the art can be easily mastered. In fact, very often it is not necessary to plot the shear diagram, since the loading diagram can be obtained directly from the moment diagram.

In order to facilitate the plotting of loading diagrams directly from moment diagrams, the following hints are given for reference, Fig. 10-9.

1. At the end of the tendons, the force F from the tendons on the concrete can be resolved into three components:

A. An axial force, $F \cos \theta_1 = F$ (since $\cos \theta = 1$), acting at the end of the anchorage. This usually has no effect on the bending moment in a continuous beam but may produce moments in a rigid frame, owing to the axial shortening effect.

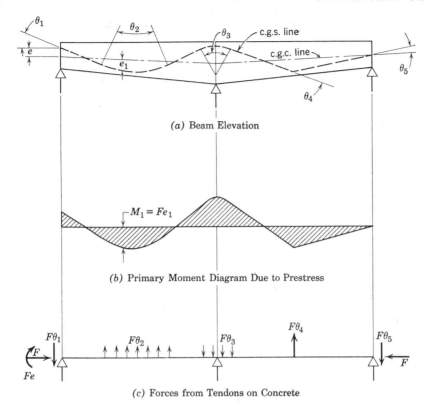

(a) Beam Elevation

(b) Primary Moment Diagram Due to Prestress

(c) Forces from Tendons on Concrete

Fig. 10-9. Obtaining loading diagrams due to prestress.

B. A transverse force, $F \sin \theta_1 = F\theta_1 = F \tan \theta$, applied at the support and balanced by the vertical reaction from the support directly beneath. This again produces no moment in a continuous beam, unless it is applied away from the support. Its effect in a rigid frame will be small.

C. A moment, $F \cos \theta_1 e = Fe$, acting at the end of the beam. This will produce moments along the entire length of the continuous beam, and it must be included when following the moment distribution procedure.

2. Along the span of a member, where the c.g.s. or the c.g.c. line of the member bends and curves, transverse loads are applied to the concrete. Two common cases can be considered:

A. When the moment diagram takes the shape of a parabolic or a circular curve (note: owing to the assumption of flat curvature, parabolic and circular curves are considered to have the same effect in producing transverse loads), a uniformly distributed load is applied to the concrete along the length of the curve. The total force for each curve is given by the change in slope between the two end tangents; thus the total force at θ_2 is given by

$$W = F \sin \theta_2 = F\theta_2$$

For practical purposes, the load W can be considered as uniformly distributed along the length of the curve.

B. When the moment diagram changes direction sharply, the force can be considered as concentrated at one point; the amount, at θ_4, for example, is

$$F \sin \theta_4 = F\theta_4$$

3. Over the interior supports, where the moment diagram changes direction, a load is applied directly over these supports. Again two cases can be considered:

A. If the moment diagram curves gradually over the support, again a uniformly distributed load is applied, as shown for θ_3. This will affect moments in the beam, and the load must be considered in performing the moment distribution.

B. If the moment diagram is bent abruptly over the supports, a concentrated load is applied thereon. Such a concentrated load is directly reacted by the support underneath and produces no moments on the beam. It can be neglected in performing the moment distribution.

Having computed the loads on the concrete, Fig. 10-9(*c*), we can proceed to determine the bending moments in the concrete, as for any continuous beam. This can be done by any method, but only the moment distribution method will be followed here. The application of moment distribution, which is also based on the elastic theory, necessarily involves other assumptions, such as the validity of Hooke's law, the principle of superposition, and linear variation of strain along the depth of a beam. Although these assumptions may not be exactly correct, the method has been considered accurate enough for reinforced concrete; because of the absence of cracks in prestressed concrete under working loads, the method can be applied with great precision and is considered sufficiently accurate for purpose of design.

The application of the above method, together with moment distribution, will be illustrated by example 10-1. Two points should be noted in the example. First, the example treats of a bonded beam. If the tendons are unbonded, the I of the net concrete area should be used, while the effect of change in prestress in the tendons due to beam curvature should be considered, although the effect is generally small, as previously mentioned. Next, a beam with a straight c.g.c. line is illustrated. Should the beam possess a curved or bent axis, it is only necessary to plot the primary moment diagram by measuring the c.g.s. eccentricity from the curved or bent c.g.c. line instead of from a straight base line.

EXAMPLE 10-1

A continuous prestressed-concrete beam with bonded tendons is shown in Fig. 10-10(*a*). The c.g.s. has an eccentricity at *A*, is bent sharply at *D* and *B*, and has a parabolic curve for the span *BC*. Locate the line of pressure (the *C*-line) in the concrete due to prestress alone, not considering the dead load of the beam. Consider a prestress of 250 k.

Solution. The primary moment diagram for the concrete is shown in (*b*). The corresponding shear diagram is computed and shown in (*c*), from which the loading diagram is drawn in (*d*). For the loading in (*d*) acting on the continuous beam, the fixed-end moments are computed: Span *AB* at *A*, in addition to 50 k-ft singular moment, we have

$$\frac{20 \times 20^2 \times 30}{50^2} = +96 \text{ k-ft}$$

at *B*,

$$\frac{20 \times 30^2 \times 20}{50^2} = -144 \text{ k-ft}$$

Span *BC*,

$$\frac{0.88 \times 50^2}{12} = \pm 183 \text{ k-ft at } B \text{ and } C$$

Moment distribution is performed in (*e*). The exterior end moments are first distributed, −96 and +183 k-ft being obtained. Together with the eccentric moment of −50 k-ft at *A*, these are carried over to *B*, obtaining −73 and +92 k-ft. Now the total unbalanced moment of +58 k-ft at *B* is distributed, obtaining −29 k-ft for each span. The resulting moment is 246 k-ft at *B*. The eccentricity of the line of pressure at *B* is, then,

$$246/250 = 0.98 \text{ ft}$$

The line of pressure for the entire beam can be computed by plotting its moment diagram and dividing the ordinates by the value of the prestress. But this is not necessary; since the line of pressure deviates only linearly from the c.g.s. line, it is only necessary to move the c.g.s. line linearly so that it will pass through the points located over the supports, (*f*). (This is known as linear transformation and will be discussed more fully in the next section.) Thus the line of pressure at *D* will be translated upward by the amount of

$$(0.98 - 0.4) \, 30/50 = 0.35 \text{ ft}$$

and is now located at 0.80 − 0.35 = 0.45 ft below the c.g.c. line. At midspan of *BC*, the line of pressure will be translated upward by the amount of (0.98 − 0.4) 25/50 = 0.29 ft and is now located at 0.61 ft below the c.g.c. line.

As an exercise, the reader may plot the entire moment diagram for the continuous beam and divide it by the amount of prestress to obtain the line of pressure. Of course, it should check exactly with the line here obtained.

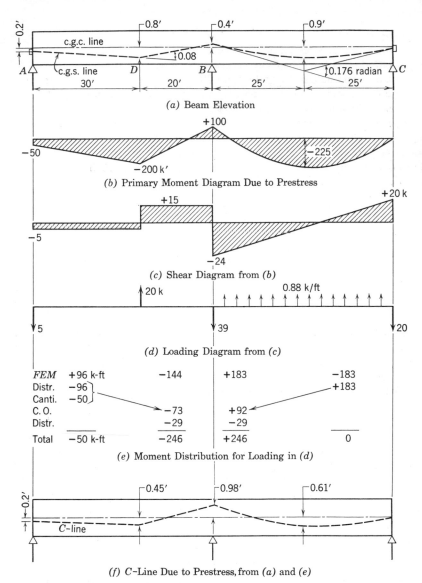

(a) Beam Elevation

(b) Primary Moment Diagram Due to Prestress

(c) Shear Diagram from (b)

(d) Loading Diagram from (c)

(e) Moment Distribution for Loading in (d)

(f) C-Line Due to Prestress, from (a) and (e)

Fig. 10-10. Example 10-1.

If desired, the secondary moment over the center support can be computed as

$$M_2 - M_1 = 246 - 100$$

$$= 146 \text{ k-ft}$$

The above procedure outlines the method for locating the line of pressure due to prestressing in a continuous beam. It is seen that the induced reactions produce moments in a continuous beam, which shift the C-line away from the c.g.s. line. Now, when external loads are applied on the beam, additional moments will be produced, and the C-line will again be shifted. Two methods of computation are possible.

1. Moments in the continuous beam due to the external loads (including the weight of the beam) are computed by the usual elastic theory, using methods such as moment distribution. These moments are added to the prestressing moments previously calculated, thus yielding the final moments in the beam. This can also be performed by shifting the C-line from that obtained for prestressing only. The amount of shifting equals the moments due to external loads divided by the prestress. For simplicity, the effective prestress and the gross concrete area can be used for all computations. This method is generally preferred when there is more than one condition of loading.

2. When there is only one condition of loading to be investigated, it may be easier to consider the effects of prestress and external loading together. Since the effect of prestressing can be reduced to a system of forces acting on the beam, it is only necessary to add these forces to the external loads to obtain the total loads on the beam. One moment distribution will then be sufficient for the two sets of forces. The load-balancing concept in Chapter 14 utilizes this method.

EXAMPLE 10-2

For the prestressed beam in example 10-1, a uniform load of 1.2 k-ft is applied to the entire length of the two spans (including the weight of the beam itself). Locate the line of pressure in the concrete due to the combined action of the prestress and the external loads. Compute the stresses in concrete at section B, if the concrete section is as shown in Fig. 10-11, with $I = 39,700$ in.^{4} and $A_c = 288$ sq in.

Solution. Two methods are possible. Since the moments and line of pressure due to prestress have been obtained in example 10-1, we shall now follow the first method, obtaining only the effect of external loads. By a simple moment distribution, see (*b*), the moment diagram can be plotted as in (*c*). (Note that for this particular case the moment diagram can be plotted by using ready-made tables from handbooks if desired.) Dividing this moment by the prestress of 250 k the shifting of C-line due to this external loading is given in (*d*). Adding

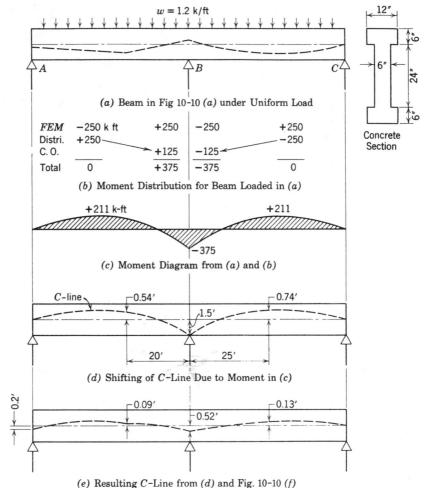

(a) Beam in Fig 10-10 (a) under Uniform Load

(b) Moment Distribution for Beam Loaded in (a)

(c) Moment Diagram from (a) and (b)

(d) Shifting of C-Line Due to Moment in (c)

(e) Resulting C-Line from (d) and Fig. 10-10 (f)

Fig. 10-11. Example 10-2.

(d) to Fig. 10-10(e) of the last example, the final location of the resulting line of pressure for both prestress and external load is given in (f).

The resulting moment in the concrete at section B is $250 \times 0.52 = -130$ k-ft, and the stresses are

Top fiber:

$$\frac{-250}{288} + \frac{130 \times 12 \times 18}{39,700} = -0.867 + 0.707 = -0.160 \text{ ksi}$$

Bottom fiber:

$$-0.867 - 0.707 = -1.574 \text{ ksi}$$

Note: The reader can try to combine the forces in Fig. 10-10(*b*) with those in Fig. 10-11(*a*) and perform one moment distribution to obtain the line of pressure. Obviously he should get the same results.

10-4   Linear Transformation and Concordancy of Cables

The previous section explains the analysis of prestressed continuous beams; the design of such beams is a more complicated problem. In analysis, the concrete section, the steel, and the location of the steel are already known or assumed. It is only necessary to compute the stresses for the given loading conditions. This is not true in design, which is essentially a trial-and-error process in an effort to reach the best proportions. The designer must be well acquainted with the method of analysis before he can perform efficiently in design. In order to design well, we must be conversant with some of the mechanics of continuous prestressed beams.

In this connection, two terms will be explained first: linear transformation and concordancy of cables.[8] After a thorough study of this section, the designer should be able to perform linear transformation with ease and skill and to obtain either concordant or nonconcordant cables to satisfy the most desirable conditions. First of all, let us define linear transformation:

When the position of c.g.s. line or of a C-line is moved over the interior supports of a continuous beam without changing the intrinsic shape (i.e., the curvature and bends) of the line within each individual span, the line is said to be linearly transformed. Linear transformation of a c.g.s. line is illustrated in Fig. 10-12(*a*).

In further explanation of the above definition, attention is called to the following points. First, the position of the line is moved only over the interior supports whenever desired, but not at the ends of a beam. Strictly speaking, a line can still be termed linearly transformed if it is moved at the ends in addition. However, for purpose of design, linear transformation without involving movement at the ends is much more useful; hence we will define it as such for the sake of convenience. Second, by linear transformation, the intrinsic shape of the line within each span remains unchanged; only the amount of bending of the line over the interior supports is changed.

It may be well to remind the reader that one use of linear transformation was described in the previous section, where we stated: "The C-line resulting from prestressing a continuous beam is a linearly transformed line from the c.g.s. line," which was explained by the fact that the secondary

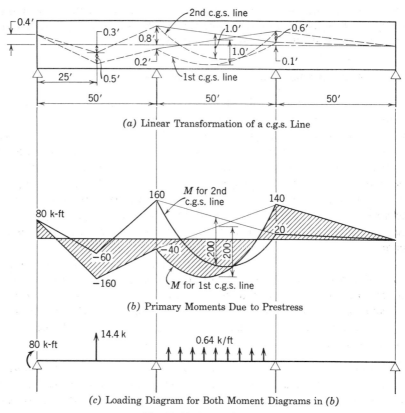

(a) Linear Transformation of a c.g.s. Line

(b) Primary Moments Due to Prestress

(c) Loading Diagram for Both Moment Diagrams in (b)

Fig. 10-12. Example 10-3.

moment that produces the deviation between the two lines varies linearly between any two consecutive supports. Now, another interesting theorem concerning linear transformation is that *in a continuous beam, any c.g.s. line can be linearly transformed without changing the position of the resulting C-line.* This means that the linear transformation of c.g.s. line does not affect the stresses in the concrete, since the *C*-line remains unchanged. Thus the two c.g.s. lines in Fig. 10-12(a) will produce the same *C*-line, and hence the same stresses in the concrete, despite their apparently divergent locations.

The proof of this theorem is as follows. C.g.s. lines having the same intrinsic shape within each individual span will produce primary moment diagrams also having same intrinsic shapes in each individual span. For moment diagrams with the same intrinsic shapes (i.e., the same curvatures and bends), the corresponding loading diagrams along the span are the same, since load is given by the curvature (or second derivative) of the moment. Since the loads are the same, the resulting moments must be the same, which means that the C-lines will have the same position. It must be noted here that, though the resulting moments are the same, the primary moments differ; hence the secondary moments will necessarily differ, since

Secondary moment = Resulting moment − Primary moment

Any bending of the c.g.s. line over the supports will produce transverse forces acting on the beam which are directly counteracted by reactions from the supports. Hence such bending will not affect the moment along the beam. Since the moment is not affected, the C-line is not affected. Thus, linear transformation involving bending of the c.g.s. line over the interior supports will not change the location of the C-line. On the other hand, any movement of the c.g.s. line at the ends of the beam changes the magnitude of the applied end moments, which do affect the moments along all spans of continuous beam and change the location of the C-line on all spans. Hence linear transformation cannot involve the movement of the c.g.s. line over the ends of the beam or over the exterior support of a cantilever, but it can involve movement of the c.g.s. line over the interior supports.

The above theorem, permitting the linear transformation of the c.g.s. line without changing the C-line, offers many possible adjustments in the location of the c.g.s. line which cannot be easily accomplished without that knowledge. Some of these possibilities are evident from the above; others will be discussed later. The validity of this theorem has been proved experimentally within the elastic range, although such a logical theory hardly needs any experimental proof. The effect of linear transformation of the c.g.s. line on the ultimate strength of continuous beams will be discussed in section 10-6.

EXAMPLE 10-3

The first c.g.s. line in the beam, Fig. 10-12(*a*), is linearly transformed to the second position. Show that the C-line in the concrete is the same for both positions. Assume prestress $F = 200$ k.

Solution. The two moment diagrams are shown in (*b*). The loading diagrams corresponding to those moment diagrams are exactly the same and are both shown in (*c*), Hence the line of pressure must also be the same for both c.g.s. lines. The only forces which are different are those directly over the intermediate and end supports. Since they do not produce any moments in the beam, they do not affect our calculations and are not shown in the figure.

Having defined "linear transformation," let us now define "concordant cable": *A concordant cable in a continuous beam is a c.g.s. line which produces a C-line coincident with the c.g.s. line.*

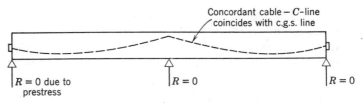

(a) Beam with Concordant Cable

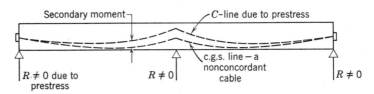

(b) Beam with Nonconcordant Cable

Fig. 10-13. Properties of nonconcordant cables.

In other words, a concordant cable produces no secondary moments. Thus, every cable in a statically determinate structure is concordant, because no external reaction is induced, and there is no secondary moment in the structure. For a continuous beam, on the other hand, external reactions will usually be induced by prestressing. These reactions will produce secondary moments in the beam, and the C-line will shift away from the c.g.s. line. When this happens, the cable is termed nonconcordant. When, by chance or by purpose, no reactions are induced in a continuous beam by prestressing, then there will be no secondary moments and the cable is a concordant one. When a concordant cable is prestressed, it will tend to produce no deflection of the beam over the supports, and hence no reactions will be induced (not considering the weight of the beam). The essential differences between a concordant and a nonconcordant cable are shown in Fig. 10-13.

Besides the fact that a concordant cable line is easier for analysis, there is seldom a necessity for using a concordant one. There were, at first, some doubts as to the behavior of a nonconcordant cable, whether its C-line would change with time or with the elastic and plastic properties of concrete. A little thinking on the subject would clear these doubts. If E_c of the entire beam changes uniformly, there will be no change in the secondary moments, since the secondary moments due to prestressing are computed independent of the E_c value, as, for example, by moment distribution. If the E_c of one portion of concrete changes at a different rate from that of another portion, slight changes in the secondary moments might result, but such effects are generally considered negligible, since the elastic theory assuming uniform E_c for a beam is believed to be sufficiently accurate for the analysis of both reinforced and prestressed concrete.

While no significant reason can be given for preferring a concordant cable, there is even less justification for locating a nonconcordant cable for the sake of nonconcordancy. The real choice of a good c.g.s. location depends on the production of a desirable C-line and the satisfaction of other practical requirements, but not on the concordancy or nonconcordancy of the cable. A concordant cable, being somewhat easier to compute, is slightly preferred, other things being equal.

A convenient procedure in design is to obtain a concordant cable that gives good positions of the c.g.s. in resisting the external moment. If that location falls outside the beam it can be linearly transformed to give a more practical location without changing its C-line. According to this procedure, the finding of locations for concordant cables becomes a useful means to an end.

Several methods have been proposed for obtaining concordant cables, but the author advocates the following method, utilizing only one basic theorem as follows. *Every real moment diagram for a continuous beam on nonsettling supports, produced by any combination of external loadings, whether transverse loads or moments, plotted to any scale, is one location for a concordant cable in that beam.* The application of this theorem is illustrated in example 10-4.

EXAMPLE 10-4

For a continuous prestressed-concrete beam loaded as shown in Fig. 10-14(a), obtain some desirable locations for concordant cables to support that loading.

Solution. Note that every moment diagram plotted to any scale is a concordant cable. If we plot the continuous beam moment diagram for the given loading, we obtain (b). Two concordant cable locations are shown in (c) and (d), both proportional to the moment diagram in (b), and hence both are concordant. (f) gives another location of a concordant cable, which is proportional to the moment diagram for loading in (e). Many similar concordant cables can be found by drawing all kinds of moment diagrams. The most desirable concordant cable will be governed by practical requirements of the particular problem as well as by the ability of the cable to resist the applied loads. For example, the location in (c) gives larger resisting arms for the steel but may overstress the concrete if the weight of the beam is light, in which case (d) may be a better location. (f) does not suit this particular loading as well but gives a symmetrical layout and may carry other loadings, such as the beam's own weight, more efficiently.

The above theorem can be easily proved. Since any moment diagram

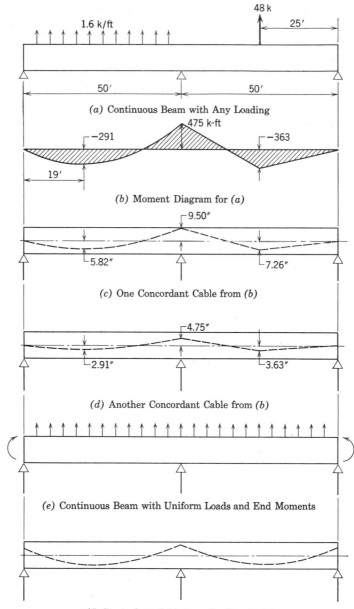

(a) Continuous Beam with Any Loading

(b) Moment Diagram for (a)

(c) One Concordant Cable from (b)

(d) Another Concordant Cable from (b)

(e) Continuous Beam with Uniform Loads and End Moments

(f) Concordant Cable from Loading in (e)

Fig. 10-14. Example 10-4.

due to the loads on a continuous beam is computed on the basis of no deflection over the supports, and since any c.g.s. line following that diagram will produce a similar moment diagram, that c.g.s. line will also produce no deflection over the supports; hence it will induce no reactions and is a concordant cable. The theorem applies not only when the beam is under a constant prestress. If the amount of prestress varies along the beam, the application of the theorem can be modified to suit. In fact, the theorem can be extended to include beams on elastic supports.

Based on this general theorem, many corollaries can be derived which will help the designer in selecting proper position for concordant cables. After the designer has mastered the theorem and its corollaries discussed herein, his work of obtaining a concordant cable is reduced to that of finding a proper moment diagram, which is a familiar operation with most engineers. Some corollaries will be stated.

1. The reverse of the theorem is also true: The eccentricity of any concordant cable measured from the c.g.c. is a moment diagram for some system of loading on the continuous beam plotted to some scale.

2. Any *C*-line is a concordant cable, since it is obtained by computing the moments due to a system of loads on the continuous beam.

3. Superposing two or more concordant cables will result in another concordant cable. Superposing a concordant and a nonconcordant cable will result in a nonconcordant one.

4. When a sudden change in direction is desired, a concentrated load is applied. When a gradual change is desired, a uniform load is applied One moment diagram can thus be modified into another by the addition of loads. Hence one concordant cable can be easily modified into another.

5. In order to obtain a concordant cable from another by linear transformation involving the moving of eccentricities over the ends of a beam, the following procedure can be used. Apply an end moment on th ; continuous beam; compute the moment diagram due to that moment. When one end is moved by a given amount, the entire cable must be transformed linearly in proportion to that moment diagram. If the movement of the eccentricities at both ends is desired, apply end moments at both ends proportional to the respective amount of movement, and shift the entire cable in proportion to the moment diagram so obtained. This will yield another concordant cable, as is illustrated in example 10-5.

Much ingenuity can be exercised in the location of concordant cables, but it should be left to the skill of the designer after he understands the basic theorem and its main corollaries. When applied to rigid frames, the effect of sidesway and rib shortening should be additionally considered. For varying prestress along the beam, the moment diagram should be divided by the corresponding prestress at each point in order to obtain the location of a concordant cable. Or the tendons may be treated separately. If each individual tendon or group of tendons forms a concordant cable, then, when acting together, they also form a concordant cable.

Like all statically indeterminate structures, it is sometimes desirable to purposely adjust the elevations of the supports in order to produce favorable moments in the beams. The moments so produced are of a different nature from the secondary moments caused by prestressing. It was previously mentioned that the secondary moments due to prestressing would not change with the value of E_c. Moments due to adjusted support elevations, on the other hand, do change with the value of E_c, because the moments induced by a given displacement are a function of E_c. Hence such moments will change with time as creep takes place and E_c changes. Therefore, when attempts are made to produce moments by support diaplacements, either the possible change in E_c must be allowed for, or the displacements must be adjusted from time to time. Thus the economy of such a manipulation, though feasible for certain large structures, may be doubtful for small and even medium-sized ones.

EXAMPLE 10-5

Obtain a new concordant cable, with its intrinsic shape the same as that of Fig. 10-14(c), but with the right end of the cable 4 in. above the c.g.c.

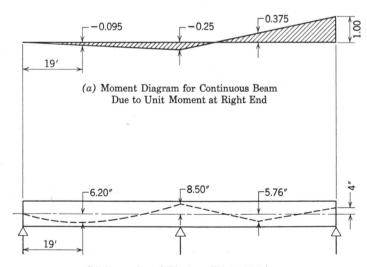

(a) Moment Diagram for Continuous Beam
Due to Unit Moment at Right End

(b) Concordant Cable from Fig. 10-14 (c)
with 4-in. Displacement at Right End

Fig. 10-15. Example 10-5.

Solution. Apply a unit moment at the right end of beam; by the method of moment distribution, plot the moment diagram as in Fig. 10-15(a). The concordant cable in Fig. 10-14(c) can now be linearly transformed in proportion to the moment diagram Fig. 10-15(a), giving a new concordant cable as in Fig. 10-15(b). Note that the same moment diagram (a) can be used to shift the end eccentricity any other amount, not only for the 4 in. illustrated here. Also, owing to the symmetry of the beam, (a) can be similarly used for moving the end eccentricity at the left. A combination of two moment diagrams due to a moment at each end will permit the simultaneous shifting of both end eccentricities.

An infinite number of concordant cables can be obtained by rotating one concordant cable about the points of inflection, because such rotation simply represents the addition of one concordant cable to another, and should result in a concordant one. The points of inflection in these moment diagrams are called "nodal points" by some European authors.

10-5 Cable Location

Here, again, by cable location is meant the location of the centroid of the tendons, that is, the c.g.s. line. After the c.g.s. line is determined, the location of the individual position of the various tendons is an easier problem which will not be discussed here.

Designing a continuous prestressed-concrete beam, like that of any other continuous structure, is essentially a procedure of trial and error. Knowledge regarding the analysis of such structures, together with a systematic approach to the solution, will aid greatly in arriving at desired results. The following steps are recommended for designing a continuous prestressed beam.

Step 1. Assume section of members for dead-load computation.

Step 2. Compute maximum and minimum moments at critical points for various combinations of dead, live, and other external loads, Fig. 10-16(a). Compute the amount of prestress required for these moments and the corresponding depth of concrete. Modify section of members, and repeat steps 1 and 2 if necessary.

Step 3. Plot top and bottom kern lines for the members, Fig. 10-16(b). From the bottom kern line, plot

$$a_{min} = \frac{M_{min}}{F} \quad \text{also} \quad a_G = \frac{M_G}{F_0}$$

where M_{min} = the algebraically smallest moment. The distances a_{min} and a_G should be plotted upward for $-M$ and downward for $+M$.

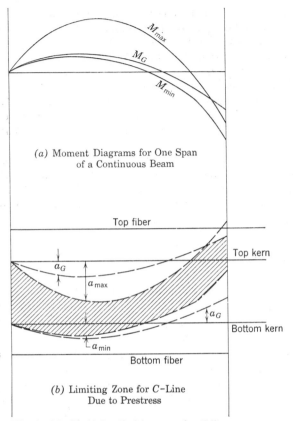

(*a*) Moment Diagrams for One Span
of a Continuous Beam

(*b*) Limiting Zone for C-Line
Due to Prestress

Fig. 10-16. Obtaining limiting zone for C-line
due to prestress.

From the top kern, plot

$$a_{\max} = \frac{M_{\max}}{F} \qquad \text{also} \qquad a_G = \frac{M_G}{F_0}$$

again upward for $-M$ and downward for $+M$.

The shaded area, between the limit of these four lines, obtained by $a_{\max}$ and $a_{\min}$ and a_G, represents the zone in which the line of pressure must lie if no tension is permitted. As in previous discussions on cable location for simple and cantilever beams, when the zone is too wide, an excess of prestress or of concrete section or of girder load is generally indicated. If the limiting line from one kern crosses a limiting line from another kern, an inadequacy is evident. An ideal layout is obtained when there exists a narrow limiting zone within the beam where the centroid of the cables can be conveniently located.

Step 4. Select a trial cable location within the above zone. Note that, if the cable follows the shape of some moment diagram, it will be a concordant cable. If this trial location is a concordant cable, it is a satisfactory solution. If it is a nonconcordant cable, the C-line can be determined by moment distribution as described in the previous section. If the C-line still lies within the limiting zone, then two locations are possible: either the trial location giving a nonconcordant cable, or a new location following the C-line, thus giving a concordant cable. If this C-line lies outside the zone, new cable locations can be tried. An attempt should be made to get a concordant cable within the zone. It is generally best to try concordant cables, because they coincide with their C-lines and give a more direct solution. Note that, after having obtained one concordant cable, it is much easier to derive from it other concordant cables by the general theorem that any moment diagram for the continuous beam is a concordant cable. Adding to the first concordant cable any form of moment diagram will give another concordant cable. The shape of the added moment diagram can be obtained by applying couples or concentrated and uniform loads anywhere along the continuous beam. Thus it is not a difficult problem to add another moment diagram to the first concordant cable to obtain another concordant one which will lie within the zone.

Step 5. The concordant cable within the limiting zone obtained in step 4 is a good location for resisting the external moment, but it may or may not be a good practical location. For example, it may be desirable to shift the c.g.s. line in order to bring the tendons within the boundaries of the beam. To achieve this without shifting the C-line, the concordant cable can be linearly transformed as desired. After this linear transformation, the cable becomes nonconcordant. This procedure is illustrated in example 10-6.

EXAMPLE 10-6

A pedestrian bridge of prestressed-concrete slab (the Harkness Avenue Bridge in San Francisco, California, of the California Division of Highways) has a three-span symmetrical continuous layout as shown, Fig. 10-17(a). The bridge is 9 ft 4 in. wide with a uniform thickness of 13 in. (neglecting curbs). The total effective prestressing force is 1,230,000 lb after deducting a loss of 15%. Design live load is 50 psf. Choose a suitable location for the cable, allowing no tension in the concrete, $f_c' = 5000$ psi.

Solution. Following the procedure described above and considering 1-ft width of slab:

Step 1. The section is already chosen, and the dead load is 162 psf or 162 plf for 1-ft width.

Step 2. The amount of prestress is already chosen; it is 1,230,000/9.33 = 132 k per ft width of slab for the effective prestress, or 156 k for the initial prestress.

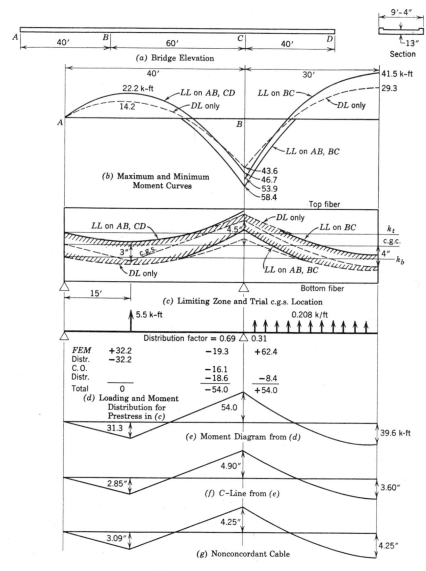

(a) Bridge Elevation

(b) Maximum and Minimum Moment Curves

(c) Limiting Zone and Trial c.g.s. Location

(d) Loading and Moment Distribution for Prestress in (c)

(e) Moment Diagram from (d)

(f) C-Line from (e)

(g) Nonconcordant Cable

Fig. 10-17. Example 10-6.

Step 3. Kern lines for a rectangular section are located at the third points. The maximum and minimum moment diagrams together with the girder moment diagrams are shown in Fig. 10-17(b) for one half of the structure. These diagrams are divided by the respective prestress, F for those with live loads, and F_0 for dead load only. The *a* values thus obtained are plotted from the kern lines as shown in Fig. 10-17(c), giving the limits for the zone within which the C-line due to prestressing must lie.

Step 4. Using the moment diagrams as guides, select a trial c.g.s. location within the zone as shown in Fig. 10-17(c). For the purpose of illustration, assume the c.g.s. line to possess the following characteristics.

1. Passing through the c.g.c. (mid-depth of slab) at end supports.
2. One sharp bend for each side span.
3. One sharp bend over each intermediate support.
4. A parabolic curve for the center span.

For this c.g.s. location, the corresponding loading on the concrete is shown in (d), moment distribution for which gives a moment diagram as in (e). Dividing the moment diagram by the prestress yields a C-line as shown in (f) which is very close to the trial location and is still within the limiting zone. Hence this C-line is a location for a satisfactory concordant cable.

Step 5. A more practical location for the c.g.s. is shown in (g), affording better protection for the steel. This is obtained by linearly transforming the concordant cable into a nonconcordant one. This nonconcordant cable will yield the same C-line as the concordant one and hence will serve the same purpose as far as stresses are concerned.

10-6 Cracking and Ultimate Strength

Tests have shown that the elastic theory can be applied to continuous prestressed-concrete beams with great accuracy[9] as long as the concrete has not cracked. Occasionally, structures are subjected to overloads beyond the point of cracking or are designed for some permissible cracking under working loads. Then it will be necessary to determine the cracking strength of such structures. In addition, knowledge regarding the ultimate strength of these beams is also of interest in providing criterion for designing.[10] Such strengths will be investigated and discussed in this section.

Since a prestressed structure is nearly a homogeneous material before cracking, the elastic theory can be applied to the calculation of strength up to that point. Even when some cracks have occurred, a prestressed structure is no less homogeneous than a reinforced-concrete structure under working loads. In fact, there is every reason to believe that the elastic theory would be more applicable to prestressed concrete at the start of cracking than reinforced concrete under working loads, since reinforced concrete usually starts to crack at about one-third the working load.

What should be the tensile stress in continuous prestressed-concrete beams at the point of cracking? Some engineers believe that the cracking tensile strength is higher than the modulus of rupture measured from plain concrete specimens. Experiments have shown, however, that the modulus of rupture is a reasonably accurate measure of the start of cracking in continuous prestressed beams. It must be realized that only hair cracks are produced when the modulus of rupture is reached. These cracks, at first, will not be easily visible to the unaided eye but can be detected by strain gages or microscopic examinations.

Before the start of actual cracking, some plastic deformation is usually exhibited in the concrete. Such deformation occurs only in limited regions and does not affect the general behavior of the structure as an elastic body. Hence the validity of the elastic theory can still be counted on, up to and perhaps slightly beyond the cracking of concrete.

Accurate determination of the ultimate strength of a continuous prestressed-concrete beam involves many difficulties. However, for design purposes, the ultimate strength can be estimated on the basis of the limit design theory,[11] if the plastic hinges are formed at critical points of maximum moment. This is true for under-reinforced sections, which deform extensively before final rupture. For over-reinforced sections, which may suddenly fail in the compressive zone of concrete before any appreciable rotation, a perfect plastic action cannot be expected. The action then is partly elastic and partly plastic.

For the purpose of design, since only an estimate of the ultimate strength is required, the solution need not be complicated. If the beam is under-reinforced, the plastic theory can be applied. If it is over-reinforced, depending on the degree of over-reinforcing, an interpolation between the plastic and the elastic theories would often give results sufficiently accurate for estimating the factor of safety.

The estimation of the ultimate capacity of a continuous prestressed beam is illustrated in example 10-7. The method is based on the plastic hinge theory (or limit design theory) together with the ultimate moment analysis for prestressed-concrete sections (see section 5-6). It is assumed, of course, that only flexural failure, but no shear or bond failure, takes place, and that the sections are under-reinforced.

EXAMPLE 10-7

For the continuous prestressed slab in example 10-6, with the c.g.s. located as finally chosen, Fig. 10-17(g), compute the ultimate load-carrying capacity for uniform load on all the spans. For effective prestress of 120 ksi, steel area per foot width of slab is $132/120 = 1.1$ sq in. f_s' for the steel wire is given as 240 ksi. $f_c' = 5000$ psi.

Solution. The probable plastic hinge locations are over the intermediate supports, at center of middle span, and near the 0.4 points E and G of the outside spans. These sections are shown in Fig. 10-18(a). Let us first determine the ultimate moment capacities of these sections. A little calculation will show that the ultimate strength of steel cannot be developed for these sections.

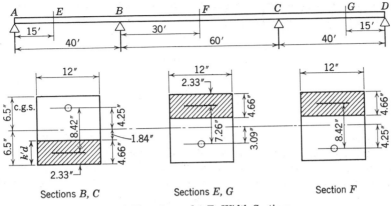

Sections B, C   Sections E, G   Section F

(a) Elevation and 1-Ft Width Sections

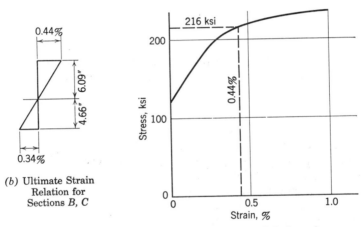

(b) Ultimate Strain
Relation for
Sections B, C

(c) Stress–Strain Relations of
Prestressed Steel

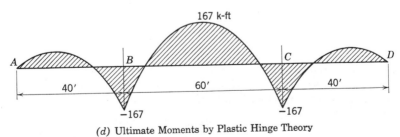

(d) Ultimate Moments by Plastic Hinge Theory

Fig. 10-18. Example 10-7.

Assume that 90% of ultimate strength of steel is developed for all these sections; the lever arm for the steel at ultimate can be computed as follows:

$$0.90 \times 240 = 216 \text{ ksi}$$
$$216 \times 1.1 = 238 \text{ k}$$
$$k'd = \frac{238}{12 \times 4250}$$
$$= 4.66 \text{ in.}$$

where $4250 = 0.85f_c'$ is the assumed average ultimate compression in concrete. With this computed $k'd$, the strain in steel can be estimated as in (b). Corresponding to that strain, the stress in steel, which is about 90% of f_s', can be obtained from the stress-strain relations as given in (c). No revised computation is necessary. The ultimate capacity of sections B, F, and C is thus

$$238 \times 8.42/12 = 167 \text{ k-ft}$$

and of sections E and G, it is

$$238 \times 7.26/12 = 144 \text{ k-ft}$$

It must be noted that both of these sections are over-reinforced and will not behave as plastically as under-reinforced sections. According to the elastic theory, maximum moment occurs over the interior supports and is given by

$$-M = 0.0747wL^2$$
$$167 = 0.0747w \times 60^2$$
$$w = 0.621 \text{ klf}$$

By the plastic hinge theory, ultimate failure will occur only when one more hinge than the number of indeterminacy is stressed to the ultimate. For this beam, when hinges form at B, F, and C, the structure will collapse. Corresponding to these hinges, the moment diagram for the center span will be as shown in (d), and the uniform weight on the beam will be

$$\frac{wL^2}{8} = 167 + 167 = 334 \text{ k-ft}$$

$$w = \frac{8 \times 334}{3600} = 0.742 \text{ klf}$$

The actual ultimate load may be somewhere between the values given by the two theories, and 700 plf would be a good guess. The factor of safety for both dead and live loads together is, hence,

$$700/212 = 3.3$$

It should be noted that according to the plastic theory the ultimate load is affected only by load on the center span and is independent of the load on the side spans in this case.

Tests have been run to prove the validity of the theory of linear transformation in the ultimate range, which can be stated as follows. *Linear transformation of the c.g.s. line does not change the ultimate load-carrying capacity of a continuous beam.* Theoretical proof of this statement has also been made but will not be attempted here. It should be mentioned, however, that the theory is valid in the ultimate range only under the following two conditions.

1. The steel must be sufficiently far from the compressive side of concrete so as not to produce sudden compression failures in the concrete. In other words, the plastic hinges must remain plastic, and the sections must remain under-reinforced.

2. The location of plastic hinges must not be changed as a result of linear transformation. For uniformly distributed loads and curved cables, linear transformation may change the location of the plastic hinge near midspan and thus modify the ultimate load-carrying capacity. In general, however, such change in location does not affect the strength seriously.

When nonprestressed steel is added to the critical points of a continuous beam, the ultimate moment capacity of these sections is increased. The amount of increase can be figured by some method such as presented in example 9-1. Using these increased ultimate strengths, and applying the theory of limit design, or the plastic hinge theory, the ultimate strength of the structure can be figured in the conventional way. Proper addition of nonprestressed steel also helps to distribute the cracks and to increase the shear strength, as well as the fatigue strength of critical sections. Design of continuous beams by ultimate strength and plastic hinge theories is often a simpler procedure than by the elastic theory. However, the elastic theory will still be needed to compute the stresses at transfer, to estimate deflections under working loads, and to compute the cracking loads. The plastic theory will permit a closer estimate of the ultimate load-carrying capacities, and it serves as a good guide for a preliminary design.

Readers interested in continuous prestressed-concrete structures are urged to study the concept of load balancing described in Chapter 11. The method presented therein will appear to be much simpler. However, both the elastic behavior and the ultimate strength described in this chapter are essential to the proper analysis and design of continuous prestressed-concrete structures and should be mastered by the designers.

References

1　*Symposium on Prestressed Concrete Continuous and Framed Structures*, Cement and Concrete Assn., London, 1951.

2 F. S. Rostasy, "Connections in Precast Concrete Structures—Continuity in Double-T Floor Construction," *PCI Journal*, August, 1962.

3 A. L. Parme and G. H. Paris, "Designing for Continuity in Prestressed Concrete Structures," *J. Am. Concrete Inst.*, September 1951 (*Proc.*, Vol. 47), pp. 45–64.

4 R. B. B. Moorman, "Equivalent Load Method for Analyzing Prestressed Concrete Structures," *J. Am. Concrete Inst.*, January 1952 (*Proc.*, Vol. 48), pp. 405–416.

5 E. I. Fiesenheiser, "Rapid Design of Continuous Prestressed Members," *J. Am. Concrete Inst.*, April 1954 (*Proc.*, Vol. 50), pp. 669–676.

6 H. Cross and N. D. Morgan, *Continuous Frames of Reinforced Concrete*, John Wiley & Sons, New York, 1932.

7 T. Y. Lin, "A Direct Method of Moment Distribution," *Trans. Am. Soc. C.E.*, 1937, pp. 561–605.

8 Y. Guyon, "Statically Indeterminate Structures in the Elastic and Plastic States," *General Report*, First Int. Congress, Int. Federation of Prestressing, London, 1953.

9 T. Y. Lin, "Strengths of Continuous Prestressed Concrete Beams under Static and Repeated Loads," *J. Am. Concrete Inst.*, June 1955 (*Proc.*, Vol. 51).

10 N. M. Hawkins, M. A. Sozen, and C. P. Siess, "Strength and Behavior of Two-span Continuous Prestressed Concrete Beams," *Structural Research Series No. 225*, Univ. of Illinois, September 1961.

11 J. A. Van den Broek, *Theory of Limit Design*, John Wiley & Sons, New York, 1948 (out of print).

load-balancing method *11*

11-1 Stress-Concept, Strength-Concept, and Balanced-Load Concept

In section 1-2, three basic concepts for prestressed concrete are discussed. Briefly, the first concept is to treat prestressed concrete as an elastic material so that it can be designed and analyzed with respect to its elastic stresses. This "stress-concept" forms the basis for methods and formulas presented in the major portion of Chapters 5 through 10. The second concept considers prestressed concrete similar to reinforced concrete, and deals with its ultimate strength. It might be termed as the "strength-concept" and is also discussed liberally in most of the above-mentioned chapters.

The third concept sees prestressed concrete as primarily an attempt to balance a portion of the load on the structure.[1,2] It was only mentioned in section 1-2 and will now be expounded upon in this chapter. While this "balanced-load-concept" often represents the simplest approach to prestressed design and analysis, its advantage over the two other concepts is not significant for statically determinate structures. When dealing with statically indeterminate structural systems, this balanced-load concept offers tremendous advantages both in calculating and in visualizing. It is noticeably simpler than the methods explained in Chapter 10 and is highly recommended. Although preliminary designs and often final analyses for indeterminate structures can be achieved far more easily using this method, it is urged that engineers also learn the other concepts, including the material presented in Chapter 10 on continuous beams.

To understand this balanced-load concept relative to the other two concepts, let us first examine the life history of a prestressed member under flexure, Fig. 11-1. While this figure is intended to describe the load-deflection relationship of a member, such as a simple beam, it also applies to a section of a member. There are several critical points in the life history, which follow.

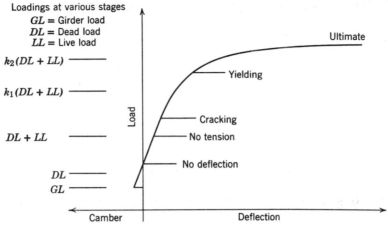

Fig. 11-1. Life history of prestressed member under flexure.

1. The point of *no deflection* which indicates a rectangular stress block across the section.
2. The point of *no tension* which indicates a triangular stress block with zero stress at the bottom fiber of a simple beam.
3. The point of *cracking* which occurs when the extreme fiber is stressed to the modulus of rupture.
4. The point of *yielding* at which the steel is stressed beyond its yield point so that complete recovery will not be obtained.
5. The *ultimate load* which represents the maximum load carried by the member at failure.

In Fig. 11-1 the various loading conditions to which a beam is subjected to are indicated as follows.

1. Girder load, *GL*
2. Total dead load, *DL*
3. The working load, made up of dead plus live load, *DL + LL*
4. A factor of safety applied to the working load to obtain the minimum yield point load, $k_1(DL + LL)$
5. Another factor of safety k_2 applied to obtain the minimum ultimate load, $k_2(DL + LL)$.

Design by stress-concept actually consists of matching the $(DL + LL)$ with the point of "no tension" (or some allowable tension) on the beam. Design by strength-concept consists of matching the $k_2(DL + LL)$ with the "ultimate strength" of the beam. Design by balanced-load concept consists of matching the $DL + k_3LL$ (where k_3 is zero or some value much less than 1) with the point of no deflection. It is clear that, depending on the relative values of the three stages of loadings as compared to the relative values of the three stages of the beam behavior (see table below), designs based on the three approaches could yield the same proportions or widely varying ones.

Applied Loadings	Stages of Beam Behavior
$DL + k_3 LL$	No deflection
$DL + LL$	No tension
$k_2(DL + LL)$	Ultimate

It is also noted that, regardless of what concept is followed in the design, it is common practice to check for the behavior of the beam at the other stages. For example, if the stress concept is used for design, the ultimate strength requirements and the deflection of the beam under dead load are usually computed in addition. We are not generally concerned with the other stages, such as the $k_1(DL + LL)$ loading, the cracking and the yielding stages, although often they could be more important and deserve careful consideration.

If the load deflection of a beam or the moment-curvature relationship of a section is of a definite shape, it is then possible to determine all critical points whenever one point is known. Actually, on account of the difference in the shape of the section, the amount and location of prestressed and nonprestressed steel, as well as different stress-strain relationships of both the concrete and the steel, these load-deflection or moment-curvature relationships may possess divergent forms. Thus it is often necessary to determine more than one critical point in order to be sure that the beam will behave properly under various loading conditions.

Which concept is the best to follow will depend on the circumstances. Generally it is desirable to choose the one which will control the proportioning of the member. If it is not certain that the other requirements will be met automatically, analysis for these other critical stages will be made, and modifications of the design may be effected. Since the balanced-load point is often representative of the behavior during the greater portion of the life span of the structure, it will deserve more consideration than either the elastic stresses or the ultimate strength.

Another consideration in the choice of the proper concept is the simplicity of analysis and design. It is believed that the balanced-load concept offers by far the simpler approach for statically indeterminate structures, especially for a preliminary design. It also gives a better picture of the structural behavior and thus enables a more intelligent approach to design and layout, as will be shown in the following sections.

A further advantage of the balanced-load approach is the convenience in the computation of deflections. Since the loading under which there will be no deflection anywhere along the beam is already known, the net deflection produced under any other condition of loading is simply computed by treating the loading differential acting on an elastic beam. Thus if the effective prestress balances the sustained loading, the beam will remain perfectly level regardless of the modulus of elasticity or the flexural creep of concrete.

11-2   Simple Beams and Cantilevers

While the load-balancing approach is not usually the best method for designing a simple beam, it can be well introduced with this simple case. Figure 11-2 illustrates how to balance a concentrated load by sharply bending the c.g.s., at midspan, thus creating an upward component,

$$V = 2F \sin \theta$$

If this V exactly balances a concentrated load P applied also at midspan, the beam is not subjected to any transverse load (neglecting the weight of the beam). At the ends, the vertical component of prestress $F \sin \theta$ is transmitted directly into the supports, while the horizontal component $F \cos \theta$ creates a uniform compression along the entire beam. Thus the stresses in the beam at any section (except for local stress concentrations) is simply given by

$$f = \frac{F \cos \theta}{A_c}$$

$$= \frac{F}{A_c}$$

for small values of θ. Any loading in addition to P will now cause bending in an elastic homogeneous beam (up to point of cracking), and the

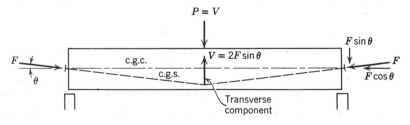

Fig. 11-2. Balancing of a concentrated load.

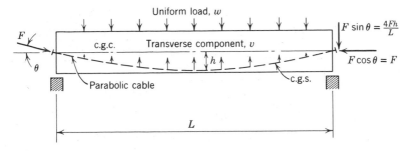

Fig. 11-3. Balancing of a uniform load.

additional stresses can be simply computed by

$$f = \frac{Mc}{I}$$

where M = the moment produced by load in addition to P.

Similarly, Fig. 11-3 illustrates the balancing of a uniformly distributed load by means of a parabolic cable whose upward component v (lb/ft) is given by

$$v = \frac{8Fh}{L^2}$$

If the externally applied load w (including the weight of the beam) is exactly balanced by the component v, there is no bending in the beam. The beam is again under a uniform compression with stress,

$$f = \frac{F}{A_c}$$

Should the external load be different from w, it is only necessary to analyze the moment M produced by the load differential and compute the corresponding stresses by the formula,

$$f = \frac{Mc}{I}$$

This procedure has already been illustrated in example 1-4 of Chapter 1.

Now consider a cantilever beam, Fig. 11-4. The conditions for load balancing become slightly more complicated, because any vertical component at the cantilever end C will upset the balance, unless there is an externally applied load at that tip. To balance a uniformly distributed load w, the tangent to the c.g.s. at C will have to be horizontal. Then the

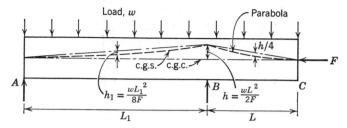

Fig. 11-4. Load balancing for a cantilever beam.

parabola for the cantilever portion can best be located by computing

$$h = \frac{wL^2}{2F}$$

and the parabola for the anchor arm by

$$h_1 = \frac{wL_1^{\,2}}{8F}$$

It soon becomes apparent that the load-balancing approach may not always be the simplest, and the same result may be achieved by locating the c.g.s. line, such that the area between the c.g.s. and the c.g.c. will be proportional to the external moment diagram.

In order to compute the transverse component of prestress for beams with curved c.g.c. (Fig. 11-5), it is necessary to use the area between the c.g.s. and the c.g.c., rather than just the curvature of the cable itself. This becomes evident when the eccentric moment created by the horizontal end component of the prestress is taken into consideration.

When exact load balancing is required, the c.g.s. line should always be located at the c.g.c. for the ends of the beam. For practical reasons, it may not be desirable to do so, as for a pre-tensioned beam of short span

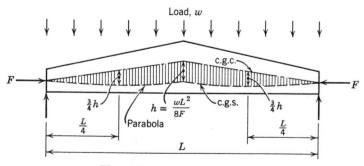

Fig. 11-5. Beam with curved c.g.c.

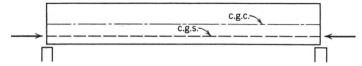

Fig. 11-6. Beam with straight cable.

(Fig. 11-6), where exact load balancing is not obtained, and other methods of analysis may be simpler.

EXAMPLE 11-1

A double cantilever beam is to be designed so that its prestress will exactly balance the total uniform load of 1.6 k/ft on the beam, Fig. 11-7. Design the beam using the least amount of prestress, assuming that the c.g.s. must have a concrete protection of at least 3 in. If a concentrated load of $P = 14$ k is added at midspan, compute the maximum top and bottom fiber stresses.

Solution. In order to balance the load in the cantilever, the c.g.s. at the tip must be located at the c.g.c with a horizontal tangent. To use the least amount of prestress, the eccentricity over the support should be a maximum, that is, $h = 12$ in. or 1 ft. The prestress required is

$$F = \frac{wL^2}{2h}$$

$$= \frac{1.6 \times 20^2}{2 \times 1}$$

$$= 320 \text{ k}$$

In order to balance the load on the center span, using the same prestress, $F = 320$ k, the sag for the parabola must be

$$h_1 = \frac{wL_1^2}{8F}$$

$$= \frac{1.6 \times 48^2}{8 \times 320}$$

$$= 1.44 \text{ ft or } 17.3 \text{ in.}$$

Hence the c.g.s. is located as shown, Fig. 11-8.

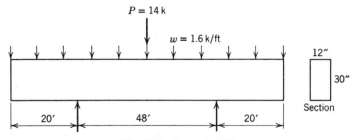

Fig. 11-7. Example 11-1.

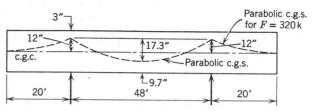

Fig. 11-8. Solution for Example 11-1.

Under the combined action of the uniform load and the prestress, the beam will have no deflection anywhere and is under uniform compressive stress of

$$f = \frac{F}{A_c} = \frac{320,000}{360} = -889 \text{ psi}$$

Owing to the $P = 14$ k, the moment M at midspan is,

$$M = \frac{PL}{4} = \frac{14 \times 48}{4} = 168 \text{ k-ft}$$

and the extreme fiber stresses are

$$f = \frac{Mc}{I} = \frac{6M}{bd^2} = \frac{6 \times 168 \times 12,000}{12 \times 30^2}$$
$$= \pm 1120 \text{ psi}$$

The resulting stresses at midspan are

$$f_{top} = -889 - 1120 = -2009 \text{ psi compression}$$
$$f_{bot} = -889 + 1120 = +231 \text{ psi tension}$$

Note that the actual cable placement may not possess the sharp bend shown over the supports, and the effect of any deviation from the theoretical position must be investigated accordingly. Also note that $F = 320$ k is the effective prestress, so that under the initial prestress there will be a slight camber at midspan and either a camber or a deflection at the tips which can be computed.

For better stress conditions under the load P, it would be desirable to relocate the c.g.s. so that it would have more sag at midspan. Then a balanced condition would not exist under the uniform load w.

11-3 Continuous Beams

Several methods are available for designing a prestressed continuous beam for balanced load. One method is to compute the actual moment diagram produced by the loading and plot the c.g.s. with an ordinate $y = M/F$ measured from the c.g.c. This involves the plotting of moment diagrams for continuous beams as a start, and it yields only a concordant cable, which is generally not the most economical one. The application of the balanced-load concept to prestressed continuous beams not only greatly simplifies their design and analysis, but also gives an approach to the use of nonconcordant cables, as well as concordant ones.

A continuous beam under the balanced action between the transverse component of the prestress and the applied external load has a uniform stress f across any section of the beam. This is given by

$$f = \frac{F}{A_c}$$

For any change from that balanced-load condition, ordinary elastic analysis (such as moment distribution) can be applied to the load differential to obtain the moment M at any section, and the resulting stresses computed from the familiar formula,

$$f = \frac{My}{I}$$

This means that, after load balancing, the analysis of prestressed continuous beams is reduced to the analysis of a nonprestressed continuous beam. Furthermore, since such analysis will be applied to only the unbalanced portion of the load, any inaccuracies in the method of analysis become a relatively insignificant factor, and approximate methods may often prove sufficient.

While analysis by this balanced-load approach is easier for continuous beams, the stress values obtained are no different than those found by the method described in Chapter 10. Design by this method, however, gives a different visualization of the problem and may yield different layouts and proportions. In order to cultivate the ability to design, it will be necessary to first learn the method of analysis. A simple case is illustrated in example 11-2.

EXAMPLE 11-2

For the symmetrical continuous beam in Fig. 11-9, prestressed with $F = 320$ k along a parabolic cable as shown, compute the extreme fiber stresses over the center support for $DL + LL = 1.6$ k/ft. Use the balanced-load method.

Solution. The upward transverse component of prestress is

$$v = \frac{8Fh}{L^2} = \frac{8 \times 320 \times 1}{50^2} = 1.03 \text{ k/ft}$$

For an applied downward load of 1.03 k/ft, the beam is balanced under a uniform stress of

$$f = \frac{320,000}{360} = -889 \text{ psi}$$

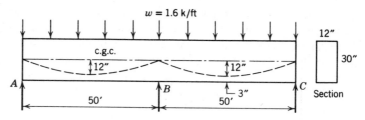

Fig. 11-9. Example 11-2.

For $w = 1.6$ k/ft, the unbalanced downward load is,

$$1.60 - 1.03 = 0.57 \text{ k/ft}$$

which produces a negative moment over the center support,

$$M = \frac{wL^2}{8} = \frac{0.57 \times 50^2}{8}$$

$$= -178 \text{ k-ft}$$

and fiber stresses,

$$f = \frac{Mc}{I} = \frac{6 \times 178 \times 12,000}{12 \times 30^2}$$

$$= \pm 989 \text{ psi}$$

The resulting stresses are

$$f_{top} = -889 + 989 = +100 \text{ psi tension}$$

$$f_{bot} = -889 - 989 = -1878 \text{ psi compression}$$

Note that we have analyzed the stresses without referring to the concordancy and linear transformation of cables as discussed in Chapter 10. Those who have studied Chapter 10 will notice that this is a nonconcordant cable, and reactions are induced by prestressing. It will be easy to compute the total reactions by the balanced-load approach. Thus, under the action of 1.03 k/ft applied load (including beam weight), the reactions are simply the vertical components of the cables:

Exterior support, reaction $R_A = 1.03 \times 25 = 25.8$ k

Interior support, reaction $R_B = 2 \times 25.8 = 51.6$ k

Under the action of the additional 0.57 k/ft load, the reactions can be computed by using ordinary continuous beam formulas:

Exterior support, $R_A = \frac{3}{8}wL = \frac{3}{8} \times 0.57 \times 50 = 10.6$ k

Interior support, $R_B = 2 \times \frac{5}{8}wL = 2 \times \frac{5}{8} \times 0.57 \times 50 = 35.6$ k

Hence the total reactions are, due to 1.60 k/ft and the effect prestress,

$$\text{Exterior support, } R_A = 25.8 + 10.6 = 36.4 \text{ k}$$
$$\text{Interior support, } R_B = 51.6 + 35.6 = 87.2 \text{ k}$$

The simple symmetrical cable profile in example 11-2 is chosen for the convenience of illustrating the method of analysis; it does not represent the most economical location. But once the principle of load-balancing is well understood, it is possible to design the beam economically and in a straightforward manner, as will be shown in example 11-3.

EXAMPLE 11-3

For the continuous beam in example 11-2, determine the prestress *F* required to balance a uniform load of 1.03 k/ft, using the most economical location of cable. Assume a concrete protection of at least 3 in. for the c.g.s. Compute the midspan section stresses and the reactions for the effect of prestress and an external load of 1.6 k/ft.

Solution. The most economical cable location is one with the maximum sag so that the least amount of prestress will be required to balance the load. As shown in Fig. 11-10, a 3-in. protection is given to the c.g.s. over the center support and at midspan (a theoretical parabola based on these clearances will have slightly less than 3 in. at a point about 20 ft in from the exterior support). The c.g.s. at the beam ends should coincide with the c.g.c. and cannot be raised, not only because such raising will destroy the load balancing, but it will not help to increase the efficiency of the cable, since unfavorable end moments will be introduced.

The cable now has a sag of 18 in. and the prestress *F* required to balance the load of 1.03 k/ft is

$$F = \frac{wL^2}{8h} = \frac{1.03 \times 50^2}{8 \times 1.5}$$

$$= 214 \text{ k}$$

The fiber stress under this balanced load condition is now

$$f = \frac{F}{A_c} = \frac{214,000}{360} = -593 \text{ psi}$$

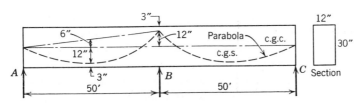

Fig. 11-10. Example 11-3.

Owing to the additional load of 0.57 k/ft, the stresses produced over center support are, as in example 11-2,

$$f = \pm 989 \text{ psi}$$

And the resulting stresses over center support are

$$f_{top} = -593 + 989 = +396 \text{ psi tension}$$
$$f_{bot} = -593 - 989 = -1582 \text{ psi compression}$$

The reactions due to 1.03 k/ft can be computed from the vertical components of the cable and are, very closely,

Exterior support, $R_A = 1.03 \times 25 - \frac{1}{50}(214) = 25.8 - 4.3 = 21.5$ k

Interior support, $R_B = 51.6 + 2 \times 4.3 = 60.2$ k

Under the action of 0.57 k/ft load, the reactions are, as obtained for example 11-2,

Exterior support, $R_A = 10.6$ k

Interior support, $R_B = 35.6$ k

Hence the total reactions due to 1.6 k/ft load and the effect of $F = 214$ k are

Exterior support, $R_A = 21.5 + 10.6 = 32.1$ k

Interior support, $R_B = 60.2 + 35.6 = 95.8$ k

Although these examples are limited to uniform loads, the same principle can be applied to concentrated loads as illustrated in example 11-1. When the cable transverse component is higher than the externally applied load, the load differential would be upward instead of downward, and computation can be made accordingly.

Since the cables in the two previous examples are nonconcordant, it will be worthwhile for the reader to compute the stresses and reactions by following the method of linear transformation explained in Chapter 10. Evidently, more work will be required even for the analysis. But what is more important is the clarity of design afforded by this method. For actual design, the load to be balanced by prestress should be chosen after individual study and with the guidance of experience.

The linear transformation of c.g.s. lines can be easily explained by the balanced load-concept. Since the transverse force applied from the cable on the concrete remains unchanged by linear transformation, it is evident that the elastic behavior of the beam remains the same. On the other hand, since the vertical components from the cable do change directly over the supports by linear transformation of c.g.s. lines, the reactions will be accordingly modified. This phenomenon has been explained in Chapter 10 and is again explained here by a new approach.

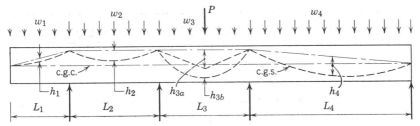

Fig. 11-11. Load balancing for irregular spans and loadings.

This method can be conveniently applied to continuous beams of multiple and unequal spans, including the use of unequal prestress in the spans. For example, the beam in Fig. 11-11 carrying various loads can have the loads in each span balanced by choosing a proper profile for the c.g.s. The cantilever span at the left has the c.g.s. tangent to the c.g.c. at the tip. The middle span has a sag h_{3a} to balance the concentrated load P and another sag h_{3b} to balance the uniform load w_3. The longer span at the right end can have higher prestress by adding more cables. The total prestress in each section is computed by using the corresponding F, w, L, and h for the section span in question. Either the F is known and the h is computed or, if h is predetermined, then F is computed.

If this is done, the entire beam is balanced due to the effect of prestress and the given loading. Then the stress at any section is computed simply by

$$f = \frac{F}{A_c}$$

where F and A_c are the prestress and the concrete area for that section.

The proper use of this method for design depends greatly on the choice of the proper loading to be balanced by the prestress. A simple uniform load for the balanced design may not be the most desirable, or the most economical. With some experience, excellent design can be obtained with such simplicity that the design of continuous prestressed-concrete structures is no longer a difficult problem.

For beams with curved or bent c.g.c., the determination of c.g.s. for a balanced load design can be made using a semi-graphical method as in Fig. 11-12. First estimate from (*a*) the controlling eccentricities (probably y_1 and y_2) as dictated by physical dimensions and prestress requirements. Transfer these eccentricities to (*b*) and join them with parabolas or other c.g.s. profiles. The sag h and the prestress F required for load balancing can now be computed. Transpose all the y values from (*b*) back into (*a*), obtaining the actual cable layout. A few trials and errors might be required to obtain the most desirable location, but no great difficulty is involved. Again, adjustments in the profile might have to be made to

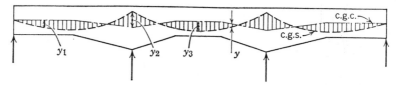

(a) Actual c.g.s. Location for Balanced Load.

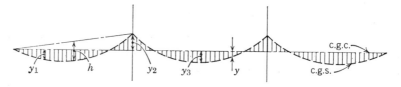

(b) Graphical Solution to Obtain c.g.s. Location

Fig. 11-12. Balanced-load design for beam with curved c.g.c.

suit certain physical requirements. These include rounding off the peaks of the profile over the interior supports, moving the c.g.s. at the ends away from the c.g.c. etc. The effect of such variations should be calculated or at least estimated.

11-4   Rigid Frames

The analysis and design of prestressed-concrete rigid frames can be made by following the method explained in Chapter 10 for continuous beams. This consists of taking freebodies of the concrete separated from the tendons and of determining the linear transformation of the tendons. Although the method is not too difficult, the designer can get lost in the mechanics of analysis so that he cannot easily visualize the problem and reach an economical design. When axial shortening and induced stresses are considered, or when precast elements are joined to form a frame, the design of rigid frames becomes much more complicated than that of continuous beams.

The balanced-load approach, on the other hand, can be applied to rigid frames quite easily, since it quickly leads to a condition of uniform stress distribution for all members of a rigid frame. Since the relatively unfamiliar effect of prestressing has been eliminated by load balancing, it is only necessary to analyze an ordinary elastic rigid frame subjected to the additional loading or to the effect of axial shortening. Since engineers are already familiar with such analysis, and since we are only concerned with the added loading or with the effect of axial shortening, without the effects of bending, the problem becomes easily controllable.

Consider a simple case of a one-story single rigid frame, Fig. 11-13. If it is desired to balance the uniform load w so that there will be no bending at all, a parabolic c.g.s. can be designed and located such that

$$F_1 = \frac{wL^2}{8h_1}$$

If the span is short and the columns long, it will be better to locate the c.g.s. of F_1 without any eccentricity with respect to the c.g.c. Then it will not be necessary to prestress the column in order to balance the loading. On the other hand, if the span is long and the columns short, it will often be economical to place the ends of F_1 as high as possible, so as to obtain a higher value for h_1 and thus a smaller value of F_1, as shown in Fig. 11-13. In this case, the prestress F_1 produces an eccentric end moment $F_1 e_1$ which must be balanced by another cable in the column placed with an eccentricity e_2 such that

$$F_2 e_2 = F_1 e_1$$

When the frame is so designed, all sections in the frame are subjected to uniform stress distribution (except at points of stress concentration) with stress in the beam equal to F_1/A_1, and stress in the column equal to $(F_2 + V_2)/A_2$ where V_2 is the vertical load on the column. A_1 and A_2 are the cross-sectional areas of the beam and the column, respectively.

The elastic shortening of the beam under prestress, as well as its shrinkage and creep, will tend to move the columns inward, thus producing bending in both the beam and the columns, even though the external loadings are balanced. Such stresses can be computed and if necessary counteracted by relocating the c.g.s. or by putting additional prestress in both the beam and the columns, or they can be resisted by nonprestressed steel.

While the above explains the design of a cast-in-place rigid frame, a slight modification will make it applicable to precast rigid frames. It is

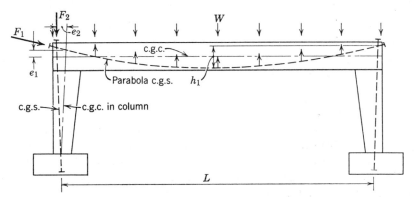

Fig. 11-13. Prestressed rigid frame.

Fig. 11-14. 120-ft precast girders, pretensioned to balance own weight and post-tensioned to balance in-place slabs, form rigid frames with post-tensioned columns—Telecomputing Facilities, Chatsworth, California (Structural Engineer T. Y. Lin and Associates).

generally desirable to first balance the weight of the beam. Then, when the beam is placed in position and more load is superimposed, additional prestress is applied to balance the load. An interesting example is shown in Fig. 11-14, where a 120-ft precast T-beam was pre-tensioned to balance its own weight, and then formed into a rigid frame by post-tensioning the beam to balance the weight of the concrete slab poured on top. High tensile bars were used to prestress the column and to supply the end moment F_2e_2 as indicated in Fig. 11-13.

Some multi-story rigid frames may require prestressing only for the beams. Balancing the load on the beams will take away the major part of the moment in the columns. Then if the value of e_1 is small, reinforcing the columns may be sufficient to carry the bending stresses. This principle was utilized in the design of the 5-story rigid frame shown in Fig. 11-15.

Fig. 11-15. Precast girders and columns form multi-story rigid frames for 75-ft span garage, Beverly Hills, California. (Architect Welton Becket and Associates; Structural Engineer T. Y. Lin and Associates) (*a*) Erection of girders. (*b*) Completed building.

11-5 Two-Dimensional Load Balancing

The principles of two-dimensional load balancing will be briefly explained in this section, including their application to a two-way slab and a
grid system. The detailed design of prestressed slabs, and particularly
flat slabs, will be presented in Chapter 12.

Two-dimensional load balancing differs from linear load balancing
for beams and columns in that the transverse component of the tendons
in one direction either adds to or subtracts from that component in the
other direction. Thus the prestress design in the two directions or dimensions are closely related, one to the other. However, the basic principle of load balancing still holds, and the main aim of the design is to
balance a given loading so that the entire structure (whether a slab or a
grid) will possess uniform stress distribution in each direction and will

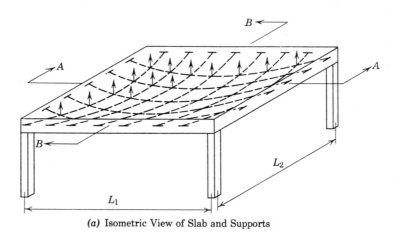

(a) Isometric View of Slab and Supports

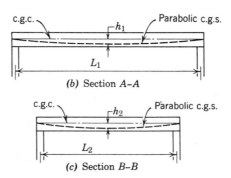

(b) Section A–A

(c) Section B–B

Fig. 11-16. Load balancing for two-way slabs.

not have deflection or camber under this loading. Any deviation from this balanced loading will then be analyzed as loads acting on an elastic slab without further considering the transverse component of prestress.

As a simple example of two-dimensional load balancing, let us consider a two-way slab simply supported on four walls, Fig. 11-16. The cables in both directions exert an upward force on the slab, and if the sum of the upward components balances the downward load w, then we have a balanced design. Thus, if F_1 and F_2 are the prestressing forces in the two directions per foot width of slab, we have

$$\frac{8F_1h_1}{L_1^2} + \frac{8F_2h_2}{L_2^2} = w$$

Note that many combinations of F_1 and F_2 will satisfy the above equation. While the most economical design is to carry the load only in the short direction (or to carry $0.50w$ in each direction in case of a square panel), practical considerations might suggest different distributions. For example, if both directions are properly prestressed, it is possible to obtain a crack-free slab.

Under the action of F_1, F_2, and the load w, the entire slab has a uniform stress distribution in each direction equal to F_1/t and F_2/t, respectively. Any change in loading from the balanced amount of w can be analyzed by the elastic theory for slabs, such as Timoshenko[3] or O'Rourke. Example 11-4 illustrates the method.

EXAMPLE 11-4

An 8-in. slab supported on four walls, Fig. 11-17, is to be post-tensioned in two directions. Design live load is 100 psf. Compute the amount of prestress,

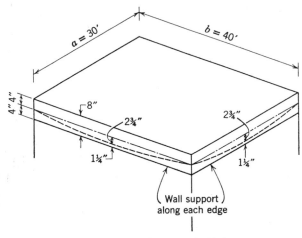

Fig. 11-17. Example 11-4.

assuming that a minimum of 200 psi compression is desired in the concrete in each direction for the purpose of getting a watertight roof slab.

Solution.   Since it is more economical to carry the load in the short direction, a minimum amount of prestress will be used in the long direction. At 200 psi compression in concrete, the prestress is,

$$200 \times 8 \times 12 = 19.2 \text{ k/ft of slab}$$

A parabolic c.g.s. with this prestress will supply a uniformly distributed upward force, as computed below, for an eccentricity of 2.75 in.,

$$w = \frac{8Fe}{L^2} = \frac{8 \times 19{,}200 \times 2.75/12}{40^2} = 21.9 \text{ psf}$$

Since the weight of slab is 100 psf, it will be necessary to supply another upward force of $100 - 21.9 = 78.1$ psf in order to balance the dead load. This will require a prestress in the 30-ft direction of

$$F = \frac{wL^2}{8e} = \frac{78.1 \times 30^2}{8 \times 2.75/12} = 38.4 \text{ k/ft}$$

and assuming an eccentricity of 2.75 in. (note that this eccentricity cannot be exactly maintained for cables in both directions where they cross each other at center portion of slab), which will give a uniform compression in the concrete of

$$\frac{38{,}400}{8 \times 12} = 400 \text{ psi}$$

Thus, under the action of dead load alone, the slab will be under uniform stress of 200 psi in the 40-ft direction and 400 psi in the 30-ft direction.

The effect of live load can now be investigated. Referring to Timoshenko's treatise,[3] for span ratio $q = \frac{40}{30} = 1.33$, we have $B = 0.0713$ and $B_1 = 0.0505$. Thus, for $w = 100$ psf and $a = 30$ ft,

$$M = Bwa^2 = 0.0713 \times 100 \times 30^2 = 6420 \text{ ft-lb/ft of slab}$$

Hence, the concrete fiber stresses are

$$f = \frac{Fe}{A} \pm \frac{Mc}{I}$$

$$= -400 \pm \frac{6420 \times 12 \times 6}{12 \times 8^2}$$

$$= -400 \pm 602$$

$$= -1002 \text{ psi compression top fiber,}$$

$$+202 \text{ psi tension bottom fiber}$$

Stresses in the 40-ft direction can be similarly computed to be -626 psi compression for top fiber and $+226$ psi tension for bottom fiber.

If uniform stress distribution and zero deflection is not essential for a structure, balanced-load design may not be the most economical approach. For example, a cable placed along the middle strips will evidently be more effective than one along the wall. If more cables are located along the middle strips than along the walls, a stronger design might be obtained than the balanced-load design suggested above. If this is done, the slab will not be level under a uniform load or under its own weight. However, it will have no deflection under a varying load intensity which is everywhere equal and opposite to the upward component of the prestress.

The same principle of load balancing for the slab just described will apply to a grid system, if at each intersection the load is balanced by the upward component of prestress. Fig. 11-18 shows a grid system (also

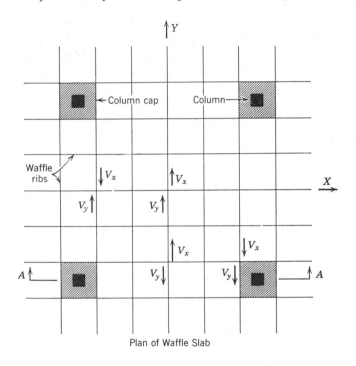

Plan of Waffle Slab

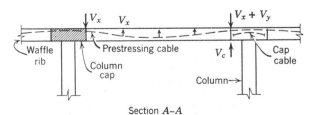

Section *A–A*

Fig. 11-18. Load balancing in a grid system.

called a waffle slab) with cables running in two directions X and Y, producing vertical components V_x and V_y. Near the center of the panel, both V_x and V_y act upward. Near the center of column line A–A, V_x acting upward is partly counteracted by V_y acting downward. Over a column capital, both V_x and V_y act downward but are balanced by another cable in the cap supplying a component V_c. Thus a prestressed grid system can be designed for a balanced-load condition with simple application of statics.

If the dead load on the grid system is 100 psf and the live load 60 psf, and the design is made to balance a load of 110 psf, then it is only necessary to analyze the elastic slab for 10 psf upward load when no live load is on and for 50 psf downward when full live load is on. This approach will enable us to design prestressed grid systems of various layouts, since the elastic analysis needs to be made only for a small fraction of the total load and can be solved by a suitable approximate method.

EXAMPLE 11-5

A square grid system with 7 beams in each direction, Fig. 11-19, is to be designed for no deflection under a uniform load of 125 psf (which includes its own weight). Compute the vertical components of the tendons for a balanced-load condition.

Solution. A solution is given in Fig. 11-20, indicating the vertical component of tendons in both directions, with a net upward force from the tendons at each interior panel point of $125 \times 16^2 = 32$ k, each exterior panel point of 16 k, and at each corner 8 k. Only half of the force from the tendons along the center lines

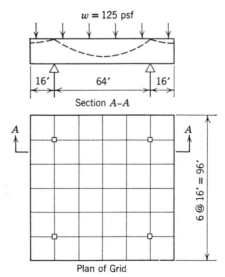

Fig. 11-19. Example 11-5.

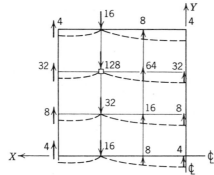

(a) Quarter Plan Showing Vertical Component
of Tendons in X Direction

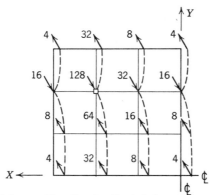

(b) Quarter Plan Showing Vertical Component
of Tendons in Y Direction

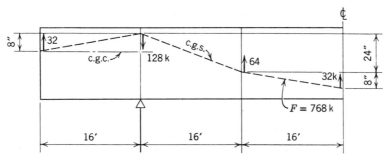

(c) Cable Profile for Half of Beam along Column Line

Fig. 11-20. Balanced solution for Example 11-5.

(on the X and Y axes) are listed in order that the diagrams will represent exactly a quadrant of the grid.

Although a balanced-load design is achieved by this arrangement, the design may not be the best, or necessarily the most economical, since the four beams passing the columns will carry very heavy loads and may have to be unusually large. Should the spans be longer than shown, some special arrangement around the columns might have to be made similar to the capital shown in Fig. 11-18.

For the purpose of illustration a tendon layout to furnish the proper vertical components is made for the beam along the column line, Fig. 11-20(c). It is noted that the c.g.s. must start from the c.g.c. at the ends of the beam in order to produce a balanced-load design. On account of the high location of c.g.c. for a waffle slab, the drape of c.g.s. for the canti-lever is limited and a large amount of prestress might be required. For the center portion, a much greater drape is possible, and the prestress required is correspondingly less. Although a broken line is shown here for the profile, a smooth curve passing through the controlling points would be a better solution, not only for obvious practical reasons, but also to balance the loads along the beam between the intersections.

Note that while other methods could also be used to solve this particular example, the balancing-load approach reveals design possibilities not so clearly indicated by others. The method can very well be used for the layout of cables in a complicated system of waffle or flat slabs. This can be accomplished either manually, using simple arithmetic, or with the help of electronic computers to solve a system of simultaneous equations. Generally, numerous sets of cable profiles can be used for each balanced-load condition, but the most economical arrangement has to be determined for each case, taking into account practical as well as theoretical require-ments.

11-6 Three-Dimensional Load Balancing

One example of three-dimensional load balancing is illustrated in Figs. 11-21 and 11-22, which show two pedestrian bridges connecting two buildings across a wide street. For architectural reasons, these bridges with a maximum span of 102 ft are limited to a structural depth of only 27 in., Fig. 11-22(c). Furthermore, the main supporting piers, Fig. 11-22(a), had to be located on the outside away from the center line of the bridges. To achieve a balanced-load condition for dead load (which included 800 lb of marbles per ft of each bridge), the bridge was prestressed in three directions, X, Y, and Z.

Fig. 11-21. Pedestrian Bridge joining two Union Oil Buildings, Los Angeles, California, has 27-inch depth spanning 102 ft. (Architect Periera and Luckman; Consultant T. Y. Lin and Associates.)

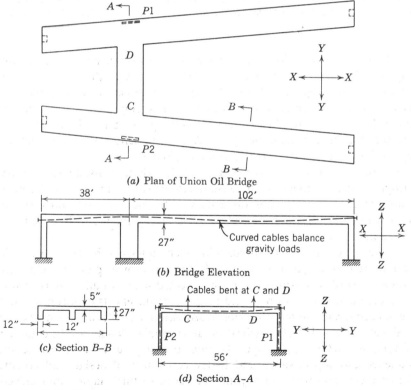

(a) Plan of Union Oil Bridge

(b) Bridge Elevation

(c) Section B-B

(d) Section A-A

Fig. 11-22. Plan, elevation, and sections of the Union Oil Bridge, Los Angeles.

Fig. 11-23. Twenty-third Avenue Over-crossing, City of Oakland, California. (Kaiser Engineers; Architect John C. Warnecke and Associates; Consultant T. Y. Lin and Associates International.)

Along the X direction, each bridge is a two-span continuous beam, Fig. 11-22(b). Parabolic cables are post-tensioned in the 12 in. $\times$ 27 in. ribs to balance the dead load. Along the Y direction, bent cables are post-tensioned in the crossover (a and d), supplying two upward concentrated forces at C and D to serve as invisible piers. Since these cables are located high at the ends, they produce end moments which are balanced by tendons in piers, $P1$ and $P2$, in the Z direction.

Another example is shown in Fig. 11-23, where a 4-span rigid frame bridge is post-tensioned in the girders (165-ft spans) to balance the dead load. Since the bridge lies on a curve, the piers are unsymmetrically loaded and hence post-tensioned both transversely and vertically to balance the cantilever action.

While these intricate load-balancing techniques can be used to enable various structural layouts, and while the basic principles are relatively simple, a word of warning should be injected here. In all designs of this type, careful consideration should be given to the effects of shrinkage and creep in concrete; to the problems of stresses camber during construction; to the amount of deflection vibration under applied loads; to the detailing of tendons, anchorages, supports, and auxiliary steel; to construction sequence and supervision; and to the economics of design and layout. All of these, however, are beyond the scope of this chapter, and indeed much of them are beyond the scope of this treatise. After the engineers have mastered the basic principles, it is up to them to learn the techniques and the application by careful study as well as actual experience.

A different application of three-dimensional load balancing lies in thin shells and folded plates.[4] It should first be pointed out that complete load balancing in all directions cannot be easily achieved for such structures. In theory, we do not know enough of shell action so as to be able to balance the loads. In practice, it may not be possible or economical to prestress the shells in all directions. However, sometimes the load-balancing approach can be used to advantage.

Consider a cylindrical shell, Fig. 11-24. Cables can be post-tensioned along the shell surface so that the vertical component will balance the gravity load. This is given by the condition that the prestressing force is

$$F = \frac{wL^2}{8h}$$

where $w = wt$ of the shell per linear ft along the Y axis. For a long shell behaving in accordance with the beam theory, a cable with a parabolic

Transverse Section at Midspan

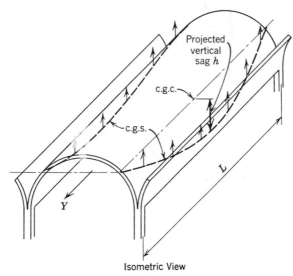

Isometric View

Fig. 11-24. Cylindrical shell prestressed for load balancing.

Fig. 11-25. Four-inch pneumatically placed concrete shell spans 120 ft for High School Gymnasium, Mira Costa, California. (Architects Flewelling and Moody; Structural Engineer Carl B. Johnson; Consultant T. Y. Lin and Associates.) (*a*) Layout of cables. (*b*) Completed building.

vertical projection will counteract the beam action. There will then be no deflection along the length of the shell, and the stress distribution will be essentially uniform. Bending stresses will still exist in the transverse direction of the shell, but they can be analyzed as strips of arches supported at different points. For the unbalanced load (generally the live load or a portion of it), ordinary shell analysis can be applied to determine the stresses.

If the deflections of the shells are minimized by load balancing, their secondary stresses are also reduced.

One example of load balancing for shell design is illustrated in Fig. 11-25, where a 4-in. thick shell spans a maximum of 126 ft, with cables post-tensioned in the shell surface to balance loads on both the main span and the cantilever (maximum 46 ft). Another example is shown in Fig. 11-26, where two continuous shell spans of 75 ft each has 3-in. lightweight cylindrical shells post-tensioned with only 0.25 lb of steel per sq ft of projected area. A third one is shown in Fig. 1-4, where 3-in. thin shells cantilever 90 ft, and the load is balanced by cables in the edge beams.[5] In all three cases, there were practically no deflections of the shells, indicating a rather accurate application of balanced-load design.

Fig. 11-26. Three-inch lightweight concrete shell with 2 continuous spans at 75-ft each is post-tensioned with *0.25 lb of steel per sq ft of projected area* to produce a balanced load design. (Division of Architecture, State of California; Consultant T. Y. Lin and Associates.)

11-7   Criteria for Load Balancing; Accuracy of the Method

Using this concept of load balancing, an important question is: What should be the loading to be balanced by the prestress? The answer to this question may not be simple. As a starting point, it is often assumed that the dead load of the structure or element be completely balanced by the effective prestress. This would mean that a slight amount of camber may exist under the initial prestress. In the course of time, when all the losses of prestress have taken place, the structure or element would come back to a level position.

Although it seems logical to balance all the dead load, such balancing may require too much prestress. Since a certain amount of deflection is always permitted for a nonprestressed structure under dead load, it is reasonable to also permit a limited amount of deflection if it would not become objectionable. However, there is a greater tendency in prestressed structures to increase their deflections as a result of creep and shrinkage. Hence the deflections should be limited to a smaller value at the beginning.

When the live load to be carried by the structure is high compared to its dead load, it may be necessary to balance some of the live load as well as the dead load. One interesting approach is to balance the dead load plus one half the live load, $(DL + \frac{1}{2}LL)$. If this is done, the structure will be subjected to no bending when one half of the live load is acting. Then, it is only necessary to design for one-half live load acting up when no live load exists, and for one-half live load acting down when full live load is on the structure. This idea of balancing dead load plus one-half live load, while theoretically interesting, could result in excessive camber if the live load consists essentially of transient load. If the live load represents actual sustained loading such as encountered in warehouses, excessive camber may not occur.

When attempting to evaluate the amount of live load to be balanced by prestressing, it is necessary to consider the real live load and not the specified design live load. If the specified design live load is higher than the actual live load, only a small amount of the live load or even no live load at all should be balanced. On the other hand, if the actual live load could be much higher than the design live load, especially if the live loading would be sustained, it would be desirable to balance a greater portion of the live load. The engineer should exercise his judgement when choosing the proper amount of loading to be balanced by prestressing. This should be done while keeping in mind the satisfaction of other requirements such as elastic stress limitations, crack control, and ultimate strength.

A balanced load design can be achieved with considerable accuracy because both the gravity load and the prestressing force can often be predicted with precision. However, variations may be encountered so that the actual loading and the actual prestress may not be as expected. For a relatively stiff member, errors in estimating the weight and the prestress will usually be negligible. For a slender member, even slight variations may result in considerable errors in the estimation of load balancing, and either camber or deflection may result.

As is well known, the modulus of elasticity of concrete and the creep characteristics cannot be predetermined with accuracy. Fortunately, neither the modulus nor the flexural creep would enter into the picture if the sustained load is exactly balanced by the prestressing component. In other words, since there is no transverse load on the member, there will be no bending regardless of the value of the modulus or the creep coefficient.

Depending on the accuracy desired in the control of camber and deflection, the amount of loading to be balanced must be chosen. If the limits of error can be estimated and if the significance of deflection or camber control can be assessed, it will not be difficult to design the member so as to possess the desired behavior.

References

1   T. Y. Lin, "A New Concept for Prestressed Concrete," *Construction Review*, Sydney, Australia pp. 21–31; (Reprinted in *PCI Journal*, December 1961, pp. 36–52.) Also T. Y. Lin, "Revolution in Concrete," *Architectural Forum Part I*, May 1961, pp. 121–127; *Part II*, June 1961, pp. 116–121.
2   T. Y. Lin, "Load Balancing Method for Design and Analysis of Prestressed Concrete Structures," *J. Am. Conc. Inst.*, June, 1963.
3   S. Timoshenko, "Theory of Plates and Shells," McGraw-Hill, 1940, p. 133.
4   T. Y. Lin, "Prestressed Concrete—Slabs and Shells—Design and Research in the United States," *Civil Engineering*, October 1958, pp. 75–77.
5   Henry M. Layne and T. Y. Lin, "Prestressed Concrete Shell for Grandstand Roofs," *J. Am. Conc. Inst.*, November 1959, pp. 409–422.

12

slabs

12-1   Introduction; One-Way Slabs

The flexural design of a simple one-way slab is usually made similar to a beam, as discussed in Chapters 5 and 6. Most continuous slabs are designed like continuous beams (Chapters 10 and 11). Balanced-load design for two-way slabs and waffle slabs is described in section 11-5. The design for punching shear in prestressed slabs is outlined in section 7-3. This chapter will be devoted to the flexural design of flat slabs and certain other special features.

A one-way slab has main reinforcement only along the length of the slab. All its supports extend the full width of the slab, Fig. 12-1, there being no isolated point-supports or supports running along the length of the slab. Occasionally, the supports may be interrupted or stopped before they reach the entire width, in which case the remaining portion should be designed for a different condition of support.

The usual procedure to design a one-way prestressed slab is to consider a typical 1-ft width of slab, and treat it as if it were a beam, as is done for a reinforced-concrete one-way slab. Whether the slab is simple, cantilever, or continuous, it is designed like a beam, with identical supports and hinges. Hence all the analysis and design of beams discussed in the previous chapters can be directly applied to slabs without any amplification. For example, the theory of linear transformation and of concordant cables for beams is also valid for one-way slabs.

Although the main prestressing steel runs only along the length of the slab, transverse steel, either prestressed or not, may be added to take care of shrinkage and to distribute any concentration of loads. The design of transverse steel, in both reinforced and prestressed structures, has always been a controversial issue, although the analysis of transverse stresses produced by concentrated loads has been solved both theoretically and experimentally for certain simple cases.[1] The main difficulties in design

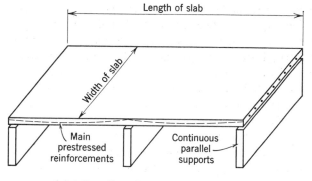

(*a*) A Two-Span Continuous Prestressed Slab

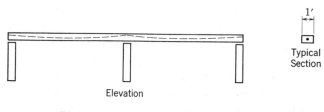

(*b*) Analysis for Slab in (*a*) Based on an
Equivalent Beam 1 Ft Wide

Fig. 12-1. One-way slabs.

are the choice of a proper amount of concentration, the combination of such concentrations, and the employment of correct allowable stresses in the design. In addition, the actual structure might have to be simplified in order to suit the conditions of analysis.

If the transverse reinforcement is prestressed, two additional questions are raised. One question is whether Poisson's ratio effect will have a significant influence on the loss of prestress in a slab prestressed in two directions. If we assume that the concrete has a Poisson's ratio of 0.15 and that the slab is subject to the same prestress in both directions, corresponding to a loss of prestress due to elastic shortening and creep in concrete of 8%, the decrease in loss due to Poisson's ratio effect will be $0.15 \times 8\% = 1.2\%$, which is not too significant as far as practical design is concerned.

Another question is whether such biaxial prestressing will change the basic strength and strain characteristics of concrete, so that they can no longer be predicted by the application of the elastic theory in conjunction with the properties obtained from ordinary test specimens. Regarding this question, there were two schools of thought. Some engineers believed that concrete as a material was more of a complex "solid-liquid" rather than a simple elastic solid, so that the laws of thermodynamics, rather than the laws of elasticity of solid, should be applied.[2] This belief was partly substantiated by several field tests in France, notably the testing of the prestressed runway at Orly. These tests brought forth the possibility that, for a slab prestressed in two directions, the cracking strength might be much higher than the value given by the elastic theory. It was proposed that, in a statically indeterminate system, there could be no relation between the appearance of cracks and the existence of tension equal to the modulus of rupture.

The second school of thought directly contradicts the first. It is believed that, when concrete is prestressed in two directions, its basic behavior and properties have not been changed. Hence the elastic theory, together with the tested values for modulus of rupture, can be applied to statically indeterminate structures, including slabs prestressed in two directions. This was shown by several laboratory tests conducted at the university of Ghent. In one test on a two-way prestressed slab, the elastic theory was shown to be quite accurate for predicting the cracking load.[3]

In another series of tests on continuous beams, the same conclusion was drawn (see reference 9, Chapter 10). More recently, tests on simple and continuous slabs prestressed in two directions[4,5] all indicated the validity of the elastic theory, and it is now generally agreed that the cracking strength is, at least, approximated by the modulus of rupture of concrete.

For narrow one-way slabs the transverse reinforcements are usually nonprestressed, because short prestressing is neither economical nor accurate. When the width is small compared to the span, any concentrated load is assumed to be carried by the entire width of the slab, and little transverse reinforcing is required for load distribution. Generally, the nonprestressed reinforcement required for shrinkage is sufficient also for load distribution.

For one-way slabs with width greater than about 50% of the span, the deflection of the different slices of the slab may vary considerably under concentrated loads. This indicates heavy transverse bending, which must be resisted by reinforcements whether prestressed or nonprestressed. If nonprestressed, the bending moments can be calculated by the usual elastic theory and the proper amount of steel provided as for any reinforced-concrete design. If economic or other considerations justify the use of transverse prestressing, the moments can also be calculated by the elastic theory and the transverse prestress designed by the ordinary procedure for designing prestressed beam sections. This is believed to be

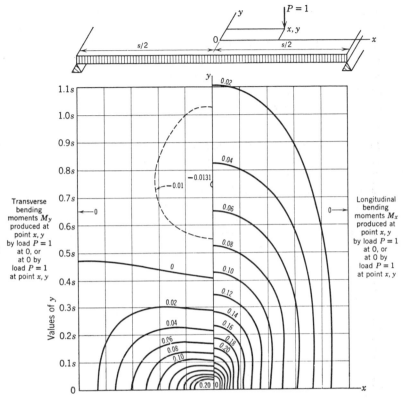

Fig. 12-2. Transverse and longitudinal moments in one-way slab due to concentrated load (see reference 1 of this chapter).

a safe procedure and, if properly applied, should give reasonable results.

In order to convey some idea of the moments in a wide slab, the longitudinal and transverse moments in a one-way slab under concentrated load[1] are given in Fig. 12-2. These are based on the elasticity theory as applied to an infinitely wide slab with a Poisson's ratio of 0.15. In such slabs, there also exist torsional moments, but the magnitude is small, and they are not often considered in design.

After the transverse moments to be resisted by prestressing have been computed, the determination of the amount of prestress is a relatively simple matter, it being remembered that, if no tension is allowed, the resisting moment is given by the prestress times its lever arm measured to the opposite kern point. This simple procedure permits the design of prestressed transverse reinforcements to be made with the same ease as nonprestressed reinforcements. The method is illustrated in example 12-1.

Concentric transverse prestressing is often preferred for slabs, although it is not as economical as eccentric prestressing. As can be seen from Fig. 12-2, the transverse positive moments are higher than the negative moments. Hence the steel should be positioned farther from the top kern than from the bottom kern, so as to possess a greater lever arm for resisting the positive moments. But such eccentric prestressing will tend to bend the slab transversely, which may be objectionable.

EXAMPLE 12-1

The Bacon Street Highway Bridge in San Francisco has a simple span of 60 ft and a width of 100 ft, Fig. 12-3. It is prestressed with an effective prestress of 196,000 lb per ft of width along the 60-ft span. Compute the amount of concentric transverse prestress required per foot of span. Design for a concentrated load of 16,000 lb and no tensile stress in the concrete.

Solution. Since the width of the bridge is greater than its span, it is close enough to use Fig. 12-2 for computing the transverse moments. For a maximum coefficient of 0.20,

$$M = 16,000 \times 0.20$$
$$= 3200 \text{ ft-lb/ft width}$$

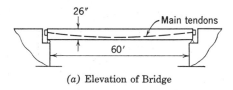

(a) Elevation of Bridge

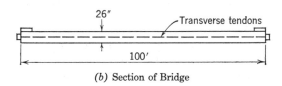

(b) Section of Bridge

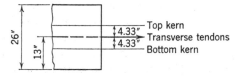

(c) Lever Arm for Resisting Moment

Fig. 12-3. Example 12-1.

In order to resist that moment without producing tension in the concrete, the most economical position for the transverse tendons is at the lower kern point. However, if the tendons are located at the lower kern point, the entire slab will be subjected to a negative transverse moment, resulting in a convex bending across the width of the bridge. Moreover, the slab may be subjected to some negative moments under concentrated load, and it would be better to place the cable within the kern. Since the amount of prestress required is small, it will be convenient to locate them through the mid-depth of the slab; then the lever arm to either kern is 4.33 in., Fig. 12-3(c). To resist the above moment, the amount of prestress required per foot is

$$\frac{3200 \times 12}{4.33} = 8860 \text{ lb}$$

Actual stress measurements on the slab of the Bacon Street Bridge indicated the accuracy of the elastic theory for load distribution and transverse moments.[6] The load distribution is apparently little affected by the presence of the transverse prestress.

12-2 Two-Way and Simple Flat Slabs

Though a one-way slab may be prestressed in two directions, it is not a two-way slab, because the transverse prestressing only serves to strengthen the concrete locally but is not intended for carrying any portion of the load to the supports. A two-way prestressed slab is one whose prestressing steels in two perpendicular directions both serve to transfer the load to its supports. Thus a two-way slab rests on continuous supports in the form of beams or walls running in two perpendicular directions. When a slab is supported by a network of columns, either with or without capitals, it can properly be called a prestressed flat slab, using that term as in reinforced-concrete construction. A prestressed flat slab can be designed using the method of load balancing as explained for the grid system in section 11-5, or the beam method as will be explained in this chapter. The two methods will yield similar resisting moment in each direction, but the distribution of tendons will be quite different. The beam method with the normal distribution between column and middle strips will not yield a balanced design for uniform loads, although slabs so designed have been found to be fairly level from a practical point of view.

One basis for the design of prestressed flat slabs is to use moment coefficients for the design of reinforced-concrete flat slabs which are available from building codes and handbooks. When applied to prestressed concrete, the procedure of design can be discussed in two parts: the acting moments due to loads, and the resisting moments provided by the prestressing steel. As far as the load moment is concerned, there is no major difference between reinforced and prestressed two-way slabs. Within the working load, they both behave according to the elastic theory, with the prestressed slabs following it more closely. Although, near the ultimate load, they behave less nearly alike, there is reason to believe that the moment coefficients for reinforced concrete, based essentially on elastic analysis, can be used for prestressed concrete without serious adjustments. This does not mean that we are satisfied with these coefficients. In fact, we are not satisfied with them even as applied to reinforced-concrete slabs themselves. However, we can with some discretion apply these coefficients to prestressed concrete.

The second part of the problem is to provide the resisting moments. As usual, the resisting moments in prestressed concrete are supplied by the steel acting with a lever arm up to around the kern point. For continuous spans, the resisting couple, instead of being measured from the steel, should be measured from the C-line produced by prestress, the determination of which is a more complicated problem, although it can be solved either by the theory of elasticity or the use of model tests. In this connection, a thorough understanding of the principles discussed in Chapter 10 is essential. Instead of the elastic theory, the application of ultimate design together with proper choice of load factors may also result in satisfactory proportions. It must be remembered that, for prestressed slabs, the initial condition at transfer could be a critical situation that must be examined for overstress in concrete. Flat slabs of prestressed concrete supported by a network of columns have already found wide application in this country. This is especially true in connection with lift slabs, where the slabs are cast on the ground and lifted along the columns to their proper height.[7,8] An interesting example is the 13-story apartment building shown in Fig. 1-8, where all the slabs were cast on the ground, post-tensioned and then lifted into position.[9] Here, an 8-inch flat slab of lightweight concrete spans a typical bay of 28 ft and a maximum of 32 ft. By proper application of the laws of statics and the theory of elasticity, plus a thorough knowledge of prestressed concrete, flat slabs can be designed with satisfactory results.

Let us first consider a flat slab supported on four columns, Fig. 12-4. This is a statically determinate system as far as the reactions are concerned. The total moments across any section, such as A–A or B–B, for example, can be readily determined from statics. But the distribution of the total moments along the length of the section is a problem in elasticity. Such distribution can be obtained theoretically by the theory of elasticity, or it can be measured experimentally by means of models. (Note that a load balancing method similar to example 11-4 could be a simpler approach.) In general, the moments along the columns strip B–B will be

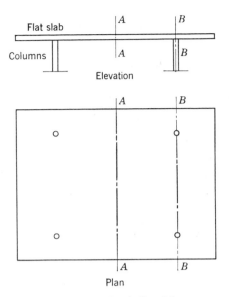

Fig. 12-4. A simple flat slab.

greater than those along the middle strip A–A since strip B–B is somewhat stiffer than A–A.

The magnitude of the slab moments at each point having been determined, the next step is to provide enough steel to resist the moments. An ideal arrangement would be to provide in both directions exactly the required amount of steel and eccentricity at each point. But this may not be possible in practice, and a reasonably satisfactory solution can be obtained by a good estimation of the distribution of the moments. So long as the total resisting moment equals the external moment, any slight error in distribution is not of serious consequence, since the transverse rigidity of the slab can be depended on to a certain extent to transfer the resistance across the slab. Again, stresses in the concrete should also be investigated for the initial condition at transfer of prestress.

An example is given in the following, illustrating the computation of steel area for a simple flat slab prestressed in two directions.
The complete design of such a slab would involve the following:

1. Locating the cable profiles.
2. Spacing the cables.
3. Checking stresses in concrete both at transfer and under working loads.
4. Computation for deflections at various stages, including the effect of plastic flow.

5. Computation of cracking and ultimate loads.
6. Design for end anchorage details.

The reader is refererd to other parts of this treatise where these are discussed.

EXAMPLE 12-2

A simple flat slab 40 ft by 30 ft is supported by four columns as shown, Fig. 12-5(a). The 6-in. concrete slab weighs 75 psf and carries a roof live load of 20 psf; $f_c' = 4000$ psi; $\frac{1}{4}$-in. wires grouped in 4 wires per unit are to be used for prestressing in two directions. The cables are greased and wrapped with paper and not bonded to the concrete. Ultimate strength of the wires is 250 ksi, with an initial prestress of 150 ksi and an effective prestress of 125 ksi. Minimum clear coverage for the cables is to be $\frac{3}{4}$ in., which is equivalent to $1\frac{1}{4}$-in. protection measured to the center line of the cables. Compute the required number of 40-ft cables per slab.

Solution.

$$DL = 75 \text{ psf}$$
$$LL = 20 \text{ psf}$$
$$\text{Total load} = \overline{95 \text{ psf}}$$

For the 40-ft direction, the average cantilever moment is

$$-wL^2/2 = (95 \times 8^2)/2$$
$$= 3.04 \text{ k-ft/ft of width}$$

and the average positive moment at midspan is

$$wL^2/8 - 3.04 = (95 \times 24^2)/8 - 3.04$$
$$= 6.84 - 3.04$$
$$= 3.80 \text{ k-ft/ft of width}$$

For the entire width of 30 ft, the moment is

$$3.80 \times 30 = 114 \text{ k-ft}$$

The resisting moment is furnished by the steel with a lever arm of 2.75 in. measured to the top kern point, allowing no tension in concrete, Fig. 12-5(d). Hence the total prestress required is, as controlled by the $+M$,

$$(114 \times 12)/2.75 = 497 \text{ k}$$

Each cable has 4 wires with $A = 0.05$ sq in.; hence A_s per cable is 0.20 sq in. For an effective prestress of 125 ksi, each cable has a total prestress of $0.20 \times 125 = 25$ k. The total number of cables required is

$$497/25 = 19.9$$

Use 20 cables.

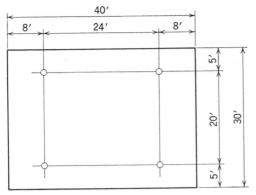

(a) Plan of Slab

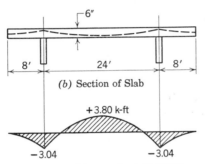

(b) Section of Slab

(c) Moment Diagram for 1-Ft Width

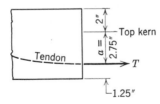

(d) Lever Arm a for Prestress at Midspan

Fig. 12-5. Example 12-2.

12-3   Continuous Flat Slabs

Continuous flat slabs are frequently constructed of prestressed concrete, especially when combined with the lifting process. A prestressed slab is lighter than a reinforced one, and its flexibility lends itself to the lifting process. When a reinforced-concrete slab is being lifted, slab levels at the columns must be more carefully controlled to avoid cracking resulting from differential levels. For prestressed concrete, even if cracks did open to some extent, they will be closed up when the lifting is completed. Besides, dead-load deflection in the slab can be largely balanced by the camber produced by prestress. Then there are the saving in formwork and other conveniences inherent in lift-slab construction.

The design of a continuous prestressed flat slab is based on a knowledge of the design of simple flat slabs as outlined in the previous section. As a result of continuity, two additional problems should be discussed: the negative moments over the interior supports due to loads, and the effect of prestressing a statically indeterminate structure, including the problems of linear transformation and cable concordancy as discussed for continuous beams.

For simple flat slabs, the total moment across any section is definitely known, because all the reactions are statically determinate. The reactions for continuous slabs, however, are statically indeterminate, and hence the total moment across a section cannot be computed from statics alone.

Since prestressed concrete can be treated as a homogeneous and elastic material in the analysis of moments, the theory of elasticity can be depended on to yield reasonably accurate results before the cracking of concrete. But to apply a rigid elastic theory to a continuous slab is a very tedious operation which would consume a great deal of time even for a simple case. Hence some easier procedure must be devised for its design.

While the method of load balancing for a grid system would be found convenient for certain cases, the beam method presented in this chapter probably offers the simplest solution, especially when combined with the concept of load balancing for continuous beams.

According to most building codes, reinforced-concrete flat slabs can be designed as continuous beams. So far as moment due to external load is concerned, there is as much justification for applying such a method to prestressed flat slabs. This beam method is illustrated in Fig. 12-6, which assumes continuous knife-edge supports along one direction when analysis is being made for moment in the other direction.

A continuous slab having been transformed into a continuous beam, the problem is greatly simplified. The effect of prestressing such a slab can then be computed as for continuous beams. On this assumption, then, it is possible to apply the method of linear transformation just as is done for a continuous beam.

If concordant cables are desired for a flat slab, a real moment surface should be computed by the elastic theory; then any set of cables producing eccentric moments proportional to the moment surface is a set of

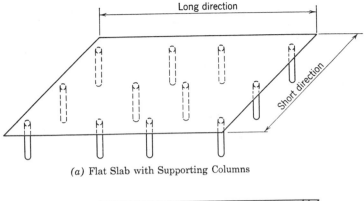

Long direction

Short direction

(a) Flat Slab with Supporting Columns

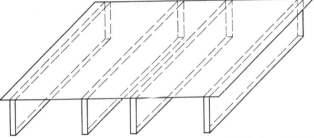

(b) Assumed Support Condition for Moment Analysis in Long Direction

(c) Assumed Support Condition for Moment Analysis in Short Direction

Fig. 12-6. Moment analysis of continuous flat slabs.

concordant cables. Although this is theoretically interesting, it usually will not give a better layout than the beam method.

By analyzing a continuous slab as a continuous beam, the total moment across any section due to loading and the average position of the C-line under prestressing can be obtained. But the distribution of the total moment and the variation of the position of C-line along the width of slab still remain to be determined. Approximations have been used, for example, assuming 45% of the total moment to be carried by the middle strip and 55% by the column strip for a simple flat slab of uniform thickness supported by 4 columns.[4] For the interior span of a slab, continuous in both directions, a better approximation seems to be 25% by the middle strip and 75% by the column strip.[5] This can also be partly explained by the balanced-load concept since at midspan of a middle strip, the cables from both directions act upward; while at midspan of a column strip, one set of cables act up with the other set acting down.

On the basis of tested high ultimate strength of reinforced-concrete flat slabs, the ACI design code permits using $0.100WL$ instead of $0.125WL$ for the numerical sum of the maximum positive and negative moments in a panel. In other words, it is permissible to design for only 80% of the theoretical moments. The author prefers to design prestressed flat slabs for 100% of the theoretical moments, although their ultimate strength is also high.[4,5] The proper approach is not to change the statical moments, but rather to modify the allowable stresses or the load factors as required. For deflection computation and for load balancing, it is clearly more realistic to deal with the real loads and moments rather than with fictitious ones.

EXAMPLE 12-3

A two-way prestressed lift slab has a plan as shown, Fig. 12-7(a). The $7\frac{1}{2}$-in. concrete slab weighs 94 psf and carries a live load of 75 psf; $f_c' = 4000$ psi; $\frac{1}{4}$-in. wires grouped in 6 wires per unit are to be used for prestressing with ultimate strength of 250 ksi; $f_0 = 150$ ksi; $f_e = 125$ ksi. Minimum coverage for the cables is $1\frac{1}{4}$ in. measured to the center line. Allowing no tension in the concrete, choose the location for the cables and compute the number of 64-ft long cables required for the slab. Use the beam method for analysis.

Solution. (a) Following the method explained in Chapter 10 using the theory of linear transformation. Assume a cable layout with the maximum possible eccentricities for both the positive and the negative moments, as shown in Fig. 12-7(b). This will result in maximum curvature for the cables, and hence the maximum upward force from the cables on the slab. A parabolic cable is used, with an eccentricity of 2.50 in. (corresponding to a concrete protection of $1\frac{1}{4}$ in.) at the points of maximum positive and negative moments. Note that the maximum $-M$ occurs at 12.4 ft from the exterior supports, which is the lowest point for the parabolic curve. This trial location is not likely a concordant cable but offers the maximum lever arm for the steel at critical points.

In order to obtain the C-line under prestressing for this cable, we can proceed as outlined in section 10-4, for continuous beams. But, for a simple problem like this one, it is not necessary to go through all the steps outlined for the procedure. The C-line here can be obtained by inspection after the principles discussed in the previous sections have been mastered. It is noted first that the C-line is a curve linearly transformed from the curve of the cable. Then it is seen that, for a parabolic cable on a beam with straight axis, the force from the cable on the slab is a uniformly distributed load. Neglecting the minor effect

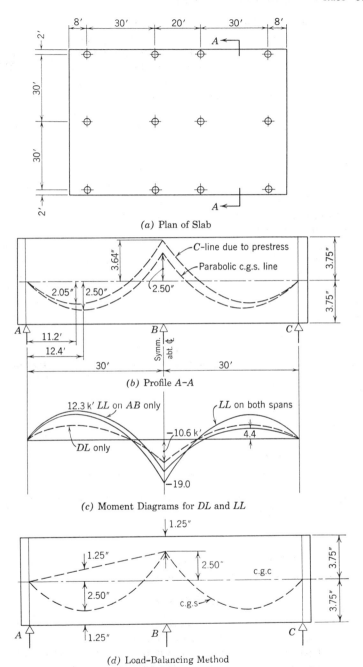

(a) Plan of Slab

(b) Profile A–A

(c) Moment Diagrams for DL and LL

(d) Load–Balancing Method

Fig. 12-7. Example 12-3.

of the 2-ft cantilevers, the moment diagram for a uniform load on two equal spans is well known, having a value of $wL^2/8$ over the center support and $9wL^2/128$ at 11.2 ft (the $\frac{3}{8}$ point) from the exterior supports. This moment diagram, when plotted to proper scale, gives the eccentricity of the C-line produced by prestress. Thus the trial parabolic cable is linearly transformed to obtain the C-line. A little geometry will show that the position of the cable over the center support is moved upward by 1.14 in. to obtain the C-line, and at the $\frac{3}{8}$ point is moved up by $\frac{3}{8} \times 1.14 = 0.43$ in., leaving an eccentricity of 2.05 in.

In other words, by the theory of prestressed continuous beams, a cable located as shown in (*b*) will produce the same effect as though it were located through the computed C-line. Since it is not practicable to locate the cable through the above C-line (too near the top surface over the center support), it is just as well to place it along the trial line, resulting in the same effect. We will see later that this line of pressure seems to lie in a very desirable location.

Next, let us compute the maximum and minimum moment diagrams, (*c*). The greatest $+M$ is obtained with live load on its own span only; the greatest $-M$ is obtained with live load on both spans. The smallest $+M$ is obtained with live load on the other span, but the smallest $-M$ with dead load only. For a final location of the cables, the graphical solution explained in section 10-5 should be used. But just to obtain the number of cables, we will compute for the critical points only, that is, the moments over the center support and near the $\frac{3}{8}$ points from the exterior supports.

First, let us design for the total moments. Over the center support, the lever arm available for the resisting couple is measured to the bottom kern point, 1.25 in. below the mid-depth, or $3.64 + 1.25 = 4.89$ in. Hence the effective prestress required is

$$(19.0 \times 12)/4.89 = 46.6 \text{ k/ft of width}$$

For the $\frac{3}{8}$ points, the lever arm available is $2.05 + 1.25 = 3.30$ in., and the effective prestress required is

$$(12.3 \times 12)/3.30 = 44.7 \text{ k/ft of width}$$

Hence the moment over the center support controls the design, and a total prestress for the entire slab should be

$$96 \text{ ft} \times 46.6 = 4480 \text{ k}$$

A 6-wire unit of $\frac{1}{4}$-in. wires will have an effective prestress of $6 \times 0.049 \times 125 = 36.8$ k; hence the total number of units required is

$$4480/36.8 = 122$$

Note that this number is not too excessive for the $+M$, which would require 117 units, indicating that this is a well-balanced layout.

Now we have to check whether the line of pressure would fall outside the kern under the action of prestress and the minimum moments. The same two critical points as above are chosen for investigation. Over the center support, the minimum *DL* moment is 10.6 k-ft per ft. The initial prestress of the 122 cables will be

$$F_0 = \frac{122 \times 6 \times 0.049 \times 150}{96} = 56.0 \text{ k/ft of width}$$

$$\frac{M_G}{F_0} = \frac{10.6 \times 12}{56.0} = 2.27 \text{ in.}$$

which means that the dead-load moment will bring the *C*-line from 3.64 in. down to $3.64 - 2.27 = 1.37$ in. above the mid-depth. Since the top kern is only 1.25 in. above the mid-depth, the *C*-line under dead load only will be $1.37 - 1.25 = 0.12$ in. outside the kern, and some tension will exist in the bottom fiber over the center support under the initial prestress, but the value is evidently small and will be reduced as soon as loss of prestress takes place. Hence, this is considered satisfactory.

Now, near the $\frac{3}{8}$ points, the minimum moment occurs when live load exists on the other span only, a total moment of 4.4 k-ft. Corresponding to the prestress of 56.0 k/ft, this moment will move the *C*-line upward by the amount of

$$4.4 \times 12/56.0 = 0.94 \text{ in.}$$

This will place the *C*-line $2.05 - 0.94 = 1.11$ in. below the mid-depth, which is within the kern, and no tension will exist.

Thus, 122 cables with critical points located as above can be considered sufficient. To make a complete design of the slab, many related problems, such as those mentioned in section 12-2 for simple flat slabs, must yet be considered. In addition, the sharp bend over the center support should be smoothed out. Also note that at the intersection of the two sets of cables in the two directions the maximum lever arm for resisting moment cannot be obtained for both sets.

(*b*). Following the load-balancing method in Chapter 11. We can start off by assuming that for optimum behavior it will be desirable to balance the 94 psf of dead load plus 15 psf of the live load, or a total of 109 psf. Referring to Fig. 12-7(*d*), the cable sag *h* is very nearly 3.75 in. Hence the effective prestress required is

$$F = \frac{wL^2}{8h} = \frac{109 \times 30^2 \times 12}{8 \times 3.75} = 39.4 \text{ k/ft}$$

and the slab is under uniform prestress of

$$f_{av} = \frac{39,400}{12 \times 7.5} = -437 \text{ psi}$$

for its dead load plus 15 psf live load.

To check the stresses under full live load, we compute the effect of $75 - 15 = 60$ psf additional live load, which will produce a maximum moment over the center support of

$$-M = \frac{wL^2}{8} = \frac{60 \times 30^2}{8} = 6750 \text{ lb-ft}$$

And the maximum bending stresses, according to the beam theory, are

$$f = \frac{Mc}{I} = \frac{6M}{bd^2} = \frac{6 \times 6750 \times 12}{12 \times 7.5^2} = 720 \text{ psi}$$

The resultant maximum fibers stresses are

$$f_{top} = -437 + 720 = +283 \text{ psi tension}$$
$$f_{bot} = -437 - 720 = -1157 \text{ psi compression}$$

These stresses are not considered excessive, and $F = 39.4$ k/ft is satisfactory. This solution is clearly much easier than (a). Note that if no tension is used as the criterion and $\frac{3}{8}L$ is used as the controlling point, the required prestress would be $F = 46.6$ k/ft as obtained in solution (a).

12-4   Flat Slabs, Some Theoretical Considerations

Although we do have a certain amount of knowledge and experience concerning the behavior and analysis of prestressed flat slabs some theoretical problems still deserve further investigation.

A. The degree of accuracy of the continuous beam analysis as applied to flat slabs. Experience has shown that, correct application of the method here presented has yielded satisfactory results, but the degree of accuracy of this method can stand further investigation.

B. The proper distribution of the cables among the column and the middle strips. This can be studied by either the elastic theory for plates or the balanced-load method explained in Chapter 11.

C. Cracking strength. The elastic theory for thin plates can be used to predict the cracking strength of flat slabs. For the use of the designing engineer a simpler method of design is needed, such as the continuous beam method. But the accuracy of such an approximate method and its limiting conditions have not been determined.

D. Ultimate strength. There are extensive data available on the ultimate strength of reinforced-concrete flat slabs, many of which have been explained by the yield-line theory.[10] It is believed that the yield-line theory could be applied to prestressed slabs as well, using the ultimate strength of the prestressed sections. This has been confirmed by some tests.[4,5]

E. Nonprestressed reinforcements. As in simple and continuous beams, nonprestressed reinforcements in slabs help to distribute the cracks and to increase the ultimate strength. If properly employed, such reinforcements can economically reduce the amount of prestressing. Although few data are available at the present, nonprestressed steel to augment the strength of prestressed slabs at sections of high moments is known to be an economical design for some flat slabs.

F. Model analysis. When the layout of the column becomes complicated, it will be almost impossible to apply either the thin plates or the continuous beam theory. Then it may be necessary to resort to model tests. Model tests will yield the elastic moments in the slab due to a given system of loads. The moments produced by prestressing can also be obtained, if the eccentricity of prestress can be reduced to a simple system of vertical loads; for example, if the cables are all of the same parabolic shape, they are equivalent to a system of uniform loads on the slab. It is possible to obtain concordant cables for slabs from such model tests. Since every moment diagram is a concordant cable, it follows that the moment diagrams for a slab obtained from the model tests are the basis for concordant cables. In the design of flat slabs, however, concordant cables usually are not the most desirable ones. As is shown in example 12-3, the nonconcordant cables give a better design. From model tests, it is possible to obtain the C-line for nonconcordant cables, provided again that their eccentricities can be reduced to a simple system of loads, which can be conveniently used for testing the model. It should be noted that all such tests hold good only within the elastic range, before the cracking of concrete.

G. Deflections. Deflections of flat slabs can be obtained by the theory of elasticity, but the time consumed for such an analysis would be enormous. When only approximate results are desired, it is possible to treat strips of the slab as beams and compute the accumulated deflection.[11] For example, the center deflection of a slab is the sum of two deflections, one due to a continuous beam along the columns, another due to a perpendicular continuous beam along the middle, Fig. 12-8. If the

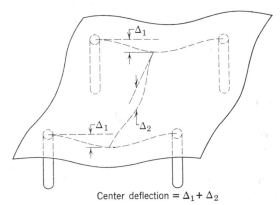

Center deflection = $\Delta_1 + \Delta_2$

Fig. 12-8. Estimating slab deflections.

moments along these two strips are known, the deflections produced by both prestress and external loads can be computed with precision. The effect of plastic flow has to be considered separately and added to the initial deflections.

12-5   Flat Slabs, Some Practical Remarks on Design

Haunched Slabs.   Most prestressed-concrete flat slabs have been built of uniform thickness. This was largely because they were used in conjunction with lifting. In order to be cast conveniently on the ground with no formwork underneath, it is desirable to employ a flat soffit. If the spans are long, and if the slabs are to be cast in place, it may sometimes be economical to design haunched slabs or slabs with drop panels similar to reinforced-concrete construction.

Hollow Slabs or Waffle Slabs.   If the spans are long, it is often economical to keep the dead load within limits. This is done by hollowing the slab, or by using waffle slabs. The sections are thus either I or T in shape and should be designed accordingly. For area over the columns, these slabs are often made solid in order to carry the heavy shear and the negative moments. Lift slabs of the waffle type should be handled with care, both in designing and during lifting. They are thicker and therefore stiffer than equivalent solid slabs and are subjected to higher stresses.

Lift Collars.   Collars for lifting the slabs are of various designs. Figure 12-9 shows a collar made by welding angles together. For other types of collars, the readers are referred to reference 12.

Partition Walls for Lift Slabs.   After the prestressed slabs are lifted in position, partition walls may sometimes be constructed beneath them. These partitions actually serve as bearing walls to some extent. The existence of such walls generally strengthens the slab and reduces its deflections. When located at odd positions, however, they may tend to increase the moments at certain points, and cracking of the slabs may result.

Long Slabs.   When the continuous slabs are too long in one direction, say much over 100 ft, special problems may arise. First, the friction in the cables may increase appreciably and thus tend to decrease the effective prestress. Next, there may be excessive shortening of the slab under prestress which may produce bending in the columns if they are rigid.

Cantilevers.   Cantilevering the slabs beyond their exterior row of columns often helps to reduce the maximum bending moment and saves prestressing steel. But the deflections of such cantilevers under various stages of loading may be excessive and should be studied.

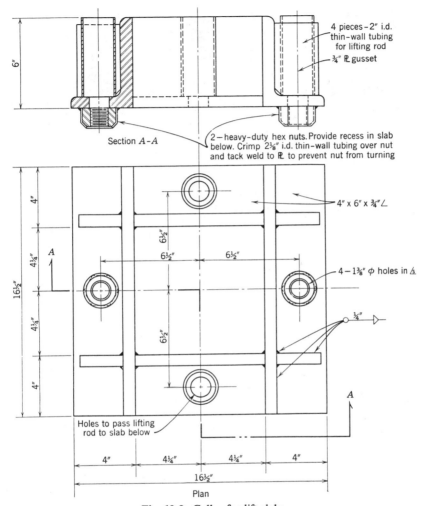

Fig. 12-9. Collar for lift slabs.

Cable Spacing. Cable spacing for flat slabs has an average of around 2 ft, Fig. 12-10, enabling easy placing of concrete. For slabs with thickness between 6 and 10 in., the maximum spacing has been about 4 ft 6 in. for roofs and 3 ft 6 in. for floors. Minimum spacing will generally vary between 6 and 8 in.

Average Prestress. Average prestress is defined as the amount of prestressing force divided by the cross-sectional area of slab concrete. A minimum average prestress is required, if it is desired to eliminate or minimize cracks in the slab. Experience indicates that this minimum

Fig. 12-10. Cable layout for a continuous prestressed lift slab, State Hospital Building, Vacaville, California. (Division of Architecture, State of California; Consultant T. Y. Lin and Associates.)

value is about 200 psi, probably ranging between 150 and 250 psi. Too high an average prestress would induce excessive creep, and should be avoided. No definite rule can be given, although 500–600 psi is considered fairly high for flat slabs.

Special Layouts. Inverted T-beams for roofs, may enable the hanging of floor slabs to the roof, Fig. 12-11, thus affording wide floor spans with thin slabs.[13]

Shear Wall Location. Stiff vertical elements, such as walls and shafts, rigidly connected to the prestress slabs should not be located so as to restrain their shortening. As a result of creep, prestressed slabs may tear themselves away from the supports or produce cracks in them.

Slabs Post-tensioned In Place. For multistory buildings, it is frequently more economical to post-tension the slabs in place. Figure 1-9 shows a

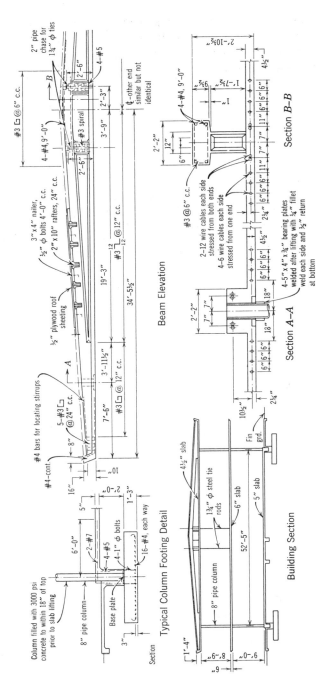

Fig. 12-11. Span 52 ft with a 6-in. post-tensioned slab (*Eng. News-Record*, April 21, 1955, p. 51). Both roof and floor slabs for this Las Vegas, Nev., hotel were lifted simultaneously. Floor slab, 6 in. thick, is hung from roof by rods. Roof slab is 4½-in. thick but has girders on top that span 52 ft between columns.

22-story building, with $8\frac{1}{2}$-in. slabs spanning 30'-6" from the interior shafts to the exterior walls. For in-place post-tensioning, proper provision should be made for the shrinkage and creep of the slabs. Fortunately, most of the floors tend to shorten together and thus will not create a serious problem.

References

1 Westergaard, "Computation of Stresses in Bridge Slabs Due to Wheel Loads," *Public Roads*, March 1930 (also *Public Roads*, March 1926, paper by Kelley giving test results).
2 E. Freyssinet, "The Deformation of Concrete," *Magazine of Concrete Research*, December 1951.
3 G. L. Rogers, "Validity of Certain Assumptions in the Mechanics of Prestressed Concrete," *J. Am. Conc. Inst.*, December 1953 (*Proc.*, Vol. 49), pp. 317–330.
4 A. C. Scordelis, K. S. Pister, and T. Y. Lin, "Strength of a Concrete Slab Prestressed in Two Directions," *J. Am. Conc. Inst.*, September 1956 (*Proc.* Vol. 53), pp. 241–256.
5 T. Y. Lin, A. C. Scordelis, and R. Itaya, "Behavior of a Continuous Slab Prestressed in Two Directions," *J. Am. Conc. Inst.*, Vol. 31, No. 6, December 1959 (*Proc.* Vol. 56), pp. 441–459.
6 A. C. Scordelis, W. Samarzich, and D. Pirtz, "Load Distribution on Prestressed Concrete Slab Bridge," *J1 PCI*, June 1960.
7 Charles Peterson and A. H. Brownfield, "Our Experience with Prestressed Lift-Slabs," *Proc. World Conference on Prestressed Concrete*, San Francisco, 1957.
8 E. K. Rice, "Economic Factors in Prestressed Lift-Slab Construction," *J. Am. Conc. Inst.*, September 1958 (*Proc.* Vol. 55), pp. 485–506.
9 H. Korner, "A 13-story Building by Lift Slab and Slip Form," *Civil Engineering*, September 1960, pp. 62–64.
10 E. Hognestad, "Yield-Line Theory for the Flexural Strength of Reinforced Concrete Slabs," *J. Am. Conc. Inst.*, March 1953 (*Proc.*, Vol. 49), pp. 637–658.
11 E. K. Rice and F. Kulka, "Design of Prestressed Lift-Slabs for Deflection Control," *J. Am. Conc. Inst.*, February 1960, pp. 681–693.
12 Joseph T. Ryerson & Son, Inc., "Lift-Slab Design & Construction," Chicago, 1962.
13 "Span 52 Ft with a 6-inch Slab," *Engineering News-Record*, April 21, 1955, pp. 51–53.

tension members; circular prestressing

13

13-1 Tension Members, Elastic Design

Prestressed tension members combine the strength of high-tensile steel with the rigidity of concrete and provide a unique resistance to tension consistent with small deformations that cannot be obtained by either steel or concrete acting alone. The rigidity of prestressed concrete serves well, especially for long tension members such as tie rods for arches or staybacks for wharves and retaining walls. When prestressed, concrete is given strength to resist any local bending and at the same time steel is stiffened and protected.

Several such members have already been designed and constructed, both in this country and abroad.[1,2] With better understanding of the strength and rigidity of such members, wider application should be found.

The basic behavior of prestressed tension members can be explained from three points of view.

1. The member can be considered as essentially made of concrete which is put under uniform compression so that it can carry tension produced by external loads. If the concrete has not cracked, it is able to carry a total tensile force equal to the total effective precompression plus the tensile capacity of the concrete itself.

2. The member can be considered as essentially made of high-tensile steel which is pre-elongated to reduce its deflection under load. From this viewpoint, the ultimate strength of the member is dependent upon the tensile strength of the steel, but the usable strength is often limited by excessive elongation of the steel which usually takes place at the cracking of the concrete.

3. The member can be considered as a combined steel and concrete member whose strains and stresses before cracking can be evaluated, assuming elastic behavior and taking into account the effect of plastic flow.

393

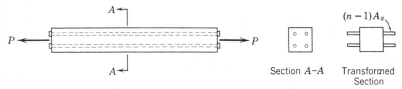

Fig. 13-1. Prestressed-concrete tension member.

Each of the three points of view furnishes some basic concepts from which the engineer can visualize his design, but the third viewpoint is most convenient for analysis by the elastic theory and will be explained first.

If the total initial prestress is F_0 and the total effective prestress F, then the stresses in the concrete will be

$$f_c = \frac{F_0}{A_c}$$

for the initial prestress and

$$f_c = F/A_c$$

for the effective prestress.

Because of a load P applied externally, Fig. 13-1, both the steel and the concrete will elongate the same amount. Hence the usual transformed-section method as applied to reinforced concrete can be applied here. Thus the cross section of the member can be transformed into an equivalent area of concrete equal to

$$A_t = nA_s + A_c \tag{13-1}$$

If the gross area of concrete A_g is used, the transformed area can be expressed as

$$A_t = nA_s + A_g - A_s = A_g + (n-1)A_s \tag{13-2}$$

This formula is valid only when the section is grouted. Otherwise the hole in the concrete will be greater than A_s and formula 13-1 can be more conveniently applied, with A_c referring to the net concrete area.

The stresses produced by P will be, for concrete,

$$f_c = \frac{P}{A_t}$$

and for steel,

$$f_s = \frac{nP}{A_t}$$

In order to be exact, it must be remembered that the value of $n = E_s/E_c$ should be chosen for the proper stress and duration of loading, taking into account the effect of creep if necessary.

Thus the resultant stresses due to the effective prestress plus the external load are, for concrete,

$$f_c = \frac{F}{A_c} + \frac{P}{A_t} \qquad (13\text{-}3)$$

and for steel,

$$f_s = f_c + \frac{nP}{A_t} \qquad (13\text{-}4)$$

If it is desired to determine the load P which will produce zero stress in the concrete, it is only necessary to put $f_c = 0$ in equation 13-3, thus

$$\frac{F}{A_c} + \frac{P}{A_t} = 0$$

$$P = -F \frac{A_t}{A_c} = -F(1 + np) \qquad (13\text{-}5)$$

It is seen that, with no stress in the concrete, the load carried by the member is somewhat greater than the effective prestress F. This is because the stress in the steel has been somewhat increased under the action of the external load P.

It is most important to investigate the strains in a prestressed-concrete member, both those due to prestressing and those due to external loads. Under the initial prestress F_0, the stress in the concrete being F_0/A_c, the corresponding instantaneous unit strain will be

$$\delta = \frac{F_0}{EA_c}$$

which will reduce to F/EA_c after the losses have taken place.

Under the action of external load P, the instantaneous strain is given by

$$\delta = \frac{P}{EA_t}$$

In all cases, the value of E must be chosen with regard to the level of stress and the age of concrete, and the effect of creep must be considered.

Let us first compare the magnitude of strains in a prestressed-concrete member with those in an ordinary steel member. For a structural steel member stressed to 20,000 psi, corresponding to a value of $E_s = 30,000,000$ psi, the unit elongation is

$$\delta = \frac{20,000}{30,000,000} = 0.00067$$

For a prestressed-concrete member, with the stresses in concrete changing from -1000 psi to 0, for an E_c of 4,000,000 psi, the unit strain is

$$\delta = \frac{1000}{4,000,000} = 0.00025$$

which is less than half of the strain in structural steel.

High-tensile steel alone cannot be used for long tension members where elongation must be limited. In order to be stressed to its working strength of 125,000 psi, the unit elongation will be

$$\delta = \frac{125,000}{30,000,000} = 0.00417$$

which is more than 6 times that of structural steel and 16 times that of prestressed concrete in the above example.

Strains in prestressed-concrete members are influenced by several factors. If the precompression in the concrete remains over a period of time, the shortening of that member due to creep could be considerable. Such creep strain, however, would be gradually recovered (though not completely) under the application of an external tension (see Chapter 2, reference 3). Since a greater portion of the creep may be eventually recovered, the lengthening of the member under sustained external load may be greater than is indicated by the elastic calculations.

On the other hand, there are ways to limit further the elongation of prestressed-concrete tension members. One obvious method is to increase the cross-sectional area of concrete. For example, if the concrete area is doubled, the stress range will be halved, and so will the strain. There is, of course, an economical limit to this method, since the area of concrete cannot be indefinitely increased. Another way to control the elongation is to time the application of prestress to the application of the external dead load. If this is carefully done, the elongation due to dead load can really be reduced to a minimum, although practical considerations may not permit such an ideal sequence of application of forces. Still another way is to use concrete possessing high modulus of elasticity. It is known that, for high strength concrete (say $f_c' > 5000$ psi) over two or three years old, the instantaneous modulus of elasticity would be as high as 8,000,000 psi (see Chapter 12, reference 6).

EXAMPLE 13-1

A straight concrete member 150 ft long is prestressed with a high-tensile steel strand through the centroid of the section. The strand is anchored to the concrete with end anchorages but separated from it by bond-breaking agents along the length. $A_c = 80$ in.^{2}. $A_s = 0.80$ in.^{2}. $f_c' = 4000$ psi, $f_s' = 250,000$ psi, $f_0 = 150,000$ psi, $f_c = 127,500$ psi, $E_c = 4,000,000$ psi, $E_s = 30,000,000$ psi.

(a) Compute the allowable external load on the member, allowing no tension in the concrete. (b) Compute the shortening of concrete due to prestress, assuming a creep coefficient of 1.5. (c) Compute the lengthening of the member due to the external load obtained in (a), neglecting creep. (d) If the member were designed of structural steel with an allowable stress of 20,000 psi, compute the lengthening under the load. (e) Compute the lengthening if the strand is used alone by itself with an allowable stress of 127,500 psi.

Solution. (a) From formula 13-5, allowable external compressive load is

$$P = F(1 + np)$$
$$= 127,500 \times 0.80(1 + 7.5 \times 0.80/80)$$
$$= 110,000 \text{ lb}$$

(b) Under the initial prestress, the shortening of concrete will be

$$\frac{F_0 L}{E_c A_c} = \frac{150,000 \times 0.80 \times 150 \times 12}{4,000,000 \times 80}$$
$$= 0.675 \text{ in.}$$

If the effective prestress is considered, the shortening will be

$$0.675 \times \frac{127,500}{150,000} = 0.573 \text{ in.}$$

If the creep coefficient is based on the effective prestress, the total elastic and creep shortening will be

$$0.573 \times 1.5 = 0.860 \text{ in.}$$

(c) Under the external load of 110 k, for a transformed area of $A_t = 80 + 7.5 \times 0.80 = 86$ in.^{2}, again using $E_c = 4,000,000$ psi, the lengthening of the member will be

$$\frac{110,000 \times 150 \times 12}{4,000,000 \times 86} = 0.575 \text{ in.}$$

this checks closely with the shortening of the concrete computed in (b).

(d) For a structural steel stressed to 20,000 psi, the elongation will be

$$\frac{20,000 \times 150 \times 12}{30,000,000} = 1.20 \text{ in.}$$

(e) For high-tensile steel stressed to 127,500 psi, the elongation will be

$$\frac{127,500 \times 150 \times 12}{30,000,000} = 7.65 \text{ in.}$$

13-2   Tension Members, Cracking and Ultimate Strengths

The previous section discusses the computation of stresses in a prestressed-concrete tension member, up to zero compression in the concrete.

The design of such a member may or may not be made on this basis, depending on the probable amount of overloading to which the member may be subjected. In order to get a sufficient factor of safety, it may be necessary to design the member so that, under working loads, there will always be some residual compression in the concrete. This will become evident after a study of the cracking and ultimate strengths of the member. Tension members are one of the typical cases in prestressed concrete where design by the allowable stress method may err very much on the dangerous side and may not yield consistent results.

Generally speaking, prestressed-concrete tension members have a very low reserve strength above the point of zero stress. If the member is not cast as one piece, for example, if it is made up of blocks, cracking may coincide with zero stress. Then any additional load on the member will be carried by the steel alone. Since the prestressing steel has a relatively small area of cross section, excessive elongation will immediately start at the cracking of concrete, and failure of other parts of the structure may result. For such a member, then, it is evident that a considerable amount of residual compression is necessary in order to ensure safety, the amount being governed by the magnitude of the probable overloads.

If the member is cast as one piece, and if shrinkage and other cracks have not occurred, it will be able to take some tension before cracking. The direct tensile strength of concrete is variable and generally ranges from 0.06 to $0.10f_c'$. Thus, for a concrete of 4000 psi, the tensile strength may be from 240 to 400 psi, which may provide a good margin of safety if the strength exists and has not been destroyed. But, once the concrete has cracked, the margin of safety is gone. In fact, failure of the entire structure may result as soon as the concrete cracks, because at this moment the tensile load carried by the concrete in tension is suddenly transferred to the steel. Thus there may be a sudden elongation of steel which may have serious effects, even though the ultimate strength of the steel is far from being reached.

The above discussion must not be construed to mean that such tension members are unsafe. They are just as safe as any other type of tension members and perhaps safer if properly designed. When heavy overloads are possible, they should not be designed on the basis of allowable stresses, but rather on the basis of the cracking or ultimate strength, with proper load factors.

Load factors should vary with the type of structure. Their choice will depend on the possibilities of overloading. If dead load predominates in a member, any serious increase in loading is not so likely. Thus, in most buildings and long-span bridges, the load factor required will be smaller than in a short bridge subject to possible heavy overloadings.

For liquid storage tanks, both the possibility and the magnitude of overloading are small, and a very low load factor is employed.

EXAMPLE 13-2

For the tension member in example 13-1, what working load can it carry, using a factor of safety of 2.0 against the cracking of concrete, assuming the direct tensile strength in concrete to be $0.08f_c' = 320$ psi? Compute the residual compression in concrete under that working load.

Solution. From formula 13-3, for $f_c = 320$ psi,

$$\frac{F}{A_c} + \frac{P}{A_t} = 320$$

From example 13-1,

$$F = -102,000 \text{ lb}$$
$$A_c = 80 \text{ sq in.}$$
$$A_t = 86 \text{ sq in.}$$

Substituting,

$$\frac{-102,000}{80} + \frac{P}{86} = 320$$
$$P = 137,000 \text{ lb}$$

which is the cracking load.

For a factor of safety of 2.0, the working load will be

$$137,000/2 = 68,500 \text{ lb}$$

Though the load factor of 2.0 is not always necessary, the great difference between this answer and the last one of 110 k should be noticed.

The residual compression can be computed using the same formula, for $P = 68,500$ lb,

$$f_c = \frac{F}{A_c} + \frac{P}{A_t} = \frac{-102,000}{80} + \frac{68,500}{86}$$
$$= -1275 + 795 = -480 \text{ psi}$$

13-3 Circular Prestressing

The term "circular prestressing" is employed to denote the prestressing of circular structures such as pipes and tanks where the prestressing wires are wound in circles. In contrast to this term, "linear prestressing" is used to include all other types of prestressing, where the cables may be either straight or curved, but not wound in circles around a circular structure. In most prestressed circular structures, prestress is applied both circumferentially and longitudinally, the circumferential prestress being circular and the longitudinal prestress actually linear. For convenience, both types of prestress as they are applied to circular structures will be discussed in this chapter.

The basic theories of circular prestressing are the same as those for linear prestressing; hence practically all the general principles presented in the previous chapters can be applied to circular structures as well, although such application necessarily involves certain details not discussed for linear structures. The practice of circular prestressing differs from linear prestressing in that the techniques of applying the prestress and of anchoring the tendons are often different.

In this chapter, the discussion will be centered on the design of tanks or circular liquid containers. Most of these principles are applicable also to the design of pipes, which will not be discussed in detail. Instead, some citations on prestressed pipes are given to which the reader can refer if he is interested in the subject.[3]

Prestressed-concrete pipes in this country can be divided into two types: those with and those without steel cylinders. The construction of those with steel cylinders is now a standardized procedure, as evidenced by the specifications[4] approved by the A.W.W.A. in 1952. These specifications cover the manufacture of such water pipes ranging in size from 16 to 54 in. and designed for static loads from 100 to 600 ft of water. A typical longitudinal section of the pipe through the joint is shown in Fig. 13-2. The pipe consists of a continuously welded sheet-steel cylinder with steel joint rings welded to its ends, the cylinder being lined on the inside with dense concrete of suitable thickness. After proper curing of concrete, high-tensile wire is wound around the outside of the steel cylinder at a specified prestress and securely fastened to it at its ends. Then a coating of mortar or concrete is deposited over the cylinder and wire for protection. A self-centering joint with rubber gasket as the sealing element is designed so as to be watertight under all conditions of service.

Pipes without steel cylinders are manufactured by simply winding prestressed wires around a concrete core and covering the wires with air-applied mortar. Longitudinal prestress is sometimes provided by

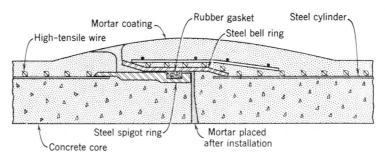

Fig. 13-2. Longitudinal section through joint of prestressed-concrete cylinder pipe.

pretensioning longitudinal wires against the inner steel form.[5] In another method, helical wire wrapping is applied in a basket-weave pattern so as to produce a longitudinal component of prestress.[6] The concrete core is often cast by the Rocla roller compaction method, by which a rotating mold rolls and places the dense concrete to form a thin-walled pipe. The Rocla firm in Australia applies pre-tensioning techniques to concrete pipes by embedding circular reinforcement in the pipe concrete which immediately after having been placed is subjected to high pressure applied to the inside of the pipe.[7] When the concrete hardens, the steel remains stretched; then the inside pressure is relieved, and the concrete becomes compressed.

In this country prestressed-concrete tanks are almost solely constructed by the Preload method, using their wire winding machines. Up to 1951, about 700 large tanks with a total capacity of more than 500 million gallons and 300 spherical shell roofs in spans up to 205 ft had been built of prestressed concrete in North America, using almost exclusively the Preload method of prestressing.[8] The Preload procedure consists of the following process. First, the walls for the tanks are built of either concrete or pneumatic mortar, mortar being generally used if the walls are less than 6 in. thick. Often, the walls are poured in alternate vertical slices keyed together. After the concrete walls have attained sufficient strength they are prestressed circumferentially by a self-propelled machine, which winds the wire around the walls in a continuous operation, stressing it and spacing it at the same time. Under favorable conditions, the machine can place the wire up to 7 miles an hour and can complete the horizontal prestressing of an average million-gallon tank in about two days.

After the circumferential prestressing is completed for each layer, a coat of pneumatic mortar is placed around the tank for protection. Two or more layers of prestressing are used for large tanks. Vertical prestressing for the tanks can be applied using any system of linear prestressing, whichever may be the most economical.

In addition to the Preload procedure, other methods have been applied in this country and abroad, though not as extensively as that using the winding machine. In the 1920's, Hewett in the United States used ordinary bars wrapped around the walls and stressed with turnbuckles.[9] But all the prestress in such bars could be lost in the course of time as a result of shrinkage and flow of concrete, although some of the tanks have remained in good service even to the present time. Mautner, of England,[10] employed high-strength steel wires wrapped around precast concrete units, between which were inserted jacks which, when extended, stretched the steel wires. Openings left for the jacks were eventually filled with concrete to maintain the compression in the walls.

The Freyssinet method of linear prestressing has been applied to tanks with the tendons in equal lengths of portions of a circle.[11] The tendons are stressed from both ends and anchored against pylons spaced uniformly around the tank. By staggering the end anchors in adjacent tendons, the frictional loss of prestress is nearly equalized around the circle.

It can be said that, similar to the Freyssinet system, most post-tensioning systems can be used for circular tanks, with the tendons along segments of the circle and anchored against pylons equally spaced. This type of tank has an advantage over the wire-winding process, whose gunite coating is not prestressed and may not give as good a protection for the tendons.

13-4   Circumferential Prestressing in Tanks

Circumferential prestress in tanks is designed to resist hoop tension produced by liquid pressure. Hence, essentially, each horizontal slice of the wall forms a ring subject to uniform internal pressure. In several

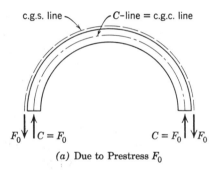

(*a*) Due to Prestress F_0

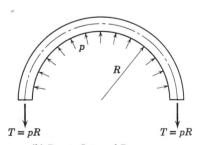

(*b*) Due to Internal Pressure p

Fig. 13-3. Forces in a horizontal slice of tank (half slice as freebody).

senses, such a ring can be regarded as a prestressed-concrete member under tension, and much of the discussion in sections 13-1 and 13-2 on tension members can be applied to the design of circumferential prestressing as well.

Consider one half of a thin horizontal slice of a tank as a freebody, Fig. 13-3(a). Under the action of prestress F_0 in the steel, the total compression C in the concrete is equal to F_0. The location of the line of pressure or the C-line in the concrete does not usually coincide with the c.g.s. line. In a circular ring under circular prestress, the C-line always coincides with the c.g.c. line. This is because a closed ring is a statically indeterminate structure, and the theory of linear transformation explained in Chapter 10 for continuous beams is applicable to such a ring. A cable through the c.g.c. is a concordant cable; any other cable parallel to it is simply that line, linearly transformed, whose line of pressure will still remain through the c.g.c. This phenomenon can also be explained by the simple fact that the effect of circular prestress is to produce an initial hoop compression on the concrete, which is always axial irrespective of the point of application of the prestress. Hence, owing to circular prestress, the stress in the concrete is always axial and is given by the formula

$$f_c = -\frac{F_0}{A_c}$$

which reduces to

$$f_c = -F/A_c$$

after the losses in prestress have taken place.

With the application of internal liquid pressure, Fig. 13-3(b), the steel and concrete act together, and the stresses can be obtained by the usual elastic theory. Using the method of transformed section, we have

$$f_c = pR/A_t$$

where p = internal pressure intensity, R = internal radius of the tank, A_t = transformed area = $A_c + (n - 1)A_s$.

The resultant stress in the concrete under the effective prestress F and the internal pressure p is

$$f_c = -\frac{F}{A_c} + \frac{pR}{A_t} \tag{13-6}$$

In order to be exact, the value of n has to be chosen correctly, considering the level of stress and the effect of creep. In practice, slight variation in the value of n may not affect the stresses very much, and an approximate value will usually suffice. If a coating of concrete or mortar is added after the application of prestress, then the area A_c under pre-stress may be the core area while the A_c sustaining the liquid pressure may include the additional coating. Such refinements in calculation may or may not be necessary, depending on the circumstances.

The criteria for designing prestressed tanks vary. The practice in this country has been to provide a slight residual compression in the concrete under the working pressure. This is accomplished by the following procedure of design.

Assume that the hoop tension produced by internal pressure is entirely carried by the effective prestress in the steel; we have

$$F = A_s f_s = pR \qquad (13\text{-}7)$$

thus the total steel area required is

$$A_s = \frac{pR}{f_s} \qquad (13\text{-}8)$$

The total initial prestress is then

$$F_0 = A_s f_0 \qquad (13\text{-}9)$$

For an allowable compressive stress f_c in concrete, the concrete area re-quired to resist the initial prestress F_0 is

$$A_c = -\frac{F_0}{f_c} \qquad (13\text{-}10)$$

From this value of required A_c, the thickness for the tank can be deter-mined.

Corresponding to the adopted value of A_c, the stresses in the concrete and steel under the internal pressure p can be obtained by

$$\text{Stress in concrete} = -\frac{F}{A_c} + \frac{pR}{A_t} \qquad (13\text{-}11)$$

$$\text{Stress in steel} = f_s + n f_c \qquad (13\text{-}12)$$

Since F is equal and opposite to pR, and A_t is always greater than A_c, it can be seen from equation 13-11 that there will be some residual compression in the concrete under the working pressure. This residual compression serves as a margin of safety in addition to whatever tension may be taken by the concrete.

Since the serviceability of a tank is impaired as soon as the concrete begins to crack, it is of utmost importance that an adequate margin of safety be provided against cracking. Where overflow pipes are installed for tanks so that there cannot exist any excessive pressure, a smaller margin of safety is required. Thus the English *First Report on Prestressed Concrete*[12] recommends a factor of safety of 1.25 against cracking. For pipes that may be subjected to much higher pressure than the working value, a greater factor of safety is necessary. For the design of prestressed concrete pipes with steel cylinders, the A.W.W.A. species that the concrete core should be sufficiently compressed to withstand an internal hydrostatic pressure equal to at least 1.25 times the designed pressure without tensile stress being induced in the core. In addition, the pressure producing elastic limit stresses in the steel cylinder and wire is sometimes required to be 2.25 times the normal operating pressure.[3]

The conventional method of design equating the effective prestress to the hoop tension may or may not provide the necessary factor of safety. If a factor of safety of m against cracking is required, the following procedure of design may be adopted.

Assuming f_t = tensile strength in concrete at cracking (which averages about $0.08f_c'$ but may be zero if the concrete has previously cracked or if precast blocks are used), we may write

$$-\frac{F}{A_c} + \frac{mpR}{A_t} = f_t \qquad (13\text{-}13)$$

At the same time, in order to limit the maximum compression in concrete to f_c, we have

$$A_c = -F_0/f_c$$

Substituting this value of A_c into equation 13-13, and noting that $A_t = A_c + nA_s$, $F = f_sA_s$, and $F_0 = f_0A_s$, we have

$$-\frac{f_sA_sf_c}{f_0A_s} + \frac{mpR}{(f_0A_s/f_c) + nA_s} = f_t \qquad (13\text{-}14)$$

Solving for A_s, we have

$$A_s = \frac{mpR}{[f_s - (f_t/f_c)f_0](1 - nf_c/f_0)} \qquad (13\text{-}15)$$

After A_s is obtained, F_0 and A_c can be computed using equations 13-9 and 13-10, and the stresses in the concrete and steel can be evaluated by equations 13-11 and 13-12.

One of the important items in the design of tanks is the evaluation of the losses of prestress. Although the details of the sources of loss are discussed in Chapter 4, the usual amount of loss occurring and allowed for in prestressed tanks will be mentioned here. Extensive experiments have been made to measure the amount of losses in prestressed tanks.[13] The average loss of prestress seems to be about 25,000 psi, resulting chiefly from the shrinkage and creep of concrete. An allowance of 35,000 psi is considered quite conservative, although, under extremely adverse conditions, losses up to 40,000 psi might take place.

Analyzing the principal sources of these losses, it might be estimated that concrete under a constant load of about 600 psi may attain a total elastic and creep deformation of about 0.0006. Since the concrete is under low compression when the tank is full, the amount of creep strain may be much smaller if the tank is kept filled most of the time. The amount of shrinkage will depend chiefly upon the moisture content in the concrete. Although the worst possible shrinkage strain can be as much as 0.0010, there have been tanks whose concrete expanded instead of contracted, thus resulting in a gain of prestress instead of a loss. For example, if a tank is prestressed after the concrete has aged for several months under dry climatic conditions, expansion will take place when it is filled with water.

The following may be taken as a safe average value.

$$\begin{aligned}
\text{Elastic and creep strain in concrete} &= 0.0005 \\
\text{Shrinkage} &= 0.0005 \\
\hline
\text{Total loss} &= 0.0010
\end{aligned}$$

which amounts to about 28,000 psi, taking E_s as 28,000,000 psi. If accurate values are desired, the possible losses must be considered for each individual tank and duly allowed for.

EXAMPLE 13-3

Determine the area of steel wire required per foot of height of a prestressed-concrete water tank 60 ft in inside diameter to resist 20 ft of water pressure. Compute the thickness of concrete required. $f_c' = 3000$ psi, $f_c = 750$ psi, $n = 10$, $f_0 = 150,000$ psi, $f_s = 120,000$ psi. Neglect the mortar coating in the calculations. Design both steel and concrete on the following two bases:

1. Assuming all hoop tension carried by the effective prestress.
2. For a load factor of 1.25, producing zero stress in concrete.

Solution. (*a*) Pressure of 20 ft of water

$$p = 20 \times 62.4 = 1248 \text{ psf}$$

Using equations 13-8 and 13-10,

$$\begin{aligned}
A_s &= pR/f_s \\
&= \frac{1248 \times 30}{120,000} \\
&= 0.312 \text{ sq in.} \\
A_c &= -F_0/f_c \\
&= \frac{-0.312 \times 150,000}{-750} \\
&= 62.5 \text{ sq in.}
\end{aligned}$$

For a height of 12 in., the thickness required is $62.5/12 = 5.2$ in. Suppose that a thickness of 5.5 in., is adopted; then, under the action of the internal pressure, equation 13-11 gives

$$f_c = -\frac{F}{A_c} + \frac{pR}{A_t}$$

$$= -\frac{0.312 \times 120,000}{5.5 \times 12} + \frac{1248 \times 30}{66 + 10 \times 0.312}$$

$$= -567 + 541$$

$$= -26 \text{ psi}$$

Note here that, the thicker the concrete, the smaller will be the residual compression under load, unless the amount of wire is proportionately increased.

(b) Using equation 13-15,

$$A_s = \frac{mpR}{[f_s - (f_t/f_c)f_0](1 - nf_c/f_0)}$$

$$= \frac{1.25 \times 1248 \times 30}{[120,000 + 0](1 - 10 \times -750/150,000)}$$

$$= 0.372 \text{ in.}^2$$

$$A_c = F_0/f_c$$

$$= 0.372 \times 150,000/750$$

$$= 74.4 \text{ in.}^2$$

Thickness required $= 74.4/12 = 6.2$ in. If a thickness of 6.5 in. is adopted, the resulting stress in the concrete under full water pressure will be

$$f_c = \frac{F}{A_c} + \frac{pR}{A_t}$$

$$= \frac{-0.372 \times 120,000}{6.5 \times 12} + \frac{1248 \times 30}{78 + 10 \times 0.372}$$

$$= -573 + 458$$

$$= -115 \text{ psi}$$

which provides a margin of safety of 25% up to zero compression in concrete.

Note that designing by this second method gives heavier sections for both concrete and steel. The design can be economized if some tension in the concrete is allowed at 25% overload.

13-5 Vertical Prestressing in Tanks

The design of prestressed-concrete structures is based on a knowledge of the behavior of nonprestressed structures plus an understanding of the effect of prestressing. This is as true for the design of tanks as for beams

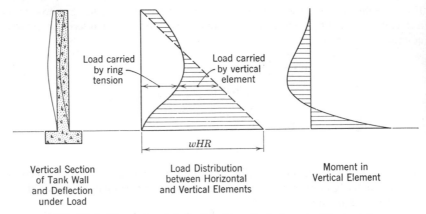

Vertical Section
of Tank Wall
and Deflection
under Load

Load Distribution
between Horizontal
and Vertical Elements

Moment in
Vertical Element

Fig. 13-4. Moment and deflection in vertical element of tank wall.

and slabs.   Before analyzing the stresses in a prestressed tank, let us consider an ordinary reinforced-concrete tank under the action of internal liquid pressure.   It is well known that, whereas the horizontal elements of the tank are subject to hoop tension, the vertical elements are under bending, Fig. 13-4.   The amount and variation of bending in the vertical elements will depend on several factors.

1. The condition of support at the bottom of the wall, whether fixed, hinged, free to slide, or restrained by friction.

2. The condition of support at the top of the wall, whether fully or partially restrained or free to move.

3. The variation of concrete thickness along the height of the wall.

4. The variation of pressure along the depth, whether triangular or trapezoidal.

5. The ratio of the height of the tank to its diameter.

Theoretical solution for several of these combinations are given by Timoshenko[14] and numerical values, convenient for application, are tabulated in some pamphlets.[15]   European books give solutions for additional cases, such as walls of varying thickness, and the results are plotted in some publications.[16]   Readers interested in the problem are referred to these and to the bibliographies listed in them.   To give an idea of such distribution of loads among the horizontal and vertical elements, two graphs are presented in Fig. 13-5.   It is evident from these graphs that the active pressure on the horizontal elements is not a direct function of depth, but often decreases with it, while the vertical elements may carry a considerable amount of load, especially if the structure is squattier than usual.

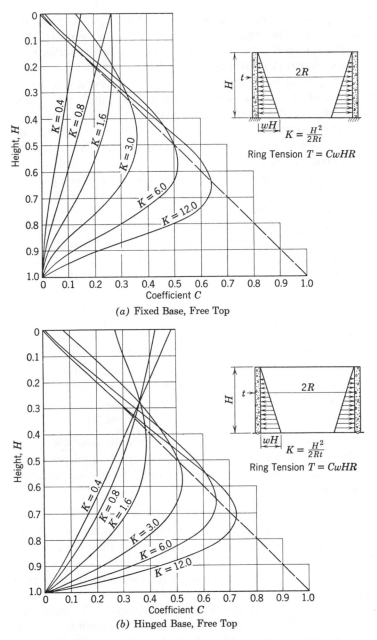

(a) Fixed Base, Free Top

(b) Hinged Base, Free Top

Fig. 13-5. Tension in tank rings, triangular load, uniform wall section.

For prestressed-concrete tanks, an additional problem is introduced: the effect of prestressing, both circumferential and vertical. Since horizontal pressure will produce vertical moments in the walls, it is evident that circumferential prestressing will also induce such moments. These vertical moments caused by circumferential prestressing will exist by themselves when the tank is empty and will act jointly with the moments produced by liquid pressure when the tank is filled. To reinforce the wall against these moments, vertical prestressing may be applied. If vertical prestress is concentrically applied to the concrete, only direct compressive stress is produced and the solution is simple. If the vertical tendons are bent or curved, the vertical prestress produces radial components which, in turn, influence the circumferential prestress. Hence the analysis can become quite complicated.

Let us investigate the effect of circumferential prestressing on the vertical moments. If the circumferential prestress varies triangularly from zero at the top to a maximum at the bottom, its effect is equal but opposite to the application of an equivalent liquid pressure. If the circumferential prestress is constant throughout the entire height of the wall, it is the same as the application of an equivalent gaseous pressure. For both cases, tables are available for the computation of vertical moments.[15] To obtain the optimum results, the circumferential prestress along the depth of the wall should be varied to suit the variation of the active pressure on the horizontal elements. However, the effect of such circumferential prestressing on vertical moments cannot be readily determined.

Vertical prestressing should be designed to stand the stresses produced by various possible combinations of the following forces.

1. The vertical weight of the roof and the walls themselves.
2. The vertical moments produced by internal liquid pressure.
3. The vertical moments produced by the applied circumferential prestress.

In addition to the above, stresses may be produced as a result of differential temperature between the inner and outer faces of the wall, and by shrinkage of the concrete walls unless they are entirely free to slide on the foundation. These forces cannot be easily evaluated and hence are often neglected or provided for indirectly in an overall factor of safety.

It must be noted that the maximum stresses in the concrete usually exist when the tank is empty, because then the circumferential prestress would have its full effect. When the tank is filled, the liquid pressure tends to counterbalance the effect of circumferential prestress and the vertical moments are smaller. Since it is convenient to use the same amount of vertical prestress throughout the entire height of the wall, the amount will be controlled by the point of maximum moment. By properly locating the vertical tendons to resist such moment, a most economical design can be obtained. However, efforts are seldom made to do so, and the amount of prestress as well as the location of the tendons is generally determined empirically rather than by any logical method of design.

EXAMPLE 13-4

A 1-ft vertical element of a water tank is shown in Fig. 13-6. It carries 1500 lb of weight from the roof. At a point 20 ft below the top, the vertical moments are: for initial circumferential prestress, $M = 3200$ ft-lb (tension on the inside fibers), which reduces to 2500 ft-lb eventually. For full liquid pressure, $M = 2400$ ft-lb (tension on the outside face). The vertical prestressing wire is located $2\frac{3}{4}$ in. from the inside face and exerts an initial prestress of 11,000 lb-ft, which reduces to 8000 lb/ft eventually. Compute stresses in the extreme vertical fibers of the concrete under the initial and final conditions, considering both an empty and a full tank.

Solution. The stresses for both the inside and outside fibers under both initial and final conditions are computed and listed as in the table. It is seen from the table that a slight tension of 36 to 41 psi exists on the inside vertical fibers when the tank is empty. Otherwise, compressive stresses are obtained throughout. (See Table 13-1.)

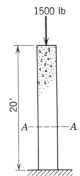

Fig. 13-6.
Example 13-4.

13-6 Dome Ring Prestressing

It is beyond the scope of this treatise to discuss the design of domes. Only the general principles and practice of dome prestressing especially as applied to tank roofs will be mentioned here. Readers interested in the subject are referred to other publications for additional details.[17,19] Generally speaking, for domes with diameter greater than 100 ft, the economy of prestressing should be seriously considered. Domes for tanks up to 230 ft in diameter have been constructed.

The dome roof itself is made of concrete or pneumatic mortar with thickness varying from 2 to 6 in. For domes of large diameter, variable thicknesses may be employed and thicknesses greater than 6 in. are used for the lower portion. Before concreting the dome, some erection bars are prestressed around the base of the dome. After the hardening of the shell concrete, wires are prestressed around it, Fig. 13-7. During this

TABLE 13-1

Computation for Stresses in Concrete (Example 13-4)

Conditions	Initial		Final	
Fiber	Inside	Outside	Inside	Outside
A. Weight of roof $\dfrac{1500}{8 \times 12} =$	-16	-16	-16	-16
B. Weight of wall $\dfrac{20 \times 150}{144} =$	-21	-21	-21	-21
C. Axial component of vertical prestress $\dfrac{11,000}{8 \times 12} =$	-115	-115		
$\dfrac{8000}{8 \times 12} =$			-83	-83
D. Eccentricity of vertical prestress $\dfrac{6M}{bd^2} = \dfrac{6 \times 11,000 \times 1.25}{12 \times 8^2} =$	-107	$+107$		
$\dfrac{6 \times 8000 \times 1.25}{12 \times 8^2} =$			-78	$+78$
E. Vertical moment due to circumferential prestress $\dfrac{6M}{bd^2} = \dfrac{6 \times 3200 \times 12}{12 \times 8^2} =$	$+300$	-300		
$\dfrac{6 \times 2500 \times 12}{12 \times 8^2} =$			$+234$	-234
Total for tank empty	$+41$	-345	$+36$	-276
F. Vertical moment due to liquid pressure $\dfrac{6M}{bd^2} = \dfrac{6 \times 2400 \times 12}{12 \times 8^2} =$	-225	$+225$	-225	$+225$
Total for tank full	-184	-120	-198	-51

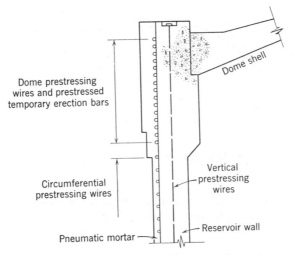

Dome prestressing
wires and prestressed
temporary erection bars

Dome shell

Circumferential
prestressing wires

Vertical
prestressing
wires

Reservoir wall

Pneumatic mortar

Fig. 13-7. Typical section of dome ring for tanks.

operation, the dome shell rises from its forms as it is compressed, thus simplifying the careful procedure of decentering required for nonprestressed domes.

Methods and formulas, though available for the analysis of dome stresses under uniform loads, are applicable only to points on the domes removed from the discontinuous edge. The computation of stresses in the edge ring becomes a very complicated problem if the edge ring is prestressed. However, for purposes of design, a conventional method is available. It consists of prestressing the ring to induce sufficient compressive stresses to counteract the tensile stresses set up in the ring under the maximum live and dead loads. With this prestress, it is usually possible to raise the dome from its false work, since only the dead load is actually acting on the dome.

Consider a spherical dome carrying loads symmetrical about the axis of rotation, that is, load with intensity constant along any given latitude, Fig. 13-8. If the total load is W, the vertical reaction per foot of length along the edge member will be

$$V = \frac{W}{2\pi R \sin \theta}$$

Since a dome is not supposed to carry any appreciable moment, the resultant reaction along the edge must be tangent to the surface. Hence the horizontal reaction per foot of length must be

$$H = V \cot \theta = \frac{W \cot \theta}{2\pi R \sin \theta}$$

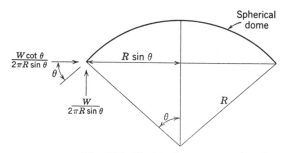

Fig. 13-8. Design for prestress in edge ring of dome.

Assuming this horizontal reaction to be entirely supplied by the prestressing force F acting in hoop tension, then,

$$F = HR \sin \theta$$

$$= \frac{W}{2\pi} \cot \theta \qquad (13\text{-}16)$$

The effective prestressing force F having been determined, the cross-sectional area of the ring concrete can be designed by

$$A_c = \frac{F_0}{f_c} \qquad (13\text{-}17)$$

where F_0 = the initial prestressing force, and f_c = the allowable compressive stress in concrete.

It is desirable to keep f_c at a relatively low value, say about $0.2f_c'$ and not greater than 800 psi. This is necessary in order to minimize excessive strain in the edge ring which might in turn produce high stresses in the shell. It must be further observed that this procedure of design is satisfactory only when there is no possibility of heavy overloads, because the

Fig. 13-9. University of Illinois Stadium, Urbana, Ill., has 400-ft dome with post-tensioned ring to deflect the membrane forces inward, forming a bowl. (Architect Harrison and Abramovitz; Structural Engineer Ammann and Whitney.)

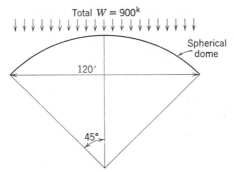

Fig. 13-10. Example 13-5.

prestressed edge ring does not possess a high factor of safety against overloads, although the factor of safety is sufficient for ordinary roof loading.

One of the world's largest concrete roofs ever built[20] is the circular dome cover for the Assembly Hall of the University of Illinois, Urbana, Fig. 13-9 The folded plate dome has a diameter of 400 ft. It is of lightweight concrete and weighs 10,700 k. The prestressing consisted of 2,503 circles of 0·236–in. wires with a total steel area of 85 sq in., stressed to about 150,000 psi, producing a stress in the edge beam of about 1000 psi at transfer.

EXAMPLE 13-5

A spherical dome, Fig. 13-10, carries a total live and dead load of 900 k. Design the prestress in the edge ring and the cross-sectional area of concrete required for the edge ring. Loss of prestress = 20%. f_c = 600 psi.

Solution. From equation 13-16, for W = 900 k and θ = 45°, we have

$$F = (W/2\pi) \cot \theta$$
$$= 900/2\pi$$
$$= 143 \text{ k}$$

which will result in zero tension in the dome ring under full live and dead load. From equation 13-17, area of concrete required, for F_0 = 143/0.8 = 179 k, is

$$A_c = F_0/f_c$$
$$= 179/0.6$$
$$= 298 \text{ in.}^2$$

References

1   A. F. Campbell, "Arch Tie Prestressed to Hold Length," *Eng. News-Rec.*, July 16, 1953, p. 48.
2   "Concrete Tied Arch Spans 236 Ft with Prestressed Hangers and Tie Girders," *Eng. News-Rec.*, Feb. 4, 1954, p. 42.

3 H. F. Kennison, "Design of Prestressed Concrete Cylinder Pipe," *J. Am. Water Works Assn.*, November 1950, p. 1049.

4 *Standard Specifications for Reinforced Concrete Water Pipe—Steel Cylinder Type, Prestressed*, Am. Water Works Assn., 1952.

5 R. M. Doull, "Prestressed Pipe without Steel Cylinders," *Eng. News-Rec.*, June 24, 1948, p. 68.

6 "New Casting and Prestressing Techniques for Ultra-Strong Concrete Pipe," *Eng. News-Rec.*, Oct. 6, 1949, p. 24.

7 "Prestressing Concrete Pipe," *Concrete*, September 1947, p. 38.

8 C. Dobell, "Prestressed Concrete Tanks," *Proc. First U.S. Conference on Prestressed Concrete*, 1951.

9 "A New Method of Constructing Reinforced Concrete Water Tanks," *Proc. Am. Conc. Inst.*, 1923, pp. 41–52.

10 K. W. Maunter, "Prestressed Concrete in Structures of Annular Cross-Sections," *Structural Engineer*, 1945, pp. 117–163 and 437–451.

11 M. R. Muzet, "Réservoirs en béton précontraint," *Précontrainte Prestressing*, 1951, No. 1, p. 87.

12 *First Report on Prestressed Concrete*, Institution of Structural Engineers, London, England, 1951.

13 J. M. Grom, "Design of Prestressed Tanks," *Proc. Am. Soc. C.E.*, October 1950, (separate No. 37).

14 S. Timoshenko, *Theory of Plates and Shells*, McGraw-Hill Book Co., New York, 1940.

15 "Circular Concrete Tanks without Prestressing," *Bull. Portland Cement Assn.*

16 W. S. Gray, *Reinforced Concrete Reservoirs and Tanks*, Concrete Publications Ltd., London, 1954.

17 "Design of Circular Domes," *Bull. Portland Cement Assn.*

18 "Principles of Prestressed Reinforcement in Design of Domes," *Concrete*, February 1939.

19 C. Dobell, "Design, Construction and Uses of Prestressed Concrete Tanks," *Public Works*, October 1949.

20 "A 400-ft Prestressed Saucer," *Eng. News-Rec.*, June 1, 1961 pp. 32–36; also May 24, 1962, pp. 44–46.

compression members; piles   *14*

14-1 Column Action Due to Prestress

The question is often brought up whether a concrete member under prestress will have a tendency to buckle like an ordinary column under compression. The answer is that, if the prestressing element is in direct contact with concrete all along its length, there will be no "column action" in the member due to prestress.

Consider an ordinary column under an external load, Fig. 14-1(*a*). When the column deflects, additional moment in a section *A–A* is created by the deflection, because the external load now acts with a different eccentricity on that section. This additional moment is the cause of column action. Now consider a member internally prestressed but not externally loaded, (*b*); so long as the steel and concrete deflect together, there is no change in the eccentricity of the prestress on the concrete, no matter how the member is deflected. Hence there is no change in moment due to any deflection of the member and no column action. When an

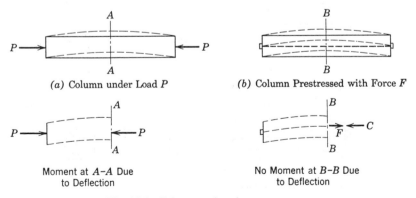

(*a*) Column under Load *P*   (*b*) Column Prestressed with Force *F*

Moment at *A–A* Due   No Moment at *B–B* Due
to Deflection   to Deflection

Fig. 14-1. Column action due to prestress.

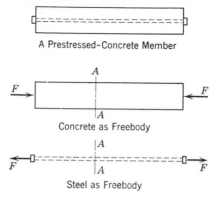

Fig. 14-2. Balancing action of concrete and steel.

external load is applied to a prestressed-concrete column, any deflection of the column will change the moment, and column action will result.

Another way to look at the problem is to separate the steel from the concrete and treat them as two free bodies, Fig. 14-2. Considering the concrete alone, it is a column under direct compression, and any slight bending of the column will result in an eccentricity on a section such as *A–A*, and hence in a tendency to buckle. But, considering the steel as a freebody, there will exist an equal eccentricity with an equal but opposite force, producing a tendency to straighten itself out. The tendency to straighten is exactly equal and opposite to the tendency to buckle, and hence the resulting effect is zero. This is not true, of course, when the member is externally prestressed, say against the abutments, because there will be no balancing effect from the prestressing element, and column action will result.

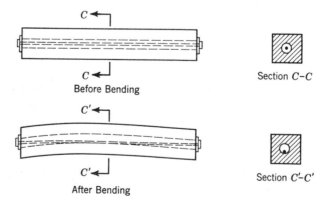

Fig. 14-3. Steel and concrete in contact after bending.

Fig. 14-4. Steel and concrete in contact at several points.

If the steel and concrete are not in direct contact along the entire length, the problem will be different, Fig. 14-3. The concrete under compression will have a tendency to deflect laterally. That deflection will not at first bring the steel to deflect together with it; hence the eccentricity of prestress on the concrete is actually changed, thus resulting in column action. After a certain amount of deflection, the steel is brought into contact with the concrete and the two will begin to deflect together. Hence the column action is limited to the differential deflection of the two materials.

If the steel is in contact with the concrete at several points, say at *E* and *F*, but not along the entire length, Fig. 14-4, then the column action is limited to the length between the points of contact. If such length is short, column action will not be serious.

Next, consider a curved or a bent member subject only to internal prestress, Fig. 14-5(*a*). If the prestress is concentric at all sections (the c.g.s. line coinciding with the c.g.c. line), then the concrete is behaving like an arch subject to axial force with the exception that the applied force from the steel will move with the deflection of the concrete and will always remain concentric. Hence there is no tendency to buckle as in an ordinary arch under external loads, whose line of pressure is determined by the loads and may not shift together with the deflection of the arch. As an extreme example, even if the member has a reverse curve, Fig. 14-5(*b*), the application of concentric prestress will not tend to straighten the member. If the prestress is eccentric, as on sections *G* and *H*, Fig. 14-6, the compression in the concrete is still equal and opposite to the tension in the steel.

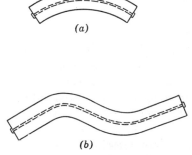

(*a*)

(*b*)

Fig. 14-5. Bent members under concentric prestress.

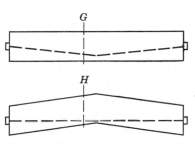

G

H

Fig. 14-6. Eccentric prestress and column action.

Any deflection of the member will still displace both of them together, and there will be no column action due to prestress. The effect of an eccentric prestress on the concrete, however, will produce deflection of the member. If the deflection is appreciable, the deflected axis of the member should be used in computing column effects due to external loads.

As far as column action is concerned, it is immaterial whether there is any frictional loss along the length of the prestressing tendon, because the tension in the steel is always balanced by the compression in the concrete at any section, whatever frictional losses may occur. Hence, whether there is frictional loss or not, there will be no column action due to prestress.

14-2   Compression Members

A prestressed-concrete compression member is one that carries external compressive load. A member that is simply compressed by its prestress is not a compression member. As explained in the previous section, a prestressed member is not under column action due to its own prestress, but it is subject to column action under an external compressive load just like a column of any other material.

It is seldom that a prestressed-concrete member is utilized to stand compression and is prestressed for compression's sake. Evidently, concrete can carry compressive load better without being precompressed by steel. And it is difficult to conceive of steel wires as adding any appreciable strength to a member carrying axial compression. However, many compression members, besides carrying direct compressive loads, are subject to transverse loads as well. Bending due to these transverse loads may more than offset the axial compressive stress at certain points, so as to produce some resulting tension in the concrete. Then it will be advisable to reinforce such columns for possible tension. In other words, some compression members are actually flexural members, and all the advantages of prestressing a beam would apply to the prestressing of those members.

Consider an industrial building of one story, for example; the columns or bearing walls may carry only light vertical loads. But they may be subject to bending during handling and erection if they are precast, or they may carry lateral force such as that due to wind and earthquake after the completion of the building. Similar conditions may exist in bridges. Then it is often feasible to precompress the member so that it can stand a certain amount of bending.

One beneficial effect of prestressing a compression member is the reduction of its deflection under transverse loads. One such pylon, 100 ft high, Fig. 14-7, was prestressed to resist an earthquake load of 2450 k

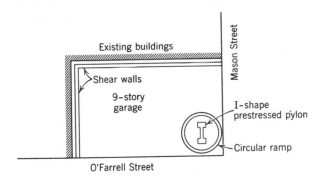

Building Plan

Fig. 14-7. Prestressed concrete Pylon resists earthquake forces in a 9-story garage.[1]

applied horizontally along the pylon.[1] Since the deflection of an uncracked section is about 40% that of a cracked section, a prestressed pylon could be about 2.5 times as stiff as an ordinary reinforced one. In this instance, the reduction of deflection at the top of the pylon minimizes the relative movements between the building floors and saves a tremendous amount of steel otherwise required to reinforce other parts of the building.

Within the working range, the stresses in a prestressed compression member due to both prestress and external loads can be analyzed by the usual elastic theory. But the design of the member is another question, because the empirical methods for designing reinforced-concrete columns cannot be directly applied to prestressed ones. The stresses ordinarily allowed for reinforced concrete are not applicable to prestressed concrete, partly because the stresses due to internal prestressing are of different nature from those due to external loads, which have column action, while internal prestressing has not. For proper design of prestressed-concrete members, one must go into basic theories of columns and prestress and choose a proper standard for the safety of the structure in each particular case.

If a section of a column is under an effective prestress F with an eccentricity e, and loaded by a concentric load P plus an external moment M, the extreme fiber stresses at that section can be computed by the following formula.

$$f_c = \frac{F}{A_c} \pm \frac{Fec}{I_c} + \frac{P}{A_t} \pm \frac{Mc}{I_t} \qquad (14\text{-}1)$$

If the column is a slender one, the deflection of the member due to both the prestress eccentricity and the external load may significantly affect the magnitude of the external moment M and must be included in it, as will be shown in the next section.

An approximate investigation of the effect of axial prestressing on the ultimate strength of columns can be made. Under the action of an external compressive load, the column will shorten and the prestress in the steel will be decreased. If, at the ultimate load, the unit compressive strain in the concrete is of the order of 0.0030, then the pre-tensioned strain in the steel will be decreased by that same amount, and the remaining prestress at the moment of failure will be less than the original effective prestress.

If the effective prestress is 120,000 psi, the remaining prestress will be only

$$f_s = f_e - 0.0030 E_s$$

$$= 120,000 - 0.0030 \times 30,000,000$$

$$= 30,000 \text{ psi}$$

In other words, the major part of the prestress may be lost at the ultimate compressive strength of the concrete. This means that the ultimate load-carrying capacity of the column is not much decreased by prestressing. On the other hand, if the column fails on the tensile side as the result of bending or buckling, the steel on that side can be stressed to near its ultimate strength.

The ultimate strength of concentrically prestressed slender columns under axial loads has been investigated both theoretically and experimentally at various universities.[2,3,4] The general conclusion is that the axial prestressing of a slender column has no effect on the superimposed axial load which will cause that column to buckle. If the prestressing exceeds the difference between the buckling stress and the ultimate strength of the concrete, the column will fail in compression before it will buckle. When the superimposed load is not axial, prestressing could increase both the cracking and the ultimate strength as will be explained in section 14-3.

The buckling of the compressive flange of prestressed beams is subject to the same reasoning. There is no danger of flange buckling produced by internal prestress in a beam. For external loads, a tendency to buckle in the flange is governed by the usual theory of elasticity, so long as there are no cracks in the concrete. After cracking or near the ultimate load, little is known about the buckling of the compressive flange in prestressed beams.

EXAMPLE 14-1

A concrete column 16 in. by 16 in. in cross section and 18 ft high, Fig. 14-8, is pre-tensioned with eight $\frac{3}{8}$-in. wires, which are end-anchored to the concrete. The effective prestress is 100,000 psi in the steel. For a concentric compressive load of 80 k and a horizontal load of 8 k at the midheight of the column, compute the maximum and minimum stresses in the column, assuming it to be hinged at the ends. Investigate the secondary moments in the column due to deflection. Discuss the safety of the column under such loads and also during handling. Assume that $n = 7$, $f_c' = 4000$ psi, $f_s' = 200,000$ psi, $E_c = 4,000,000$ psi.

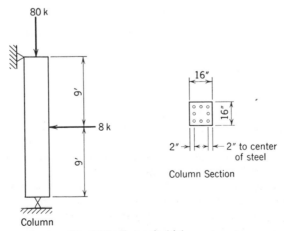

Fig. 14-8. Example 14-1.

Solution. Stress in the concrete due to prestress is

$$\frac{F}{A_c} = \frac{8 \times 0.11 \times (-100,000)}{256 - (8 \times 0.11)}$$

$$= -344 \text{ psi}$$

Stress due to the axial load of 80 k, disregarding deflection of column, is

$$\frac{P}{A_t} = \frac{-80,000}{256 + (7-1)8 \times 0.11}$$

$$= -80,000/261$$

$$= -306 \text{ psi}$$

The maximum bending moment occurs at the midheight of column, and is

$$8 \times 18/4 = 36 \text{ k-ft}$$

The I_t of the transformed section is

$$\frac{16^4}{12} + 6 \times 0.11 \times (7-1) \times 6^2$$

$$= 5460 + 142$$

$$= 5602 \text{ in.}^4$$

The extreme fiber stresses are

$$\frac{Mc}{I_t} = \frac{36,000 \times 12 \times 8}{5602}$$

$$= \pm 616 \text{ psi}$$

The maximum and minimum stresses are hence

$$-344 - 306 - 616 = -1266 \text{ psi compression}$$
$$-344 - 306 + 616 = -34 \text{ psi compression}$$

The maximum deflection of the column due to the horizontal load is

$$\frac{PL^3}{48E_cI_t} = \frac{8000 \times 18^3 \times 12^3}{48 \times 4,000,000 \times 5602}$$

$$= 0.075 \text{ in.}$$

This will increase the moment due to axial load by the amount of 80,000 × 0.075 = 6000 in.-lb = 0.5 k-ft. This moment will produce more deflection and further increase the eccentric moment in the column, but the magnitude is seen to be quite small and may be neglected. Hence the above-computed stresses can be considered sufficiently correct. The maximum compressive stress of 1266 psi would appear high for a reinforced-concrete column but is not excessive for a prestressed member which is more a beam than a column in this example.

The safety of the column can be determined only if we know the ultimate strength of the column under such combined axial and transverse loads and also if we know the possibilities of overloading, that is, to what extent the axial or the horizontal loads may be increased, and whether eccentricity of the applied axial load may be possible.

For the purpose of investigation, let us assume that both the horizontal and the axial load are increased by 50% while, in addition, there will be an eccentricity of 2 in. for the axial load. Then the stresses will be

Due to axial load, $1.5 \times 306 = -459$ psi.

Due to eccentricity of axial load, $1.5 \times 80 \times 2$ in. $= 240$ k-in. $= 20$ k-ft, which will produce stresses of

$$616 \times 20/36 = \pm 342 \text{ psi}$$

Due to horizontal load, $1.5 \times 616 = \pm 924$ psi.

Resulting stress:

$$-344 - 459 - 342 - 924 = -2069 \text{ psi}$$
$$-344 - 459 + 342 + 924 = +463 \text{ psi}$$

Note that the compressive stress of 2069 psi is only about $0.52f_c'$ while the tensile stress is below the modulus of rupture of about $0.12f_c' = 480$ psi. Hence the column would not have cracked, and the midheight deflection can still be computed by the elastic theory to be not more than 0.2 in., which is not a significant value. Thus it can be concluded that the column is safe.

For investigating handling stresses, let us assume that the column is picked up at the midheight.

The moment produced will be

$$\frac{wL^2}{2} = \frac{256 \times (150/144) \times 9^2}{2}$$
$$= 10.8 \text{ k-ft}$$

which will produce a maximum tensile stress of

$$\frac{Mc}{I_t} = \frac{10.8 \times 12,000 \times 8}{5602} = +185 \text{ psi}$$

This is much less than the precompression of 344 psi, and the column is safe during handling.

14-3 Columns under Eccentric Load

Precast bearing walls and columns can be prestressed to improve their elastic behavior and handling characteristics, and to increase their resistance to lateral forces both in the elastic and the ultimate ranges. They cannot be designed following rules of thumb applied to reinforced concrete walls and columns. But they can be properly designed on basic principles of mechanics and properties of materials. The behavior and strength of prestressed columns under eccentric loading, Fig. 14-9, can be predicted with fair precision, although they have been confirmed only by a limited number of tests.[5] The degree of accuracy will depend on the choice of values for the modulus of elasticity. the modulus of rupture, and the compressive strength of the concrete. Before cracking, the stresses and deflections can be calculated assuming the column to behave elastically. The stress at any section is the sum of the stresses due to prestress, direct axial load, moment due to the eccentricity, and the moment due to the deflection.

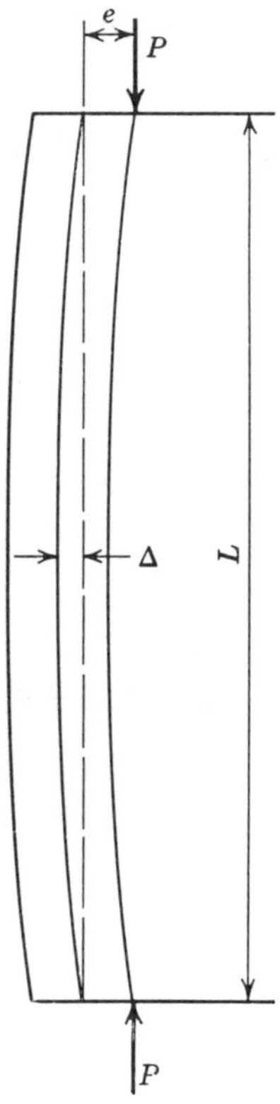

$$f_{\substack{\max \\ \min}} = -\frac{F}{A_t} - \frac{P}{A_t} \pm \frac{Pec}{I_t} \pm \frac{P\,\Delta c}{I_t} \qquad (14\text{-}2)$$

where F = effective total prestress including all losses except elastic shortening of concrete due to superimposed load

P = superimposed load

e = eccentricity of load from the centroid of the section

c = distance to the extreme fiber from the centroid of the section

A_t = area of transformed section

I_t = moment of inertia of transformed section

Δ = deflection of column at the section

Critical stresses occur at the midheight of the column, where the deflection is given by the well-known secant formula:

$$\Delta = e\left(\sec\sqrt{\frac{PL^2}{4E_cI_t}} - 1\right) \qquad (14\text{-}3)$$

Fig. 14-9. Column under eccentric load.

By the elastic theory, cracking can be assumed to occur when the fiber stress reaches the modulus of rupture. Beyond cracking, the elastic theory is no longer accurate. An estimation of the ultimate load can be made by the elastic theory, assuming it to be the load at which the extreme fiber stress reaches the compressive strength of the concrete. Since such approximate analysis can be way off (by perhaps some 10% even for ordinary cases), it is desirable to apply plastic analysis, taking into account the cracking of concrete under tension, the plasticity of concrete under compression, and the plasticity of steel. Furthermore, while the elastic analysis mentioned above will generally err on the conservative side, it is conceivable that, under unusual conditions, erratic conclusions could be reached unless plastic analysis is applied.

Elastic analysis for a prestressed column under eccentric load is illustrated in example 14-2.

EXAMPLE 14-2

A pre-tensioned concrete pin-ended column has elevation and section as shown, Fig. 14-10. The effective prestress in the six $\frac{3}{8}$-in. 7-wire strands ($A_s = 0.08$ in.^{2} each) is 150,000 psi or 12,000 lb per strand. $E_s = 30,000,000$ psi. Concrete has cylinder strength of 5700 psi, modulus of rupture of 600 psi, and $E_c = 4,000,000$ psi. It is loaded by load P with an eccentricity of 1.5 in. along the weak direction. Compute the cracking and the ultimate value of P using the elastic theory, assuming noncracked section.

Solution. (*a*) Compute properties of the section,

$$n = \frac{30,000,000}{4,000,000} = 7.5$$

$$A_t = 8 \times 12 + 0.48 \times (7.5 - 1) = 96 + 3 = 99 \text{ sq in.}$$

$$I_t = \frac{12 \times 8^3}{12} + 0.48 \times (7.5 - 1) \times 2.5^2$$

$$= 512 + 19 = 531 \text{ in.}^4$$

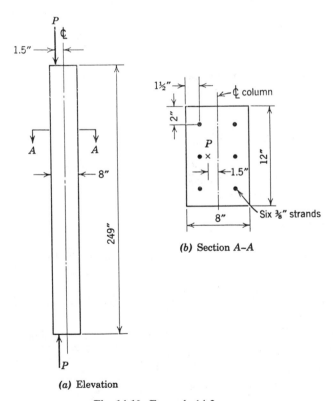

(*a*) Elevation

(*b*) Section A–A

Fig. 14-10. Example 14-2.

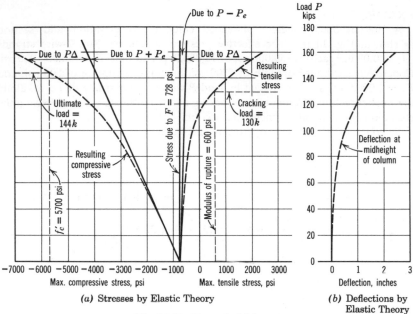

Fig. 14-11. Example 14-2.

(b) Compute deflection of the column at midheight by formula 14-3 for various values of P, say $P = 50, 100, 120, 140,$ and 160 k. Only calculation for $P = 120$ k will be given here:

$$\Delta = e\left(\sec\sqrt{\frac{PL^2}{4E_cI_t}} - 1\right)$$

$$= 1.5\left(\sec\sqrt{\frac{120{,}000 \times 249^2}{4 \times 4{,}000{,}000 \times 531}} - 1\right)$$

$$= 1.5(\sec 0.935 - 1)$$

$$= 1.5(\sec 53°.7 - 1)$$

$$= 1.5(1.688 - 1)$$

$$= 1.03 \text{ in.}$$

(c) Compute stresses in concrete at midspan section by formula 14-2.

$$f_{\substack{\max \\ \min}} = -\frac{F}{A_t} - \frac{P}{A_t} \pm \frac{Pec}{I_t} \pm \frac{P\,\Delta c}{I_t}$$

Assuming $F = 72$ k is not reduced by the presence of P, and using $P = 120$ k with $\Delta = 1.03$ in., we have

$$f_{\substack{\max \\ \min}} = -\frac{72{,}000}{99} - \frac{120{,}000}{99} \pm \frac{120{,}000 \times 1.5 \times 4}{531} \pm \frac{120{,}000 \times 1.03 \times 4}{531}$$

$$= -728 - 1210 \pm 1355 \pm 930$$

$$f_{\max} = -4223 \text{ psi compression}$$

$$f_{\min} = +347 \text{ psi tension}$$

Elastic stresses and deflections for various loads P are calculated and plotted in Fig. 14-11, assuming noncracked sections. From the graph, it can be seen that the cracking load located at f_{min} = modulus of rupture of 600 psi corresponds to $P = 130$ k, and the ultimate load located at $f_{max} = 5700$ psi gives $P = 144$ at ultimate. (Although the actual tested values were 130 k at cracking and 155 k at ultimate, it should be mentioned that any correctness of this ultimate-load analysis by the elastic theory is only coincidental. Should the eccentricity be greater and more cracking occur, the assumption of noncracked section could lead to rather nonconservative estimates.)

The ultimate strength of a section under combined axial load and moment can be estimated by the following relationship. Thus, in Fig. 14-12, static equilibrium of the section requires that for $\Sigma V = 0$,

$$P = C - T_1 - T_2$$

and for $\Sigma M = 0$,

$$M = (T_1 - T_2)\frac{y_t}{2} + Cy_c$$

By assuming a location for the neutral axis at ultimate load, setting ε_c as the ultimate strain in concrete and f_c' as the ultimate stress of concrete,

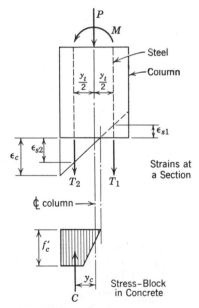

Fig. 14-12. Ultimate strength under combned axial load and moment.

and by assigning ultimate stress distribution curves for concrete, it is possible to compute the combination of P and M that results in this ultimate failure.

For slender columns, the value of M just computed should include the effect of deflection, which can be computed by a numerical procedure provided the load-moment curvature relationship of the column section is known. Ultimate load analysis taking into account the effect of cracking and the plasticity of concrete and steel is explained in references 5 and 6.

EXAMPLE 14-3

For the column section shown in example 14-2, if the ultimate neutral axis were located at 3 in. from one edge, compute the combined P and M producing that failure.

Solution. Assume $\varepsilon_c = 0.0030$, by proportion, changes in strain for the steel are shown as $+0.0009$ for T_1 and -0.0021 for T_2, which gives stresses in steel (for $E_s = 30{,}000{,}000$ and $A_s = 3 \times 0.08 = 0.24$ sq in.),

$$T_1 = 150{,}000 + 0.0009 \times 30{,}000{,}000 = 177{,}000 \text{ psi} \times 0.24 = 42.5 \text{ k}$$

$$T_2 = 150{,}000 - 0.0021 \times 30{,}000{,}000 = 87{,}000 \text{ psi} \times 0.24 = 20.8 \text{ k}$$

Using trapezoidal stress distribution for concrete with ultimate strength at $0.85 \times 5700 = 4850$ psi, we have

$$C = 4850 \times 12 \times (3 + 2/2) = 232{,}000 \text{ lb}$$

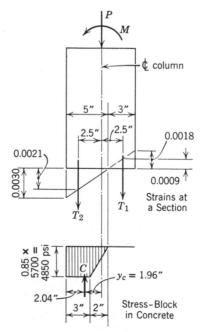

Fig. 14-13. Example 14-3.

acting at 2.04 in. from the edge. Hence,

$$P = C - T_1 - T_2 = 232 - 42.5 - 20.8 = 169 \text{ k}$$
$$M = (T_1 - T_2)2.5 + C(1.96)$$
$$= 21.7 \times 2.5 + 169 \times 1.96$$
$$= 54 + 331 = 385 \text{ k-in.}$$
$$e = \frac{M}{P} = \frac{385}{169} = 2.28 \text{ in.}$$

which indicates that a load of 169 k with a total eccentricity of 2.28 in. (including the column deflection if any) will produce failure of the column, when the ultimate neutral axis is assumed located at 3 in. from the edge. By locating the neutral axis at various places, other combinations of P and M to produce failure can be obtained.

This example indicates how simple it is to compute the ultimate P and M for a given location of ultimate neutral axis. On the other hand, it would be a major mathematical problem to determine the neutral axis, if either P or M or both are given.

Thus the resisting capacity of a given section can be best obtained by computing the interaction curve for ultimate P and M for various assumed locations of ultimate neutral axis. This method can be extended to include the presence of nonprestressed steel in prestressed columns and is indeed a simple approach to the solution of combined ultimate strength of columns.

The ultimate strength of prestressed columns may be controlled by the tensile strength of steel or by the compressive strength of concrete, depending on the amount of reinforcement, the eccentricity of loading, etc. For slender columns, deflections may appreciably affect the ultimate load. When the eccentricity of the load is small, column deflections may be predicted by the elastic theory, assuming noncracked sections. When moment predominates, it would be necessary to estimate the deflections on the basis of cracked sections. If the loading on a column is sustained, creep and shrinkage could become a major problem and should be carefully considered.

14-4 Piles*

Since piles are subjected to tensile stresses during transportation, driving, and under certain service conditions, the desirability of prestressing is evident. Post-tensioned concrete piles, essentially of the Raymond

* Material in this section is essentially taken from the article "Pretensioned Concrete Piles—present knowledge summarized," by T. Y. Lin and W. J. Talbot, *Civil Engineering*, May 1961, pp. 53–58.

cylinder type, have been produced since 1949.[6] About 1953, pre-tensioned concrete piles were developed; they are now readily available because of the establishment of hundreds of pretensioning plants throughout the country, and indeed all over the world.[7]

In common with many construction materials and techniques, pre-tensioned concrete piles were developed by the industry rather than by the profession. A process of trial and error, rather than a rational approach, was employed during their development. At present, enough experience has been accumulated to permit safe and economical utilization of these piles.

Discussion follows under five headings: design, details, manufacture, driving, and special applications.

Design. Experience seems to indicate that a prestress of about 700 psi in the piles will insure safety during handling and driving under normal conditions. While the amount of prestress required will vary with the size and shape of the pile, the hammer blow, and the cushioning effects, as well as the soil conditions, it is obviously impractical to vary the prestress in each pile. Of course, higher or lower values than 700 psi may be desirable for special cases.

The bearing capacity of concrete piles is seldom if ever controlled by their strength under direct compression, but it is convenient to express the bearing capacity in terms of the compressive strength or stresses. Strictly speaking, if the bearing capacity were limited by the compressive stress, there would be no need for prestressing. Therefore, current formulas are empirical in nature. For reference, they are outlined as follows.

The design load on such piles is often based on the ultimate strength, using an arbitrary factor of safety of about 4. Such a high factor of safety is hardly necessary so far as the service load is concerned, but it is believed that, for piles so designed, the compressive stresses during driving will seldom be critical, and it should be possible to attain the desired bearing value without damaging the pile.

If the cylinder strength of the concrete is f_c', the ultimate strength of the concrete in a pile can be safely assumed as $0.85f_c'$. At ultimate load, the amount of prestress remaining in the tendons is approximately 60% of the effective prestress. Thus, if a 6000-psi concrete pile is prestressed to an effective prestress of 700 psi, the ultimate strength can be computed by the formula,

$$N' = (0.85 \times 6000 - 0.60 \times 700)A_c = 4680A_c$$

where A_c is the cross-sectional area of the concrete pile in sq in. Using a factor of safety of 4, the design load, N, is one fourth of this, or $1,170A_c$.

Joint standards set up by the American Association of State Highway Officials and the Prestressed Concrete Institute state that the maximum compressive stress f_{pc} on prestressed concrete piles (in addition to the effective prestress) for $f_c' = 5000$ psi shall not exceed the following:

$$f_{pc} = 1000 \text{ psi for } L/D = 0 \text{ to } 10$$
$$f_{pc} = 1160 - 16L/D \text{ for } L/D = 10 \text{ to } 25$$

where L = effective length of pile, taken as the actual length of pile when both ends are hinged

D = diameter or width of pile

For f_c' between 5000 and 6000 psi, these stresses may be increased in direct proportion to the design concrete strength. The buckling load of a pre-tensioned concrete pile can be computed by Euler's formula,

$$N_{cr} = \frac{\pi^2 EI}{L^2}$$

where N_{cr} = critical buckling load, lb

E = modulus of elasticity for concrete, psi

I = moment of inertia of concrete pile section, in.[4]

L = length of pile, in.

The above formula assumes hinged supports for both ends and can be modified for other end conditions. The value of E should be chosen to fit the duration of loading—that is, a higher value should be used for dynamic load and a reduced value for sustained load. Since the possibility of an increase in actual load is remote, a factor of safety of 2 is considered sufficient. Thus the allowable load is often set at

$$N = \frac{N_{cr}}{2} = \frac{\pi^2 EI}{2L^2}$$

If no tensile stress is allowed, a high factor of safety is obtained for concentrically prestressed members subjected to bending. It is therefore often permissible to allow tensile stresses in the concrete under design moments.

The Joint AASHO-PCI Standards allow 250 psi tension for normal design loads, while values up to 600 psi have been permitted for earthquake and other infrequent loads. Thus, if f_e is the effective prestress in the pile concrete, the allowable moment under earthquake loading, in in.-lbs, will be

$$M = (f_e + f_t)(I/c)$$

where I = moment of inertia of concrete section, in.

c = distance from neutral axis to extreme fiber, in.

The ultimate moment, in inch-pounds, for a pretensioned pile can be computed by the methods in section 5-6 or approximated by

$$M_{ult} = CA_s f_s' d$$

where C = a coefficient depending on shape of pile section, etc., varying
usually from 0.32 to 0.38
 A_s = total area of prestressing steel, sq in.
 f_s' = ultimate strength of steel, psi
 d = diameter or size of pile, in.
The design moment, based on the ultimate, should have a factor of safety of 2, while a factor of 1.5 to 1.7 will be sufficient for earthquake and wind loads.

According to the elastic theory, the existence of direct external loads delays the cracking of the concrete pile and thereby increases the moment-carrying capacity. On the other hand, the ultimate moment capacity is reduced by the presence of direct external loads. Hence, when the design is for combined moment and direct loads, the moment capacity of the pile should be checked by both the elastic and the ultimate-load theories, as described in section 14-3.

Details and Connections.   Some typical pre-tensioned pile sections are given in Fig. 14-14. These piles are usually pre-tensioned with 7-wire strands, from $\frac{3}{8}$ to $\frac{1}{2}$ in. in diameter. The spacing of spiral steel also was established by experience. Its design has not been rationalized, but it is generally agreed that steel of No. 5 gage about 0.2 in. in diameter, at a 6 in. pitch, will suffice for the middle part of the pile, while a 3-in. pitch is used for the end portions. Four or five tight turns at about a 1-in. pitch are usually extended to within 1 in. from the end.

Where the pile tops are encased in a heavy footing, very often no connection other than sufficient embedment is required. In this case, the pile can be either driven to grade or cut off to the desired level with ordinary concrete chipping hammers.

If additional anchorage is required, one or more of the following types of connections can be used.

The prestressing strand can be extended from the pile head and used as reinforcement. Actual tests have shown that an embedment of 18 in. is adequate to develop the full strength of a strand of $\frac{3}{8}$-in. diameter. The strands may be exposed by stripping off the concrete after driving. If the piles are to be driven to grade, the strand extension must be allowed for at the time of casting.

If the pile reinforcement consists of more than 12 or 14 strands, threading the projecting steel through the driving head becomes costly and time consuming. Since most precast piles are ordered slightly on the long side,

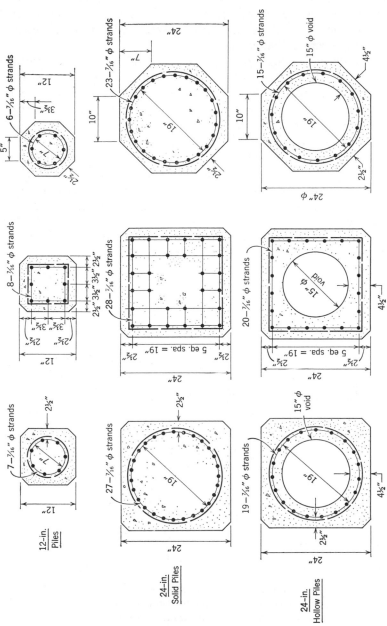

Fig. 14-14. Typical pre-tensioned pile sections (AASHO-PCI Standard).

it may be simpler to cut off the pile after driving and expose the reinforcing for anchorage. It should be noted that the full working strength of the strands cannot be developed as unprestressed reinforcement, owing to the excessive elongation that could be produced.

To post-tension a dozen or more small strands through the cap or footing is difficult and costly so that this method has not been used to any extent for pre-tensioned piles. In the post-tensioned pile, particularly where alloy bars of large diameter are used for reinforcement, a tensioned connection is easier to make and has been used in Europe, where fixity or full anchorage is required at the pile head.

Probably the most versatile and widely used connection of pile to cap is the simple reinforcing-bar anchorage similar to that used for many years in conventionally reinforced piles, Fig. 14-15. The reinforcing can be cast in the head of the prestressed pile where the piles can be driven reasonably close to final elevation, but a special driving head or follower must be used. Bars can be grouted into either precast holes or holes drilled after driving. If precast holes are to be used, the pile must be driven within 1 or 2 ft of final grade. With greater variations, the field-drilled holes may prove to be cheaper.

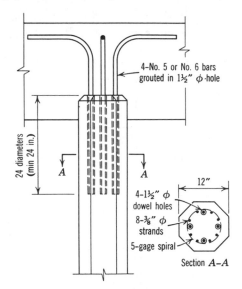

Fig. 14-15. Holes drilled or formed $\frac{3}{4}$ in. or 1 in. larger than dowels, by lightweight tubing (without bond breaker or lubricant), provide adequate bond for reinforcing when carefully grouted. Section *A-A* shows method of ensuring load transfer for piles with $\frac{3}{8}$-in. strand.

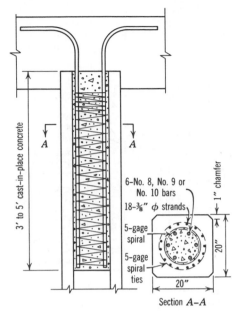

3' to 5' cast-in-place concrete

6-No. 8, No. 9 or No. 10 bars

18-⅜" φ strands

5-gage spiral

5-gage spiral ties

1" chamfer

20"

20"

Section *A–A*

Fig. 14-16. Connection of a hollow pile to footing or bent, using steel dowels. The poured-in-place plug can be put at any depth by suspending an expendable form at the proper depth.

Pull-out tests have indicated that special grouting mixtures are not required to develop the full bond strength. A good plastic sand-and-cement grout with an ultimate strength equal to that of the pile, properly worked into place and cured, will be satisfactory. A water-reducing plasticizing admixture is desirable to reduce shrinkage.

For a pile with a hollow core, the connection can be made by using a poured-in-place concrete plug with an embedded reinforcing-steel cage placed inside the core and extended into the cap or footing, Fig. 14-16. Where welded connections are desired, they are provided by grouting a plate or other steel section into the pile with extended steel reinforcing bars attached. The connection is completed by welding to the superstructure.

Splicing of precast piles can be rather difficult. The splice or extension should be at least as durable as the prestressed concrete section; it should have equivalent load-carrying capacity, bending, and shear strength. The splice must be economical and must allow driving to be resumed within a reasonable time. Several methods have been developed and successfully used for splicing prestressed concrete piles.

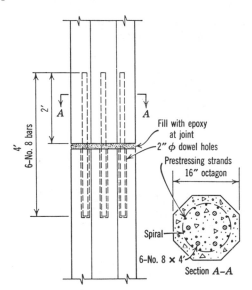

Fig. 14-17. Pile splice detail. Dowels are secured with epoxy.

A splice recently developed in Connecticut consists of two pre-tensioned sections joined by means of reinforcing steel dowels and a plasticized cement. The lower section is first driven and the head drilled to receive reinforcing bars cast in the upper section. The jointing compound is placed in a molten state and fills the dowel holes and the space between the pile sections. Because of the high strength and fast set of the cementing compound, the spliced section can be driven after a very short curing time. On the Pacific Coast, similar experimental splices have been made using a slower setting epoxy compound, Fig. 14-17.

A splice can be made by welding the two sections in the field using steel pipe sleeves or anchored plates embedded in the prestressed sections at the time of casting. An epoxy compound can be used between the concrete sections for load transfer.

Where full moment-carrying splices are not necessary, simpler connections can be used. In Honolulu, long piles composed of three prestressed sections were spliced by driving the upper section into a snugly fitting steel sleeve that had previously been driven over the lower section. A center dowel was used to align the two sections.

Manufacture. Pre-tensioned piles are usually manufactured by the long-line method, Fig. 14-18; multiple sections are cast in a single stressing line up to perhaps 600 ft in length. Pre-tensioning is used for piles up to about 30 in. in cross-section, although it is possible to pre-tension larger sections if it is economical to set up the heavier tensioning bed and auxiliary equipment.

The pre-tensioning bed should be strong enough to resist the maximum stressing force to be applied, rigid enough to prevent excessive deflections, and accurately level so that the strands and the final product will be in true alignment. The strands can be stressed as a group by large-capacity jacks, or individually by single-strand jacks.

Forms for the piles should be preferably of steel, sufficiently rigid to eliminate distortion. Joints between sections, or at end forms, should be accurately fitted so that offsets or openings are eliminated. Thermal movements, particularly with high-temperature curing, can produce cracking at points where large offsets or fins restrict movement. Forms should be so constructed as to permit movement of the pile without damage during release of the prestressing force. The form at the pile ends should be perfectly square with the pile axis and reasonably plane. To form the core for hollow piles, either paraffin-treated cardboard tubes or inflatable rubber mandrels are used.

Most pre-tensioned piles made in the United States have a square or octagonal cross section. The square section is perhaps somewhat easier to form and pour; the octagonal section is often preferred because of its smaller area and weight for a given least dimension. The octagonal pile requires a slightly more complicated form process, but generally requires less complicated spiral ties. Both fixed and collapsible-type steel forms are used for either type of pile.

Low-slump concrete with a cement content of $6\frac{1}{2}$ to 8 sacks per cu yd is generally used to provide a 28-day strength of 4500 to 7000 psi. A water-reducing admixture of some kind is usually added. Calcium chloride should not be used. Most piling specifications require Type II low-alkali cement, particularly where piles are used in sea water, although cements of Types I and III are occasionally permitted. Aggregates usually are $\frac{3}{4}$ to 1 in. in maximum size.

When the concrete is placed, particular care should be taken to insure that the head and tip are well vibrated as these areas usually have close spiral or tie spacing and may have dowels or tubes for preformed holes at the head. In the case of piles with a hollow core formed with paper tubes or inflated rubber tubes, it is necessary to provide external hold-downs at intervals close enough to prevent flotation or deflection of the tube. Attempts to secure the tube by means of the encircling strands usually result in excessive flotation or deflection on all but very short piles.

Since economy in manufacture requires a rapid turnover of piles on the casting bed, most producers of pre-tensioned piles employ accelerated curing. Low-pressure steam, radiant heat, and hot air are all used for curing. Curing is usually done at temperatures ranging from 130 to 165°F for 10 to 18 hours. In hot, arid areas, additional water or membrane curing may be required for an additional 7 to 10 days. In most cases air curing will develop the required ultimate strengths before 28 days.

Since pre-tensioned piles employ concentric prestressing seldom exceeding 1000 psi, the primary consideration is bond rather than compression or tension in the concrete at stress transfer. Concrete strengths for stress release are generally set at 3500 psi as a minimum for $\frac{7}{16}$ and $\frac{3}{8}$-in. strands. Minimum transfer strengths are usually adequate for handling of the section so that piles can be removed from beds immediately after stress transfer.

Driving. Prestressed concrete piles have proven their ability to take an unbelievable amount of punishment without structural damage. They are very strong in bending but are not indestructible. Experience has shown that if the criteria of no tension in the concrete is used for handling and transporting, a sufficient factor of safety against cracking is available to take care of impact and shock loads for all but extreme cases. When no extra loads are expected, tensile stresses may be permitted during handling.

As previously mentioned the pile head must be truly perpendicular to the pile axis and reasonably plane. Irregular or inclined heads tend to concentrate the driving blow and may cause spalling or cracking at the head. The wire strands should be burned flush with the pile head. Projecting wire stubs, even when covered by a cushion block, have been known to cause spalling at the head. A chamfered edge at the head also helps to prevent spalling. If jetting is required, the internal-type jet has proved superior to the external type in preventing wandering of the pile tip and consequent eccentricity during driving.

One of the most important details in connection with the driving operation is the cushion block. Generally the best performance has been obtained with 4 to 8 in. of laminated softwood, such as Douglas fir, placed directly between the pile head and the driving helmet. Hardwood blocks have proven unsatisfactory. Plywood cushion blocks are sometimes used, but in more than a few cases these have caused trouble until replaced with thicker laminations of softwood. Cushion blocks should be replaced frequently; once they are fully compressed, they cease to perform their function.

The type of cushion block directly affects the magnitude of the driving stresses. In severe cases, the use of a reduced hammer blow during the soft driving stage may also help.

In one instance, what was originally thought to be tensile cracking was directly traced to torsional stresses induced by the twisting of the pile head in the driving helmet. The solution to the problem in this case was to round the pile head so as to eliminate restraint at the driving head. The pile head should not be completely restrained against rotation.

It has been found that pile hammers with an energy within the limits shown below are usually adequate for driving in the moderate to hard driving range. These values are listed for reference rather than for absolute guidance:

Pile Size, in.	Ft-lb of Energy
10	8000–15,000
12	15,000–19,000
14	15,000–24,000
16–18	24,000–32,000
20–21	24,000–36,000
24 and over	32,000–38,000

Large-diameter cylinder piles have been driven with hammers having a rated energy up to 50,000 ft-lb.

Properly designed prestressed concrete piles can be used economically for almost all types of foundations, piers, wharves, mooring and fender dolphins, marine ways, bulkheads, sea walls, and other structures.

When very long piles are used, the problem of handling and transporting may be a critical one. Hollow-core piles can be used to reduce the handling weight; 20-in. octagonal hollow-core piles up to 132 ft long were driven for a waterfront structure in San Francisco.

Special Applications. Where batter piles are used in marine structures in deep water, critical bending stresses may occur during setting and driving when the pile may be cantilevered far below the pile driver leads. A pile with higher prestress or one of greater section modulus may be required.

When the pile tip is to be seated in rock or other hard material, a steel H-pile section may be embedded in the prestressed concrete pile. For example, hollow-core piles 26 in. square, with 14-in. steel H-pile tips, were driven to rock for the foundation of the Petaluma Creek Bridge near San Francisco. The design load on these piles was 200 tons.

Prestressed sheetpiles, Fig. 14-18, are being used for marine installations where corrosion resistance is important. Since the sheetpile is primarily a bending member, the effective prestress may vary depending on design moments. The efficiency of a sheetpile in bending can be substantially increased by using eccentric prestressing, Fig. 14-19. Where moment reversals may occur, this is not feasible and somewhat greater concentric prestressing should be used.

The use of prestressed-concrete soldier piles for bulkheads, sea walls, and retaining walls is another application as a bending member. These piles

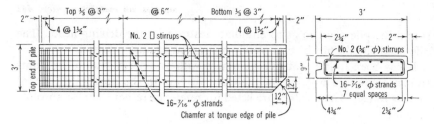

Fig. 14-18. A typical prestressed concrete sheetpile.

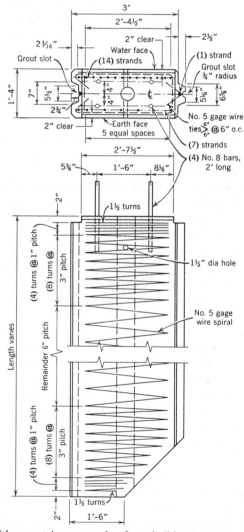

Fig. 14-19. Sheetpile with eccentric prestressing for a bulkhead wall in Long Beach, Calif. Slight eccentricity does not affect the driving characteristics of the pile.

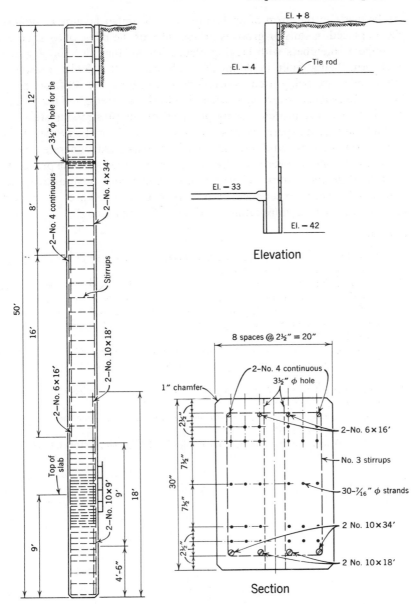

Fig. 14-20. Soldier piles with reinforced and prestressed steel, to take care of peak moment in different parts of the pile.

can be made in the form of an H-section with timber lagging or concrete planks placed in slots or grooves on the sides of the piles, or as square or rectangular members with lagging placed behind the pile. On a graving dock now being built in Alameda, California, 20 × 30-in. prestressed soldier piles are being used as a retaining wall for a cut 40 ft deep, Fig. 14-20. Mild-steel reinforcing is used for additional strength at the moment peaks, the main reinforcing being provided by the prestressing steel.

While sufficient experience has been accumulated for the proper design, production, driving, and utilization of pre-tensioned concrete piles, it must be admitted that very little has been done to rationalize the procedures or to analyze the results. If economical applications have already been obtained by sheer experience, it is only natural to expect even better performance with a more refined and scientific approach.

References

1 W. H. Ellison and T. Y. Lin, "Parking Garage Built for $5.28 per sq. ft," *Civil Engineering*, June 1955, pp. 37–40.
2 R. A. Breckenridge, *A Study of the Characteristics of Prestressed Concrete Columns*, Engineering Center, University of Southern California, Los Angeles, 1953.
3 A. M. Ozell and A. M. Jernigan, *Some Studies on the Behavior of Prestressed Concrete Columns*, Florida Engineering and Industrial Experiment Station, University of Florida, July 1956.
4 Paul Zung-Tsh Zia, *Ultimate Strength of Slender Prestressed Concrete Columns*, Florida Engineering and Industrial Experiment Station, University of Florida, July 1957.
5 T. Y. Lin and R. Itaya, "A Prestressed Concrete Column under Eccentric Loading," *PCI Journal*, December 1957.
6 A. S. Hall, *Buckling of Prestressed Columns*, Cement and Concrete Association, Sydney, Australia, 1961.
7 N. H. E. Weller, "Prestressed Concrete Piles." *PCI Journal*, October 1962.

economics; structural types
15

15-1 General Considerations

When prestressed concrete was first used in this country in the early 1950's, the problem of the relative economy of this type of construction as compared to others was a controversial issue. Some zealous advocates held an optimistic outlook on its saving in materials; other conservative engineers overestimated the additional labor involved and condemned its popular adoption in this country. That period is now concluded. With the numerous prestressed-concrete structures built all over the country, its economy is no longer in doubt. Like any new promising type of construction, it will continue to grow as more engineers and builders master its technique. But, like any other type of construction, it has its own limitations of economy and feasibility so that it will suit certain conditions and not others.

The time is also past when one or two specific instances of the relative economy of prestressed concrete as against other types could be cited as positive proof either for or against its adoption. Hence no attempt will be made to refer the reader to the many early articles and discussions on the economy of certain particular prestressed structures. Basic quantity data are now known for prestressed concrete, and the unit price for prestressing is gradually becoming stabilized. Hence a general discussion is possible at this time, although some of the values should be modified with further developments.

In prestressed concrete we have materials that are much stronger than those for ordinary reinforced concrete. At the same time, these materials cost more and require more labor and better technique for placement. Speaking in general, the working stress in prestressing steel is 5 to 7 times as high as mild steel, and its unit price in place is 2 to 5 times as much. Concrete is 2 times stronger than reinforced concrete, and costs about 15% more, not including formwork which may cost from 0% to 100%

445

more than that for reinforced concrete. Between the various possible combinations of strength and cost of these materials, it can be readily seen that the net result can be either for or against the use of prestressed concrete.

From an economic point of view, conditions favoring prestressed construction can be listed as follows:

1. Long spans, where the ratio of dead to live load is large, so that saving in weight of structure becomes a significant item in economy. A minimum dead-to-live-load ratio is necessary in order to permit the placement of steel near the tensile fiber, thus giving it the greatest possible lever arm for resisting moment. For long members, the relative cost of anchorages is also lowered.

2. Heavy loads, where large quantities of materials are involved so that saving in materials becomes worthwhile.

3. Multiple units, where forms can be reused and labor mechanized so that the additional cost of labor and forms can be minimized.

4. Precasting units, where work can be centralized so as to reduce the additional cost of labor and to obtain better control of the products.

5. Pre-tensioning units, where the cost of anchorage, sheathing, and grouting can be saved.

There are other conditions which, for certain locale, are not favorable to the economy of prestressed concrete but which are bound to improve as time goes on. These are:

1. The availability of builders experienced with the work of pre-stressing. This will stimulate keener competition and supply skilled workmen at smaller cost.

2. The availability of equipments for post-tensioning and of plants for pre-tensioning. This will obviously reduce the unit cost of prestressing.

3. The availability of engineers experienced with the design of pre-stressed concrete, and the familiarity of architects with the possibilities of overall economic design using prestressed concrete. This will permit more prestressed-concrete structures to be designed and built and thereby their cost will be lowered.

4. The reduction of the cost of materials and installation for pre-stressed concrete. This has already been taking place, and the trend will continue as new methods and materials are developed and as the demand and supply both grow with time.

5. The promulgation and improvement of a set of codes for prestressed concrete. This should put prestressed-concrete structures on an equal footing with other types and encourage their design and construction.

It is perhaps unnecessary to repeat that there will always be situations where prestressed concrete cannot compete economically with other types of construction, whether timber, steel, or reinforced concrete. Each type has its advantages as well as limitations.

15-2 Quantity of Materials

As compared to reinforced concrete, the basic economy of prestressed concrete lies in the saving of materials, because it utilizes concrete and steel of much higher strength. A general comparison of the quantity of materials required for the two types of construction can be made, based on their strength ratios.

First, let us compare the quantity of concrete. The economical strength of concrete for ordinary reinforced work is generally 2500 to 3000 psi in this country. The use of higher strength for ordinary reinforced concrete will result in smaller sections, and will increase the amount of reinforcing steel, and hence is not economical. In prestressed concrete, the average strength used is 5000 psi. Considering 3000 psi for reinforced concrete, the allowable stress at $0.45f_c'$ is 1350 psi; similarly, for 5000 psi in prestressed concrete, the allowable stress at $0.40f_c'$ is 2000 psi. Under working loads, the stress blocks for the two types are shown in Fig. 15-1. For reinforced concrete, the resisting moment is given by the well-known formula

$$M = \tfrac{1}{2}f_ckjbd^2$$

Using a value of $k = 0.40$, and of $j = 0.87$, we have

$$M = \tfrac{1}{2} \times 1350 \times 0.40 \times 0.87 \times bd^2$$

$$= 235bd^2 \tag{15-1}$$

For prestressed concrete, the resisting moment at working load is given by

$$M = \tfrac{1}{2}f_cbha$$

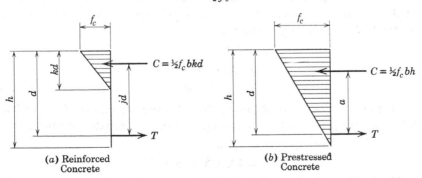

(a) Reinforced Concrete

(b) Prestressed Concrete

Fig. 15-1. Comparison of concrete stress blocks in beams (under working loads).

Assuming that $h = 1.1d$, and $a = 0.6d$, we have

$$M = \tfrac{1}{2} \times 2000 \times b \times 1.1d \times 0.6d$$
$$M = 660bd^2 \qquad\qquad (15.2)$$

Comparing equation 15.2 with equation 15-1, it is seen that, for the same resisting moment, the ratio of bd^2 required for the two is

$$\frac{bd^2 \text{ for prestressed concrete}}{bd^2 \text{ for reinforced concrete}} = \frac{235}{660} = 0.36$$

If d is kept the same for both sections, the ratio of the areas is 0.36; if b is kept the same, the ratio is $\sqrt{0.36} = 0.6$. Hence it would be proper to say that, as an average, the quantity of concrete required for prestressed is only about one-half of that for reinforced work.

The above comparison does not take into account the fact that the lighter dead weight of the prestressed design would further decrease the quantity required. Also the value of a for the prestressed beam can vary greatly and throw the advantage one way or the other. Again, the above computed saving in concrete is possible with prestressed work only because the principal tension produced by shear is reduced as a result of prestressing. Otherwise smaller concrete sections might require excessive web reinforcement.

In order to get an optimum value of a for prestressed beams, it is often necessary to use I- or T-sections instead of rectangular ones. This means more complicated formwork. When rectangular sections are used for prestressed beams, the formwork can be a little less than for reinforced beams, since the sectional area is smaller.

The ultimate strength for concrete in reinforced work cannot be used as basis for economic comparison because the factor of safety is unnecessarily high. But the quantity of steel for the two types of construction can be compared on the basis either of working stress or of ultimate strength. On the basis of working stresses, reinforcing bars of intermediate grade are designed for 20,000 psi, and, with a lever arm of $jd = 0.87d$, the resisting moment is

$$M = f_s A_s jd$$
$$= 20,000 A_s \times 0.87d$$
$$= 17,400 A_s d \qquad\qquad (15\text{-}3)$$

Taking an average value of design stress for prestressing steel as 145,000 psi, and with $a = 0.7d$ for an average section, the resisting moment is

$$M = f_s A_s a$$
$$= 145,000 A_s \times 0.7d$$
$$= 101,000 A_s d \qquad\qquad (15\text{-}4)$$

Comparing equation 15-4 with equation 15-3, it is seen that the materials required to resist the same moment will be in the ratio of

$$\frac{\text{Prestressed steel}}{\text{Reinforced steel}} = \frac{17,400}{101,000} = 0.17$$

On the basis of ultimate strength, at the rupture of the beams, prestressed steel will be stressed to about 230,000 psi on the average, while reinforcing bars will be stressed only to about 40,000 psi. Owing to the increase in the lever arm for the prestressing steel at the ultimate range, the ultimate lever arm is about the same for both reinforced and prestressed work; hence the ratio of materials required will be equal to the inverse ratio of their strength, thus

$$\frac{\text{Prestressed steel}}{\text{Reinforced steel}} = \frac{40,000}{230,000} = 0.174$$

Hence an average quantity ratio for the two materials will be just about 0.17 in favor of prestressing steel.

The amount of web reinforcement is not included in the above. Because of the presence of precompression, web reinforcement is much less in prestressed beams even though they have smaller concrete sections. However, the ratio of web reinforcement for the two types of construction varies greatly and generalizations are not easy.

It must be noticed that the above two ratios of materials, 0.50 for concrete and 0.17 for steel, apply only to the critical section of a member. For reinforced-concrete beams, the concrete section is often kept constant while the amount of reinforcing steel can be varied along the length of the beam, thus effecting some saving in steel. For prestressed-concrete beams, the area of steel cannot be so conveniently varied.

In prestressed concrete, various accessory materials are required which add greatly to the cost. Depending on the method of prestressing used, the quantities of end anchorages, sheathing, and grouting vary to a great extent. The cost of plant and overhead varies with the amount of work involved; the cost per unit decreases with the increase in the amount of work. For convenience in discussion, these factors will be analyzed in the next section.

15-3   Unit Cost

Section 15-2 describes the saving in material for prestressed as against reinforced concrete because of the higher strength of materials employed.

It is only natural that materials of higher strength will cost more per unit volume. Whereas the relation of strength to volume of material is a matter of mechanics, the cost of materials per volume is dependent on time and place. However, it is possible to take an average case as a basis for comparison, keeping in mind that these values must be modified for local and individual conditions if they differ from the so-called average case.

Concrete. On the average, about $1\frac{1}{2}$ more bags of cement are required per cubic yard of 5000-psi concrete as compared to 3000-psi concrete. At a cost of $1.00 per bag, this means an additional cost of $1.50 per cu yd. If ready-mixed concrete is available at $12.50 per cu yd for the ordinary mix, it may cost about $14 for the prestressed concrete. The cost for placing the concrete will also be a little higher for the stronger concrete, since it will be less workable. Assuming $5.50 per cu yd for the placing of ordinary concrete, $7 may be required for prestressed work. Hence the total cost will be

Cost per cu yd of concrete in place, exclusive of forms:
Reinforced concrete at 3000 psi = $18
Prestressed concrete at 5000 psi = $21

Thus the unit cost of concrete for prestressed work is about 15% higher than that for ordinary reinforced work, assuming average conditions.

Formwork and Falsework. The unit cost of formwork for slabs is virtually the same for prestressed and reinforced concrete. For beams, depending on the shape of the concrete section, the unit cost per square foot of contact area will be 40% to 100% higher than for reinforced work. Assuming $0.50 per sq ft for reinforced concrete, it will average about $0.70 for prestressed beams. The number of square feet of contact area per cubic yard of concrete varies greatly with the size and shape of beams. As an average value, we may assume 40 sq ft per cu yd of reinforced concrete, and 90 sq ft per cu yd of prestressed concrete. Then the average cost of formwork, assuming the forms to be not reusable, will be

Cost of formwork per cu yd of concrete:
Reinforced concrete 40 × $0.50 = $20
Prestressed concrete 90 × $0.70 = $63

If the forms are reusable, the cost will be much lower.

The amount of falsework supporting the concrete will vary greatly. For an average job, it will be a little cheaper for prestressed concrete, because less weight is to be supported. But, expressed in terms of dollars per cubic yard, it will be higher for prestressed work, since the total quantity involved is less. When precast elements or composite sections are used for prestressed concrete, the saving may be quite appreciable. Just for the purpose of discussion we may assume:

Cost of falsework per cu yd of concrete:
Reinforced concrete = $5.00
Prestressed concrete = $8.00

For precast prestressed concrete, the cost of falsework can be much lower, although cost for transportation, erection, and connection must be added.

Steel. For both ordinary reinforced concrete and for nonprestressed reinforcement in prestressed concrete, reinforcing bars cost an average of about $0.065 per lb of raw material. Adding to it the cost of transportation, fabrication, and installation, the contract cost in place averages about $0.12 per lb in this country.

High-tensile wires average about $0.14 per lb of material. Cost of transportation, cutting, straightening, and tensioning may average about $0.20 per lb. This will yield an average contract cost of $0.34 per lb for pre-tensioned unanchored wires. Cost of end anchorages may average about $0.10 per lb of wire, with cost of sheathing and grouting another $0.06 per lb of wire. Hence post-tensioned wires will average about $0.50 per lb, a little higher for the bonded and a little lower for the unbonded reinforcement.

Large high-tensile wire strands for post-tensioning cost about $0.20 per lb of material. Cost of end anchorages together with cutting and fitting which are done in the shop may amount to another $0.16 per lb, depending chiefly on the length of the strands. Installation, tensioning, and transportation may total another $0.08 per lb, while sheathing and grouting, if used, may average $0.06 per lb. Hence the average cost of steel in place for the usual beams may run about $0.50 per lb for post-tensioned bonded type. Seven-wire strands of $\frac{3}{8}$-in. to $\frac{1}{2}$-in. size used for pre-tensioning cost about $0.15 per lb. Since no anchorages, sheathing, or grouting is required for pre-tensioning, their cost in place may be no more than $0.25 per lb.

High-tensile bars cost about $0.18 per lb of material. Cost of end anchorages and splices, if required, may be about $0.05 per lb. Transporting, installation, and tensioning may total $0.10 per lb, and sheathing and grouting another $0.08 per lb. This will yield a total of $0.41 per lb of bar in place for the post-tensioned bonded type.

It is evident that the above average values may vary greatly, depending on the particular conditions, and the designer is advised to obtain his own data for an accurate assessment. It is further necessary to note that while the average unit cost differs for the wires, strands, and bars, when the matter of strength and suitability is taken into account, each of the three materials will have its own field of economy and it is not possible to condemn or to favor one material for all conditions.

If it is desired to express the cost of steel in terms of unit yardage of concrete, we can assume an average amount of 60 lb of high-tensile steel per cubic yard of concrete: For unit cost at $0.50 per lb, an approximate total cost of $30 of high-tensile steel in place including accessories is indicated for each cubic yard of post-tensioned work. For pre-tensioning, 60 lb of strands at $0.25 indicates $15 per cu yd. It must be realized, of course, that values like this should be taken with a grain of salt, since the percentage of steel varies greatly with different designs. The amount of mild steel also varies with each job; a value of $5 of mild steel per cubic yard of prestressed concrete may be taken as an average.

Accessories. Although the cost of accessories has been included in the last paragraph and expressed in terms of cost per pound of steel, for more accurate estimates it would be desirable to separate such cost from that of steel, since cost does not always vary directly with the weight of steel.

End anchorages for wires cost about $3 to $5 apiece, capable of anchoring 6 to 18 wires of about $\frac{1}{4}$-in. size. End anchorages for bars cost $1 to $2 apiece, for $\frac{1}{2}$-in. to $1\frac{1}{8}$-in. bars. Those for large strands cost from $5 to $30 apiece, for steel cross-sectional areas of 0.2 sq in. to 2 sq in., including the cost of cutting and swaging but excluding the cost of steel bearing plates. These should be used only for preliminary estimates; more accurate values can be obtained from the respective manufacturers.

Metallic sheathing costs $0.05 to $0.20 per ft of length, enclosing from 6 to 32 wires. Plastic sheathing used for unbonded work costs $0.05 to $0.10 per ft; paper enclosure costs only $0.01 to $0.02 per ft but involves more labor in wrapping. Retractible rubber tubes of about $1\frac{1}{2}$ in. by $2\frac{1}{2}$ in. size cost about $1.00 per ft but can be reused many times.

The cost of grouting varies markedly with the size of the job. When the plant is set up and the work systematized, grouting should not cost more than $0.01 to $0.02 per lb of steel.

EXAMPLE 15-1

Eighty prestressed-concrete roof girders, each 75 ft long, are to be built for a warehouse, using concrete of 5000-psi and wires of 240,000-psi strength. The midspan section of the girders is shown in Fig. 15-2. Cables in the web are curved; those in the bottom flange are to remain straight. The girders are to be precast at the building site and to be lifted to place. Allow 100 days for casting and prestressing the girders. Estimate and analyze the cost of the girders: (a) using 11 bonded cables of twelve 0.196-in. wires per cable; (b) using 14 unbonded cables of six 0.250-in. wires per cable. Assume unit costs as necessary. All cables are to be post-tensioned.

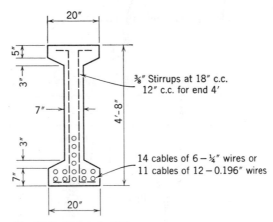

Fig. 15-2. Example 15-1.

Solution.   Quantities of materials required for one girder are estimated as follows:

Concrete	12 cu yd
Wires, 11 cables of 12–0.196-in. wires	1050 lb
14 cables of 6–0.250-in. wires	1100 lb
Mild steel bars	500 lb
End anchorages, for 11 cables	22 units
for 14 cables	28 units
Metal hose for bonded cables	830 ft
Paper wrapping for unbonded cables	1050 ft
Formwork, bottom contact area	125 sq ft
side contact area	780 sq ft

Contract unit prices for the various items are assumed as follows:

Concrete, 5000 psi, in place	= $22/cu yd
Wires, material and warehousing	= $0.17/lb
Straightening, cutting, placing at 0.04 hr/lb	
and at $2.50 per man-hour	= $0.10/lb
Total	$0.27/lb
Metallic hose, material and labor	= $0.12/ft
Paper wrapping, and grease	= $0.03/ft
Anchorage for twelve 0.196-in. wires	= $4.80/pc
Anchorage for six 0.250-in. wires	= $4.50/pc
Labor for tensioning at $2.50/hr:	
6-wire units @ 1.5 hr per anchorage	= $3.75/pc
12-wire units @ 1.8 hr per anchorage	= $4.50/pc
Equipment and plant, 100 days at $20 a day	= $2000
Grouting, 0.4 hr/cable at $2.50/hr	= $1.00/cable
Formwork, bottom, reused 5 times	= $0.20/sq ft
side, reused 10 times	= $0.15/sq ft

The cost per girder can now be tabulated.

Item	Unit	Quantity	Unit Price	Total Price Design (a)	Total Price Design (b)
Concrete	cu yd	12	$22.00	$264	$264
Wires	Lb	1050	$0.27	$283	
		1100	0.27		$297
Sheathing	Ft	830	0.12	100	
		1050	0.03		32
Anchorage	Piece	22	4.80	106	
		28	4.50		126
Tensioning	Unit	22	4.50	99	
		28	3.75		105
Equipment and plant				25	25
Grouting	Cable	22	1.00	22	
		Cost of steel and prestressing		$635	$585
Formwork, bottom	Sq ft	125	$0.20	$25	$25
side	Sq ft	780	0.15	117	117
Lifting	Girder			50	50
		Cost of formwork and erection		$192	$192
		Total cost per girder		$1091	$1041

The cost analysis is performed as follows:

	Design (a)	Design (b)
Cost per lb of steel	$ 0.605	$ 0.532
Cost per cu yd of concrete		
steel	$53	$49
concrete	22	22
formwork and lifting	16	16
	$91	$87

15-4   Cost Comparison with Reinforced Concrete

On the basis of the unit quantities discussed in section 15-2 and the unit prices in section 15-3, it is possible to make an overall cost comparison between prestressed and reinforced concrete for an average case. Since it is almost impossible to define the exact meaning of the term "average" it must be admitted that such a comparison merely serves as a qualitative guide, although for the sake of presentation it is expressed in quantitative terms.

The comparison can be made by two methods, depending on the degree of accuracy desired. The first method of comparison is to consider the three main cost items separately: concrete, formwork and falsework, and steel. The second method, more approximate, is to compare the cost per cubic yard of concrete, everything included.

Method (a). Considering the three main items separately, and referring to sections 15-2 and 15-3, we have

Concrete:

$$\text{Average quantity ratio} \quad \frac{\text{P.C.}}{\text{R.C.}} = 0.5$$

$$\text{Average unit price ratio} \quad \frac{\text{P.C.}}{\text{R.C.}} = \frac{21}{18} = 1.17$$

$$\text{Average overall cost ratio} \quad \frac{\text{P.C.}}{\text{R.C.}} = 0.5 \times 1.17 = 0.58$$

in favor of P.C.

Formwork. Formwork, assuming that, for every cubic yard of P.C., 2 cu yd of R.C. are required:

$$\text{Average quantity ratio} \quad \frac{\text{P.C.}}{\text{R.C.}} = \frac{90}{40 \times 2} = 1.12$$

$$\text{Average unit price ratio} \quad \frac{\text{P.C.}}{\text{R.C.}} = \frac{0.70}{0.50} = 1.4$$

$$\text{Average overall cost ratio} \quad \frac{\text{P.C.}}{\text{R.C.}} = 1.12 \times 1.4 = 1.6$$

in favor of R.C.

Falsework. Owing to the smaller dead weight of prestressed construction and the possibilities for precasting work, it can be assumed that the average cost ratio will be

$$\frac{\text{P.C.}}{\text{R.C.}} = 0.8 \text{ in favor of P.C.}$$

Steel:

$$\text{Average quantity ratio} \quad \frac{\text{P.C.}}{\text{R.C.}} = 0.20$$

$$\text{Average unit price ratio} \quad \frac{\text{P.C.}}{\text{R.C.}} = \frac{0.50}{0.12} = 4.2$$

$$\text{Average overall cost ratio} \quad \frac{\text{P.C.}}{\text{R.C.}} = 4.2 \times 0.20 = 0.84$$

in favor of P.C.

Method (b). When all materials and labor are expressed in cost per cubic yard of concrete, an average case for post-tensioned beams and girders is as follows:

	R.C.	P.C.
Concrete	$18	$21
Formwork	10	32
Falsework	4	3
Steel	16	30
Total per cu yd	$48	$86

The above cost does not include overhead and profit. Since the cost per cubic yard is nearly doubled for prestressed work, while the quantity of concrete required for a structure will be about one-half of that for reinforced beams, the overall cost works out to be a close competition between the two types of construction, with a slight favor for prestressed beams, considering an "average" case. For pre-tensioning, the cost of formwork and of steel will be much lower, and the economy will become more obvious.

15-5   General Economic Considerations in Design

Economy and safety are the two major goals in structural design. The problem of designing prestressed-concrete structures economically is actually discussed in every chapter of this treatise. However, it may be well to summarize the major issues involved so that the designer can grasp the vital points of economy and not lose himself in a maze of minor details.

The first and foremost decision to be made is whether the structure can be economically designed for prestressed concrete or whether it might be better to employ some other type of construction, be it timber, steel, or reinforced concrete. There are, of course, other problems besides economy, such as aesthetic or functional requirements, which might force the choice one way or another, but by far the majority of structures will be decided on an economic basis. There are structures where prestressed concrete would be most suitable, but there are also those where it simply cannot compete with other types. Therefore the first motto for the designer is to employ prestressed concrete only where it belongs and not to use it as a cure-for-all.

The choice for prestressed-concrete construction must be considered together with the possible change in layout of the entire structure. Since most engineers are more familiar with other types of construction, span lengths and proportions are usually laid out with those in mind, the designer not realizing that, with prestressed concrete, radical changes may be possible and often desirable. For example, longer spans, smaller depth, thinner members, bold cantilevers, precasting procedures, reuse of forms not contemplated for reinforced concrete, may be embodied in the layout when prestressed concrete is used.

Once the use of prestressed concrete has been decided upon, the next important decision concerns the right type of prestressed construction. Should the members be pre-tensioned or post-tensioned? Should they be precast or cast-in-place, or should composite construction be adopted? Is bonded reinforcement necessary for the job, or would the unbonded type suffice for the service? These questions must be answered first, although often not until some preliminary work has been done on the design.

Engineers seldom realize an important prerequisite in design, namely, that the design loadings for structures must be chosen with care and judgment. Too often the loadings are specified for the structures by certain code requirements, and the engineer simply takes them for granted. Such specified loadings can be either too heavy or too light. Although they may have proved to be satisfactory for other types of construction whose methods of design have been empirically devised to suit such loadings, they may not be directly applicable to a new type of construction like prestressed concrete. If such loadings are used, the designer should exercise his care in employing a suitable set of allowable stresses and load factors so as to attain a proper but not excessive degree of safety in the structure.

Having settled these essential premises, the engineer can now proceed to design the members in detail. The first item to be settled, then, is usually the depth or thickness of the member. This is an individual item which must be determined for each particular structure. But, speaking in general, the economical depth of beams and thickness of slabs would be about 70% to 80% that of reinforced concrete. The depth having been chosen, the concrete section can be designed, taking into account the cost of formwork, ease in concrete placing, as well as stress requirements. At the same time, the strength of concrete for the job can be decided on. Often it is not the 28-day strength but the strength at transfer that controls the economy, since it is frequently necessary to obtain high strength fast in order to permit prestress transfer at an early age and thus speed up the production and construction.

Although prestressing steel is an item peculiar to prestressed work, its choice ranks least in importance when compared to the major considerations mentioned above. When the layout of a member is fixed, there will result a certain amount of prestress required, which is often beyond the control of the designer. Sometimes, the adoption of a particular system of prestressing may modify the sectional dimensions of the members, but such modifications are minor when compared to the major decisions. In this country, it is often unnecessary and sometimes undesirable to fix a particular system of prestressing for the job, because this will rule out competition which will help to lower the cost. Hence it is best to design a structure so that several systems, using different steels, may fit into it with very little modification, so that the problem of selecting an economic system is left to the competition of the bidders. There are, however, some obvious cases when one system is definitely superior to the others, and then the engineer should design on that basis.

One of the vital problems in the design of prestress steel is the positioning of the steel so as to give it a maximum resisting lever arm. In order that such a position of steel will not overstress the concrete at transfer, it it sometimes necessary to add superimposed weight to the member previous to prestressing, or first to partially tension the steel and to retension it to its final prestress after some superimposed load is put on the structure. Another economic method is to place nonprestressed reinforcements at strategic points in order to increase the ultimate and fatigue strengths. Means such as those must be kept in mind and applied when conditions warrant.

15-6 Building Types and Economics

Prestressed concrete can be economically applied to many types of buildings, whether of long or short spans, multi-story apartments or single-story industrial buildings. But it should not be concluded that it is the most economical construction for all buildings. Each individual structure must be studied by itself, with respect to its particular functions, environment, facilities, and other requirements.

Generally speaking, the following conditions will enhance the economy of prestressed-concrete construction in buildings, as compared to the more conventional materials.

1. Repetition of elements, enabling the reuse of forms whether for precast or cast-in-place construction.

2. Availability of prestressing and precasting plants, or of builders with experience in prestressing.

3. Availability of engineers and of architects who are not only versed in prestressed design, but also able to visualize the significance of related factors, such as architectural, mechanical, occupancy, and operational economies.

It is often argued that prestressed concrete, while saving material, does require more labor; hence it may not be economical in countries with high labor cost. This is true only to a certain extent. Mechanization is often more advanced in a country with high labor cost; hence new labor-saving devices will be easily developed to meet the requirement of the industry. As a result, there is universality in the economy of basically sound materials and methods such as prestressed concrete.

Prestressed Slabs. Concrete slabs can be economically post-tensioned in place for buildings. Solid slabs post-tensioned in place are economical from 20-ft to about 35-ft. in span For solid slabs with span from 30 to about 45 ft, haunches can be added to form various patterns. Waffled slabs can be made to span about 100 ft without excessive concrete or steel, if suitable structural depth can be obtained. However the shrinkage, creep, and elastic shortening of concrete must be allowed or compensated for when prestressed in place. This can be accomplished by arranging the vertical elements to permit movement in the direction of the shortening: Either the elements are made slender, or sliding joints and hinges can be provided. For a multi-story building, only the shortening of the second floor relative to the ground floor needs to be considered, while the relative shrinkage and creep between the various floors are usually small.

Pre-tensioned hollow slabs of various sizes and designs are produced in the United States. They are about 8-in. thick with 5-in. round or oval holes.

Pre-tensioned solid slabs over continuous spans are occasionally employed. Such long and thin slabs over several spans reduce the number of joints and may prove economical when they can be transported and erected without special equipment.

Another type of construction utilizes precast pre-tensioned slabs as the form on which the top concrete can be poured in place. This type of monolithic precast construction is economical when the live load is heavy or when an in-place topping is required.

Lift Slabs. The lift-slab type of construction resulted from an effort to reduce the cost of concrete construction by eliminating the expense of soffit forming and shoring. This method of construction has been greatly improved by prestressing the slabs, as described in Chapter 12. These slabs are cast and prestressed at ground level and then lifted into position by hydraulic jacks mounted on top of the columns. The prestressing of the slab reduces the slab's thickness, controls the deflection, eliminates cracks in the slab, and cuts down the cost.

When spans get much over 30 ft, solid slabs, even when prestressed, become too heavy for economical lifting and prestressing. For example, a 25-ft span prestressed slab would have a thickness of 6 to 8 in. for the usual loading, but a 35-ft span would need a 10 to 12-in. slab. For these longer spans the flat beam and joist type, or the waffled slab can be used. The flat beams generally span the short distance between columns, with the joists spanning the long direction. Bays of 35 by 60 ft are economical with this scheme.

The waffled slab, is more economical than the flat beam and joist type when the spans are almost equal in the two directions. These slabs can be cast on cardboard boxes and prestressed in two directions. One of the construction problems with the boxes is that they disintegrate very rapidly when exposed to sun and rain. Boxes exposed to the elements could collapse during the placing of the concrete.

When a flat roof slab with long spans in one direction is required, a dropped beam and slab type is used. The beam can be formed by leaving slots in the grade slab. These slots are filled in after the roof slabs have been lifted. For roof parking on factories and commercial buildings, this type of framing can be made to yield watertight roofs without conventional roofing or membrane, since the concrete is prestressed in two directions.

When long clear spans with a flat soffit are required, slabs with inverted beams are used. Spans of 120 ft or more, can be economically designed. When clear spans are desired on the ground floor such as for parking or merchandizing, the second floor can be hung from an inverted beam on the roof.

Precast Panels. Various types of precast prestressed panels are developed in different countries. In the United states, the double-tee type has found wide acceptance. The economy of the double-tee lies in the utilization of the top slab to carry the major portion of the compressive

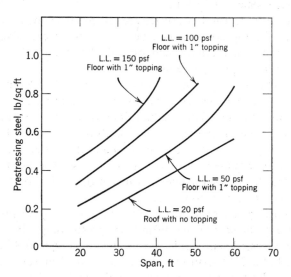

Fig. 15-3. Quantity of prestressing steel for double-tee panels.

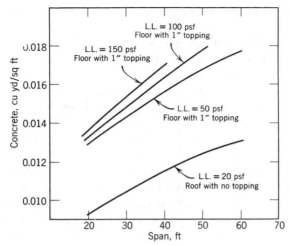

Fig. 15-4. Quantity of concrete for double-tee panels.

force, in combination with the narrow stems, which house the prestressing tendons, acting in tension.

Figures 15-3 and 15-4 give the quantities of concrete and steel required for double-tee sections for different spans and live loads. Simply by iucreasing the depth of the stems, the double-tee sections can be made to span greater distance, say 50 to 60 ft, with little additional material.

In order to provide greater fire protection and more flexibility, the single-tee section has been developed. By concentrating two stems in one, greater coverage is given to the tendons. The forms for single-tee can be easily stripped and adjusted to accommodate any variation in stem depth and thickness.

The channel section has also been successfully employed for buildings in the United States. When spans are short, say below 20 ft, reinforced concrete channels are often used. For long spans, prestressed sections are preferred, both for their lighter weight and for better deflection characteristics.

A large cored section is shown in Fig. 6-24(*c*) and is further illustrated in section 16-1.

When used for floors, these panels are topped with a thin layer of cast-in-place concrete. Such a topping is employed to smooth out any uneven camber, to encase conduits in the floor, and to provide a diaphragm for earthquake or wind loads.

Beams. Beams post-tensioned in place are economical only when carrying heavy loads over long spans. Precasting the beams in a plant or at the site will be found to be cheaper, if they can be transferred and lifted into position.

Joists of rectangular sections can be precast and erected to receive a poured-in-places slab. This is generally not as economical as single or double-tee panels discussed previously.

I-beams can be economically employed to support in-place floor slabs. One of the interesting features is the relative simplicity with which a number of large holes for ducts and conducts can be provided in the prestressed beam web, without damaging its shear strength, if properly designed.

In order to provide supports for precast panels and to integrate them, sometimes only the bottom portion of the beam is precast and pre-stressed. They are then supported on temporary shoring, and the panels positioned on them. Concrete is then placed for the top portion of the beam, also serving to connect the panels together. Such composite action is often economical when the beam spans over 30 ft.

Continuity for these composite beams can be obtained in several ways. Often, mild steel bars are embedded in the concrete over the supports to carry the negative moments. This type of combined action, with mild steel reinforcing bars carrying the negative moments and the prestressing wires carrying the positive moments, is best designed by the plastic theory, with their deflections checked by the elastic theory. The usual values of allowable stresses cannot serve as a proper guide.

Continuity for the beams can also be achieved by post-tensioning over the columns. Many methods have been employed, including the lapping of cables previously embedded in the beams. A perfect control of deflection can be obtained if properly designed and constructed.

Columns and Wall Panels.   Although it is seldom necessary to prestress cast-in-place building columns, there are cases when such a design may be desirable and economical. If a column carries only direct compression, there is no need for prestressing. However, there are columns which serve as anchors—for example, of a cantilever anchor arm—then pre-stressing gives a definite hold-down and limits the deflections of the cantilever. Some columns carry high lateral loads and are therefore subject to bending, resulting in tensile stresses on certain portions. Prestressing is then desirable for both strength and rigidity. A typical example is the Downtown Garage in San Francisco whose 9-story column was prestressed to carry earthquake loads, a horizontal force of 2,400 k. During the 1957 earthquake the building was totally unhurt, while some others were seriously damaged. Prestressing such a column will often relieve other elements from carrying lateral forces and result in overall economy.

Building louvers generally built of reinforced concrete can be made more economically with prestressed ones. The thickness of such louvers can be almost cut by half, thus saving both concrete and the dead load of the louvers.

Precast columns which are subject to bending either during transportation or after erection can be economically built of prestressed concrete. This was done for a number of lift-slab buildings, where the columns had to be designed for lateral forces during lifting.

Wall panels can be economically prestressed to permit easier handling, to minimize cracking, as well as to increase the bending resistance.

Trusses. Pre-tensioned trusses of shorter spans have been used in Europe for buildings. While there is a great saving in materials, their formwork, which also serves as the pre-tensioning bed, is costly and cannot be justified unless there are sufficient repetitions of the same design. In the U.S.S.R., where standardized trusses are mass-produced, they are pre-tensioned with continuous wires.

Post-tensioned trusses are economical when used for medium and long spans, say from 100 ft up. The truss members and the joints are precast and then they are joined together at the site.

Tied arches can also be made of precast elements post-tensioned together (Fig.15-5). The bottom chord is made of a post-tensioned tie, while the vertical hangers are also of post-tensioned concrete. Precast panels may be placed either on the top or the bottom chord. Thus a long warehouse can be constructed with a width of 200 ft or more with no interior columns. This results in the saving of columns and footings.

Cantilever trusses of the Vierendeel type can also be post-tensioned economically for long span airplane hangars. Such trusses cannot be economically designed when the live load is heavy, but for light roof loading, secondary stresses are limited in the members.

Thin Shells. The prestressing of thin shell roofs opens up a completely new field for long span building construction, in which, with ingenuity,

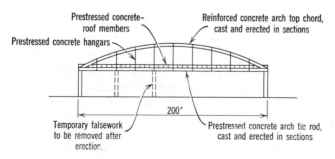

Fig. 15-5. Precast tied arch, post-tensioned.

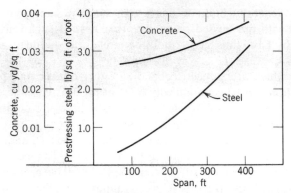

Fig. 15-6. Quantities of steel and concrete for prestressed cylindrical shell roof.

great economy can be developed. It is possible to use the minimum practical shell thickness, say 3 in., to span 200 ft simple spans or 100-ft cantilevers, completely eliminating structural interferences. The economy results from the balancing of gravity forces by prestressing, thus nullifying all vertical loads, leaving only direct compression in the concrete shell. Thus, the only additional cost for long span is in the prestressing steel, which, when properly designed, forms only a minor part of the cost (Fig.15-6).

The major part of the cost of a prestressed thin shell lies in its formwork. Means must be devised to reduce its cost if economy in construction is to be obtained.

There are three methods to economize the cost of formwork. First, the shells can be precast on the ground so that a set of forms can be used many dozens of times. This, of course, limits the span of shell to dimensions that can be handled and erected. Sometimes a long shell can be precast in parts and joined by post-tensioning.

Secondly, traveling falsework can be used. One such scheme is proposed for cylindrical shells, with the formwork moving along the length of the barrel. Temporary shores will be installed at intervals to support the edge beams before the final post-tensioning is applied. This arrangement avoids the more difficult problem of supporting the exterior edge of the shells if they are concreted with construction joint along the edge.

Domes can be precast with prestressed elements. Designs have been made for a 400-ft inverted dome, using such precast elements. Here again, economy is achieved by reuse of forms and simplification of falsework.

Folded plates of prestressed concrete have been built for roofs. For economy, it would be desirable to pre-tension and precast such slabs and then properly join them.

Thin shells of the hyperbolic paraboloid type are economical, in that straight timbers can be used for the formwork. Many designs are possible for utilizing this type of layout. Shorter spans can be precast or cast with movable formwork. Long single spans necessarily involve high cost of formwork, but yet can be cheaper when compared to similar designs using other materials.

When spans get really long, it might be economical to use shells with ribbed stiffeners, or of the corrugated type, so as to limit the thickness and weight of concrete. For long spans, prestressing is also essential in order that the cracks and deflections in an ordinary reinforced shell could be brought within control.

Connections. A major task in the design of precast-prestressed buildings lies in the detailing of the connections. In addition to the usual problems encountered in detailing a precast building, prestressing introduces additional ones. Prestressed elements tend to shrink and creep more than ordinary reinforced ones. Whereas reinforced members have their shrinkage cracks spread throughout their length, prestressed members concentrate their shrinkage and creep at the connections. Prestressed members are usually more slender and subject to greater rotation at the ends. When subject to temperature differential, they also camber and deflect more than conventional designs. Hence the connections should be designed to permit both longitudinal and rotational movements, unless the supporting members are flexible enough. The Prestressed Concrete Institute has prepared a tentative set of connection details for precast-prestressed buildings, which should be ready in final form in 1963. It includes some fifty designs for column base, beam-to-column, beam-to-girder, and bearing-wall details and should serve as an excellent reference.

Conclusions. So many different types of prestressed concrete construction are now available for building construction that economical types can be chosen to fit various conditions. While it cannot be always cheaper than other materials, its adaptability will be greatly enhanced by the knowledge and experience of engineers and builders. Standardization of certain products will help to reduce the cost; but individual attention must always be given to each case, taking into account the local and specific requirements.

Finally, no building should be judged and designed solely on the basis of first cost. The cost of maintenance, of insurance, and of operation must be simultaneously considered. The value of the building, its earning power, its rental income, its appearance, its adaptability and lastingness all play an important part which should affect the decision of the engineer.

15-7   Bridge Types and Economics

As stated in Chapter 1, 12% of the highway bridges in the United States were of prestressed concrete during the years 1959–61. For this same period, about 80% of all bridges between the spans of 50 to 300 ft were built of prestressed concrete in West Germany. It is now hardly necessary to prove the economy of prestressed concrete for bridge construction. Although prestressed concrete may not be the most economical material for all bridges, it has certainly taken its place among the family of major construction materials.

The saving of materials by using prestressed concrete for bridges, is shown in Figs. 15-7 and 15-8. Figure 15-7 indicates that the weight of prestressing steel per sq ft of bridge is about $\frac{1}{5}$ that of the reinforcing steel in a reinforced-concrete bridge, and about $\frac{1}{8}$ the structural steel in a steel bridge. Figure 15-8 indicates the saving in the volume of concrete, when compared to a conventionally reinforced-concrete bridge. However, the saving in materials alone may not result in overall economy, unless the cost of forming and falsework is also minimized.

In order to save forming costs, the forms must be reused either at the site or in the production plant. Mass-production techniques were best

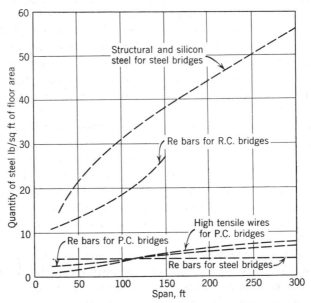

Fig. 15-7. Average quantity of steel for bridge superstructure (H20-S16 loading).

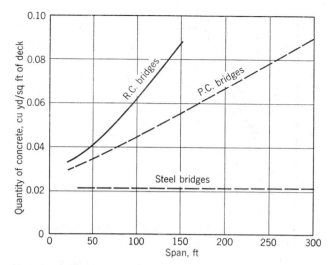

Fig. 15-8. Average quantity of concrete for bridge super-structure (H20-S16 loading).

exemplified in the 24-mile long Lake Pontchartrain Bridge (Fig. 1-12), where thousands of identical spans were produced, with each span precast as a unit, 56 ft long and 33 ft wide. To save falsework, erecting methods and procedures must be carefully planned for each project, making full use of the potentialities of precasting, of joinery by prestressing, and of the capabilities of erection equipments

In the United States, the most common shapes for spans from 40 to 120 ft are approximately in the following order: I-sections, box-sections, T-sections, hollow cores, and channel sections. While there are inherent advantages to each section, its availability and the local economic factors often determine the adoption of one type or the other. Precast spans can be made continuous by placing reinforcement over the piers to obtain further economy. One such example is described in section 16-5.

What has not yet been realized in this country is the tremendous potential of prestressed concrete for long span bridges, ranging from 120 ft up to 400 and perhaps 1000 ft. For long spans, the saving in materials becomes more pronounced. However, it is often necessary to resort to new concepts in design, in production, and in construction. Long simple spans of prestressed concrete are economical only when they can be erected without excessive cost.

For span length exceeding about 150 ft, Fig. 15-9, continuous spans are definitely lighter than simple spans. However, the economical span

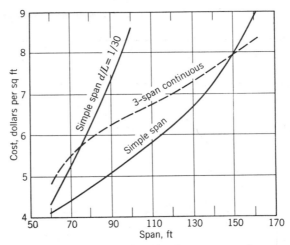

Fig. 15-9. Cost study: simple versus continuous spans (H20-S16 loading).

Fig. 15-10. Tee sections for Feather River Bridge, Marysville, California, two continuous spans at 152-ft. (Structural Engineer T. Y. Lin and Associates.)

limit between simple and continuous types will vary with local conditions. Figure 15-10 shows a 2-span continuous bridge at 152-ft each, where economy in continuity partly results from savings in anchorage and stressing operations.

For long bridges requiring expansion joints, cantilever spans are often convenient. Cantilever construction will also make possible the elimination of falsework for the main spans. The use of movable scaffold enables the concrete to be placed section-by-section as the scaffold is moved outward. Prestress is applied to the completed section before proceeding to the next. Figure 15-11 shows the Nibelungen Bridge at Worms, Germany, with a center span of 375 ft. This span has two closed box sections with a depth of 8.2 ft at midspan and 21.3 ft over supports. A similar bridge over the Rhine now under construction at Bendorf, Germany, has a center span of 682 ft. Figure 15-12 shows the Medway Bridge at Kent, England, with a main span of 500 ft where the center-suspended span was lifted into position.

Prestressing of piers is often economical, because it enables slender piers to carry sizable lateral loads. When piers are prestressed to the superstructure, rigid frames are obtained. Rigid frames reduce the deflections and help to carry unbalanced live load. However, deck shortening results in secondary stresses and must be provided for. Hinges located at the bottom of the piers will cut down the effect of shrinkage and creep.

Fig. 15-11. Nibelungen Bridge, Worms, Germany, uses cantilever construction. Main spans 334-375-342 ft. Completed 1953. (Dywidag-Spannbeton Dyckerhoff-Widmann.)

Fig. 15-12. Medway Bridge, Kent, England, has 500-ft center span. (Courtesy Cement and Concrete Association, London.)

Stress control can also be obtained by jacking the lower ends of the piers in a horizontal direction.

Figure 11-22 shows a rigid frame bridge designed to carry a pedestrian load of 100 psf plus an architectural load of 840 plf of bridge. It has a main span of 102 ft, with a structural depth of only 27 in. The two parallel spans are connected by a crosswalk, which forms a rigid frame with the

Fig. 15-13. 300-ft span Zaza River Bridge uses precast trusses, Las Villas, Cuba. (Courtesy Stressteel Corp.)

prestressed piers on the outside of the spans. Owing to its shallow depth and heavy load, the amount of prestressing steel was 7 lb per sq ft of floor.

An interesting example of a precast prestressed truss bridge is the 300-ft span Zaza River Bridge in Las Villa, Cuba, consisting of two 117-foot long cantilevers extending from each abutment carrying a 66-ft suspended span, Fig. 15-13. Each cantilever is made up of 4 parallel trusses, and each truss is composed of 5 panels approximately 23 feet long. Total amount of concrete for the superstructure was 1.6 cu ft per sq ft of roadway bridge, and prestressing steel 5.1 psf plus reinforcing steel at 17.8 psf. This type of design is economical when there is not sufficient number of spans to warrant the installations of expensive plants and equipment for production and erection of larger segments.

By prestressing the bottom chord, a tied-arch bridge can be economically built of prestressed concrete. Prestressing will control the rib shortening and shrinkage of the arch ribs. Hangars for the arch can also be made of prestressed concrete to obtain rigidity and to facilitate maintenance.

In Moscow, precast components are assembled and prestressed to make tied arches spanning 354 ft in a bridge across the Moscow River,[3] Fig. 15-14. Both the curved ribs and the horizontal ties were made of precast parts. They were assembled in two pieces along the shore, and floated into position by barges with each piece weighing 5500 tons. During erection, the two flanking spans of 150 ft each were connected to the main span by prestressing cables over the top of the ribs. The 300-ft main span

Fig. 15-14. Main spans of Moscow River Bridge are precast prestressed in 5500-ton pieces and floated into position.

Fig. 15-15. Prestressed suspension span of 328 ft, Merelbeke Bridge, Ghent, Belgium. (Courtesy of Dr. D. C. Vandepitte.)

of the high-level bridge over Rudkoebing Sound in Denmark is a concrete bow string arch with a prestressed tie.[4]

Prestressed concrete suspension bridges make use of the force in the external cables by anchoring them into the concrete girders, thus prestressing them.[5] This may be visualized as self-anchored suspension bridges using concrete girders instead of steel ones, or it may be viewed as a continuous prestressed bridge using external cables. A notable bridge of this type is the Merelbeke Bridge near Ghent, Belgium, with a center span of 328 ft, Fig. 15-15.

The Maracaibo Bridge in Venezuela has five main spans of 771-ft each.[6] It is of the prestressed suspender or stayed-girder type of construction, with long prestressed girders cast on preassembled steel-erection trusses weighing 250 tons apiece.

When the idea of precast long panels is applied to suspension designs, different layouts are obtained. Figure 15-16 shows a 700-ft center span, with two 280-ft side spans. Precast elements 140-ft long each are erected on temporary supports. Then they are suspended to the top of the towers

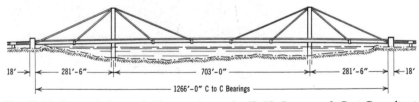

Fig. 15-16. Suspended span bridge—prestressed. (J. H. Pomeroy & Co., Consultant, T. Y. Lin and Associates.)

by post-tensioned inclined suspenders. The amount of prestressing steel required for this bridge is only 12 lb per square ft of floor area, and the concrete only 3.0 cu ft, including the towers. When considered together with the saving in formwork and falsework, this is truly an economical design for long spans.

References

1   T. Y. Lin and E. K. Rice, "Economics of Prestressed Concrete Buildings," *Indian Construction News*, August 1958

2   T. Y. Lin, "Economics of Prestressed Concrete Bridges," *Proc. Eighth California Street and Highway Conference*, 1956; also reprinted by Portland Cement Association, Chicago.

3   "Soviet Precast Arch in Parts," *Eng. News-Rec.*, August 14, 1958, p. 54.

4   "Bow String Has Prestressed Tie," *Eng. News-Rec.*, July 26, 1962, pp. 48–49.

5   D. C. C. Vandepitte, "Prestressed Concrete Suspension Bridges," *Proceedings, World Conference on Prestressed Concrete*, San Francisco, 1957; also "Suspended Span is Prestressed Concrete," *Eng. News-Rec.*, April 21, 1960, p. 40–42.

6   Maracaibo Bridge Opens to Traffic," *Eng. News-Rec.*, August 30, 1962, p. 30.

16   *design examples*

In order to integrate various subjects discussed in previous chapters, and to illustrate the application of the principles of analysis, five examples are given in this chapter to cover different types of structures and phases of design. They deal essentially with flexural members. It is fully realized that these examples form only a small portion of the possible range of applicability, and represent only the simplest beginning of prestressed-concrete design. They should be useful to the readers to serve as a guide for design procedures. For easier reference, subject matters and chapters specifically illustrated in each example are listed in the following table.

TABLE 16-1

Topics Illustrated in the Examples

Topics	Chapters	Example 16-1	Example 16-2	Example 16-3	Example 16-4	Example 16-5
Pre-tensioning	3	x	x		x	x
Post-tensioning	3			x	x	
Pre-tensioning + post-tensioning	3				x	
Loss of prestress	4	x		x		
Preliminary beam design	5, 6		x		x	
Elastic flexural design	5, 6	x	x	x		x
Ultimate strength design	5, 6	x		x		x
Composite action	5, 6			x	x	x
Shear	7	x	x	x		
Camber, deflections	8	x		x		
Cable layout	8	x	x	x	x	x
Partial prestress	9					x
Continuous beams	10				x	x
Load balancing	11				x	
Rigid frames	11				x	
One-way slabs	12				x	
Buildings	15	x	x		x	
Bridges	15			x		x

16-1 Design Example, Pre-tensioned Cored Section

A pre-tensioned cored section (the Dynacore Section, Fig. 6-24c), Figs. 16-1 and 16-2, is to be used for roof construction carrying an added dead load of 10 psf and a design live load of 30 psf on a simple span of 70 ft. It is made of lightweight concrete at 110 pcf, precast in a factory with a transfer strength of $f_{ci}' = 4000$ psi and a minimum 28-day strength of $f_c' = 5000$ psi. Design the tendons, using $\frac{7}{16}$-in. 7-wire strands (Appendix B with $A_s = 0.1089$ sq in. per strand, $f_s' = 250,000$ psi, $f_i = 175,000$ psi, $f_t = 165,000$ psi, and $f_e = 145,000$ psi. Check the loss of prestress, both immediately at transfer and eventually, say at the end of 3 years.

Fig. 16-1. Erecting a Dynacore section. (Courtesy of Material Service Division of General Dynamics, Chicago.)

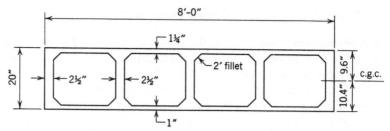

Fig. 16-2. Dynacore section. Example 16-1.

Note that this section is pre-tensioned transversely both in the top and the bottom flanges, with an average concentric transverse prestress of about 200 psi. The flange slabs spanning between the webs can be analyzed for concentrated or uniform loads and has been tested successfully, but will not be treated in this example, which is devoted to the design of the longitudinal prestressing and reinforcement. Follow PCI Building Code Requirements when applicable, Appendix D.

   Solution. Referring to section 6-9, the location of c.g.c. and other properties are obtained: $c_b = 10.4$ in., $A_c = 470$ sq in., $I_c = 27100$ in.^{4}, $w_G = 358$ plf. On a simple span of 70 ft, the maximum bending moments are

$$M_G = \frac{358 \times 70^2}{8} = 219,000 \text{ ft-lb}$$

$$M_S = \frac{8 \times 10 \times 70^2}{8} = 49,000 \text{ ft-lb}$$

$$M_L = \frac{8 \times 30 \times 70^2}{8} = 147,000 \text{ ft-lb}$$

$$M_D = 219,000 + 49,000 = 268,000 \text{ ft-lb}$$

$$M_T = 268,000 + 147,000 = 415,000 \text{ ft-lb}$$

   Elastic Design. To determine the prestress and c.g.s. location for midspan section by the elastic theory, top and bottom kerns are computed:

$$r^2 = \frac{I_c}{A_c} = \frac{27,100}{470} = 57.5 \text{ in.}^2$$

$$k_t = \frac{r^2}{c_b} = \frac{57.5}{10.4} = 5.53 \text{ in.}$$

$$k_b = \frac{r^2}{c_t} = \frac{57.5}{9.6} = 5.99 \text{ in.}$$

Since the girder load is relatively heavy, the c.g.s. can be placed as low as possible. Assuming a clear concrete protection of 1.5 in. for fire resistance and a protection to c.g.s. of 2.4 in., we have total available lever arm from c.g.s. to top kern,

$$10.4 - 2.4 + 5.53 = 13.53 \text{ in.}$$

This will give a resisting moment of $13.53F_e$ up to zero tension in bottom fiber.

Allowing a maximum tension of $6\sqrt{f_c'} = 6\sqrt{5000} = 423$ psi [PCI Code Art. 203(b)2], we have resisting moment from zero tension to 423-psi tension,

$$M = \frac{fI}{c} = \frac{423 \times 27,100}{10.4} = 1,100,000 \text{ in.-lb}$$
$$= 91,600 \text{ ft-lb}$$

This value of 91,600 ft-lb may be found to be too high since it constitutes 22% of the total moment of 415,000 ft-lb. If fully utilized in design, it will appreciably reduce the required amount of prestressing steel and hence the ultimate moment. Furthermore, we will be using a great deal of tension in the bottom flange concrete, which, once cracked, may not be able to resist that tension. Hence, it would be well to use perhaps only half of that value in our first attempt to determine the required prestress; thus

$$\frac{13.53F_e}{12} = 415,000 - \frac{91,600}{2} = 369,200 \text{ ft-lb}$$
$$F_e = 318,000 \text{ lb}$$
$$A_s = \frac{F_e}{145,000} = 2.20 \text{ in.}^2$$

No. of $\frac{7}{16}$ in. strands required $= 2.20/0.1089 = 20.2$. Using 20 strands, we can check the stresses at transfer and under total load as follows.

$$F_t = 20 \times 0.1089 \times 165,000 = 359,000 \text{ lb}$$
$$F_e = 20 \times 0.1089 \times 145,000 = 316,000 \text{ lb}$$
$$e = 10.4 - 2.4 = 8.0 \text{ in.}$$

At transfer,

$$f = \frac{F_t}{A_c} \pm \frac{F_t ec}{I_c} \mp \frac{M_G c}{I_c}$$
$$= \frac{-359,000}{470} \pm \frac{359,000 \times 8.0 \times (9.6 \text{ or } 10.4)}{27,100} \mp \frac{219,000 \times 12 \times \binom{9.6}{10.4}}{27,100}$$
$$= -765 \pm \frac{1015}{1100} \mp \frac{930}{1007}$$
$$= \begin{array}{l} -680 \text{ psi top fiber compression} \\ -858 \text{ psi bottom fiber compression} \end{array}$$

These stresses indicate a near-rectangular stress block, and a small amount of camber under the girder's own weight, which is usually desirable.

Under total design load,

$$f = \frac{F_e}{A_c} \pm \frac{F_e ec}{I_c} \mp \frac{M_T c}{I}$$

$$= \frac{-316,000}{470} \pm \frac{316,000 \times 8.0 \times \left(\dfrac{9.6}{10.4}\right)}{27,100} \mp \frac{415,000 \times 12 \times \left(\dfrac{9.6}{10.4}\right)}{27,100}$$

$$= -672 \pm \frac{893}{968} \mp \frac{1770}{1915}$$

$$= \begin{matrix} -1549 \text{ psi top fiber compression} \\ +275 \text{ psi bottom fiber tension} \end{matrix}$$

The top fiber compression is well within the allowable $0.45f_c' = 2250$ psi, and the bottom fiber tension is also less than the permissible 423 psi; this is as expected when choosing the 20 $\frac{7}{16}$-in. strands.

To locate the strands at the ends of the section, we assume that the strands are spaced at the minimum of $1\frac{3}{4}$-in. c.c. Depending on the hardware available and the practice at the plant, this spacing may vary considerably. Further, we will assume that one-point harping is preferred for simplicity in production (actually it frequently happens that 2-point or 3-point harping may be used, then the profile may be easily arranged both for camber control and for stress control along the entire length of the span), then we can make a tentative arrangement. In order to produce no tension in the top fiber, the c.g.s. at the ends should be within the kern. In order to produce a rectangular stress block at the ends, the c.g.s. should be at the c.g.c. In order not to have the intermediate points control the design the c.g.s. should be located within a limiting zone. The c.g.s. at the end should also be located so as to produce the best camber effect. Taking all this into consideration and using 4 strands for each web, we have a tentative arrangement as shown in Fig. 16-3.

The stresses at the ends can only be critical at transfer and will be computed as follows, assuming no external moment.

$$f = \frac{F_t}{A_c} \pm \frac{F_t ec}{I}$$

$$= \frac{-359,000}{470} \pm \frac{359,000 \times (10.4 - 6.63)(9.6 \text{ or } 10.4)}{27,100}$$

$$= -765 + 479 \text{ or } -765 - 519$$

$$= \begin{matrix} -286 \text{ psi compression top fiber} \\ -1284 \text{ psi compression bottom fiber} \end{matrix}$$

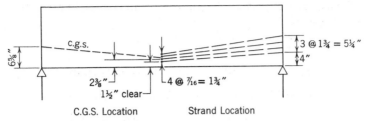

C.G.S. Location   Strand Location

Fig. 16-3. Strand and c.g.s. location.

These stresses are all well within the allowable range. Further check on the stresses at or the quarter-span points will show that they are also under control. Hence the design is considered satisfactory so far as the flexural elastic stresses are concerned.

Ultimate Strength. To check the ultimate strength requirements, we compute the ultimate moments:

$$1.8(D + L) = 1.8 \times 415{,}000 = 747{,}000 \text{ ft-lb} - \text{controlling}$$

$$1.2D + 2.4L = 1.2 \times 268{,}000 + 2.4 \times 147{,}000 = 675{,}000 \text{ ft-lb}$$

The expected actual ultimate resisting moment strength of the section may be estimated following the method outlined in section 5-6 as follows:

$$T' = 20 \times 0.1089 \times 250{,}000 = 545{,}000 \text{ lb}$$

$$A_c' = \frac{545{,}000}{0.85 \times 5{,}000} = 128 \text{ in.}^2$$

For width $b = 96$ in. and thickness of 1.25 in., flange area $= 120$ in.^{2}, with only 8 in.^{2} to be additionally furnished by the web and the fillets. Hence the center of compression can be assumed at $1.25/2 = 0.63$ in., the section is not over-reinforced, and $f_{su} = 250{,}000$ psi can be developed. The ultimate lever arm is approximately $20 - 2.4 - 0.63 = 16.97$ in., and

$$M' = 545{,}000 \times 16.97/12 = 770{,}000 \text{ ft-lb}$$

which is slightly greater than the required amount of 747,000 ft-lb and indicates that $20 - 7/16$-in. strands are just about right, while 19 strands would not have been sufficient.

Ultimate strength at other sections can be shown to be more than adequate, since the reduction in ultimate lever arm away from midspan is slower compared to the reduction in the parabolic moment diagram.

Camber and Deflection.   Camber at transfer due to prestress only, from section 8-1, is

$$E = 2,500,000 \text{ psi}$$

$$F_t = 20 \times 0.1089 \times 165,000 = 359,000 \text{ lb}$$

$$M_1 = 359,000[10.4 - 6.63] = 1,355,000 \text{ in.-lb}$$

$$M_2 = 359,000[6.63 - 2.4] = 1,520,000 \text{ in.-lb}$$

$$\Delta = \frac{L^2}{8EI}\left[M_1 + \frac{2}{3}M_2\right]$$

$$\Delta = \frac{(70 \times 12)^2}{8 \times 2,500,000 \times 27,100}[1,355,000 + \tfrac{2}{3} \times 1,520,000]$$

$$= \frac{2,363,000}{766,000} = 3.09 \text{ in.}$$

Deflection due to beam own weight.

$$Mg = \frac{wL^2}{8} = 219,000 \text{ ft-lb}$$

$$\Delta = \frac{L^2}{8EI}[\tfrac{5}{6}Mg]$$

$$= \frac{5}{6} \times \frac{219,000 \times 12}{766,000}$$

$$= 2.86 \text{ in.}$$

Hence the net camber at transfer, 1-day old, is $3.09 - 2.86 = 0.23$ in. camber upward.

Depending on the age of concrete at which the additional dead load is placed, the deflection will vary. If the dead load is added early, then after one year the amount of deflection or camber can be approximated by using an average value of $E = 3,500,000$ psi and a creep factor of 1.8 for the effects of prestress and the dead load. (Note these values will vary greatly for the type of aggregates and concrete.) Using the effective prestress of $f_e = 145,000$ psi, we can compute the resulting deflection as follows:

$$M_D = 268,000 \text{ ft-lb}$$

$$F_e = 20 \times 0.1089 \times 145,000 = 316,000 \text{ lb}$$

$$M_1 = 316,000(10.4 - 6.63) = 1,190,000 \text{ in.-lb}$$

$$M_2 = 316,000(6.63 - 2.4) = 1,330,000 \text{ in.-lb}$$

$$\Delta = \frac{L^2}{8EI}(M_1 + \tfrac{2}{3}M_2 - \tfrac{5}{6}M_D) \times (\text{creep} = 1.8)$$

$$= \frac{(70 \times 12)^2}{8 \times 3,500,000 \times 27,100}$$

$$\times [1,190,000 + \tfrac{2}{3}(1,330,000) - \tfrac{5}{6}(268,000) \times 12] \, 1.8$$

$$= \frac{1}{1,075,000}[1,190,000 + 886,000 - 2,680,000]1.8$$

$$= -1.01 \text{ in.}$$

which indicates that, in the course of one year, the member will have a maximum downward deflection of 1.01 in., which probably will not be objectionable on a span of 70 ft. But it does indicate that either a more careful study of the camber and deflection history is desirable, or that some means to reduce the deflection is needed, such as placing the c.g.s. at ends further below the present location.

The instantaneous deflection due to live load may be estimated using a high value of $E_c =$, say, 3,800,000 psi,

$$M_L = 147,000 \text{ ft-lb}$$

$$\Delta = \frac{L^2}{8EI}(\tfrac{5}{6}M_L)$$

$$= \frac{(70 \times 12)^2}{8 \times 3,800,000 \times 27,100}[\tfrac{5}{6}(147,000) \times 12]$$

$$= \frac{1,470,000}{1,165,000} = 1.26 \text{ in.}$$

which is $\dfrac{1.26 \text{ in.}}{70 \times 12} = \dfrac{1}{667}$ of the span length and is not considered excessive.

Design for Shear. Shear is critical only under the total load, hence,

$$V_T = \frac{wL}{2} = \frac{(358 + 80 + 240) \times 70}{2} = 23,700 \text{ lb}$$

Vertical component from the tendons, for $F_e = 316,000$ lb, is

$$316,000\left(\frac{6.63 - 2.4}{35 \times 12}\right) = 3200 \text{ lb}$$

Net shear, assuming the prestress is already transmitted to the concrete, is

$$V_c = V - V_s = 23,700 - 3200 = 20,500 \text{ lb}$$

At c.g.c., we have,

$$Q = \text{top flange } 120 \times 8.97 \quad = \quad 1075$$
$$\text{fillet } 16 \times 7.68 \quad = \quad 123$$
$$\text{web } 104 \times 4.18 \quad = \quad 435$$
$$Q = \quad \overline{1633} \text{ in.}^3$$

$$v = \frac{V_c Q}{Ib}$$

$$= \frac{20{,}500 \times 1633}{27{,}100 \times 12.5} = 99 \text{ psi}$$

For average prestress

$$\frac{F_e}{A_c} = \frac{316{,}000}{470} = 672 \text{ psi}$$

Principal tension is

$$S_t = \sqrt{v^2 + \left(\frac{f_c}{2}\right)^2} - \frac{f_c}{2}$$

$$= \sqrt{99^2 + \left(\frac{672}{2}\right)^2} - \frac{672}{2}$$

$$= 350 - 336 = 14 \text{ psi}$$

which is very low.

However, the end block stresses should be considered and a certain amount of web reinforcement used near the ends.

Loss of Prestress. The loss of prestress will now be studied for this design. First, the elastic shortening can be estimated using the average prestress at transfer of $359{,}000/470 = 765$ psi, $E_c = 2{,}500{,}000$ psi, and $E_s = 27{,}000{,}000$ psi:

$$\Delta f_s = 765 \times \frac{27{,}000{,}000}{2{,}500{,}000} = 8250 \text{ psi}$$

The loss at the level of the tendons at midspan may be slightly higher since the fiber stress in concrete is somewhat higher. This also indicates that the estimated loss of 10,000 psi from the initial prestress of 175,000 psi to 165,000 psi at transfer is a fairly good estimation.

Loss of prestress due to creep may be estimated at 2 times the elastic shortening, thus,

$$\Delta f_s = 2 \times 8250 = 16{,}500 \text{ psi}$$

Loss of prestress due to shrinkage may be estimated, assuming a coefficient of 0.0003, at

$$\Delta f_s = 0.0003 \times 27{,}000{,}000 = 8100 \text{ psi}$$

Total loss of prestress, excluding loss or gain due to bending of member, is,

$$8250 + 16,500 + 8100 = 32,850 \text{ psi}$$

which is fairly close to the assumed loss of 30,000 psi in the problem statement.

16-2 Design Example, Pre-Tensioned Roof Beam

This example illustrates the design of a tapered roof beam, precast and pre-tensioned. The design was used in a warehouse, San Diego, California, Fig. 16-4. Since this roof beam is not likely to be subjected to any overload, checking for ultimate strength was not required. However, one of the

Fig. 16-4. Erecting a 66-ft pre-tensioned roof beam. (Southwest Structural Concrete Corp., San Diego, California.)

beams was tested to failure and showed a factor of safety of 1.3 (girder + D + L) against cracking and a factor of 2.2 (girder + D + L) at ultimate.

This precast pre-tensioned roof beam is to span a clear distance of 64 ft with an additional length of 1 ft over each support. The beam carries a superimposed dead and live load of 520 plf, in addition to its own weight. The top chord of the beam is to be tapered so that the depth of beam is 40 in. at midspan and 16 in. at the ends, the bottom of the beam to remain straight. Use concrete with $f_c' = 4500$ psi at 28 days and $f_{ci}' = 4000$ psi at transfer. Steel for pre-tensioning will have an ultimate strength of 200,000 psi. Further assume that $\frac{3}{8}$-in. wires with Dorland anchorages for pre-tensioning are to be used. Allowable stresses are as follows.

	At Transfer	Under Working Load
Concrete:		
Compressive fiber	$f_b = 0.60f_{ci}' = 2400$	$f_t = 0.45f_c' = 2025$ psi
Tensile fiber	$f_t' = 0.06f_{ci}' = 240$	$f_b' = 0$
Principal tension		
without web steel		$s_t = 0.03f_c' = 135$ psi
Steel:		
Initial prestress	$f_i = 130{,}000$ psi	
Prestress just after		
transfer	$f_o = 120{,}000$ psi	
Effective prestress		$f_e = 110{,}000$ psi

(a) Make a preliminary design for the beam.

(b) Design the beam for flexure, and locate the profile for the c.g.s.

(c) Design the beam for shear, and provide necessary web reinforcement.

Solution.   (a) *Preliminary Design.*   For this tapered beam carrying a uniform load, the controlling section for flexure is not at midspan but is nearly at the third point. For $w_S = 520$ plf,

$$M_S = \frac{w_S L^2}{8} = \frac{520 \times 65^2}{8} = 274 \text{ k-ft}$$

The weight of the beam is estimated by an empirical formula

$$A_c = \frac{5M}{hf_c} = \frac{5 \times 274 \times 12}{40 \times 2.025} = 203 \text{ in.}^2$$

Hence, $w_G =$ about 220 plf. The total load on the beam is $520 + 220 = 740$ plf. Since the ratio of M_G/M_T is not too high, critical stresses may be found both at transfer and under the working load; hence an I-shape is considered economical. The moments at midspan and third points are, for span of 65 ft,

			Midspan	Third Points
$M_S = 520 \times 65^2/8$	=		274 k-ft $\times$ 8/9 = 244	
$M_G = 220 \times 65^2/8$	=		116 k-ft $\times$ 8/9 = 103	
M_T	=		390 k-ft	347 k-ft

The depth of beam at the third points is nearly 32 in. Using formulas 6-1 and 6-4, we have

$$F = \frac{M_T}{0.65h} = \frac{347 \times 12}{0.65 \times 32} = 200 \text{ k}$$

and

$$F = \frac{M_L}{0.50h} = \frac{244 \times 12}{0.50 \times 32} = 183 \text{ k}$$

Corresponding to $F = 200$ k and $f_c = 2025$ psi, we have, from formula 6-3

$$A_c = F/0.50f_c$$
$$= 200/(0.50 \times 2.025) = 198 \text{ sq in.}$$

A trial midspan section is sketched as in Fig. 16-5, with $A_c = 208$ sq in. at the third point. In order to maintain a uniform flange section throughout the entire length of the beam, a trial layout for the beam is now sketched as shown. The end 3 ft of the beam is made rectangular in section in order to distribute the stress at anchorage and to provide sufficient area for the end shear.

For a section 3 ft from the end of beam, the shear is

$$V_T = 740 \times 30 = 22,200 \text{ lb}$$

Neglecting the shear taken by steel, the maximum unit shear stress in concrete can be approximated by

$$v = 1.2 \frac{V}{A_{\text{web}}}$$

$$= 1.2 \frac{22,200}{4 \times 18.2} = 366 \text{ psi}$$

for a web 4 in. thick and a depth of beam = 18.2 in. Corresponding to a compressive fiber stress of about 600 psi, this would indicate a principal tension of

$$\sqrt{366^2 + 300^2} - 300 = 173 \text{ psi}$$

which is somewhat above the allowable value of 135 psi. Hence it seems desirable to thicken the web near the support. A gradual increase from

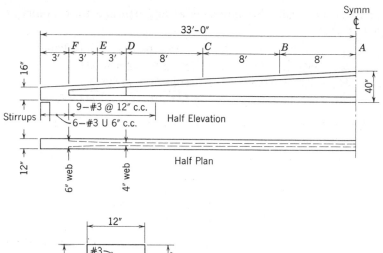

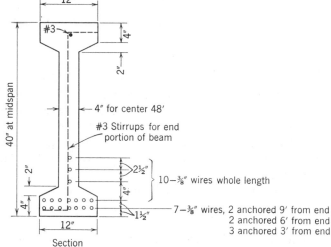

Fig. 16-5. Example 16-2.

4 in. to 6 in. within a distance of 6 ft is thus adopted as shown. This also increases the A_c near the ends so as to keep the flexural stress within limits.

(*b*) *Design for Flexure.* To provide for effective prestress of about 200 k, seventeen ⅜-in. wires will be used, furnishing total effective prestress

$$F = 17 \times 0.11 \times 110 = 206 \text{ k}$$

Although the initial prestress in the steel is 130 ksi, immediately after transfer, the creep in steel and the elastic shortening of concrete would have already taken place, and the steel stress at that time can be considered to be 120 ksi. Hence,

$$F_0 = 206 \times 120/110 = 225 \text{ k}$$

Now, again considering the section at 3 ft from end of beam, the A_c is 169 sq in., and the maximum compression can be as high as

$$(225/169) \times 2 = 2660 \text{ psi} = 2.66 \text{ ksi}$$

which is somewhat too high. It would be desirable to cut off bond between concrete and wires before they reach the ends. After some trial, it is decided to cut off 3 wires at F, 2 at E, and another 2 at D, Fig. 16-5.

In order to determine the location of the c.g.s., a procedure similar to that of example 8-3 is followed. Since both A_c and A_s vary along the beam, it will be convenient to tabulate the computations as shown.

Section	F		E		D		C	B	A
x, ft from center of support	2.5		5.5		8.5		16.5	24.5	32.5
h, in.	18.2		20.3		22.5		28.4	34.2	40.0
Web thickness, in.	12	6	5		4		4	4	4
A_c, in.^{2}	218	169	171		170		193	217	240
I, in.^{4}		5700	7700		10,000		18,800	30,500	46,000
r^2, in.^{2}		34	45		60		98	141	192
$k_t = k_b$, in.	3.0	3.8	4.4		5.4		6.9	8.2	9.6
No. of $\frac{3}{8}''$ wires	10	13	13	15	15	17	17	17	17
F_0 at 120 ksi	132	172	172	198	198	225	225	225	225
F at 110 ksi	121	158	158	182	182	206	206	206	206
M_T, k-ft	59		121		179		294	368	390
M_G, k-ft	17		36		53		87	109	116
M_T/F, in.	5.9	4.5	9.2	8.0	11.8	10.4	17.1	21.4	22.7
M_G/F_0, in.	1.5	1.2	2.5	2.2	3.2	2.8	4.6	5.8	6.2
$f_t'A_tk_b/F_0$, in. ($f_t' = 0.24$ ksi)	1.2	0.9	1.1	1.0	1.1	1.0	1.4	1.9	2.5
e_b, in.	1.7	0.9	2.2	1.4	2.3	1.4	2.1	2.2	1.8
$f_b = \dfrac{F_0}{A_c}\left(\dfrac{h}{c_t} - \dfrac{e_b}{k_t}\right) + 0.24$, ksi	1.11	2.03	1.74	2.19	2.08	2.54	2.29	2.04	1.94
e_t, in.	1.5	3.9	1.1	2.7	0.9	2.5	0.4	0.4	3.4
$f_t = \dfrac{F}{A_c}\left(\dfrac{h}{c_b} - \dfrac{e_t}{k_b}\right)$, ksi	0.83	0.91	1.62	1.48	1.96	1.86	2.07	1.85	1.42

Values from the table are plotted in Fig. 16-6, which shows a half profile of the beam. First, the kern points are plotted from the c.g.c.; then, from the respective kern lines, the values of M_T/F and $M_G/F_0 + f_t'A_ck_b/F_0$ are plotted to obtain the limiting zone for c.g.s. If the c.g.s. is located within this zone, there will be no tension in the bottom fiber under working load and the tension in the top fiber will be no greater than 240 psi at transfer.

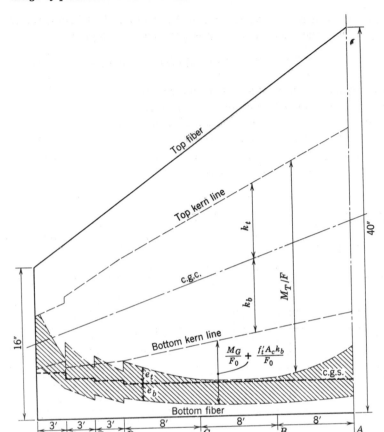

Fig. 16-6. Example 16-2. Location of c.g.s.

The actual location of c.g.s. is given by the heavy dotted line in Fig. 16-6, with the wires placed and cut off as indicated in Fig. 16-5. For this profile of c.g.s., the bottom compressive stress at transfer is

$$f_b = \frac{F_0}{A_c}\left(\frac{h}{c_t} - \frac{e_b}{k_t}\right) + 0.24$$

and the top fiber compressive stress under working load is

$$f_t = \frac{F}{A_c}\left(\frac{h}{c_b} - \frac{e_t}{k_b}\right)$$

where e_b and e_t are the distances of c.g.s. within the limiting zone measured from the bottom and top limits, respectively. These values of f_b and f_t are computed and listed in the table. It will be observed that the greatest compressive stress occurs at D at transfer; its magnitude of 2.54 ksi slightly exceeds that of the allowable of 2.40 ksi but is not considered serious. The greatest compressive stress under working load is 2.07 ksi, very close to the allowable of 2.03 ksi, and is considered satisfactory.

The percentage of reinforcement at D is

$$(17 \times 0.11)/170 = 1.1\%$$

which indicates that the beam is somewhat over-reinforced and compression failure in concrete may occur without too much elongation in the wires.

Actual test showed a live load deflection of $7\frac{1}{2}$ in. at rupture.

(*c*) *Design for Shear.* After a little investigation, it is seen that the critical section for shear is a 3 ft from the end of beam, where we have a 6-in. web and a shear of

$$30 \times 740 = 22,200 \text{ lb}$$

which is also very nearly the shear perpendicular to the c.g.c. line. The prestressing steel makes an angle of $1/33$ with the c.g.c. line and hence will carry some of the shear. The 10 wires at this section with a prestress of 121 k carry a shear of

$$121,000/33 = 4000 \text{ lb}$$

leaving $V_c = 22,200 - 4000 = 18,200$ lb to be carried by the concrete. The maximum shearing stress at the c.g.c. is

$$v = \frac{V_c Q}{Ib} = \frac{18,200(48 \times 7.1 + 6 \times 4.4 + 30.6 \times 2.55)}{5700 \times 6}$$

$$= 240 \text{ psi}$$

The compressive stress at this point is $121,000/169 = 716$ psi. Hence the principal tension is

$$\sqrt{240^2 + 358^2} - 358 = 72 \text{ psi}$$

Although this is well within the allowable of 135 psi, it is desirable to provide some web steel to increase the shear resistance of the beam. For the end 3 ft, $\frac{3}{8}$-in U-stirrups at 6-in. spacing are used to distribute the load, Fig. 16-5. For the next 9 ft, single stirrups at 12-in. spacing are employed. No stirrups are used for the remainder of the beam.

16-3 Design Example, Post-Tensioned Bridge Girder

This example illustrates the design of a precast post-tensioned girder for composite action in a highway bridge. It can be easily modified for pre-tensioning as may be desired.

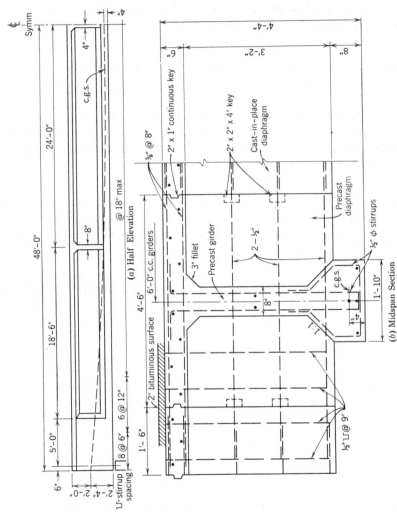

Fig. 16-7. Example 16-3. Girder layout.

Precast girders of a highway bridge are to be post-tensioned, grouted, then lifted to the bridge site to be connected together by concrete poured in place, Fig. 16-7. The two-lane bridge is to carry H20-S16-44 loading, and the girders are spaced 6 ft on centers. Overall length of girder is 96 ft, with 95 ft between centers of supports. Following the 1961 AASHO Specifications for Highway Bridges, (Appendix E) when applicable, design an interior girder as follows:

(*a*) Design the midspan section, indicating the required amount of prestressing steel.

(*b*) Design the end section, showing the mild-steel stirrups.

(*c*) Design a longitudinal layout of the girder showing the profile for c.g.s. and the intermediate and end diaphragms.

(*d*) Investigate the factor of safety of the girder at cracking and ultimate strengths.

(*e*) Compute the deflection of the girder at transfer and under the working load.

(*f*) Detail the midspan and the end sections using the Freyssinet system. Compute the loss of prestress due to friction and the initial prestress required at the jack.

Strength of concrete is to be 4500 psi at 28 days and 4000 psi at transfer.

The high-tensile steel used is to have a minimum ultimate tensile strength of 250,000 psi and a minimum yield point of 200,000 psi at 0.2% plastic set. The steel stress at transfer will be 160,000 psi, and the effective prestress at 25,000 psi loss (Appendix E) is 135,000 psi. $E_s = 28,000,000$ psi. $E_c = 4,000,000$ psi. Use intermediate-grade reinforcing bars for the mild-steel reinforcement.

Solution. (*a*) From Appendix A of the AASHO Specifications for Highway Bridges, the maximum moment for one lane of H20-S16-44 loading on a span of 95 ft is found to be 1433 k-ft. The proportion of lane load carried by an interior stringer can be approximated by the AASHO formula $S/10$ for interior stringers (Art. 1.3.1 of 1961 AASHO Specifications). Note that this formula is considered conservative for spans as long as 95 ft. For spacing $S = 6$ ft, the moment per girder is

$$LLM = 1433 \times 6/10 = 860 \text{ k-ft}$$

Impact on highway bridges is given by the formula

$$I = 50/(L + 125)$$
$$= 50/(95 + 125)$$
$$= 0.227$$

$$\text{Impact moment } IM = 860 \times 0.227 = 195 \text{ k-ft}$$
$$LLM + IM = 860 + 195 = 1055 \text{ k-ft}$$

Note the above value of maximum moment actually does not occur at midspan, but for all practical purposes it can be assumed to occur there.

After some preliminary design and trials, a section is assumed as in Fig. 16-7, from which

$$
\begin{aligned}
\text{Bituminous paving 2 in. at 150 pcf} &= 25 \text{ psf} \times 6 \text{ ft} = 150 \text{ plf} \\
\text{In-place concrete slab and diaphragms} &= 133 \text{ plf} \\
\text{Total added } DL &= \overline{283 \text{ plf}}
\end{aligned}
$$

Added DL moment $= (283 \times 95^2)/8 = 319$ k-ft
Weight of girder and diaphragms $= 940$ plf
Girder load moment $M_G = (940 \times 95^2)/8 = 1060$ k-ft
Total moment $M_T = 1055 + 319 + 1060 = 2434$ k-ft
The c.g.c. of the section, using the gross area, is as follows.

$$
\begin{aligned}
6 \times 54 = 324 \times 3 &= 972 \\
3 \times 3 = 9 \times 7 &= 63 \\
38 \times 8 = 304 \times 25 &= 7600 \\
7 \times 7 = 49 \times 41.67 &= 2040 \\
22 \times 8 = 176 \times 48 &= 8450 \\
\overline{862} \qquad \qquad \qquad 19{,}125 &\div 862 = 22.5 \text{ in.} = c_t \\
52 - 22.5 &= 29.5 \text{ in.} = c_b
\end{aligned}
$$

The moment of inertia of the concrete section about the c.g.c. is

$$
\begin{aligned}
324(6^2/12 + 19.5^2) &= 124{,}000 \\
9(3^2/18 + 15.5^2) &= 2{,}200 \\
304(38^2/12 + 2.5^2) &= 38{,}600 \\
49(7^2/18 + 19.17^2) &= 18{,}000 \\
176(8^2/12 + 25.5^2) &= 115{,}000 \\
\overline{297{,}800} &\div 862 = 345 = r^2
\end{aligned}
$$

$$
k_t = r^2/c_b = 345/29.5 = 11.7 \text{ in.}
$$
$$
k_b = r^2/c_t = 345/22.5 = 15.4 \text{ in.}
$$

Owing to the relatively large ratio of M_G/M_T, it is evident that the c.g.s. can be located as low as practicable without producing any tension in the top fiber. Assuming that the c.g.s. is located 4 in. above the bottom fiber, the total arm for the internal resisting moment is

$$
a = 11.7 + 29.5 - 4 = 37.2 \text{ in.}
$$

The total effective prestress required is

$$
F = M_T/a = (2434 \times 12)/37.2 = 786 \text{ k}
$$

For a loss of prestress at 15%, the initial prestress required will be

$$
F_0 = F/0.85 = 786/0.85 = 925 \text{ k}
$$

To limit the top fibers to a maximum stress of 1.8 ksi, we must have

$$A_c = \frac{Fh}{f_t c_b} = \frac{786 \times 52}{1.8 \times 29.5} = 770 \text{ in.}^2$$

To limit the bottom fibers to a maximum of 2.2 ksi, we must have

$$
\begin{aligned}
A_c &= \frac{F_0}{f_b}\left(1 + \frac{e - (M_G/F_0)}{k_t}\right) \\
&= \frac{925}{2.2}\left(1 + \frac{25.5 - 1060 \times 12/925}{11.7}\right) \\
&= 841 \text{ in.}^2
\end{aligned}
$$

The actual gross area furnished is 862 sq in., which seems to be just about sufficient for the required area of 841 in.². The top fibers will not be stressed to the allowable value, but the width and thickness of the top flange are governed by the slab requirements, which will not be discussed here. Also note that the in-place concrete will further reduce the stress in the top fibers, and may be included in the computation if desired. Hence the section is considered satisfactory and is adopted without further changes. Note that it generally takes two or three trials to arrive at this adopted section rather than just one trial as illustrated here.

To supply the effective prestress of 786 k at an allowable stress of 135 ksi, steel area required will be

$$786/135 = 5.83 \text{ in.}^2$$

(*b*) Shearing stresses can be checked for two sections, one at the support and another 5 ft from the support where the web is 8 in. thick. At the support, the web is 22 in. thick; shear is evidently not controlling. The shear at 5 ft from support is

LL shear, from AASHO Specifications	= 61.3 k/lane	
61.3 × 6/10	= 36.8 k/girder	
Impact shear = 0.227 × 36.8	= 8.4 k	
Bituminous paving and in-place concrete 0.283 × 42.5	= 12.0 k	
Girder own wt 0.940 × 42.5	= 40.0 k	
Total shear	97.2 k	

Shear V_s carried by the tendons at end of span, assuming a parabolic rise of $h = 2$ ft on a length of $L = 96$ ft, is given by

$$
\begin{aligned}
V_s &= 4Fh/L \\
&= (4 \times 786 \times 2)/96 \\
&= 65.5 \text{ k}
\end{aligned}
$$

At 5.5 ft from end of girder,

$$V_s = (42.5/48)65.5$$
$$= 58.0 \text{ k}$$

Hence V_c by concrete is

$$97.2 - 58.0 = 39.2 \text{ k}$$

Maximum shearing stress in concrete occurs at c.g.c. and is given by

$$v = V_c Q/Ib$$

Since Q, the statical moment of the area above the c.g.c. about it, is $(324 \times 19.5) + (9 \times 15.5) + (8 \times 16.5^2/2) = 7550$,

$$v = \frac{39{,}200 \times 7550}{297{,}800 \times 8} = 124 \text{ psi}$$

The compressive fiber stress at c.g.c. is given by F/A_c

$$f_c = F/A_c$$
$$= 786{,}000/862$$
$$= 912 \text{ psi}$$

The principal tensile stress is

$$S_t = \sqrt{v^2 + (f_c/2)^2} - f_c/2$$
$$= \sqrt{124^2 + 456^2} - 456$$
$$= 20 \text{ psi}$$

The moment is relatively small at this section of maximum shear; hence the fiber stress is nearly uniform throughout the depth of the section, and the maximum principal tensile stress at the c.g.c. represents rather closely the greatest tensile stress. This maximum principal tension does not exceed the allowable value of $0.03f_c' = 0.03 \times 4500 = 135$ psi. Hence no stirrups are required under the working load. To investigate the ultimate strength for shear, from AASHO Specification, we have ultimate shear

$$V' = 1.5D + 2.5(L + I)$$
$$= 1.5 \times 52.0 + 2.5 \times 45.2$$
$$= 191 \text{ k}$$

Shear carried by the tendons can be conservatively approximated by $V_s = 58.0$ k. Hence,

$$V_u = V' - V_s' = 191 - 58 = 133 \text{ k}$$

Shear carried by the concrete V_c can be approximated by

$$V_c = vbjd$$

where v can be assumed at 90 psi, $b = 8$ in., $j = 0.87$, and assuming $d = h = 52$ in.,

$$V_c = 90 \times 9 \times 0.87 \times 52 \div 1000 = 36.6 \text{ k}$$

The stirrup area required for $f_y' = 40$ ksi is

$$A_v = \frac{(V_u - V_c)s}{2f_y'jd}$$

$$= \frac{(133 - 36.6)s}{2 \times 40 \times 0.87 \times 52}$$

$$= 0.0266s \text{ in.}^2$$

Using $\frac{1}{2}$ in. U-stirrups with $A_v = 0.40$ in.², the permissible spacing is

$$s = 0.40/0.0266 = 15 \text{ in.}$$

Similar computation can be made for other points along the girder. So far as shear alone is concerned, more stirrups are required near the ends than along the middle portion of the girder, but the reverse is true when considering the effect of combined moment and shear. Hence judgment should be exercised in the actual spacing of the stirrups.

Again, AASHO Specifications require a minimum of web reinforcement

$$A_v = 0.0025b's$$

For $b' = 8$ in. and $A_v = 0.40$ in.², we have

$$s = \frac{0.40}{0.0025 \times 8} = 20 \text{ in.}$$

indicating that the spacing of $\frac{1}{2}$-in. U-stirrups shall not exceed 20 in. (Note that the 1963 ACI Code has different requirements.)

For the end section, stirrups are required to distribute the anchorage stresses. Since the anchorages are to be fairly uniformly distributed, the computed tensile stresses in the anchorage zone will be low and analysis is not required. Nominal stirrups, however, are provided as shown on Fig. 16-7.

(c) A half elevation of the girder is shown in Fig. 16-7. The midspan section is adopted for the entire girder, except the 5 ft near the ends where a uniform web thickness equal to the bottom flange width of 22 in. is used in order to accommodate the end anchorages, to permit the curving up of some tendons, and to distribute the prestress. Three intermediate diaphragms are placed along the length of the span. Sometimes transverse prestressing is employed to bind the girders together. But, for this design. transverse dowels are provided in these diaphragms to be joined together by in-place concrete. In either case, the theoretical calculation for the steel in these diaphragms can be a complicated problem. But the amount of steel is not excessive for these girders; some nominal reinforcement is employed as shown.

The most common location of c.g.s. for a simple beam is a parabola with c.g.s. near the c.g.c. at the ends. Such a profile will give ample moment resistance along the entire beam. If the c.g.s. is above the c.g.c. at the ends, the tendons will carry greater shear but lose some of the reserve moment resistance. If the c.g.s. is below the c.g.c. at the ends, the tendons will carry less shear, but the positive prestressing moment at the ends will tend to decrease the principal tension. Also note that the c.g.c.'s for the midspan and the end sections actually differ slightly. For this design, the c.g.s. will be placed a little below the c.g.c. of the end section.

(d) The cracking moment is computed as follows. The resisting moment up to zero stress in the bottom fiber is given by

$$Fa = 786 \times 37.2/12 = 2434 \text{ k-ft}$$

Assuming the modulus of rupture at bottom fiber to be $0.14 f_c' = 0.14 \times 4500 = 630$ psi, the additional resisting moment from zero stress to 630 psi is

$$M = fI/c_b = \frac{630 \times 297{,}800}{12{,}000 \times 29.5}$$

$$= 530 \text{ k-ft}$$

Total resisting moment at cracking is

$$M_{cr} = 2434 + 530 = 2964 \text{ k-ft}$$

Overall factor of safety against cracking is

$$2964/2434 = 1.22$$

Factor of safety for live load and impact is

$$\frac{M_{cr} - (M_G + DLM)}{LLM + IM} = \frac{2964 - (1060 + 319)}{1055} = 1.50$$

which indicates that the girder will begin to crack only when the live load plus impact is increased by as much as 50%.

The ultimate resisting moment will be computed by the procedure used in section 5-6, as follows.

Assuming the ultimate strength of steel to be developed, the ultimate tensile force is

$$f_s' A_s = 250 \times 5.83 = 1460 \text{ k}$$

Assuming an average stress in concrete of $0.85f_c' = 0.85 \times 4500 = 3.82$ ksi, the total concrete area under compression is

$$1460/3.82 = 382 \text{ in.}^2$$

Neglecting the in-place concrete, the ultimate neutral axis can be located at about 9 in. below the top fiber. Thus the distance from the ultimate neutral axis to the c.g.s. is about 39 in., indicating that, at rupture of the girder, the steel is stressed to very near its ultimate strength. The centroid of the 382 in.² of concrete is located at

$$(324 \times 3 + 9 \times 7 + 49 \times 9.0)/382 = 3.8 \text{ in.}$$

below top fiber, and the ultimate lever arm is

$$52 - 4 - 3.8 = 44.2 \text{ in.}$$

Hence the ultimate moment is

$$1460 \times 44.2/12 = 5360 \text{ k-ft}$$

If computed by the AASHO Specifications formulas, the ultimate moment will be somewhat smaller than 5360 k-ft. However, the ultimate moment capacity required by the AASHO Specifications is only

$$1.5D + 2.5(L + I) = 1.5 \times 1379 + 2.5 \times 1055$$
$$= 4706 \text{ k-ft}$$

Hence the ultimate strength is considered sufficient.

(e) Referring to Fig. 16-8, it is seen that the deflection due to the initial prestress of 925 k can be computed as due to a uniform moment of $M_1 = 116$ k-ft for the whole length of the beam plus a parabolic moment with $M_2 = 1850$ k-ft at midspan. Downward deflection due to M_G is given by a parabolic moment with 1060 k-ft at midspan. Thus the instantaneous upward deflection due to prestress is given by

$$\frac{M_1L^2}{8EI} + \frac{5M_2L^2}{48EI} = \left(\frac{116}{8} + \frac{5 \times 1850}{48}\right)\frac{96^2 \times 12^2 \times 12,000}{4,000,000 \times 297,800}$$
$$= 2.78 \text{ in.}$$

To simplify the numerical work, gross I for the concrete is used for all computations. Owing to the loss of prestress, this deflection will reduce to

$$0.85 \times 2.78 = 2.36 \text{ in.}$$

Downward deflection due to M_G is

$$\frac{5M_GL^2}{48EI} = \left(\frac{5 \times 1060}{48}\right)\frac{96^2 \times 12^2 \times 12,000}{4,000,000 \times 297,800}$$
$$= 1.47 \text{ in.}$$

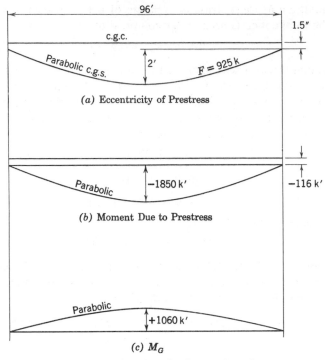

(a) Eccentricity of Prestress

(b) Moment Due to Prestress

(c) M_G

Fig. 16-8. Example 16-3. Deflection computation.

Hence the immediate upward deflection of the girder at transfer will be

$$2.78 - 1.47 = 1.31 \text{ in.}$$

The added dead load will produce a downward deflection of

$$(319/1060) \times 1.47 = 0.44 \text{ in.}$$

Not considering the composite action of in-place concrete, the eventual upward deflection will be decreased by the effect of loss of prestress, but increased by the creep effect of concrete. Assuming creep coefficient of 2 for the period considered, we have the resultant upward deflection after loss of prestress

$$(2.36 - 1.47 - 0.44)2 = 0.90 \text{ in.}$$

The instantaneous downward deflection due to the design live load and impact, assuming parabolic moment diagram, is

$$(1055/1060)1.47 = 1.46 \text{ in.}$$

(*f*) The above design will be applicable to most prestressing systems now used in this country, although minor modifications may be desirable for certain cases. For purpose of illustration, detailed arrangement of the tendons will be shown for the Freyssinet system, as in Fig. 16-9. Using cables of eighteen 0.196-in. wires, 11 tendons are required (see Appendix B). They will supply a steel area of 5.97 in.² which is more than the 5.83 in.² required in part (*a*) of this solution. The midspan and end sections are drawn showing the arrangement of tendons to give the required locations of c.g.s. Curving of the tendons in both horizontal and vertical planes is necessary to conform with the required location of c.g.s. It is noted that some deviation from the required parabola is permissible, because it will not affect the strength of the girder. A recommended order for tensioning the cables is indicated as shown.

Loss for the anchorage slip in Freyssinet cones may be assumed to average 0.2 in., which, if averaged throughout the entire length of 96 ft, indicates a loss of prestress equal to

$$[0.2/(96 \times 12)] \times 28,000,000 = 4900 \text{ psi}$$

To estimate the frictional loss, let us assume a coefficient of friction = 0.35 for Freyssinet cables in metal sheathing and a $K = 0.0010$ per ft for wobble effect. The average change in direction for the cables is given by $8 \times 2/96 = 0.167$ radian, for a parabolic rise of 2 ft in a span of 96 ft. Hence the maximum frictional loss at the far end, if tensioned only from one end, can be computed as

$$u\theta + KL = 0.35 \times 0.167 + 0.0010 \times 96$$
$$= 0.058 + 0.096$$
$$= 15.4\%$$

The controlling point is the midspan which has a loss equal to half of $15.4\% = 7.7\%$. 7.7% of 160,000 = 12,300 psi. If the tendons are over-tensioned by 12,300 psi at the anchorages, the anchorage loss of 4900 psi

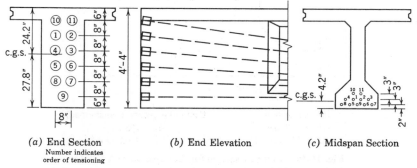

(*a*) End Section
Number indicates
order of tensioning

(*b*) End Elevation

(*c*) Midspan Section

Fig. 16-9. Example 16-3. Cable location for Freyssinet system.

will automatically be balanced. Using the Freyssinet jack, there is an additional loss at the jack of about 8000 psi. Hence the maximum initial stress at the jack should be

$$160,000 + 12,300 + 8000 = 180,300 \text{ psi}$$

According to AASHO Specifications this temporary jacking stress should not exceed $0.80f_s' = 0.80 \times 250,000 = 200,000$ psi. The effective prestress should not exceed $0.60f_s' = 0.6 \times 250,000 = 150,000$ psi, or $0.80f_y' = 0.8 \times 200,000 = 160,000$ psi. Hence the stress in the steel is considered safe under all conditions. In fact, the tendons can be more highly stressed so as to reduce the required steel area if desired.

Note: It is suggested that the reader try to rework this example using some of the following possible modifications:

(1) For comparison in detailing, try the Freyssinet system, but using tendons with either twelve 0.276 in. wires or with twelve ½-in. 7-wire-strands.

(2) For comparison of post-tensioning systems, try the Roebling, the BBRV, or the Prescon system (Appendix B) instead of the Freyssinet system.

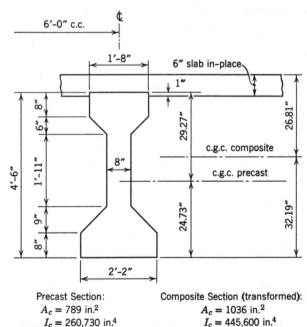

Precast Section:
$A_c = 789$ in.^{2}
$I_c = 260,730$ in.^{4}

Composite Section (transformed):
$A_c = 1036$ in.^{2}
$I_c = 445,600$ in.^{4}

Fig. 16-10. Alternate section for Example 16-3 (AASHO-PCI type IV I-beam).

(3) For comparison of different girder sections and the use of pretensioning instead of post-tensioning, try the AASHO Type IV I-girder (section 6-9) spaced at 6-ft centers with a 6-in. poured in-place slab. A section of this girder together with its properties are shown in Fig. 16-10. The composite section properties are computed for slab concrete with $f_c' = 3000$ psi and girder concrete with $f_c' = 5000$ psi, using a transformed section considering $3000/5000 = 0.6$ of the slab area. Also note that for these pre-tensioned sections, no end blocks are used with the girder, but additional mild steel is added as described in section 7-8. A continuous end block is usually poured after the girders are in place. Seven-wire strands of $\frac{7}{16}$-in. or $\frac{1}{2}$-in. size are commonly used in the United States for girders of this size. To approximate a parabola, try 2-point harping for these pre-tensioned strands.

16-4 Design Example, Precast Rigid Frame—Preliminary Design

A one-story rigid-frame building is to be made up of precast 90-ft girders and precast columns. The frames are spaced 20 ft centers to be roofed with concrete slab, post-tensioned in place with unbonded wires, Fig. 16-11. The girders are pre-tensioned with 7-wire strands to carry their own weight and are then post-tensioned with bonded or unbonded wires to balance the added weight of the in-place concrete slab. The columns are post-tensioned with high-tensile rods to form rigid frames with the girders. It is intended to obtain a water-tight concrete roof without additional roofing. Live load $= 50$ psf. Use lightweight concrete at 110 pcf; $f_c' = 5000$ psi; $f_{ci}' = 3500$ psi for girders and columns; $f_c' = 4000$ psi, and $f_{ci}' = 3000$ psi for the slab. For both pre-tensioning strands and post-tensioning wires, $f_s' = 250,000$ psi, $f_i = 175,000$ psi, and $f_e = 145,000$ psi. For high-tensile rods, $f_s' = 160,000$ psi, $f_i = 112,000$ psi, and $f_e = 96,000$ psi. Use intermediate grade steel for reinforcing bars. Design a typical interior bay for the building as follows:

(*a*) Make a preliminary design for the slab, including amount of prestress and cable profile.

(*b*) Make a preliminary design for a girder, including its pre-tensioning and post-tensioning.

(*c*) Make a preliminary design of a column for its post-tensioning.

(*d*) Discuss various considerations and procedure required for the final design of this typical bay.

Solution. (*a*) *Preliminary Design for Slab.* To achieve economy, a minimum slab thickness will be chosen consistent with fire-resistant and rigidity requirements. For a continuous one-way slab of lightweight

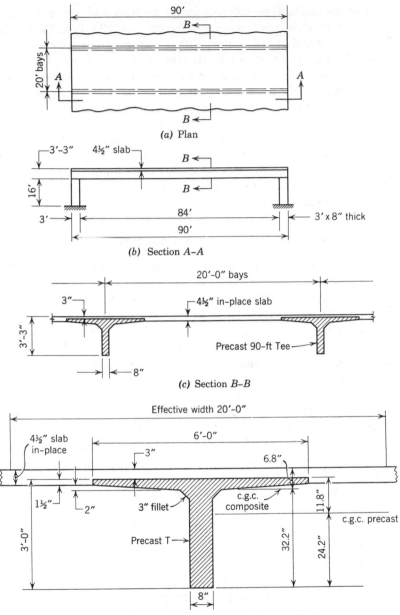

(a) Plan

(b) Section A–A

(c) Section B–B

(d) Precast and Composite T-Section

Fig. 16-11.

concrete, a limiting depth/span ratio is $\frac{1}{52}$ for roof and $\frac{1}{48}$ for floor (see section 8-5). Since the specified live load of 50 psf could indicate possible future use of the slab as a floor or for parking purposes, it will be well to keep within the $\frac{1}{48}$ ratio. Thus the minimum thickness for 20-ft span is

$$20 \times \tfrac{12}{48} = 5 \text{ in.}$$

Since the slab thickness near the girder web is 2 in. thicker, Fig. 16-11(*d*), using 4.5 in. for the central portion of the slab is considered sufficient.

As a preliminary design, we may assume that it is intended to balance the weight of the slab on an interior continuous span of 20 ft, using optimum location for the c.g.s. This will be on the safe side, since the actual clear span is less than 20 ft and since the haunch of the slab is neglected. Assuming the tendons to be $\frac{3}{4}$-in. in diameter and to require a minimum concrete protection of $\frac{3}{4}$-in., we have a midspan sag of the cable $h = 2.25$ in., Fig. 16-12. For weight of the slab $w = 110 \times 4.5/12 = 41.2$ psf, effective prestress required per ft width of slab to balance its weight is, referring to Sections 11-2 and 11-3,

$$F_e = \frac{wL^2}{8h}$$

$$= \frac{41.2 \times 20^2}{8 \times 2.25/12}$$

$$= 11,000 \text{ lb/ft width of slab}$$

which would indicate an average prestress of

$$11,000/(4.5 \times 12) = 204 \text{ psi}$$

This value of 204 psi may not be sufficient to produce a watertight slab, since experience indicates that a value of 250 psi compression is often necessary. For an average prestress of 250 psi, the required total effective prestress per foot-width of slab is

$$250 \times 4.5 \times 12 = 13,500 \text{ lb/ft}$$

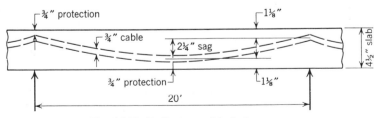

Fig. 16-12. Preliminary slab design.

This will be good for the end spans where the sag is smaller. For the interior spans, this prestress will result in a slight camber if the sag of 2.25 in. is maintained. Hence it may be desirable to modify the cable profile after a more exact final analysis, taking into account the effect of clear span and slab haunches, actual cable profile, cable friction, etc.

Solution. (*b*) *Preliminary Design for Girder.* The choice of the girder shape will depend on the local availability of forms. The single tee is chosen here partly because of its economy for this type of construction (saving of some slab forming and the provision of haunches for the slab) and partly for its convenience in accommodating the curved and bent tendons within the relatively thick web. For rigidity requirements, the depth of the section should have a minimum of $\frac{1}{32}$ span (Section 8-5), or

$$84 \times \tfrac{12}{32} = 31.4 \text{ in.}$$

It is generally economical to employ a girder depth greater than the minimum, since the additional web concrete is quite nominal, while the saving in prestress is appreciable. On the other hand, deeper girder does mean a higher building and all the added costs. For this example, it is assumed that a 36-in. tee form is available and is chosen also to get better rigidity and shear resistance. A total depth of 39 in. is thus obtained for the composite girder.

Section properties for the precast single tee are given:

$$c_b = 24.2 \text{ in.}$$
$$A_c = 457 \text{ in.}^2$$
$$I_c = 61,000 \text{ in.}^4$$
$$w_G = 457 \times \tfrac{110}{144} = 348 \text{ plf}$$

For clear span of 84 ft, the maximum moment at midspan is

$$M_G = \frac{w_G L^2}{8} = \frac{348 \times 84^2}{8} = 308,000 \text{ ft-lb}$$

Assuming 4-in. concrete cover to the c.g.s. at midspan and uniform stress distribution with center of compression at c.g.c., we have a lever arm of $c_b - 4 = 24.2 - 4 = 20.2$ in., and the amount of prestress required is

$$F_e = \frac{M_G}{a} = \frac{308,000}{20.2/12}$$
$$= 183,000 \text{ lb}$$

Using $\frac{1}{2}$-in. 7-wire strands with $A_s = 0.1438$ in.^{2} and $F_e = 0.1438 \times 145,000 = 20,800$ lb per strand, we need $183,000/20,800 = 8.8$ strands. Assuming that 10 strands be used for the final design, the corresponding

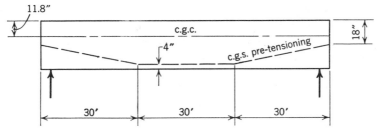

Fig. 16-13. Preliminary location of c.g.s. for girder pre-
tensioning.

camber should be calculated. For a long span like this, two-point harping
may be desirable, in order to more closely approximate a parabola. The
location of c.g.s. at the ends of a girder should preferably be below the
c.g.c. and above the bottom kern. A tentative profile for c.g.s. is thus
chosen as shown, Fig. 16-13, with or without the help of a limiting zone
diagram (section 8-3). This profile may be modified after analyzing for
camber and stress conditions at various controlling points, such as the
harping points and the ends of span. However, detailed calculations may
not be necessary, since the location of the C-line is not too far from the
c.g.c. at all points along the girder. Ultimate strength of the girder need
not be analyzed at this stage, since the pre-tensioning is designed essentially
to produce a more or less level girder for transporting and erecting.

After the girders are erected onto the columns, they will be shored
underneath at two or three points. The shoring may be just snug under
the soffit to prevent deflection of the girder under the added load of the
slab; they also may be propped slightly so that composite action may be
obtained for part of the girder weight. Calculations should be made to
determine the stress and camber conditions at various stages, if propping
is employed.

Post-tensioning of the girders will be designed to essentially balance the

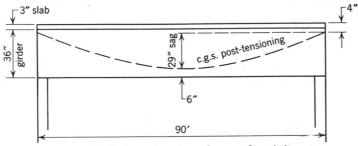

Fig. 16-14. Preliminary location of c.g.s. for girder post-
tensioning.

weight of the in-place slab. Maximum sag will be obtained for the parabolic c.g.s., Fig. 16-14, in order to minimize the amount of post-tensioning
force. Assuming 4 in. from the top of slab to the center of end anchorage,
and 6 in. from the bottom of girder to c.g.s. of tendons, we have a sag of

$$39 - 6 - 4 = 29 \text{ in.}$$

The weight of slab to be balanced by post-tensioning has a cross-sectional area of

$$(240 \times 4.5) - (72 \times 1.5) = 972 \text{ in.}^2$$

and a weight of $972 \times \frac{110}{144} = 743$ plf, producing a maximum simple beam
moment of

$$\frac{wL^2}{8} = \frac{743 \times 84^2}{8} = 655,000 \text{ ft-lb}$$

which requires an effective prestress of

$$F_e = \frac{M}{a} = \frac{655,000}{29/12} = 271,000 \text{ lb}$$

or a steel area of

$$A_s = \frac{F_e}{f_e} = \frac{271,000}{145,000} = 1.87 \text{ in.}^2$$

If $\frac{1}{4}$-in. wires are used, the total number of wires required will be

$$1.87/0.05 = 38 \text{ wires}$$

For example, the Prescon or the BBRV system of 2 cables at $20 - \frac{1}{4}$-in.
wires per cable would likely be right. This will produce an average compressive prestress of

$$40 \times 0.05 \times 145,000/1429 = 203 \text{ psi}$$

in the slab and will increase the average compression in the girder by
the same amount (1429 in.^{2} = total concrete area per bay).

In order to determine section properties for the composite section, the
slab concrete area may be reduced to obtain an equivalent area of girder
concrete. Since the ratio of f_c' of slab to f_c' of girder is 0.80, and since
the slab concrete will not be as old as the girder concrete at time of post-
tensioning, it may be assumed that E_c for the slab is 80% of the E_c for the
girder. The section properties for the composite section are listed below:

$$\text{Actual concrete area} = 972 + 457 \qquad = 1429 \text{ in.}^2$$
$$\text{Equivalent area } A_c = 972 \times 0.80 + 457 = 1236 \text{ in.}^2$$
$$c_b \text{ for equivalent area} \qquad\qquad = 32.2 \text{ in.}$$
$$I_c \text{ for equivalent area} \qquad\qquad = 108,700 \text{ in.}^4$$

This indicates that the post-tensioning c.g.s. at ends of girder is above the c.g.c. of the composite section by

$$6.8 - 4 = 2.8 \text{ in.}$$

Thus the post-tensioning will place an end moment on the frame girder with a 2.8-in. eccentricity, which must be balanced by an eccentric prestress in the columns, as will be discussed in the next section. Note that it is also possible to lower the c.g.s. at the ends of the girder to the c.g.c. of the composite section so that the column may be concentrically prestressed, or mild steel bars may be placed at the corners to obtain rigid frame action with no post-tensioning in the columns.

Solution. (c) *Preliminary Design for Column—Prestress.* The size of the column 3 ft × 8 in., is chosen to give sufficient rigidity to the frame and to increase its ultimate strength. The prestress in the column serves two purposes: to balance the eccentric moment on the girder ends from its post-tensioning cables, and to create rigid connection between column girder so as to carry the negative live-load moment. For this latter purpose, the live-load moment may be computed for the rigid frame as follows.

For tributary area of 90 × 20 = 1800 sq ft, the design live load of 50 psf may be reduced to 25 psf when designing for the rigid frame. Thus we have 25 × 20 = 500 plf of girder. Using moment distribution, Fig. 16-15, we have

$$\text{Fixed end moment} = \frac{wL^2}{12} = \frac{500 \times 84^2}{12} = 294,000 \text{ ft-lb}$$

and the relative stiffnesses are,

$$\text{Girder } I/L = 108,700/(84 \times 12) = 108$$

$$\text{Column } I/L = (8 \times 36^3)/(12)(16 \times 12) = 162$$

For symmetrical loading, girder I/L can be modified by one-half to enable one-step moment distribution, giving the resulting corner moment as

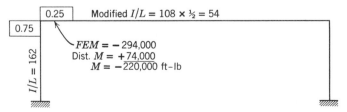

Fig. 16-15. Moment distribution for live load.

220,000 ft-lb. Part of this moment can be resisted by permitting some tension in the concrete, say 300 psi, giving a resisting moment of

$$M = \frac{fI}{c} = \frac{fbd^2}{6} = 300 \times 8 \times \frac{36^2}{6} = 518,000 \text{ in.-lb}$$

$$= 43,200 \text{ ft-lb}$$

with $220,000 - 43,200 = 176,800$ ft-lb. to be carried by post-tensioning, with a lever arm equal to the kern distance of 12 in. (column width = 3 ft). Hence the amount of post-tensioning required is

$$176,800/1 = 176,800 \text{ lb}$$

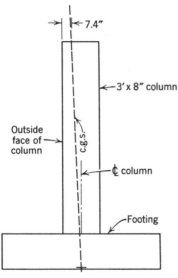

Fig. 16-16. Column prestress.

To further balance the eccentric moment from the girder of

$$(40 \times 0.05 \times 145,000) \times 2.8$$
$$= 812,000 \text{ in.-lb}$$

the c.g.s. of tendons in the column can be placed outside the kern by

$$812,000/176,800 = 4.6 \text{ in.}$$

or $12 - 4.6 = 7.4$ in. within the outer edge, Fig. 16-16. The location of the c.g.s. along the column will depend on the shrinkage and of the roof and other considerations, and will not be discussed here.

To produce the required effective prestress of 176,800 lb and to simplify construction, two high-tensile rods 1-$\frac{1}{8}$ in. diameter can be used, with $A_s = 0.994$ in.² per rod, at a stress of 96,000 psi; total prestress supplied is

$$2 \times 0.994 \times 96,000 = 190,800 \text{ lb}$$

Solution. (*d*) *Procedure for Final Design.* Solution (*c*) presents only the preliminary design for the typical bay insofar as prestressing is concerned. It should indicate the feasibility and the economy of the design and should establish sufficient dimensioning and prestressing so that we can now proceed with a final design. The final design should include the following steps.

1. Review of the slab design for stress conditions under design live load for ultimate strength with plastic-hinge action. Addition of mild

steel if required. Computation of frictional loss and establishing sequence of construction and tensioning. Consideration of actual slab profile and haunches for the slabs. Special case for the end span.

2. Review of the girder design for stress conditions at various sections under design live load. Actual location of the cable profile after choosing a suitable system. Choice of bonded or unbonded tendons. Check for shear resistance and design for stirrups. Check for loss of prestress due to shrinkage, creep, and friction. Check for ultimate strength and the addition of mild steel bars if required.

3. Final design for the column reinforcement. Detailing for the rigid joints between girder and column. Check for shear, moment, and direct stress in columns. Camber in girder resulting from eccentric prestressing of columns.

4. Check for the effects of shrinkage and creep on the frame moments. Estimate the effect of temperature on camber and deflections.

16-5 Design Example, Continuous Bridge with Precast Beams

This example describes a four-span highway bridge using precast pre-tensioned beams made continuous for live load by placing reinforcing steel in the slab over the piers. Figure 16-17 shows this East 12th Street Underpass located in Travis County, Texas. The design and construction supervision of this bridge were performed by the Texas Highway Department. Completed in 1961, the itemized contract cost of this bridge is given in Table 16-2. The solution given here represents only the essential part of the prestressed design and is not intended to cover the design of

Fig. 16-17. East 12th Street Underpass, Travis County, Texas. (Design and construction supervision by Texas Highway Dept.)

TABLE 16-2

Contract cost for Bridge in Example 16-5

	Bid Unit	Super-structure	3-Bents	2-Abut-Bents	Total	Bid Price	Total Price
Struct. Excav.	C.Y.			58	58	5.00	$290.00
Drilled Shaft							
(30″ Dia.)	L.F.		96	24	120	11.50	1,380.00
Conc. (Bent)	C.Y.		108.8	82.0	190.8	43.00	8,204.40
Conc. (Slab)	C.Y.	385.0			385.0	42.00	16,170.00
Prestr. Conc. Bm.	L.F.	1800.5			1,800.5	11.50	20,705.75
Riprap	C.Y.			200	200	30.00	6000.00
Reinf. Steel	Lbs.	103,121	18,644	10,520	132,285	0.095	12,567.08
Struct. Steel	Lbs.	2432			2,432	0.14	340.48
Railing	L.F.	396.5			396.5	9.00	3,568.50
Rigid Metal							
Conduit (2″)	L.F.	470.0			470.0	1.65	775.50
						Total	$70,001.71

$346.54/linear ft of bridge
$4.70/sq ft of bridge

the entire bridge. An elevation and half section of the bridge are shown in Fig. 16-18.

Solution.

Loading—AASHO loading H2O-44.

Specifications—*AASHO Specifications for Highway Bridges*, 1957, ed., except that prestressed design is essentially based on 1961 AASHO Specifications as reproduced in Appendix E.

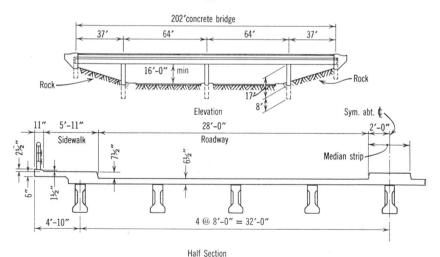

Half Section

Fig. 16-18. Elevation and section for bridge in Fig. 16-17.

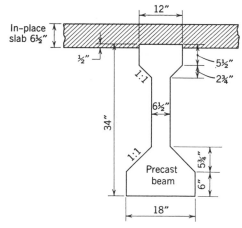

Fig. 16-19. Texas Standard Type-B beam.

Precast Beams—Use Texas Standard Type B, Fig. 16-19, with properties as follows:

$A_c = 361$ in.^{2}

$I_c = 43,300$ in.^{4}

$c_t = 19.1$ in.; $c_b = 14.9$ in.

$k_t = \dfrac{43,300}{361 \times 14.9} = 8.1$ in.

$k_b = 6.3$ in.

Prestressing Steel—$\frac{7}{16}$-in. 7-wire strands with $A_s = 0.1089$ in.^{2} per strand, $f_i = 175,000$ psi, $f_e = 140,000$ psi, $f_s' = 250,000$ psi.

Precast Concrete—$f_{ci}' = 5000$ psi; $f_c' = 6000$ psi.

In-Place Slab Concrete—$f_c' = 3000$ psi.

Composite Section—For beams spaced 8-ft c.c., properties of the composite section are computed, Fig. 16-20. Corresponding to $f_c' = 3000$ psi for the slab and 6000 psi for the beam, and referring to Fig. 2-2, the slab can be approximately transformed by a factor of $\frac{2}{3}$.

$A_c = 361 + \frac{2}{3}(620) = 775$ in.^{2}

$I_c = 137,000$ in.^{4}

$c_t = 13.5$ in.; $c_b = 26.5$ in.

Reinforcing Steel—intermediate grade $f_y = 40,000$ psi.

Construction Sequence—Pre-tensioned beams erected without shoring, slab concrete placed first over midspans and then over piers. All dead load carried by simple beam action, while $LL + I$ will act on a continuous structure having top steel in slabs over the piers.

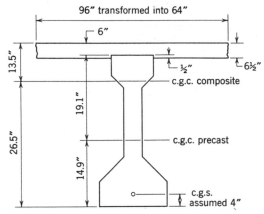

Fig. 16-20. Composite section.

Dead-Load Moments—For typical interior beam use simple span c.c. beam supports of 62.75 ft; beam weight = 377 plf; 6½-in. slab 8-ft wide, wt = 650 plf of beam.

$$M_G = 0.377 \times 62.75^2/8 = 186 \text{ k-ft}$$

$$M_S = 0.650 \times 62.75^2/8 = 320 \text{ k-ft}$$

Live-Load Moments—Maximum $+M$ and $-M$ on this 4-span continuous beam are computed, using 37-ft and 64-ft spans with uniform

TABLE 16-3

Maximum *LL* moment per lane, k-ft

	$+M$ near Midspan of 37' Span	$+M$ near Midspan of 64' Span	$-M$ over Outer Pier	$-M$ over Center Pier
Lane load	251	364	373	445
Truck load	273	374	243	199

moment of inertia. This is first done for the lane loading of 640 plf plus one concentrated load of 18,000 lb for $+M$ and two such concentrated loads for $-M$. Then it is done for one H20-44 truck having two concentrated loads of 32,000 lb and 8000 lb spaced at 14-ft c.c. These moments are tabulated above, with controlling moments for design underlined. It is noted that the truck load produces bigger $+M$ while the lane load produces bigger $-M$. Computation for these moments follow usual methods for structural analysis and will not be shown here.

Impact factors are:

37-ft span—for $+M$, $\dfrac{50}{125 + 37} = 30\%$

for $-M$, $\dfrac{50}{125 + 50.5} = 28\%$

64-ft span—for both $+M$ and $-M$,

$$\dfrac{50}{125 + 64} = 26\%$$

Since beams are spaced 8-ft c.c., each beam carries 0.8 lane (AASHO Code) and the $LL + I$ moment per beam is

37-ft span— $+M = 273 \times 0.8 \times 1.30 = 284$ k-ft

64-ft span— $+M = 374 \times 0.8 \times 1.28 = 384$ k-ft

Outer pier— $-M = 373 \times 0.8 \times 1.26 = 379$ k-ft

Center pier— $-M = 445 \times 0.8 \times 1.26 = 452$ k-ft

Design of Prestress.   Now we will design the prestress for the 64-ft span as follows: $M_G = 186$ k-ft; $M_s = 320$ k-ft; hence total moment for precast portion $M_P = 186 + 320 = 506$ k-ft. $LL + I$ moment on composite section is $M_C = 384$ k-ft, which can be reduced to an equivalent moment on the precast section by the method explained in section 6-7, using a factor m_b for the bottom fiber:

$$m_b = \frac{I/c_b}{I'/c_b'} = \frac{43{,}300/14.9}{137{,}000/26.5} = \frac{2910}{5150} = 0.565$$

Using equation (6-21a) for allowable bottom fiber tensile stress $= 0$,

$$F = \frac{M_P + m_b M_C}{e + k_t}$$

$$= \frac{(506 + 0.565 \times 384)12}{10.9 + 8.1} = 456 \text{ k}$$

for eccentricity of prestress assumed at 10.9 in. (c.g.s. located at 4 in. above bottom fiber), and $k_t = 8.1$ in. for precast section. Readers may check to find out that about 19% more prestress would be required if the beam were not made continuous for live load.

This indicates that we may employ 30 strands of $\frac{7}{16}$-in. with prestress at 15.2 k per strand, or total $F = 456$ k; $F_0 = \frac{175}{140} 456 = 570$ k. The top

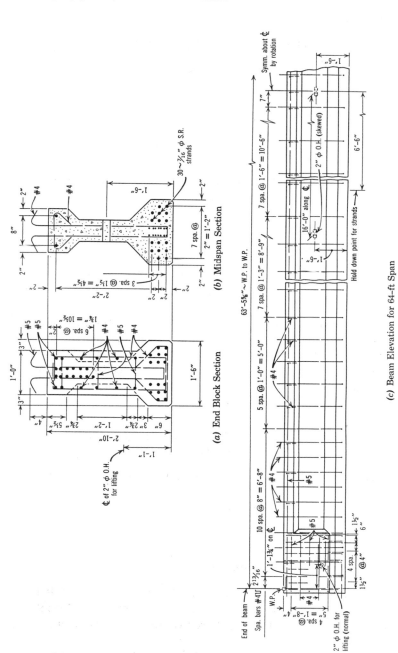

(a) End Block Section

(b) Midspan Section

(c) Beam Elevation for 64-ft Span

Fig. 16-21. Typical beam details for 64-ft spans.

and bottom fiber stress at transfer can be checked by eq. 6-22 as follows:

$$f_t = \frac{F_0}{A_c} - \frac{F_0 e - M_G}{A_c k_b}$$

$$= \frac{-570}{361} - \frac{-570 \times 10.9 + 186 \times 12}{361 \times 6.3}$$

$$= -1.58 + 1.75 = +0.17 \text{ ksi tension,}$$

$$f_b = \frac{F_0}{A_e} + \frac{F_0 e - M_G}{A_c k_t}$$

$$= \frac{-570}{361} + \frac{-570 \times 10.9 + 186 \times 12}{361 \times 8.1}$$

$$= -1.58 - 1.36 = -2.94 \text{ ksi compression}$$

which requires $f_{ci}' = 5000$ psi, with an allowable stress of $0.60 f_{ci}' = 3$ ksi at transfer.

A trial arrangement for the 30 strands at midspan can now be made, as shown in Fig. 16-21(a) and the actual eccentricity computed. In order to limit the transfer stresses at the ends of the beam, to reduce the beam bottom compressive stress over the piers, and to minimize the camber of the beam, some of the strands should be harped to a higher position at the ends. An arrangement is shown in Fig. 16-21(b). An elevation of the beam is shown in Fig. 16-21(c).

The 37-ft spans are made of the same beam section, but fewer strands are required, Fig. 16-22. Calculation for these will not be given here. It is noted that the new AASHO specifications will not require end blocks

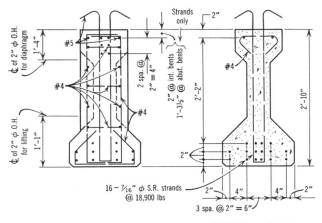

(a) End Block Section   (b) Midspan Section

Fig. 16-22. Typical beam sections for 37-ft spans.

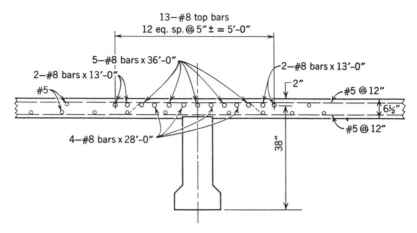

Fig. 16-23. Arrangement of reinforcing bars over center pier.

for pre-tensioned beams. An extensive series of tests carried out by the Portland Cement Association of Chicago[1] indicated that plastic behavior of concrete would actually permit much higher compressive stresses in this region.

Reinforcing Steel over Piers—To provide for the $-M$ over piers, we have for the center pier, $-M = 452$ k-ft. Although this $-M$ is computed by the elastic theory it can best be designed to meet ultimate strength requirements with the specified minimum load factors,

$$1.5D + 2.5(L + I)$$

Applying the usual formula for reinforced concrete design,

$$A_s = \frac{M}{f_y j d}$$

$$= \frac{2.5 \times 452 \times 12}{40 \times 0.875 \times 38} = 10.2 \text{ in.}^2$$

assuming a yield point stress of 40,000 psi, $j = 0.875$, and $d = 38$ in.

Use thirteen No. 8 bars of varying length with $A_s = 10.2$ in.² and arrange them as shown in Fig. 16-23. Details of end bearings using neoprene pads are shown in Fig. 16-24.

Ultimate Load Capacity. *Ultimate Load Capacity of a 64-ft Span.* By limit design theory, the ultimate load capacity of a 64-ft beam can be computed assuming three plastic hinges, one at midspan and two at the ends.

Ultimate moment capacity of hinge at end of span, using Whitney's method, is

$$A_s f_y = 10.2 \times 40 = 408 \text{ k}$$

$$k'd = \frac{A_s f_y}{0.85 f_c' b} = \frac{408}{0.85 \times 6 \times 18} = 4.4 \text{ in.}$$

where $f_c' = 6$ ksi used, neglecting compression due to the strands.

$$M' = A_s f_y (d - k'd/2) = 408 \times (38 - 2.2)/12$$
$$= 1210 \text{ k-ft}$$

Ultimate moment capacity of hinge at midspan:

$$A_s f_{su} = 3.27 \times 250 \text{ ksi} = 816 \text{ k}$$

assuming $f_{su} = 250$ ksi (note that a lower value of f_{su} will be obtained by formula in Section 1.13.10 of ASSHO Specifications, Appendix E).

$$k'd = \frac{816}{0.85 \times 3 \times 96} = 3.4 \text{ in.}$$

$$M' = \frac{816(36 - 3.4/2)}{12} = 2330 \text{ k-ft}$$

Total resisting moment = $1210 + 2330 = 3540$ k-ft. For dead load moment at 506 k-ft (using 62.75 ft span), capacity for $LL = 3540 - 506 = 3034$ k-ft. From AASHO Specifications, moment table for H20-44, lane moment = 616 k-ft on a 64-ft span. For 0.8 lane load and 28 % impact, moment per beam = 630 k-ft. Load factor provided for $LL + I$ is,

$$3034/630 = 4.82.$$

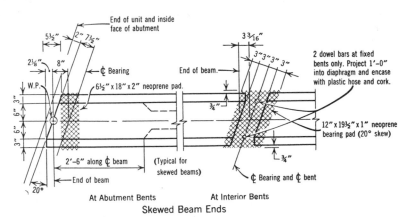

Fig. 16-24. End bearing details.

Note that at the failure of one beam, much more load will be carried by the adjacent beams, hence the use of 0.8 lane for beams at 8-ft spacing is too conservative. The bridge as a whole has 9 beams capable of carrying $9 \times 0.8 = 7.2$ lane loads, whereas the bridge actually accommodates only 4 lanes. Hence an additional load factor is obtained, thus raising the real live-load factor to

$$\frac{7.2}{4}(4.82) = 8.66$$

which is indeed a very high factor and indicates that this bridge has plenty of reserve strength.

To make a complete design for this bridge would require the following additional items:

1. Check for the stresses at the supports and other points along the beam.

2. Design the stirrups to meet beam shear and end block stress requirements, also design for bond between beam and slab.

3. Computation of camber and deflection at various stages.

4. Positive moments over supports produced by live load away from adjacent spans.

5. Checking of exterior beams, considering effect of sidewalks and loadings; checking of center beam considering the effect of medium strip.

6. Design of end bearings, roadway slab, bents, foundations, railings, and other details.

Reference

1 "Precast-Prestressed Concrete Bridges," Journal of the PCA Research and Development Laboratories (in 6 parts), May 1960, September 1960, January 1961, May 1961, and September 1961 issues; also published as PCA Development Department Bulletins *D34, D35, D43, D45, D46*, and *D51*.

design criteria; codes and specifications

17

17-1 Design Criteria—Deflection, Stress, Strength

As discussed in Section 11-1 there are three approaches to the design of prestressed concrete, one based on deflection, one based on stresses, and a third based on strength. These are known as the balanced-load method, the allowable-stress method and the ultimate-strength method, respectively.

According to the balanced-load method, a chosen amount of loading is balanced by prestressing so that no bending exists under this condition. Frequently, the dead load is fully balanced. But, when live load is small, some portion of the dead load may be left unbalanced; and when the live load is heavy, part of it must be balanced together with the dead load. Safety in the structure so designed is provided on the knowledge that anticipated variation of loadings from the balanced condition will not produce undesirable effects.

According to the allowable-stress method, a normally maximum service load is specified as the design load, the elastic theory is generally applied in the computation of stresses, and a set of allowable values is set up as the maximum limits. In following such a procedure, a margin of safety is provided almost entirely in the allowable stresses, the choice of whose values determines the degree of safety of the structure and its ability to carry overloads.

According to the ultimate-strength method, allowable stresses are ignored. Instead, the ultimate or rupture strength of the members is obtained and often expressed in semiempirical formulas. Then the specified service load is multiplied by a load factor and equated to the ultimate strength of the member. Here, the margin of safety is provided almost entirely in the load factors.

All three methods of design can be applied to prestressed-concrete structures, while only the last two methods are applied to other types. Because of the peculiar nature of prestressed concrete, wherein stress may not be a correct representation of safety and strength is not often the controlling factor, deflection and camber become the main criterion. When the balanced-load approach is used for design, it will usually be necessary to study the behavior of the structure under its working load, as well as its ultimate strength. The effect of repeated loads and of high local stresses must also be investigated for some structures.

Because of our engineers' familiarity with both the working-stress and the ultimate-strength methods of design, it has been the practice to adopt either of these approaches, rather than the balanced-load approach. As pointed out in section 11-1, by suitable choice of the amount of load to be balanced, of the allowable stresses for design load, or of the load factors for ultimate design, we can arrive at similar dimensioning of a structure. For engineers not familiar with prestressed concrete, whichever method is used for design, checking by the other two is highly desirable. With the accumulation of experience, the relation between the three methods of design will become better known, and then the application of any one method will often suffice, and checking by the other methods may become unnecessary.

17-2   Design Loadings and Methods of Computation

The conventional methods of elastic stress design and of ultimate strength design are often unrealistic because the specified design live load is not well related to the actual live load. For example, highway bridges in this country are designed on the basis of the H-loadings, but the actual heavy vehicles over the highways are known to exceed these loadings greatly. The bridges are safe because the allowable stresses used in design are sufficiently low, and the assumptions for load distribution are very conservative.[1] In buildings for human occupancy, the actual live load is often far below the specified values. Dead load on a structure, on the other hand, is often very realistic, and thus becomes a more significant criterion for design, especially when the effect of creep is considered. Since it is beyond the scope of this treatise to discuss the design loadings for various structures, it will be assumed that the present specified loadings for bridges and buildings are acceptable for the design of prestressed-concrete structures. Such an acceptance does not necessarily signify the approval of these loadings presently in use, but it will permit prestressed-concrete structures to be designed on the same basis as other types of construction as far as loadings are concerned.

The method of computation used in obtaining the stresses is another important consideration. For ordinary types of construction, such as steel or reinforced concrete, methods of computation are well understood and standardized. Even though most of these methods do not yield the actual stresses in structures, proper application will usually result in satisfactory dimensions. For example, the actual stresses in structural rivets are seldom the same as those indicated by the design formulas; the elastic theory in reinforced concrete only occasionally gives correct stresses. Yet, by following such accepted methods of computation, together with the specified loadings and allowable stresses, engineers have designed and built thousands of structures without too many failures. Similarly, in prestressed concrete, methods of computation for simple structures are well known and accepted and can be applied in a routine manner. For complicated structures, no standardized method is available for computation, and care must be exercised in their design.

17-3 Choice of Values

A simple initial approach to the establishment of proper allowable stresses and load factors for prestressed concrete is to compare them with those for reinforced concrete. Generally speaking, there is enough similarity between the two types of construction so that one can be conveniently discussed in terms of the other. Yet, specifically, the two types differ in so many respects that it is dangerous to pattern one exactly after the other.

The specific features of prestressed concrete, as distinguished from reinforced concrete, have been discussed elsewhere in this treatise. Their effect on the values of allowable stresses and load factors will now be summarized:

1. Use of high-strength materials highly stressed. Both high-strength concrete and steel are less ductile than their counterparts in reinforced concrete. Under high stresses, fatigue-resisting properties differ from those at low stresses, elastic and creep strains become more significant, and the Poisson's ratio effect is more pronounced.

2. Effect of prestress on bending. When the design load is exceeded in a prestressed-concrete beam, the neutral axis of the beam shifts appreciably upward as the bending moment is further increased. This shifting of the neutral axis decreases the compressive area of concrete on the one hand but lengthens the lever arm of the tensile steel on the other. Hence, both the compressive stress in the concrete and the tensile stress in the steel are not directly proportional to the external moment, as they are in reinforced concrete.

3. Effect of prestress on shear and principal tension. Shear in reinforced concrete is used as a direct measure of diagonal tension. In prestressed

concrete, diagonal tension is greatly reduced by precompression, and the principal tensile plane is shifted to a more nearly horizontal position. The principal tensile stress in prestressed concrete is much smaller than the diagonal tension in reinforced concrete, but it increases rapidly as the amount of shear or of moment is increased at the section.

4. Effect of prestress on direct compression. As stated in section 14-1, column action in a prestressed member generally is not accentuated by the prestressing force. The resultant compressive stress in prestressed columns is not directly proportional to the external load. For example, when the external load is doubled, the resultant compressive stress is less than doubled, because the compression due to prestress is not increased but somewhat decreased.

5. Bond and bearing stresses. The conditions of bond and bearing stresses at end anchorage in prestressed concrete are not met with in reinforced concrete.

6. Girder load effect. Whereas dead and live loads in a reinforced-concrete beam have similar effects in producing compressive stress in the top fibers, dead load on a prestressed beam applied before the transfer of prestress can be made to result in zero compressive stress or even tensile stress in the top fibers. Although this is an advantage in prestressed concrete from an economic point of view, it renders the compressive fiber stress in prestressed beams more sensitive to the increase of live load.

Because of these differences, allowable stresses and load factors for prestressed concrete cannot be directly based on those for reinforced concrete. They must be chosen with regard to the basic considerations which underlie the choice of such values. These considerations are:

1. The ratio of overloads to design loads. Since it is the practice to design the service loads for the allowable stresses, overloads are to be carried at stresses exceeding the allowable values. Hence the allowable stresses must be determined with respect to the ratio of overloads to design loads. Load factor must be chosen so that the actual overloads will not impair the serviceability of the structure.

2. Frequency and magnitude of repeated loads. Allowable stresses and load factors must be chosen so as to avoid failures under repeated loads.

3. Variation in the properties of materials. Materials having greater variation should be given lower values of allowable stresses and perhaps higher values of load factors.

4. Inaccuracies in design methods and formulas. Whenever the accuracy of the methods and formulas is in doubt, a greater margin of safety will be needed.

5. Variations in the dimensions of materials and possibilities of deterioration. Allowances should differ for different structures.

6. Seriousness and suddenness of failure. Brittle failures are usually given a greater margin of safety. Main members and important structures are also accorded greater safety.

7. Secondary effects. Allowable stresses are sometimes kept sufficiently low to avoid undesirable secondary effects, such as excessive creep and undesirable vibrations.

8. Economics of proportioning. Where safety can be obtained at relatively low cost, it is usually more liberally provided.

Some of these factors can be analyzed quantitatively; others do not lend themselves to mathematical treatment. Hence the choice of proper values for allowable stresses and load factors often can be based only on good and experienced judgment.

It is not a simple matter to assign a value to an allowable stress or load factor. These values vary with:

1. Types of structures. Allowable stresses and load factors may differ for different types of structures (as is presently true for bridges and buildings). The probability of overloads, the repetition of loadings, the possibilities of deterioration, and the requirement for water-tightness differ for different types.

2. Grades of materials. In prestressed concrete, different kinds of reinforcement are employed, including high-tensile wires, strands, and alloy bars. There may be several grades in each of these types. The materials may differ in ductility, creep, and fatigue characteristics. Concrete may have strength varying from 3000 to perhaps 10,000 psi. Beams may be built of blocks cemented by grout or mortar. All these may call for a variety of values for allowable stresses and load factors.

3. Methods of construction. It is known, for example, that under similar conditions a bonded prestressed beam usually has a higher ultimate strength than the unbonded one; post-tensioned members have smaller loss of prestress than pre-tensioned members; precast, cast-in-place, and composite construction may possess different strengths. To be consistent, different values should be assigned for each case.

4. Stages of loading. Load factors and allowable stresses may differ for different stages of loading. For example, at jacking, stresses in steel are rather definite, and there is little danger of overstress; hence a small margin of safety will be sufficient.

A comprehensive set of values must include all the possible variations just described. However, for practical reasons, only a comparatively simple set is provided in codes and specifications. Hence these specified values must always be taken with a grain of salt.

17-4 Codes and Specifications

In England a First Report on Prestressed Concrete[2] was published by the Institution of Structural Engineers in 1951 and "The Structural Use of Prestressed Concrete in Buildings"[3] was adopted as a British standard code of practice in 1959. A circular giving provisional instructions concerning prestressed concrete[4] was published by the French Ministry of Public Works in 1953. Belgium issued her Instructions on Prestressed Concrete[5] in 1954. Germany, under the leadership of Dr. Rusch, revised their tentative code seven times and finally formulated it into a German Standard[6] as early as 1953. Russia formalized its code on prestressed concrete in 1957.

In the United States the Bureau of Public Roads issued its Criteria for Prestressed Concrete Bridges[7] in 1954. The Joint Committee of ACI-ASCE published its Tentative Recommendations for Prestressed Concrete[8] in 1958. The Prestressed Concrete Institute issued its specifications for pretensioned prestressed concrete in 1957 and for post-tensioned prestressed concrete in 1958. A Tentative Building Code for Prestressed Concrete[9] was issued by the PCI in 1959, with a formalized version printed in 1961. Based on recommendations from the California Structural Engineers' Association, the Uniform Building Code[10] included prestressed concrete in its 1961 edition. The 1963 ACI Code[11] includes a set of requirements concerning prestressed concrete, which will be essentially identical with the PCI Code of 1961 (Appendix D). The AASHO Standard Specifications for Highway Bridges[12] has a section on prestressed concrete based on the ACI-ASCE Tentative Recommendations.[8]

For a relatively new material and technique such as prestressed concrete, progress and changes are apt to come faster than usual. Codes and specifications can easily become out-of-date and not apply. Good engineers should utilize the latest findings and make necessary deviations from specified values when justified with knowledge and experience.

17-5 Allowable Stresses for Concrete

Allowable stresses for prestressed concrete have been specified on a more or less empirical basis. Although considerations have been given to stress conditions, strength requirements, as well as the effects of cracking and creep, judgment and tradition prevail in their determination. Fortunately, the usual allowable stresses coupled with the usual design loads and the so-called recognized methods of computation will generally yield fairly satisfactory results. It is therefore wise for a beginner to follow these rules. When unusual structures are being designed or when more refinement and economy is needed, deviations are often necessary. Some of the common allowable stresses will now be discussed.

Extreme Fiber Compressive Stress. At jacking or at transfer of prestress the amount of prestress is rather accurately known, there is little likelihood of excessive loading, and there is no danger of fatigue; hence a relatively high stress is permissible. Most codes set $0.60f_c'$ as the maximum allowable compressive stress. Here the stress is not controlled by the consideration of overload capacities but rather by the possibility of excessive creep, camber, or other local strains. So far as strength and safety are concerned, values as high as $1.00f_c'$ may not result in failure.[14]

When considering the structure under service loads, there is a possibility of fatigue effect and occasional excessive overloads; hence lower values must be allowed. Generally $0.40f_c'$ for bridges and $0.45f_c'$ for buildings are the maximum. Higher values can be justified only after careful investigations of fatigue and ultimate strength. The value of f_c' is usually based on the 28-day strength but may occasionally be based on the strength of concrete at the time of service if such strength can be assured. Depending on the shape of the section, the above allowable value will usually yield a factor of safety of about 2.5 to 3, which is ample. Occasionally, a factor of safety of only about 2 is atttained, which seems inadequate for concrete except where overloads and repeated loadings are not at all likely.

Axial Compressive Stress. As explained in Chaper 14, axial compressive stress is produced by two sources: prestress and external load. Compressive stress produced by prestress decreases as the external load is increased; that produced by external load generally increases faster than the load, on account of bending or buckling. The different nature of these two types of compressive stresses, must be recognized when specifying allowable stresses for prestressed columns. In most cases, a column should be checked for its strength and behavior, rather than just for its stresses.

Bearing Stress. Depending on the type of anchorage and the methods of stress analysis, allowable bearing stress at the anchorage has been accorded widely different values. Most conventional methods of analysis yield only fictitious stresses; hence the allowable values must be varied accordingly. Moreover, the strength of concrete in local bearing depends greatly upon the surrounding conditions; for example, a confined high bearing stress may not be harmful at all. Hence, in general, allowable bearing values are rather high—in fact, so high that more failures in prestressed concrete have occurred in bearing under prestress than any other type of failure. Fortunately, such failures, generally resulting from poor concrete, are noticeable during prestressing, so that means may be immediately taken to remedy the situation in order to ensure safety under service.

For direct bearing under anchorage plates, a value of $0.60f_c'$ is often permitted. This is much higher than that allowed for support bearing in reinforced concrete, but it is justified by the fact that the bearing load comes only from the prestressing steel, and there is no need for providing a greater margin of safety than that given the force in the steel. Since the usual allowable prestress in steel is $0.60f_s'$, the allowable bearing stress in concrete can be as high as $0.60f_c'$. In fact, there is little likelihood of any serious increase in the bearing force on the concrete at the anchorage, even if the load on the beam is greatly augmented. This is especially true for bonded beams.

Bearing stress at places other than the anchorage is similar to that for reinforced concrete, and little reason can be found to allow different values, although it is known that the usual allowable bearing stress for concrete is quite conservative.

Extreme Fiber Tensile Stress. The average modulus of rupture for high-strength concrete is about $0.12f_c'$. Hence an allowable tensile fiber stress such as $0.05f_c'$ is considered to be on the safe side, especially for the stress at transfer when no overload is expected. Actually, the allowable tension at transfer should vary with many factors, such as the shape of section, the amount of nonprestressed reinforcement, and the possibility of overload.[14] Under service, structures may be subjected to overloads resulting in cracking of concrete, and objections have been raised as to whether any tensile stress should be allowed in designing, since the concrete would have cracked and would not be able to carry any tension. Actually, whether the concrete has cracked or not has little to do with allowable tensile stress. Consider reinforced concrete, for example. Under the design load concrete always cracks on the tensile side, which means that tensile stress is always allowed in design, although it is neglected in the analysis. If the same criterion is applied to prestressed concrete, high tensile stress can also be allowed provided that it is neglected in the analysis. However, allowing too high a tensile stress in a prestressed beam would tend to lower the ultimate strength of the beam and to increase its deflection under overloads. Also, cracking in prestressed concrete may expose the wires to corrosion and subject them to possible fatigue failures. When proper behavior and safety can be assured, high tensile stresses up to and beyond cracking can be permitted in prestressed as in reinforced concrete.

Axial Tensile Stress. The actual direct tensile strength of concrete varies widely, say from $0.06f_c'$ to $0.10f_c'$. For computing cracking load under direct tension, a value of $0.06f_c'$ is recommended by the German code. This appears to be a reasonable value, assuming that the member has not been previously cracked. When designing tension members, some residual compression under design loads is often necessary in order to provide a sufficient margin of safety against cracking unless an appreciable amount of nonprestressed steel has been provided. It is considered best not to specify any allowable direct tensile stress. Instead, the member should be designed for its ultimate or serviceable strength with a proper load factor.

Principal Tensile Stress. Comparing the allowable principal tensile stress in prestressed concrete to the allowable diagonal tension in reinforced concrete, a value of $0.03f_c'$ seems to be reasonable. It is generally assumed that, if the principal tension under working load does not exceed that allowable value, no web reinforcement is theoretically needed, although some nominal stirrups are often provided. Since the principal tension in a prestressed beam increases rapidly with the increase of the external shear and moment, and since the flexural cracking of concrete will affect its shear resistance, it is believed that ultimate strength would be a better basis for the shear design of structures subject to heavy overloads.

17-6 Allowable Stresses for Steel

Allowable stresses for steel are expressed as a percentage of either the ultimate strength f_s' or the yield point f_y; sometimes they are expressed in terms of both, and the smaller value thus obtained is used as the allowable. During tensioning and immediately after, the yield point f_y is often a more significant value, because it is an indication of the creep and elastic limits, tensioning near or beyond which might produce excessive creep and plastic deformations. At that same stage, the ultimate strength f_s' is important only as an indication of the existing safety against breakage of the steel. Current allowable value for steel stress during jacking is about $0.70f_s'$. In order to overcome frictional loss, a temporary jacking stress of $0.80f_s'$ is often permitted.

The allowable stress for design loads is determined by two conditions. First, it is limited by the allowable stress at jacking which, after deducting all losses, becomes automatically the design stress. Hence, often the design stress is not specified but is computed from the stress at transfer by deducting all the losses. There is a second condition, however, which often constitutes a good reason for specifying an upper limit for the design stress. The ratio of the ultimate strength of a member to its design strength is lowered when the design stress is raised in the steel. This explains why some authorities prefer to set a maximum allowable stress for design in addition to one for the stress at transfer. Furthermore, allowance must be made for the possibility of fatigue and creep effects, which may be more serious at higher stresses. This is another reason for limiting the design stress to a certain level.

The above general discussion has not included possible differentiation between bonded and unbonded reinforcement, since the two types of construction possess different ultimate strengths. Again, for new materials which possess widely different elastic and strength properties from those currently in use, allowable stresses must be necessarily modified. It is more important that the designer understand the basis for fixing the allowable values so that he can exercise his judgment when encountering new situations.

The design of nonprestressed reinforcement can hardly be performed by the allowable stress method since the steel is often in compression under the design load. However, elastic design is sometimes carried out on the assumption that the tensile stress block in concrete is carried by the steel acting at $0.50f_y$ (e.g., at 20,000 psi for immediate grade steel bars). Although incorrect, the thinking is that the steel will bridge over the cracks at that stress. The German code calls for design on the ultimate strength basis, using the yield point of mild steel as the maximum stress developed at rupture. The design for nonprestressed high-tensile wires must also be based on the ultimate strength method, keeping in mind that such wires will not appreciably increase the cracking strength of the members.

17-7 Load Factors

Load factors are dimensionless values by which the working load must be multiplied in order to be equated to the ultimate strength of a member under design. Instead of using the ultimate strength, the cracking strength is sometimes employed; it should then be stated that the factor is for the cracking strength. Cracking strength is important only for liquid containers, tension members, or structures subject to fatigue loading and corrosion. For most other cases, safety is related to the ultimate rather than the cracking strength.

The various bases for the choice of load factors have been discussed in section 17-3. The most important item is the ratio of the maximum overload to the design or working load. But, since a structure is rendered unserviceable long before its total rupture, it is evident that the maximum possible overload cannot be equated to the ultimate strength but only to the maximum usable strength. Hence load factors can be expressed as a product of two ratios:

$$\frac{\text{Maximum possible load}}{\text{Working load}} \times \frac{\text{Ultimate strength}}{\text{Maximum usable strength}}$$

In addition, they must be chosen so that, in general, no excessive stresses or deflections or fatigue failures will occur under the working load. This is desirable in order that structures designed by the ultimate-strength method will not need serious revisions when checked for stresses, deflections, and fatigue effects.

When specified for the total load, load factors generally range between 1.8 for buildings to 2.0 for bridges. They may also vary depending on the mode of failure, for example, higher factors are desirable for such brittle failures as shear or compression. The 1963 ACI Code specifies an under-strength factor to be applied to each ultimate-strength formula, while lower load factors are applied to the design loadings.[11]

Since the chance of overloading is higher for live load L than for dead load D, different factors are employed. For buildings, $(1.2D + 2.4L)$ is often specified for ultimate design; for bridges, $(1.5D + 2.5L)$. When wind or earthquake load W is considered, together with live and dead load, a lower factor will be considered sufficient, such as $1.4(D + L + W)$. When dead load produces stresses opposite to the live load, it is sometimes suggested that only a portion of the dead load be considered effective.

Similar to allowable stresses, load factors have been specified on an empirical basis. In general, they work quite well, but they are not sacred values and should be subject to modification as the conditions may require.

References

1 T. Y. Lin, "Load Factors for Prestressed Concrete Bridges," *Journal of Structural Division (Proc. ASCE)*, July 1957, Paper 1315.

2 *First Report on Prestressed Concrete*, Institution of Structural Engineers, London, England, 1951.

3 "The Structural Use of Prestressed Concrete in Buildings," *British Standard Code of Practice*, CP 115, 1959, British Standards Assn., London, England.

4 *Instructions provisoires relatives à l'emploi du béton précontraint*, Ministère des Travaux Publiques, des Transports et du Tourisme, France, Circulaire 141, October 1953.

5 *Instructions relatives au béton précontraint*, Bureau de contrôle pour la sécurité de la construction en Belgique, 1954.

6 H. Ruesch, *Design Specifications for Structural Members in Prestressed Concrete*, 7th Draft, Cement and Concrete Assn., London, England, 1950. The original German edition revised and made the national standard DIN 4227, July 1953.

7 *Criteria for Prestressed Concrete Bridges*, Bureau of Public Roads, Superintendent of Documents, Washington, D.C., 1954.

8 "Tentative Recommendations for Prestressed Concrete," *ACI-ASCE Joint Committee 323, J. Am. Conc. Inst.*, January 1958, pp. 545–578.

9 *Prestressed Concrete Building Code Requirements*, Prestressed Concrete Institute, 1961 (reproduced in Appendix D).

10 *Uniform Building Code*, International Conference of Building Officials, 1961, Vol. III, pp. 274–279.

11   Proposed Revision of Building Code Requirements for Reinforced Concrete, ACI Committee 318, *J. Am. Conc. Inst.*, February 1962, pp. 253–263; also see Amendments in December 1962 issue. to above, Jl. ACI Dec., 1962.

12   *Standard Specifications for Highway Bridges*, Am. Assn. of State Highway Officials, 1961, pp. 126–134 (reproduced in Appendix E).

13   T. Y. Lin, "Allowable Stresses and Load Factors for Prestressed Concrete," *Proc. Western Conference on Prestressed Concrete*, University of California, Los Angeles, 1952.

14   A. C. Scordelis, T. Y. Lin, and H. R. May, "Flexural Strength of Prestressed Concrete Beams at Transfer," *Proc. World Conference on Prestressed Concrete*, San Francisco, 1957.

15   T. Y. Lin, "Load Factors in Ultimate Design of Reinforced Concrete," *J. Am. Conc. Inst.*, June 1952 (*Proc.*, Vol. 48), pp. 881–900.

special topics

18

18-1 Fire Resistance

One approach to evaluate the fire resistance of prestressed concrete is to compare it with that of reinforced concrete, whose fire-resistance characteristics are well known. Basically, concrete is a good insulating material and serves to protect the steel. It is therefore possible to study the thermal properties of concrete,[1] the temperature-strength relations for the steel, and to correlate them for predicting the fire resistance of the combination.

Concrete used in prestressed work is often mechanically compacted, dense in texture, subjected to higher compressive stresses, and possesses higher strength. Questions have been raised as to whether such concrete is a better conductor of heat, whether it easily results in spalling, and whether it rapidly loses its strength at high temperatures. From the many fire tests conducted on prestressed concrete, it can now be stated that the answer is negative to all these questions.

The sensitivity of high-tensile steel to temperature can be compared with that of mild steel bars. Results of some tests on the strength of high-tensile wires and strands[1] under high temperature show that, up to about 300°F, there is a slight increase in strength, which begins to drop from there on down to a value of about 50% at 750°F. Since in general there is a factor of safety of 2 in our designs and since the ultimate strength of a prestressed member in bending is proportional to the ultimate strength of steel, that limit of 750°F in the steel may be considered as the point of impending failure, provided that full live load is on the structure.

The strength of structural reinforcing bars at 550°F is about 25% higher than at normal temperature. At 800°F its strength is about the same as at normal temperature, but it drops sharply after that, losing about half its strength at 1200°F. Since the failure of reinforced-concrete members under flexure usually starts at the yield point of steel, it is more important to determine the variation of the yield point with high temperature than the variation of the ultimate strength. Data in this country seem to indicate that the yield point of mild steel is about halved at 1000°F, whereas French tests have indicated that the limit is halved at about 750°F.

The residual strength of prestressing steels, after heating and then cooling, depends on the temperature to which they have been heated, whereas the strength of conventional reinforcing bars remains almost unchanged, even after heating to 1200°F. If prestressing steel is cooled from 850°F, its residual strength is about 80 to 90 % of its original value, and the higher the temperature the greater the strength reduction.

The fact that high-tensile steel is more sensitive to heat does not necessarily mean that prestressed-concrete members are less fire resistant, because the resistance of the member will depend on the thickness of protection afforded by the concrete. Whereas all steel bars for most reinforced work are placed near the surface of concrete with the minimum permissible protection, steel tendons for prestressed concrete are distributed along the depth so that, while the exterior layer may be subjected to high temperature, other layers may be only slightly heated and may still possess sufficient strength to prevent collapse. Hence the fire resistance of prestressed members, while basically similar to that of reinforced concrete, needs to be evaluated, taking other factors into account.

To determine the fire resistance of an element of any type of construction, Standard Fire Test E119 is specified by the ASTM. This fire test is conducted according to a prescribed procedure which covers all details such as size of specimen, loading conditions, edge or end restraint, deflections, and observation of furnace temperatures. Most important of all, a standard time-temperature curve is required to be reproduced in the furnace, rising very rapidly to 1399°F at 15 minutes and thereafter more gradually to 2000°F at 4 hours. This standard fire may not represent an actual fire, since the actual exposure of an element in an actual fire will depend on a number of factors, including kind and amount of combustibles in the area, availability of enough oxygen to support combustion, and the promptness of the response of the fire department. However, it is generally agreed that the ASTM standard fire test is a more or less equitable means for evaluating fire resistance of various types of construction. It represents a rather severe fire even for a small area. Over a large area, such an intense fire does not frequently occur.

Many tests on the fire resistance of prestressed concrete have been carried through, both in the United States and elsewhere.[3,4,5] In the United States many tests have been conducted at the Underwriters' Laboratories in Northbrook, Illinois; the Portland Cement Association Laboratories in Skokie, Illinois; the National Bureau of Standards in Washington,

D.C.; and the Fire Prevention Research Institute in Gardena, California.

Up to 1961, about 35 individual beams mostly 20-ft long, but a few up to 40-ft long, as well as about 19 types of floor systems on spans of about 17 ft, have been tested in these laboratories. Some 80 beams up to 26-ft long and several types of floor systems have been tested in England and Holland. Since their standard fire tests are quite similar to the ASTM E119 Standard, the results obtained can be easily compared to those obtained in the United States.

Results of these tests have shown that the fire resistance of prestressed concrete depends on several factors:

1. The principal factor is the clear cover of concrete which protects the steel. In a series of tests conducted in England, it was shown that approximately two hours of additional fire resistance can be provided by $\frac{7}{8}$-in. thick vermiculite-gypsum plaster, or by $\frac{3}{4}$-in. thick sprayed asbestos. Tests in England have also indicated that when the protective cover of concrete exceeds about $2\frac{1}{2}$ in., a light reinforcement should be used to ensure that the concrete will remain in place to protect the steel tendons. With an adequate concrete cover many tests have shown that prestressed concrete can readily withstand standard fires lasting up to 4 hours.

2. The shape of the element may appreciably affect the fire resistance. In a slab, all heat must penetrate to the steel from the lower surface only, whereas in a beam or joist, it may penetrate from the two sides, as well as from the bottom surface. For cored slabs with tendons hidden in the webs, heat transfer is also considerably cut down. Thus the required clear coverage for steel in a slab is considerably less than for a beam.

3. The cross-sectional size of the element is another factor, since with increased size its heat absorption capacity is increased; this helps its fire resistance. Thus the actual fire resistance of a full-sized beam will be greater than a smaller one tested in the furnace.

4. The positioning of tendons away from the exposed surfaces, whether across a section or along the length of a member, will increase the fire resistance.

5. In one series of tests it was shown that fire resistance for lightweight concrete was about 26% better than for the normal weight concrete—as the former having better insulation characteristics.

6. Amount of end restraint for the element may appreciably affect its fire resistance. When no end restraint is provided the fire resistance of a simple beam or slab is controlled by its steel at midspan. When end moment restraint is provided, additional strength is given to the member. When axial restraint is provided, the expansion of concrete increases the

prestress and often adds greatly to the resisting capacity. On the other hand, if the axial restraint is excessive, concrete could fail in compression as a result of expansion under high temperature.

Apart from controlled fire tests, there have been at least nine known fires in prestressed-concrete structures in the United States. In none of these were any lives lost due either to the failure of the structure or to flame spread within the structure. In only one fire did any part of the structure collapse, and that occurred only after many hours of uncontrolled fire with no water available to extinguish the fire. This experience with actual fires, although limited in scope, gives a good indication of the resistance of prestressed concrete to fire damage.[6]

The Fire Rating Committee of the Prestressed Concrete Institute in 1963 suggested the following code provisions:

1. Where standard fire test results are available for the type of unit to be rated, the rating shall be as established by test results or by the requirements for label service of Underwriters' Laboratories, Inc.

2. Where there are no specific test results or label service requirements, the following criteria shall apply:

(*a*) To resist transmission of heat, the thickness of floors, roofs, or walls shall be the same as for reinforced concrete.

(*b*) For simply supported, unrestrained beams, floor units, or roof units, the thickness of either normal weight or structural lightweight concrete protection of reinforcement shall be no less than that given in Table 18-1.

(*c*) Cover for anchorage devices for unbonded tendons shall be 50% greater than those given in Table 18-1.

TABLE 18-1
Cover for Various Fire Resistance Ratings*

Type of Unit	Cross-sectional Area†, (in.²)	Rating			
		1 hr	2 hr	3 hr	4 hr
Girders, beams, and	40–150	$2''$	...	...	...
joists	150–300	$1\frac{1}{2}''$	$2\frac{1}{2}''$	...	...
	over 300	$1\frac{1}{2}''$	$2''$	$3''$‡	$4''$‡
Slabs, solid or cored with flat undersurface		$1''$	$1\frac{1}{2}''$	$2''$	...

* Cover for an individual tensile reinforcing element (tendon) is the minimum thickness of concrete between the tendon and the nearest exposed surface. For members in which several tendons are used the cover is the average of those of the individual tendons.

† In computing the cross-sectional area for joists, the area of the flange shall be added to the area of the stem, but the total width of the flange assumed in the calculations, shall not exceed three times the average width of the stem.

‡ Adequate provisions against spalling of cover shall be provided by means of light U-shaped or hoop reinforcement. Spacing of such transverse reinforcement shall not exceed the depth of the unit and the concrete cover shall be approximately 1 in.

On the effect of low temperatures on both prestressed and reinforced concrete, tests at the University of Ghent[7] indicated the following:

1. The crushing strength of concrete is considerably higher at $-40°F$ than at normal temperature of $68°F$, about twice for ordinary-strength concrete and $1\frac{1}{3}$ times for high-strength concrete.
2. The modulus of rupture of concrete is even more increased, becoming about 3 times for ordinary-strength concrete, and 2 times for high-strength concrete.
3. The modulus of elasticity is slightly increased to about 1.2 times for ordinary-strength concrete and 1.1 for high-strength concrete.
4. Loading tests on both types of beams confirm the above results; their cracking and ultimate loads were higher at $-40°F$ and their deflection was smaller.

18-2 Corrosion Resistance and Durability

Past performance of prestressed-concrete has definitely proved its durability and its high resistance to corrosive environments. It is generally believed that, owing to the absence of cracks, prestressed concrete protects its steel better than reinforced concrete, although the tendons are more sensitive to corrosion.

Several methods are employed for protecting prestressed steel against corrosion. The most common one is to bond the steel to the concrete, as is done for pre-tensioning work and for grouted post-tensioning. When steel is surrounded by concrete, oxidation does not take place. Even though the concrete may contain moisture or the grouting may be imperfect, there is enough evidence to show that bonded steel does not corrode under ordinary circumstances.

Unbonded tendons are either galvanized or greased. Like wires used in suspension bridges, galvanized prestressing wires seldom need additional painting. When not galvanized, the tendons are greased and encased in paper or metallic wrapping. Occasionally, galvanized tendons may be greased in addition. Ends of unbonded tendons are either painted or covered with epoxy before encased in concrete, in order to guard against possible corrosion resulting from cracks in nonprestressed concrete.

When steel is subjected to high-tensile stress, it is known to be more sensitive to corrosion. Hence the term "stress corrosion" is often used to denote the overall corrosive effects caused by the interaction of superimposed mechanical stress and chemical reaction with an environment.[8] The mechanism of stress-corrosion is not exactly known; it is surmised that local corrosion may produce high-stress concentration, which tends to pull the molecules apart and hasten the corroding process. The phenomenon of stress corrosion is identified by corrosion cut directly across the wire or by corrosion splitting along the length of it, often termed as "stress-corrosion cracking."

A method for determining the susceptibility of steel to stress-corrosion cracking is described in a German article.[9] The method consists in using a corrosive solution containing 60 gm per liter $Ca(NO_3)_2 \cdot H_2O$ with 4 gm per liter NH_4NO_3, maintained at a temperature of approximately 165°F. The wires are stressed by bending to various radii of curvature, and are then suspended into the corrosive media for accelerated corrosion.

John A. Roebling's Sons Company of New Jersey applied this method of testing to different kinds of wires and strands. Their preliminary tests, though not conclusive, seemed to indicate the following (see also reference 10):

1. Wires bent to smaller radii, consequently under higher tension, fail in corrosion sooner than straight wires or wires bent to greater radii.
2. Oil-tempered wires are less resistant to corrosion than cold-drawn prestressing wires and strands.
3. Stress-relieved wires and strands are less susceptible to corrosion than non-stress-relieved ones, possibly owing to the lessening of internal stresses in the wires as a result of stress relieving.

A survey of the failures of prestressed-concrete structures resulting from corrosion revealed practically no failure among the tens of thousands of linear prestressed concrete structures.[11] The only five failures on record took place in Holland, Germany, and Austria and all involved the use of "hot-rolled tempered" steel wire. In each case ruptures of the wires occurred either while the wire was still in the coils or so soon after tensioning that the concrete had not been placed. These failures were attributed to a high susceptibility to stress corrosion of hot-rolled tempered wire, coiling of these wires in small-diameter rolls, and their storage in corrosive environments. These wires are not used for prestressing in the United States.

For circularly prestressed concrete, there were more failures. The corrosion of post-tensioned cables in the Richmond water reservoir in California resulted from leaving the cables in the conduits, stressed, ungrouted, and unprotected for 5 months under humid conditions. Corrosion in the cables around a tank in England occurred at the base of the wall where water had penetrated by capillary action between the pneumatically placed coating and the parent concrete, with very poor bond between the two.

A circular tank in Algeria and another in New York using the wire-winding process protected by pneumatic concrete failed as a result of stress corrosion. The widely known case of pipe failures in Regina, Canada, 1952, was attributed at least partly to the presence of calcium chloride, although opinions varied as to what other factors might have been involved. Several other cases of pipe failures are described in reference 11.

Studies in several countries[11,12] indicate that the use of 2% or more calcium chloride (by weight of cement) will result in appreciable corrosion of high-tensile steel. Although the hazards of using small amounts of calcium chloride have not been evaluated, it is recommended that calcium chloride not be used in prestressed concrete when direct contact exists between the mortar and the steel.

To summarize, it may be stated that corrosion in prestressed concrete steel is practically nonexistent for linear prestressing, including beams with curved or bent tendons. It has occurred more frequently with circular prestressing, but even then not to an alarming extent. Furthermore, the cause of corrosion can be attributed to one or more of the following.

1. The use of oil-tempered wires.
2. The addition of calcium chloride to the mortar.
3. The exposure of steel to air and moisture because of lack of protection or cracking of concrete coating.

Since the above conditions can be properly controlled, it can be concluded that the chance of corrosion of prestressing steel is exceedingly small.

At the University of California, Berkeley, research is being carried on concerning the effect of galvanizing on prestressed and nonprestressed steel reinforcement, under the direction of Professors B. Bresler and I. Cornet, and sponsored by the Zinc and Iron Institute. It is expected that some useful new steels will soon be ready.

At the Portland Cement Laboratories, concretes suitable for prestressing were tested for resistance to freezing and thawing in water and resistance to de-icer scaling.[13] Some of the conclusions are listed below:

1. Intentionally entrained air increased the resistance of concretes to freezing and thawing and de-icer scaling.
2. Concretes made with Type I and Type III Portland cements were equally durable.
3. Curing at an elevated temperature to attain high-early strength did not impair the durability of concrete, provided some drying followed the

elevated curing cycle prior to exposure. A few days of yard storage at above freezing temperatures should be ample for this purpose.

4. A prestressing force providing a compressive stress of 350–400 psi in the concrete had no significant influence of the resistance to freezing and thawing.

Another series conducted at Purdue University,[14] on the other hand, indicated significant improvement in the durability of 5000 psi concrete under a constant compresive stress of about 2000 psi. Prestressed specimens showed better durability than unstressed concrete made of the same mix and also better than unstressed concrete made of a leaner mix. It was indicated that continuously stressed concrete is effectively more durable than intermittently stress-released concrete, which is generally more durable than unstressed concrete of the same mix. Hence it can be concluded that the durability of concrete is generally enhanced by prestressing.

18-3 Fatigue Strength

The fatigue strength of prestressed concrete can be studied from three approaches: that of concrete itself, that of high-tensile steel, and that of the combination. It may also be studied by utilizing our knowledge on the fatigue strength of reinforced concrete, since so much data has already been accumulated.[15] There are, however, some differences between prestressed and reinforced concrete. For example, in prestressed concrete, compression in the extreme fibers is frequently near zero under dead load and increases to a maximum under live load, thus varying throughout a wide range. Furthermore, high-strength steel is prestressed to a high level, while its stress range is relatively small.

For prestressed members under the action of design live loads, the stress in steel wires is seldom increased by more than 10,000 psi from their effective prestress of about 140,000 psi. It is safe to say that, so long as the concrete has not cracked, there is little possibility of fatigue failure in steel, even though the working load is exceeded. After the cracking of concrete, high stress concentrations exist in the wires at the cracks. These high stresses may result in a partial breakage of bond between steel and concrete near the cracks. Under repeated loading, either the bond may be completely broken or the steel may be ruptured.

Numerous tests have been conducted on prestressed-concrete members, giving considerable data on their fatigue strength. The results of these tests confirm the ability of the combination to stand any number of repeated loads within the working range. Failure started invariably in the wires near the section of maximum moment and often directly over the separators where the wires had a sharp change in direction.

No tests are available concerning the fatigue bond strength between high-tensile steel and concrete. But, from the results of tests on prestressed-concrete beams, it seems safe to conclude that, if properly grouted, bond between the two materials can stand repeated working loads without failure. This is true because, before the cracking of concrete, bond along the length of the beam is usually low. For unbonded members, the problem of bond is clearly not an issue.

Fatigue failures at anchorage of end-anchored tendons are hardly known. When the tendons are bonded to the concrete, stress in the tendons near the end is not affected by live load. Hence there is no danger of fatigue failure, even though high localized stresses may exist in the wires at the anchorage. When unbonded, stress near the end of wires will change under live loads, but the range of stress under working loads is small so that fatigue failures are not likely.

Few data on the fatigue strength of unbonded beams are available, but there is some evidence to indicate that the use of mild-steel reinforcement may greatly increase such strength.[16] Fatigue tests on partially-prestressed concrete members incorporating nontensioned wires show that such wires can stand repeated loads somewhat higher than the working loads without decreasing their eventual load-carrying capacity.[17] This sounds quite reasonable, since the untensioned wires would be subject to the same stress range as the tensioned ones, while their stress would be at a much lower level and hence there is less danger of fatigue failure.

A rational method for predicting the fatigue strength of prestressed concrete beams in bending has been developed by Professor Ekberg.[18] It utilizes fatigue-failure envelopes for prestressing steel and concrete, and relates them to the stress-moment diagram for a beam.

A typical failure envelope for prestressing steel is shown in Fig. 18-1(a). This envelope indicates how the tensile stress can be increased from a given lower level to a higher level to obtain failure at one million load-cycles. Note that all values are expressed as a percentage of the static tensile strength. Thus the steel may resist a stress range amounting to $0.27f_s'$ if the lower stress limit is zero, but only a stress range of $0.18f_s'$ if the lower stress limit is increased to $0.40f_s'$. At a lower stress limit of $0.90f_s'$ or over, it takes only a negligible stress increase to fail the steel at one million cycles. While this fatigue envelope varies for different steels,[19] the curve given here may be considered a typical one.

The fatigue-failure envelope for concrete is given in Fig. 18-1(b). This is analogous to (a) for steel, except it is drawn to cover both tensile and compressive stresses. This diagram indicates that if the lower stress limit

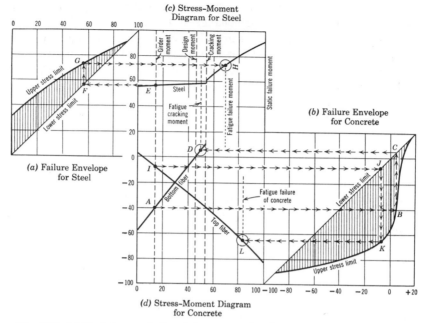

Fig. 18-1. Method for predicting fatigue strength of prestressed concrete beams.

is zero, a compressive stress of $0.60f_c'$ may be repeated one million cycles. If the lower stress limit is $0.40f_c'$, the stress range can be $0.40f_c'$. If the compressive stress limit is $0.20f_c'$, the tensile stress limit, to produce cracking, is $0.05f_c'$.

A typical stress-moment diagram for steel is given in Fig. 18-1(c), which again expresses nondimensionally both the stress and the moment by relating them to the static strength and the ultimate static moment. For example, when the external moment is 70% of the ultimate static moment, the stress in the steel is shown to be $0.80f_s'$. Similarly, Fig. 18-1(d) gives the concrete fiber stresses relative to the moment. It is noted that under certain loading conditions, either the top or bottom fibers can be under tension rather than compression.

Combining these four portions (Fig. 18-1) it is possible to determine the fatigue-cracking moment and the fatigue-ultimate moment as limited by steel or concrete. Starting on the stress-moment diagrams at the point of dead-load stress, which represent the lowest possible stress level, we can trace three paths as follows.

Steel: *E-F-G-H*
Concrete top fiber: *I-J-K-L*
Concrete bottom fiber: *A-B-C-D*

The point H indicates that for a maximum moment of $0.68M_{ult}$, the steel will fail in tension at one million cycles. The point L indicates, for a maximum moment of $0.84M_{ult}$, the top fiber will fail in compression at one million cycles. The point D indicates that the fatigue-cracking moment is $0.50M_{ult}$.

Using this analytical approach, Ekberg studied the effect of the level of prestress, the effect of over- and under-reinforcing, and the cracking characteristics. The following conclusions were reached:

1. Other conditions being equal, reducing the level of prestress considerably reduces the fatigue-failure moment. This becomes evident when it is realized that cracking would occur sooner for the lower level of prestress and a wider stress range would occur for the steel.

2. Since fatigue failure in concrete is not the controlling criterion, over-reinforcing will generally increase the fatigue strength. The optimum-fatigue moment occurs for a percentage of steel higher than that indicated for a static balanced design.

3. The ratio of dead-load moment to live-load moment has very little effect on the fatigue-cracking moment. Although repetitive loading necessarily reduces the cracking moment, prestressing does delay the occurrence of cracks very substantially.

It is clear that the shape of the member and the location of the steel also have to do with the fatigue strength. When reliable fatigue resistance is to be found, it is desirable that the stress-moment curves and the fatigue-failure envelopes be obtained for the given case and the analytical method outlined above be followed for its determination.

18-4 Dynamic Loadings

The behavior of prestressed-concrete members under dynamic loadings can be discussed in two parts: the energy-absorption capacity and the response characteristics.

The resisting capacity of a prestressed member to suddenly applied loads, also termed the impact resistance, is measured by the amount of energy that can be absorbed by the member as it deforms under the action of the loading. Consider a concentrated static load gradually applied to a simple beam; a load-deflection curve is obtained as in Fig. 18-2. The elastic energy absorbed by the beam is measured by the area below its load-deflection curve up to the point of cracking (shaded area A). The total energy that can be absorbed by the beam up to rupture is given by the entire area below the curve (areas A plus B). This approach has been generally confirmed by a series of tests conducted by the British

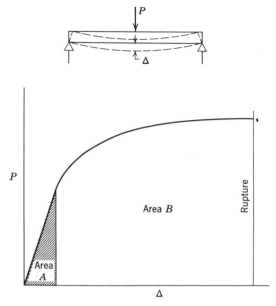

Fig. 18-2. Load-deflection curve of a simple beam.

Building Research Station,[20] which additionally brought out the following observations.

1. Load deflection relations given by static tests can generally be used as a measure of the impact resistance. When failure starts in the steel and ends with the crushing of concrete, this measure is somewhat on the safe side. When failure is due to the breaking of wires or when the wires are nonprestressed, this measure errs a little on the dangerous side.

2. There are three types of failures under impact load as under static load: bond, shear, and flexural. Flexural failure may start in steel or in concrete, depending on the percentage of reinforcement and the prestress in it.

3. Resistance to repeated blows is not decreased by repetition if cracking or crushing of concrete has not taken place; otherwise, the strength may be decreased, especially when modes of failure other than flexural are developed.

4. For each beam, there appears to be optimum values for the percentage of steel, the prestress in it, and the strength of concrete so far as impact resistance is concerned. For example, either too high or too low a percentage of reinforcement may reduce the impact resistance.

5. The greatest resistance to the impact of a single blow will normally be obtained by the use of reinforced concrete, whereas the greatest resistance to repeated impact may be provided by prestressed-concrete construction.

6. The presence of shear reinforcement in the form of stirrups has an important influence on the impact resistance of reinforced concrete and may be expected to be of similar importance for prestressed-concrete members.

This series of tests also included some reinforced-concrete beams designed for the same static strength as some of the prestressed ones. For all these reinforced beams, failure started at the yield point of steel. And it is pointed out that, as for the prestressed ones, the resistance calculated from the results of the static test slightly underestimated the impact resistance. It is further concluded that, for these beams, the reinforced ones were superior to the prestressed ones under these particular test conditions. This was primarily due to the fact that the ultimate deflections of these prestressed beams were less than the corresponding reinforced ones, under either static or impact loads.

Another series of tests were conducted at the University of Ghent on post-tensioned members of 13- to 20-ft spans.[21] These tests were continued in 1954 on prestressed slabs and beams with and without mild steel bars, the results of which are not yet published. These tests proved that, because of the big deflections of prestressed beams, the impact resistance of post-tensioned anchored beams is much higher than those of ordinary reinforced concrete of the same static strength.

Although, on the surface, the two series of tests seem to yield conflicting verdicts regarding the relative impact strength of prestressed versus reinforced concrete, upon careful examination it can be seen that they in fact gave the same findings. Both actually agreed that resilience of the beams as given by static tests is a rather good measure of the impact strength. In the first series of tests, the reinforced beams were designed so that they deflected more than the prestressed ones at the ultimate load; in the second series, the prestressed ones deflected more. Whether a beam is reinforced or prestressed, the one with the greater resilience will have the greater impact resistance. In other words, the ability of prestressed beams to stand impact load can be estimated by the usual theory of resilience, just as that of reinforced beams.

Another series of tests were performed at U.S. Naval Civil Engineering Laboratory on concrete beams post-tensioned with straight unbonded bars to determine their dynamic resistance, their natural period of vibration, and their rebound characteristics.[22] Some of their major conclusions are listed here:

1. The beams exhibited a very high capacity for recovery, with 85 to 90% recoverability at incipient collapse. Thus essentially all of the energy-absorbing ability can be utilized without incurring serious permanent damage.

2. Natural periods as given by free-vibration tests agree well with the calculated period using the sonic modulus of elasticity.

3. The maximum rebound (negative deflection) for any given load curve $P(t)$ may be obtained (for loads in the elastic range) by considering an elastic beam with viscous-type damping, provided its natural period and damping factor can be predicted. The shorter the load duration, the more serious the rebound problem and the more important damping becomes.

A procedure for dynamic design for blast loadings is recommended as a result of these tests.[22] The method suggests a preliminary design section by any conventional method using a dynamic load factor of 2.0 (100% impact), then compute the stiffness, the natural period, and the maximum deflection and rebound under the given loading. Then design the amount and location of prestress required to keep the maximum fiber stresses within the allowable limits. If the section should be modified, the process can be repeated until a satisfactory design is obtained. This elastic approach is believed to be rather conservative, unless high-tensile and compressive stresses are allowed. Since the plastic-energy absorption is so much higher than the elastic energy, advantage must be taken of this reserve capacity when designing for dynamic loads. Care must be taken so that rebound effect can be taken care of by adding nonprestressed reinforcement on the tension side during rebound. For beams under high shear, the addition of stirrups should also be considered.

The damping characteristics of prestressed concrete were investigated by Professor Penzien at the University of California.[23] Twenty concrete beams of size 6 in. × 6 in. × 90 in. were post-tensioned to various stress levels and to result in various stress distributions. Three significant conclusions are pointed out in the report:

1. Under steady state conditions, internal damping in prestressed concrete members may be less than one percent of critical if the initial prestress is sufficient to prevent tension cracks from developing. If tension cracks are allowed to develop, but on a microscopic scale, damping can be expected of the order of two percent of critical. If larger (visible) cracks are permitted to develop, one should expect higher damping.

2. Under transient conditions, the amount of internal damping present in prestressed concrete members depends to a great extent on the past history of

loading and on the amplitude of displacements produced. For those cases where members have been dynamically loaded only a few times to a given stress level which produces considerable cracking, damping can be expected anywhere in the range of 3–6 percent of critical.

3. Magnitude and type of prestress in concrete members have an indirect influence on internal damping only because these parameters control the amount of cracking which can take place.

It is therefore noted that critical damping for prestressed concrete is smaller than for reinforced concrete under the design loadings because of the absence of cracking, but is probably comparable to reinforced concrete in the post-cracking range.

Because of the slender proportions of prestressed concrete as compared to reinforced concrete, the natural frequencies are relatively low and vibration problems are more likely to arise. This is further aggravated by the low critical damping factor for prestressed concrete within the working loads. Up to now, fortunately, there have not been too many cases of objectionable vibrations in prestressed-concrete structures. This can be partly explained by comparing them with steel structures which generally possess smaller stiffness and smaller damping but do not yet present too many problems of vibration. It is, however, desirable to study the vibration characteristics of a prestressed-concrete structure when unusual proportions and unconventional loadings are encountered. Readers interested in this subject are referred to an extensive report by the Netherlands Committee for Concrete Research[24] and another article by Marshall and Ozell.[25]

18-5 Torsional Strength

Because of the high shear strength of concrete coupled with its low tensile strength, the failure of concrete beams in torsion seldom results from shearing stresses as such, but rather from principal tensile stress produced by the shearing stress. When the shearing stress v is combined with direct stress f_c, the principal tensile stress is given by the familiar formula (refer to section 7-2),

$$S_t = \sqrt{v^2 + (f_c/2)^2} - f_c/2 \qquad (18\text{-}1)$$

Consider the simple case of a round plain concrete bar subject to pure torsion. Like other brittle materials, it fails along the plane of principal tension, at a spiral line 45° to the axis. This failure can be delayed by nonprestressed spiral and longitudinal reinforcement. However, such steel does not begin to act until the concrete has cracked, hence the elastic torsional strength of the concrete beam is not affected, although the ultimate failure resistance and the postcracking resilience of the member are increased.

Since the value of f_c in formula 18-1 can be considerably increased by prestressing along the length of the member, the principal tensile stress S_t is reduced for the same value of v. Hence the torsional resistance of a concrete member can be increased several-fold by prestressing, as has been proved experimentally by several investigators.[26-29] It is also evident that prestressing the member along its depth and width will further increase its torsional resistance, although the economics of such 2- and 3-dimensional prestressing may limit its practicality for the present.

Confining our discussion to one-dimensional prestressing and rectangular sections, we can simply apply the general theory of torsion developed by St. Venant. According to St. Venant's theory, the maximum shearing stresses occur on the periphery at the middle of the sides, the absolute maximum v_{max} being at the middle of the longer sides of the rectangle,

$$v_{max} = \gamma b G \theta \tag{18-2}$$

and

$$M_T = \beta b^3 D G \theta \tag{18-3}$$

where b = the width (smaller dimension) of the rectangle
$\quad\quad\quad D$ = the depth (greater dimension) of the rectangle
$\quad\quad\quad G$ = the shear modulus of the concrete
$\quad\quad\quad \theta$ = angle of twist in radians
$\gamma \ \alpha$ and β = constant, depending on the proportion of the rectangle (Table 18-2)

TABLE 18-2[27]

St. Venant's Constants for the Design of Rectangular Sections Subject to Torsion

D/b	α	β	γ
1.0	0.208	0.141	0.675
1.2	0.219	0.166	0.759
1.4	0.227	0.187	0.822
1.6	0.234	0.204	0.869
1.8	0.240	0.217	0.904
2.0	0.246	0.229	0.930
2.5	0.258	0.249	0.968
3.0	0.267	0.264	0.985
5.0	0.292	0.291	0.999
10.0	0.312	0.312	0.100
110.0	0.331	0.331	1.000
∞	0.333	0.333	1.000

Letting $\alpha = \beta/\gamma$, Table 18-2 we have

$$M_T = \alpha b^2 D v_{max} \qquad (18\text{-}4)$$

or

$$v_{max} = \frac{M_T}{\alpha b^2 D} \qquad (18\text{-}5)$$

Then the principal tensile stress can be calculated from formula 18-1. When this principal tensile stress reaches the ultimate tensile strength of the concrete, cracking starts and the section may fail immediately without much warning. In fact, the torsional failure of prestressed concrete can often be accompanied by considerable noise and flying debris, owing to the release of the prestressing force upon the formation of the cracks.

In contrast to the mode of failure in torsion, a prestressed concrete beam under bending generally fails gradually and possesses much reserve strength and ductility after the appearance of the first cracks. This becomes evident when it is realized that the bending failure is dependent on the tensile stress and strain of steel, together with the compressive stress and strain of concrete, whereas the torsional strength is exhausted when the tensile limit is reached in concrete, and there is no ductility in concrete under tension.

The behavior of concrete beams subject to combined bending and torsion is intermediate between that of beams subject to pure torsion and pure bending. For prestressed beams with relatively low ratios of bending moment M_B to torsional moment M_T, the formation of the first crack results in failure of the beam in a sudden and destructive manner, such as beams subject to pure torsions. With higher ratios of M_B/M_T, the failure becomes more gradual, and the ultimate load becomes higher than the load causing the formation of the first cracks.

The resistance of prestressed concrete under combined torsion and bending is discussed in reference 26. It is noted therein that concentrically prestressed beams are considerably stronger than plain concrete beams, and a theoretical interaction relation between the bending and the torsional resistance can be obtained. For eccentrically prestressed beams, a bending moment giving a uniform stress block across the section is usually the ideal for its torsional resistance.

18-6   Ties, Pavements, Masts

Brief mention will be made of some recent applications of prestressed concrete in the United States. Readers interested in their details are referred to the listed references for further information.

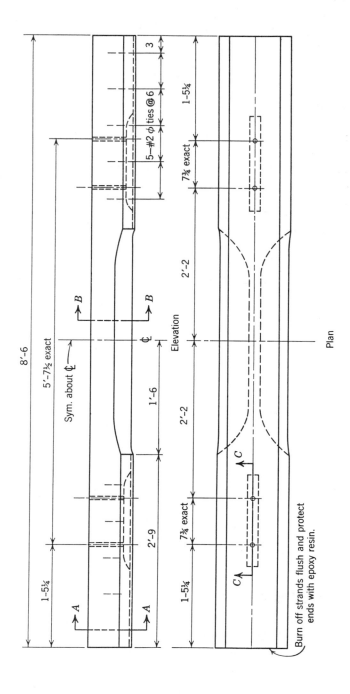

Elevation

Plan

Burn off strands flush and protect
ends with epoxy resin.

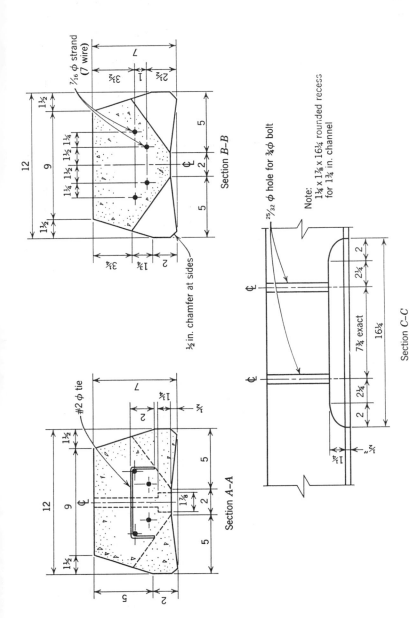

Fig. 18-3. Prestressed concrete railroad tie—Prestressing strand: All strands shall be 7/16ϕ, 7 wire uncoated, stress-relieved, meeting ASTM A416-57T specification with a minimum breaking strength of 27,000 lb. Initial prestress shall be 75% of minimum breaking strength = 20,250 lb per strand. The concrete shall consist of Portland cement, mineral (granite) aggregate and water and shall have a minimum ultimate strength of 6000 psi in 28 days, with maximum water-cement ratio of 5 gallons of water per sack of cement. Concrete shall be air-entrained. (Association of American Railroads.)

Railroad Ties. An extensive series of laboratory investigation and field performance testing on prestressed-concrete railroad ties has been carried out by the American Association of American Railroads.[30,31] A preliminary study to replace one wood tie with one concrete tie, both spaced at 20 in., indicated satisfactory performance from a technical standpoint but was not desirable from an economic point of view. By increasing the concrete tie spacing to 30 in., it was found that the rail stresses would be increased by only 10%, that the tie loading would be increased from 40% of the axle load to 50%, and that the pressure of the 12-in. concrete tie on the ballast would be the same as that under the 9-in. wide-wood ties.

Consequently, experimental ties were designed, Fig. 18-3, and subjected to both static and repeated loads in the laboratory. Four $\frac{7}{16}$-in. 7-wire strands were used to apply a total initial prestress of 81,000 lb on the tie. An important feature of this tie design is its wedge shape for the central 3-ft portion, reducing the direct bearing surface on the ballast to only 2 in. This practically eliminates "center binding," which results when the ballast supporting the tie under the rails is pounded and shifted until the tie is supported only at its midlength. It is also noted that the bottom surface of the tie under the rails is slightly concave, thus helping to hold the supporting ballast in place.

While these test ties made with lime-rock aggregates were not satisfactory, those made with granite were able to meet the design criteria of a static bending moment of 150,000 in.-lb at center line of rail and to sustain without failure 2,000,000 cycles of repeated load, producing a bending moment of 200,000 in.-lb at center line of rail. Suitable rail fastenings, such as rail clips, insulating pads, anchor bolts, and thimbles for electrical insulation were also developed. A successful design using the channel-type fastener is shown in Fig. 18-4.

Field tests on several miles of track have indicated the general satisfactory performance of these ties under actual service conditions. The data secured will undoubtedly help to further improve the design, and to indicate proper installation and maintenance procedures.

Airfield and Highway Pavements. Little has been done in the United States in the development of prestressed-concrete highway pavements. It is generally believed that, although cheaper in maintenance, a prestressed slab of 4 or 5 in. cannot compete in initial cost with the commonly used 8-in. pavement of plain concrete. This situation, however, may change if suitable design for prestressed pavements can be evolved and if economical methods of construction can be developed.

The foremost problem confronting the design of prestressed pavements is the loss of prestress through friction between the slab and the ground.

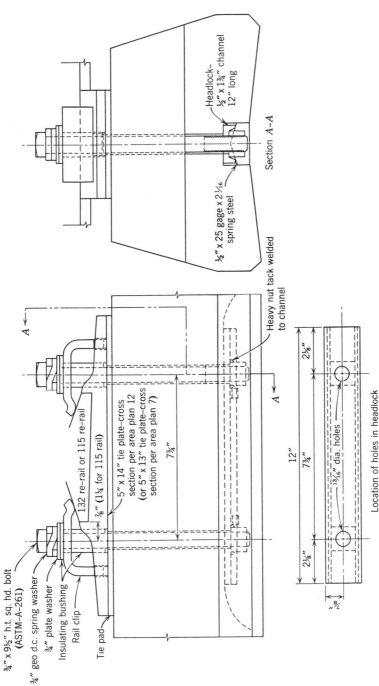

Section A–A

Headlock–
½" x 1¾" channel
12" long

½" x 25 gage x 2 1/16"
spring steel

Heavy nut tack welded
to channel

A

A

5" x 14" tie plate–cross
section per area plan 12
(or 5" x 13" tie plate–cross
section per area plan 7)

132 re-rail or 115 re-rail

7¾"

⅞" (1¼ for 115 rail)

¾" x 9½" h.t. sq. hd. bolt
(ASTM-A-261)

¾" geo d.c. spring washer

¾" plate washer

Insulating bushing

Rail clip

Tie pad

12"

2⅛"

7¾"

2⅛"

13/16" dia. holes

7/8"

Location of holes in headlock

Fig. 18-4. Channel-type fastener (for tie in Fig. 18-3).

Another problem is the devising of a reliable and economical expansion joint, although it is required only every few hundred feet. Construction costs could be lowered if cheap methods for prestressing the steel can be devised. It does appear that chemical prestressing by expansive cements may eventually provide a solution, since the labor for stressing operations is eliminated, and the friction developed during slab expansion could help to precompress the concrete.

For airfield pavements, an 8-in. prestressed slab could economically replace a 24-in. plain concrete one, if maintenance is taken into consideration. Prestressed-concrete pavements possess several advantages compared to a conventional type;[32,33] cracks are practically eliminated, the number of transverse joints are reduced, a more watertight pavement and a smoother surface are provided, and a longer life is expected. All these advantages point to further development of prestressed pavements, particularly those made with expansive cements.

Power Masts. While prestressed concrete poles and masts have found wide acceptance in European and Mediterranean countries, their adoption in the United States has so far been limited. Prestressed concrete masts are lighter than those of conventionally reinforced concrete, they are more durable than timber, and require less maintenance than steel. When produced on a massive scale, they will likely compete favorably with other conventional types.[34] An experimental tower for high voltage transmission up to 750,000 volts has been constructed by the General Electric Company.[35] This tower 100-ft high is made of two columns of hollow box section 18 × 36 in., with 5-in. wall thickness. These columns are cross-braced by 12 × 12 in. solid sections.

References

1 A. P. Carman and R. A. Nelson, "The Thermal Conductivity and Diffusivity of Concrete," *Bull.* 122, University of Illinois, 1921.
2 M. S. Abrams and C. R. Cruz, "The Behavior at High Temperature of Steel Strands for Prestressed Concrete," *PCA Journal of Research and Development Laboratories,* Portland Cement Assn, September 1961, Chicago.
3 A. W. Hill and L. A. Ashton, "The Fire-Resistance of Prestressed Concrete," *Proc. World Conference on Prestressed Concrete,* 1957, San Francisco.
4 A. H. Gustaferro and C. C. Carlson, "An Interpretation of Results of Fire Tests of Prestressed Concrete Building Components" J. Prestressed Conc. Inst., Oct. 1962.
5 G. E. Troxell, "Fire Resistance of Prestressed Concrete," Symposium on Fire Resistance of Concrete, ACI Publication, *SP-5,* 1962.
6 C. C. Zollman, M. G. Garavaglia, and A. Rubin, "Prestressed Concrete Resists Fire Damage," *Civil Engineering,* December 1960, pp. 36–41.
7 G. Huyghe, "Essais à basses températures sue des poutres en béton armé et en béton précontraint," *Précontrainte Prestressing,* No. 1, 1952, p. 31.
8 E. C. Roberts, "A Review of Stress-Corrosion Cracking," *The Trend in Engineering,* Univ. of Washington, Seattle, January 1962.

9   W. Raedeker, "Verbesserung der Pruefung von Stahl auf Empfindlichkeit gegen Spannungsrisskorrosion," *Stahl und Eisen*, April 1953, pp. 485–492.

10 W. O. Everling, "Stress Corrosion in High-Tensile Wire," *Wire Products*, Vol. 30, 1955, p. 316.

11 G. E. Monfore and G. J. Verbeck, "Corrosion of Prestressed Wire in Concrete," *Journal PCA Research and Development Laboratories*, November 1960.

12 M. H. Roberts, "Effect of Calcium Chloride on the Durability of Pre-tensioned Wire in Prestressed Concrete," *Magazine of Concrete Research*, CACA, London, November 1962.

13 P. Kleiger, "Some Aspects of Durability and Volume Change of Concrete for Prestressing," *Journal PCA Research and Development Laboratories*, September 1960.

14 F. E. Musleh, "The Effects of Freezing and Thawing on Prestressed Concrete," Purdue Univ., *Report Joint Highway Research Project*, 1959.

15 G. M. Nordby, "Fatigue of Concrete—A Review of Research," *Proc. of the American Concrete Institute*, Vol. 55, 1958–1959.

16 T. Y. Lin, "Strength of Continuous Prestressed Concrete Beams Under Static and Repeated Loads," *J. Am. Conc. Inst.*, June 1955.

17 P. W. Abeles, "Fatigue Tests on Partially Prestressed Concrete Members," *Final Report, Fourth Congress, Int. Assn. Bridge and Structural Eng.*, 1953; also "Fatigue Tests of Prestressed Beams," presented at ACI Convention at Denver, 1954.

18 C. E. Ekberg, Jr., R. E. Walther, and R. G. Slutter, "Fatigue, Resistance of Prestressed Concrete Beams in Bending," *Journal of the Structural Division of the American Society of Civil Engineers* (Vol. 83, No. ST4), July 1957.

19 R. E. Lane, and C. E. Ekberg, Jr., "Repeated Load Tests on 7-Wire Prestressing Strands," Lehigh Univ., *Fritz Laboratory Report*, January 1959; E. J. Ruble and F. P. Drew," Railroad Research on Prestressed Concrete," *PCI Journal*, December 1962; R. F. Warner and C. L. Hulsbos," Probable Fatigue Life of Prestressed Concrete Flexural Members," Fritz Engineering Laboratory Report, Lehigh Univ., July 1962.

20 S. C. C. Bate, "Strength of Concrete Members under Dynamic Loading," *Symposium on the Strength of Concrete Structures* (Session D, Paper No. 2), Building Research Station, Garston, Watford, Herts, England.

21 G. Magnel, "Essai au choc sur poutres en béton armé et en béton précontraint," *Le béton précontraint*, Gand, Belgium, 3rd ed., 1953, pp. 289–321.

22 "Blast Load Tests on Post-tensioned Concrete Beams," U.S. Naval Civil Engineering Laboratory, Fort Hueneme, Calif., *Technical Report 116*, May 1961.

23 J. Penzien, *Damping Characteristics of Prestressed Concrete*, Institute of Engineering Research, Univ. of Calif., January 1962.

24 "Vibration Problems in Prestressed Concrete," Netherlands Committee for Concrete Research, *Report 17*, 1960.

25 P. W. Marshal, and A. M. Ozell, "Behavior of Prestressed Concrete under Dynamic Loading," *PCI Journal*, December 1960.

26 H. J. Cowan, "Experiments on the Torsional Strength of Prestressed Concrete," *Third Congress of FIP*, Berlin, 1958.

27 H. J. Cowan and S. Armstrong, "The Torsional Strength of Prestressed Concrete," *Proc. World Conference on Prestressed Concrete*, 1957, San Francisco.

28 R. Humphreys, "Torsion Properties of Prestressed Concrete," *Structural Engineer* June 1957.

29 P. Zia, "Torsional Strength of Prestressed Concrete Members," *J. Am. Conc. Inst.*,

April, 1961; J. S. Reeves, "Prestressed Concrete Tee Beams under Combined Bending and Torsion," *Technical Report*, CACA, London, December 1962.

30 "Prestressed Concrete Tie Investigation," Association of American Railroads, Engineering Research Division, *Report No. ER-20*, November 1961.

31 G. M. Magee and E. J. Ruble, "Service Tests of Prestressed Concrete Ties," *Railway Track and Structures*, September 1960.

32 F. M. Mellinger, "A Summary of Prestressed Concrete Pavement Practices," *Journal of the Air Transport Division (Proc. ASCE*, Vol. 87, No. AT2), August 1961.

33 J. P. McIntyre and F. M. Mellenger, "Prestressed Concrete Taxiway Biggs Air Force Base, Texas, U.S.A.," *Fourth Congress International Federation for Prestressing*, Rome, May 1962; C. F. Renz and P. L. Melville, "Experience with Prestressed Concrete Airfield Pavements in the United States," *PCI Journal*, March 1961; Y. Osawa. "Strength of Prestressed Concrete Pavements," *Journal of the Structural Division (Proc. ASCE*, Vol. 88, No. 575) October 1962.

34 Robert J. D. Finfrock, "Prestressed Concrete Masts for Power Lines," *Proc. World Conference on Prestressed Concrete*, San Francisco, 1957.

35 M. Schupack, "Design of an Extra-high Voltage Transmission Tower 100 Feet High," *PCI Journal*, February 1962.

definitions, notations, abbreviations

definitions, notations,   *appendix* A
abbreviations

Definitions

1 *Pre-tensioning and post-tensioning.* Any method of prestressing concrete members in which the reinforcement is tensioned before (after) the concrete is placed.

2 *Full and partial prestressing.* Degree of prestress applied to concrete in which no tension (some tension) is permitted in the concrete under the working loads.

3 *Circular and linear prestressing.* Circular prestressing refers to prestressing in round members like tanks and pipes; prestressing in all other members is termed linear.

4 *Transfer.* The transferring of prestress to the concrete. For pretensioned members, transfer takes place at the release of prestress from the bulkheads; for post-tensioned members it takes place after the completion of the tensioning process.

5 *Bonded and unbonded reinforcement.* Reinforcement bonded (not bonded) throughout its length to the surrounding concrete.

6 *Anchored and non-end-anchored reinforcement.* Reinforcement anchored at its ends (not anchored) by means of mechanical devices capable of transmitting the tensioning force to the concrete.

7 *Prestressed and nonprestressed reinforcement.* Reinforcement in prestressed-concrete members, which are elongated (not elongated) with respect to the surrounding concrete.

8 *Tendons.* Another name for prestressed reinforcement, whether wires, bars, or strands.

9 *Cables.* A group of tendons, or the c.g.s. of all the tendons.

10 *Concordant and nonconcordant cables.* Cables or c.g.s. lines which produce a *C*-line or line of pressure coincident (noncoincident) with the c.g.s. line itself.

11 *Linear transformation.* Moving the position of a c.g.s. line over the

interior supports of a continuous beam without changing the intrinsic shape of the line within each individual span.

12 *Girder load, working load, service load, cracking load, and ultimate load.* GIRDER LOAD: The weight of the beam or girder itself plus whatever weight is on it at the time of transfer. WORKING LOAD OR SERVICE LOAD: The normally maximum total load which the structure is specified or expected to carry. CRACKING LOAD: The total load required to initiate cracks in a prestressed-concrete member. ULTI-MATE LOAD: The total load which a member or structure can carry up to total rupture.

13 *Load factor.* The ratio of cracking or ultimate load to the working or service load (sometimes considering only the live load when so specified).

14 *Creep.* Time-dependent inelastic deformation of concrete or steel resulting solely from the presence of stress and a function thereof.

15 *Shrinkage of concrete.* Contraction of concrete due to drying and chemical changes, dependent on time but not directly dependent on stresses induced by external loading.

Notations
Greek Letters

Δ = deflection of beams.

Δ_a = total deformation of anchorage

Δ_s = total strain in steel.

δ = unit strain

δ_i = initial unit strain in concrete, due to elastic shortening.

δ_t = final unit strain in concrete, including the effect of creep but not of shrinkage.

δ_s = unit strain in steel.

μ = coefficient of friction.

θ or α = change in angle of tendons; angles in general.

α, β, γ = torsional constants.

English Letters

A = cross-sectional area in general.

A_c = net cross-sectional area of concrete; or area of precast portion.

A_{c1}, A_{c2} = compressive portion of A_c at transfer or under working load, respectively.

A_g = gross cross-sectional area of concrete.

A_s = cross-sectional area of steel, generally in square inches.

A_{sb} = steel area for a balanced section, in square inches.

A_t = gross cross-sectional area of concrete, including steel transformed by ratio n.

A_v = cross-sectional area of one set of steel stirrups.

a = lever arm between the centers of compression and tension in a beam section.

a' = a at ultimate load.

a_1, a_2, a_G = a at various stages as defined in text.

b = width of beam or its flange; or width of a rectangle.

b' = width of web of beam.

C = center of compressive force, center of pressure, or center of thrust; or carry-over moment, in moment distribution.

C' = C at ultimate load.

C_c = coefficient of creep = δ_t/δ_i.

c = distance from c.g.c. to extreme fiber.

c_b, c_t = c for bottom (top) fibers; $c_{b1}, c_{t1}, c_{b2}, c_{t2}$ for compressive portion at transfer or under working load, respectively; c_b', c_t' for composite sections.

c.g.s. = center of gravity of steel area.

c.g.c. = center of gravity (centroid) of concrete section; c.g.c.' for composite section.

D = diameter of bars or wires; or distributed moment, in moment distribution; or depth of a rectangle.

DL = dead load.

d = depth of beam measured to c.g.s., generally in inches.

e = eccentricity in general.

e_1, e_2, e_b, e_t = various eccentricities as defined locally in text.

e_x, e_y = eccentricities along X-axis (Y-axis).

E = modulus of elasticity in general.

E_c = modulus of elasticity for concrete.

E_s = modulus of elasticity for steel.

F = total effective prestress after deducting losses.

F_a = average prestress in steel for a given length.

F_1, F_2 = total prestress at points 1 and 2, respectively.

F_i = total initial prestress before transfer.

F_0 = total prestress, just after transfer.

FEM = fixed-end moment, in moment distribution.

f = unit stress in general.

f_1, f_2 = unit stresses at stages or points 1 and 2, respectively.

f' = modulus of rupture of concrete.

f_a = average unit stress in steel for a given length.

f_c = unit stress in concrete.

f_c' = ultimate unit stress in concrete, generally at 28 days old.

f_{ci}' = ultimate unit stress in concrete, at time of transfer.

f_{cs} = average concrete stress along the c.g.s. line.

f_i = initial unit prestress in steel before transfer.

f_0 = unit prestress in steel, just after transfer.

f_e = effective unit prestress in steel after deducting losses.

f_s = unit stress in steel, generally; or effective unit prestress in steel after deducting losses.

f_s' = ultimate unit stress in steel.

f_{sa} = additional unit stress in steel, which is the increase from the effective stress up to the stress at ultimate load.

f_{su} = unit stress in steel at ultimate load on the section.

f_{s1} = initial unit stress in steel to overcome slack.

Δf_s = change in f_s.

f_t, f_b = fiber stress at top (bottom) fibers.

f_t', f_b' = tensile fiber stress at top (bottom) fibers.

f_v = unit stress in steel stirrups.

$f_v' = f_v$ at ultimate load.

f_y = yield point of steel; or f along Y-axis.

f_1, f_2 = unit prestress at stage 1 (2).

f_A, f_B = unit stress at point A (B).

H = horizontal reaction.

h = overall depth of beam; h_1, h_2 for compressive portion at transfer or under working load, respectively.

I = moment of inertia of section; I' for composite section; I_1, I_2 for compressive portion at transfer or under working load, respectively.

IL = impact load.

I_t = I for transformed section.

I_x, I_y = I about Y-axis (X-axis).

j = for resisting lever arm jd in a beam section.

K = coefficient for wobble effect of tendons in a prestressed member.

k = coefficient for depth of compressive area kd in a beam section; or as defined locally.

k' = k at ultimate load.

k_1 = ratio of average stress in ultimate compression area of beam to f_c'.

k_t, k_b = kern distances from c.g.c. for top (bottom) = $r^2/c_b(r^2/c_t)$; $k_{t1}, k_{b1}, k_{t2}, k_{b2}$ for compressive portion at transfer or under working load, respectively; k_t', k_b' for composite section.

L = length of member, or length in general; L_t = length of transfer.

LL = live load.

M = bending moment in general.

M' = ultimate moment.

M_A, M_B = moment at point A (B).

M_C = moment acting on composite section.

M_{cr} = cracking moment

M_L = moment due to total live load only.

M_G = moment due to girder load, including any load on the beam or girder at time of transfer.

M_0 = moment at midspan.

M_P = moment on precast portion of composite section.

M_S = moment due to superimposed load.

M_T = moment due to total load.

M_1, M_2 = primary (resulting) moments in a continuous beam.

m = load factor or factor of safety.

m_b, m_t = ratio of section moduli of precast portion to composite section for bottom (top) fiber.

n = modular ratio E_s/E_c.

o = perimeter of bars or wires.

P = concentrated load.

p = percentage of steel, ratio of A_s/A_c; or unit pressure in tank or pipe. For rectangular sections, $p = A_s/bd$.

p_b = value of p for a balanced section = A_{sb}/bd for rectangular sections.

R = radius of curvature, or radius of tanks and pipes.

r = radius of gyration = $\sqrt{I/A}$.

s = stirrup spacing.

S_c = principal compressive stress.

S_t = principal tensile stress.

T = total tension in prestressed steel or center of total tension.

T' = T at ultimate load.

T_1 = T in nonprestressed steel.

T_1' = T' in nonprestressed steel.

t = thickness of beam flange.

u = unit bond stress.

u' = u at ultimate load.

v = unit shear; or vertical component.

V = total shear in beam.

V_c = total shear carried by concrete.

V_s = total shear carried by steel.

V', V_c', $V_s' = V$, V_c, V_s at ultimate load, respectively.

$W =$ total weight.

$W_0 =$ total weight carried by plain concrete section up to cracking.

$w =$ load or weight per length.

$w' = w$ at ultimate load.

w_c, $w_c' = w$ and w' for continuous beams, respectively.

$w_G =$ girder load, plf.

$w_S =$ superimposed load, plf.

$y =$ perpendicular distance from c.g.c. line to said fiber.

$y_0 = y$ for certain points, as defined in text.

$Z =$ section modulus I/c.

Abbreviations

cm = centimeter(s)

cu = cubic

F = Fahrenheit

ft = foot (feet)

in. = inch(es)

k = kip(s) = 1000 pounds

ksi = kip(s) per square inch

kg = kilogram(s)

lb = pound(s)

mm = millimeter(s)

plf = pound(s) per linear foot

psf = pound(s) per square foot

psi = pound(s) per square inch

P.C. = prestressed concrete

R.C. = reinforced concrete

sq = square

yd = yard(s)

data for some prestressing systems

appendix B

B-1 Addresses of Some Post-Tensioning Systems

Anderson system, Concrete Technology Corp., 1123 Port of Tacoma Rd., Tacoma 2, Wash.

Atlas system, Atlas Service Corp., 14809 Calvert St., Van Nuys, Calif.

BBRV system, Joseph T. Ryerson & Son, P.O. Box 8000-A, Chicago 80, Ill.

Freyssinet system, Intercontinental Equipment Co., Prestressed Concrete Div., 120 Broadway, New York 5, N.Y.

General Prestressing system, Western Concrete Structures, 19113 S. Hamilton Gardena, Calif.

Gifford-Udall system, Holly-Edwards Sales, P.O. Box 4818, Jacksonville, Fla.

Magnel-Blaton system, Precompressed Concrete Engineering Co. Ltd., 5012 Western Ave., Montreal, Quebec, Canada

PI system, Prestressing, Inc., 8546 Broadway, San Antonio, Texas.

Preload system, The Preload Co., Inc., 837 Old Country Road Westbury, Long Island, N.Y.

Prescon system, The Prescon Corp., P.O. Box 4186, Corpus Christi, Texas

Roebling system, Construction Materials Div., John A. Roebling's Sons, 640 S. Broad St., Trenton 2, N.J.

Stressrods system, Rods, Inc., 706 Folger Ave., Berkeley, Calif.

Stressteel system, Stressteel Corp., 221 Conyngham Ave., Wilkes-Barre, Pa.

VSL system, Colcrete Structures, 10 East 40th St., New York 16, N.Y.

B-2   Seven-Wire Uncoated Stress-Relieved Strands for Pre-Tensioning

ASTM A-416 Grade

Nominal Diameter in.	Weight per 1000 Ft, lb	Approximate Area, in.^{2}	Ultimate Strength, lb	Tensioning Load, lb
$\frac{1}{4}$	122	0.0356	9,000	6,300
$\frac{5}{16}$	198	0.0578	14,500	10,150
$\frac{3}{8}$	274	0.0799	20,000	14,000
$\frac{7}{16}$	373	0.1089	27,000	18,900
$\frac{1}{2}$	494	0.1438	36,000	25,200

270K Grade

Nominal Diameter, in.	Weight per 1000 Ft, lb	Approximate Area, in.^{2}	Ultimate Strength, lb	Tensioning Load, lb
$\frac{3}{8}$	292	0.085	23,000	16,100
$\frac{7}{16}$	400	0.117	31,000	21,700
$\frac{1}{2}$	525	0.152	41,300	28,910

Addresses of some United States' Suppliers:

Colorado Fuel and Iron Corp., Continental Oil Bldg., Denver, Colorado

Leschen Wire Rope Division, H. K. Porter Co., 2727 Hamilton Ave., St Louis 12, Mo.

John A. Roebling's Sons, 640 S. Broad St, Trenton 2, N.J.

Union Wire Rope Corp., 21st and Manchester Ave., Kansas City 26, Mo.

American Steel & Wire Division, U.S. Steel Corp., Cleveland 13, Ohio.

B-3 BBRV System

Almost any number of $\frac{1}{4}$-in. wires up to 40 and over can be made into a cable. Typical data are given for two types as shown on pp. 564–567.

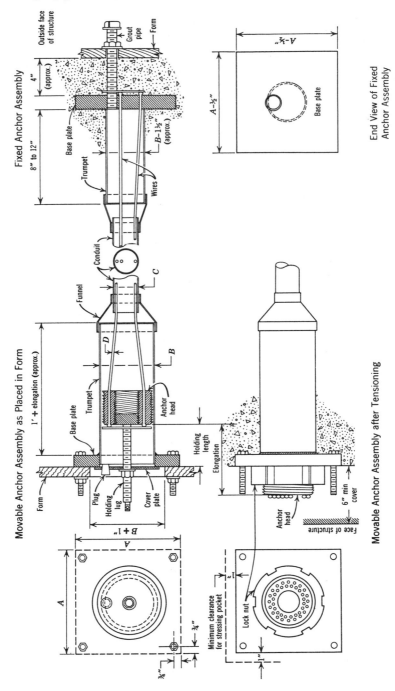

Fixed Anchor Assembly

End View of Fixed Anchor Assembly

Movable Anchor Assembly as Placed in Form

Movable Anchor Assembly after Tensioning

(A) Grout-Type Tendons; Screw-Type Head

Dimensional Data

		14 mf or mm	28 mf or mm	40 mf or mm
Tendon designation*				
Wire diameter, in.	$D =$	$\frac{1}{4}$	$\frac{1}{4}$	$\frac{1}{4}$
Base plate size ($A \times A$), in.	$A =$	$6\frac{3}{4}$	$9\frac{1}{4}$	11
Trumpet diameter (B), in.	$B =$	4	5	$5\frac{3}{4}$
Conduit diameter (C), in.	$C =$	$1\frac{5}{8}$	$2\frac{1}{8}$	$2\frac{1}{2}$

Engineering Data

	1	14	28	40
Number of wires	1	14	28	40
Section area of wires, in.²	0.04909	0.687	1.3744	1.963
Final force (60% of ultimate), lb	7,070	98,980	197,960	283,000
Initial force (70% of ultimate), lb	8,250	115,500	231,000	330,000
Overstressing force (80% of ultimate), lb	9,420	131,880	263,760	376,800
Ultimate strength, lb	11,780	164,920	329,840	471,200

* mm Signifies two movable heads on tendon. mf signifies one fixed, one movable.

BBRV System

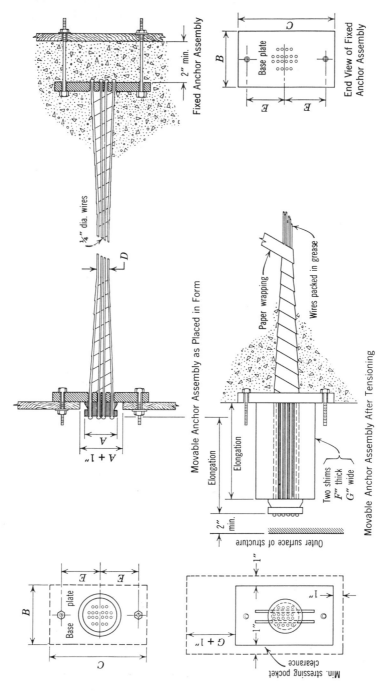

(B) Greased and Paper-wrapped Tendons; Grip-Type Head

Dimensional Data

Tendon designation*	7 mm or mf	14 mm or mf	20 mm or mf	27 mm or mf
A = Anchor diameter, in.	$2\frac{1}{4}$	3	$3\frac{1}{2}$	4
B = Base plate width, in.	4	$5\frac{1}{2}$	6	7
C = Base plate length, in.	6	9	10	11
D = Tendon diameter, in.	$\frac{3}{4}$	$1\frac{1}{8}$	$1\frac{1}{4}$	
E = Plate mount bolt location, in.	$2\frac{1}{2}$	$3\frac{3}{4}$	4	$4\frac{1}{2}$
F = Shim thickness, in.	$\frac{3}{8}$	$\frac{1}{2}$	$\frac{1}{2}$	$\frac{5}{8}$
G = Shim width, in.	4	$5\frac{1}{2}$	6	7

Engineering Data

Number of wires	1	7	14	20	27
Sectional area of wires, in.^{2}	0.04909	0.3436	0.687	0.9818	1.3254
Final force (60% of ultimate), lb	7,070	49,490	98,980	141,500	190,990
Initial force (70% of ultimate), lb	8,250	57,750	115,500	165,000	222,750
Overstressing force (80% of ultimate), lb	9,420	65,940	131,880	188,500	254,440
Ultimate force, lb	11,780	82,460	164,920	236,000	318,460

* $mf \rightarrow$ movable head both ends of tendon. $mf \rightarrow$ one end movable, one fixed.

BBRV System

B-4   Freyssinet System

(a) Wires.   (0.196-in. and 0.276-in. diameters)

Cable Characteristics

Cable Size	12/0.196	18/0.196	12/0.276
Nominal steel area, in.^{2}	0.362	0.543	0.718
Ultimate strength, lb	90,000	135,000	168,500
Max. tensioning load, lb (80% ultimate)	72,000	108,000	135,000
Max. design load, lb (60% ultimate)	54,000	81,000	101,100
Cable weight—sheath not included, lb/ft	1.23	1.85	2.45
Recommended hole diameter	$1\frac{1}{8}$ in.	$1\frac{1}{2}$ in.	$1\frac{1}{2}$ in.

Anchorage Dimensions

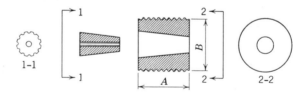

Dimensions of Cones

Cable Size No. wires/Wire diam., in.	A	B
12/0.196	4″	$3\frac{7}{8}″$
18/0.196	$4\frac{7}{8}″$	$4\frac{7}{8}″$
12/0.276	$4\frac{7}{8}″$	$4\frac{7}{8}″$

Assembled View

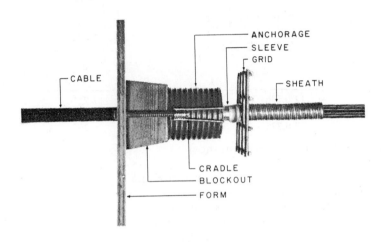

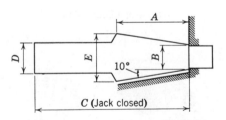

C (Jack closed)

Jack Clearances

Anchorage Type	A	B	C	D	E
12/0.196	11″	4″	23″	5″	6″
18/0.196 & 12/0.276	17″	$5\frac{1}{2}$″	36″	7″	11″

End Zone Details

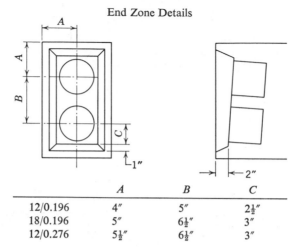

	A	B	C
12/0.196	4″	5″	2½″
18/0.196	5″	6½″	3″
12/0.276	5½″	6½″	3″

(b) Strands   ($\frac{1}{2}$-in. 7-wire strands)

Cable Characteristics

1. Nominal steel area   1.73 in.²
2. Ultimate cable strength (1.73 × 250,000 psi)   432,000 lb
3. Maximum tensioning load (75% of ultimate)   324,000 lb
4. Maximum design load (60% of ultimate)   259,000 lb
5. Cable weight (sheath not included)   5.93 lb
6. Recommended hole diameter (I.D.) $2\frac{5}{8}$ in.

Anchorage Dimensions

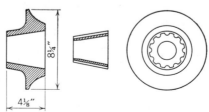

Assembled View

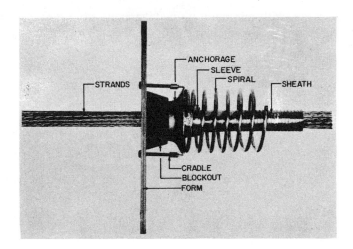

Jack Clearances

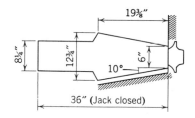

End Zone Details

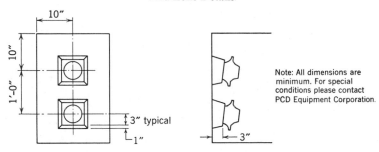

Note: All dimensions are minimum. For special conditions please contact PCD Equipment Corporation.

B-5 P.I. System

All ¼-in. wires, with minimum ultimate strength at 11,780 lb, nominal area of 0.0491 in.² and approximate modulus of elasticity of 29,000,000 psi.

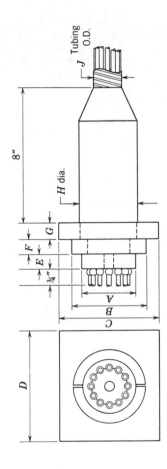

PI Assembly Number	A	B	C	D	E	F	G	H	Tubing O.D.	No. of Wires	Wire Area, in.^{2}	Weight, lb/ft	Working Force, lb (144,000 psi)	Initial Force, lb (168,000 psi)	Ultimate Strength, lb (240,000 psi)
6	$2\frac{1}{4}''$	$3\frac{1}{2}''$	$5''$	$5''$	$\frac{3}{4}''$	$\frac{1}{2}''$	$\frac{1}{2}''$	$2\frac{1}{2}''$	$1\frac{1}{2}''$	6	0.294	1.00	42,414	49,482	70,692
8	$2\frac{5}{8}''$	$4''$	$6''$	$6''$	$\frac{3}{4}''$	$\frac{5}{8}''$	$\frac{5}{8}''$	$2\frac{7}{8}''$	$1\frac{1}{2}''$	8	0.392	1.33	56,552	65,976	94,256
10	$3\frac{1}{8}''$	$4''$	$6''$	$6''$	$\frac{3}{4}''$	$\frac{3}{4}''$	$\frac{3}{4}''$	$3\frac{3}{8}''$	$1\frac{3}{4}''$	10	0.491	1.67	70,690	82,470	117,820
12	$3\frac{1}{4}''$	$4\frac{1}{2}''$	$6''$	$6\frac{1}{2}''$	$\frac{7}{8}''$	$\frac{7}{8}''$	$1''$	$3\frac{1}{2}''$	$1\frac{3}{4}''$	12	0.589	2.00	84,828	98,964	141,384
16	$3\frac{3}{8}''$	$5\frac{1}{4}''$	$7''$	$7\frac{1}{2}''$	$\frac{7}{8}''$	$1''$	$1\frac{1}{8}''$	$4\frac{1}{8}''$	$2\frac{1}{8}''$	16	0.784	2.67	113,104	131,952	188,512

Tendon Size Chart

Note: Prescon Prestressing Tendons are identified as to number of wires; coated or grouted; and stressed from both ends.
Example:
6M1
6—Number ¼″ Diameter Wires Per Tendon — *M*—Coated Wires Wrapped in Paper — 1—Stressed From One End Only
10G2
10—Number ¼″Diameter Wires Per Tendon — *G*—Wires Enclosed in Flexible Metal Conduit For Grouting — 2—Stressed From Both Ends

No. 0.250″ Wires Either *M* or *G*	Prestress Force, k $0.6f'_s$	*A*	*B*	*C*	*D*	*E**	*F*†	*G* Dia. Coated Tendon	*H*‡ Cond. Size O.D. Grouted Tendon	*J*§	f_c'§
2	14.1	3	4	2	1¼	3	3¾	½	1	¾	3000
3	21.2	3	4	2	1¼	3	4½	½	1	¾	3000
4	28.3	3	4½	2	1¼	3½	5	⅝	1⅜	1¼	4000
5	35.3	3	5½	2	1¼	4½	5½	¾	1⅜	1¼	4000
6	42.4	4	6	2½	1¼	5	5½	¾	1⅜	1¼	4000
7	49.5	4	6	2½	1¼	5	6½	¾	1⅜	1¼	4000
8	56.6	4	7	2½	1¼	6	6¾	⅞	1⅝	1¼	4000
9	63.6	4	7½	3	1¼	6	6¾	1	1⅝	1¼	4000
10	70.7	4	8½	3	1¼	7	6¾	1	1⅝	1¼	4000
11	77.8	5	7½	3	1¼	6½	7	1⅛	1⅝	1¼	4000
12	84.8	5	8	3	1¼	7	7	1⅛	1⅝	1½	4000
13	91.9	6	7½	3	1¼	6½	7	1⅛	1⅝	1½	4000
14	98.9	6	8½	3½	1¼	7	8¼	1⅛	1⅞	1½	4000
15	106.0	6	8½	3½	1¼	7	8¼	1⅛	1⅞	1½	4000
16	113.1	6	9½	3½	1¼	7	8¼	1¼	1⅞	1½	4000
17	120.2	6	9½	3½	1¼	7	8¼	1¼	1⅞	1½	4000
18	127.2	6	10	3½	1½	8½	8¼	1¼	2	1½	4000
19	134.3	6	11	3½	1½	8½	8¼	1⅜	2	1½	4000
20	141.4	6	11	3½	1½	8½	8¼	1⅜	2	1½	4000
21	148.5	6	11½	4	1⅞	9	8¼	1⅜	2	1½	4000
22	155.5	6	11½	4	1⅞	9	8¼	1⅜	2	1½	4000
23	162.6	6	12	4	1⅞	9	8¼	1½	2	1½	4000
24	169.7	6	12	4	1⅞	9	8¼	1½	2	1½	4000
25	176.8	7	11½	4	1⅞	9	10	1⅝	2⅛	1½	5000
26	183.8	7	11½	4	1⅞	9	10	1⅝	2⅛	1½	5000
27	190.9	7	12	4	1⅞	9	10	1⅝	2⅛	1½	5000
28	197.9	7	12	4	1⅞	9	10	1⅝	2⅛	1½	5000
29	205.0	7	12½	4	1⅞	9	10	1¾	2⅛	1½	5000
30	212.0	8	12	5¼	2¼	9	10¾	1¾	2⅛	1½	5000

* Anchor holes are ⅝″ for 14 wire tendons and larger, ½″ for all others.
† Clear dimensions required on one side only for inserting shims, measured in the direction of the long dimension of the plate.
‡ I.D. of tubing is ⅛″ less than this value.
§ If either *J* or f_c' are less than the values shown on table, then bearing plates must be increased in size to prevent excess bearing stresses in concrete.

Tendons are readily available to 42 wires with larger tendons available on special order. Due to varying applications of larger tendons, terminal hardware will be custom designed to fit the application.

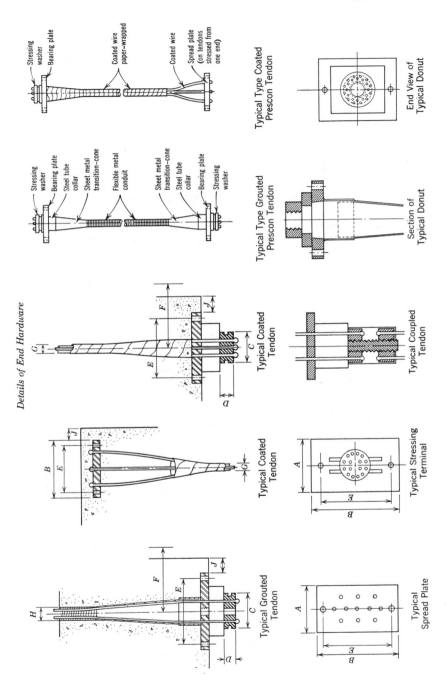

Details of End Hardware

Stressing washer
Bearing plate
Coated wire paper-wrapped
Coated wire
Spread plate (on tendons stressed from one end)

Typical Type Coated Prescon Tendon

End View of Typical Donut

Stressing washer
Bearing plate
Steel tube collar
Sheet metal transition-cone
Flexible metal conduit
Sheet metal transition-cone
Steel tube collar
Bearing plate
Stressing washer

Typical Type Grouted Prescon Tendon

Section of Typical Donut

Typical Coated Tendon

Typical Coupled Tendon

Typical Coated Tendon

Typical Stressing Terminal

Typical Grouted Tendon

Typical Spread Plate

B-7   Roebling System

Galvanized Strands for Post-Tensioning

Diameter, in.	Weight per Foot, lb	Area, in.^{2}	Minimum Guaranteed Ultimate Strength, lb	Recommended Design Load, lb
0.600	0.737	0.215	46,000	26,000
0.835	1.412	0.409	86,000	49,000
1	2.00	0.577	122,000	69,000
$1\frac{1}{8}$	2.61	0.751	156,000	90,000
$1\frac{1}{4}$	3.22	0.931	192,000	112,000
$1\frac{3}{8}$	3.89	1.12	232,000	134,000
$1\frac{1}{2}$	4.70	1.36	276,000	163,000
$1\frac{9}{16}$	5.11	1.48	300,000	177,000
$1\frac{5}{8}$	5.52	1.60	324,000	192,000
$1\frac{11}{16}$	5.98	1.73	352,000	208,000

The average modulus of elasticity of the strands in the above table is 25,000,000 psi.

Dimension of Anchorage Fittings

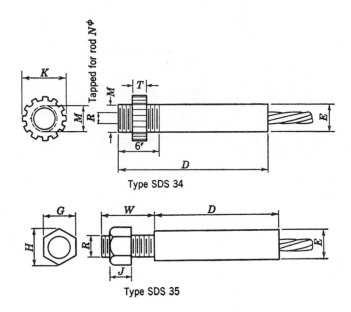

Type SDS 34

Type SDS 35

Measurements in Inches											Total Weight, lb	
Diameter Strand	D	W	E	M	R	G	H	J	K	T	Type SDS34	Type SDS35
0.600	$9\frac{1}{2}$	8	$1\frac{11}{16}$	12N	$1\frac{1}{4}$–12N	$1\frac{11}{16}$	$1\frac{15}{16}$	1	$2\frac{3}{4}$	$\frac{3}{4}$	7	$9\frac{1}{4}$
0.835	$12\frac{1}{2}$	10	$2\frac{1}{4}$	12N	$1\frac{5}{8}$–12N	$2\frac{1}{4}$	$2\frac{9}{16}$	$1\frac{5}{16}$	$3\frac{3}{4}$	1	$16\frac{1}{2}$	21
1	$14\frac{1}{8}$	11	$2\frac{3}{4}$	8N	$2\ \ –8N$	$2\frac{13}{16}$	$3\frac{3}{16}$	$1\frac{5}{8}$	$4\frac{3}{8}$	$1\frac{1}{4}$	$24\frac{3}{4}$	$32\frac{1}{2}$
$1\frac{1}{8}$	$16\frac{1}{2}$	11	3	8N	$2\frac{1}{4}$–8N	3	$3\frac{7}{16}$	$1\frac{3}{4}$	$4\frac{3}{4}$	$1\frac{1}{2}$	$39\frac{1}{2}$	50

N = American National thread series.

For fittings Type SDS35, standard studs having dimension W, shown above, are carried in stock.

Other stud lengths must be fabricated to order. All SDS 34 and 35 fittings are proof-loaded to a stress in excess of the recommended design stress after being attached to the strand.

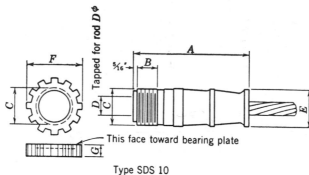

Type SDS 10

Strand Diameter	Measurements, In.					Total Weight, lb
	A	C	D	F	G	
1	10	$3\frac{1}{2}$–4N	2–4$\frac{1}{2}$NC	$5\frac{3}{8}$	$1\frac{1}{4}$	29
$1\frac{1}{8}$	$10\frac{3}{4}$	4–4N	$2\frac{1}{4}$–4$\frac{1}{2}$NC	6	$1\frac{3}{8}$	38
$1\frac{1}{4}$	$11\frac{3}{8}$	$4\frac{3}{8}$–4N	$2\frac{1}{2}$–4NC	$6\frac{1}{2}$	$1\frac{5}{8}$	45
$1\frac{3}{8}$	$11\frac{3}{4}$	$4\frac{7}{8}$–4N	3–4NC	7	$1\frac{5}{8}$	54
$1\frac{1}{2}$	$12\frac{3}{8}$	$5\frac{1}{4}$–4N	3–4NC	$7\frac{5}{8}$	$1\frac{3}{4}$	74
$1\frac{9}{16}$	$12\frac{3}{4}$	$5\frac{1}{2}$–4N	$3\frac{1}{2}$–4NC	$7\frac{7}{8}$	$1\frac{3}{4}$	77
$1\frac{5}{8}$	13	$5\frac{5}{8}$–4N	$3\frac{1}{2}$–4NC	8	$1\frac{3}{4}$	84
$1\frac{11}{16}$	$13\frac{1}{4}$	$5\frac{7}{8}$–4N	$3\frac{1}{2}$–4NC	$8\frac{3}{8}$	$1\frac{3}{4}$	88

N = American National thread series.

NC = American National coarse-thread series.

Fittings Type SS-2 can also be supplied with permanent studs and no external threads when necessary.

Details for Post–Tensioned Strands

Bearing Plate Assembly

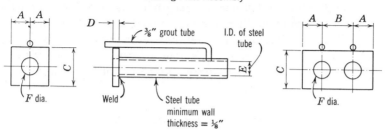

Type of Fitting	Strand Dia. in.	A^*	B^*	C^*	D	E Min.	E Max.	F
SDS 34	0.835	3	$5\frac{1}{4}$	6	$\frac{7}{8}$	$2\frac{3}{8}$	$2\frac{1}{2}$	$E + \frac{1}{16}$
	1	3	$5\frac{1}{2}$	6	$\frac{7}{8}$	$2\frac{7}{8}$	3	$E + \frac{1}{16}$
	$1\frac{1}{8}$	$3\frac{1}{2}$	$6\frac{1}{4}$	7	1	$3\frac{1}{4}$	$3\frac{1}{4}$	$E + \frac{1}{16}$
	0.600	2	$3\frac{1}{4}$	4	$\frac{5}{8}$	$1\frac{3}{4}$	$1\frac{7}{8}$	$1\frac{1}{2}$
SDS 35	0.835	3	$4\frac{1}{2}$	6	$\frac{7}{8}$	$2\frac{3}{8}$	$2\frac{1}{2}$	$1\frac{7}{8}$
	1	3	$4\frac{7}{8}$	6	$\frac{7}{8}$	$2\frac{7}{8}$	3	$2\frac{1}{4}$
	$1\frac{1}{8}$	$3\frac{1}{2}$	$5\frac{1}{2}$	7	1	$3\frac{1}{8}$	$3\frac{1}{4}$	$2\frac{1}{2}$

Type of Fitting	Strand Dia. in.	A^*	B^*	C^*	D	E Min.	E Max.	F
SS2	1	4	7	8	$\frac{7}{8}$	$3\frac{3}{4}$	$3\frac{7}{8}$	$E + \frac{1}{16}$
	$1\frac{1}{8}$	$4\frac{1}{4}$	$7\frac{1}{2}$	$8\frac{1}{2}$	1	$4\frac{1}{4}$	$4\frac{3}{8}$	$E + \frac{1}{16}$
	$1\frac{1}{4}$	$4\frac{1}{2}$	8	9	$1\frac{1}{4}$	$4\frac{5}{8}$	$4\frac{3}{4}$	$E + \frac{1}{16}$
	$1\frac{3}{8}$	$4\frac{3}{4}$	$8\frac{1}{2}$	$9\frac{1}{2}$	$1\frac{1}{4}$	$5\frac{1}{8}$	$5\frac{1}{4}$	$E + \frac{1}{16}$
	$1\frac{1}{2}$	$5\frac{3}{8}$	$9\frac{1}{2}$	$10\frac{3}{4}$	$1\frac{3}{8}$	$5\frac{1}{2}$	$5\frac{5}{8}$	$E + \frac{1}{16}$
	$1\frac{9}{16}$	$5\frac{7}{8}$	$10\frac{1}{4}$	$11\frac{3}{4}$	$1\frac{3}{8}$	$5\frac{3}{4}$	$5\frac{7}{8}$	$E + \frac{1}{16}$
	$1\frac{5}{8}$	$5\frac{7}{8}$	$10\frac{1}{4}$	$11\frac{3}{4}$	$1\frac{1}{2}$	$5\frac{7}{8}$	6	$E + \frac{1}{16}$
	$1\frac{11}{16}$	6	$10\frac{1}{2}$	12	$1\frac{1}{2}$	$6\frac{1}{8}$	$6\frac{1}{4}$	$E + \frac{1}{16}$

* These are standard minimum dimensions. They can be reduced slightly by using special jack bases. Bearing pressure under above plates does not exceed 2500 psi.

B-8   Stressteel System

Stressteel Bars are now available in two grades: *Regular* Stressteel with a guaranteed minimum ultimate strength of 145,000 psi and *Special* Stressteel with a guaranteed minimum ultimate strength of 160,000 psi. The *special bar* was developed to meet the ever increasing needs for higher strength materials in prestressed concrete construction. *Special* bars are slightly more expensive than *regular* bars because of higher alloy content and more extensive treatment.

Design Properties of Stressteel Bars

Bar Size ø"	Weight Pounds lin/ft	Area in.²	Ultimate Strength Guaranteed Minimum		Initial Tensioning Load—0.7f_s' *		Design Load—0.6f_s'	
			REGULAR	SPECIAL	REGULAR	SPECIAL	REGULAR	SPECIAL
			(All values in units of 1000 pounds)					
$\frac{3}{4}$	1.50	0.442	64.1	70.7	44.9	49.5	38.5	42.4
$\frac{7}{8}$	2.04	0.601	87.1	96.2	61.0	67.3	52.3	57.7
1	2.67	0.785	113.8	125.6	79.7	87.9	68.3	75.4
$1\frac{1}{8}$	3.38	0.994	144.1	159.0	100.9	111.3	86.5	95.4
$1\frac{1}{4}$	4.17	1.227	177.9	196.3	124.5	137.4	106.7	117.8
$1\frac{3}{8}$	5.05	1.485	215.3	237.6	150.7	166.3	129.2	142.6

* Losses due to creep, shrinkage and plastic flow of concrete and steel relaxation should be deducted from this value. Overtension to 0.8f_s' is permitted to account for friction loss and/or wedge seating loss.

Couplers and Coupler Shields

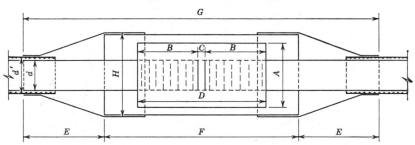

| Part No. | | Bar Ø" | Flex. Tube I.D." | Dimensions, In. | | | | | | | | Weight, lb each |
Coupler	Coupler Shield	d	d'	A	B	C	D	E	F†	G	H	Coupler
HC-6	CS-6*	$\frac{3}{4}$	1	$1\frac{1}{2}$	$1\frac{3}{8}$	$\frac{1}{4}$	3					1.1
HC-7	CS-7	$\frac{7}{8}$	$1\frac{1}{8}$	$1\frac{3}{4}$	$1\frac{5}{8}$	$\frac{1}{4}$	$3\frac{1}{2}$	2	10	14	$2\frac{1}{2}$	1.8
HC-8	CS-8	1	$1\frac{1}{4}$	$1\frac{3}{4}$	$1\frac{3}{4}$	$\frac{1}{4}$	$3\frac{3}{4}$	2	10	14	$2\frac{1}{2}$	1.9
HC-9	CS-9	$1\frac{1}{8}$	$1\frac{3}{8}$	2	$1\frac{7}{8}$	$\frac{1}{2}$	$4\frac{1}{4}$	2	10	14	$2\frac{1}{2}$	2.5
HC-10	CS-10	$1\frac{1}{4}$	$1\frac{1}{2}$	$2\frac{1}{4}$	$2\frac{1}{8}$	$\frac{1}{2}$	$4\frac{3}{4}$	3	10	16	3	3.7
HC-11	CS-11	$1\frac{3}{8}$	$1\frac{5}{8}$	$2\frac{1}{4}$	$2\frac{1}{4}$	$\frac{1}{2}$	5	3	10	16	3	3.5

* CS-6 on special request only.
† Standard—can be made any length required for coupler movement.

Wedges, Nut and Plates

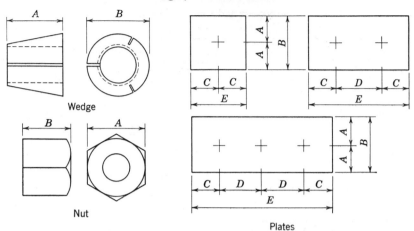

Wedge

Nut

Plates

Bar Ø"	Part No.	Wedges Dimensions, In.		Weight, lb each	Part No.	Nuts Dimensions, In.		Weight, lb each
		A	B			A	B	
$\frac{3}{4}$	W-6	$1\frac{3}{16}$	$1\frac{1}{4}$	0.22	HN6	$1\frac{3}{8}$	$1\frac{1}{4}$	0.5
$\frac{7}{8}$	W-7	$1\frac{1}{2}$	$1\frac{1}{2}$	0.32	HN7	$1\frac{5}{8}$	$1\frac{7}{16}$	0.7
1	W-8	$1\frac{1}{2}$	$1\frac{3}{4}$	0.50	HN8	$1\frac{7}{8}$	$1\frac{5}{8}$	1.0
$1\frac{1}{8}$	W-9	$1\frac{3}{4}$	2	0.70	HN9	$2\frac{1}{8}$	$1\frac{13}{16}$	1.5
$1\frac{1}{4}$	W-10	2	$2\frac{1}{4}$	0.80	HN10	$2\frac{3}{8}$	2	2.0
$1\frac{3}{8}$	W-11	$2\frac{3}{16}$	$2\frac{1}{2}$	1.10	HN11	$2\frac{3}{8}$	2	2.0

Bar Ø"	Part No. WT, TP or P*	No. of Holes	Plates Dimensions, In.						Weight, lb each
			A	B	C	D	E	Thickness	
$\frac{3}{4}$	6	1	2	4	2		4	1	4.5
$\frac{7}{8}$	7	1	$2\frac{1}{4}$	$4\frac{1}{2}$	$2\frac{1}{2}$		5	$1\frac{1}{2}$	9.5
1	8	1	$2\frac{1}{2}$	5	$2\frac{3}{4}$		$5\frac{1}{2}$	$1\frac{1}{2}$	11.7
$1\frac{1}{8}$	9	1	3	6	3		6	$1\frac{3}{4}$	17.8
$1\frac{1}{4}$	10	1	3	6	$3\frac{1}{2}$		7	$1\frac{3}{4}$	20.8
$1\frac{3}{8}$	11	1	$3\frac{1}{2}$	7	$3\frac{3}{4}$		$7\frac{1}{2}$	2	29.7
2 @ $\frac{3}{4}$	6-2	2	2	4	2	4	8	1	9.1
2 @ $\frac{7}{8}$	7-2	2	$2\frac{1}{2}$	5	$2\frac{1}{2}$	4	9	$1\frac{1}{2}$	19.0
2 @ 1	8-2	2	$2\frac{1}{2}$	5	3	5	11	$1\frac{1}{2}$	23.4
2 @ $1\frac{1}{8}$	9-2	2	3	6	$3\frac{1}{2}$	5	$11\frac{1}{4}$	$1\frac{3}{4}$	34.2
2 @ $1\frac{1}{4}$	10-2	2	$3\frac{1}{2}$	7	$3\frac{1}{2}$	5	$12\frac{1}{2}$	$1\frac{3}{4}$	43.4
2 @ $1\frac{3}{8}$	11-2	2	$3\frac{1}{2}$	7	$4\frac{1}{4}$	6	$14\frac{1}{2}$	2	57.5
3 @ $\frac{3}{4}$	6-3	3	2	4	2	4	12	1	13.6
3 @ $\frac{7}{8}$	7-3	3	$2\frac{1}{2}$	5	$2\frac{1}{2}$	4	13	$1\frac{1}{2}$	27.6
3 @ 1	8-3	3	$2\frac{1}{2}$	5	3	5	16	$1\frac{1}{2}$	34.0
3 @ $1\frac{1}{8}$	9-3	3	3	6	$3\frac{3}{4}$	5	$17\frac{1}{2}$	$1\frac{3}{4}$	52.0
3 @ $1\frac{1}{4}$	10-3	3	$3\frac{1}{2}$	7	$3\frac{3}{4}$	$5\frac{1}{2}$	$18\frac{1}{2}$	$1\frac{3}{4}$	64.2

* WP = Wedge Plate; TP = Threaded Plate; P = Plate with drilled hole.

Notes:

1. Dimensions are subject to change as new developments or improvements occur.
2. Parts for $\frac{1}{2}''$ and $\frac{5}{8}''$ Ø bars available on special request.
3. Drilled holes in P type plates are $\frac{1}{4}''$ larger than bar Ø.
4. Plate sizes conform to allowable bearing stress provisions of latest ACI-ASCE Recommended Practice and PCI Building Code, assuming that $f'c = 5000$ psi, and $\frac{Ac}{Ap}$ or $\frac{A'b}{Ab} = 1.0$. For lower strength concrete a larger bearing area should be provided. For higher strength concrete, or 5000 psi concrete where $\frac{Ac}{Ap}$ exceeds 1.0, smaller plates may be used. Consult Stressteel Corporation, Engineering Department for our recommendations on plate design.
5. Plates to anchor a larger number of bars, plates to anchor bars of different diameters, or plates of nonrectangular shape may be designed to meet the needs of the structural engineer.

appendix *C* constants for beam sections

TABLE 1

Constants for T-Sections

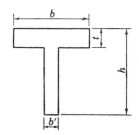

Section	b'/b	t/h	A^*	c_b†	c_i†	I‡	r^2§	k_t†	k_b†
1–a	0.1	0.1	$0.19bh$	$0.714h$	$0.286h$	$0.0179bh^3$	$0.0945h^2$	$0.132h$	$0.333h$
1–b	0.1	0.2	0.28	0.756	0.244	0.0192	0.0688	0.0910	0.282
1–c	0.1	0.3	0.37	0.755	0.245	0.0193	0.0520	0.0689	0.212
1–d	0.1	0.4	0.46	0.735	0.265	0.0202	0.0439	0.0597	0.165
1–e	0.2	0.1	0.28	0.629	0.371	0.0283	0.1010	0.161	0.272
1–f	0.2	0.2	0.36	0.678	0.322	0.0315	0.0875	0.129	0.272
1–g	0.2	0.3	0.44	0.691	0.309	0.0319	0.0725	0.105	0.234
1–h	0.2	0.4	0.52	0.684	0.316	0.0320	0.0616	0.090	0.195
1–i	0.3	0.1	0.37	0.585	0.415	0.0365	0.0985	0.169	0.237
1–j	0.3	0.2	0.44	0.626	0.374	0.0408	0.0928	0.148	0.248
1–k	0.3	0.3	0.51	0.645	0.355	0.0417	0.0819	0.127	0.231
1–l	0.3	0.4	0.58	0.645	0.355	0.0417	0.0720	0.112	0.203
1–m	0.4	0.1	0.46	0.559	0.441	0.0440	0.0954	0.171	0.216
1–n	0.4	0.2	0.52	0.592	0.408	0.0486	0.0935	0.158	0.229
1–o	0.4	0.3	0.58	0.609	0.391	0.0499	0.0860	0.141	0.220
1–p	0.4	0.4	0.64	0.612	0.388	0.0502	0.0785	0.128	0.205
1–q	1.0	1.0	1.00	0.500	0.500	0.0833	0.0833	0.167	0.167

* Given as a function of bh.
† Given as a function of h.
‡ Given as a function of bh^3.
§ Given as a function of h^2.

TABLE 2
Constants for I-Sections

Section	b'/b	t/h	A*	c_b†	c_t†	I‡	r^2§	k_t†	k_b†
2-a	0.1	0.1	$0.21bh$	$0.650h$	$0.350h$	$0.0260bh^3$	$0.1236h^2$	$0.190h$	$0.354h$
2-b	0.1	0.2	0.32	0.675	0.325	0.0345	0.1080	0.160	0.332
2-c	0.1	0.3	0.43	0.672	0.328	0.0387	0.0900	0.134	0.274
2-d	0.2	0.1	0.29	0.610	0.390	0.0316	0.1090	0.179	0.280
2-e	0.2	0.2	0.38	0.647	0.353	0.0378	0.0994	0.153	0.282
2-f	0.2	0.3	0.47	0.655	0.345	0.0402	0.0856	0.131	0.248

* Given as a function of bh.
† Given as a function of h.
‡ Given as a function of bh^3.
§ Given as a function of h^2.

TABLE 3
Constants for I-Sections

Section	b'/b	t/h	A*	c_b†	c_t†	I‡	r^2§	k_t†	k_b†
3-a	0.1	0.1	$0.23bh$	$0.597h$	$0.403h$	$0.0326bh^3$	$0.1420h^2$	$0.238h$	$0.352h$
3-b	0.1	0.2	0.36	0.611	0.389	0.0464	0.1288	0.210	0.331
3-c	0.1	0.3	0.49	0.606	0.394	0.0535	0.1090	0.180	0.274
3-d	0.2	0.1	0.31	0.572	0.428	0.0373	0.1204	0.210	0.282
3-e	0.2	0.2	0.42	0.595	0.405	0.0488	0.1160	0.195	0.286
3-f	0.2	0.3	0.53	0.599	0.401	0.0540	0.1020	0.170	0.254
3-g	0.3	0.1	0.39	0.557	0.443	0.0430	0.1103	0.198	0.250
3-h	0.3	0.2	0.48	0.582	0.418	0.0510	0.1065	0.183	0.255
3-i	0.3	0.3	0.57	0.592	0.408	0.0553	0.0970	0.164	0.238

* Given as a function of bh.
† Given as a function of h.
‡ Given as a function of bh^3.
§ Given as a function of h^2.

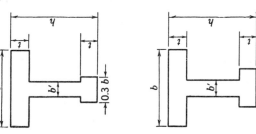

TABLE 4
Constants for I-Sections

Section	b'/b	t/h	$A*$	c_b†	c_i†	I‡	r^2§	k_i†	k_b†
4-a	0.1	0.1	$0.25bh$	$0.554h$	$0.446h$	$0.0381bh^3$	$0.1525h^2$	$0.276h$	$0.342h$
4-b	0.1	0.2	0.40	0.560	0.440	0.0560	0.1391	0.248	0.316
4-c	0.1	0.3	0.55	0.557	0.443	0.0651	0.1182	0.212	0.267
4-d	0.2	0.1	0.33	0.540	0.460	0.0425	0.1290	0.239	0.280
4-e	0.2	0.2	0.46	0.552	0.448	0.0578	0.1258	0.228	0.281
4-f	0.2	0.3	0.59	0.553	0.447	0.0657	0.1113	0.202	0.249
4-g	0.3	0.1	0.41	0.534	0.466	0.0467	0.1140	0.214	0.244
4-h	0.3	0.2	0.52	0.546	0.454	0.0598	0.1150	0.210	0.254
4-i	0.3	0.3	0.63	0.550	0.450	0.0663	0.1051	0.191	0.234

* Given as a function of bh.
† Given as a function of h.
‡ Given as a function of bh^3.
§ Given as a function of h^2.

TABLE 5
Constants for I-Sections

Section	b'/b	t/h	$A*$	c_b†	c_i†	I‡	r^2§	k_i†	k_b†
5-a	0.1	0.1	$0.21bh$	$0.350h$	$0.650h$	$0.0260bh^3$	$0.1236h^2$	$0.354h$	$0.190h$
5-b	0.1	0.2	0.32	0.325	0.675	0.0345	0.1080	0.332	0.160
5-c	0.1	0.3	0.43	0.328	0.672	0.0387	0.0900	0.274	0.134
5-d	0.2	0.1	0.29	0.390	0.610	0.0316	0.1090	0.280	0.179
5-e	0.2	0.2	0.38	0.353	0.647	0.0378	0.0994	0.282	0.153
5-f	0.2	0.3	0.47	0.345	0.655	0.0402	0.0856	0.248	0.131

* Given as a function of bh.
† Given as a function of h.
‡ Given as a function of bh^3.
§ Given as a function of h^2.

TABLE 6
Constants for Symmetrical I- and Box-Sections

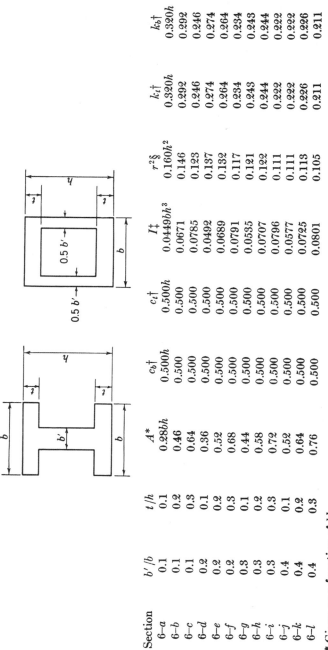

Section	b'/b	t/h	A*	c_b†	c_t†	I‡	r^2§	k_t†	k_b†
6–a	0.1	0.1	$0.28bh$	$0.500h$	$0.500h$	$0.0449bh^3$	$0.160h^2$	$0.320h$	$0.320h$
6–b	0.1	0.2	0.46	0.500	0.500	0.0671	0.146	0.292	0.292
6–c	0.1	0.3	0.64	0.500	0.500	0.0785	0.123	0.246	0.246
6–d	0.2	0.1	0.36	0.500	0.500	0.0492	0.137	0.274	0.274
6–e	0.2	0.2	0.52	0.500	0.500	0.0689	0.132	0.264	0.264
6–f	0.2	0.3	0.68	0.500	0.500	0.0791	0.117	0.234	0.234
6–g	0.3	0.1	0.44	0.500	0.500	0.0535	0.121	0.243	0.243
6–h	0.3	0.2	0.58	0.500	0.500	0.0707	0.122	0.244	0.244
6–i	0.3	0.3	0.72	0.500	0.500	0.0796	0.111	0.222	0.222
6–j	0.4	0.1	0.52	0.500	0.500	0.0577	0.111	0.222	0.222
6–k	0.4	0.2	0.64	0.500	0.500	0.0725	0.113	0.226	0.226
6–l	0.4	0.3	0.76	0.500	0.500	0.0801	0.105	0.211	0.211

* Given as a function of bh.
† Given as a function of h.
‡ Given as a function of bh^3.
§ Given as a function of h^2.

appendix D *prestressed concrete building code requirements**

building code committee

T. Y. LIN, *Chairman*
ROSS H. BRYAN
HARRY H. EDWARDS
BEN C. GERWICK, JR.
MORRIS SCHUPACK
IRWIN J. SPEYER
PETER J. VERNA, JR.

CHAPTER I
GENERAL

101—Notation

A_b = bearing area of anchor plate of post-tensioning steel
A'_b = maximum area of the portion of the anchorage surface that is geometrically similar to and concentric with the area of the anchor plate of the post-tensioning steel
A_s = area of prestressed tendons
A'_s = area of unprestressed reinforcement
A_{sf} = steel area required to develop the ultimate compressive strength of the overhanging portions of the flange
A_{sr} = steel area required to develop the ultimate compressive strength of the web of a flanged section
A_v = area of web reinforcement placed perpendicular to the axis of the member

* Courtesy of the Prestressed Concrete Institute, 1961.

b = width of compression flange of a flanged member or width of a rectangular member

b' = width of web of a flanged member

D = design dead load

d = distance from extreme compressive fiber to centroid of the prestressing force

E_c = flexural modulus of elasticity of concrete

E_s = modulus of elasticity of prestressing steel

e = base of Naperian logarithms

f'_c = compressive strength of concrete at 28 days

f'_{ci} = compressive strength of concrete at time of initial prestress

f'_{ct} = compressive strength of concrete at time considered

f_{cp} = permissible compressive concrete stress on bearing area under anchor plate of post-tensioning steel

f_{cs} = average concrete stress at level of centroid of prestressing steel

f'_s = ultimate strength of prestressing steel

f_{se} = effective steel prestress after losses

f_{si} = initial stress in prestressing steel after transfer has taken place

f_{su} = stress in prestressing steel at ultimate load

f_{sy} = nominal yield point stress of prestressing steel

f'_y = yield point stress of unprestressed reinforcing steel

I = moment of inertia about the centroid of the cross-section

j = ratio of distance between centroid of compression and centroid of tension to the depth d

K = friction wobble coefficient per foot of prestressing steel

L' = length of prestressing steel element from jacking end to any point x

L = design live load

p = A_s/bd; ratio of prestressing steel

p' = A'_s/bd; ratio of unprestressed steel

Q = statical moment of cross-section area, above or below the level being investigated for shear, about the centroid

M_u = ultimate bending moment

s = longitudinal spacing of web reinforcement

T_o = steel stress at jacking end

T_x = steel stress at any point x

t = average thickness of the compression flange of a flanged member

V_c = shear force carried by concrete

V_u = shear force due to specified ultimate load and effect of prestressing

W = design wind or earthquake load.

v = shearing stress

μ = friction curvature coefficient

α = total angular change of prestressing steel profile in radians from jacking end to any point x

102—Definitions

(a) Anchorage—The means by which the prestress force is permanently delivered to the concrete

(b) Bonded tendons—Tendons which are bonded to the concrete either directly or through grouting. Unbonded tendons are free to move relative to the surrounding concrete.

(c) Composite construction—Construction in which part of a load-carrying member is precast and part is cast in place.

(d) Effective prestress—The stress remaining in the tendons after all losses have occurred, excluding the effect of superimposed loads.

(e) Friction: Curvature friction—Friction resulting from bends or curves in the specified cable profile.

Wobble friction—Friction caused by the unintentional variation of the prestressing steel from its specified profile.

(f) Jacking force—The temporary force exerted by the device which introduces the tension into the tendons.

(g) Post-tensioning—A method of prestressing in which the tendons are tensioned after the concrete has hardened.

(h) Pretensioning—A method of prestressing in which the tendons are tensioned before the concrete is placed.

(i) Tendon—A tensioned steel element used to impart prestress to the concrete.

(j) Transfer—The action of delivering the tendon force to the concrete.

103—Scope

(a) This code covers the use of prestressed concrete in any structure to be built under the provisions of the general building code. It is intended to supplement the provisions of the general code in order to provide for the incorporation of prestressed concrete. In all matters pertaining to materials, design and construction of prestressed concrete, this code shall govern.

(b) Provisions in this code apply to linear, flexural members prestressed with high tensile steel. Pavements, shells, piles, and circular prestressing, such as for tanks and pipes, are not included in this code. The absence of provisions relative to types other than those specifically mentioned in this code shall not be construed to mean any restrictions on such types.

(c) Structures or components of structures embodying both prestressed and reinforced concrete are subject to the provisions of this code, with the exception that independent elements or portions containing no prestressing shall be subject to the code for reinforced concrete.

104—New Materials and Methods of Design and Construction

(a) New materials and their design and construction methods, pertaining to prestressed concrete structures, which are proven to be safe, (either by analytical or experimental methods), to the satisfaction of the Building Official, are considered acceptable under the provisions of this code.

(b) When materials, design and construction methods as submitted by the engineer pertaining to prestressed concrete are in conflict with the provisions of this code, the sponsors of such materials and methods shall have the right to present the supporting data to a "Board of Examiners for Special Construction" appointed by the Building Official. This Board shall be composed of registered engineers and architects familiar with prestressed concrete, and shall have the authority to investigate the data so submitted and to decide on the acceptance of the proposed deviations.

105—Load Tests

Load tests on precast units, completed structures or parts thereof shall be made if required by the specification or if there is reasonable doubt as to its structural adequacy. When such load tests are made, the applicable sections of the ACI Building Code Requirements for Reinforced Concrete, (ACI 318), latest edition, shall be followed.

CHAPTER II

DESIGN

201—General Considerations

(a) Stresses shall be investigated at service conditions and at all load stages that may be critical during the life of the structure from the time prestress is first applied.

(b) Stress concentrations due to the prestressing or other causes shall be taken into account in the design.

(c) The effects on the adjoining structure of elastic and plastic deformations caused by the prestressing shall be provided for. When the effect is additive to temperature and shrinkage effects, they shall be considered simultaneously.

(d) The possibility of buckling of a member between points of contact between concrete and prestressing steel and of buckling of thin webs and flanges shall be considered.

202—Basic Assumptions

The following assumptions shall be made for purposes of design:

(a) Strains vary linearly with depth through the entire load range.

(b) At cracked sections, the ability of the concrete to resist tension is neglected.

(c) In calculations of section properties prior to bonding of tendons, areas of the open ducts shall be deducted unless relatively small. The transformed area of bonded tendons may be included in pretensioned members and in post-tensioned members after grouting.

(d) Modulus of elasticity of concrete in psi shall be assumed as follows:
   1. Standard-weight concrete, when not determined by test:
$$E_c = 1,800,000 + 500 \, f'_{ct}$$
   2. Lightweight concrete:
E_c to be established by tests

(e) The modulus of elasticity, E_s, of prestressing steel shall be determined by tests or supplied by the manufacturer.

203—Allowable Stresses in Concrete

(a) Temporary stresses immediately after transfer, before losses due to creep and shrinkage, shall not exceed the following:
   1. Compression .... $0.60 \, f'_{ci}$
   2. Tension in members without auxiliary
      reinforcement in the tensile zone .... $3 \sqrt{f'_{ci}}$

Where the calculated tensile stress exceeds this value, reinforcement shall be provided to resist the total tensile force in the concrete computed on the assumption of an uncracked section. See 204 (c).

(b) Stresses at design loads, after allowance for all prestress losses, shall not exceed the following:
   1. Compression .... $0.45 \, f'_c$
   2. Tension in the precompressed tensile zone:
      Members, not exposed to a corrosive environment,
      which contain bonded prestressed or unprestressed
      reinforcement located so as to control cracking .... $6 \sqrt{f'_c}$
      All other members 0

These values may be exceeded when not detrimental to proper structural behavior as provided in Section 104.

(c) The bearing stress on the concrete created by the anchorage in post-tensioned concrete with adequate reinforcement in the end regions shall not exceed the following:

$$f_{cp} = 0.6\ f'_{ci}\ \sqrt[3]{A'_b/A_b}\ \text{ but not greater than } f'_{ci}$$

204—Allowable Stresses in Steel

(a) Temporary stresses
   1. Due to temporary jacking force: .... 0.80 f'_s
      but not greater than the maximum value recommended by the manufacturer
   2. Pretensioning tendons immediately after transfer, or post-tensioning tendons immediately after anchoring: .... 0.70 f'_s

(b) Effective prestress: .... 0.60 f'_s or 0.80 f_{sy}
      whichever is smaller

(c) Stress in auxiliary unprestressed reinforcement provided in accordance with 203(a)2: .... 20,000 psi

205—Loss of Prestress

(a) To determine the effective prestress allowance for the following losses shall be deducted from the transfer prestress:
   1. Elastic shortening of concrete
   2. Creep of concrete
   3. Shrinkage of concrete
   4. Relaxation of steel stress
   5. Frictional loss due to intended or unintended curvature in the tendons.

(b) Friction losses in post-tensioned steel shall be calculated in accordance with the following formulas and on experimentally determined wobble and curvature coefficients,* and shall be verified during stressing operations. The values of coefficients assumed for design, and the acceptable ranges of jacking forces and steel elongations shall be shown on the plans.

$$T_o = T_x e^{(KL' + \mu\alpha)} \tag{a}$$

When $(KL + \mu\alpha)$ is not greater than 0.3, formula (b) may be used in lieu of formula (a):

$$T_o = T_x {}^{(1 + KL + \mu\alpha)} \tag{b}$$

(c) When prestress in a member may be lost through its connection with adjoining elements, such loss shall be allowed for in the design.

(d) Where a slip of the tendons is expected to take place in seating the anchorage device, the resulting loss of prestress shall be allowed for.

*Values of K and μ vary appreciably with duct material and method of construction. The following table may be used as a guide.

Type of Steel	Type of duct or sheath	Unusual range of observed values		Suggested design values	
		K	μ	K	μ
Wire Cables	Bright metal sheathing	0.0005-0.0030	0.15-0.35	0.0020	0.30
High Strength Bars	Bright metal sheathing	0.0001-0.0005	0.08-0.30	0.0003	0.20
Galvanized strand	Bright metal sheathing	0.0005-0.0020	0.15-0.30	0.0015	0.25

206—Load Factors

(a) The value by which the design load is multiplied to be equated to the ultimate load is termed the load factor.

(b) For ultimate flexural strength calculations load factors indicated by the following formulas shall be used:

$$1.8 \ (D + L)$$
$$\text{or } 1.2D + 2.4L$$
$$\text{or } 1.4 \ (D + L + W)$$

whichever is controlling. In the above, D = design dead load, L = design live load, and W = design wind or earthquake load.

(c) When ultimate strength is governed by shear or bond, the load factors for shear or bond only in Article 206(b) shall be increased a minimum of 20%.

207—Ultimate Flexural Strength

The required ultimate load on a member, determined in conformance with Section 206 shall not exceed the ultimate flexural strength computed by the formulas in the following:

1. Rectangular sections, or flanged sections in which the neutral axis lies within the flange,

$$M_u = A_s f_{su} d \left(1 - \frac{0.6 \ pf_{su}}{f'_c} \right)$$

2. Flanged sections in which the neutral axis falls outside the flange:*

$$M_u = A_{sr} f_{su} d \ (1 - 0.6 \frac{A_{sr} f_{su}}{b' d f'_c}) + 0.85 \ f'_c \ (b - b') t \ (d - 0.5t)$$

where

$$A_{sr} = A_s - A_{sf}$$
$$A_{sf} = \frac{0.85 \ f'_c \ (b - b') t}{f_{su}}$$

3. Where information for the determination of f_{su} is not available, and provided that f_{se} is not less than 0.5 f'_s, the following values shall be used:

Bonded members $\quad f_{su} = f'_s \ (1 - 0.5 \ pf'_s / f'_c)$

Unbonded members $f_{su} = f_{se} + 15,000 \ psi$

4. Non-prestressed reinforcement, in combination with prestressed steel, may be considered to contribute to the tensile force in a member at ultimate moment an amount equal to its area times its yield point, provided

$$\frac{pf_{su}}{f'_c} + \frac{p'f'_y}{f'_c} - \text{does not exceed } 0.3.$$

*Usually where the flange thickness is less than 1.4 dpf_{su}/f'_c

208—Limitations on Steel Percentage

(a) Except as provided in Section 208 (b), the ratio of prestressing steel used for calculations of M_u shall be such that

$$pf_{su}/f'_c \text{ is not more than } 0.30.$$

For flanged sections, p shall be taken as the steel ratio of only that portion of the total tensile steel area which is required to develop the compressive strength of the web alone. ($A_{sr}f_{su}/b'df'_c$)

(b) When a steel ratio in excess of that specified in Section 208 (a) is used, the ultimate moment shall be taken as not greater than the following:

Rectangular sections, or flanged sections in which the neutral axis lies within the flange

$$M_u = 0.25 \, f'_c b d^2$$

Flanged sections in which the neutral axis falls outside the flange

$$M_u = 0.25 \, f'_c b'd^2 + 0.85f'_c \, (b - b')t \, (d - 0.5t)$$

(c) The amount of prestressing steel shall be adequate to ensure that ultimate load in flexure will be at least equal to 1.2 times the cracking load. Cracking load may be computed on the basis of a modulus of rupture (assume $7.5\sqrt{f'_c}$.)

209—Shear

(a) Except as provided in Sections 209 (b) and (c), the area of shear reinforcement placed perpendicular to the axis of a member shall not be less than:

$$A_v = \frac{1}{2} \frac{(V_u - V_c) \, s}{f'_y jd}$$

$$\text{or } A_v = 0.0025 \, b's$$

whichever is larger. V_c shall be assumed equal to .06 $f'_c b'jd$ but not more than 180 b'jd. (assume $j = \frac{7}{8}$)

The factor ½ shall apply only where the effective prestress f_{se} is not less than $0.5f'_s$, and where the prestressing steel is designed to resist 100 percent of the required ultimate bending moment at all sections. It shall be increased linearly to 1.0 for the case where none of the required ultimate moment is resisted by the prestressing steel (ordinary reinforced concrete).

(b) The steel area required in Section 209 (a) may be reduced or omitted where it is demonstrated by tests that a member with the lesser amount of web reinforcement is capable of developing the required ultimate flexural strength, and the provisions of Section 104 are satisfied.

(c) The amount of web reinforcement provided in the middle third of the span length of a simple beam shall not be less than that required at its third point.

(d) The amount of web reinforcement required at the section of a simple beam where the extreme fiber tensile stress equals $7.5\sqrt{f'_c}$ at ultimate load shall be provided from that point to the nearest end of the member, provided concentrated loads do not occur in the region so reinforced.

(e) Web reinforcement shall be spaced not further apart than three-fourths of the depth of the member nor 24 inches, whichever is smaller.

(f) Sections of combined high moment and shear shall be given special attention and the effects of flexural cracking taken into account.

210—Bond

In pretensioned members particularly in which flexural cracking is antici-

pated in or near the region of prestress transfer, the influence of transfer length°
on the design shall be taken into account.

211—Repetitive Loads

(a) The possibility of bond failure due to repeated dynamic loads shall be
investigated in regions of high bond stress and where flexural cracking is expected at design loads.

(b) In unbonded construction, special attention shall be given to the possibility of fatigue in the anchorages.

(c) The possibility of inclined diagonal tension cracks forming under repetitive loading at appreciably smaller stresses than under static loading shall be
taken into account in the design.

212—Composite Construction

(a) Shear Transfer.

Shear shall be transferred along the contact surface either by bond or entirely by shear keys. Except as provided in (a) 1, separation of elements shall
be prevented by steel ties or other suitable mechanical anchorage. The following
is a list of recommended bond capacities. The capacity of bond at ultimate
shall be taken as twice the recommended value.

1) For members where the transverse width of the contact surface coincides with the width of compression block, mechanical anchorages may be
eliminated provided shear stresses at service load on the contact surface does not
exceed 40 psi and that the precast surface is rough, clean and free of foreign
material and loose or scaling particles.

2) When minimum steel requirements of 212 (b) are followed and the
contact surface of the precast element is smooth (a smooth surface is one which
has been cast against a form, trowelled, or floated) .... 40 psi.

3) When minimum steel requirements of 212 (b) are followed and the
contact surface on the precast element is rough and clean ....160 psi.

4) When additional vertical ties are used the allowable bond stress on a
rough surface may be increased at the rate of 75 psi for each additional area of
steel ties equal to 1% of the contact area.

(b) Vertical Ties.

Mechanical anchorage in the form of vertical ties to prevent separation of
the component elements in the direction normal to the contact surfaces shall be
provided. Spacing of such ties shall not exceed four times the thickness of the
slab nor 24 in. The minimum cross-sectional area of steel ties supplied in each
foot of span shall be 0.15% of the contact area, but not less than 0.20 sq. in. shall
be provided. It is preferable to provide all ties in the form of extended stirrups.

213—End Regions

(a) End blocks shall be provided as required for end bearing and as
necessary to distribute concentrated prestressing forces safely from the anchorages to the cross-section of the member.

(b) End blocks may be omitted where adequate reinforcement is pro-

°Under normal conditions, bond transfer lengths for strand may be assumed
to be between 25 and 50 times the nominal strand size, depending on the
surface conditions of the strand, concrete strength at transfer, and method of
release.

vided and where their omission is justified by tests or indicated by common usage.

(c) Reinforcement shall be provided in the anchorage zone to resist bursting and spalling forces induced by the concentrated loads of the prestressing steel. Points of abrupt change in section shall be adequately reinforced.

214—Continuity

(a) For continuous girders and other statically indeterminate structures, moments, shears, and thrusts produced by external loads and prestressing shall be determined by elastic analysis. The effects of creep, shrinkage, axial deformation, and restraint of attached structural elements shall be considered in the design.

(b) In the application of ultimate load factors where effects of dead and live loads are of opposite sign, the case of a dead load factor of unity shall be included in the investigation.

215—Concrete Cover

(a) The following minimum thicknesses of concrete cover shall be provided for prestressing steel, ducts and non-prestressed steel:

	Cover, inches
Formed concrete surfaces in contact with ground........	2
Beams and girders	
Prestessing steel and main reinforcing bars	1½
Stirrups and ties	1
Slabs and joists exposed to weather	1
Slabs and joists not exposed to weather	¾

216—Placement of Prestressing Steel

(a) All pretensioning steel and ducts for post-tensioning shall be accurately placed and adequately secured in position.

(b) The minimum clear spacings between pretensioning steel at each end of the member shall be four times the diameter of individual wires or three times the diameter of strands, but not less than 1⅓ times the maximum size of the coarse aggregate.

(c) Prestressing steel or ducts may be bundled together in the middle portion of the span, provided the requirements of Section 216(b) are satisfied.

(d) Ducts may be arranged closely together vertically when provision is made to prevent the steel, when tensioned, from breaking through into an adjacent duct. Horizontal disposition of ducts shall allow proper placement of concrete.

(e) Where concentration of steel or ducts tends to create a weakened plane in the concrete cover, suitable reinforcement shall be provided against cracking.

(f) The inside diameter of ducts shall be at least ¼ in. larger than the diameter of the post-tensioning bar or strand.

CHAPTER III

MATERIALS AND CONSTRUCTION

301—Concrete

(a) Portland Cement shall conform to one of the following:
Specifications for Portland Cement (ASTM C150)
Specifications for Air-Entraining Portland Cement (ASTM C175)
Specifications for Portland Blast Furnace Slag Cement (ASTM C205)
Specifications for Portland-Pozzolan Cement (ASTM C340)
(b) Concrete aggregates shall conform to one of the following:
Specifications for Concrete Aggregates (ASTM C33)
Specifications for Lightweight Aggregates for Structural Concrete (ASTM C330)

(c) Water for mixing concrete shall be clean and free of injurious quantities of substance harmful to the concrete or to the tendons. Sea water shall not be used.

(d) Suitable admixtures to obtain high early strength or to increase the workability of low-slump concrete may be used if known to have no injurious effect on the steel or the concrete. Calcium chloride or an admixture containing calcium chloride shall not be used where it may come in contact with prestressing steel.

(e) The strength of the concrete required at given ages shall be indicated on the plans. The strength at transfer shall be adequate for the requirements of the anchorages or of transfer through bond. The minimum strength at transfer for 7 wire strands shall be 3,000 psi for ⅜-inch strands and smaller, and 3,500 psi for ⁷⁄₁₆-inch and ½-inch strands.

302—Grout

(a) Portland cement and water shall conform to the provisions of Section 301 (a) and (c) respectively. Suitable admixtures, known to have no injurious effects on the steel or the concrete, may be used to increase workability and to reduce shrinkage.

(b) Sand, if used, shall conform to "Tentative Specifications for Aggregate for Masonry Mortar" (ASTM C144) except that gradation may be modified as necessary to obtain proper placeability.

(c) Proportions of grouting materials shall be based on results of tests made on fresh and hardened grout prior to beginning work. The water contents shall be the minimum necessary for proper placement but in no case more than 5½ gallons per sack. When permitted to stand until setting takes place, grout shall neither bleed nor segregate.

(d) Grout shall be mixed in a high-speed mechanical mixer and then passed through a strainer into pumping equipment which provides for recirculation.

(e) Just prior to grouting, the ducts shall be made free of water, dirt, and other foreign substances. The method of grouting shall be such as to ensure the complete filling of all voids between the prestressing steel and the duct and anchorage fittings.

303—Steel Tendons

(a) Wires for prestressing shall conform to ASTM Specification A421.

Wires for pretensioning shall be uncoated and shall be of a size and type such as to insure sufficient prestress transfer bond. Oil tempered wires shall not be used.

(b) Seven-wire strands for pretensioning shall conform to ASTM Specification A416.

(c) Wires used in making strands for post-tensioning shall be cold-drawn and either stress-relieved, in the case of uncoated strands, or hot-dip galvanized, in the case of galvanized strands.

(d) High-strength alloy steel bars for post-tensioning shall be proof-stressed to 90 per cent of the guaranteed ultimate strength. After proof-stressing, the bars shall conform to the following minimum properties:

Ultimate strength f'_s	145,000 psi
Yield strength (0.2% set)	$0.90 f'_s$
Elongation at rupture in 20 diameters	4%
Reduction of area at rupture	25%

(e) Prestressing steel shall be clean and free of excessive rust, scale, and pitting. A light oxide is permissible. Unbonded steel shall be permanently protected from corrosion unless accessible for maintenance.

(f) Burning and welding operations in the vicinity of prestressing steel shall be carefully performed, so that the prestressing steel shall not be subjected to excessive temperatures, welding sparks, or ground currents.

304—Application and Measurement of Prestressing Force

(a) Prestressing force shall be determined (1) by measuring tendon elongation and also (2) either by checking jack pressure on a calibrated gage or by the use of an accurately calibrated dynamometer. The cause of any discrepancy which exceeds 5 per cent shall be ascertained and corrected. Elongation requirements shall be taken from load-elongation curves for the steel used.

(b) Transfer of force from the bulkheads of the pretensioning bed to the concrete shall be carefully accomplished, by proper choice of cutting points and cutting sequence. Release of pretensioning may be effected by gradual means or by burning of tendons. Long lengths of exposed strands shall be cut near the member to minimize shock to the concrete.

(c) If several wires or strands are stretched simultaneously, provision must be made to induce approximately equal stress in each.

(d) Occasional breakage of single wires in a member prestressed with multiple strands or wires need not require replacement, provided the total loss so caused is less than 2 per cent of the total prestress.

(e) Where there is a considerable temperature differential between the concrete and the tendons, its effect shall be taken into account.

305—Post-tensioning Anchorages and Couplers

(a) Anchorages, couplers, and splices for post-tensioned reinforcement shall be capable of developing the ultimate strength assumed for the tendons in the design. Couplers and splices shall be placed in areas approved by the Engineer and enclosed in housings long enough to permit the necessary movements. They shall not be used at points of sharp curvature.

(b) Anchorage and end fittings shall be permanently protected against corrosion.

306—Formwork

(a) Form construction and removal shall conform to the requirements of the appropriate sections of ACI code 318.

(b) Forms for pretensioned members shall be constructed to permit movement of the member without damage during release of the prestressing force.

(c) Forms for post-tensioned members shall be constructed to minimize resistance to the shortening of the member. Deflection of members due to the prestressing force and deformation of falsework shall be considered in the design.

(d) Form supports may be removed when sufficient prestressing has been applied to carry dead load, formwork carried by the member, and anticipated construction loads.

307—Fabrication of Precast Units

(a) The loss of prestress which results from shortening of a pretensioning bed shall be considered and, when significant, allowed for in the stressing operation.

(b) Lifting eyes or other similar devices shall be designed for 100 per cent impact. They shall be made of materials sufficiently ductile to ensure obvious deformation before fracture.

(c) When lifting members from pretensioning beds, care shall be taken to avoid undue stresses resulting from binding in forms. If necessary, members shall be freed from forms by suitable means before lifting.

308—Joints and Bearings for Precast Members

(a) Design and detailing of the joints and bearings shall be based on the forces to be transmitted, and on the effects of dimensional changes due to shrinkage, elastic deformation, creep and temperature. Joints shall be detailed so as to allow sufficient tolerances for manufacture and erection of the members.

(b) Bearings shall be detailed to provide for stress concentrations, rotations, and the possible development of horizontal forces by friction or other restraints.

1.13.1 General

The design of prestressed concrete members of highway bridges shall conform to the requirements of Section 7, Concrete Design, insofar as the requirements of that section apply and are not specifically modified by requirements set forth herein. The specifications of this section are intended for use in the design of simple-span structures of moderate length. Large or unusual structures require special study and detailed consideration of effects that can be neglected or assigned arbitrary values in the design of structures to which this section is intended to apply.

1.13.2 Notation

A_b = bearing area of anchor plate of post-tensioning steel.
A_c = maximum area of the portion of the anchorage surface that is geometrically similar to and concentric with the area of the bearing plate of post-tensioning steel.
A_s = area of main prestressing tensile steel.
A_s' = area of conventional steel.
A_{sr} = steel area required to develop the ultimate compressive strength of the web of a flanged section.
A_v = area of web reinforcement.
b = width of flange of flanged member or width of rectangular member.
b' = width of web of a flanged member.
d = distance from extreme compressive fiber to centroid of the prestressing force.

* Courtesy of the American Association of State Highway Officials.

I = moment of inertia about the centroid of the cross section.

I = impact load.

j = ratio of distance between centroid of compression and centroid of tension to the depth d.

$p = A_s/bd$, ratio of prestressing steel.

$p' = A_s'/bd$, ratio of conventional reinforcement.

s = longitudinal spacing of web reinforcement.

t = average thickness of the flange of a flanged member.

Q = statical moment of cross section area, above or below the level being investigated for shear, about the centroid.

D = effect of dead load.

L = effect of design live load including impact, where applicable.

V_c = shear carried by concrete.

V_u = shear due to ultimate load and effect of prestressing.

E_c = flexural modulus of elasticity of concrete.

E_s = modulus of elasticity of prestressing steel.

f_c' = compressive strength of concrete at 28 days.

f_{ci}' = compressive strength of concrete at time of initial prestress.

f_s' = ultimate strength of prestressing steel.

f_{se} = effective steel prestress after losses.

f_{su} = average stress in prestressing steel at ultimate load.

f_{sy} = nominal yield point stress of prestressing steel (at 1.0 per cent extension).

f_y' = yield point stress of conventional reinforcing steel.

n = ratio of E_s/E_c.

e = base of Naperian logarithms.

K = friction wobble coefficient per foot of prestressing steel.

T_0 = steel stress at jacking end.

T_x = steel stress at any point x.

μ = friction curvature coefficient.

α = total angular change of prestressing steel profile in radians from jacking end to point x.

l = length of prestressing steel element from jacking end to point x.

1.13.3   Design Theory

The elastic theory shall be used for the design of prestressed concrete members under design loads at working stresses. The members shall be checked by ultimate strength theory for compliance with specified load factors.

1.13.4 Basic Assumptions

The following assumptions are made for design purposes:
- (a) Strains vary linearly over the depth of the member throughout the entire load range.
- (b) Before cracking, stress is linearly proportional to strain.
- (c) After cracking, tension in the concrete is neglected.

1.13.5 Loading Stages

The state of stress shall be investigated under each loading condition that is anticipated in the manufacture, handling and service life of the structure. The following are some of the conditions that may exist:

(*A*) *Initial Prestress.* The concrete and steel stresses in the initial stressing of the member before the dead load from other members is effective and before losses due to length changes of the concrete and steel have taken place. The condition of manufacture shall be taken into account, particularly as to whether the dead load of the member itself is effective.

(*B*) *Transportation and Erection.* Precast members that are to be moved from their place of manufacture shall be designed so that handling is practicable.

(*C*) *Design Load.* Stresses in effect after losses and under dead load and the assumed working live load.

(*D*) *Cracking Load.* Complete freedom from cracking may or may not be necessary at any particular loading stage. Type and function of the structure and type, frequency, and magnitude of live loads should be considered.

(*E*) *Ultimate Load.* The ultimate load that a member can withstand without failure shall be the sum of the multiples of live and dead loads specified in the formulas given in Article 1.13.6. The ultimate load capacity shall be that producing moments equal to the ultimate moment of the concrete or steel as given in Article 1.13.10.

1.13.6 Load Factors

Load factors are multiples of the design load applied to the structure to insure its safety.

The computed ultimate load capacity shall not be less than
$$1.5D + 2.5(L + I)$$
These load factors are intended for simple spans of moderate length. For long spans, continuous spans and unusual designs, special investigation is advisable with probable increase in the ultimate load factors.

1.13.7 Allowable Stresses

In general the design of prestressed members shall be based on a maximum concrete strength of 5000 psi. In exceptional cases on individual projects justified by the availability of suitable materials and the assured establishment of rigid control of mixing, placing and curing, this maximum may be increased to 6000 psi.

(A) Prestressing Steel.

(1) Temporary stress before losses due to creep and shrinkage, $0.70f_s'$ (Overstressing to $0.80f_s'$ for short periods of time may be permitted provided the stress, after seating of the anchorage, does not exceed $0.70f_s'$.)

(2) Stress at design load (after losses) $0.60f_s'$ or $0.80f_{sy}$ whichever is smaller.

(B) Concrete.

(1) Temporary stresses before losses due to creep and shrinkage:
Compression
Pretensioned members, $0.60f_{ci}'$
Post-tensioned members, $0.55f_{ci}'$
Tension
Members without nonprestressed reinforcement:
Single element, $3\sqrt{f_{ci}'}$
Segmental element, zero
Members with nonprestressed reinforcement sufficient to resist tensile force in the concrete without cracking when computed on the basis of an uncracked section:
Single element, $6\sqrt{f_{ci}'}$
Segmental element (within the element itself), $3\sqrt{f_{ci}'}$

(2) Stress at design load after losses have occurred:
Compression, $0.40f_c'$
Tension (in precompressed tensile zone), zero

(3) Cracking stress:
Modulus of rupture from tests or if not available, $7.5\sqrt{f_c'}$

(4) Anchorage bearing stress:
Post-tensioned anchorage (but not to exceed f_{ci}'), $0.6f_{ci}'\sqrt[3]{A_c/A_b}$

1.13.8 Loss of Prestress

(A) Friction Losses. Friction losses in post-tensioned members occur from angle change in draped cables and from wobble of the ducts. These losses can be estimated by the following formula:

$$T_0 = T_x e^{(Kl + \mu\alpha)}$$

using the following average values of K and μ

Type of steel	Type of Duct	K	μ
Wire cables	Bright metal sheathing	0.0020	0.30
	Galvanized metal sheathing	0.0015	0.25
	Greased or asphalt-coated and wrapped	0.0020	0.30
	Direct contact with concrete	0.0015	0.45
High-strength bars	Bright metal sheathing	0.0003	0.20
	Galvanized metal sheathing	0.0002	0.15
	Direct contact with concrete	0.0005	0.40
Galvanized strand	Bright metal sheathing	0.0015	0.25
	Galvanized metal sheathing	0.0010	0.20
	Direct contact with concrete	0.0015	0.50

Friction losses occur prior to anchoring but should be estimated for design and checked during stressing operations.

(B) Prestress Losses. Losses of prestress due to all causes except friction may be assumed to be as follows:

Pretensioned members, 35,000 psi
Post-tensioned members, 25,000 psi

(When data are available for losses due to above-cited causes, more exact prestress losses may be estimated. Reference is made to ACI-ASCE Joint Committee Report.)

(C) Lightweight Concrete. When lightweight aggregates are used, prestress losses should be estimated from tests on concrete made with the aggregates to be used.

1.13.9 Flexure

Prestressed concrete members may be assumed to act as uncracked members subjected to combined axial and bending stresses within specified design loads. The transformed area of bonded reinforcement may be included in pretensioned members and in post-tensioned members after grouting.

1.13.10 Ultimate Flexural Strength

(A) Rectangular Sections. For rectangular or flanged sections in which the neutral axis lies within the flange, the ultimate flexural strength shall be assumed as

$$M_u = A_s f_{su} d \left(1 - 0.6 \frac{p f_{su}}{f_c'}\right).$$

(B) Flanged Sections. If the neutral axis falls outside the flange (usually if the flange thickness is less than $1.4 dp f_{su} f_c'$), the ultimate flexural strength shall be assumed as

$$M_u = A_{sr} f_{su} d \left(1 - 0.6 \frac{A_{sr} f_{su}}{b' d f_c'}\right) + 0.85 f_c'(b - b')t(d - 0.5t)$$

where

$A_{st} = A_s - A_{sf}$ = the steel area required to develop the ultimate compressive strength of the web of a flanged section.

$A_{sf} = 0.85 f_c'(b - b')t/f_{su}$ = steel area required to develop the ultimate compressive strength of the overhanging portions of the flange.

(C) Steel Stress. Unless the value of f_{su} can be more accurately known from detailed analysis, the following value may be used:

Bonded members $\qquad f_{su} = f_s'\left(1 - 0.5 \frac{p f_s'}{f_c'}\right)$

Unbonded members $\qquad f_{su} = f_{se} + 15,000$

provided that
  (1) The stress-strain properties of the prestressing steel approximate those specified in Article 2.4.43.
  (2) The effective prestress after losses is not less than $0.5 f_s'$.

1.13.11 Maximum and Minimum Steel Percentage

Prestressed concrete members shall be designed so that failure of the steel rather than of the concrete will occur at ultimate load. In general the percentage of steel shall be such that $p \dfrac{f_{su}}{f_c'}$ for rectangular sections and $A_{sr} \dfrac{f_{su}}{b' d f_c'}$ for flanged sections does not exceed 0.30. For steel with percentages greater than this, the ultimate flexural strength shall not be assumed as greater than

$M_u = 0.25 f_c' b d^2$ for rectangular sections, or

$M_u = 0.25 b' d^2 f_c' + 0.85 f_c'(b - b')t(d - 0.5t)$ for flanged sections.

In prestressed concrete members reinforced with tendons of high-tensile-strength steel wire or high-tensile-strength strand in which the anchorage of the tendons is by bond alone, the cross sectional area of the tendons shall be not less than 0.3 per cent of the cross sectional area of the member at the time of the transfer of stress from the prestressing bed to the member.

1.13.12 Nonprestressed Reinforcement

Nonprestressed reinforcement may be considered as contributing to the tensile strength of the beam at ultimate strength in an amount equal to its area times its yield point, provided that

$$\frac{pf_{su}}{f_c{}'} + \frac{p'f_y{}'}{f_c{}'}$$

does not exceed 0.3 for rectangular sections, or

$$A_{sr}\frac{f_{su}}{b'df_c{}'} + \frac{A_s{}'f_{sy}{}'}{b'df_c{}'}$$

does not exceed 0.3 for flanged sections.

1.13.13 Shear

Prestressed concrete members shall be reinforced for diagonal tension stresses. Shear reinforcement shall be placed perpendicular to the axis of the member. The area of web reinforcement shall be

$$A_v = \frac{(V_u - V_c)s}{2f_y{}'jd}$$

but shall not be less than

$$A_v = 0.0025b's.$$

The spacing of web reinforcement shall not exceed three-fourths the depth of the member and shall provide transverse reinforcement across the bottom flanges.

The critical sections for shear will usually not be near the ends of the span where the shear is a maximum but at some point away from the ends in a region of high moment.

For the design of web reinforcement in simply supported members carrying moving loads, it is recommended that shear be investigated only in the middle half of the span length. The web reinforcement required at the quarter points should be used throughout the outer quarters of the span.

For simply supported beams carrying only uniformly distributed load, the maximum web reinforcement may be taken as that required at a distance from the support equal to the depth of the member. This amount of web reinforcement should be provided from this point to the end of the member. In the middle third of the span length, the amount of web reinforcement provided should not be less than that required at third-points of the span.

1.13.14 Composite Structures

(*A*) *General.* Composite structures in which the deck is assumed to act integrally with the beam shall be interconnected to transfer shear along the contact surfaces and to prevent separation of the elements. Transfer of shear shall be by bond or by shear keys. The elements shall be tied together by extension of the web reinforcement or by dowels.

(*B*) *Shear Capacity.* The shear connection shall be designed for the ultimate load and may be computed by the formula $v = V_u Q/I$.

(*C*) *Bond Capacity.* The following values for ultimate bond resistance at the contact surfaces shall be used in determining the need for shear keys:

> When the minimum steel tie requirements of (*D*) of this article are met, 75 psi.
>
> When the minimum steel tie requirements of (*D*) of this article are met and the contact surface of the precast element is artificially roughened, 150 psi.
>
> When steel ties in excess of the requirements of (*D*) of this article are provided and the contact surface of the precast element is artificially roughened, 225 psi.

If bond capacity is less than the computed shear, shear keys shall be provided throughout the length of the member. Keys shall be proportioned according to the concrete strength of each component of the composite member.

(*D*) *Vertical Ties.* All web reinforcement shall extend into cast-in-place decks. The spacing of vertical ties shall not be greater than four times the minimum thickness of either of the composite elements and in any case not greater than 24 inches. The total area of vertical ties shall not be less than the area of two No. 3 bars spaced at 12 inches.

(*E*) *Shrinkage Stresses.* In structures with a cast-in-place slab on precast beams, the differential shrinkage tends to cause tensile stresses in the slab and in the bottom of the beams. Stresses due to differential shrinkage are important only insofar as they affect the cracking load. When cracking load is significant, such stresses should be added to the effect of loads.

1.13.15   End Blocks

End blocks shall have sufficient area to allow the spacing of the pre-stressing steel as specified in Article 1.13.16. Preferably they shall be as wide as the narrower flange of the beam. They shall have a length at least equal to three-fourths of the depth of the beam and in any case 24 inches. In post-tensioned members a closely spaced grid of both vertical and horizontal bars shall be placed near the face of the end block to resist bursting and closely spaced reinforcement shall be placed both vertically and horizontally throughout the length of the block.

1.13.16   Cover and Spacing of Prestressing Steel

(*A*) *Minimum Cover.* The following minimum concrete cover shall be provided for prestressing and conventional steel:

>Prestressing steel and main reinforcement, $1\frac{1}{2}$ inches
>Slab reinforcement, 1 inch
>Stirrups and ties, 1 inch

In locations where members are exposed to salt water, salt spray or chemical vapor, additional cover should be provided.

(*B*) *Minimum Spacing.* The minimum clear spacing of prestressing steel at the ends of beams shall be as follows:

Pre-tensioning steel: three times the diameter of the steel or $1\frac{1}{3}$ the maximum size of the concrete aggregate, whichever is greater.
Post-tensioning ducts: $1\frac{1}{2}$ inches or $1\frac{1}{2}$ times the maximum size of the concrete aggregate, whichever is the greater.

The inside diameter of post-tensioning ducts shall be at least one-fourth inch greater than the diameter of the prestressing steel.

(*C*) *Bundling.* When prestressing steel is draped or deflected, not to exceed three ducts may be bundled in the middle third of the beam length provided that the spacing specified in (*B*) is maintained in the end three feet of the member.

1.13.17   Embedment of Prestressing Strand

To insure proper bond in pre-tensioned members designed to resist flexure, the following minimum length of embedment of seven-wire strand, measured from the free end of the strand to the point of maximum steel stress at ultimate flexural strength, shall be as follows:

$\frac{1}{2}$-inch strand	135 inches
$\frac{7}{16}$-inch strand	120 inches
$\frac{3}{8}$-inch strand	100 inches
$\frac{1}{4}$-inch strand	65 inches

1.13.18 Concrete Strength at Stress Transfer

Unless otherwise specified, stress shall not be transferred from strand to concrete in pre-tensioned members until the compressive strength of the concrete as indicated by test cylinders cured by methods identical with the curing of the members is at least 4000 psi.

index

Modulus of elasticity, of concrete, 36, 591
of steel, 50, 591
Modulus of rupture, 36, 45
Morandi system, 79

Non-end-anchored tendons, 24, 555
Nonprestressed reinforcements, 284, 287, 290, 295, 555, 606
Notations, 555, 588, 600

Over-reinforced beams, 147, 281

Partial prestress, 25, 175, 280, 555
Patents, 59
Pavements, 547
Piles, 431
Pipes, joints of, 400
prestressed-concrete, 400
PI system, 80, 561, 572
Plastic sheathing, 55
Poles, 552
Post-tensioning, 24, 68, 555
anchorages, 75, 79, 81, 84, 598
couplers, 561, 598
jacks, 69
systems, 561
Precast construction, 25, 599
Preflex method, 75
Preliminary design, 161, 190
Preload anchorages, 77
Preload Company, 5, 561
Prescon system, 79, 80, 561
Prestressed concrete, definition, 11
Prestressed Concrete Institute, 6, 9, 56, 560, 588
Prestressed reinforcements, 555, *see also* Steel; Tendons
Prestressed steel, 8
Prestressing, external and internal, 23
full and partial, 25, 555
linear and circular, 24, 555
Prestressing bed, 62
Prestressing force, measurement of, 598
Prestressing systems, 59
addresses of some, 561
comparison of, 87
table of, 61
Pre-tensioning, 24, 555
end anchorages, 62
strands, 562
systems, 62

Principal stresses, 211
Protection for prestressed reinforcement, 190

Reinforced concrete, combination of prestressed and, 298
cost comparison with, 454
prestressed vs., 30
Retensioning, 27
Rigid frames, 352, 501
Roebling, anchorages, 84, 243, 576
jacks, 71
system, 561, 576
Roof beam, 483

Safety, factor of, 31
Secondary moments, 312
Shapes of concrete section, 195, 584
Shear, 207, 594, 606
combined moment and, 226
principal tensile stress, 211
ultimate strength, 218
web reinforcement, 221, 594, 606
Shorer system, 65
Sign conventions, 120
Slabs, continuous flat, 379
flat, 386, 388
lift, 9, 382, 388
load-balancing method, 356, 385
one-way, 370
two-way, 356, 375
Span depth ratios, 277
Stages of loading, 26
Steam curing of concrete, 43
Steel, arrangement of, 203, 596
chemical composition, 49
conduits for, 54
modulus of elasticity, 50
percentage, 594, 605
for prestressing, 48
Steiner, C. R., 2
Stirrups, 221, 227
Strands, high-tensile, 51
Strescon system, *see* Prescon system
Stresses, in concrete, 121, 128
in steel, 132
Stress-relieving process, 49
Stressrods system, 561
Stressteel system, 71, 82, 561
Structural types, 445